Collectibles
PRICE GUIDE 2004

Collectibles
PRICE GUIDE 2004

Judith Miller
with Mark Hill

DK PUBLISHING

LONDON, NEW YORK,
MELBOURNE, MUNICH, AND DELHI

A joint production from DORLING KINDERSLEY
and THE PRICE GUIDE COMPANY

THE PRICE GUIDE COMPANY LIMITED

Publisher Judith Miller

Collectibles Specialist Mark Hill

Publishing Manager Julie Brooke

European Consultant Martina Franke

Managing Editor Claire Smith

Project Editor Carolyn Wilmot

Assistant Editors Sara Sturgess, Megan Watson

Editorial Assistants Sandra Lange, Christine Allinger, Daniel Dunlavey, Katie Lamble, Kirsty Miller, Alex Higham, Lucie Baird

Design and DTP Tim Scrivens, TJ Graphics

Additional Design Colin Loughrey

Digital Image Co-ordinator Cara Miller

Marketing and Advertising Consultant Richard Tidsall

Photographers Graham Rae, Bruce Boyajian, John McKenzie, Byron Slater, Steve Tanner, Ellen McDermott, Elizabeth Field, Dave Pincott, Mike Molloy, Martin Spillane

Indexer Hilary Bird

Workflow Consultant Edward MacDermott

Business Advisor Nick Croydon

DORLING KINDERSLEY LIMITED

Category Publisher Jackie Douglas

Managing Art Editor Heather McCarry

Managing Editor Julie Oughton

Designer Martin Dieguez

DTP Designer Mike Grigoletti

Production Controller Rita Sinha

Production Manager Sarah Coltman

While every care has been taken in the compilation of this guide, neither the authors nor the publishers accept any liability for any financial or other loss incurred by reliance placed on the information contained in *Collectibles Price Guide 2004*

First American Edition 2003
00 01 02 03 04 05 10 9 8 7 6 5 4 3 2 1

Published in the United States by
DK Publishing Inc.
375 Hudson Street
New York, New York 10014

The Price Guide Company Ltd
info@thepriceguidecompany.com

A CIP catalog record for this book is available from the Library of Congress.

ISBN 0 7894 9657 7

Printed and bound in Germany by GGP Media GmbH

Discover more at
www.dk.com

CONTENTS

Welcome to my second annual Collectibles Price Guide, published in association with Dorling Kindersley. Over the past 25 years that I have been writing about antiques, books have come a long way, as our book demonstrates, being laden with specially commissioned full-color illustrations. But it's not just the pictures that are important, it's also the expertise contained in the text that guides you to understand more about a collectible. That's why, in addition to over 5,000 beautiful full-color illustrations, we include features such as "Collectors' Notes" which give you a basic grounding in the subject and our "Closer Look" features which take one object and help you understand why it is more desirable and valuable than another.

Having said this, books aren't everything and although they form the basis for much of our learning, the most important aspect is interacting with other people who are passionate about collecting. So always remember to balance curling up on a comfortable chair reading a book with visiting auctions, fairs, dealers' shops and society meetings.

Judith Miller.

LIST OF CONSULTANTS

Advertising

Rick and Sharon Corley
Toy Road Antiques
Winchester OH

Joe and Sharon Happle
Sign of the Tymes
Lafayette NJ

Americana

Glenn Hart
Mitch Michener
Bucks County Antiques Center
Lahaska PA

Books

Abby Schoolman
Bauman Rare Books
New York NY

Ceramics

David Rago
Craftsman Auctions
Lambertville NJ
info@ragoarts.com

Judith Miller
The Price Guide Company (UK) Ltd

Comics

Vincent Zurzolo Jnr
Metropolis Collectibles Inc
New York NY

Computer Games

Hugo Lee Jones
electroniccollectables@hotmail.com

Costume Jewelry

Roxanne Stuart
gemfairy@aol.com

Glass

Dudley Brown
James D Julia Auctioneers Inc
Fairfield ME
lampnglass.juliaauctions.com

Marbles

Bob Block
AuctionBlocks
Huntington Station CT
auctionblocks@aol.com

Optica , Technical & Scientific Instruments and Plastics

Mark Hill
The Price Guide Company (UK) Ltd

Posters

Sam Sarowitz
Posteritati, New York NY
mail@posteritati.com

Toys

Noel Barrett
Noel Barrett Antiques & Auctions
Ltd, Carversville PA
toys@noelbarrett.com

Sewing

Christina Bertrand
tineke@rcn.com

Sporting

David Hunt
Hunt Auctions Inc
Exton PA

We are also very grateful to our friends and experts who gave us so much help – Beth & Beverley Adams, Michael Bennett-Levy of Early Technology, James Bricges, Dr Graham Cooley, Leo Harrison of Biblion, John Mackie of Lyon & Turnbull, Vernon Martin of Alderfer Auction Company, Jean Scott, Russell Singler of The Animation Art Gallery and Simon Smith of Vectis Auctions Ltd.

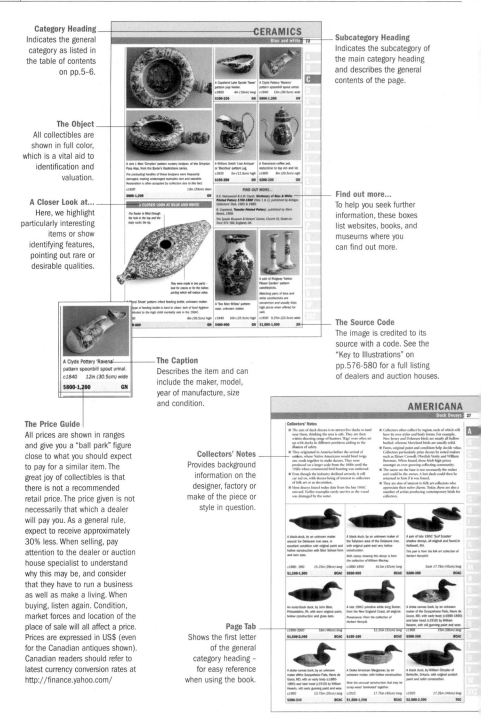

Category Heading
Indicates the general category as listed in the table of contents on pp.5–6.

Subcategory Heading
Indicates the subcategory of the main category heading and describes the general contents of the page.

The Object
All collectibles are shown in full color, which is a vital aid to identification and valuation.

A Closer Look at...
Here, we highlight particularly interesting items or show identifying features, pointing out rare or desirable qualities.

Find out more...
To help you seek further information, these boxes list websites, books, and museums where you can find out more.

The Source Code
The image is credited to its source with a code. See the "Key to Illustrations" on pp.576–580 for a full listing of dealers and auction houses.

The Caption
Describes the item and can include the maker, model, year of manufacture, size and condition.

The Price Guide
All prices are shown in ranges and give you a "ball park" figure close to what you should expect to pay for a similar item. The great joy of collectibles is that there is not a recommended retail price. The price given is not necessarily that which a dealer will pay you. As a general rule, expect to receive approximately 30% less. When selling, pay attention to the dealer or auction house specialist to understand why this may be, and consider that they have to run a business as well as make a living. When buying, listen again. Condition, market forces and location of the place of sale will all affect a price. Prices are expressed in US$ (even for the Canadian antiques shown). Canadian readers should refer to latest currency conversion rates at http://finance.yahoo.com/

Collectors' Notes
Provides background information on the designer, factory or make of the piece or style in question.

Page Tab
Shows the first letter of the general category heading – for easy reference when using the book.

Collectors' Notes

- Coca-Cola was developed in and sold from 1886 and was named after the extracts of coca leaves and kola nuts that John Pemberton used to make it.
- It began as a medicinal 'pick me up' drink, sold through pharmacists. Its 'restorative' properties were due to the coca leaf extracts – coca leaves are also used to make the narcotic cocaine. A slogan used in 1907 advised 'Delicious Coca-Cola, Sustains, Refreshes, Invigorates'.
- The first magazine advertisement appeared in 1902 and shortly after, a huge range of associated advertising and accessories could be found, including drip trays, glasses and signs, often showing people enjoying themselves drinking Coke.
- By the 1920s and 1930s, when sales were slow due to the Depression and the coca leaf extracts had been replaced with caffeine, Coca-Cola revitalized itself by furthering the theme of group enjoyment and marketed its product as being suitable for the whole family. Since then, the drink has relied on images of enjoyment, togetherness and tradition.
- The well-known 'Santa Claus' images still used today were developed in the early 1930s by a Swedish artist called Haddon Sundblom. Santa's red coat is the same color as the cans, with this red itself being a special, patented color owned by the company.
- Memorabilia from the late 1880s and 1890s is scarce and valuable. Collectors should be aware that since the 1970s, Coca-Cola has actively produced items that were made to look old, including some reproductions of vintage designs. Examine pieces carefully to discern their true age. Condition and availability (rarity) control demand and desirability.
- Coca-Cola celebrated its centenary in 1986, look for unopened or unused items related to that event and bearing the centenary logo, which are still affordable. Also look for branded items produced for special events, such as political rallies, which are slowly rising in value. Again, these must be unopened and in mint condition.

A Coca-Cola advertising 'WW1 Girl' tin tip tray.

c1916   6in (15cm) long

$300-400   SotT

A rare Coca-Cola advertising 'The Soda Jerk' tin serving tray.

This tray is rare and more valuable than others as it is very unusual for a man to be used in the artwork.

c1928   13in (33cm) long

$1,200-1,800   SotT

A Coca-Cola advertising 'Bather with the Glass' tin serving tray.

It is hard to find this particular image in good condition.

c.1929   13in (33cm) long

$400-600   SotT

A Coca-Cola advertising tray, dated.

1941   13in (35cm) high

$180-220   DH

A Coca-Cola advertising 'Girls in the Car' tin serving tray.

c1942   13in (33cm) long

$300-400   SotT

A Coca-Cola advertising tray, from a set of three.

c1950   13in (33cm) long

$80-120   DH

A scarce 1950s Mexican Coca-Cola tin advertising tray

13.25in (33.5cm) high

$350-400   AtA

A very rare 1930s card Coca-Cola advertising standee showing Lupe Velez, printed by the Niagara Litho Ltd of Buffalo & New York.

Lupe Velez was a beauty and film star during the 1920s, 1930s and 1940s, and starred in 'The Mexican Spitfire' in 1939. This example has been restored, if it was in excellent and unrestored condition, its value would be nearer $2,500.

20.5in (52cm) high

$1,000-1,500   **AtA**

A plastic and card Coca-Cola miniature novelty billboard store display.

6in (15.5cm) wide

$60-90   **AtA**

A Coca-Cola advertising miniature card six-pack, with glass bottles.

$60-90   **SotT**

A Coca-Cola amber glass, straight-sided bottle, marked "Norfolk, Virginia".

c1910

$80-120   **SotT**

A 1950s Coca-Cola advertising Christmas carton stuffer, with cut-out Santa Claus doll.

7.25in (18.5cm) high

$70-100   **SotT**

An American Coca-Cola tin advertising sign, with thermometer.

c1941   15.⁷5in (40cm) high

$350-400   **AtA**

A 1950s painted plywood Coca-Cola advertising sign, made by Kay Displays Inc of 230 Park Avenue New York City.

27.75in (70.5cm) high

$1,000-1,500   **AtA**

A 1950s Coca-Cola advertising porcelain push plate.

$300-400   **SotT**

A metal Coca-Cola advertising display thermometer, shaped as a large Coke bottle.

29.25in (74.5cm) high

$120-180   **TA**

A rare 1940s box of Coca-Cola advertising straws.

8.75in (22cm) high

$150-200   **SotT**

A 1950s Coca-Cola toy drinks dispenser, boxed with plastic cups.

It is rare to find these dispensers still retaining the plastic cups.

11in (28cm) wide

$100-150   **SotT**

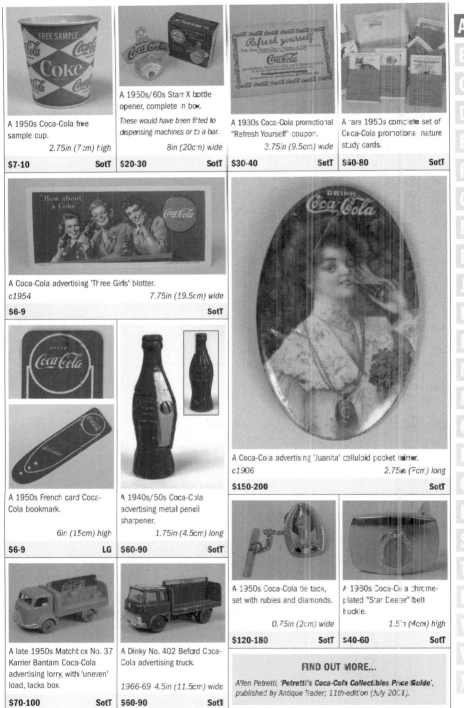

A 1950s Coca-Cola free sample cup.

2.75in (7cm) high

$7-10   SotT

A 1950s/60s Starr X bottle opener, complete in box.

These would have been fitted to dispensing machines or to a bar.

8in (20cm) wide

$20-30   SotT

A 1930s Coca-Cola promotional "Refresh Yourself" coupon.

3.75in (9.5cm) wide

$30-40   SotT

A rare 1950s complete set of Coca-Cola promotional nature study cards.

$50-80   SotT

A Coca-Cola advertising 'Three Girls' blotter.

c1954   7.75in (19.5cm) wide

$6-9   SotT

A 1950s French card Coca-Cola bookmark.

6in (15cm) high

$6-9   LG

A 1940s/50s Coca-Cola advertising metal pencil sharpener.

1.75in (4.5cm) long

$60-90   SotT

A Coca-Cola advertising 'Juanita' celluloid pocket mirror.

c1906   2.75in (7cm) long

$150-200   SotT

A 1950s Coca-Cola tie tack, set with rubies and diamonds.

0.75in (2cm) wide

$120-180   SotT

A 1960s Coca-Cola chrome-plated "Star Dealer" belt buckle.

1.5in (4cm) high

$40-60   SotT

A late 1950s Matchbox No. 37 Karrier Bantam Coca-Cola advertising lorry, with 'uneven' load, lacks box.

$70-100   SotT

A Dinky No. 402 Beford Coca-Cola advertising truck.

1966-69   4.5in (11.5cm) wide

$60-90   SotT

FIND OUT MORE...

Allen Petretti, *'Petretti's Coca-Cola Collectibles Price Guide'*, published by Antique Trader; 11th edition (July 2001).

Collectors' Notes

■ Pepsi-Cola was developed in 1898 in North Carolina and was named after the beneficial effects its maker, pharmacist Caleb Bradham, claimed drinking it had on dyspepsia. However, for a number of decades after its invention, it was far less popular than Coca-Cola.

■ When Coca-Cola began advertising in earnest, Pepsi responded and slowly became more prominent. Although Pepsi-Cola went bankrupt twice in 1921 and 1931, it was the first soft drink company to have a celebrity endorser, racing driver Barney Oldfield, in 1909, and it had the first radio jingle in 1939. In 1934, Pepsi also threatened Coca-Cola's dominance with a successful 12ounce bottle priced at only a nickel.

■ Since then, the two companies have shown a leading, cutting edge in their competitive advertising, with Pepsi relying more on the appeal of celebrities, pop music and young people. During the 1970s, the taste of Pepsi was preferred over Coca-Cola, causing more competitive advertising from both companies.

■ As with Coca-Cola memorabilia, look for early pieces in unused condition, but also for pieces that show celebrities or popular icons, such as Michael Jackson, Madonna and Joe Montana.

An early 1940s Pepsi-Cola glass, with syrup level.
4.25in (11cm) high

$30-50   **SotT**

A late 1940s Pepsi-Cola glass, with applied color label.
5.25in (13.5cm) high

$10-15   **SotT**

A rare 1940s Fepsi crown top tin can.
5.5in (14cm) high

$220-280   **SotT**

A 1960s Keisler gold-plated ballpoint pen, with Pepsi decal.
5.25in (13.5cm) long

$50-80   **SotT**

A 1950s Pepsi-Cola miniature card six-pack, with glass bottles.
2.5in (6.5cm) wide

$70-100   **SotT**

A Pepsi-Cola card advertising sign.
c1906   *14in (35.5cm) wide*

$280-320   **SotT**

Four Pepsi-Cola advertising matchboxes, each with a different Disney character on the reverse.

These characters were designed by the Walt Disney Co. and were used as army unit mascots during WWII. There are 48 different covers in total.

2in (5cm) high

$8-12   **SotT**

A 1950s Pepsi-Cola celluloid 'bottle cap' sign, in good condition.

9in (23cm) wide

$150-200   **SotT**

A 1940s Linemar Pepsi-Cola advertising toy truck.
3.75in (9.5cm) wide

$100-150   **SotT**

A 1960s Pepsi-Cola advertising toy truck, made in Japan.
3.5in (9cm) wide

$15-25   **SotT**

Collectors' Notes

- Guinness has employed brand-building advertising techniques since 1928, when they appointed advertising company S.H. Benson Ltd. to advertise and market their product.
- Benson employed the artist John Gilroy (1898–1985), whose designs have now become recognizable across the world. Gilroy thought up the famous toucan character, which was introduced in 1935, and also introduced a range of other animals including a seal and a kangaroo.
- Other famous designers and artists, such as Abram Games, also designed for Guinness and they soon became known for innovative, colorful and fun campaigns. Carlton ware was also appointed to make a series of models in the 1950s, which are highly desirable and have been reproduced.
- Look for the Carlton ware range of animals in particular, but beware of reproductions, which are collectible but much less valuable. Most advertising featured black and white, reflecting the colors of the beer, but also often red, due to the ruby tint it has when held to the light. Also look for pieces that epitomize popular campaigns such as 'Guinness for Strength' and 'My Goodness My Guinness'.

A Carlton ware Guinness toucan advertising lamp base.

These figures, along with the toucan wall plaques have been much copied in recent years. Copies typically have cream necks, and the graduation between the orange and red color or the beak is either marked too clearly or is smudged.

12in (30.5cm) high

$400-600 — **Bev**

A Carlton ware Guinness toucan advertising figure.

3.25in (8.5cm) high

$400-600 — **Bev**

A 1950s set of Carlton ware Guinness flying toucan wall plaques.

Largest 9.75in (25cm) wide

$500-700 — **BonS**

A Carlton ware 'Draught Guinness' penguin, on turquoise base.

3.75in (9.5cm) high

$700-1,000 — **D**

A plastic pull-along Guinness penguin.

3in (7.5cm) high

$120-180 — **D**

A Carlton ware Guinness kangaroo advertising figure.

4in (10cm) high

$300-400 — **Bev**

A Carlton ware Guinness ostrich advertising figure.

4in (10cm) high

$300-500 — **Bev**

A Carlton ware Guinness seal advertising figure.

3.5in (9cm) high

$350-400 — **Bev**

A Carlton ware Guinness turtle advertising figure.

3in (7.5cm) high

$180-220 — **Bev**

A Carlton ware Guinness man with joey advertising figure.

4in (10cm) high

$180-220　　　　**Bev**

A pair of ceramic Guinness canisters.

$70-100　　　　**D**

A Guinness ceramic cruet set.

$80-120　　　　**D**

A 1960s Guinness advertising plastic cruet set.

5in (12.5cm) high

$20-30　　　　**DH**

A blue Guinness tankard.

$40-60　　　　**D**

A 1950s Guinness advertising tray.

10.5in (26.5cm) diam

$70-100　　　　**DH**

A 1950s Guinness advertising wooden brush.

8in (20cm) high

$20-30　　　　**DH**

A card Guinness beer mat, probably 1950s.

4in (10cm) wide

$4-6　　　　**LG**

A 1930s card Guinness beer mat.

4in (10cm) wide

$4-6　　　　**LG**

A card Guinness menu.

9.75in (25cm) high

$10-15　　　　**LG**

A 1990s set of Guinness playing cards, the major cards with reproductions of 1930s Guinness advertising.

$10-15　　　　**LG**

A wooden Guinness advertising cribbage board.

c1913　　　*10.75in (27.5cm) wide*

$30-40　　　　**DH**

FIND OUT MORE...

'The Book of Guinness Advertising', by Jim Davies, published by Guinness Publishing Ltd, 1998.

Website: www.guintiques.com

Collectors' Notes

- Advertising clickers are sometimes known as 'tin crickets' because squeezing the two flaps together makes a clicking sound. They have been produced since the late 19thC in Europe, Japan and the US, initially from color-lithographed tin and later in hard plastic.

- As they were colorful and cheap to produce in quantity, they were ideal for advertising purposes. Many were aimed at children, featuring bright graphics and characters. They were also given away as candidates in political campaigns.

- Collectors look for certain companies or political personalities, as well as figural examples, such as frogs. Condition is important, with no rusting or scratches to the lithograph.

A color-lithographed tin advertising clicker for "Instantly Prepared Gelatin Dessert Jack & Jill".

1.75in (4.5cm) long

$70-100 TRA

A color-lithographed tin advertising clicker for "New & True Coffee".

2.25in (5.5cm) long

$30-50 TRA

A yellow color-lithographed tin advertising clicker for "Weatherbird Shoes".

1.5in (4cm) long

$30-50 TRA

A color-lithographed tin advertising clicker for "Allen's Parlor Furnace".

1.75in (4.5cm) long

$50-80 TRA

A color-lithographed tin advertising clicker for "All Leather Weatherbird Shoes".

1.75in (4.5cm) long

$40-60 TRA

A dark green color-lithographed tin advertising clicker for "Twinkle Shoes".

1.75in (4.5cm) high

$70-100 TRA

A color-lithographed tin advertising clicker for "Peter's Weatherbird Shoes".

1.75in (4.5cm) long

$20-30 TRA

A color-lithographed tin advertising clicker for "Humpty Dumpty Shoes".

2in (5cm) high

$70-100 TRA

A Dutch color-lithographed tin advertising clicker for "Het Melkmeisje Karnemelk Zeep".

1.5in (4cm) long

$80-120 TRA

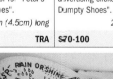

A color-lithographed tin advertising clicker for "Flavor Kist Saltines".

1.75in (4.5cm) long

$30-40 TRA

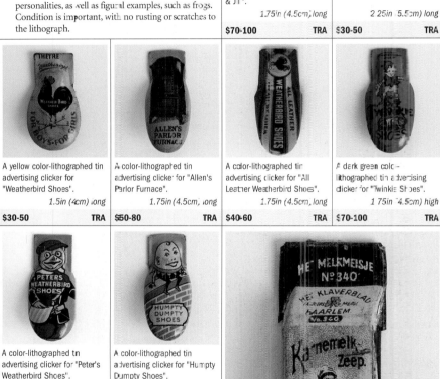

A
B
C
D
E
F
G
H
I
J
K
L
M
N
O
P
Q
R
S
T
U
V
W
XYZ

Collectors' Notes

- The 'golden age' of tins is between the 1860s and the 1930s, when more inexpensive packaging superseded them. Tins practically and decoratively housed perishable goods including tobacco, cookies and gramophone needles. These are among the most popular collecting areas today.

- Tins with advertising in bright colors and intricate printed designs are desirable. They often document the development of graphic advertising past the turn of the 20th century and onwards. Novelty shapes such as books, carriages and figurative designs are also highly sought after, especially if they have moving parts such as wheels.

- Date is also important and early examples in good condition will fetch a premium, especially as many were thrown away after use, or used to store other goods, often in poor conditions.

- Condition is very important, examples in mint or near mint condition will always be worth more than damaged examples. Rust, dents, scratches to the lithography or loss to the paper label will devalue a tin. Do not immerse a tin in water to clean it as this can cause rust and will often damage the printing.

A Lèfevre-Utile tin biscuit barrel, with Art Nouveau artwork by Alphonse Mucha.

Alphonse Mucha (1860-1939) was one of the most famous illustrators and designers working in the Art Nouveau style. He is best known for his poster designs. A similar tin can be found in the Mucha museum in Prague, Czech Republic.

c1905   6.5in (16.5cm) high

$1,800-2,200   **DH**

A CLOSER LOOK AT A BISCUIT TIN

These bucket-shaped tins were given to children as sand pails so are often damaged or in poor condition. This example is in excellent condition.

The colors are bright and cheerful and the design of children is charming.

Novelty shaped tins are always popular with collectors as fewer were produced.

The artwork is finely detailed, well drawn and printed.

A Red Seal Brand Peanut Butter bucket-shaped tin, by the Newton Tea & Spices Co. of Cincinnati, Ohio, showing Little Jack Horner.

1900-1910   3.25in (8cm) high

$700-1,000   **TRA**

A Huntley & Palmer "The Shell" biscuit tin.

c1912   7in (18cm) long

$500-700   **DH**

A 1920s FFV Hors d'Oeuvres biscuit tin, for Southern Biscuit Company Inc, of Richmond, Virginia.

FFV is a popular American name for biscuit tin collectors. Although they produced a large range of biscuits and tins are commonly found, this is one of the harder tins to find.

6in (15.5cm) high

$70-100   **TRA**

A 1920s FFV Lemon Wafers biscuit tin.

6in (15.5cm) high

$30-40   **TRA**

A 1920s FFV Vanilla Wafers biscuit tin.

6in (15.5cm) high

$20-30   **TRA**

A
B
C
D
E
F
G
H
I
J
K
L
M
N
O
P
Q
R
S
T
U
V
W
XYZ

A 1920s American Biscuit Co. 'American Snow Flakes' biscuit tin.

The Swastika was a Nordic symbol for good luck before it became associated with the German Nazi party in the 1930s.

9in (23cm) wide

$100-150 TRA

Two views of a 1920s Sunshine Martini Butter Crackers biscuit tin, by the Loose-Wiles Biscuit Co.

Although for the same biscuits as the next tin, the design including the 'Busy Bazer' shows the period as being the 1920s.

6.75in (17cm) high

$80-120 TRA

A Sunshine Martini Butter Crackers biscuit tin, by the Loose-Wiles Biscuit Co.

See the difference in design from the previous tin, showing this tin to be later

c1950s 6.75in (17cm) high

$40-60 TRA

A 1920s American Rudolph Valentino biscuit tin, with artwork by Henry Clive.

7.5in (19cm) diam

$40-60 DH

A 1950s Huntley & Palmer soldier-shaped biscuit tin.

8in (20cm) high

$200-250 DH

A Rowntree's Cachous cricket bat-shaped sweet tin.

c1910 4.5in (11.5cm) long

$80-120 DH

A Lovell & Covel Co. Candies bucket-shaped tin, by Lovel & Covel of Boston USA, showing Little Red Riding Hood.

1900-1910 2.75in (7cm) high

$500-700 TRA

A Hudson Scott & Son sentry box-shaped candy tin.

c1910 6.5in (16.5cm) high

$250-350 DH

A Dunn's Chocolate miniature clock tower tin.

c1910 2.25in (5.5cm) high

$250-350 DH

A Lyons Assorted Toffee book-shaped tin, titled "British Railway Engines" and featuring the "Royal Scot" LMS.

This was one of six railway 'books' produced by Lyons.

1929 5.5in (14cm) high

$300-350 DH

A 1930s French Midy 'Pastilles de Cocaine' cough pastille tin.

2.25in (5.5cm) wide

$30-50   **DH**

A 1920s 'Melrose Marshmallows' tin.

This is the smallest in a range of sizes, the largest having a glass top.

4.25in (11cm) wide

$70-100   **TRA**

A rare 1920s 'Handbag Cut Plug Tobacco' color lithographed purse-shaped tin, manufactured by Laurus & Bro. Co. of Richmond, VA.

7in (18cm) wide

$500-600   **TRA**

An early 20thC Salmon & Gluckstein's 'Dandy Fifth' Cigarettes tin.

5.75in (14.5cm) wide

$100-150   **TRA**

An early 20thC 'Ram's Horn' color lithographed tobacco tin.

6in (15.5cm) wide

$200-250   **TRA**

A late 19thC brown and gold printed 'Sextons Cocoa' tin, for John Sexton & Co., Wholesale Grocers, of Chicago, Illinois.

This is a very early tin, hence its comparatively high price.

9.5in (24cm) high

$180-220   **TRA**

An early 20thC 'Fairway Cocoa' tin, with paper label.

$120-180   **TRA**

A 1920s 'Banner Baking Powder' tin, by Geo. Hubbard & Co. of Pittsburgh PA.

4.5in (11.5cm) high

$80-120   **TRA**

A 1930s 'Sultana Peanut Butter' bucket-shaped tin, by The Quaker Maid Co. Inc.

4.25in (10.5cm) high

$100-150   **TRA**

A 1950s American Cadette Borated Baby Talcum Powder tin.

7in (18cm) high

$180-220   **DH**

An early 20thC Bickmore 'Morticians Powder' tin, 'Allay all Disagreeable Odors', by the Bickmore Company, Old Town, Maine.

6in (15cm) high

$80-120   **TRA**

Collectors' Notes

- Pocket tobacco tins primarily date from the late 19th to the early 20thC, when cardboard took over. They were made to fit into a gentleman's pocket easily, with rounded sides. There are different varieties, some flat and some with rounded backs as well as fronts. Tins with paper labels date from before the 1870s as after then lithography could be applied directly to the tin.

- Many thousands of brands were sold, making the variety of these attractively and brightly colored tins immense. They are currently highly collectible, with certain extremely rare examples fetching over $10,000 when offered for sale. Their small size makes them easy to store and trade.

- Look for superior artwork with elaborate designs using ten colors or more. Patriotic, character and animal subjects are often popular themes. Tax stamps will help with providing an accurate date.

- Condition is very important. Examples in mint condition will fetch higher prices as they were mass-produced and used. Dents, scratches or loss of the paper label will devalue a pocket tin.

A Big Ben smoking tobacco pocket tin.

4.25in (11cm) high

$100-150 TRA

A Briggs Pipe Mixture tobacco pocket tin, manufactured by P. Lorillard Company.

4.25in (11cm) high

$50-80 TRA

A City Club Crushed Cubes tobacco pocket tin.

4.5in (11.5cm) high

$100-150 TRA

An Epicure Shredded Plug Tobacco shaped pocket tin.

4.25in (10.5cm) high

$350-400 TRA

A Hi-Plane Smooth Cut Tobacco pocket tin.

4.25in (11cm) high

$150-200 TRA

An early 20thC Holiday Pipe Mixture 'Aromatic in the Pack, Aromatic in the Pipe' pocket tin.

4.25in (11cm) high

$60-90 TRA

An early 20thC Maryland Club Mixture tobacco pocket tin.

Pocket tins are currently enjoying a boom in popularity, possibly related to their small and convenient size and colorful designs that sum up the period.

4in (10cm) high

$600-900 TRA

A Stag Tobacco pocket tin.

6in (15.5cm) high

$100-150 TRA

A US Marine Flake Cut tobacco pocket tin.

4.25in (11cm) high

$600-900 TRA

A Q Boid Finest Quality Granulated Plug tobacco pocket tin, manufactured by Larus & Bro. Co. Richmond, VA.

4in (10cm)

$100-150 TRA

Collectors' Notes

- Trade cards are distinct from the late 20thC sport themed 'trading cards' and advertised the services or products of tradesmen and manufacturers.
- Although few cards can be found from the 18thC, most date from the late 19thC, following the development of color lithography in the 1870s which allowed large quantities of colored cards to be easily produced.
- They are small, were produced for many thousands of products or services and are easy to store and display. They are comparatively inexpensive, allowing an interesting collection to be built rapidly.
- Look for cards with intricate, colorful printing. Novelty shapes are desirable, as are examples featuring well-known brands, amusing characters or products.
- Colors should be bright and unfaded. Tears, scuffs and folds will devalue a card.

A color lithographed Thurber's No.41 coffee advertising trade card.

c1900   4.25in (11cm) wide

$10-15   TRA

A novelty palette-shaped advertising trade card, for John E. Kaughran & Co, of Broadway, New York.

1900-1910 10.5in (26.5cm) high

$70-100   TRA

A color lithographed palette-shaped Levering's Roasted Coffee advertising trade card.

c1900   5in (13cm) high

$50-80   TRA

A color lithographed Libby, McNeill & Libby's Cooked Corned Beef advertising trade card.

c1900   4.75in (12cm) high

$40-60   TRA

A color lithographed and embossed advertising trade card, for Heinz soups, pickles and sauces.

c1900   5in (12.5cm) high

$25-35   TRA

A color lithographed Colburn's Phila. Mustard advertising trade card, the reverse stating "King of condiments" and "Always Reliable for Table & Medicinal Uses".

c1900   3.25in (8.5cm) high

$20-30   TRA

A color lithographed advertising trade card, for Wells' of Jersey City, NJ corn remedy.

c1900   5in (13cm) high

$50-80   TRA

A color lithographed advertising trade card, for James Pyles' Pearline washing compound.

c1900   5in (13cm) high

$30-40   TRA

Collectors' Notes

■ Broadsides are advertisements printed on one side that conveyed messages such as the sale of merchandize, the launch of a new product or an event. They were used in the 19th and early 20thC, before mass media communication methods, and were an inexpensive way to reach a large audience, being pasted onto surfaces in prominent locations. They usually favor text over imagery and were truly ephemeral in nature, being intended for short-term immediate use and then discarded.

A 19thC perfume broadside with price list, for William K. David, Practical Perfumer, 39 South Second Street, Philadelphia

1850   9.75in (25cm) high

$100-150   **AAC**

A 19thC perfume broadside, for John G. O'Brien, Perfumery Manufacturer, 86 North Fifth Street, Philadelphia, printed on yellow stock, printed by Gartland Garren, Hineline, 38 Apple-Tree Alley.

1850   7.5in (19cm)

$50-80   **AAC**

A 19thC graphic perfume and ink broadside, for Harrison's Columbian Perfumery and Ink, South 7th Street, Philadelphia, with various vignettes of exterior and interior of premises.

24in (60cm) wide

$1,000-1,500   **AAC**

A color lithographic broadside, for the Lambertville Rubber Co. of Lambertville, NJ, by Ketterlinus of Philadelphia, featuring a rubber boot and shoes being attached by Brownies.

24in (35.5cm) high

$1,000-1,500   **AAC**

A color lithographic broadside for the Nichols & Shepherd Company, Battle Creek, Michigan Threshing Machinery, by Ketterinus of Philadelphia, with scene titled 'Dinner Time on Threshing Day'.

1890   25in (66cm)

$2,200-2,800   **AAC**

Other Advertising & Packaging

A 1920s color printed and embossed tin Orange Julep shop display sign.

13.5in (34cm) high

$120-180   **TRA**

A color lithographed Konjola shop display sheet, "A Splendid Medicine of Proven Merit".

c1920   27.75in (70.5cm) wide

$250-300   **TRA**

A circular color printed tin sign for Heart & Orange juice drink.

1935-1945   14.25in (36cm) wide

$400-600   **TRA**

A 1940s color printed 'Popsicle Pete's Frozen Goodies' paper store decal.

8in (20cm) wide

$50-80   **TRA**

A color lithographed and embossed tin sign, for Sunbeam Bread, manufactured by Bakers of American Cooperative.

c1961   29.75in (75.5cm) wide

$320-380   **TRA**

A 1940s 'Orange Crush' drink color-printed card standee.

11.5in (29cm) high

$120-180   **TRA**

An American color lithographed and embossed card standee, for Pear's Soap.

Pear's is a very desirable name amongst collectors and this standee has a combination of high quality printing and embossing.

1880-1890   12.5in (31.5cm) high

$220-280   TRA

A late 19thC color lithographed novelty card standee, for Hecker's Buckwheat baby food.

4.75in (12cm) high

$60-90   TRA

A color lithographed advertising calendar, for the Liberty Restaurant.

1929   23.25in (59cm) high

$350-400   TRA

A color lithographed hanging calendar, for Cowlands Department Store of New Philadelphia, Ohio.

1936   10.5in (26.5cm) high

$60-90   TRA

A Dingman's Soap bookmark.

c1900   7in (18cm) high

$15-25   TRA

A celluloid owl-shaped advertising bookmark, for Maltine constipation remedy.

On the reverse, the maker's recipe list recommended drinking the remedy mixed with creosote!

c1900   3.25in (8.5cm) high

$15-25   TRA

A Hires Rootbeer promotional folding checkerboard.

The reverse is a checkerboard for chess or draughts.

c1892   12in (30.5cm) wide

$400-600   TRA

A 1920s Fisk Tire advertising blotter.

6in (15.5cm) high

$50-80   TRA

A 1920s Lucky Strike advertising punchcard.

Punchcards were issued as a form of game, much like today's lottery scratchcards.

5.5in (14cm) high

$30-50   TRA

An American The Boye Needle Company, Chicago tinplate thimble shop display unit, for thread cutting thimbles.

c1910   9.5in (24cm) wide

$40-60   CBe

A 1950s cast plastic or resin countertop display, for Nalcedon-CX cough remedy.

5in (13cm) high

$80-120   TRA

A Kasco Feeds brass hanging scale, with black painted highlights, back is rusted.

12in (30.5cm) long

$20-30   TWC

Collectors' Notes

■ 'Mr Peanut' was adopted as a trademark for Planters Peanuts in 1916 and has been used in its national advertising campaigns ever since. Planters was founded by Polish immigrant Amedeo Obici in 1908. He revolutionized the peanut industry, realizing that strong, colorful branding encouraged customer loyalty.

■ Jars are plentiful and make good display pieces. Pieces produced before the 1970s are highly desirable amongst collectors. Pieces made after the 1970s are usually more affordable. Rarities include memorabilia associated with Planters' short-lived Canadian factory and rare pieces such as a papier-mâché 'Mr Peanut' window display figure, holding a cane that tapped the window.

A metal 'Mr Peanut' advertising nut spoon.
5.25in (13.5cm) high
$15-25   **AIS**

A gold-plated metal 'Mr Peanut' advertising nut spoon.
5in (13cm) high
$20-30   **CEC**

A metal 'Mr Peanut' advertising knife.
7in (17.5cm) high
$15-25   **AIS**

A printed glass Planters 'Mr Peanut' advertising nut jar, lacking lid.
7.5in (19cm) high
$20-25   **AIS**

A silver-colored plastic 'Mr Peanut' advertising salt shaker.

This is also available in a gold-colored finish, which has the same value.
3.25in (8cm) high
$25-30   **CEC**

A fabric 'Mr Peanut' advertising soft toy.
20.5in (52cm) high
$20-30   **AIS**

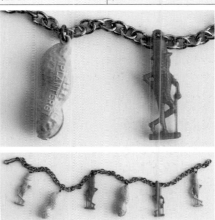

A plush 'Mr Peanut' advertising soft toy.
18in (45.5cm) high
$20-30   **CEC**

A 1960s Japanese ceramic 'Mr Peanut' advertising ashtray.

Similarly shaped metal ashtrays are not authentic.
4in (10cm) high
$50-80   **CW**

A plastic and metal 'Mr Peanut' novelty bracelet.
5in (13cm) long
$40-60   **BB**

A plastic 'Mr Peanut' advertising ballpoint pen.
5.25in (13.5cm) high
$20-30   **CEC**

FIND OUT MORE...

Planters Peanut Collectibles, by Jan Lindenberger and Joyce Spontak, Schiffer Publishing, 1997.

Collectors' Notes

- The Zeppelin was a large propelled, hydrogen filled rigid framed balloon developed by the German Graf von Zeppelin. The first Zeppelin flew in 1900. From then, they increased in popularity, making flights to the Arctic, transatlantic passenger flights to the US and Brazil, as well as famously being used in the First World War.
- The tragic destruction of the 'LZ129 Hindenburg' on May 6, 1937 and the onset of war ended public interest in Zeppelins and airships until the late 20thC. Look for artefacts relating to transatlantic voyages, or to the Hindenburg itself, particularly advertising and relics.
- Other countries including the US and Britain used similar airships.
- Ballooning memorabilia is scarce and desirable. During the 18th and 19thC, when it was pioneered, it was a wealthy man's hobby and ascensions drew large crowds.
- A large number of souvenirs were made and sold to commemorate flights. Today these are rare, with fans, objects of vertu and ceramics depicting balloons being especially sought after. Look for pieces that can be tied into particular flights by known aeronauts. Pieces relating to flights towards the end of the 19th and into the 20thC are still affordable.

A European silver box commemorating the Hindenburg's first flight to North America on June 14, 1936, with applied enameled plaque and Swastika and inscription reading "Zur Erinnerung an die erste Fahrt des Luftschiffes nach Nordamerika am 14.06.36", also stamped "EHW 850".

4.75in (12cm) wide

$1,200-1,800   **COB**

A piece of outer fabric from the Graf Zepplin, mounted on a descriptive card reading "Certified genuine piece of aluminized outer fabric of the Graf Zeppelin from a sheet presented to Clara Adams, the only woman passenger on the 1st flight to America, given to her by Dr. Hugo Eckener in October 1928".

Fabric 0.5in wide (1.5cm) wide

$150-200   **AGI**

An aluminium girder recovered from the L-33 Zepplin.

This airship was damaged by anti-aircraft shelling and forced to land in Little Wigborough, Essex on September 24, 1916.

11in (28cm) long

$100-150   **AGI**

A Burgoyne's Australian Wines menu, with an image of an airship.

A Graf Zeppelin metal match book cover.

c1905   *2.25in (5.5cm) wide*

$150-200   **DH**

A German sweet bag, with an image of an airship.

c1905   *9.25in (23.5cm) high*

$12-18   **DH**

A Eugen Riemer airship sweet tin.

c1905   *2.75in (7cm) wide*

$350-400   **DH**

c1905   *7.75in (19.5cm) high*

$20-30   **DH**

A 'Graf Zeppelin's Weltreise' board game, by Klee.

c1928   *12in (30.5cm) wide*

$300-400   **DH**

An American Zeppelin game.

William Randolph Hearst promoted the first global flight of the Graf Zeppelin to raise public awareness and Lakehurst, New Jersey was the offical starting point.

1929   *3.5in (9cm) wide*

$50-80   **DH**

An airship air rifle pellet tin.

c1920s   *3in (7.5cm) diam*

$30-40   **DH**

A set of 12 photographs of the Graf Zeppelin.

c1928   3.5in (9cm) wide

$30-50   **DH**

A 1933 commemorative Zeppelin calendar, the cover and each page showing a photograph of the Graf Zeppelin in flight or landing at its destinations, retailed by Otto Kummer of Wien.

8.75in (22.5cm) high

$600-900   **ET**

An early 19thC Sunderland pink lusterware jug, one side printed with the ascent of the Aerial Balloon, the other with a South East view of the iron bridge over the Wear, marks including Dixon & Co. and Hylton Pottery, damaged.

19thC ceramics showing balloons are rare and highly desirable to collectors.

8.75in (22cm) high

$1,200-1,800   **WW**

A cast bronze medallion with balloon motifs and wording reading "Souvenir de mon ascension dans le grand ballon captif a vapeur de Mr Henry Giffard".

1878   2in (5cm) diam

$120-180   **COB**

Celiere, Paul, "The Startling Exploits of Dr. Quies", first American printing, translated from the French, cover has some wear with warping at the very bottom, insides show traces of water soak.

This adventure story includes ballooning.

1887

$700-1,000   **AGI**

A rare A. Nichols, Jr. ballooning flyer, discussing the use of a balloon as an advertising medium, excellent condition.

9in (23cm) high

$600-900   **AGI**

A rare American flier for Schenevus Fair advertising "The Big Air Ship", for Thursday, Friday, Saturday, Sept. 16, 17 & 18 97, printed by Brown's, Schenevus, New York.

1897

$100-150   **CHAA**

A collection of relics from the National Geographic stratospheric balloon flight of July 1934, including a piece of rope, insulation from the batteries, lead sheathing from the radio cables and ballast, together with the two National Geographic magazines detailing the planned flight and the failure of the balloon.

1934

$700-1,000   **CHAA**

A Breitling Orbiter 2 first day cover, autographed by the pilots Bertrand Piccard, Wim Verstraeten and engineer Andy Elson with the launch, landing distance and duration noted in ink.

This was the second attempt by the Breitling team at going non-stop, around the world in a balloon. Although they set two new time records, it was the Breitling Orbiter 3 which completed the journey in March 1999.

1998

$80-120   **AGI**

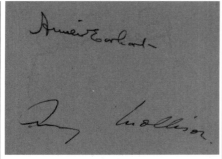

Amelia Earhart and Amy Johnson, an album page signed in blue ink, with Johnson signing her married name of "Amy Mollison", mounted, framed and glazed.

$3,200-3,800 FA

Amy Johnson, an album page signed in black ink by Johnson, signing her married name "Amy Mollison".

Amy Johnson was a British aviator who flew solo from England to Australia in 1930, to Japan in 1931 and Cape Town in 1932, setting new records in each case.

$350-400 FA

Glenn Curtiss, signed on white card and mounted together with photo of him in his plane.

One of the first aviators, Curtiss (1878- 1930) ran a successful bicycle and motorcycle business from his teens and became involved in aviation in 1904. In 1907 he became director of experiments at the Aerial Experiment Association formed by Dr. Alexander Graham Bell. He won a large number of trophies and world records and his aviation company was hugely successful, supplying the US Army during WWI.

21in (53.5cm) high

$30-40 AGI

Chuck Yeager, signed lithograph. As a test pilot, Yeager, (b 1923) was the first man to fly faster than the speed of sound on October 14, 1947. In 1956 he took command of the Air Force Aerospace Research Pilots School to train pilots for the US space program.

10in (25.5cm) wide

$400-600 AGI

A cast metal bust of Charles Lindbergh, marked with illegible artist's name.

6in (15cm) high

$20-30 AGI

A cast bronze bust of Charles Lindbergh, with plaque reading "La Ville de Paris a Charles Lindbergh en commemoration de la Première Taversee de L'Atlantique en Avion".

1927

$20-30 AGI

A copy of "Aviation Stories and Mechanics" July 1927, Vol. 1, No. 1, featuring Lindbergh's Trans-Atlantic flight, excellent overall condition.

$20-30 AGI

An aluminium hood ornament in the form of 'The Spirit of St Louis', wtih attached radiator bracket.

The Spirit of St Louis was the name of the plane that took Lindbergh on the first trans-Atlantic flight in 1927.

c1927   11in (28cm) long

$30-50 AGI

A brass petrol table lighter, in the form of a Spitfire.

1940-2   5.5in (14cm) high

$70-100 COB

A cast bronze plaque, with wording reading "Navigation Aerienne" and low relief design showing an airship and an aeroplane on one side and industrial themes on the other and inscription reading "'Ville de Meudon Exposition du Travail", signed "A. Morlon".

Pierre Andre Morlon (1878-1951) was well known for his cast designs for coins and medals. This plaque was designed and made in 1920 but used with this inscription in 1936.

3.25in (8.5cm) wide

$100-150 COB

A German WWII V-2 rocket head igniter, consisting of a metal rod set into a threaded wooden base with a nail-like needle projecting from the base.

20in (51cm) long

$350-400 AGI

Collectors' Notes

- The aim of duck decoys is to attract live ducks to land near them, thinking the area is safe. They are then within shooting range of hunters. 'Rigs' were often set up with ducks in different positions adding to the illusion of safety.
- They originated in America before the arrival of settlers, where Native Americans would bind twigs and reeds together to make decoys. They were produced on a larger scale from the 1800s until the 1920s when commercial bird hunting was outlawed.
- Even though the industry declined severely, it still carried on, with decoys being of interest to collectors of folk art or as decoration.
- Most decoys found today date from the late 19thC onward. Earlier examples rarely survive as the wood was damaged by the water.

- Collectors often collect by region, each of which will have its own styles and body forms. For example, New Jersey and Delaware birds are nearly all hollow bodied, whereas Maryland birds are usually solid.
- Form, original paint and condition help decide value. Collectors particularly prize decoys by noted makers such as Elmer Crowell, Obediah Verity and William Bowman. When found, these fetch high prices amongst an ever-growing collecting community.
- The name on the base is not necessarily the maker and could be the owner. A lost duck could then be returned to him if it was found.
- They are also of interest to folk art collectors who appreciate their naïve charm. Today, there are also a number of artists producing contemporary birds for collectors.

A black duck, by an unknown maker around the Delaware river area, in excellent condition with original paint and hollow construction with Blair School form and tack eyes.

c1880-1890   15.25in (39cm) long

$1,200-1,800   **BCAC**

A black duck, by an unknown maker of the Tuiytown area of the Delaware river, with original paint and very hollow construction.

With stamp showing this decoy is from the collection of William Mackey.

c1880-1890   16.5in (42cm) long

$850-950   **BCAC**

A pair of late 19thC Surf Scoter shadow decoys, all original and found in Hollowell, MA.

This pair is from the folk art collection of Herbert Hemphill.

Each 17.75in (45cm) long

$200-300   **BCAC**

An early black duck, by John Blair, Philadelphia, PA, with worn original paint, hollow construction and glass eyes.

c1890-1900   18in (46cm) long

$1,500-2,500   **BCAC**

A late 19thC primitive white wing Scoter, from the New England Coast, all original.

Provenance: From the collection of Herbert Hemphill.

12.25in (31cm) long

$100-150   **BCAC**

A drake canvas back, by an unknown maker of the Susquehana Flats, Havre de Grace, MD, with early body (c1880-1890) and later head (c1910) by William Heverin, with old gunning paint and wear.

c1900   15in (38cm) long

$300-350   **BCAC**

A drake canvas back, by an unknown maker of the Susquehana Flats, Havre de Grace, MD, with an early body (c1880-1890) and later head (c1910) by William Heverin, with early gunning paint and wear.

c1900   13.75in (35cm) long

$300-350   **BCAC**

A Drake American Merganser, by an unknown maker, with hollow construction.

Note the unusual construction that may be scrap wood laminated' together.

c1910   17.75in (45cm) long

$1,000-1,500   **BCAC**

A black duck by William Chrysler of Belleville, Ontario, with original scratch paint and solid construction.

c1920   17.25in (44cm) long

$2,000-2,500   **TGC**

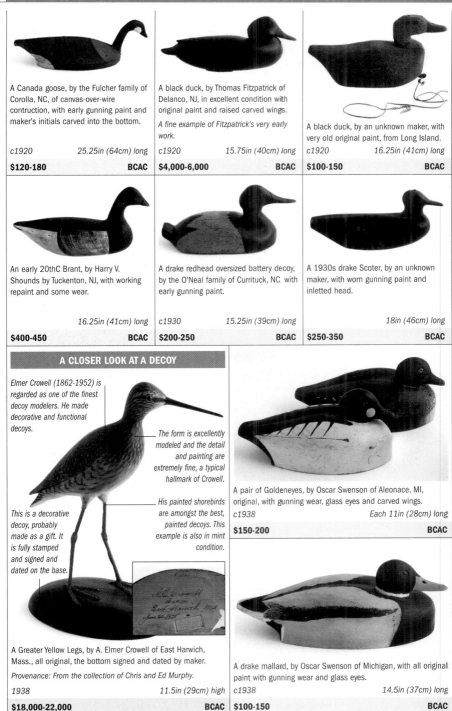

A Canada goose, by the Fulcher family of Corolla, NC, of canvas-over-wire contruction, with early gunning paint and maker's initials carved into the bottom.

c1920   25.25in (64cm) long

$120-180   **BCAC**

A black duck, by Thomas Fitzpatrick of Delanco, NJ, in excellent condition with original paint and raised carved wings.

A fine example of Fitzpatrick's very early work.

c1920   15.75in (40cm) long

$4,000-6,000   **BCAC**

A black duck, by an unknown maker, with very old original paint, from Long Island.

c1920   16.25in (41cm) long

$100-150   **BCAC**

An early 20thC Brant, by Harry V. Shounds by Tuckenton, NJ, with working repaint and some wear.

16.25in (41cm) long

$400-450   **BCAC**

A drake redhead oversized battery decoy, by the O'Neal family of Currituck, NC with early gunning paint.

c1930   15.25in (39cm) long

$200-250   **BCAC**

A 1930s drake Scoter, by an unknown maker, with worn gunning paint and inletted head.

18in (46cm) long

$250-350   **BCAC**

A CLOSER LOOK AT A DECOY

Elmer Crowell (1862-1952) is regarded as one of the finest decoy modelers. He made decorative and functional decoys.

The form is excellently modeled and the detail and painting are extremely fine, a typical hallmark of Crowell.

His painted shorebirds are amongst the best, painted decoys. This example is also in mint condition.

This is a decorative decoy, probably made as a gift. It is fully stamped and signed and dated on the base.

A Greater Yellow Legs, by A. Elmer Crowell of East Harwich, Mass., all original, the bottom signed and dated by maker.

Provenance: From the collection of Chris and Ed Murphy.

1938   11.5in (29cm) high

$18,000-22,000   **BCAC**

A pair of Goldeneyes, by Oscar Swenson of Aleonace, MI, original, with gunning wear, glass eyes and carved wings.

c1938   Each 11in (28cm) long

$150-200   **BCAC**

A drake mallard, by Oscar Swenson of Michigan, with all original paint with gunning wear and glass eyes.

c1938   14.5in (37cm) long

$100-150   **BCAC**

A drake redhead, by Charles 'Couper' Burkley, of Bordontown, NJ, excellent condition with original paint, hollow construction and applied raised wings.
c1940   15.25in (39cm) long

$1,500-2,000   BCAC

An oversized black duck, by William Hammarstrom of Burnaget, NJ, with original paint and hollow construction.

c1940   20in (51cm) long

$150-200   BCAC

A 194Cs black duck, by an unknown maker with a cork body, wooden bottom board and head, with original paint and glass eyes.
                    19in (48cm) long

$100-150   BCAC

A 1940s blue winged teal, by Caleb Ridgway Marter of Burlington, NJ, with original paint, hollow construction and glass eyes.
                                12.25in (31cm) long

$2,000-2,500   BCAC

A drake mallard, by an unknown maker, found in New York, with worn original paint, tack eyes and folky appearance, together with a weight and line.
                    15.25in (39cm) long

$100-150   BCAC

A white winged Scoter, by an unknown maker, hollow construction with old gunning paint.
                    17.25in (44cm) long

$100-200   BCAC

A pair of canvas backs by R. Madison Mitchell of Havre de Grace, MD, with worn original paint and hand-cast weights.
c1940   Each 15.75in (40cm) long

$700-1,000   BCAC

A Greenwing Teal hen, by Paul Gibson of Havre de Grace, MD, with original paint and gunning wear.
c1940   12.5in (32cm) long

$250-350   BCAC

A 1940s drake redhead, by an unknown maker in New Jersey, with old gunning paint and hollow construction.
                    13.75in (35cm) long

$100-150   BCAC

A Loon decoy, by an unknown maker, solid construction and old gunning paint.
1940   12.5in (32cm) long

$50-70   BCAC

A 1940s black duck, by an unknown maker of New York state, with worn original paint, solid construction.
                    16.25in (41cm) long

$100-150   BCAC

A 1950s signed drake pintail, by Eldridge Tyler of Crisfield, MD, with original paint and solid construction.

The unusual colors and shapes are typical of this maker and are very folk arty.

15.75in (40cm) long

$150-200 | **BCAC**

A 1950s miniature mallard, by Eldridge Tyler of Crisfield, MD, with original paint and solid construction.

$150-250 | **BCAC**

A 1950s brightly painted miniature widgeon, by Eldridge Tyler of Crisfield, MD, with original paint and solid construction.

These jaunty ducks are currently still inexpensive.

6.25in (16cm) long

$60-90 | **BCAC**

A white swan, Delaware River style, of hollow construction with raised wings, all original.

Swans were used as confidence decoys, attracting ducks who thought the area was safe as a swan was there.

$800-1,200 | **BCAC**

A black swan decoy, by an unknown maker, from the Delaware river with hollow construction and unusual head position and color.

32in (81cm) long

$800-1,200 | **BCAC**

A Canada goose, by Bid Furnase of Camden, NJ, with worn original paint and hollow construction.

This is the only known goose decoy by this maker.

c1941 | 24in (61cm) long

$1,500-2,500 | **BCAC**

A 1960s Canada goose, by John Egeli of New Jersey, with hollow construction, Delaware river style with raised wings, original paint, some gunning wear and glass eyes.

Talented John Egeli's career was cut short by his untimely death.

25.5in (65cm) long

$800-1,200 | **BCAC**

A contemporary curlew decoy, by Ken Kirby of South Carolina, in excellent original condition.

13in (33cm) long

$100-160 | **BCAC**

A contemporary robin, by Virginia folk artist and decoy carver Frank Finney, with original paint and glass eyes.

5.5in (17cm) long

$200-250 | **BCAC**

A 20thC American carved and painted figure of a rotund bellhop, inscription on underside of base "Found in Sherman Oaks, Ca, 1987, made in the 1920s".

10in (25.5cm) high

$280-320   **FRE**

A mid-20thC carved and painted folk art figure of a businessman, from Nova Scotia, possibly Collins Eisenhauer.

10in (25.5cm) high

$600-900   **WAD**

A 20thC American carved and painted figure of a conductor.

10.5in (27cm) high

$350-450   **FRE**

An American carved and painted figure of an archer, inscribed on underside of base, "Found in Portland, Oregon, carved from a double branch limb 1947", with leather belt, quiver and quiver strap.

12.5in (32cm) high

$350-400   **FRE**

A rare 19thC Mark Twain marionette with carved wood head and limbs, cloth body, clothed in period dress with strings and armature, in very good original condition, together with a painted child's rocker.

Samuel Langhorne Clemens (1835-1910) used the pen-name 'Mark Twain' to write a number of classic American novels including 'The Adventures of Tom Sawyer' and 'The Adventures of Huckleberry Finn'. Immensely successful as both a novelist and a humorist, he is considered a national icon. Depictions of him such as this are rare and have immense popular appeal, particularly if contemporary.

35in (89cm) high

$2,200-2,800   **TA**

An American chalkware pigeon, some damage.

11.5in (29cm) high

$30-40   **Daw**

An American wax figure of a cat, with a glass come on wood stand, dome has crack.

6in (15cm) high

$500-700   **Daw**

A carved and painted wood bird.

c1930-40   *3.5in (9cm) high*

$60-90   **BCAC**

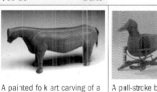

A painted folk art carving of a steer.

15.5in (39cm) long

$120-180   **WAD**

A pull-stroke bell toy, with felt dove and wire-spoke wheels.

$350-400   **TA**

A
B
C
D
E
F
G
H
I
J
K
L
M
N
O
P
Q
R
S
T
U
V
W
XYZ

An American folk art wood and metal whirligig, in the shape of a cardinal bird with bright painted body.

20in (51cm)

$180-220   **TA**

A folk art sheet metal figure of a horse, mounted on a later pole stand.

32in (81cm) high

$220-280   **WAD**

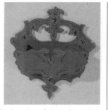

An American folk art letter box, with cut-out back, painted ocher with green details.

11in (28cm)

$180-220   **TA**

An American painted locking box, with iron strap hardware.

$120-180   **TA**

An American Folk Art candle box, with two holders, cut-out back, painted red with and white details.

The extra detailing, both in terms of the painting and carving, make this a more valuable candle box.

12in (30.5cm) wide

$400-450   **TA**

A wood and glass bower lantern.

c1810   *9.5in (24cm) high*

$250-300   **BCAC**

A hooked rug.

$400-600   **BCAC**

An early 20thC folk art circular hooked rug.

35.5in (90cm) diam

$200-250   **WAD**

A pieced, appliqued and embroidered sunbonnet babies quilt, Pennsylvania, solid and printed cotton pieces arranged in forty figures of "Sunbonnet Sue", each with a different embroidered object, animal or toy.

This quilt was made from a kit, the publication of Bertha L. Corbett's 'Sunbonnet Babies' in 1900 established the figure of the little girl with the big bonnet known as "Sunbonnet Sue". The character became extremely popular with printed quilt patterns showing the figure being available by mail order throughout the country by the 1920s.

c1925   *79in (200cm) long*

$800-1,200   **FRE**

An American leaded stained glass window, featuring an American flag and another, fanciful flag crossed, the frame not original.

44in (112cm) high

$850-950   **CHAA**

Collectors' Notes

- Black dolls were made in the Southern States of America from the 1920s until the 1950s as souvenirs for visitors and tourists. Now many consider that they form an important part of American social history and have become desirable amongst collectors.

- They were made from local produce, such as cotton, apples and pecan nuts, as well as fabric. Fruit and nuts were dried and used as heads, with carved or painted faces.

- Look for different types of basic material being used as bodies, for example, glass bottles, card tubes and stuffed fabric shapes. The style of stands and shoes can often help identify specific manufacturers.

- As prices have risen over the past five years, fakes have appeared. Look at the fabric, which should show signs of age, such as fading, and stress at the stitching. If in doubt, compare a suspicious example to a genuine doll.

A 1920s American black cotton doll, with a pecan nut face.

The fabric used here is older than the one on the right.

10.75in (27cm) high

$320-380　　**BCAC**

A 1930s American black cotton doll, with black-painted pecan nut face.

Note that the feet are similar here to the 1920s black doll (left), showing that they were by the same manufacturer.

10.25in (26cm) high

$300-350　　**BCAC**

A 1930s painted walnut-head black doll, of a fishing boy.

8.5in (22cm) high

$200-250　　**BCAC**

A 1930s painted walnut-headed black doll, in a black felt and fabric suit.

11.5in (29cm) high

$200-300　　**BCAC**

A CLOSER LOOK AT A BLACK SOUVENIR DOLL

The preacher is a popular and specific character subject, rather than being a generic lady or man.

The detailing is excellent, for example the prayer book is made from cut newspaper, so has pages containing words.

There is a hole in his shoe through which his sock protrudes, showing great thought has been given to the detailing.

The stand helps to identify a particular manufacturer.

A 1930s stuffed-cloth black doll, of a preacher with a prayer book, on a mock asphalt stand.

8.5in (22cm) high

$300-500　　**BCAC**

A 1930s dried apple-headed black doll, with a pink petticoat and paper-covered card tube body.

9.5in (24cm) high

A 1930s apple-faced black matron doll, with stuffed rag body.

10.25in (26cm) high

$300-350　　**BCAC**

A 1930s American black doll, with bottle body and black dried apple head.

9.5in (24cm) high

$320-380　　**BCAC**

$220-280　　**BCAC**

A 1930s black doll table bell.

4in (10cm) high

$70-100 BCAC

A 1920s black doll, with paper-covered card tube body.

9.75in (25cm) high

$200-300 BCAC

A 1930s American black doll, with painted nut head, head bundle and purse.

10.25in (26cm) high

$280-320 BCAC

A dried fruit-faced black cloth doll, in the form of a seated granny.

The nose on this example is carved.

9.75in (25cm) high

$100-150 BCAC

A 1930s apple head black doll, of a granny in painted wooden rocker, with pipe-cleaner limbs.

7.5in (19cm) high

$220-280 BCAC

A 1940s stuffed stockinette black doll, with blue gingham dress.

7.5in (19cm) high

$100-150 BCAC

A 1930s stuffed pin cushion black doll, with a fabric head.

4.25in (11cm) high

$100-150 BCAC

A 1930s American black rag doll, with a painted face.

16.5in (42cm) high

$500-700 BCAC

A 1930s 'Souvenir Cotton Novelty' of a carved and painted wooden black boy, by A. Hirchwitz MFR. of New Orleans, LA, eating a slice of watermelon and seated on a cotton bale with a cotton ball behind him, in original box.

Box 5.5in (14cm) high

$100-150 BCAC

A 1930s painted, cast iron souvenir soap dish.

5in (13cm) high

$220-280 BCAC

Two black souvenir painted chalk wall plaques.

c1949 Each 5in (13cm) high

$60-90 BCAC

A Native American sterling, turquoise, coral and bear claw bolo, with matching ring, clear blue and green turquoise with nice matrix.

$50-70 TA

A 1930s Native American sterling bolo, with turquoise and coral lizard, possibly Navajo Moreno turquoise,

$120-180 TA

A Native American sterling bolo, with massive turquoise eagle figure, possibly Stormy Mountain.

$80-120 TA

A Native American sterling and turquoise bolo, with large turquoise terminals, smokey matrix, probably New Mexico made.

$100-150 TA

A Navajo bracelet, with three turquoise stones set in beaded and stamped "Silver".

$350-400 TA

A Navajo bracelet, with two stones carved as masks set into silver wire mount on cuff decorated with tourist motif.

$50-70 TA

A 1930s Native American sterling bolo, with turquoise and coral lizard, possibly Navajo Moreno turquoise.

$120-180 TA

A Navajo sterling Squash Blossom necklace, with red coral and turquoise, with similar ring.

$150-200 TA

A Native American Squash Blossom necklace, matching earrings and ring, with bezel-mounted coral and turquoise, silver blossoms and stamped leaves, with large horse-shoe shaped pendant on silver beaded double strand, ring signed "M. Yazzie".

$350-450 TA

A Navajo pendant, with turquoise in a tear-drop shape, signed and stamped "Sterling".

$180-220 TA

A massive Navajo sterling belt buckle, with turquoise, coral and bear claw, and similar ring.

$70-100 TA

A Navajo bracelet, with large turquoise, set in freeform silver mount, signed.

$180-220 TA

A pair of Southern Plains beaded hide moccasins, Arapaho, resoled.

c1890   10in (25.5cm) long

$350-400   **FRE**

A pair of late 19thC Northeast Woodlands beaded child's moccasins, Iroquois, decorated with cloth and trade beads, wear to fabric.

4.5in 11.5cm) long

$300-350   **FRE**

A 20thC Southern Plains beaded and fringed hide pipebag, Arapaho, yellow pigmented hide body, with lazy stitch glass beading, slat-style tin suspensions on fringe.

14in (35.5cm)

$500-550   **FRE**

A Southern Plains beaded hide belt pouch, 'Strike-a-light' bag, tin-cone danglers suspended along flap and bottom.

4.5in (11.5cm)

$500-600   **FRE**

Two 20thC Plains-style beaded hide fetishes, the first in the form of a horse, trimmed in horse hair, the second in the form of a turtle with quilled decoration.

5in (13cm) long

$500-550   **FRE**

A Plains beaded hide umbilical fetish, in the form of a turtle decorated with multi-colored glass seed beads and bead and tine cone suspensions.

c1900   5in (13cm) long

$200-250   **FRE**

A Navajo woven wool rug, with red and brown stepped decoration on a beiged ground, on wall-mount stretcher.

50in (127cm) long 30in (76cm) wide

$200-300   **TA**

A wax native American figure, from the Osceola tribe of Florida, dressed in beaded and animal hide attire, standing on rock holding a long gun, loss to beading/jewelry, loss of fingers, detached arm, cracks to the wax rock base, housed in plexiglass display case.

16in (40.5cm) high

$450-550   **AAC**

A An American Tilden-Hendricks 'clean sweep' pin, from the disputed election of 1876, a hollow shell badge in the form of a broomstick embossed with "Tilden & Hendricks" and "Reform", coppered brass, original pin intact.

Following the financial crisis of 1873, and the chaos that ensued, 'hard money' supporter Samuel J. Tilden became the leading Presidential nominee for the Democratic party. However, to balance his hard line, fellow Democrat Thomas Hendricks, who supported 'soft money' and agrarian reform, was nominated by the party as Vice-President. In the election, Republican candidate Rutherford B. Hayes, who controlled every Midwestern state except Hendrick's Indiana appeared to have lost, with both parties claiming control of three Southern states. Deadlock ensued over counting votes and the issue was resolved by a special electoral commission. This was won by the Republicans 8-7 and Hayes was voted in as President.

1876　　　　　　　　4in (1.5cm) long

$700-1,000　　　　　　　　**CHAA**

A 'Roosevelt The American' campaign badge.

c1904　　　*0.75in (2cm) wide*

$60-90　　　　　　　**HGS**

An oval Roosevelt campaign pin.

c1904　　　*1.25in (3cm) high*

$80-120　　　　　　　**HGS**

A rare 'Roosevelt Spectacle Pin', a campaign novelty with two celluloid covered photographs.

Retailing at 10 cents, this pin was seen advertised in 'Playthings' magazine, August 1904, the form being modeled after Roosevelt's 'trademark' pince-nez type spectacles.

c1904　　　*2in (5cm) high*

$500-600　　　　　　　**HGS**

A leather and metal Teddy Roosevelt watch fob.

c1904　　*5in (12cm) high*

$200-250　　　　　　　**HGS**

A campaign badge for Theodore Roosevelt, reading "Employment for Labor A Full Dinner Bucket Prosperity Sound Money - Good Market", made by The Whitehead & Hoag Company, Newark, NJ.

c1904　　*1.25in (3cm) wide*

$120-180　　　　　　　**HGS**

A Republican campaign pin, for November 4, 1941.

1941

$10-15　　　　　　　**AnaA**

A Pennsylvania Council of Republican Women ribbon.

3.5in (9cm) long

$8-12　　　　　　　**AnaA**

A boutonnière photographic McKinley/Roosevelt button, with fabric rim and center featuring silver gelatin photograph.

0.75in (2cm) diam

$200-250　　　　　　　**AAC**

An Alf Landon campaign lapel button.

Alf Landon ran against Roosevelt in 1936.

1936　　*0.5in (1.5cm) wide*

$20-25　　　　　　　**AnaA**

A Staffordshire ceramic commemorative plate for Theodore Roosevelt, by Rowland & Marsellus & Co.

9.75in (25cm) wide

$100-150 BCAC

A color lithographed commemorative plaque, showing the British and American flag.

8.75in (22.5cm) wide

$80-120 BCAC

A WWI calendar plate, by D.E. McNichol of East Liverpool.

c1917 *9in (23cm) wide*

$100-150 BCAC

A rare American opalescent blue glass candy dish, with a central paper portrait of McKinley affixed to the interior of the pedestal, minor damage to the portrait.

8in (20.5cm) wide

$150-200 CHAA

An American chromolithographed tin tray, promoting the candidacy of Taft and Sherman in 1908, with pictures of Lincoln, Hayes, Arthur, Harrison, Roosevelt, McKinley, Blaine, Garfield, Grant and Freemont in the center and the "Grand Old Party 1856-1908 Standard Bearers" around the border, slight wear to the edge, the color still strong.

9.5in (24cm) diam

$180-220 CHAA

An American solid 'back-to-back' ferrotype of Douglas and Johnson, by DeWitt, No.1860-38, minor vertige on metal frame, small loss to portrait of Herschel Vespasian Johnson.

1in (2.5cm) diam

$120-180 CHAA

A carte-de-visite of General Byron Root Pierce (1829-1924) 3rd Michigan Infantry, WIA Gettysburg, unknown photographer.

$350-400 AAC

An outdoor carte-de-visite of General Sherman mounted on a horse, image incorrectly identified on front at bottom as General Meade, no photographer backmark.

$30-50 AAC

A rare American flashlight bulb, a glass-dome covered portrait of Teddy Roosevelt on a silvered base with turn-screw base, probably designed for a flashlight cane, conductivity ring missing, one small dimple in the glass.

1in (2.5cm) wide

$220-280 CHAA

An early 19thC political cartoon titled 'Panama Canal', signed "Bert Cobb", showing two children representing Honduras and Nicaragua fighting over the Panama Canal with Uncle Sam approaching in the background to stop the fight, exhibits edge staining and overall toning.

19in (48cm)

$120-180 AAC

A political cartoon titled 'Lodge', signed "Norman", showing Senator Lodge and problems arising from a gold basis platform, exhibits rubs and toning

$100-150   **AAC**

An early 19thC political cartoon titled 'Rai roads', signed "Bert Cobb", depicting Edward Henry Harriman, railroad magnate standing in front of J.P. Morgan and others, staining at lower right side with some rubs and toning.

$100-150   **AAC**

A Penmanship print featuring George Washington, designed by Benjamin O. Tyler and engraved by P. Maverick, image features penmanship text with angels and eagles and central vignette of George Washington, exhibits surface toning.

22in (55cm)

$220-280   **AAC**

An American small folio Currier lithograph, commemorating the nomination of James K. Polk for president, framed.

1845

$120-180   **CHAA**

An American pass to the 1880 Democratic Convention in Cincinnati, "National Democratic Convention Cincinnati June 22 1880" minor damage to lower right corner.

4.25in (11cm) wide

$700-1,000   **CHAA**

A 'Facts About The Candicate' campaign book for Theodore Roosevelt, by Byron Andrews, given out by the New York Tribune, giving facts about Roosevelt's life and political career.

1904   *2.25in (5.5cm) high*

$40-60   **HGS**

A pair of Abraham Lincoln commemorative patinated bronze bookends, "The Emancipator", manufactured by the Pompeian Bronze Co.

5.5in (14cm) high

$60-90   **Daw**

A large American cast iron commemorative plaque, with gilding, featuring a bust of U.S. Grant and inscribed "1822 / U.S. Grant / 1885" below the portrait, much of the original gilding remains.

1885   *19in (48.5cm) diam*

$400-600   **CHAA**

An Abraham Lincoln commemorative porcelain tile, by Sherwin & Cotton, framed, losses.

9in (23cm) high

$220-280   **Daw**

A Centennial Presidential Game, by McLoughlin Bros., New York, with a 54 card deck, each with a different American president.

c1876

$1,200-1,800   **TK**

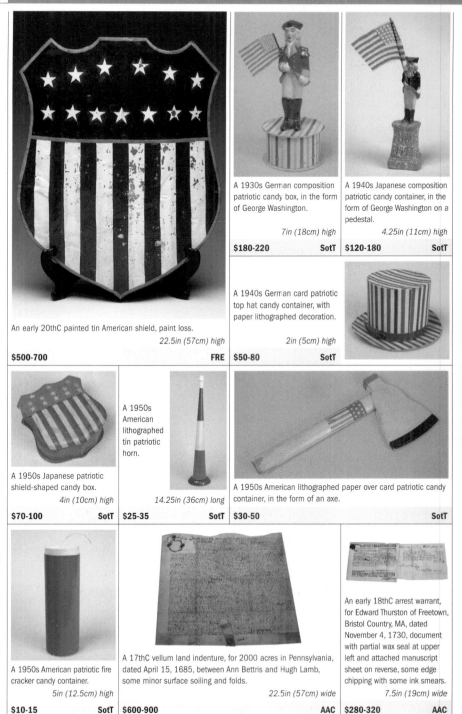

An early 20thC painted tin American shield, paint loss.

22.5in (57cm) high

$500-700 FRE

A 1930s German composition patriotic candy box, in the form of George Washington.

7in (18cm) high

$180-220 SotT

A 1940s Japanese composition patriotic candy container, in the form of George Washington on a pedestal.

4.25in (11cm) high

$120-180 SotT

A 1940s German card patriotic top hat candy container, with paper lithographed decoration.

2in (5cm) high

$50-80 SotT

A 1950s Japanese patriotic shield-shaped candy box.

4in (10cm) high

$70-100 SotT

A 1950s American lithographed tin patriotic horn.

14.25in (36cm) long

$25-35 SotT

A 1950s American lithographed paper over card patriotic candy container, in the form of an axe.

$30-50 SotT

A 1950s American patriotic fire cracker candy container.

5in (12.5cm) high

$10-15 SotT

A 17thC vellum land indenture, for 2000 acres in Pennsylvania, dated April 15, 1685, between Ann Bettris and Hugh Lamb, some minor surface soiling and folds.

22.5in (57cm) wide

$600-900 AAC

An early 18thC arrest warrant, for Edward Thurston of Freetown, Bristol Country, MA, dated November 4, 1730, document with partial wax seal at upper left and attached manuscript sheet on reverse, some edge chipping with some ink smears.

7.5in (19cm) wide

$280-320 AAC

An 18thC US Port inspection document, for one chest of tea from Canton, China entering the port of New York on the ship "America", document dated "New York 1794" and signed by John Gasher as Inspector of Revenue.

1794 8.25in (21cm)

$80-120 AAC

An 18thC auction broadside, for sundry articles consisting of young trees, necessary, gate etc , to be sold on February 23, 1799 on Market Street, Philadelphia, exhibits edge chipping with some tears and ink manuscript note on reverse with bleed through to front.

Advertisements for auctions are extremely scarce and collected by a small, but dedicated band of collectors. They were printed cheaply and handed out in quantity, but as they advertised such ephemeral, single day events, they were thrown away. Advertisements for early book or private library auctions are particularly sought after.

10in (25.4cm)

$700-1,000 AAC

An early 19thC patriotic paper label, for one ream of paper by I. Anderson, American Manufacturer of Paper from Milton, Massachussets, featuring an eagle stand of arms with flags in background, is trimmed at the edges and exhibits horizontal fold weakness.

1810 9in (23cm) nigh

$150-200 AAC

An unissued certificate for United Bowman, Philadelphia, signed by the club's president, secretary and treasurer features vignette of tent and target with archery equipment and exhibits some foxing.

1850 15.5in (39cm)

$150-200 AAC

A stock certificate for one share of the Pennsylvania Land and Marble Company, features vignette of quarry scene with steam engine and vignettes of allegorical women, dated February 9, 1857.

12in (30.5cm)

$220-280 AAC

An illustrated coach maker's receipt, issued by Harrison Dickinson, Practical Coach Maker of Norristown, Pennsylvania, dated August 22, 1860, receipt details repairs to coach and wheels totaling $9.65, document has illustrated logo upper left and some folding.

8in (20cm)

$70-100 AAC

A 1933 Druggist's Convention badge, from the 35th Annual Convention, Chicago.

1.75in (4.5cm) wide

$80-120 SotT

A 14ct gold-plated and enameled 'God Bless America' pin, with the liberty bell.

2in (5cm) long

$25-35 AnaA

A National Association of Letter Carriers delegate badge, for the 17th Annual Convention , Feb 22nd, 1935.

1935 4.75in (12cm) high

$8-12 AnaA

A bronze plaque commemorating the destruction of the USS Maine, depicts Columbia holding shield with text "In Memoriam USS Maine destroyed in Havana Harbor February 15 1898 This Tablet is Cast From Metal Recovered From the USS Maine," by John William.

1913 17.5in (44.5cm)

$700-1,000 AAC

Collectors' Notes

- There are two main varieties of animation art, and the type dictates price, availability and desirability.
- A production cel (celluloid) or drawing is produced by hand for the creation of the animation, but be aware that this does not mean that the image appeared in the eventual film. Cels that feature the main or popular characters in the cartoon are the most sought after, even more so if they come from key scenes.
- Limited editions are fairly new to the market and are issued by the animation studios specifically for collectors. They are produced in a number of formats.
- Hand-painted (non-production) cels are unlikely to be painted by the animators, although they may have had some input, and the cels are often signed. They are produced in small editions, fewer than 500.

- Serigraphs or sericels are machine-produced using a screen-silking process and come in larger editions, so are more affordable than hand-painted limited editions.
- Giclees (from the French for 'spray of ink') use a new technique to produce high quality, affordable prints on archive quality paper or even canvas.
- Before 1991 and the production of Walt Disney's "Beauty and the Beast", all production artwork was done by hand, but now characters and backgrounds are drawn by hand and then scanned into a computer. Color is added and the finished scene is transferred straight onto film, with no production cels being produced. This means that only special limited edition cels are available for all subsequent films and for current popular TV shows such as "The Simpsons".

Walt Disney

A Walt Disney Studios serigraph cel "Bonjour Belle" from "Beauty and the Beast".

1991   *26in (66cm) wide*

$100-150   AAG

A Walt Disney Studios original storyboard of Donald Duck.

8in (20cm) wide

$1,200-1,800   AAG

A Walt Disney Studios original production cel from "Mickey's 60th Birthday".

1970   *14.25in (36cm) high*

$1,200-1,800   AAG

A Walt Disney Studios original storyboard of Goofy.

8in (20cm) wide

$1,200-1,800   AAG

A limited edition Walt Disney Studios ser cel "Portrait of a Hero" from "Hercules".

1997   *19in (48.5cm) high*

$300-500   AAG

A Walt Disney Studios original production cel from "The Jungle Book", featuring Mogli and Kaa.

1967   *10.75in (27.5cm) wide*

$1,500-2,000   AAG

A limited edition Walt Disney Studios hand-painted cel "Mono a Mano" from "Lilo and Stitch".

2002   *18.25in (46.5cm) wide*

$1,500-2,000   AAG

A limited edition Walt Disney Studios serigraph "On Ice", from an edition of 9,500, featuring Mickey and Minnie Mouse skating, taken from a 1935 original production cel.

1990   13in (33cm) wide

$300-500   **AAG**

A Walt Disney Studios original production cel from "The Rescuers", featuring Evinrude the dragonfly.

1977   13.75in (35cm) wide

$400-600   **AAG**

A limited edition Walt Disney Studios hand-painted cel of Cruella de Vil from "101 Dalmatians", from an edition of 350 with lithograph model background sheet, signed by Disney artist Marc Davis.

17.75in (45cm) high

$2,800-3,200   **AAG**

A Walt Disney Studios original storyboard of Mickey Mouse.

8in (20cm) wide

$1,000-1,500   **AAG**

A Walt Disney Studios original production cel from "Robin Hood", featuring Prince John.

1977   18in (45.5cm) wide

$1,000-1,500   **AAG**

A Walt Disney Studios original production cel from "Robin Hood", featuring Friar Tuck, John "Piglet" Fiedler and Beulah Bondi.

1973   16in (40.5cm) wide

$500-700   **AAG**

A Walt Disney Studios original production cel from "Robin Hood", featuring Prince John and Maid Marian.

14.75in (37.5cm) wide

$1,000-1,500   **AAG**

A Walt Disney Studios original production cel, featuring Scrooge McDuck, signed by his creator Carl Barks.

Scrooge McDuck first appeared in 1967 in "Scrooge McDuck And Money".

13.25in (33.5cm) wide

$800-1,200   **AAG**

A Walt Disney Studios original production cel from Snow White and The Seven Dwarfs, featuring Doc, with Courvoisier background, dated "May 1937".

5.5in (14cm) wide

$4,000-6,000   **AAG**

A Walt Disney Studios original production cel from "Snow White and the Seven Dwarfs", featuring Happy, with Courvoisier background, dated "May 1937".

5.5in (14cm) wide

$4,000-6,000   **AAG**

A Walt Disney Studios original production cel of Winnie the Pooh.

16in (40.5cm) wide

$700-1,000   **AAG**

A Walt Disney Studios original production cel of Winnie the Pooh.

14.5in (37cm) wide

$700-1,000   **AAG**

Hanna Barbera

A Hanna Barbera original production cel from "The Flintstones", featuring Fred doing a dance.

A limited edition Hanna Barbera hand-painted cel "Fred's Windscreen Wipers" from "The Flintstones", from an edition of 300, signed by Bill Hanna and Joe Barbera.

1961 *12in (30.5cm) wide*

$1,500-2,000 **AAG**

1989 *14in (35.5cm) wide*

$1,000-1,500 **AAG**

A Hanna Barbera original production cel and background artwork from "The Flintstones", featuring Barney and Betty Rubble, signed by Bill Hanna and Joe Barbera.

13.25in (33.5cm) wide

$600-900 **AAG**

A Hanna Barbera original production cel of "Hong Kong Phooey, Number 1 Super Guy".

12.25in (31cm) wide

$700-1,000 **AAG**

A Hanna Barbera original production cel and photo background art from "Johnny Bravo", featuring Johnny in front of the mirror, checking his hair.

14in (35.5cm) wide

$400-600 **AAG**

A limited edition Hanna Barbera hand-painted cel "Classic Scooby Doo", from an edition of 500, signed by Scooby creator Iwao Takamoto.

2000 *13.5in (34.5cm) high*

$600-900 **AAG**

A limited edition hand-painted cel of Scooby Doo and the gang, from an edition of 50, with model background sheet, signed by Joe Barbera and Iwao Takamoto.

16.5in (42cm) wide

$700-1,000 **AAG**

A limited edition Hanna Barbera hand-painted cel "Yankee Doodle Mouse", from an edition of 300, taken from a 1943 original production cel, signed by Bill Hanna, Joe Barbera and Iwao Takamoto.

12in (30.5cm) wide

$1,200-1,800 **AAG**

A Hanna Barbera original production cel from "Tom and Jerry: The Movie", featuring Tom, signed by Bill Hanna and Joe Barbera.

1992 *11.75in (30cm) wide*

$400-600 **AAG**

A Hanna Barbera original production set-up from "The Secret Squirrel Show".

12in (30.5cm) wide

$1,200-1,800 **AAG**

A limited edition Hanna Barbera hand-painted cel 'Mouse Trouble', signed by Bill Hanna, Joe Barbera and Iwao Takamoto.

12in (30.5cm) wide

$1,200-1,800 **AAG**

A Hanna Barbera original production cel and background art from "Wacky Races", featuring Mutley, signed by Bill Hanna and Joe Barbera.

12in (30.5cm) wide

$600-900 AAG

A Hanna Barbera original production cel from Wacky Races, featuring Dick Dastardly, signed by Bill Hanna and Joe Barbera.

12.5in (31.5cm) wide

$600-900 AAG

A Hanna Barbera original production cel from "Yogi Bear", featuring Yogi and Boo Boo, signed by Bill Hanna and Joe Barbera.

1989   14.5in (37cm) wide

$600-900 AAG

A 1970s Hanna Barbera original production cel of Yogi Bear.

10.75in (27.5cm) wide

$600-900 AAG

GENNDY TARTAKOVSKY

■ Genndy Tartakovsky was born in Moscow, Russia in 1970. In 1977 he and his family moved to the US and he soon became fascinated by comic books and TV.

■ Genndy and his brother Alex started to copy and then draw their own cartoons and Genndy realized that this was the career for him. He studied at Chicago's Columbia College and then Valencia's Cal Arts in Los Angeles. One of his student pieces told the story of a young boy genius called Dexter, his annoying older sister Dee Dee and the secret laboratory in his bedroom.

■ This pilot was taken up by Hanna Barbera, where Tartakovsky was also put to work on "Two Stupid Dogs". "Dexter's Laboratory" became an instant hit with the public and went on to be nominated for a number of awards and won an 'Annie'. He then went on to work with college friend Craig McCracken's show "The Powerpuff Girls".

■ In 2001 Tartakovsky launched "Samurai Jack" for the Cartoon Network, an Anime/Manga-styled story of an avenging warrior flung into the far future, which has proved very popular with both critics and fans.

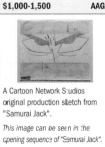

A Hanna Barbera original production cel and background art from "Dexter's Laboratory".

17in (43cm) wide

$400-600 AAG

A Cartoon Network original production cel and background art from "The Powerpuff Girls", featuring Bubbles, Buttercup and Blossom.

15.25in (38.5cm) wide

$1,000-1,500 AAG

A Cartoon Network Studios hand-painted cel of "Samurai Jack".

12.75in (32.5cm) wide

$700-1,000 AAG

A Hanna Barbera original production cel and background art from "The Powerpuff Girls", featuring Mojo Jojo

17in (43cm) wide

$700-1,000 AAG

A Cartoon Network Studios original production sketch from "Samurai Jack".

This image can be seen in the opening sequence of "Samurai Jack".

2001   12.25in (31cm) wide

$220-280 AAG

A B C D E F G H I J K L M N O P Q R S T U V W XYZ

Cosgrove Hall Productions

■ Cosgrove Hall Productions, based in Manchester, UK, was formed in 1976 by former art students Brian Cosgrove and Mark Hall and is one of the largest animation studios in Europe.

■ They are best known for their hugely popular "Danger Mouse" cartoon but also produced classic series such as "Jamie and his Magic Torch", "Chorlton and the Wheelies", and "The Wind in the Willows" and unique productions including the award-winning Roald Dahl's "The B.F.G" and "The Fool of the World and the Flying Ship".

■ Their shows have been sold to over 70 countries worldwide.

A Cosgrove Hall original production cel from the "Danger Mouse" episode "Once Upon a Time Slip", featuring Danger Mouse.

1984　　　*12.75in (32.5cm) wide*

$220-280　　　**AAG**

A Cosgrove Hall original production cel from the "Danger Mouse" episode "Cat-Astrophe", featuring Danger Mouse and Baron Greenback's mechanical cat.

1985　　*16in (40.5cm) wide*

$320-380　　**AAG**

A Cosgrove Hall original production cel from the "Danger Mouse" episode "Once Upon a Time Slip", featuring Danger Mouse and Penfold, signed by the voice of Danger Mouse - David Jason.

1984　　*15.5in (39.5cm) wide*

$800-1,200　　**AAG**

A Cosgrove Hall original production cel from the "Danger Mouse" episode "Once Upon a Time Slip", featuring Baron Greenback, Colorel K and Stiletto.

1984　　*16in (40.5cm) wide*

$500-700　　**AAG**

A Cosgrove Hall original production cel from the "Danger Mouse" episode "Remote Controlled Chaos", with original production background, featuring Baron Greenback.

16in (40.5cm) wide

$400-600　　**AAG**

A Cosgrove Hall original production cel from "Count Duckula", featuring the Count, Nanny and Igor.

1988-93　*12.25in (31cm) wide*

$220-280　　**AAG**

A Cosgrove Hall promotional artwork from "Count Duckula", featuring the Count, Igor and Nanny.

"Count Duckula" was a spin-off from "Danger Mouse".

15.25in (38.5cm) wide

$400-600　　**AAG**

Superheroes

A limited edition Bob Kane artwork of "Batman", from an edition of 1284.

$400-600　　**AAG**

A limited edition Warner Bros hand-painted cel from "Batman: The Animated Series" episode "The Cat and the Claw", with Batman and Catwoman.

$1,000-1,500　　**AAG**

A Warner Bros original production cel from "Batman: The Animated Series", featuring Batman and Mr Freeze.

9.75in (25cm) wide

$500-700   AAG

A Warner Bros original production cel from "Batman: The Animated Series", featuring the Joker and Harley Quinn.

9.75in (25cm) wide

$600-900   AAG

A limited edition Warner Bros hand-painted cel from "Batman: The Animated Series", featuring Batman and Poison Ivy.

10in (25.5cm) high

$1,000-1,500   AAG

A limited edition Warner Bros hand-painted cel from "Batman Beyond", featuring Bruce Wayne and Terry McGinnis.

16.75in (42.5cm) high

$600-900   AAG

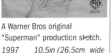

A Warner Bros original "Superman" production sketch.

1997   10.5in (26.5cm) wide

$280-320   AAG

A Marvel Studios official 'Marvel Collectors Edition' hand-painted cel of "Spiderman".

This cel was given away free in a magazine.

10.75in (27.5cm) wide

$280-320   AAG

A limited edition hand-painted cel "The New JLA" from "Justice League of America: The Animated Series", taken from original production cels, featuring Martian Manhunter, Hawkgirl, Green Lantern, Wonder Woman, The Flash, Superman and Batman.

12.75in (32.5cm) wide

$1,500-2,000   AAG

A hand-painted cel from "Justice League of America: The Animated Series", together with the two original production drawings, featuring Superman, J'onn J'onzz, The Martian Manhunter and Batman.

$1,200-1,800   AAG

A limited edition Marvel Comics "The Thing" sericel, from an edition of 1,000.

10.25in (26cm) wide

$180-220   AAG

A Marvel Comics original production cel and background art from "Iron Man".

14.75in (37.5cm) wide

$700-1,000   AAG

An original production cel of "The Beast".

14.25in (36cm) wide

$500-700   AAG

A B C D E F G H I J K L M N O P Q R S T U V W XYZ

An American hooked rug, showing a 1906 Cadillac worked in shades of green, blue, gray, red and yellow on a burlap ground, mounted for hanging.

c1930   24in (61cm) high

$280-320   **FRE**

An early 20thC American photograph, showing a Ford (Ewing Tup with NJ licence plate) with driver, dog and human passenger, in a carved wood frame.

Image 5.5in (17cm) wide

$70-100   **BCAC**

A colored print, 'Busy French provincial street with early automobiles', by Georges Lepape, in its first state, showing cars and their drivers preparing for journeys, pedestrians and a rider on horseback, signed on plate "G. Lepape" and dated "06", and another print of the same image, in the final state.

1906   13.75in (35cm) wide

$300-500   **DN**

A poster advertising Castrol Motor Oil, depicting a Lotus Cortina, a Mini-Cooper and a Rover 2000 set in a steering wheel.

19.75in (50cm) high

$15-25   **SAS**

A mid-20thC racing car teapot, the car and driver detailed in silver luster, the number plate "OK T42", impressed marks.

These novelty teapots came in a range of colors. The silvering is easily damaged, particularly on the helmet knop, and those in less than immaculate condition are worth much less than this excellent example.

9in (23cm) high

$120-180   **Chef**

A painted plaster model of a streamlined 1940s Scarab automobile, covered in gray, black and dark brown paint, with some minor chips and touch-ups.

15in (38cm) long

$2,200-2,800   **DRA**

An AA membership certificate.

1925   3in (7.5cm) wide

$10-15   **COB**

A gold-painted tin weathervane, in the form of a car with driver, lacks pieces.

This is a very unusual subject for a weathervane.

17.25in (44cm) wide

$700-1,000   **BCAC**

A Michelin tire compressor, in the shape of an artillery shell, surmounted by a painted, cast aluminum figure of the Michelin Man, all mounted on a wooden base, a top-mounted gauge inscribed "Michelin & Cie, Clermont Ferrand".

$300-500   **DN**

A French polished metal one-liter dispenser can, with hinged cover.

$30-40   **D**

An Auto Racing Game, by Bradley's, with four lead cars and four game counters, lacks front board of cover.

c1925

$100-150   **ATK**

Collectors' Notes

- The first edition of a book is the closest version to the author's original vision and it is this that makes them desirable. Later editions and reprints can also be collected if they have sought-after alterations or additions such as illustrations.

- Within a first edition, you will also find a number of printings, again the first print of a first edition is worth more than a second or later printing although it can often be difficult to determine which printing a book comes from.

- Always look for examples in good condition, as this can greatly affect the value and the presence of the original dust jacket or wrapper also has a huge influence. Books in 'as-new' condition attract a premium.

- While the author's signature, dedication or doodle can make a book more desirable, owner inscriptions or notes decrease the value unless the owner is famous or connected to the author.

- Titles by popular authors such as Agatha Christie, Ian Fleming, Ernest Hemingway or John Steinbeck, are generally sought-after. However, a classic title, written at the height of an author's career will often be worth less than an early and less well received piece as these are usually produced in much smaller numbers.

Michener, James A., "Chesapeake", first trade edition, published by Random House, New York, signed by the author.
This edition was preceded by a deluxe edition of 500 copies earlier the same year.
1978
$300-400   BRB

Agee, James, "A Death in the Family", first edition, second issue, published by McDowell, Obolensky, New York.
1957
$100-150   BRB

Albee, Edward, "Who's Afraid of Virginia Woolf?", first edition, published by Atheneum, New York, signed by the author.
1962
$1,500-2,000   BRB

Alexie, Sherman, "Reservation Blues", published by The Atlantic Monthly Press, New York signed by the author.
1995
$120-180   BRB

Bellow, Saul, "Dangling Man", first edition, published by Vanguard Press, New York signed by the author.
1944
$4,000-6,000   BRB

Bradbury, Ray, "The Martian Chronicles", first edition, published by Doubleday & Company, Inc., Garden City, New York, signed by the author.
1950
$2,200-2,800   BRB

Bradbury, Ray, "A Graveyard for Lunatics", first edition, published by Alfred A. Knopf, New York, signed by the author.
1990
$150-200   BRB

Burgess, Anthony "The Right To An Answer", first English edition, by Heinemann, London.
1960
$70-100   Bib

Burgess, Anthony, "A Clockwork Orange", first English edition, published by Heinemann London.
1962
$3,500-4,000   Bib

Burroughs, William, "The Naked Lunch", first edition, published by The Olympia Press, Paris.
1959
$2,000-2,500   BRB

A B C D E F G H I J K L M N O P Q R S T U V W XYZ

BOOKS

Capote, Truman, "Breakfast at Tiffany's: A Short Novel and Three Stories", first edition, published by Random House, New York.

1958

$1,800-2,200   **BRB**

Carr, Caleb, "The Alienist", first trade edition, published by Random House, New York, signed by the author.

This trade edition was issued in the same year as a signed limited edition by the Franklin Library.

1994

$100-150   **BRB**

Carver, Raymond, "Cathedral", first edition, published by Alfred A. Knopf, New York.

1983

$200-250   **BRB**

Christie, Agatha, "Death On the Nile", first English edition, published by Collins Crime Club, London, in scarce dustjacket.

1937

$5,000-5,500   **Bib**

Christie, Agatha, "Evil Under the Sun", first English edition, published by Collins Crime Club, London.

1941

$2,200-2,800   **Bib**

Christie, Agatha, "Towards Zero", first English edition, published by Collins Crime Club, London.

1944

$250-300   **Bib**

Christie, Agatha, "Death Comes as the End", first English edition, published by Collins Crime Club, London.

1945

$200-250   **Bib**

Christie, Agatha, "The Mirror Crack'd From Side To Side", first English edition, published by Collins Crime Club, London.

1962

$70-100   **Bib**

Christie, Agatha, "A Caribbean Mystery", first English edition, published by Collins Crime Club, London.

1964

$50-80   **Bib**

Clancy, Tom, "The Hunt for Red October", first edition, published by Naval Institute Press, Annapolis.

This true first edition was following by another, practically identical edition printed for a book club. The only way to tell the two apart is by weight, the original weighs 2lbs, the book club edition only 1lb.

1984

$800-1,200   **BRB**

Dinsen, Isak, "Out of Africa", first American edition, published by Random House, New York.

1938

$850-950   **BRB**

Ellis, Bret Easton, "Less Than Zero", first edition, published by Simon and Schuster, New York.

1985

$250-300   **BRB**

Faulkner, William, "The Sound and the Fury", first edition, published by Jonathan Cape and Harrison Smith, New York.

1929

$20,000-26,000 | **BRB**

Faulkner, William, "Absalom, Absalom!", first trade edition, published by Random House, New York.

1936

$3,200-3,800 | **BRB**

Fitzgerald, F. Scott, "Taps at Reveille", first edition, published by Scribner's, New York, signed by 'Ellery Queen' and "Barnaby Ross".

Ellery Queen and Barnaby Ross were the pseudonyms of renowned detective writers Frederic Dannay and Manfred Lee who later published Fitzgerald's 'The Mystery of the Raymond Mortgage' in "Ellery Queen's 15th Mystery Annual".

1935

$5,200-5,800 | **BRE**

Fleming, Ian, "Moonraker", first English edition, published by Jonathan Cape, London, extremely scarce, particularly with the dustjacket.

1955

$5,500-6,500 | **Bib**

Fleming, Ian, "Diamonds Are Forever", first English edition, published by Jonathan Cape, London.

1956

$2,500-3,000 | **Bib**

Fleming, Ian, "Dr. No", first English edition, published by Jonathan Cape, London.

1953

$2,000-2,500 | **Bib**

Fleming, Ian, "Gold Finger", first English edition, published by Jonathan Cape, London.

1959

$80-120 | **Bib**

Fleming, Ian, "For Your Eyes Only", first English edition, published by Jonathan Cape, London.

1960

$850-950 | **Bib**

Fleming, Ian, "Thunderball", first English edition, published by Jonathan Cape, London.

1961

$180-220 | **Bib**

Fleming, Ian, "The Spy Who Loved Me", first English edition, published by Jonathan Cape, London.

1962

$400-600 | **Bib**

Fleming, Ian, "The Man With the Golden Gun", first English edition, published by Jonathan Cape, London.

A first edition version without the gold-blocked revolver on the front cover was also produced, but is worth considerably less.

1955

$4,500-5,000 | **Bib**

Frazier, Charles, "Cold Mountain", first edition, published by Atlantic Monthly Press, New York, signed by the author.

1997

$500-600 | **BRB**

Garcia Marquez, Gabriel, "One Hundred Years of Solitude", first English language edition, published by Harper & Row.

1970

$4,000-4,500 BRB

Greene, Graham, "Loser Takes All", first English edition, published by Heinemann, London.

1955

$220-280 Bib

Greene, Graham, "In Search of a Character: Two African Journals", first English edition, published by Bodley Head, London.

1961

$40-60 Bib

Greene, Graham, "May We Borrow Your Husband?", first English edition, published by Bodley Head, London.

1967

$50-80 Bib

Greene, Graham, "Travels with my Aunt", first English edition, published by Bodley Head, London.

1969

$30-50 Bib

Hammett, Dashiell, "The Thin Man", first edition, published by Alfred A. Knopf, New York, lacks scarce dust jacket.

1934

$1,000-1,400 BRB

Harris, Thomas, "The Red Dragon", first edition, published by G.P. Putman's Sons, New York.

1981

$200-250 BRB

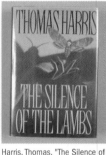

Harris, Thomas, "The Silence of the Lambs", first edition, published by St Martin's Press, New York.

1988

$180-220 BRB

Hemingway, Ernest, "To Have and Have Not', first edition, published by Charles Scribner's Sons, New York.

1937

$1,800-2,200 BRB

Hemingway, Ernest, "The Fifth Column", first edition, published by Charles Scribner's Sons, New York.

1938

$2,000-2,500 BRB

Hemingway, Ernest, "For Whom the Bell Tolls", first edition, published by Charles Scribner's Sons, New York.

1940

$1,000-1,500 BRB

Hemingway, Ernest, "The Old Man and the Sea", first edition, published by Charles Scribner's Sons, New York.

1952

$2,000-3,000 BRB

Hemingway, Ernest, "A Moveable Feast", first edition, published by Charles Scribner's Sons, New York.

1964

$320-380 | **BRB**

Herbert, Frank, "Dune", first edition, published by Chilton Books, Philadelphia and New York.

"Dune" won the first Nebula award for best science fiction novel in 1965.

1965

$7,500-8,500 | **BRB**

Highsmith, Patricia, "The Talented Mr. Ripley", first edition, published by Coward-McCann, Inc., New York.

1955

$2,000-2,500 | **BRB**

Irving, John, "The World According to Garp", first edition, published by E.P. Dutton, New York.

1978

$400-600 | **BRB**

Kerouac, Jack, "Excerpts from Visions of Cody", signed limited first edition of 750, published by New Directions, New York.

1959

$3,500-4,000 | **BRB**

King, Stephen, "The Shining", first edition, published by Doubleday & Company, Garden City, New York.

1977

$750-850 | **BRB**

King, Stephen, "The Stand", first edition, published by Doubleday and Company, Garden City, New York.

1978

$600-700 | **BRB**

King, Stephen, "The Dead Zone", first edition, published by The Viking Press, New York, signed by the author.

1979

$500-600 | **BRB**

King, Stephen, "Firestarter", first trade edition, published by The Viking Press, New York

A signed limited edition of this book was also published earlier the same year.

1980

$180-220 | **BRB**

Kovic, Ron, "Born on the Fourth of July", first edition, published by McGraw Hill, New York.

1976

$120-180 | **BRB**

Lee, Harper, "To Kill a Mockingbird", first edition, 36th printing, published by J.B. Lippincott Company, Philadelphia and New York, signed by the author.

c1961

$5,500-6,500 | **BRB**

Mailer, Norman, "The Naked and the Dead", first edition, published by Rinehart and Company, Inc., signed by the author on the title page.

1948

$2,200-2,300 | **BRB**

A B C D E F G H I J K L M N O P Q R S T U V W XYZ

Michener, James A., "Caravans", first edition, published by Random House, New York, signed by the author.

1963

$400-450 BRB

Morrison, Toni, "Song of Solomon", first edition, published by Alfred A. Knopf, New York, signed by the author.

1977

$700-800 BRB

Nabakov, Vladimir, "Lolita", first edition, in two volumes, published by Olympia Press, Paris.

1955

$8,000-9,000 BRB

O'Brien, Tim, "The Nuclear Age", first edition, published by Alfred A. Knopf, New York, signed by the author.

1972

$220-280 BRB

O'Hara, John, "Butterfield 8", first edition, published by Harcourt, Brace and Company, New York.

1935

$2,800-3,200 BRB

Ondaatje, Michael, "The English Patient", first American edition, published by Alfred A. Knopf, New York, signed by the author.

1992

$300-400 BRB

O'Neill, Eugene, "The Iceman Cometh", first edition, published by Random House, New York, signed by the author.

1946

$6,000-7,000 BRB

Pynchon, Thomas, "V", first edition, published by J.B. Lippincott, New York and Philadelphia.

1963

$3,000-3,300 BRB

Puzo, Mario, "The Dark Arena", first edition, published by Random House, New York, inscribed by the author to his editor on "The Godfather".

1955

$800-1,200 BRB

Rice, Anne, "Interview with the Vampire', first edition, published by Knopf, New York.

1976

$700-800 BRB

Roth, Philip, "Portnoy's Complaint", signed limited first edition of 600, published by Random House, New York.

1969

$800-900 BRB

Salinger, J.D., "The Catcher in the Rye", first edition, published by Little, Brown and Company, Boston.

1951

$10,000-15,000 BRB

Salinger, J.D., "Franny and Zooey", first edition, published by Little, Brown and Company, Boston.

1961

$750-850 BRB

Saroyan, William, "Here Comes There Goes You Know Who", first edition, published by Simon and Schuster, New York, signed by the author.

1961

$250-300 BRB

Sebold, Alice, "The Lovely Bones", first edition, published by Little, Brown and Company, Boston, signed by the author.

2002

$280-320 BRB

Steinbeck, John, "The Grapes of Wrath", first edition, published by Viking Press, New York.

1939

$5,200-5,800 BRB

Steinbeck, John, "Cannery Row", first edition in canary yellow second state cloth binding, published by The Viking Press, New York, signed by the author.

Cannery Row was first issued with light buff colored cloth and when, due to wartime rationing, it ran out, this yellow cloth was used to finish the production.

1945

$3,500-4,000 BRB

Tyler, Anne, "A Patchwork Planet", first edition, published by Alfred A. Knopf, New York, signed by the author.

1998

$60-80 BRB

Vonnegut, Kurt, "Welcome to the Monkey House", first edition, published by Delacorte Press, signed and inscribed by the author.

1968

$1,800-2,200 BRB

Vonnegut, Kurt, "Slaughterhouse-Five", first edition, published by Delacorte Press, New York, signed by the author.

1969

$3,200-3,800 BRB

Warhol, Andy, "The Philosophy of Andy Warhol (From A to B and Back Again)", first edition, published by Harcourt Brace Jovanovich, New York, initialed by the author.

1975

$750-850 BRB

Williams, Tennessee, "A Streetcar Named Desire", first edition, published by New Directions, New York.

1947

$2,200-2,800 BRB

A
B
C
D
E
F
G
H
I
J
K
L
M
N
O
P
Q
R
S
T
U
V
W
XYZ

Baum, L. Frank, "Rinkitink in Oz", first edition with illustrations by John R. Neill, published by Reilly & Britton, Chicago.

1916

$1,000-1,500 **BRB**

Baum, L. Frank, "The Lost Princess of Oz", first edition with illustrations by John R. Neill, published by Reilly & Britton, Chicago.

1917

$700-1,000 **BRB**

Baum, L. Frank, "The Tin Woodman of Cz", first edition with illustrations by John R. Neill, published by Feilly & Britton, Chicago.

1918

$700-1,000 **BRB**

Blyton, Enid, "Noddy and the Bumpy Dog", published by Sampson Low, Marston & Co, London.

1957

$60-90 **Bib**

Blyton, Enid, "Five On Finniston Farm", first English edition, published by Hodder & Stoughton, London.
1960

$80-120 **Bib**

Blyton, Enid, "Five Go To Demon's Rock", first English edition, published by Hodder & Stoughton, London.
1961

$100-150 **Bib**

Blyton, Enid, "Noddy's New Big Book", published by Sampson Low, Marston & Co., London.
1960

$50-80 **Bib**

Dahl, Roald, "James and the Giant Peach", first English edition, published by Allen & Unwin, London.
1967

$180-220 **Bib**

Duvoisin, Roger, "Petunia", first edition, published by Alfred A. Knopf, New York.
1950

$180-220 **BRB**

Johns, Captain W.E, "Biggles & Co.", first English edition, published by Oxford University Press.

1936

$180-220 **Bib**

Johns, Captain. W.E, "Biggles In Mexico", first English edition, published by the Brockhampton Press, Leicester.

1959

$70-100 **Bib**

Johns, Captain. W.E., "Biggles and the Plane That Disappeared", first English edition, publisned by Hodder and Stoughtor, London.

1963

$320-380 **Bib**

Johns, Captain. W.E., "Biggles Takes A Hand", first English edition, published by Hodder and Stoughton.

1963

$70-100 **Bib**

Potter, Beatrix, "The Tailor of Gloucester", first English trade edition, published by F. Warne.

An edition of 500 was privately printed in 1903. A first edition of the first printing is worth up to $7,000.

$500-700 | **Bib**

Potter, Beatrix, "The Tale of Squirrel Nutkin", first English edition, published by F. Warne and Co., London.

1903

$320-380 | **Bib**

Potter, Beatrix, "The Tale of Two Bad Mice" first English edition, published by F. Warne and Co., London, mint copy and in original slip case.

1904

$50-80 | **Bib**

Potter, Beatrix, "The Tale of Timmy Tiptoes", first English edition, published by F. Warne and Co., London.

1911

$500-700 | **Bib**

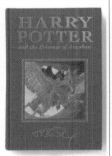

Rowling, J.K., "Harry Potter and the Prisoner of Azkaban", first English edition, second imprint, published by Bloomsbury, London.

1999

$80-120 | **Bib**

Rowling, J.K., "Harry Potter and the Goblet of Fire", first English edition, published by Bloomsbury, London.

2000

$50-80 | **Bib**

Rowling, J.K, "Harry Potter and the Philosopher's Stone", large print edition, first English edition, published by Bloomsbury, London.

This book is known as "Harry Potter And The Sorcerer's Stone" in the US.

2000

$150-200 | **Bib**

Schulz, Charles M., "It's a Mystery, Charlie Brown", first edition, eighth printing published by Random House, New York, signed by the author.

1975

$600-900 | **BRB**

Seuss, Dr., "Horton Hears a Who!", first edition, published by Random House, New York.

1954

$700-1,000 | **BRB**

Seuss, Dr., "How the Grinch Stole Christmas!", first edition, Random House, New York.

1957

$2,200-2,800 | **BRB**

Seuss, Dr., "The Lorax", first edition later printing, published by Random House, New York, signed with drawing by author.

1971

$1,800-2,200 | **BRB**

BOOKS

Travel Books

Cassell, "The Official Guide To the London and South Western Railway", illustrated, printed in Great Britain.

$70-100   Bib

"Cook's Travellers Handbook, Norway, Sweden and Denmark", first edition, published by Thos. Cook & Son, Ludgate Circus.
1923

$180-220   Bib

Fox, Frank, "Australia", first edition, with illustrations by Percy F.S. Spence, published by A. & C. Black, London.
1910

$150-200   Bib

Fox, Frank, "Italy", with illustrations by Alberto Pisa, published by A. & C. Black, London.
1918

$70-100   Bib

Heer, J.C., "Guide to Lucerne, the Lake and its Environs", first edition.
1906

$15-20   Bib

Leyland, John, "The Thames Illustrated, A Picturesque Journeying From Richmond To Oxford", undated, published by Newnes, London.

$60-90   Bib

Menpes, Mortimer, "The Thames", published by Black.
1906

$150-200   Bib

Cookery Books

Beeton, Mrs., "Every Day Cookery and Housekeeping Book", first edition, published by Ward Lock and Co., London.
c1880

$70-100   Bib

Henderson, Mrs Mary, "Practical Cooking and Dinner Giving", first reprint, published by Harper & Bros., New York.
1878

$60-90   Bib

Sala, George Augustus, "The Thorough Good Cook", first edition, published by Cassell and Company Ltd., London.

1895

$120-180   Bib

Ranhofer, Charles, "The Epicurean: A Complete Treatise of Analytical and Practical Studies on the Culinary Art", published by The Hotel Monthly Press, Chicago.
1920

$500-700   BRB

A 19thC Sheraton-style tea caddy, in dark mahogany inlaid with a satinwood shell and paterae, central partition removed.

9.75in (25cm)

$350-400   **BonS**

A 19thC mahogany oval tea caddy, with marqueterie satinwood panel to the hinged lid and with boxwood stringing.

5in (15cm) wide

$600-900   **L&T**

A Victorian coromandel come-top tea caddy, applied with gilt metal strapwork, the hinged lid enclosing named caddies, "Black" and "Green", with spring-action lids.

The combination of brass 'straps' and coromandel wood, with its deep and rich mottled coloring, is typically late Victorian in style.

c1870   *9in (23cm) high*

$400-600   **BonS**

A 19thC walnut domed top two-sectional tea caddy, having two bands of Tunbridge-like decoration including satinwood, ebony, tulipwood and opening to reveal two mahogany lidded sections with traces of original zinc lining present.

9in (22.5cm) wide

$400-600   **D**

A Victorian coromandel wood and brass-mounted domed top stationary box, with hinged cover and fitted interior.

c1870

$350-400   **D**

A Victorian calamander and brass-bound writing box, by Edwards, London, the hinged lid enclosing a tooled leather writing slope and divisions for inkwells and pens.

17.5in (44cm) wide

$400-600   **DN**

An early to mid-19thC mahogany jewel box, lined in crimson velvet and fitted with removable boxes and trays, together with open compartments, bearing the original paper label for "William Dobson, 133 The Strand", listing the numerous items stocked, flush brass side handles.

c1825   *11.5in (29cm) wide*

$300-400   **BorS**

A mid-19thC mother-of-pearl jewelry box, the top opening to reveal ivory outer lining and a damask silk-lined interior the whole standing on four bone feet.

5.5in (14cm) wide

$70-100   **D**

A European silver and enameled rectangular compact, depicting in naturalistic colors and Watteau-esque manner, an amorous couple in a woodland setting, the remainder of the case with engine-turning, with London import marks for 1928.

2.25in (5.5cm) wide

$120-180   **DN**

A B C D E F G H I J K L M N O P Q R S T U V W XYZ

BOXES

A Victorian mother-of-pearl card case, with concertina interior.

c1840   4.25in (10.5cm) wide

$120-180   **MB**

A 19thC silver inlaid tortoiseshell wallet, with silk interior.

$280-320   **PSA**

A Victorian mother-of-pearl cheroot case, with gilt-edged silk interior.

c1870   5.5in (14cm) wide

$120-180   **MB**

A 19thC tin tobacco box, the hinged cover with painted battle scene decoration.

4.75in (12cm) wide

$30-50   **Clv**

A 19th/20thC Russian lacquer box, decorated with a troika group.

10.5in (27cm) long

$400-600   **SI**

A Victorian gilt metal games box, of rectangular form, the hinged lid inlaid with black slate, alabaster and mother-of-pearl, depicting gaming cards and counters, above a frieze set with roundels similarly inlaid with card suits, with fitted rosewood interior with trays, on a plinth base.

The technique of using slabs of differently colored stone cut to shape and inlaid into an object is also known as 'pietra dura'. It was perfected in Italy during the Renaissance, and is still being used today as a decorative technique, although the choice of stone and detailing is often poorer on later examples.

c1870   13in (33cm) wide

$800-1,200   **BonS**

A 19th/20thC Russian lacquer box, decorated with a troika group.

5.5in (13.5cm) long

$300-400   **SI**

A Mauchline photographic ware box, the top with photograph of Wells House, the catch at fault.

4in (10cm) wide

$30-40   **B**

A rare set of three pre-WWII Japanese wooden boxes, they sit in one another.

$150-200   **V**

A miniature chest of drawers, bracket feet, dovetailed drawers, original wooden knobs and hardware, probably a cabinet maker's sample.

c1810   11.5in (29cm) high

$1,000-1,500   **RAA**

A Berning & Co., 'Robot I' Federwerkkamera camera, version five with working spring motor, unreliable shutter, good condition, with case.

1936

$300-350 ATK

A Compass 35mm rangefinder camera, by Le Coultre Co. Switzerland, with anastigmatic 3.5/35 lens.

The Compass was one of the most sophisticated miniature cameras made, with many features packed into a tiny body that is just over 1in (3cm) deep and 2.75in (7cm) wide when closed.

1938

$1,800-2,200 ATK

A Franke & Heidecke Tele-Rolleiflex, with Sonnar 4/135 Synchro-Compur lens, "Telos" label for the French importer, finder relacquered

This was the first Tele-Rolleiflex model released and is valuable due to this telephoto feature.

1959

$400-600 ATK

A Franke & Heidecke Rolleiflex T, gray body with Tessar 3.5/75 Synchro-Compur lens, cased.

1958

$300-350 ATK

A Franke & Heidecke Rolleiflex 2.8f, worn but working.

$180-220 ATK

A Ticka 'pocket watch' camera, by Houghton Ltd, London, with spool, viewfinder, box, French language instructions and enlarger.

A much rarer and more desirable and valuable version of this camera has a dummy watch face and was produced in 1908. It typified the late 19thC and early 20thC trend for disguised cameras and was invented by Swede Magnus O'Niell in 1904. This example is valuable as it had its rare box and instructions.

$700-1,000 ATK

A Concava Tessina 35, with 2.8/25 lens, original box, film loader and nine film cartridges.

The Tessina also came with a watch strap accessory so it could be worn on the wrist. Black versions are rarer and are usually worth twenty percent more, gold versions are rarer still and usually worth fifty percent more.

1960

$600-900 ATK

A Franke & Heidecke Rolleiflex 3.5f, with Planar 3.5/75 Synchro-Compur lens, in Rolleiflex card box.

1960

$700-1,000 ATK

A Goerz 'Tenax' 6x9 camera, with Dogmar 4.5/10cm compound lens.

c1922

$70-100 ATK

An Ihagee Exakta B, chrome body with rare Meyer Makro Plasmat 2.7/7.5cm lens, cased.

1936

$600-900 ATK

A Leitz Leica 1 (A), with Elmar 3.5/50 lens, excellent condition with case and lens cap.

$1,000-1,500 ATK

A limited edition Leica M6 J, with Elmar-M 2.8/50 lens, lens hood, ever-ready case, wooden case, presentation carton and Leica certificate of authenticity.

This limited edition was produced to celebrate the 40th anniversary of the Leica 'model M'.

1994

$3,500-4,000 ATK

A Chinese Shanghai 58-II camera, with collapsible 3.5/50 lens.

The immense popularity of the Leica camera caused many companies to copy its appearance and design, like this Shanghai. Some of these 'copies' have a value approaching authentic Leicas, such as the English-made Reid & Sigrist cameras. Russian and Far Eastern imitations are usually the least valuable.

1958

$280-320 ATK

A Russian spy camera, disguised as a packet of John Player cigarettes, metal body with box and Cyrillic language information sheet.

$180-220 ATK

A round subminiature camera, by Petal, Japan, in wooden case with instructions.

1948

$180-220 ATK

An '1890 Instantograph' tropical quarter-plate camera, by Lancaster & Son, Birmingham, brass fittings, red bellows and Retigraph lens.

$700-1,000 ATK

A Sanderson half-plate field camera, with brass and mahogany body, Ross No. 2 Wide Angle Symmetric 4in lens and Thornton Pickard roller blind shutter.

1898

$320-380 ATK

A Voigtländer green 'Bergheil' camera, luxury version, with some supplements.

1933   3.5in (9cm) high

$180-220 ATK

A Kodak No. 2 roll film camera, with string pull.

The No. 2 was larger in size than the No. 1.

1889-1897 10in (25.5cm) long

$700-1,000 ET

An early 20thC Marion & Co. reflex camera and case.

This camera is important for two reasons. Firstly, it is in mint condition with no signs of wear and secondly, it was once owned by the wealthy steel magnate Andrew Carnegie, then resident at Skibo Castle, Scotland. Without the provenance, it would be worth around $350-450 in this condition.

$1,200-1,800 ET

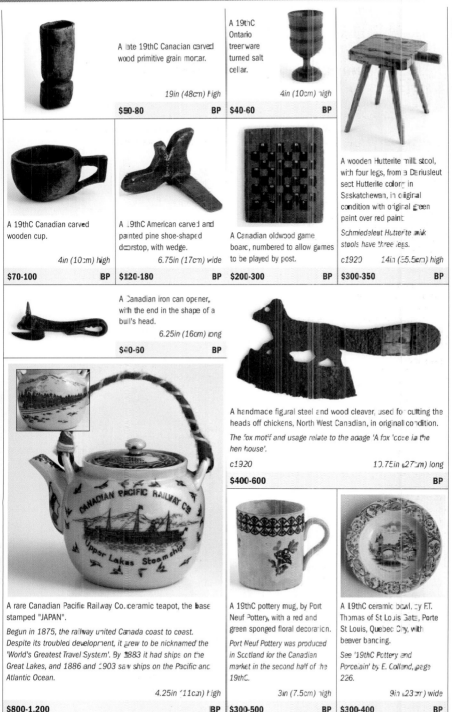

A late 19thC Canadian carved wood primitive grain mortar.

19in (48cm) high

$50-80 **BP**

A 19thC Ontario treenware turned salt cellar.

4in (10cm) high

$40-60 **BP**

A wooden Hutterite milk stool, with four legs, from a Deriusleut sect Hutterite colony in Saskatchewan, in original condition with original green paint over red paint.

Schmiedeleut Hutterite milk stools have three legs.

c1920 14in (35.5cm) high

$300-350 **BP**

A 19thC Canadian carved wooden cup.

4in (10cm) high

$70-100 **BP**

A 19thC American carved and painted pine shoe-shaped doorstop, with wedge.

6.75in (17cm) wide

$120-180 **BP**

A Canadian oldwood game board, numbered to allow games to be played by post.

$200-300 **BP**

A Canadian iron can opener, with the end in the shape of a bull's head.

6.25in (16cm) long

$40-60 **BP**

A handmade figural steel and wood cleaver, used for cutting the heads off chickens, North West Canadian, in original condition.

The fox motif and usage relate to the adage 'A fox 'cose in the hen house'.

c1920 10.75in (27cm) long

$400-600 **BP**

A rare Canadian Pacific Railway Co. ceramic teapot, the base stamped "JAPAN".

Begun in 1875, the railway united Canada coast to coast. Despite its troubled development, it grew to be nicknamed the 'World's Greatest Travel System'. By 1883 it had ships on the Great Lakes, and 1886 and 1903 saw ships on the Pacific and Atlantic Ocean.

4.25in (11cm) high

$800-1,200 **BP**

A 19thC pottery mug, by Port Neuf Pottery, with a red and green sponged floral decoration.

Port Neuf Pottery was produced in Scotland for the Canadian market in the second half of the 19thC.

3in (7.5cm) high

$300-500 **BP**

A 19thC ceramic bowl, by F.T. Thomas of St Louis Gate, Porte St Louis, Quebec City, with beaver banding.

See '19thC Pottery and Porcelain' by E. Colland, page 226.

9in (23cm) wide

$300-400 **BP**

An Anglo-Indian elephant ivory L-shaped cane, the two pieces forming a highly stylized elephant's head with scrollwork on the lower portion, mounted on a tapered black palm shaft with a nickel and steel ferrule.

36.5in (93cm) high

$100-150   **CHAA**

Collectors' Notes

■ Canes reached the height of popularity from the mid-19thC to the early 20thC, falling out of use by the end of WWI. A gentleman may have had a number of canes for day, evening, town and countryside uses, and the designs often displayed his social standing and wealth.

■ Collectible canes can be placed into two categories: decorative and gadget. Look for fine materials and well-executed, intricate detailing on decorative canes, and well-machined, complex or hidden tools or accessories on gadget canes. Modern canes tend to be of lower value and little interest to collectors.

A carved walrus ivory cane, in the form of a cat clenching a goose in its jaws, the handle with a brown stain highlighting carved detail, mounted on an ivory-painted tapered wood shaft with amber glass eyelets and a horn ferrule.

38.25in (97cm) high

$300-500   **CHAA**

An early stacked shark vertebrae walking stick, with a black horn ferrule, three horn discs separate the top three vertebrae, slight shrinkage to vertebrae.

34.75in (87cm) high

$400-600   **CHAA**

An American Folk Art carved cane, with partial bark covering on a knobby hardwood single-piece shaft, top section carved with openwork caged wood spheres, the lower portion with relief-carved fish and fox, dated, with original patinated red paint.

1936   *39.5in (100.5cm) high*

$220-280   **CHAA**

A California gold quartz cane, with an unmarked yellow gold knob, engraved with a floral scroll surrounding four panels for initials, a piece of smoky California gold quartz inset into the top of the knob, mounted on a tapered rosewood shaft with a brass ferrule, minor damage and wear.

34in (86.5cm) high

$3,000-5,000   **CHAA**

A carved wood scrimshaw cane, in the form of a sea monster's head, with baleen and ivory segments below the handle, and a whalebone and baleen ferrule, a crack in the carved handle, which is filled with old resin, possibly original to the cane, the rhinestone eyes not original, one missing.

35.25in (89.5cm) high

$320-280   **CHAA**

A 19thC Meissen porcelain tau staff, with mask head finial of a periwigged gentleman, with ebony stick.

36.5in (93cm) long

$600-900   **CIv**

A nickel-plated brass 'cheroot' cane, in the form of a naval cannon with a 22-caliber barrel, cast with a pedestal mount, set on a tapered ebonized hardwood shaft, barrel reattached, married shaft and handle, and losses.

31.5in (80cm) high

$400-600   **CHAA**

An air rifle walking cane, by J.B. Lissett & Sons, London, the three section cane rescrewing to form the rifle, with key to wind spring, and fitted, felt lined case.

c1880

$700-1,000   **ET**

Collectors' Notes

- The Beswick Pottery was founded in 1894 by John Beswick and his father, James Wright Beswick. The pottery was based at Loughton in Stoke-on-Trent, England, and started by producing domestic bone china and earthenware.

- In the 1930s the studio expanded production to include animal figures for which it became renowned. In 1948, at the suggestion of Lucy Beswick, the wife of the Managing Director, a series of ten Beatrix Potter figures was launched. The first was 'Jemima Puddle-Duck', designed by chief modeler Arthur Gredington.

- The success of this range convinced Beswick to expand further and it added Disney characters such as Mickey Mouse and Winnie the Pooh, which remain extremely popular with collectors today.

- In 1969, Beswick was bought by Royal Doulton but the Beswick backstamp was used until 1989 when it was replaced with the Royal Albert backstamp.

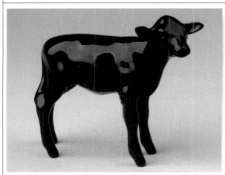

A rare Beswick 'Aberdeen Angus Calf' special commission gloss figure.

$1,800-2,200 PSA

Animals

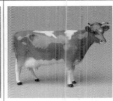

A Beswick 'Highland Bull' gloss figure, No. 2008.

$280-320 PSA

A Beswick 'Hereford Bull' first version gloss figure, No. 1363A.

$220-280 PSA

A Beswick 'Aberdeen Angus Calf' gloss figure, No. 1406A.

$400-600 PSA

A Beswick 'Guernsey Cow' version one, gloss figure, No. 1248A.

$320-380 PSA

A Beswick 'Ayrshire Cow Champion Ickham Bessie' gloss figure, No. 1350

$220-280 PSA

A Beswick 'Dairy Shorthorn Calf' figure, No. 1406C, restored ear.

$500-700 PSA

A CLOSER LOOK AT A BESWICK ANIMAL FIGURE

This figure was designed by Arthur Galloway.

Unlike the common breeds which are still made today, the Galloway had a short run, making it much sought-after today.

It was produced for only seven years, between 1963 and 1969.

Two other variations were made, including a more valuable all-black version and a less valuable version in fawn and brown.

A Beswick 'Belted Galloway Bull' figure, No. 1746B.

$3,000-4,000 PSA

A Beswick 'Lesser Spotted Woodpecker' gloss figure, No. 2420.

$220-280 PSA

A Beswick 'Eagle on a Rock' figure, No. 2307, restored wing tip.

$120-180 PSA

A Beswick 'Tawny Owl' gloss figure, No. 3272.

$50-80 PSA

A Beswick 'Mallard Duck' large gloss figure, No. 817.

$300-350 PSA

A Beswick 'Mallard Duck' large gloss wall plaque, No. 596/0.

$220-280 PSA

A Beswick set of graduated 'Kingfisher' wall plaques, No. 729, smallest restored.

$180-220 PSA

A Beswick set of three graduated 'Seagull' wall plaques, No. 922/1/2/3.

$280-320 PSA

A graduated set of three Beswick models of penguins, the largest with a parasol, each decorated in colored enamels, printed marks in black.

4in (10cm) high

$60-90 LFA

A Beswick 'Cowboy on Horseback', No. 1377, 'Ghost Rider', restored ears.

$1,000-1,500 PSA

A Beswick Thelwell Pony 'Kickstart' gray gloss figure, No. 2769A.

$220-280 PSA

A Beswick 'Girl on a Pony' gloss figure, No. 1499.

$280-320 PSA

A Beswick Thelwell Pony 'An Angel on Horseback' bay gloss figure, No. 2704B.

$220-280 PSA

A Beswick Thelwell Pony 'Express' gray gloss figure, No. 2789A.

$220-280 PSA

A Beswick 'Zebra' gloss figure, No. 845b.

$180-220   PSA

A Beswick 'Faracre Viscount 3rd' saddleback boar gloss figure, No. 1512.

$300-400   PSA

A Beswick 'Wall Queen 46th' sow champion gloss figure No. 1452a.

$30-40   PSA

A Beswick 'Pig' gloss figure, No. 832.

$30-40   PSA

A Beswick 'Piggy Back' pig and piglet gloss figure, No. 2746.

$50-80   PSA

A Beswick 'Endon Black Rod' smooth-haired terrier gloss figure, No. 964.

$400-600   PSA

A Beswick 'Corgi' large gloss figure, No. 1299b.

$60-90   PSA

A Beswick 'Fireside Black Labrador' gloss figure No. 2314.

$320-380   PSA

A rare Beswick 'Cat' dark pewter satin gloss figure, lying with its left front paw up, No. 1542.

$600-900   PSA

Beatrix Potter

A Beswick Beatrix Potter 'Tom Kitten' figure, BP9C, with gold backstamp

$30-50   PSA

A Beswick Beatrix Potter 'Tom Kitten' figure, BP3B, with brown stamp.

$50-80   AOY

A Beswick Beatrix Potter 'Tabitha Twitchett' figure, BP3B.

$60-90   PSA

A Beswick Beatrix Potter 'Miss Moppet' figure, BP3B.

$50-80   PSA

A Beswick Beatrix Potter 'Tabitha Twitchett and Miss Moppet' figure, BP3B.

$70-100   PSA

A Beswick Beatrix Potter 'Susan' figure, BP3B.

$300-350   PSA

A Beswick Beatrix Potter 'Simpkin' figure, BP3B.

$400-600 PSA

A Beswick Beatrix Potter 'Ribby', figure, BP3B.

$50-80 PSA

A Beswick Beatrix Potter 'Ginger' figure BP3B.

$300-400 PSA

A Beswick Beatrix Potter 'Benjamin Bunny' figure, BP2 GBS, ears out, shoes out.

$220-280 PSA

A Beswick Beatrix Potter 'Mr Benjamin Bunny' figure, BP2 GBS, pipe out.

$280-320 PSA

A Beswick Beatrix Potter 'Mr Benjamin Bunny and Peter Rabbit' figure, BP3B.

$70-100 PSA

A Beswick Beatrix Potter 'Mrs Rabbit' figure, BP2 GBS, umbrella out.

$180-220 PSA

A Beswick 'Mrs Rabbit' large figure, BP6, boxed.

$50-80 PSA

A Beswick Beatrix Potter 'Mrs Rabbit and Bunnies' figure, BP3B.

$50-80 PSA

A Beswick Beatrix Potter 'Flopsy, Mopsy and Cottontail' figure, BP2 GBS.

$100-150 PSA

A Beswick Beatrix Potter 'Amiable Guinea Pig' figure, BP2 GBS.

$320-380 PSA

A Beswick Beatrix Potter 'Johnny Townmouse Eating Corn' figure, BP10, boxed.

$50-70 PSA

A Beswick Beatrix Potter 'Mrs Tiggywinkle takes Tea' figure, BP3B.

$50-80 PSA

A Beswick Beatrix Potter 'Old Woman who Lived in a Shoe' figure, BP2 GBS.

$70-100 PSA

A Beswick Beatrix Potter 'Anna Maria' figure, BP2 GBS.

$220-280 PSA

A Beswick Beatrix Potter 'Hunca Munca' figure, BP3.

$50-80 AOY

A Beswick 'Foxy Whiskered Gentleman' large figure, BP6, boxed.

$50-80   PSA

A Beswick Beatrix Potter 'Pig Wig' figure, BP3B.

$220-280   PSA

A Beswick Beatrix Potter 'Jemima Puddleduck' figure, BP3B.

$30-50   PSA

A Beswick Beatrix Potter 'Sir Isaac Newton' figure, BP3B.

$220-280   PSA

A Beswick Beatrix Potter 'Duchess with Pie' figure, BP3B, small nip to ear.

$180-220   PSA

A Beswick Beatrix Potter 'Tommy Brock' figure, 3P3B.

$50-80   PSA

Other Figures

A Beswick Alice in Wonderland 'The Cheshire Cat' figure, 2480.

$300-350   PSA

A Beswick Alice in Wonderland 'The King of Hearts' figure.

$60-90   PSA

A Beswick Alice in Wonderland 'Alice' figure, 2476.

$180-220   PSA

A Beswick Alice in Wonderland 'White Rabbit' figure, 2477.

$150-220   PSA

A Beswick Alice in Wonderland 'Mad Hatter' figure, 2479.

$100-150   PSA

A Beswick Alice in Wonderland 'Queen of Hearts' figure, 2490.

$60-90   PSA

A Beswick 'Martha Cunn' miniature toby jug, 1;113.

$70-100   PSA

A Beswick miniature toby jug, 1;114.

$80-120   PSA

A Beswick 'Laurel and Hardy' novelty cruet, on a shaped stand impressed "375".

3.75in (9.5cm) wide

$60-90   F

FIND OUT MORE...

'Beswick Quarterly', Laura Rock-Smith, 10 Holmes Court, Sayville, N.Y. 11782-2408, U.S.A.

The Charlton Standard Catalogue of Beswick Animals', Diana Callow, The Charlton Press, Toronto, Ontario, 1996.

'Royal Doulton Beswick Storybook Figurines' (6th edition), Jean Dale, Charlton International Inc, U.S.A. 2000.

A B C D E F G H I J K L M N O P Q R S T U V W XYZ

Collectors' Notes

- Blue and white patterns were first used by the Chinese during the Ming Dynasty and were hand-painted. The majority of the blue and white ware found and collected today is English and dates from late 18th century onwards, when the development of transfer-printing led to a huge expansion in production.

- Chinese scenes, floral motifs, scenes incorporating classical architecture and pastoral themes are prevalent.

- Blue and white ware was not made by a single maker, but was produced by many factories, with Spode being one of the most prolific.

- Plates are probably the most widely collected form as the surface shows the pattern to its best advantage. Platters and dishes are also popular for the same reason.

- The pattern depicted will affect value and desirability – a plate with the 'Willow' pattern will be worth less than one with a rarer design. Consult a reference book to learn which patterns are the most desirable.

- Size is also important – large pieces are usually more valuable, but certain shapes are rarer and therefore more desirable.

- Examine pieces carefully for damage or restoration as this will reduce value. Brown stains caused by frost damage or bleach cannot be removed. Be careful not to use sprung metal wall hangers as they can damage delicate rims.

An Adams plate, from the 'South American Sporting' series.
c1840   8.5in (21.5cm) diam
$120-180   GN

An S. Alcock 'Commerce and Free Trade' plate.
c1840   10in (25.5cm) diam
$180-220   GN

A Copeland late Spode 'Botanical' pattern plate.
c1850   9.5in (24cm) diam
$80-120   GN

A Copeland 'Filigree' pattern plate.
c1850   9.75in (25cm) diam
$80-120   GN

A B. Godwin 'The Peacock' child's plate.
c1840   5.75in (14.5cm) diam
$70-100   GN

A Hollins & Co. 'Fisherman and Castle' pattern dished plate.
c1820   9in (23cm) diam
$100-150   GN

A Minton 'Pinwheel' pattern plate.
c1820   9.5in (24cm) diam
$120-180   GN

A Riley 'Floral Basket' pattern plate, with the arms of the Drapers Company.
c1820   9.75in (25cm) diam
$280-320   GN

A Leeds Pottery 'Scene after Claude Lorraine' plate, with impressed mark.

Claude Lorraine (c1604-1682) was a painter known for his expansive and dramatic landscapes, often incorporating Classical themes and ruins.

1818-20   9.5in (24cm) diam
$150-200   GN

A Spode 'Net' pattern tart dish.

c1815   7in (18cm) diam

$100-150   **GN**

A rare Spode 'Floral' pattern plate.

c1825   9.75in (25cm) diam

$320-380   **GN**

A Spode 'Trophies Etruscan' cheese plate.

c1820   7.25in (18.5cm) diam

$120-180   **GN**

A Spode 'Temple' pattern cheese plate

c1820   8in (20cm) diam

$100-150   **GN**

A Spode 'Greek' pattern cheese plate.

c1820   8in (20cm) diam

$150-200   **GN**

An 'Angry Lion' pattern plate, unknown maker.

c1815   9.5in (24cm) diam

$350-400   **GN**

A Stevenson 'Rural Scenery' plate, semichina warranted

c1820   10in (25.5cm) diam

$350-400   **GN**

A 'Boy Piping' pattern plate, unknown maker.

c1820   9.5in (24cm) diam

$220-280   **GN**

A plate, 'Proposal', from the 'Cherub Border' series, unknown maker.

c1820   9in (23cm) diam

$180-220   **GN**

A 'The Grazing Rabbits' pattern plate, unknown maker.

c1820   9.5in (24cm) diam

$320-380   **GN**

A 'The Beemaster' pattern plate, unknown maker

This pattern was taken from a watercolor called The Swarm of Bees in Autumn' by George Robertson (1742-1788). Pieces bearing this rare pattern are desirable and fetch high prices.

10in (25.5cm) diam

$500-700   **GN**

A B C D E F G H I J K L M N O P Q R S T U V W XYZ

CERAMICS

A Copeland and Garrett 'View of Venice' platter, from the 'Byron's View' series.

1833-47 19.5in (49.5cm) wide

$700-1,000　　　　**GN**

A rare Stubbs 'Italian' pattern platter, with 'Wild Rose' border.

c1822　　20.5in (52cm) wide

$1,200-1,800　　　　**GN**

A Ridgway 'The Old Oak Tree' platter, from the 'Stafford Gallery' series.

c1820　　19in (48cm) wide

$1,200-1,800　　　　**GN**

A Spode 'Trophies' or 'Etruscan' pattern shaped comport.

c1825　　10in (25.cm) wide

$400-600　　　　**GN**

A Spode 'The Horse and the Loaded Ass' platter, from the Aesops Fables series.

Patterns showing Aesop's Fables were introduced by Spode in 1830 and continued to be produced by Copeland & Garrett. They bear a clear, identifying backstamp and inspired many other patterns.

c1825　　　　20.5in (52cm) wide

$1,500-2,000　　　　**GN**

A Spode 'Marble' pattern platter.

c1820　　16.5in (42cm) wide

$350-400　　　　**GN**

A Copeland 'Italian' pattern cusped dish.

c1900　　8in (20cm) diam

$150-200　　　　**GN**

A Hollins 'Conversation' pattern dessert comport.

c1900　　9in (23cm) diam

$150-200　　　　**GN**

A Davenport 'Tudor Mansion' or 'Bisham Abbey' pickle dish.

$200-300　　　　**GN**

A Robinson & Wood 'Venetian Scenery' pattern sauce tureen.

c1830　7.25in (18.5cm) wide

$220-280　　　　**GN**

A Spode 'Net' pattern chestnut basket.

c1820　　8in (20.5cm) wide

$400-600　　　　**GN**

A 'Bridge of Lucarno' cheese cradle, attributed to Swansea, one end restored.

c1820　　20in (51cm) wide

$1,800-2,200　　　　**GN**

A Poutney & Allies 'View of Bristol Harbor' toilet box, from the Bristol Views series.

c1825　　7.5in (19cm) wide

$400-600　　　　**GN**

A Copeland Late Spode 'Tower' pattern pap feeder.
c1850   4in (10cm) long
$180-220   GN

A Clyce Pottery 'Ravena' pattern spoonbill spout urinal.
c1340   12in (30.5cm) wide
$800-1,200   GN

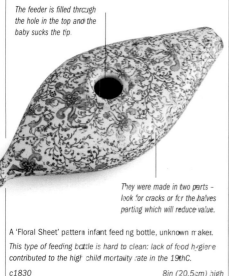

A rare J. Meir 'Simplon' pattern nursery bedpan, of the Simplon Pass Alps, from the Byron's Illustrations series.

The protruding handles of these bedpans were frequently damaged, making undamaged examples rare and valuable. Restoration is often accepted by collectors due to this fact.

c1830   13in (33cm) diam
$800-1,200   GN

A William Smith 'Lion Antique' or 'Bacchus' pattern jug.
c1835   5in (12.5cm) high
$150-200   GN

A Stevenson coffee pot, restoration to top rim and lid.
c1800   8in (20.5cm) high
$280-320   GN

FIND OUT MORE...

R.K. Henrywood & A.W. Covsh, **'Dictionary of Blue & White Printed Pottery 1780-1880'** *(Vols 1 & 2), published by Antique Collectors' Club, 1982 & 1989.*

R. Copeland, **'Transfer Printed Pottery'**, *published by Shire Books, 1999.*

The Spode Museum & Visitors' Centre, Church St, Stoke-on-Trent ST4 1BX, England, UK.

A CLOSER LOOK AT BLUE AND WHITE

The feeder is filled through the hole in the top and the baby sucks the tip.

They were made in two parts - look for cracks or for the halves parting which will reduce value.

A 'Floral Sheet' pattern infant feeding bottle, unknown maker.

This type of feeding bottle is hard to clean: lack of food hygiene contributed to the high child mortality rate in the 19thC.

c1830   8in (20.5cm) high
$400-600   GN

A 'Two Man Willow' pattern vase, unknown maker.
c1840   10in (25.5cm) high
$400-600   GN

A pair of Ridgway 'Italian Flower Garden' pattern candlesticks.

Matching pairs of blue and white candlesticks are uncommon and usually fetch high prices when offered for sale.

c1830   9.25in (23.5cm) wide
$1,000-1,500   GN

CERAMICS

Collectors' Notes

- The Bunnykins series began in a similar way as Hummel figures, when a young nun began to draw pictures of characters to entertain school children during the 1930s. However, Sister Barbara Vernon concentrated on drawing bunnies rather than people. Her father, Cuthbert Bailey, was Managing Director of Royal Doulton, Burslem, England, at that time.

- He appreciated her attractive drawings and, in 1934, launched her characters as nursery ware for children. They became popular and, in 1939, Royal Doulton's legendary modeler Charles Noke created the first Bunnykins figurines.

- The advent of WWII limited the character designs to just six, including Billy Bunnykins, Mother Bunnykins and Farmer Bunnykins. Unsurprisingly, they are very scarce and much sought-after today, usually fetching over $1,500 each. The range was not restarted until 1972 when Royal Doulton's Albert Hallam modeled 12 characters between 1972 and 1973, including 'Family Photograph' and 'Billie Bunnykins Cooling Off'.

- From then, Harry Sales took over with Graham Tongue as head modeler. They were responsible for introducing a wider range of characters, including sporting characters and the 'Collector' Bunnykins, aimed at the growing community of collectors.

- Despite this, relatively few characters were produced and by the mid-1980s, the complete set consisted of just 28 figures. Since then however, at least one figure has been released every year.

- All characters from 1972 have a 'DB' number which helps to identify and date them. Look for rare prewar figures which are very popular with collectors. With characters from 1972 onwards, look for those that have popular appeal or were produced in smaller-sized limited editions, such as the second edition of the Royal Family, or for shorter periods of time. Scarcer editions are more valuable.

- Condition is very important. Cracks or chips will reduce the value and make a figure less desirable.

A Royal Doulton 'Bunnykins' Family Photograph', DB1.

This example is the first of three color variations.

1972-1988 4.5in (11.5cm) high

$70-100 PSA

A Royal Doulton 'Billie and Buntie Sleigh Ride' Bunnykins figure, DB4.

1972-1997 3.5in (9cm) high

$20-30 PSA

A Royal Doulton 'Mr Bunnykins Autumn Days' figure, DB5, underglaze chip to ear.

1972-1982 4.25in (10.5cm) high

$100-150 PSA

A Royal Doulton 'Mrs Bunnykins Clean Sweep' figure, DB6.

1972-1991 4in (10cm) high

$70-100 PSA

A Royal Doulton 'Daisy Bunnykins, Spring Time' figure, DB7.

1972-1983 3in (7.5cm) high

$120-180 PSA

A Royal Doulton 'Dollie Bunnykins Playtime' figure, DB8.

1972-1993 4in (10cm) high

$60-90 PSA

A Royal Doulton 'The Artist' Bunnykins figure, DB13.

1975-1982 3.75in (9cm) high

$180-220 PSA

A Royal Doulton 'Mr Bunnykins at the Easter Parade' figure, DB18, boxed.

1982-1993 5in (12.5cm) high

$70-100 PSA

A Royal Doulton 'Mrs Bunnykins at the Easter Parade' figure, DB19, boxed.

1982-1996 4.5in (11.5cm) high

$50-80 PSA

A Royal Doulton 'Knockout' Bunnykins figure, D330, with Jubilee backstamp, boxed.

1984-1988 4.25in (10.5cm) high

$150-200 PSA

A Royal Doulton 'Bogey' Bunnykins figure, DB32.

1984-1992 4in (10cm) high

$70-100 PSA

A Royal Doulton 'Happy Birthday' Bunnykins music box, DB36.

1984-1993 7in (18cm) high

$100-150 PSA

A Royal Doulton 'Home Run' Bunnykins figure, DB43, boxed.

1986-1993 4.25in (10.5cm) high

$70-100 PSA

A Royal Doulton 'White Santa' Bunnykins Christmas ornament, DB32.

1987 3.75in (9cm) high

$180-220 PSA

A Royal Doulton 'Collector' Bunnykins figure, DB54.

This figure was exclusive to members of the Royal Doulton International Collectors' Club in 1987.

1987   4.5in (11.5cm) high

$320-380 PSA

A Royal Doulton 'Paperboy' Bunnykins figure, DB77.

$70-100 PSA

A Royal Doulton 'Tally Ho' Bunnykins figure, DB78, from a limited edition special colorway.

1988   4in (10cm) high

$120-180 PSA

A Royal Doulton Ice-cream Seller' Bunnykins figure DB82.

1990-1993 4.75in (12cm) high

$100-150 PSA

A Royal Doulton 'King John' Bunnykins figure, DB91.

This is part of the desirable second series of the Bunnykins Royal Family. Each figure was released in a limited edition of 250 in 1990 only. Designed by Harry Sales and modeled by David Lyttleton and with a UKI Ceramics Special backstamp, they were issued without certificates.

1990   4in (10cm) high

$300-400   **PSA**

A Royal Doulton 'Queen Sophie' Bunnykins figure, DB92, from a limited edition of 250.

1990   4in (10cm) high

$320-380   **PSA**

A Royal Doulton 'Princess Beatrice' Bunnykins figure, DB93, from a limited edition of 250.

1990   3.5in (9cm) high

$300-350   **PSA**

A Royal Doulton 'Prince Frederick' Bunnykins figure, DB94, from a limited edition of 250.

1990   3.25in (8cm) high

$300-350   **PSA**

A Royal Doulton 'Harry the Herald' Bunnykins figure, from a limited edition of 250, DB95.

1990   3.5in (9cm) high

$300-350   **PSA**

A Royal Doulton 'Halloween' Bunnykins figure, DB132.

1993-1997   3.25in (8cm) high

$50-80   **PSA**

A Royal Doulton '60th Anniversary' Bunnykins figure, DB137, boxed.

1994   4.75in (12cm) nigh

$30-40   **PSA**

A Royal Doulton yellow 'Cheerleader' Bunnykins figure, DB143, from a limited edition of 1,000.

1994   4.5in (11.5cm) high

$120-180   **PSA**

A Royal Doulton 'Partners in Collecting' Bunnykins figure, DB151, Collectors' Club Exclusive, boxed.

1999   3in (7.5cm) high

$70-100   **PSA**

A Royal Doulton 'Boy Skater' Bunnykins figure, DB152.

1995-1998 3.75in (9.5cm) high

$20-30   **PSA**

A limited edition Royal Doulton 'Fortune Teller' Bunnykins toby jug, DB157.

2000   5.5in (12.5cm) high

$120-180   **PSA**

A Royal Doulton 'Jester' Bunnykins figure, DB161, from a limited edition of 1,500.

1995   4.25in (10.5cm) high

$180-220   PSA

A Royal Doulton 'Joker' Bunnykins figure, DB171, boxed.

1997   4.25in (10.5cm) high

$80-120   PSA

A Royal Doulton 'Sweet Heart' Bunnykins figure, DB174, from a limited edition of 3,500.

1997   3.75in (9.5cm) high

$60-90   PSA

A Royal Doulton 'Ballerina' Bunnykins figure, DB176, boxed.

1998-present   3.5in (9cm) high

$20-30   PSA

A Royal Doulton 'Scotsman' Bunnykins figure, DB180, boxed with certificate.

1998   4in (10cm) high

$80-120   PSA

A Royal Doulton 'Banjo' Bunnykins figure, DB182, boxed, with certificate.

1999-2000 4.5in (11.5cm) high

$70-100   PSA

A Royal Doulton 'Fireman' Bunnykins figure, DB183.

This figure is from a second series produced in a limited edition of 3,500 and released in 1998. Although it does not come with a certificate, each figure bears an etched number. This figure has been recently re-released in a limited edition of 2001 with a black jacket and yellow trousers to honor the firemen after the World Trade Center tragedy on September 11, 2001.

1998   4.25in (10.5cm) high

$50-80   PSA

A Royal Doulton 'Saxophone' Bunnykins figure, from a limited edition of 2,500, boxed, with certificate, DB186.

1999   4.5in (11.5cm) high

$60-90   PSA

A Royal Doulton 'Sydney' Bunnykins figure, DB195, from a limited edition of 2,500.

1999   4.75in (12cm) high

$100-150   PSA

A Royal Doulton 'Judge Bunnykins' figure, DB188.

Judge Bunnykins was produced by Royal Doulton to be given away as a membership gift when joining the Royal Doulton International Collectors' Club.

1999   4.25in (10.5cm) high

$15-20   PSA

A Royal Doulton 'Statue of Liberty' Bunnykins figure, DB198, from a limited edition of 3,000, boxed.

1999   5in (12.5cm) high

$60-90   PSA

A Royal Doulton 'Piper' Bunnykins figure, DB191, from a limited edition of 3,000, boxed.

1999   4in (10cm) high

$60-90   PSA

FIND OUT MORE...

'Royal Doulton Bunnykins, A Charlton Standard Catalogue', by Jean Dale & Louise Irvine, published by Charlton Press, 2002.

CERAMICS

Collectors' Notes

- The Carlton Works was established at Stoke-on-Trent, England in 1890 by Wiltshaw & Robinson. The name became Carlton Ware Ltd. in 1958.
- During the 1920s and 1930s, the company became known for its richly decorated luster wares which were aimed at emulating the success enjoyed by the Wedgwood 'Fairyland' Luster' range designed by Daisy Makeig Jones and launched in 1916.
- Typically, luster wares have dark, lustrous backgrounds, in blue, red or black, which were then decorated with Oriental, Egyptian or Persian style scenes or motifs in bright, jewel-like enamels that are raised to the touch. As well as these themes being inspirations for the Art Deco style, they helped define the style. They also used Oriental ceramics as an inspiration.
- Their geometrically designed pieces, like the jug on this page, were very popular and are much sought after today. Look particularly for large pieces or pieces that are Oriental in form and decoration, such as ginger jars. Pieces in the Egyptian style are currently fetching very high prices.

A Carlton ware 'Devil's Corpse' pattern ginger jar and cover, of ovoid form printed and painted in gilt and colored enamels, printed and painted marks "3787".

7.75in (20cm) high

$500-700   **L&T**

A Carlton ware Rouge Royale ginger jar and cover, of ovoid form, decorated with chinoiserie scenes, printed marks.

9in (23cm) high

$300-400   **L&T**

A Carlton ware 'Starflower' ginger jar and cover, transfer-printed in gilt and painted in vivid colors with geometric star-shaped flowers and spiky foliage against a pale mottled blue and turquoise ground, factory marks and original paper retail label.

7.75in (20cm) high

$600-900   **DN**

A Carlton ware Noire Royale 'Kingfisher' small vase, with ribbed lower section, tapering neck and twin gilt handles, painted in colors and gilt with a kingfisher on a grapevine peering into a lily pond against a black ground, damaged.

4.75in (12cm) high

$70-100   **DN**

A 1920s Art Deco Carlton ware 'Bell' pattern jug, on rouge ground.

Geometrically patterned pieces such as this jug are highly desirable and usually very valuable. The angular handle, the use of gilding and 'flat' frieze-like handling of the flower motifs typifies both Carlton ware's high quality production of the period in the Art Deco style, as do the bright, jewel-like colors.

8in (20cm) high

$1,000-1,500   **TDG**

A Carlton ware 'Secretary Bird' luster vase, of oviform with a broad cylindrical neck, decorated in vivid colors with the exotic creature by a black-trunked tree with pendant, highly stylized flowers and foliage in colors heightened with gilding, against a predominantly coral-colored ground, printed factory marks on base.

6in (15.5cm) high

$500-700   **DN**

A Carlton ware 'Secretary Bird' luster vase, decorated in vibrant colors with the exotic bird against pendant foliage. with stylized flowers and foliage on the back, reserved against a coral, green and black ground with gilt detailing, and looped and gilded handles, printed factory marks.

5in (12.5cm) high

$500-700   **DN**

A Carlton ware footed gondola, transfer printed and painted in colors with an exotic bird, butterflies and a tree against a muted butterscotch ground with a gilt interior and handles, and black and gilt border.

13.5in (34cm) wide

$600-900 **DN**

A pair of Carlton ware baluster-shaped vases, each decorated in gilt and turquoise in Chinese style with landscapes, on a powder blue ground, printed marks, one with small rim chip.

10.25in (26cm) high

$150-200 **LFA**

A Carlton ware Rouge Royale 'Spider Web' coffee set, comprising: a coffee pot and cover; a sugar pot and cover; a milk jug and six cups and saucers; each piece painted with a gilt painted spider's web suspended from a fruiting bough above a bed of flowers against a mottled dark red ground, the cups and jug with gilt interiors, some damage to coffee pot neck.

Coffee pot 8in (20cm) high

$280-320 **DN**

A CLOSER LOOK AT A CARLTONWARE CHARGER

The 'Handcraft' range was hand painted with freehand designs.

The design of certain elements shows a strong Art Deco style.

The fairy and entire 'fairy tale' scene shows the influence of Wedgwood's highly successful 'Fairyland Luster' range, which Carlton ware aimed to mimic.

This is a large example, chargers like this, which are easy to display, show off the pattern extremely well.

A Carlton ware 'Handcraft' charger, painted with a seated faun playing pipes in an exotic floral and foliate landscape, printed marks.

15in (38cm) diam

$1,500-2,000 **L&T**

1930S CARLTON WARE

- During the 1930s, Carlton ware launched a range which was very different in style to its 'chinoiserie' luster ranges, and that was to become a mainstay of the factory for nearly two decades.
- Flowers and leaves were key design elements, and these were either used for the shape of the piece or as decorative motifs. 'Oak Tree' introduced in 1934 in cream and blue, was one of the most popular ranges. Look for less popular ranges like 'Cherries' that were produced for a shorter time and are rarer.
- Colors were bright and again based on flowers including yellow, green and pink. 'Buttercup' was popular in yellow but is more desirable in pink.
- Condition is very important. As so many were made, only those in excellent condition without damage will be of interest to collectors. Lids are often damaged, as are rims and bases. Also look for boxed gift sets and the boxes themselves, which add value.
- During the 1950s, colors and forms became more sophisticated and 'modern' to appeal to the new, post war taste. Two-tone colors with clean, lined forms were common. The 'Orbit' range is very popular with collectors and was produced during the 1960s, when outer space and science fiction were public obsessions.

Floral

A 1930s Carlton ware yellow 'Buttercup' pattern jug.

2.5in (6.5cm) high

$80-120 **Bev**

A 1930s Carlton ware yellow 'Fruit Basket' pattern jug.

4in (10cm) high

$120-180 **Bev**

A 1930s Carlton ware yellow 'Rose' pattern teapot.

Teapots are easily damaged, particularly the spouts, handles and finials, and so undamaged examples will fetch a premium.

4.25in (11cm) high

$220-280 **Bev**

A 1930s Carlton ware yellow 'Apple Blossom' pattern bowl.
9.25in (23.5cm) wide

$60-90 Bev

A 1930s Carlton ware 'Daffodil' pattern posy holder.
4.5in (11.5cm) high

$100-150 Bev

A 1930s Carlton ware green 'Waterlilies' pattern jug.
3.75in (9.5cm) high

$120-180 Bev

A 1930s Carlton ware 'Tomatoes' pattern salad bowl.
10.75in (27.5cm) diam

$80-120 Bev

A 1930s Carlton ware green 'Foxglove' pattern toast rack.
4.5in (11.5cm) wide

$80-120 Bev

An unusual 1930s Carlton ware 'Flower and Basket' pattern jam pot.
4.5in (11.5cm) high

$100-150 Bev

A 1930s Carlton ware 'Fruit Basket' pattern trefoil dish.
8.75in (22cm) high

$60-90 Bev

A 1930s Carlton ware pink 'Lily' pattern posy holder.
3.5in (9cm) diam

$50-80 Bev

A 1930s Carlton ware 'Raspberry' pattern bowl.

From 1935-1961, a new backstamp was added reading 'Registered Australian Design'. This was due to Japanese factories copying successful Western designs and selling them cheaply. Designs registered in Australia could not be copied by the Japanese, so Carlton Ware Ltd chose to register their designs there to prevent damage to their business.

10.5in (26.5cm) high

$100-150 Bev

A 1930s Carlton ware pink 'Buttercup' pattern trefoil dish.

This pattern is rare in the pink colorway, and more desirable than in the yellow colorway.

10.5in (26.5cm) wide

$220-280 Bev

A 1930s Carlton ware 'Hydrangea' pattern vase.

5in (12.5cm) high

$120-180 Bev

A pair of Carlton ware 'Geometric' pattern book ends.
5.5in (14cm) high

$400-600 Bev

A 1930s cream-colored Carlton ware jug, with gilt painted Art Deco styled handle and foot.

5.5in (14cm) high

$40-60 **AOY**

A light green Carlton ware jug, with gilt detailing and rare factory foil sticker.

5in (12.5cm) high

$40-60 **AOY**

1950s & 1960s

A 1960s Carlton ware 'Orbit' pattern cruet set.

9.25in (23.5cm) wide

$50-70 **Bev**

A 1960s Carlton ware 'Orbit' pattern jam pot.

5.25in (13.5cm) high

$50-80 **Bev**

A 1960s Carlton ware 'Orbit' pattern cheese dish.

8in (20cm) wide

$70-100 **Bev**

A 1960s Carlton ware 'Orbit' pattern teapot.

6in (15cm) high

$80-120 **Bev**

A 1950s curved Carlton ware dish, with link rim and green leaf design.

4.75in (12cm) wide

$12-18 **AOY**

A Carlton ware Rouge Royale leaf-shaped dish.

6.75in (17cm) wide

$40-60 **AOY**

Two Carlton ware napkin rings, dish-shaped on oval bases and decorated in peach, yellow and green glazes.

$20-30 **D**

FIND OUT MORE...

'**Collecting Carlton Ware**, by David Serpell, published by Krause Publications: 1999.

'**Collecting Carlton Ware**, by Francis Joseph & Francis Salmon, published by Kevin Francis Publishing, 1994.

A large Carlton ware Rouge Royale leaf-shaped dish.

13.75in (35cm) long

$40-60 **AOY**

A light blue and gilt leaf-shaped Carlton ware dish.

13.75in (35cm) long

$30-50 **AOY**

A B C D E F G H I J K L M N O P Q R S T U V W XYZ

CERAMICS

Collectors' Notes

- Character jugs are based on toby jugs, which first appeared in the early 18thC. Toby jugs feature the whole body of the figure, while character jugs just show the head and sometimes the shoulders.

- Doulton began making toby jugs in 1815, but it was Doulton artist and modeler Charles J Noke (1858-1941) who developed the company's colorful character jugs over a period of nearly ten years from c1925. The first of these jugs was based on 'John Barleycorn', who represents alcohol, and was released in 1934. Royal Doulton went on to produce jugs representing other fictional and historical characters and is still producing them today.

- Other early examples are 'Old Charley', 'The Night Watchman', 'Sairey Gamp', 'Parson Brown' and 'Dick Turpin'. In 1936, fellow Doulton designer Harry Fenton introduced the first jug based on a real person, John Peel, the best friend and subject of John Woodcock Graves famous poem 'D'ye ken John Peel'.

- While Doulton is one of the most prolific producers of character jugs, other manufacturers include Beswick, SylvaC, Kevin Francis and Royal Worcester.

Royal Doulton

A Royal Doulton 'Athos' small character jug, D6452.

1956-91

$60-90   PSA

A Royal Doulton 'Britannia' limited edition small character jug, D7107, with box and certificate.

$60-90   PSA

A Royal Doulton 'John Doulton' small character jug, with clock face reading eight o'clock, D6656.

Designed by Eric Griffiths for the Royal Doulton International Collectors' Club, founded in 1980. On pieces from the first year of production, Big Ben shows a time of eight o'clock, and from 1981 onwards, it shows a time of two o'clock. The first version is rarer and can fetch up to 50 per cent more.

1980

$70-100   PSA

A Royal Doulton 'Chopin' large character jug, D7030, from the Composers series, boxed.

£70-100   PSA

A Doulton 'Gladiator' miniature character jug, D6556.

1961-67

$280-320   PSA

A Royal Doulton 'Falstaff' large character jug, printed 'D6287' in green.

1950-95   *6.25in (16cm) high*

$50-80   LFA

A Royal Doulton 'Granny' translucent character jug, D5521.

c1935-83   *5.75in (14.5cm) high*

$50-80   Clv

A Royal Doulton 'Old King Cole' small character jug, D6037, with orange crown.

1939-60

$60-90   **PSA**

A Royal Doulton 'Lobster Man' small character jug, D6320.

1968-92

$50-80   **PSA**

A Royal Doulton 'Mad Hatter' small character jug, D6602.

1965-83

$70-100   **PSA**

A Royal Doulton 'Old Mack' translucent character jug, D5823.

1937-85 5.75in (14.5cm) high

$50-80   **Clv**

A Royal Doulton double-sided character jug 'Mephistopheles', by Harry Fenton, D5758.

1937-48   *3.25in (8.5cm) high*

$600-900   **DN**

A Royal Doulton 'The Mikado' miniature character jug D6525.

1960-69

$280-320   **PSA**

A Royal Doulton 'Catherine Parr' miniature character jug, D6752.

1986-89

$120-180   **PSA**

A Royal Doulton 'Catherine Parr' small character jug, D6751.

1986-89

$100-150   **PSA**

A rare Royal Doulton 'Pearly Boy' miniature character jug, with factory and 'A' mark on base.

This is a rare variation of the 'Arry' jug but with small buttons on his hat. Four color variations exist – this example has brown colored buttons.

2.25in (6cm) high

$600-900   **DN**

A Royal Doulton 'Pearly Queen' small character jug, D6843.

1987-91

$60-80   **PSA**

A Royal Doulton 'Robinson Crusoe' miniature character jug, D6546.

1960-83

$50-80   **PSA**

A Royal Doulton 'Sir Walter Raleigh' large character jug, D7169, with box and certificate.

This jug was jug of the year for 2002.

$150-200   **PSA**

CERAMICS

A Royal Doulton 'Sancho Panza', large character jug, D6456.
1957-83
$60-90 PSA

A Royal Doulton 'The Snowman' miniature character jug, D7158, with Christmas cracker handle, with box and certificate.

This character jug was sold exclusively by UK retailer John Sinclairs as a limited edition of 2,000.
c1997
$60-90 PSA

A Royal Doulton 'The Viking' miniature character jug, D6526.
1959-75
$70-100 PSA

Other Factories

Two views of a SylvaC bright glaze painted 'George Bernard Shaw' character jug, stamped "3279".
6in (15.5cm) high
$70-100 MCol

A SylvaC cellulose painted 'Neville Chamberlain' character jug, stamped "1463".
This jug was also available with a green glaze.
6.5in (16.5cm) high
$120-180 MCol

A 1960s SylvaC 'John F. Kennedy' character jug, stamped "2899".
6.25in (16cm) high
$70-100 MCol

A 1970s SylvaC 'Maid Marian' character jug, stamped "5117".
7in (18cm) high
$60-90 MCol

A 1970s SylvaC 'Robin Hood' character jug, stamped "5114".
6.25in (16cm) high
$60-90 MCol

A 1960s SylvaC 'Uncle Sam' character jug, stamped "2888".
6.75in (17cm) high
$70-100 MCol

FIND OUT MORE...

Graham McLaren, **'Toby and Character Jugs'** Shire Books, 2000.

David Fastenau & Stephen Mullins, **'Toby and Character Jugs of the Twentieth Century'**, Kevin James, 1999.

An Ashtead Potters' Guild 'Lloyd George' character jug, designed by Percy Metcalfe, numbered "298-1000", printed marks.
7.5in (19cm) high
$180-220 Chef

Collectors' Notes

- Chintzware has been produced since the 19thC, when toilet sets, jugs and dressing table sets were decorated with allover floral patterns. It reached two peaks in popularity, in the 1920s and again in the 1950s.

- Royal Winton (owned by the Grimwade Brothers) is one of the most popular names and prolific makers, and the style of a Royal Winton mark can help date a piece to a decade. Also look for Lord Nelson Ware, James Kent and Crown Ducal.

- Patterns are not hand-painted, but applied by transfer. Many patterns are only minutely different so look closely. The pattern name is often written on the bottom of the piece. Impressed or stamped words, such as 'Ascot', indicate the name of the shape.

- Value is based on the pattern and the item it is applied to – certain patterns are more popular with collectors. The most popular items are those that are covered as much as possible with transfer work.

- Certain patterns were exported in bulk to different countries, for example, 'Sweet Pea' went to Australia and 'Summertime' to the USA.

- Damage, such as chips, cracks, smudged transfers and restoration, reduces value substantially. It can usually be seen by examining and feeling the pattern. Pieces in excellent condition that also retain a bright gold rim are more desirable to collectors.

A 1940s Royal Winton Chintz 'Balmoral' pattern sandwich tray.

These trays would have had six small plates on top of them.

10.25in (26cm) wide

$70-100   FJA

A 1940s/50s Royal Winton Chintz 'Summertime' pattern sandwich tray.

12.25in (31cm) wide

$70-100   FJA

A 1940s/50s Royal Winton Chintz 'Sweet Pea' pattern sandwich tray.

12.25in (31cm) high

$120-180   FJA

A 1940s/50s Royal Winton Chintz 'Kew' pattern sandwich plate.

12.25in (31cm) wide

$80-120   FJA

A Royal Winton Chintz 'Marion' pattern dish.

c1950   10.25in (26cm) wide

$80-120   FJA

A 1940s/50s Royal Winton Chintz 'Cheadle' pattern plate.

9in (23cm) wide

$70-100   FJA

A 1940s/50s Royal Winton Chintz 'Old Cottage Chintz' pattern plate.

9in (23cm) wide

$60-90   FJA

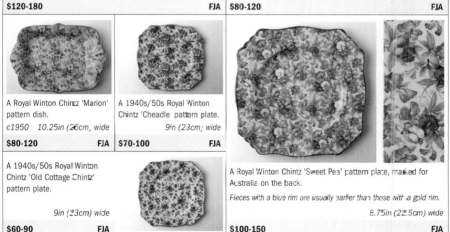

A Royal Winton Chintz 'Sweet Pea' pattern plate, marked for Australia on the back.

Pieces with a blue rim are usually earlier than those with a gold rim.

8.75in (22.5cm) wide

$100-150   FJA

CERAMICS

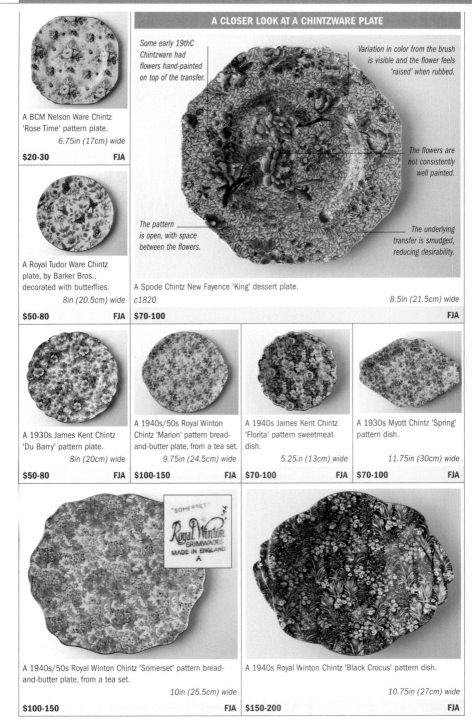

A BCM Nelson Ware Chintz 'Rose Time' pattern plate.

6.75in (17cm) wide

$20-30   **FJA**

A Royal Tudor Ware Chintz plate, by Barker Bros., decorated with butterflies.

8in (20.5cm) wide

$50-80   **FJA**

A CLOSER LOOK AT A CHINTZWARE PLATE

Some early 19thC Chintzware had flowers hand-painted on top of the transfer.

Variation in color from the brush is visible and the flower feels 'raised' when rubbed.

The flowers are not consistently well painted.

The pattern is open, with space between the flowers.

The underlying transfer is smudged, reducing desirability.

A Spode Chintz New Fayence 'King' dessert plate.

c1820   *8.5in (21.5cm) wide*

$70-100   **FJA**

A 1930s James Kent Chintz 'Du Barry' pattern plate.

8in (20cm) wide

$50-80   **FJA**

A 1940s/50s Royal Winton Chintz 'Marion' pattern bread-and-butter plate, from a tea set.

9.75in (24.5cm) wide

$100-150   **FJA**

A 1940s James Kent Chintz 'Florita' pattern sweetmeat dish.

5.25in (13cm) wide

$70-100   **FJA**

A 1930s Myott Chintz 'Spring' pattern dish.

11.75in (30cm) wide

$70-100   **FJA**

A 1940s/50s Royal Winton Chintz 'Somerset' pattern bread-and-butter plate, from a tea set.

10in (25.5cm) wide

$100-150   **FJA**

A 1940s Royal Winton Chintz 'Black Crocus' pattern dish.

10.75in (27cm) wide

$150-200   **FJA**

A Royal Winton Chintz 'Sweet Pea' pattern compote.
6.75in (17cm) wide

$150-200 FJA

A 1940s/50s Royal Winton Chintz 'June Rose' pattern musical cake stand, the base fitted with a Thorens clockwork mechanism.
8in (20.5cm) wide

$220-280 FJA

A Royal Winton Chintz 'Cranstone' pattern two-tier cake stand.
8.75in (22cm) high

$100-150 FJA

COMPARE AND CONTRAST CHINTZWARE JUGS

The ornate shape of the handle and rim indicate 19thC styling.

Patterns produced from the 1920s onwards were 'tighter' with an allover pattern and no spacing.

The shape and handle are clean and geometric – indicative of 1930s styling.

19thC and early Chintzware has a more 'open' design, with space between the flowers.

Colors tend to be darker and more muted, highlighted with a few, brighter flowers.

Bright, attractive colors.

An 1840s Chintzware 'Sheet Patterned' jug.
7.25in (18.5cm) high

$180-220 FJA

A Wedgwood & Co. Ltd. Chintz jug, with Art Deco-style handle.
4.75in (12cm) high

$150-200 FJA

A 1930s Royal Winton 'Hazel' pattern jug.

Note the difference between the 1930s mark on this piece and the 1950s mark on the 'Somerset' plate on the previous page.
5in (12.5cm) high

$220-280 FJA

A 1930s Royal Winton Chintz 'Cromer' pattern Cambridge-shape milk jug, with impressed shape name.
4.25in (11cm) high

$50-70 FJA

A 1930s Leighton Chintz 'Chinese Rose' pattern pottery jug.
5.5in (14cm) high

$150-200 FJA

A 1930s Royal Winton Chintz 'Fireglow' pattern milk jug.
3.25in (8cm) high

$80-120 FJA

A 1930s Wade Chintzware milk jug.

Note the pattern covers the whole of the handle, not just the outside. Examples such as this are more desirable.

4.25in (10.5cm) high

$80-120 FJA

A 1930s Crown Ducal Chintz 'Peony' pattern mint sauce boat.

Tray 5.5in (14cm) wide

$100-150 FJA

A 1930s Royal Corona Ware Chintz 'Rosetta' pattern jug, by Hancock & Sons.

6.25in (16cm) high

$180-220 FJA

A rare 1930s Royal Winton Chintz 'Kinver' pattern Ascot-shape teapot.

6in (15cm) high

$350-400 FJA

A 1940s Royal Winton Chintz 'White Crocus' pattern coffee pot.

8.25in (21cm) high

$400-600 FJA

A 1930s James Kent Chintz 'Hydrangea' pattern 'tennis' tea set.

Tray 8.75in (22cm) wide

$100-150 FJA

A 1940s/50s Royal Winton Chintz 'Old Cottage Chintz' pattern 'tennis' tea set.

9.5in (24cm) wide

$70-100 FJA

A 1940s/50s Royal Winton Chintz 'Old Cottage Chintz' pattern bedside set, or tea for one set.

Look at the bottom of each piece to check that they are all of the same period. Pieces were often broken and replaced, or sets 'made up'. Also ensure that the pattern is identical.

Tray 10.5in (26.5cm) wide

$500-700 FJA

A 1930s Crown Ducal 'Ivory Chintz' pattern small candlestick.

Candlesticks came in two sizes, the smaller ones were sold as part of dressing table sets, the larger ones were sold separately.

7in (17.5cm) high

$120-180 FJA

One of a pair of Mintons Chintzware candlesticks.

Candlesticks are rare. Matched pairs are very desirable and fetch high prices.

1890-95 8.75in (22cm) high

$150-200 (pair) FJA

A Royal Winton Chintz 'Fireglow' pattern Ascot-shape sugar bowl.

4.75in (12cm) wide

$50-80 FJA

A Royal Winton Chintz 'Estelle' pattern butter-dish.

6.5in (16.5cm) wide

$120-180 FJA

A 1940s/50s Royal Winton Chintz 'Joyce Lynn' pattern butter-dish.

6.75in (17cm) wide

$150-200 FJA

A 1940s/50s Royal Winton Chintz 'Mayfair' pattern cheese dish.

Tray 6.5in (16.5cm) wide

$180-220 FJA

A Royal Winton Chintz 'Sweet Pea' cruet set, items missing

8.5in (21.5cm) long

$70-100 AOY

A Royal Winton Chintz 'Cranstone' pattern cruet set.

This set is in an unusual pattern and is particularly nice as the pattern covers the whole piece, including the sides

6in (15.5cm) long

$150-200 FJA

A 1930s Crown Ducal Chintz 'Primula' pattern sugar sifter.

5.25in (13.5cm) high

$150-200 FJA

A Royal Winton Chintz 'Royalty' pattern sugar sifter, with original metal top.

6in (15cm) high

$180-220 FJA

A 1930s Royal Winton Chintz 'Summertime' pattern Rheims-shape jam pot.

Although original, examples with metal parts are not as desirable as those with transfer-decorated ceramic parts.

4.25in (11cm) high

$80-120 FJA

A 1940s Royal Winton Chintz 'Kew' pattern sweetmeat basket.

5in (12.5cm) wide

$180-220 FJA

A 1930s James Kent Chintz 'Apple Blossom' pattern toast rack.

7in (18cm) long

$120-180 FJA

A 1940s/50s Royal Winton Chintz 'Shrewsbury' pattern ashtray.

This late example of Chintzware is unusual as the pattern is spaced out

4.75in (12cm) wide

$50-80 FJA

A 1920s Copeland late Spode Chintz toothbrush holder, with transfer-printed decoration.

These toothbrush holders were sold as part of a toilet set and are often mistaken for vases.

4.75in (12cm) high

$80-120 FJA

A Crown Ducal Chintz 'Ivory Chintz' pattern toothbrush holder, by A.G. Richardson, from a toilet set.

$120-180 FJA

An unusual 1930s Royal Corona Ware Chintz 'Rosetta' pattern vase, by Hancock & Sons.

11in (28cm) high

$180-220 FJA

A B **C** D E F G H I J K L M N O P Q R S T U V W XYZ

A 1930s Keeling & Co. Losol Ware Chintz jardinière.
10in (25.5cm) diam

$320-380 FJA

A 1940s/50s Royal Winton Chintz 'Black Crocus' pattern Nita-shape wall pocket.
8.5in (21.5cm) high

$400-600 FJA

A 1940s/50s Royal Winton Chintz 'Sweet Pea' pattern wall pocket, Art Deco shape.
8.75in (22cm) high

$500-700 FJA

A 1930s Royal Winton Chintz 'Cotswold' pattern lamp base, with replaced fittings.
13in (33cm) high

$400-600 FJA

A Staffordshire Chintz lamp.

Beware of vases that have been converted to lamps, look at the shape of the base to check if it is actually a converted vase and check for modern fittings.
7.75in (19.5cm) high

$120-180 FJA

A Royal Winton Chintz 'Hazel' pattern box.
4.5in (11.5cm) wide

$100-150 FJA

A Crown Ducal Chintz 'Ivory Chintz' pattern ring stand, from a dressing table set.
4.5in (11.5cm) high

$60-90 FJA

An unnamed Chintzware soap dish, originally part of a toilet set.
c1880
5.25in (13.5cm) wide

$120-180 FJA

FIND OUT MORE...

'Chintz: The Charlton Standard Catalogue', Susan Scott, *Charlton International Inc, 1997.*

Collectors' Notes

- Clarice Cliff was born in the north of the Staffordshire potteries. After earning enameling and freehand painting at Linguard Webster & Co, Cliff joined A.J. Wilkinson Ltd. of Burslem in 1916.

- By the late 1920s her talent had been recognized and in 1927 she was given her own studio in the newly acquired Newport Pottery. Her early pattern experiments were brightly colored, geometric and quite unlike patterns produced before. They were named 'Bizarre Ware' and launched in 1928.

- The range was successful and soon the entire pottery was taken over by 'Bizarre Girls' decorating items with her colorful designs inspired by art of the period, flowers and botany.

- Value is determined by shape, pattern, size and rarity, condition is also important with damage or wear usually reducing value unless the piece is extremely rare.

- Look for bright, colorful and geometric shapes which are popular with collectors. Chargers, 'Lotus' shape jugs, vases and plates display the pattern well so are very popular and fetch high prices.

- Fakes do exist – look for poor-quality painting but do not mistake this for visible brushstrokes which are a hallmark of some of Cliff's best work. Smudged designs and thick, uneven glaze also usually indicate a fake.

Vases

A Clarice Cliff Fantasque Bizarre 354 'Umbrellas' pattern vase, printed mark, Lawleys mark, minor restoration to the rim.

c1929   6in (15cm) high

$400-600   **WW**

A large Clarice Cliff Bizarre 'Orange Roof Cottage' pattern ribbed ovoid vase, with molded "ISIS" mark, a large section of the neck re-glued and a rim chip.

Look for a version with a pink roof which is rarer and more valuable.

c1932

$700-1,000

9.75in (25cm) high

WW

A Clarice Cliff 'Limberlost' pattern vase.

1932   8.5in (21.5cm) high

$1,000-1,500   **SCG**

A Clarice Cliff 451 'Nasturtium' pattern cylindrical vase, with castellated rim, marks.

c1932   7.75in (20cm) high

$400-600   **L&T**

A Clarice Cliff Bizarre 569 'Jonquil' pattern vase, printed mark, faint glaze star crack to base.

6in (15cm) high

$300-500   **WW**

A Clarice Cliff Bizarre Isis 'Patina Country' vase, printed mark.

This pattern was complicated to produce and did not sell well.

c1932   10in (25.5cm) high

$700-1,000   **WW**

A Clarice Cliff 358 'Capri' pattern vase, printed marks and molded marks.

1933-34   8in (20cm) high

$400-600   **L&T**

A Clarice Cliff Fantasque Bizarre 342 'Alton' pattern vase, printed mark.

1933-34   8.25in (21cm) high

$700-1,000   **WW**

A Clarice Cliff Fantasque Bizarre 342 'Secrets' pattern vase, printed mark.

1933-c1935 8in (20cm) high

$1,200-1,800   **WW**

Bowls & Barrels

A Clarice Cliff 'Idyll' pattern bowl, with original EPNS overlaid rim.

1930-36   8in (20.5cm) diam

$400-600   **SCG**

A Clarice Cliff 'Summerhouse' pattern rose bowl, printed marks.

1931-33   9in (23cm) diam

$300-500   **L&T**

A Clarice Cliff Bizarre 'Tennis' pattern cauldron, printed mark, minor scratches.

c1931   3in (7.5cm) high

$700-1,000   **WW**

A Clarice Cliff 'Delecia Pansies' pattern bowl.

1933-34   7in (18cm) diam

$400-600   **SCG**

A Clarice Cliff 'Tulip' pattern cauldron, printed mark.

1934-1935   3in (7.5cm) high

$400-600   **WW**

A Clarice Cliff 'Forest Glen' pattern bowl.

1936-37   7in (18cm) diam

$400-600   **SCG**

A Clarice Cliff 'Newlyn' pattern bowl.

1935-36   8.5in (21.5cm) diam

$700-1,000   **SCG**

A Clarice Cliff 'Autumn' pattern preserve jar and cover, printed marks.

1931-1933   3.5in (9cm) high

$400-600   **L&T**

A Clarice Cliff 'Rodanthe' pattern 'Bon Jour' biscuit barrel and cover, printed mark.

During the second half of the 1930s this pattern overtook Crocus as the top selling design.

1934-39   6in (15cm) high

$280-320   **L&T**

A Clarice Cliff Bizarre 'Pine Grove' pattern preserve pot and cover, printed mark.

c1935   3.5in (9cm) high

$300-400   **WW**

A Clarice Cliff 'Forest Glen' pattern preserve jar and cover, printed marks.

1936-1937   4in (10cm) diam

$300-500   **L&T**

Sifters & Plates

A Clarice Cliff 'Crocus' pattern conical sugar sifter, printed marks.

1928-69   5.25in (13.5cm) high

$350-400   **L&T**

A Clarice Cliff Fantasque 'Secrets' pattern three-footed sugar caster.

1933-c1937 6.75in (17cm) high

$400-600   **Clv**

A 1930s Clarice Cliff Bizarre 'Clematis' pattern sifter, with electroplated mount, printed mark

5.5in (14cm) high

$400-600   **WW**

A Clarice Cliff Fantasque Bizarre 'Orange Chintz' pattern conical sugar sifter, printed mark, restored tip.

c1933   5.5in (14cm) high

$400-600   **WW**

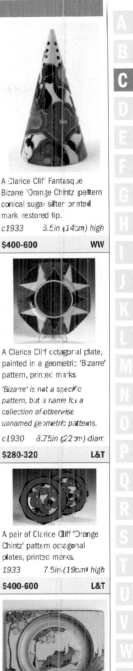

A Clarice Cliff 'Mowcop' pattern conical sugar sifter, printed mark.

1937   5.5in (14cm) high

$300-400   **WW**

A Clarice Cliff octagonal plate, painted in a geometric 'Bizarre' pattern, printed marks.

'Bizarre' is not a specific pattern, but a name for a collection of otherwise unnamed geometric patterns.

c1930   8.75in (22cm) diam

$280-320   **L&T**

A Clarice Cliff Bizarre 'Windbells' pattern conical sugar sifter, printed mark, restored.

1933-34   5.5in (14cm) high

$600-900   **WW**

A Clarice Cliff 'Farmhouse' pattern bowl.

1931-32   9.5in (24cm) wide

$1,200-1,800   **SCG**

A pair of Clarice Cliff 'Orange Chintz' pattern octagonal plates, printed marks.

1933   7.5in (19cm) high

$400-600   **L&T**

A Clarice Cliff 'Comets' pattern plate.

This is an early abstract pattern, the comets have small floral shapes at their heads.

1929-30   10in (25.5cm) diam

$1,000-1,500   **SCG**

A Clarice Cliff 'Secrets' pattern Biarritz shape plate.

Plates with decoration inside the center as well as around the rim are more desirable.

1933-37   9in (23cm) wide

$700-1,000   **SCG**

Jugs & Miscellaneous

A Clarice Cliff 'Luxor' pattern water jug.

This early landscape pattern is very rare.

1929-30   6.25in (16cm) high

$800-1,200   **SCG**

A Clarice Cliff 'Sliced Fruit' pattern ovoid Perth jug, printed mark.

c1930   5in (13cm) high

$220-280   **L&T**

A Clarice Cliff Bizarre Athens 'Delecia Pansies' pattern jug, printed mark.

1933-34   6in (15.5cm) high

$500-700   **WW**

A Clarice Cliff Bizarre George 'Coral Firs' jug, printed mark.

1935-39   7in (17.5cm) high

$500-700   **WW**

An early Clarice Cliff geometric pattern trio set.

Plate 6in (15cm) diam

$500-700   **Bev**

A CLOSER LOOK AT A CLARICE CLIFF CANDLESTICK

The stepped shape is very Art Deco. Look at steps for damage or cracks, this example is undamaged so is valued highly.

Floral chintz was popular in the 1930s, and this is Cliff's typically styled interpretation of that design.

The pattern works very well and the hand-painted colors are bright and show brushmarks, typical of Cliff's style.

Clarice Cliff candlesticks are not common items.

A Clarice Cliff 'Blue Chintz' pattern stepped candlestick.

1932-33   6.75in (17cm) high

$1,200-1,800   **SCG**

A Clarice Cliff Bizarre 'Rudyard' pattern clog, printed mark.

This pattern was named after the village of Rudyard, just north of Stoke.

1933-34   5.5in (14cm) wide

$500-700   **WW**

A Clarice Cliff 'Coral Firs' pattern, Biarritz shape trio set.

1935-39

$500-700   **SCG**

A Clarice Cliff Bizarre reel-shaped pepper-pot, painted with yachts under sail, worn, and a saltcellar painted with stylized flowers.

Salt 3.25in (8cm) high

$180-220   **BonS**

An Eva Croft for Clarice Cliff tea set, comprising teapot, sugar and milk jug.

$350-400   **Bev**

Collectors' Notes

- Susie Cooper (1902-1995) started work in 1922 as a paintress, decorating wares for A.E. Gray & Co. in Hanley, Staffordshire. In 1929, she left to set up her own company, decorating ceramics.
- Plain white 'blanks' were made locally and decorated by her team of six paintresses. In 1931, she moved and expanded production to Crown Works, part of Woods & Sons, in Burslem. In 1932, she began to design her own shapes as well as designs, unlike fellow designer, Clarice Cliff.
- In 1958, the Susie Cooper Company merged with R.H. and S.L. Plant, before being acquired by the Wedgwood Group in 1966. The Crown Works were closed in 1980. Cooper designed in the Potteries until 1986 and died in 1995.
- Her work in the Art Deco style, with bold, geometric patterns and bright colors, is the most popular amongst collectors. Designs were painted freehand or applied by lithographed transfer. Close examination for variations in the application of the paint caused by brush strokes will reveal the difference between these decorative forms.
- As well as pattern, look for Cooper shapes, particularly the streamlined 'Kestrel', her first shape, and 'Curlew' shapes. Pieces made from 1932 until just after the war are marked with her famous 'Leaping Deer' mark.
- Postwar production, with its more muted colors and patterns inspired by natural objects, is currently less popular amongst collectors, as are the dinner services produced from the 1950s onwards.
- Fakes exist, look for fuzzy marks and poor quality decoration, as do later reproductions such as The Bradford Exchange's series of geometric decorated plates, released in 1999.

A Susie Cooper for A.E. Gray stylized floral coffee set.

1928   Coffee pot 8in (20.5cm) h

$700-1,000   SCG

A Susie Cooper for A.E. Gray stylized floral trio.

1928   6in (15cm) diam

$150-200   SCG

A Susie Cooper for A.E. Gray stylized floral box.

1928   2.5in (6.5cm) high

$300-350   SCG

A Susie Cooper for A.E. Gray fruit bowl

1929   9.25in (23.5cm) diam

$400-600   SCG

A Susie Cooper for A.E. Gray tall jug.

1928   6.75in (17cm) high

$400-600   SCG

A Susie Cooper Ross's Belfast' dish.

1929   5in (13cm) diam

$300-350   SCG

A Susie Cooper jug. 'Bronze Chrysanthemum Dutch' pattern.

1930   4.75in (12cm) high

$400-600   SCG

A Susie Cooper hand-painted 'Geometric' coffee pot.

1928   8in (20.5cm) high

$400-600   CG

A Susie Cooper jug.

1930   5.75in (17cm) high

$400-600   SCG

A Susie Cooper 'Symphony Dutch' pattern jug.
1931 *5in (12.5cm) high*
$400-600 **SCG**

A Susie Cooper hand-painted chocolate pot.
1931
$180-220 **SCG**

A Susie Cooper hand-painted stylized floral plate.
1932 *8.5in (22cm) diam*
$60-90 **SCG**

A Susie Cooper 'Rodeo' pattern plate
1933 *7.75in (20cm) diam*
$220-280 **SCG**

A rare Susie Cooper wall charger.
1933 *15.75in (40cm) diam*
$1,200-1,800 **SCG**

A Susie Cooper 'Pig' divided dish.
1933-34 *8in (20.5cm) diam*
$350-400 **SCG**

A Susie Cooper 'Guardsman' divided dish.
1933 *7.75in (20cm) diam*
$400-600 **SCG**

A Susie Cooper 'Jeremy Goose' mug.
People paid to have their names painted on these mugs, making each one effectively unique.
1933 *3in (7.5cm) high*
$300-400 **SCG**

Two Susie Cooper porcelain 'Jockey' mugs.
1933-34 *3in (7.5cm) high*
$120-180 (each) **SCG**

A Susie Cooper 'Pear in Pompadour' plate.
1934 *7.75in (20cm) diam*
$70-100 **SCG**

A Susie Cooper 'Tree of Life' trio.
1934 *Largest 6.75in (17.5cm) diam*
$350-400 **SCG**

A Susie Cooper hand-painted 'Bells' square dish.
1936 *7.5in (19cm) diam*
$280-320 **SCG**

A Susie Cooper 'Printemps' lithographed plate.
1937 *10in (25.5cm) diam*
$50-80 SCG

A Susie Cooper 'April' lithographed plate.
1937 *8.75in (22.5cm) diam*
$50-80 SCG

A Susie Cooper 'Panel Spray' oval platter.
1937 *11.75in (30cm) wide*
$70-100 SCG

A Susie Cooper 'Modernist' trio.
1937 *Largest 6.75in (17.5cm) diam*
$80-120 SCG

A Susie Cooper green 'Dresden Spray' pattern, Rex shape tea set.
'Dresden Spray' was the most prolific pattern, having been in production for a long time.
1938 *Teapot 4.75in (12cm) high*
$320-380 SCG

A Susie Cooper 'Gardenia Tree' trio.
1937 *Plate 6.75in (17cm) d*
$80-120 SCG

A Susie Cooper hand-painted coffee set, comprising six cups, a coffee pot, milk jug and sugar bowl.
1938
$500-700 (set) SCG

An extensive Susie Cooper 'Dresden Spray' pattern part tea and dinner service, comprising 19 fish plates, eight soup plates, 15 side plates, five soup bowls and stands, a sauce boat, eight tea cups and three saucers, three coffee cans and three saucers, a muffin dish and cover, two vegetable dishes and covers and seven further assorted pieces, printed marks.
$700-1,000 (set) L&T

A Susie Cooper 'Acorn' pattern part dinner service, comprising a vegetable tureen and cover, four graduated ashes, six dinner plates, five fish plates, four side plates, three smaller plates, two saucers and a sauceboat.
An ashet is a meat-platter
$220-280 (set) L&T

A Susie Cooper 'Green Feather' pattern coffee service, comprising a coffee pot and cover, a milk jug, a cream jug, six cups and six saucers, printed marks.
$300-500 (set) L&T

A Susie Cooper 'Patricia Rose' lithographed plate.
1940 *8.5in (21.5cm) diam*
$60-90 SCG

FIND OUT MORE...

The Potteries Museum & Art Gallery, Bethesda Street, Hanley, Stoke-on-Trent, Staffordshire ST1 3DE, England. A good collection which spans her production, including pieces donated by Cooper herself.

'Susie Cooper: A Pioneer of Modern Design', by Andrew Casey and Ann Eatwell, published by Antique Collectors' Club, 2002.

A Bristol coffee cup and saucer, with molded borders, painted with swags of flowers, unmarked.

c1770

$300-500 WW

A Chamberlain cup and saucer.

5.25in (13.5cm) diam

$1,200-1,800 TBk

A Coalport cup and saucer, with serrated edge, pattern no. 996.

c1830

$120-180 MH

A Coalport cup and saucer, pattern no.10.

c1845

$70-100 MH

A Coalport cup and saucer, pattern no. Y2665.

c1905

$60-90 MH

A Susie Cooper Pottery 'Azalea' pattern bone china trio set, transfer-printed with hand-painted banding.

c1950 *Plate 6in (15cm) diam*

$30-50 FFM

A Davenport 'Longport' pattern cup and saucer.

1870-1886 *Saucer 5.75in (14.5cm) wide*

$120-180 AOY

A Doulton 'Clifton' pattern cup and saucer.

Saucer 5.5in (14cm) wide

$30-50 AOY

A Foley trio set, decorated with thistles and stylized flowers.

Plate 5.75in (14.5cm) wide

$80-120 AOY

A Hammersley trio set, decorated with violets, pattern no. 11202.

$30-50 MH

A Hammersley trio set, pattern no. E265.

c1940

$300-400 MH

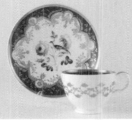

An early 19thC Hicks and Meigh cup and saucer, painted with birds and roses with gilded cobalt bands.

$50-80 BonS

A Hilditch & Hopwood cup and saucer.
c1830

$70-100 MH

A George Jones plate, cup and saucer.
c1910

$60-90 MH

A W. Lowe cup and saucer, pattern no. 5741.
c1930

$30-50 MH

A 1930s Mason's Ironstone 'Regency' pattern cup and saucer.
Saucer 5in (12.5cm) wide

$30-50 AOY

A 1950s Alfred Meakin plate, cup and saucer, decorated with cacti.

$15-25 MH

A Midwinter Fashion shape 'Pastel Cherokee' pattern trio set, designed by Jessie Tait, hand-painted.
c1960 *Plate 6in (15.5cm) diam*

$30-50 FFM

A Midwinter Fashion shape 'Border Stripe' pattern trio set, designed by Jessie Tait, hand-painted.
c1960 *Plate 6in (15.5cm) diam*

$30-50 FFM

A Midwinter 'Savannah' pattern trio set, designed by Jessie Tate.
Plate 5.5in (14cm) wide

$60-90 Bev

A Minton cup and saucer.

c1835

$70-100 MH

A Scottish Nautilus porcelain trio set, with crimped pink edges and floral designs.

Plate 6.75in (17cm) wide

$180-220   AOY

A John Ridgway porcelain cup and saucer.

c1825-30

$150-200   MH

A John Ridgway London-shape trio, pattern no. 2/549.

$80-120   MH

A Noritake hand-painted trio set, with floral and gilt details.

Plate 6in (15.5cm) wide

$80-120   BAd

A Quimper cup and saucer.

Saucer 5.5in (14cm) wide

$30-40   AOY

A John Ridgway cup and saucer, pattern no. 3794.

c1840

$70-100   MH

An early Victorian tea cup and saucer, possibly John Ridgeway, decorated with the 2-1373 pattern of gilt blue and yellow bands about central flowers.

$30-50   Chef

A Paragon cup and saucer.

c1912

$60-90   MH

A Thomas Rathbone 'The Milk Maid' pattern cup and saucer.

c1820   *Saucer 5.25in (13.5cm) diam*

$220-280   GN

A John Ridgway cup and saucer.

c1850

$60-90   MH

A Royal Crown Derby Imari pattern trio set, No. 2434 1885/7.

$70-100   Clv

A Royal Doulton cup and saucer.

$30-50 — MH

A Royal Doulton trio set.

$50-80 — MH

A Royal Doulton trio set, pattern no. V2105.

$80-90 — MH

A Royal Doulton trio set, pattern no. V166.

$30-50 — MH

A Royal Worcester trio set.
c1930

$120-180 — MH

An American blue spatter cup and saucer, with rose pattern.

$150-200 — Pook

A Spode cup and saucer.

c1815-25

$180-220 — MH

A Spode 'Two Temples' pattern cup and saucer, with gilt highlights.
c1820   Saucer 5.25in (13.5cm) wide

$100-150 — GN

A Spode cup and saucer.

c1825

$100-150 — MH

A 19thC Carl Thieme porcelain cup and saucer, painted with Deutsche Blumen, within a basket molded border and gilt lined rims, painted mark in underglaze blue.

$50-80 — Chef

A Wileman & Co. plate, cup and saucer.

c1890

$220-280 — RH

A Worcester yellow scale trio set, crossed swords and "9" marks.

$3,500-4,000 — TBk

CERAMICS

Collectors' Notes

- Doulton & Watts was founded by John Doulton in 1815 in Lambeth, South London, UK and primarily produced chimney pots and pipes for industrial or commercial use.
- His son Henry influenced the company's future success by introducing a range of art pottery. It became very popular in the late 1860s, after it was shown at the Paris Exhibition in 1867 and again at the International Exposition in London 1871. By the 1880s, 200 people were employed at the factory.
- Doulton had close ties with the Lambeth School of Art, which provided many of its best decorators and designers, including sisters Florence and Hannah Barlow, and brothers Arthur and George Tinworth.
- As well as Lambeth stoneware, which was often made in an Art Nouveau style, a 'faience' range with naturalistic hand-painting and a 'Silicon' ware range with stone bodies were made. In 1877, Henry Doulton acquired a stake in – and eventually took over – Pinder, Bourne & Co. of Burslem, which produced earthenware and bone china.
- Production ended at Lambeth in 1956 but continued at the Burslem factory, which is still active today.
- Condition affects the value of Doulton pieces, as does the intricacy and detailing of any handmade features. Examine the bases for inscribed initials relating to the artists, which may increase the value of a piece.

A Doulton Lambeth jug by Hannah Barlow, of tapering cylindrical form, incised with a frieze of cattle within a foliate beds and with silver band on the rim, hallmarked Birmingham, impressed and incised marks.

Hannah Barlow was born in 1851 and was the first female artist to be taken on by a major British pottery. She joined Doulton in 1871, and was soon followed by her sister Florence. They brought their love of animals and the countryside to their designs. Hannah specialized in animals and Florence in flowers and birds.

9.5in (24cm) high

$800-1,200   **L&T**

A pair of Doulton Lambeth vases, by George Tinworth, incised with applied boss decoration, incised initials on the body, impressed factory marks.

9.5in (24cm) high

$700-1,000   **L&T**

A Doulton Lambeth stoneware bottle vase, incised with a frieze of flowering foliage with a beaded border, impressed and incised marks for the Art Union of London.

8.25in (21cm) high

$180-220   **L&T**

A CLOSER LOOK AT A DOULTON LAMBETH VASE

This vase was decorated by Florence Barlow who, along with her sister Hannah, joined Doulton from the Lambeth School of Art.

The palette is muted, using browns, beiges and blues, but with an elaborate border, like most of the pieces Doulton produced at this time.

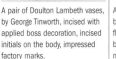

Birds are one of Florence Barlow's most typical and favorite motifs.

The sgraffito decoration over a colored slip is also typical of Florence Barlow.

A Doulton Lambeth bottle vase, by Florence Barlow, decorated pâte-sur-pâte with panels of ducklings with foliate and geometric banding, impressed and incised marks.

10in (26cm) high

$600-900   **L&T**

A Doulton Lambeth stoneware jug, decorated by Georgina Burr, dated, artist's initials, numbered "975".

1884   7.25in (18.5cm) high

$80-120   **DN**

A Doulton Lambeth stoneware tyg, by Louisa J. Davis, dated and with artist's monogram, the collar with indistinct London hallmarks.

1881   6in (15cm) high

$350-400   **DN**

A Doulton Lambeth bottle-shaped vase, inlaid with a Moorish pattern in teal, blue and ivory, stamped "Doulton/ Lambeth", incised "ED".

9.75in (25cm) high

$320-280   **DRA**

A large Doulton Lambeth vase by Florence Barlow, painted with pâte-sur-pâte with flying cranes among foliage on a textured ground, impressed and incised marks.

14.5in (37cm) high

$400-600   **L&T**

A Doulton Lambeth stoneware dressing table set, by Emily E. Stormer, impressed factory marks, dated and with a 'fist's initials "E.E.S."

c1885 Tray 10in (25.5cm) wide

$600-900   **DN**

A Doulton stoneware ashtray, with vesta stand, raised leaf decoration.

The central rectangular protrusion would have held a card matchbox.

4in (10cm) diam

$50-80   **LC**

A pair of Doulton Lambeth candlesticks, by Florence Barlow, each with turned and leaf decorated nozzles, raised on a broad incised base.

8.25in (21cm) high

$600-900   **L&T**

Two Doulton Lambeth 'Faience' vases, one of ovoid form, with impressed date marks, and one of baluster form, impressed and painted marks.

c1880 Taller 10in (26cm) high

$120-180 (each)   **L&T**

A Doulton Lambeth twin-handled vase, decorated with blossom and foliage, the neck with white daisies and birds in flight, factory marks on base.

8.75in (22cm) high

$120-180   **DN**

A Doulton Lambeth stoneware whisky flask, with transfer decoration "Ye Olde Cheshire Cheese, BA Moore & Son".

9.75in (25cm) high

$30-50   **Clv**

A pair of Doulton Lambeth art pottery tapered cylindrical vases, with painted foliate decoration, bases with printed marks and monogram for Emily J. Gillman.

13.5in (34cm) high

$150-200   **Clv**

A late 19thC pair of Doulton faience cylindrical vases, with bases on round foot-rims, printed marks and artist's monogram, one repaired.

14.5in (37cm) high

$500-800   **DN**

A Royal Doulton Series ware 'The Jackdaw of Rheims' fruit bowl, badly damaged.

8in (20.5cm) diam

$7-10   **AS&S**

A 19thC Doulton blue and white transfer-decorated punch bowl, printed mark under the foot reading "Watteau/Eurslen Doulton England", cracks, light staining.

14.25in (36cm) diam

$300-500   **FRE**

Two of a set of 12 Doulton dinner plates, 'Persian Spring' pattern, each in underglaze blue, gilt border with shaped edge, around a similarly decorated center, two damaged.

9.5in (24cm) diam

$320-380 (set)   **FRE**

A Royal Doulton stoneware vase, by Francis C. Pope, of broad oviform tapering to a flared neck, incised decoration, impressed factory marks and incised "F.C.P." numbered "46", restored on neck.

12in (30.5cm) high

$350-400   **DN**

A tall Royal Doulton bulbous vase, decorated by Bessie Newberry, with chains of green and blue ovals around a fluted neck, on a mottled green ground, stamped "Royal Doulton/BN".

11.25in (28.5cm) high

$320-380   **DRA**

A Royal Doulton Burslem baluster vase, decorated in underglaze blue with irises and gilt detailing against a shaded gilt ground, the neck and foot-rim transfer decorated with golden foliage against deep blue, factory marks on base.

9in (23cm) high

$320-380   **DN**

A Royal Doulton ovoid jug, with loop handle, printed and painted with a huntsman, in continuous wooded landscape, within stiff leaf bands, on round base, impressed and printed marks in brown, handle reattached.

c1860-70   *8in (20.5cm) high*

$180-220   **LFA**

A Royal Doulton jardinière, of almost globular shape, transfer-printed with a dark-blue outline of highly stylized flowers and foliage, colored pale blue, green and pale brown, factory mark on base.

6.5in (16.5cm) high

$150-200   **DN**

A Royal Doulton charger, 'Under the Greenwood Tree', painted with Robin Hood and his men within an oak leaf barrier, printed marks and painted pattern number "Q5623".

15.25in (39cm) diam

$150-200   **BonS**

A set of twelve early 20thC Royal Doulton painted porcelain fish plates, each gilt rimmed plate realistically painted with an underwater scene of various fish, signed "C. Halloway", and the fish identified by the artist on the reverse, with green-painted "Royal Doulton/Made in England" under a lion, retailed by Tiffany and Company, impressed numerals.

9.75in (23.5cm) diam

$1,500-2,000 (set)   **SI**

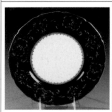

A 20thC set of twelve Royal Doulton dinner plates with raised gilt decoration on a cobalt rim, printed, impressed and enameled marks.

10in (25.5cm) diam

$1,200-1,800 (set)   **SI**

A Royal Doulton Penguin Books advertising figure, raised on a square base, inscribed 'Best Wishes', printed factory marks.

4.75in (12cm) high

$120-180   **L&T**

One of a set of three Royal Doulton plates, boldly printed in blue with flowers amongst sponged gilt grounds, the blue rim bands gilt with oriental flowers, printed marks and impressed dates.

c1925

$120-180 (set)   **Chef**

FIND OUT MORE...

'Doulton for the Collector' by Jocelyn Lukins, published by Venta Books, 1993.

'The Doulton Lambeth Wares', by Desmond Eyles, published by Richard Dennis, 2002.

Collectors' Notes

- Although Doulton had produced figures from the mid-19thC, production did not really take off until c1913 under modeler C.J. Noke, when the HN (for Harry Nixon, head of figure painting department) model numbering system was introduced for a new collection.

- During the 20thC production mushroomed under the guidance of Noke and Leslie Harradine. Take care as some models have variations in color and size which will have different HN numbers and will often have different values.

- Dates given in captions represent the dates between which the figurine was in production. Some have been produced for long periods, such as 'Top o' the Hill', first issued in 1937, which is still being made.

- Fair ladies are the most popular collecting area, and some collectors focus on collecting figures in different colorways which can vary significantly in value. Leslie Harradine's work also forms an important collecting area.

- Condition is of key importance to value. Only figures in mint condition will command the highest prices. Scratches, wear to paint and especially cracks and other similar serious damage, will reduce value dramatically.

Lesley Harradine

A Royal Doulton 'Autumn Breezes' figure HN1934, designed by Leslie Harradine.

Leslie Harradine was one of Royal Doulton's key modelers. He released his first figure in 1920 and, for 30 years, designed at least one figure per month. He is renowned for his stylish ladies which dominated 1930s production.

1940-97   8in (19cm) high

$100-150   Clv

A Royal Doulton 'Top o' the Hill' figure HN1834, designed by Leslie Harradine.

This model, introduced in 1937, is one of Harradine's most enduringly popular designs.

1937-present 7.5in (19cm) high

$120-180   Clv

A Royal Doulton 'Paisley Shawl' figure HN1392, by Leslie Harradine.

This figure in purple HN1707 can fetch twice the value of this version.

1930-1949   8.5in (21.5cm) high

$220-280   D

A rare Royal Doulton 'Colinette' figure HN1998, by Leslie Harradine.

1947-1949   7.25in (18.5cm) h

$220-280   DN

A Royal Doulton miniature figure 'Sweet Anne' M5, designed by Leslie Harradine.

1932-1945   4in (10cm) high

$180-220   DN

A Royal Doulton 'The Mask Seller' figure HN2103, designed by Leslie Harradine, boxed.

1953-1995   8.5in (21.5cm) h

$150-200   D

A Royal Doulton 'Mr Pickwick' figure style 3 HN2099, by Leslie Harradine and from the Dickens series.

1952-1967 7.5in (19cm) high

$100-150   **DN**

A Royal Doulton 'Marie' figure HN1370, designed by Leslie Harradine, restored.

1930-1988 4.75in (12cm) h

$30-50   **PSA**

A rare Royal Doulton 'Erminie' miniature figure M40, designed by Leslie Harradine.

1933-1945   *4¹in (10cm) high*

$500-700   **PSA**

A Royal Doulton miniature 'Robin' figure M38, designed by Leslie Harradine.

1933-1945 2.5in (6.4cm) h

$350-400   **PSA**

A Royal Doulton 'Dreamland' figure HN1481, designed by Leslie Harradine, mounted on wooden base incorporating lamp fitments.

1931-1938 6.25in (16cm) w

$2,200-2,800   **DN**

Mary Nicholl

A Royal Doulton 'Past Glory' figure HN2484, designed by M. Nicholl.

1973-1979 7.5in (19cm) high

$180-220   **PSA**

A Royal Doulton 'Omar Khayyam' figure HN2247, designed by M. Nicholl.

1965-1983 6.25in (16cm) h

$180-220   **Clv**

A Royal Doulton 'A Good Catch' figure HN2258, designed by M. Nicholl, from the Sea Characters series.

1966-1986 7.5in (19cm) high

$120-180   **D**

A Royal Doulton 'The Captain' figure HN2260, designed by M. Nicholl and from the Sea Characters series.

1965-1982 9.5in (24cm) high

$220-280   **PSA**

A Royal Doulton 'Shore Leave' figure HN2254, designed by M. Nicholl, from the Sea Characters series, boxed.

Mary Nicholl joined Doulton as a modeler in the mid-1950s. Her talent made her one of the foremost modelers during the 1950s and 1960s, along with Peggy Davies. Her series of nautical personalities was introduced in 1955 as part of a range of character models including street entertainers and historical personalities. She died in 1974.

1965-1979 7.5in (19cm) high

$150-200   **D**

Margaret Davies

A Royal Doulton 'The Young Master' figure HN2872, designed by M. Davies, boxed.

1980-1989 7.5in (19cm) high

$180-220 D

A Royal Doulton 'Sweet Sixteen' figure HN2231, designed by M. Davies and from the Teenagers series.

Margaret 'Peggy' Davies produced her first figure in 1946 and, working on a contract basis, produced around 250 designs until her retirement in 1984. Dominating the collection as Harradine moved towards retirement, she is known for her 1950s figures in contemporary dress, historical characters and studies of children.

1958-1965 7.25in (18.4cm) h

$120-180 PSA

A Royal Doulton 'Elyse' figure HN2474, designed by M. Davies.

Issued in 1986 in North America, followed by the rest of the world from 1987-1999.

5.75in (14.6cm) high

$120-180 PSA

Other Designers

A Royal Doulton 'St George' figure HN2051, designed by M. Davies.

1950-1985 7.5in (19cm) high

$350-400 PSA

A Royal Doulton 'Welcome' figure HN3764, designed by N. Pedley, boxed.

This figure was a club membership figure for 1996.

5.75in (14.6cm) high

$30-40 PSA

A Royal Doulton 'Take Me Home' figure HN3662, designed by N. Pedley, boxed.

1995-1999 7.5in (19cm) high

$50-80 D

A Royal Doulton 'Christine' figure HN3767, designed by N. Pedley.

1996-1998 8in (20cm) high

$100-150 Clv

A Royal Doulton 'The Jester' miniature figure HN3335, designed by C.J. Noke and remodeled by R. Tabbenor.

This figurine was a Royal Doulton International Collectors Club exclusive in 1990.

1990 4in (10cm) high

$150-200 PSA

A Royal Doulton 'The Genie' figure HN2989, designed by R. Tabbenor, boxed.

1983-1990 10in (25.5cm) h

$120-180 D

A Royal Doulton 'The Auctioneer' figure HN2988, designed by R. Tabbenor.

This figure was made exclusively for the Royal Doulton International Collectors Club and was issued in 1986.

1986 8.5in (21.6cm) high

$220-280 PSA

A Royal Doulton 'Barbara' figure HN3441, from a limited edition of 9,500, designed by P. Gee.

7.5in (19cm) high

$100-150 D

A B C D E F G H I J K L M N O P Q R S T U V W XYZ

A Royal Doulton 'Amy' figure HN3316, designed by P. Gee. This figure was 'Figure of the Year' in 1991.

1991   *8in (20.5cm) high*

$400-600   **PSA**

A Royal Doulton 'Tomorrow's Dream' figure HN3665, designed by P. Gee, from Images Series, boxed.

1995-present

$50-80   **D**

A Royal Doulton 'Sisterly Love' figure HN3130, designed by P. Parsons, from Reflections Series, boxed.

1987-1995   9in (23cm) high

$70-100   **D**

A Royal Doulton 'Susan' figure HN3050, designed by P. Parsons, boxed.

1986-1995   8.5in (21.6cm) h

$120-180   **PSA**

A Royal Doulton 'The Wizard' character figure HN2877, designed by A. Maslankowski.

1979   9.75in (24.8cm) high

$120-180   **PSA**

A Royal Doulton 'Partners' figure HN3119, designed by A. Maslankowski and from the Clowns series.

1990-1992 6.75in (17.2cm) h

$220-280   **PSA**

A Royal Doulton 'The Clown' figure HN2890, designed by W.K. Harper.

1979-1999   9in (23cm) high

$180-220   **PSA**

A Royal Doulton 'Grace Darling' limited edition figure HN3089, designed by E.J. Griffiths.

This model was commissioned by 'Lawleys By Post' in a limited edition of 9,500 and was issued in 1987.

1987   9in (23cm) high

$220-280   **PSA**

A Royal Doulton 'Little Lord Fauntleroy' figure HN2972, designed by A. Hughes.

As this example is a factory flawed 'second', the value is lower.

1982-1985 6.25in (15.9cm) h

$60-90   **PSA**

A Royal Doulton 'Barliman Butterbur' figure HN2923, designed by D. Lyttleton and from the 'Middle Earth' series.

This series was inspired by J.R.R. Tolkien's 'The Lord of The Rings' series.

1982-1984   5.25in (13.3cm) h

$400-600   **PSA**

A
B
C
D
E
F
G
H
I
J
K
L
M
N
O
P
Q
R
S
T
U
V
W
XYZ

A CLOSER LOOK AT A ROYAL DOULTON FIGURINE

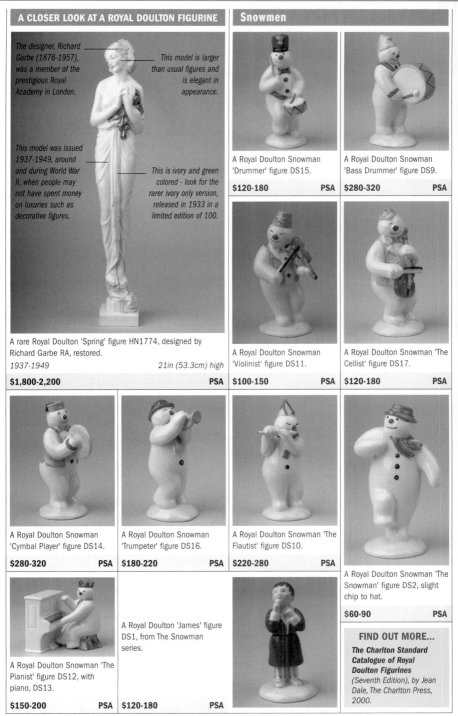

The designer, Richard Garbe (1876-1957), was a member of the prestigious Royal Academy in London.

This model is larger than usual figures and is elegant in appearance.

This model was issued 1937-1949, around and during World War II, when people may not have spent money on luxuries such as decorative figures.

This is ivory and green colored - look for the rarer ivory only version, released in 1933 in a limited edition of 100.

A rare Royal Doulton 'Spring' figure HN1774, designed by Richard Garbe RA, restored.

1937-1949   *21in (53.3cm) high*

$1,800-2,200   **PSA**

Snowmen

A Royal Doulton Snowman 'Drummer' figure DS15.

$120-180   **PSA**

A Royal Doulton Snowman 'Bass Drummer' figure DS9.

$280-320   **PSA**

A Royal Doulton Snowman 'Violinist' figure DS11.

$100-150   **PSA**

A Royal Doulton Snowman 'The Cellist' figure DS17.

$120-180   **PSA**

A Royal Doulton Snowman 'Cymbal Player' figure DS14.

$280-320   **PSA**

A Royal Doulton Snowman 'Trumpeter' figure DS16.

$180-220   **PSA**

A Royal Doulton Snowman 'The Flautist' figure DS10.

$220-280   **PSA**

A Royal Doulton Snowman 'The Snowman' figure DS2, slight chip to hat.

$60-90   **PSA**

A Royal Doulton Snowman 'The Pianist' figure DS12, with piano, DS13.

$150-200   **PSA**

A Royal Doulton 'James' figure DS1, from The Snowman series.

$120-180   **PSA**

FIND OUT MORE...

The Charlton Standard Catalogue of Royal Doulton Figurines (Seventh Edition), by Jean Dale, The Charlton Press, 2000.

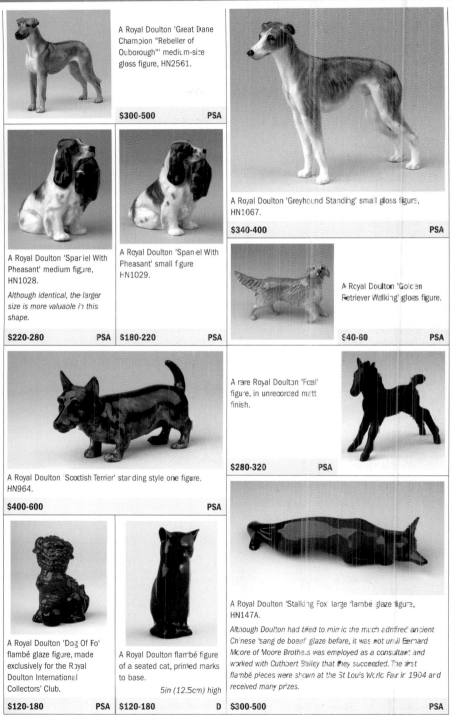

A Royal Doulton 'Great Dane Champion "Rebeller of Ouborough"' medium-size gloss figure, HN2561.

$300-500 — PSA

A Royal Doulton 'Greyhound Standing' small gloss figure, HN1067.

$340-400 — PSA

A Royal Doulton 'Spaniel With Pheasant' medium figure, HN1028.

Although identical, the larger size is more valuable in this shape.

$220-280 — PSA

A Royal Doulton 'Spaniel With Pheasant' small figure HN1029.

$180-220 — PSA

A Royal Doulton 'Golden Retriever Walking' gloss figure.

$40-60 — PSA

A Royal Doulton 'Scottish Terrier' standing style one figure, HN964.

$400-600 — PSA

A rare Royal Doulton 'Foal' figure, in unrecorded matt finish.

$280-320 — PSA

A Royal Doulton 'Dog Of Fo' flambé glaze figure, made exclusively for the Royal Doulton International Collectors' Club.

$120-180 — PSA

A Royal Doulton flambé figure of a seated cat, printed marks to base.

5in (12.5cm) high

$120-180 — D

A Royal Doulton 'Stalking Fox' large flambé glaze figure, HN147A.

Although Doulton had tried to mimic the much admired ancient Chinese 'sang de boeuf' glaze before, it was not until Bernard Moore of Moore Brothers was employed as a consultant and worked with Cuthbert Bailey that they succeeded. The first flambé pieces were shown at the St Louis World Fair in 1904 and received many prizes.

$300-500 — PSA

CERAMICS

Collectors' Notes

- Fiesta ware was manufactured by the Homer Laughlin China Company of Newell, West Virginia. The factory was originally founded in 1871 in Liverpool, Ohio.
- Noted ceramicist Frederick Rhead joined the company in 1927 and was responsible for the design of Fiesta, which was first released in 1936. After changes to the materials and some of the shapes and colors, production of 'vintage' Fiesta ceased in 1969, with all related production ending in 1973.
- Bright glaze colors were introduced in defiance of the Great Depression and to reflect the desire for colorful objects during the 1930s and 1950s. Styling is typically Art Deco, with a concentric circle design as the main design element, which is best seen on the range of pitchers and plates.
- When Fiesta ware was first brought out, there were five colors: red (orange), ivory, cobalt blue, yellow and green. In 1937, turquoise was introduced. Rose, gray, forest green and chartreuse were introduced in 1951, and further colors were added during the period after 1986.
- Values depend on color and shape. Some shapes were changed over time, and some shapes are rare in certain colors. Not all pieces are marked, particularly smaller items where the mark would not fit on the base.
- Collectors can tell newer Fiesta from old Fiesta primarily through the color – consult a reference book to learn which were introduced later. New Fiesta is also made from a different clay. New pitchers have a large dimple inside where the handle joins to body, and old versions have a small dimple. Newer plates bear a mark stating that the glaze is lead free.

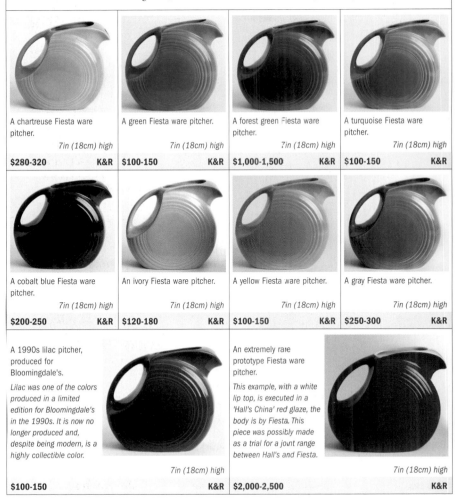

A chartreuse Fiesta ware pitcher.
7in (18cm) high
$280-320   **K&R**

A green Fiesta ware pitcher.
7in (18cm) high
$100-150   **K&R**

A forest green Fiesta ware pitcher.
7in (18cm) high
$1,000-1,500   **K&R**

A turquoise Fiesta ware pitcher.
7in (18cm) high
$100-150   **K&R**

A cobalt blue Fiesta ware pitcher.
7in (18cm) high
$200-250   **K&R**

An ivory Fiesta ware pitcher.
7in (18cm) high
$120-180   **K&R**

A yellow Fiesta ware pitcher.
7in (18cm) high
$100-150   **K&R**

A gray Fiesta ware pitcher.
7in (18cm) high
$250-300   **K&R**

A 1990s lilac pitcher, produced for Bloomingdale's.

Lilac was one of the colors produced in a limited edition for Bloomingdale's in the 1990s. It is now no longer produced and, despite being modern, is a highly collectible color.

7in (18cm) high
$100-150   **K&R**

An extremely rare prototype Fiesta ware pitcher.

This example, with a white lip top, is executed in a 'Hall's China' red glaze, the body is by Fiesta. This piece was possibly made as a trial for a joint range between Hall's and Fiesta.

7in (18cm) high
$2,000-2,500   **K&R**

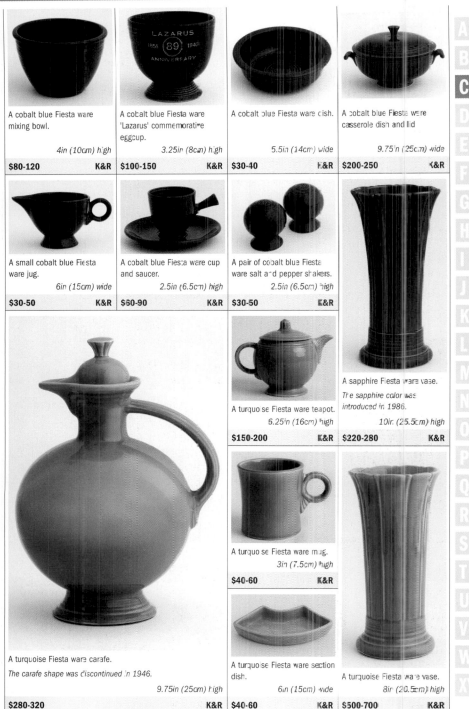

A cobalt blue Fiesta ware mixing bowl.

4in (10cm) high

$80-120 K&R

A cobalt blue Fiesta ware 'Lazarus' commemorative eggcup.

3.25in (8cm) high

$100-150 K&R

A cobalt blue Fiesta ware dish.

5.5in (14cm) wide

$30-40 K&R

A cobalt blue Fiesta ware casserole dish and lid

9.75in (25cm) wide

$200-250 K&R

A small cobalt blue Fiesta ware jug.

6in (15cm) wide

$30-50 K&R

A cobalt blue Fiesta ware cup and saucer.

2.5in (6.5cm) high

$60-90 K&R

A pair of cobalt blue Fiesta ware salt and pepper shakers.

2.5in (6.5cm) high

$30-50 K&R

A sapphire Fiesta ware vase.

The sapphire color was introduced in 1986.

10in (25.5cm) high

$220-280 K&R

A turquoise Fiesta ware teapot.

6.25in (16cm) high

$150-200 K&R

A turquoise Fiesta ware mug.

3in (7.5cm) high

$40-60 K&R

A turquoise Fiesta ware carafe.

The carafe shape was discontinued in 1946.

9.75in (25cm) high

$280-320 K&R

A turquoise Fiesta ware section dish.

6in (15cm) wide

$40-60 K&R

A turquoise Fiesta ware vase.

8in (20.5cm) high

$500-700 K&R

A red Fiesta ware sauce boat.

8in (20.5cm) long

$70-100   **K&R**

A red Fiesta ware sauce boat.

$50-80   **K&R**

A red Fiesta ware small covered bowl.

4.25in (11cm) high

$300-400   **K&R**

A red Fiesta ware bud vase.

6.25in (16cm) high

$100-150   **K&R**

A red Fiesta ware breakfast bowl.

8.25in (21cm) wide

$50-80   **K&R**

A gray Fiesta ware oval platter.

12.5in (32cm) wide

$40-60   **K&R**

A gray Fiesta ware dinner plate.

9.5in (24cm) wide

$20-30   **K&R**

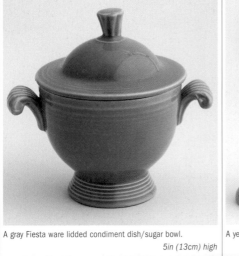

A gray Fiesta ware lidded condiment dish/sugar bowl.

5in (13cm) high

$50-80   **K&R**

A yellow Fiesta ware bud vase.

6.25in (16cm) high

$80-120   **K&R**

A yellow Fiesta ware mixing bowl.

7.5in (19cm) wide

$120-180   **K&R**

A turf green Fiesta ware dinner plate.

9.5in (24cm) wide

$20-30   **K&R**

A green Fiesta ware ashtray.

5.25in (13.5cm) wide

$40-60   **K&R**

A forest green Fiesta ware bowl.

8.25in (21cm) wide

$50-80   **K&R**

An ivory Fiesta ware dinner plate.

9.5in (24cm) wide

$15-25   **K&R**

A rose Fiesta ware small dish.

4.75in (12cm) wide

$30-40   **K&R**

A pair of modern chartreuse Fiesta ware candlesticks.

Chartreuse was the third of the three colors produced as limited editions for Bloomingdale's in the 1990s. Lilac came first, followed by medium blue and then chartreuse.

c1996-1998

$50-80   **K&R**

A rare Homer Laughlin China Company advertising mug for Fiesta.

3.25in (8.5cm) high

$120-180   **K&R**

An ivory Fiesta ware stacking dish set.

4.5in (11.5cm) high

$200-250   **K&R**

A 1990s lilac Fiesta ware butterdish, produced for Bloomingdale's.

Fiesta did not make butterdishes between the 1930s and the 1970s, so all butterdishes are of later manufacture.

7in (18cm) long

$70-100   **K&R**

A Laughlin Fiesta ware anniversary mug.

3.25in (8.5cm) high

$30-50   **K&R**

FIND OUT MORE...

'Fiesta: Homer Laughlin China Company's Colorful Dinnerware', by Jeffrey B. Snyder, published by Schiffer Publishing, 1999.

'Collector's Encyclopaedia of Fiesta', by Bob Huxford & Sharon Huxford, published by Collector Books, 2000.

CERAMICS

Collectors' Notes

- The Fulper Pottery began as the Samuel Hill Pottery in 1815, manufacturing drain pipes in Flemington, New Jersey, where they utilised the local heavy clay.
- Abraham Fulper (1815-1881), an employee since the 1820s, became a partner in 1847 and then took over the running of the company two years after Hill's death in 1858. When Fulper died, the company was incorporated as the Fulper Pottery Company and produced a range of utility ware.
- Fulper's grandson was running the pottery by the turn of the century and was experimenting with colored glazes.
- Pieces are almost always molded, with early examples showing Germanic influence, followed by Oriental and lastly Art Deco styling.
- The factory's output was inconsistent and later pieces are lightweight and are of poorer quality. Look for early pieces, with interesting finishes such as the flambé, mirrored and crystalline glazes.

A Fulper bullet-shaped vase, in 'Cat's Eye' flambé glaze, with three buttressed handles, vertical mark.

6.5in (16.5cm) high

$400-450   **CR**

A Fulper bulbous two-handled vase, covered in 'Cat's Eye' flambé glaze, vertical ink stamp, several shallow scratches overall.

7.75in (19.5cm) high

$250-300   **CR**

A Fulper three-sided corseted vase, covered in a fine 'Cat's Eye' flambé glaze, vertical mark.

8in (20.5cm) high

$350-400   **CR**

A Fulper lotus bowl, covered in 'Cat's Eye' flambé glaze, vertical mark.

9.5in (24cm) diam

$200-250   **CR**

A Fulper corseted vase, covered in a frothy matte amber glaze, with buttressed handles, horizontal mark.

8in (20.5cm) high

$200-250   **CR**

A Fulper low bowl, covered in a dripping mahogany-over-speckled mustard glaze, vertical ink stamp.

9.5in (24cm) diam

$120-180   **CR**

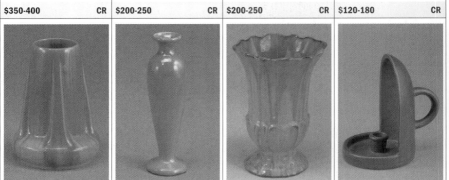

A Fulper tapered vase, covered in glossy amber and turquoise glaze, with four buttresses, vertical mark, short tight line to rim.

8.5in (21.5cm) high

$180-220   **CR**

A Fulper baluster bud vase, covered in an amber and celadon flambé glaze, vertical mark.

6.5in (16.5cm) high

$200-250   **CR**

A Fulper flaring Classical vase, covered in mottled blue and beige flambé glaze, horizontal mark.

7.5in (19cm) high

$70-100   **CR**

An early Fulper chamber sconce, covered in a fine dark brown matte crystalline glaze, vertical mark, small shallow chip to bottom ring.

7.5in (19cm)

$150-200   **CR**

A Fulper bulbous vase, covered in a mirrored blue and green frothy glaze, vertical mark.

7.25in (18.5cm) high

$300-350 CR

A Fulper gourd-shaped two-handled vase, covered in mottled blue and amber glaze, some glaze bubbles, horizontal mark.

7.5in (19cm) high

$400-450 CR

An early Fulper three-handled vase, covered in purple microcrystalline glaze, marked.

4.25in (11cm) high

$220-280 CR

A fine Fulper baluster vase, covered in Chinese Blue flambé glaze, vertical mark.

6.5in (16.5cm) high

$220-280 CR

A Fulper twisted candlestick, covered in a Chinese Blue flambé glaze, vertical ink mark.

8in (20.5cm)

$100-150 CR

A Fulper baluster vase, with prunts, covered in blue crystalline glaze, vertical mark and paper label, minute fleck to rim.

7in (18cm) high

$280-320 CR

A Fulper tall bulbous vase, with flaring neck, covered in a mottled matte blue glaze, touch-up to tight lines from rim, vertical stamp mark.

12.5in (32cm) high

$150-200 CR

A Fulper three-handled vase, covered in turquoise crackled glaze, horizontal mark.

6.75in (17cm) high

$150-200 CR

A Fulper floriform bowl, covered in a sheer turquoise glaze, vertical stamp mark.

3.5in (9cm) high

$80-120 CR

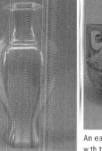

A Fulper faceted vase, covered in an ocher and sheer turquoise crystalline glaze, vertical mark obscured by glaze.

10.75in (27.5cm) high

$150-200 CR

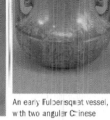

An early Fulper squat vessel, with two angular Chinese handles, covered in a fine Leopard Skin Crystalline glaze, vertical mark, small flake to handle.

4.75in (12cm) high

$300-350 CR

A
B
C
D
E
F
G
H
I
J
K
L
M
N
O
P
Q
R
S
T
U
V
W
XYZ

A Fulper squat ridged urn, covered in Leopard Skin Crystalline glaze, horizontal mark.

7.5in (19cm) high

$280-320 CR

A Fulper low bowl, the exterior covered in a frothy ocher to Flemington Green glaze, the interior in ivory crystalline and green glaze, vertical ink stamp, dark crazing lines to interior.

10.75in (27.5cm) diam

$120-180 CR

A Fulper spherical vessel, with closed-in rim, covered in Leopard Skin Crystalline glaze, vertical mark.

5.5in (14cm) high

$280-320 CR

A fine Fulper bullet-shaped bud vase, covered in Flemington Green flambé glaze, illegible mark.

5.5in (14cm) high

$350-400 CR

A fine Fulper bud vase, with squat base, covered in Flemington Green flambé glaze, vertical mark.

5.25in (13.5cm) high

$300-350 CR

A Fulper 'Colonial Ware' pitcher, covered in mottled green glaze, vertical mark.

5in (12.5cm) high

$80-120 CR

A Fulper two-handled bulbous vase, covered in a Moss-to-Wistaria flambé glaze, vertical mark.

7in (18cm) high

$380-420 CR

A Fulper bud vase, with tall narrow neck, covered in Chinese Blue flambé glaze dripping over a speckled matte green ground, vertical mark.

8.5in (21.5cm) high

$350-400 CR

A fine and early Fulper tapering vase, with two buttressed handles, covered in a fine Moss-to-Rose flambé glaze, paper label, tight line to top of handle.

11.25in (28.5cm) high

$350-400 CR

A large Fulper bulbous vase, covered in Famille Rose matte glaze, vertical stamp mark, a couple of deep crazing lines around rim.

11.5in (29cm) high

$350-400 CR

Two Fulper low candlesticks, one in Famille Rose, the other in Wistaria matte glaze, marked, two small chips to first candlestick.

3in (7.5cm) high

$100-150 CR

A Fulper footed flaring bowl, covered in a frothy blue and white glaze dripping over Famille Rose ground, vertical stamp mark.

10in (25.5cm) diam

$150-200 CR

Collectors' Notes

- James S. Taft and his uncle James Burnap began making redware and later utilitarian stoneware at the Hampshire Pottery in 1872. It was based in Keene, New Hampshire.

- Taft's brother-in-law Cadmon Robertson joined the company in 1904 and introduced a large number of glazes including the matte finishes.

- When Robertson died in 1914, Taft sold the pottery to George Morton of Grueby who continued production for a year. After WWII, the pottery started manufacturing again, making mostly hotel china and tiles and was finally closed for good in 1923.

- Matte green glazed pieces are the most common, followed by matte blue and others. Shapes and decoration is very similar to that of the Grueby Pottery who Hampshire unashamedly copied. Unlike Grueby, the pieces were molded rather than hand thrown with decoration applied in-mold.

A Hampshire bulbous vase, with lotus leaves and buds under a smooth matte green glaze, marked.

7in (18cm) high

$1,000-1,500   **CR**

A fine Hampshire bulbous vase, embossed with tulips under a smooth matte green glaze, marked, 0.25in (0.5cm) kiln kiss to leaf.

8.5in (21.5cm) high

$600-700   **CR**

A fine Hampshire vase, embossed with leaves and buds under a superior green and brown frothy matte glaze, marked, tight inner line, does not go through.

6.75in (17cm) high

$700-800   **CR**

A Hampshire vase, embossed with full-height leaves under a fine matte blue-green feathered glaze, marked.

7in (18cm) high

$1,000-1,500   **CR**

An unusual Hampshire vase, with full-height leaves, covered in mottled and veined café-au-lait glaze against a darker brown ground, marked, hairline to rim.

7in (18cm) high

$300-350   **CR**

A Hampshire squat vessel, embossed with trees under veined matte green glaze, dark crazing lines to bottom, marked.

5.5in (14cm) diam

$220-280   **CR**

A Hampshire squat low bowl, embossed with geometric pattern under a matte green glaze, marked.

5.5in (14cm) diam

$350-400   **CR**

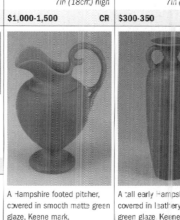

A Hampshire footed pitcher, covered in smooth matte green glaze, Keene mark.

6in (15cm) high

$150-200   **CR**

A tall early Hampshire urn, covered in leathery matte green glaze, Keene stamp.

14.5in (37cm) high

$1,500-2,000   **CR**

A Hampshire bulbous vase, in a brownish gray matte glaze, marked.

6.25in (16cm) high

$400-450   **CR**

CERAMICS

Collectors' Notes

- Berta Hummel was born in 1909 in Bavaria, Germany. A talented artist, she studied art before befriending two nuns and joining the Franciscan convent of Siessen, where she became Sister Maria Innocenti.

- In 1934, Franz Goebel, owner of the Goebel porcelain factory saw her charming drawings of children and was inspired to produce them as figurines. Finally gaining Hummel's permission, Goebel introduced the first figurines to his production line in 1935.

- Since then, over 500 figurines have been designed, the first of which was named 'Puppy Love'. Figurines are still being produced today, so collectors of vintage pieces should familiarize themselves with the marks on figurines which help to date a piece.

- Collectors should study the bases closely. All pieces bear Hummel's name, 'M.I. Hummel'. Impressed numbers, sometimes including a '/', indicate the mold or shape number. An impressed date indicates the date the mold was made and not necessarily the figurine's date of manufacture.

- Backstamps are very important too. The earliest mark includes a crown and dates pieces between 1935-1949. After 1950, a motif incorporating a bee and a V shape was used. The bee becomes smaller and moves inside the V shape from the 1950s through to the 1970s. Wording including 'Goebel' indicates a date of manufacture after 1964.

- The condition of a piece is vital. Hummel figurines graze and chip very easily and such damage reduces value significantly. Look closely at protruding or thin parts, such as small birds or pigtails, as these break easily and may have been reglued.

A Goebel Hummel 'School Girl' figurine, stamped "81 2/0".

4.5in (11.5cm) high

$120-180   **GCA**

A Goebel Hummel 'Little Gardener' figurine, stamped "74".

4.25in (11cm) high

$100-150   **MAC**

A Goebel Hummel 'Autumn Harvest' figurine, stamped "355".

5in (12.5cm) high

$150-200   **MAC**

A Goebel Hummel 'Happy Pastime' figure, stamped "69".

3.25in (8.5cm) high

$120-180   **GCA**

A Goebel Hummel 'Chimney Sweep' figurine, stamped "12 2/0".

This model was originally modeled by sculptor Arthur Moeller in 1935 but was remodeled many times following this. The other vintage version on this page has differences including a different mold number and a turned head and is more valuable than this version.

4in (10cm) high

$100-150   **MAC**

A Goebel Hummel 'Chimney Sweep' figurine, stamped "12/I".

5.5in (14cm) high

$180-220   **GCA**

A Goebel Hummel 'Trumpet Boy' figurine, stamped "97".

c1940   *4.25in (11cm) high*

$80-120   **MAC**

A Goebel Hummel 'Little Pharmacist' figurine, stamped "322".

c1955   5.75in (14.5cm) high

$220-280   MAC

A Goebel Hummel 'Puppy Love' figurine, with some damage.

c1955   4.75in (12cm) high

$180-220   MAC

A Goebel Hummel 'Strolling Along' figurine, stamped "5".

5in (13cm) high

$320-380   GCA

A Goebel Hummel 'Friends' figurine, stamped "136/1".

c1945   5in (13cm) high

$180-220   GCA

A Goebel Hummel 'Good Friends' figurine, stamped "182".

4in (10cm) high

$180-220   GCA

A Goebel Hummel 'Prayer before Battle', stamped "20".

4.25in (11cm) high

$180-220   GCA

A Goebel Hummel 'Favourite Pet' figurine, stamped "361".

c1960   4.25in (11cm) high

$300-400   MAC

A Goebel Hummel 'Goose Girl' figurine, stamped "47 3/C".

4in (10cm) high

$150-200   MAC

A Goebel Hummel 'Wayside Harmony' figurine, stamped "111 3/0".

4.25in (10.5cm) high

$120-180   MAC

A Goebel Hummel 'Just Resting' figurine, stamped "112 3/0".

3.75in (9.5cm) high

$120-180   MAC

A Goebel Hummel 'Out of Range' figurine, stamped "56/A".

6.5in (16.5cm) high

$300-400   MAC

A Goebel Hummel figurine, of a Scottie dog with a slipper and a girl up a tree.

5.25in (16cm) high

$150-200   GCA

A Goebel Hummel 'Little Bookkeeper' figurine, stamped "306".

c1955   4.5in (11.5cm) high

$300-500   GCA

A Goebel Hummel 'Max and Moritz' figurine, stamped "123".

Max and Moritz are two popular German children's characters developed by Wilhelm Busch. Their educational stories appeared in illustrated books and or television.

5in (12.5cm) high

$180-220   MAC

CERAMICS

Collectors' Notes

- Originally conceived as a therapeutic pastime for his patients, Dr Herbert J. Hall established the pottery near his Marblehead sanitorium, based in Massachusetts, in 1904.

- Arthur Baggs joined soon after and by 1908 the pottery had become a commercial enterprise with profits going back into the hospital. By 1915, Dr Hall had sold the business to Baggs after moving his sanitorium.

- Pieces are usually hand-thrown and simple in form with satin matte glazes in a range of colors including blue, gray, green brown and pink. Damage is uncommon, particularly on undecorated ware and any minor marks do not affect the value greatly.

A Marblehead bulbous vessel, covered in smooth matte blue glaze, impressed ship mark.

5.25in (13.5cm) diam

$500-600 CR

A Marblehead barrel-shaped vase, covered in matte blue glaze, faint ship mark.

4in (10cm) high

$500-600 CR

A Marblehead spherical vessel, covered in dark indigo speckled glaze, mark obscured by glaze.

3.25in (8.5cm) high

$380-420 CR

A Marblehead bud vase, covered in speckled indigo glaze, circular stamp mark, bruise and hairline from rim.

4in (10cm) high

$120-180 CR

A Marblehead corseted bud vase, covered in smooth matte gray glaze, circular stamp mark.

4.5in (11.5cm) high

$300-350 CR

A Marblehead small spherical bud vase, covered in smooth matte green glaze, circular stamp mark.

3.75in (9.5cm) high

$400-500 CR

A Marblehead small squat two-handled vessel, covered in curdled and speckled matte ocher glaze, circular stamp mark.

2.5in (6.5cm) high

$500-600 CR

A Marblehead beaker-shaped vase, covered in speckled green glaze, impressed ship mark, several flecks to rim, tight interior line does not appear to go through.

3.75in (9.5cm) diam

$420-480 CR

A Marblehead ovoid vase, covered in speckled blue-gray matte glaze, obscured mark, nick to rim.

5in (12.5cm) high

$280-320 CR

A Marblehead flaring bowl, covered in speckled brown glaze impressed ship mark, cracks through body.

7in (18cm) diam

$70-100 CR

A Marblehead low bowl, covered in smooth matte pink glaze, impressed ship mark.

6in (15cm) diam

$180-220 CR

Collectors' Notes

- The Midwinter factory was founded in 1910 in Burslem, Stoke-on-Trent, England by William Robinson Midwinter. His son Roy joined in 1946 and set about revolutionizing British tableware with innovative designs, many from up-and-coming, young designers.
- Jessie Tait is the most prolific and considered one of the most important of these designers, executing her best work during the 1950s. Terence Conran and Hugh Casson are also notable for their designs.
- Production was aimed at a younger market with affordable, modern shapes and patterns that departed from the austerity of the postwar period.
- The 'Stylecraft' range was released in 1953 and was followed in 1955 by 'Fashion', inspired by Eva Zeisal's work which Roy Midwinter saw on a visit to America.
- Look for designs and patterns that are typical of the tastes of the time. Modern abstract patterns in bright colors are generally more popular and valuable. Condition is important as these pieces were functional and often show signs of wear.

A Midwinter Fashion shape 'Bali H'ai' pattern plate, designed by John Russell, with printed and enameled decoration.
c1960   8.75in (22.5cm) diam
$7-10   FFM

A Midwinter Stylecraft shape plate, unnamed designer, transfer-printed with hand-painted banding.
c1950   6in (15.5cm) diam
$5-8   FFM

A Midwinter Stylecraft shape 'Ming Tree' pattern platter, designed by Jessie Tait, with printed and enameled decoration.
c1950   12in (30.5cm) wide
$30-50   FFM

A Midwinter Fashion shape 'Magnolia' pattern plate. designed by John Russell, transfer-printed.
c1955   6in (15.5cm) diam
$5-8   FFM

A Midwinter Fashion shape 'Falling Leaves' pattern plate, designed by Jessie Tait, with unusual hand-painted background texture and transfer-printed decoration.
c1955   7.5in (19.5cm) diam
$30-50   FFM

A Midwinter Fashion shape 'Bouquet' pattern meat plate, unnamed designer, transfer-printed.
c1960   13.75in (35cm) diam
$20-30   FFM

A Midwinter 'Vegetable' pattern plate, designed by Sir Terence Conran, transfer-printed.
c1955   7.75in (19.5cm) diam
$80-120   REN

A hand-painted Midwinter Stylecraft shape 'Primavera' pattern plate, designed by Jessie Tait.
c1955   9.5in (24.5cm) diam
$30-50   FFM

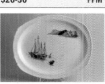

A Midwinter Stylecraft shape 'Riviera' pattern meat platter, designed by Sir Hugh Casson, with printed and enameled decoration.
c1955   12in (30.5cm) wide
$30-50   FFM

A Midwinter Fashion shape 'Whispering Grass' pattern plate, designed by Jessie Tait, with printed and enameled decoration.
c1960   9.5in (24.5cm) diam
$20-30   FFM

A Midwinter Pottery 'Chequers' pattern plate, designed by Sir Terence Conran.

c1960   8.75in (22cm) diam

$100-150   **GGrt**

A Midwinter Pottery 'Chequers' pattern oval platter, designed by Sir Terence Conran.

Conran's 'Chequers' pattern began in 1951 as a textile pattern for David Whitehead, having featured in the Festival of Britain.

c1960   *13.75in (35cm) wide*

$220-280   **GGrt**

A Midwinter Pottery 'Mosaic' pattern dish, designed by Jessie Tait.

c1960   7.75in (19.5cm) wide

$150-200   **GGrt**

A Midwinter Pottery 'Patio' pattern plate, designed by Jessie Tait.

c1960   9.5in (24cm) diam

$100-150   **GGrt**

A Midwinter Pottery 'Magic Moments' pattern plate, designed by Jessie Tait.

c1950   9.5in (24.5cm) wide

$150-200   **GGrt**

A Midwinter Pottery 'Caribbean' pattern plate, designed by Jessie Tait.

This was the first Midwinter pattern to utilise the innovative Murray Curvex printing method.

c1955   9.5in (24.5cm) diam

$100-150   **GGrt**

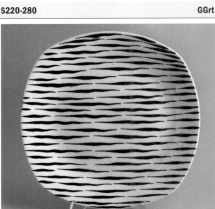

A hand-painted Midwinter Fashion shape 'Zambesi' pattern plate, designed by Jessie Tait.

This pattern was introduced in 1956 and was so popular that it was widely copied. Beswick's 'Zebrette' range is very similar.

c1955   *8.5in (22cm) diam*

$15-25   **FFM**

A Midwinter Pottery 'Hollywood' pattern plate, designed by Jessie Tait.

c1950   9.5in (24.5cm) wide

$80-120   **GGrt**

A Midwinter Pottery 'Savanna' pattern plate, designed by Jessie Tait.

c1955 9.75in (24.5cm) diam

$60-90   **GGrt**

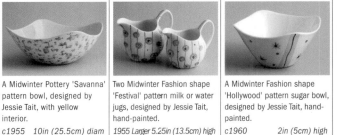

A Midwinter Pottery 'Savanna' pattern bowl, designed by Jessie Tait, with yellow interior.

c1955   10in (25.5cm) diam

$120-180   **GGrt**

Two Midwinter Fashion shape 'Festival' pattern milk or water jugs, designed by Jessie Tait, hand-painted.

1955 Larger 5.25in (13.5cm) high

$30-50 (each)   **FFM**

A Midwinter Fashion shape 'Hollywood' pattern sugar bowl, designed by Jessie Tait, hand-painted.

c1960   2in (5cm) high

$15-25   **FFM**

Collectors' Notes

- Charles Meigh manufactured pottery at the Old Hall Pottery, Hanley, UK. He succeeded his father Job Meigh in the family business in 1835, adding good quality stoneware with Gothic Revival motifs to the range. He won a medal at the Great Exhibition in 1885 for two gilt stoneware vases.

- Pieces can usually be dated from the registration numbers and stampings. From 1835-1849, a variety of marks incorporating his name or initials were used. From 1850-1851, he was in partnership under the name 'Charles Meigh, Son & Pankhurst', using the initials 'CMS & P' and between 1851 and 1861, he traded under the name Charles Meigh & Son.

- Following this, he traded under the name 'Old Hall Earthenware Co Ltd' until 1886 and finally 'Old Hall Porcelain Works Ltd' until 1902, when the factory closed. Look carefully for damage to the relief and missing lids as these will lower the value.

A large Charles Meigh 'Bacchanalian Dance' jug, relief-molded in buff stoneware, molded mark incorporating registration diamond.

c1844   *11.75in (30cm) high*

$300-400   **DN**

A Charles Meigh 'Minster' jug, relief-molded in buff stoneware, applied mark incorporating registration diamond.

c1856   *9.25in (23.5cm) high*

$120-180   **DN**

A Charles Meigh 'Apostle' teapot and cover, relief-molded in buff stoneware, applied royal arms mark incorporating registration date.

c1842   *6in (15.5cm) high*

$120-180   **DN**

A Charles Meigh 'Julius Caesar' jug, relief-molded in buff stoneware and fitted with a Britannia metal lid, applied publication mark, dated.

1839   *6.75in (17cm) high*

$80-120   **DN**

A Charles Meigh 'Gothic Windows' jug, relief-molded in white stoneware and fitted with a Britannia metallic, applied royal arms mark incorporating registration, dated.

1839   *9in (23cm) high*

$150-200   **DN**

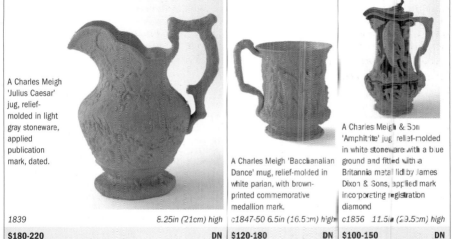

A Charles Meigh 'Julius Caesar' jug, relief-molded in light gray stoneware, applied publication mark, dated.

1839   *8.25in (21cm) high*

$180-220   **DN**

A Charles Meigh 'Bacchanalian Dance' mug, relief-molded in white parian, with brown-printed commemorative medallion mark.

c1847-50   *6.5in (16.5cm) high*

$120-180   **DN**

A Charles Meigh & Son 'Amphitrite' jug, relief-molded in white stoneware with a blue ground and fitted with a Britannia metal lid by James Dixon & Sons, applied mark incorporating registration diamond.

c1856   *11.5in (29.5cm) high*

$100-150   **DN**

A Moorcroft 'Florian' ware candlestick, of tapering form with knopped and slightly swollen sconce, decorated with fine tube-lining and painted in various blues with sinuous flowers and foliage, brown "Florian Ware" mark and signed in green "W.M. des", broken across the middle.

William Moorcroft's 'Florian' ware designs for Staffordshire art pottery MacIntyre & Co. are considered to be one of the most important contributions to Art Nouveau ceramics. Inspired by Middle Eastern patterns, he used the tube-lined decoration technique (fine lines of slip applied to the surface in a pattern) and took it to new heights by covering the entire vessel.

11.75in (30cm) high

$220-280 | **DN**

A Moorcroft 'Pansies' pattern miniature ovoid vase, on a mottled pale blue ground, impressed mark, initialed in green.

3.5in (9cm) high

$600-900 | **L&T**

A Moorcroft 'Pomegranate' pattern ovoid bowl, impressed mark, initialed in blue.

3.25in (8cm) high

$320-380 | **L&T**

A Moorcroft 'Orchid' pattern vase, of shouldered form with everted rim, impressed mark, applied "By Appointment" paper label.

5in (12.5cm) high

$280-320 | **L&T**

A Moorcroft oviform vase, with an inverted rim painted with an orchid design against a dark blue ground, signed "W M" and impressed mark.

5.25in (13cm) high

$150-200 | **DN**

A Moorcroft straight tapering vase with a handle, decorated with irises against a blue and cream ground, impressed marks and "No. 267".

9.5in (24cm) high

$280-320 | **DN**

A Moorcroft Carousel ginger jar and cover, designed by and signed "Rachel Bishop", impressed marks and "No. 232", certificate and original box.

Rachel Bishop is inspired by William Morris' designs.

6.25in (16cm) high

$280-320 | **DN**

A Moorcroft bud vase, designed by Rachel Bishop, the round vase with tall tapering with a peacock, signed "Rachel Bishop", impressed marks, original box.

8.5in (20.5cm) high

$280-320 | **DN**

A Moorcroft rectangular box and cover, decorated to a design by Walter Moorcroft with red hibiscus and a leaf against a mottled blue green ground, impressed "Moorcroft" and "Made in England" with attached paper label.

4.75in (12cm) long

$120-180 | **DN**

A Moorcroft limited edition circular charger, decorated with "H. M. S. Syrius", impressed and painted marks "31/150".

14.25in (36cm) diam

$300-500 | **L&T**

Collectors' Notes

- Considered a pioneer of the Art Deco style, Keith Murray was born in 1892 in New Zealand and trained as an architect. After working for British glassmakers Stevens &Williams, he was approached by Wedgwood in 1932 and his first ceramics were released in Spring 1933.

- His architectural training is evident in his simple, Modernist designs produced for Wedgwood during the 1930s and 1940s. His forms are typically simple, bold and clean. Decoration is usually integral to the form, rather than being painted on or applied, and ribbing and fluting are common. The one exception is a series of tableware, which was patterned.

- The matt, semimatt or celadon satin glazes are also a characteristic and important aspect of his work. Colors include green, white, straw yellow and blue.

- Nearly all of Murray's pieces bear a backstamp; if one is not marked, double-check to ensure that it is a Murray design. Signatures help to date a piece – see the thumbnails of signatures for further information.

- Postwar pieces tend to have a crazed surface, whereas those pieces from before the war tend to be smoother.

- Production of Murray's designs was reduced dramatically during the 1950s, but a few pieces were produced until the late 1960s. Murray retired in 1967 but remained a consultant until c1969.

A Keith Murray for Wedgwood matt green fluted vase, with signature mark.

This shape, known as 3802, was introduced in 1933.

1930s   9in (23cm) high

$700-1,000   SCG

A Keith Murray for Wedgwood matt green bulbous ribbed vase, with signature mark.

c1932   6in (15cm) high

$800-1,200   SCG

A Keith Murray for Wedgwood matt green ribbed vase, with signature mark.

c1932   6.5in (16.5cm) high

$700-1,000   SCG

A Keith Murray for Wedgwood matt green, tall, fluted vase, with "KM" mark.

c1934   9.5in (24cm) high

$800-900   SCG

A Keith Murray for Wedgwood matt green, tall, fluted vase, with signature mark.

c1932   12in (30.5cm) high

$700-1,000   SCG

A Keith Murray for Wedgwood 'Etruscan' white-lined green tall vase, with "KM" mark.

c1934   8in (20.5cm) high

$500-700   SCG

A Keith Murray for Wedgwood matt green ribbed vase, with "KM" mark.

This is a rare shape.

c1934   5in (12.5cm) high

$700-1,000   SCG

A Keith Murray for Wedgwood matt green vase, "KM" mark.

c1934   6.5in (16.5cm) diam

$400-600   SCG

A Keith Murray for Wedgwood matt green plain bowl, with signature mark.

c1932   11in (28cm) diam

$600-900   SCG

A Keith Murray for Wedgwood matt green sweet dish, with signature mark.

c1932   4in (10cm) diam

$60-90   SCG

A B C D E F G H I J K L M N O P Q R S T U V W XYZ

A Keith Murray for Wedgwood matt green lidded jar, with signature mark.

c1936 5in (12.5cm) high

$600-900 SCG

A Keith Murray for Wedgwood matt green lidded sugar bowl, with signature mark.

c1932 4in (10cm) diam

$280-320 SCG

A Keith Murray for Wedgwood matt green ashtray, with signature mark.

c1932 4.5in (11.5cm) diam

$70-100 SCG

A Keith Murray for Wedgwood matt green dinner plate, with "KM" mark.

c1934 8in (20.5cm) diam

$30-50 SCG

A Keith Murray and others for Wedgwood matt green tea cup and saucer.

Saucer 5in (12.5cm) diam

$60-90 SCG

A Keith Murray for Wedgwood matt green desk tray, with signature mark.

The value is considerably reduced if the lid or the liners are missing or damaged.

c1932 10in (25.5cm) wide

$1,500-2,000 SCG

A Keith Murray for Wedgwood moonstone ribbed vase, with "KM" mark.

c1934 6.5in (16.5cm) high

$400-600 SCG

A Keith Murray for Wedgwood moonstone ribbed vase, with "KM" mark.

c1934 7.25in (18.5cm) high

$600-900 SCG

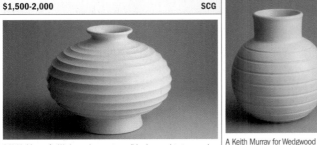

A Keith Murray for Wedgwood moonstone ribbed vase, signature mark.

This shape is hard to find.

c1932 6in (15cm) high

$1,000-1,500 SCG

A Keith Murray for Wedgwood moonstone bulbous vase, with "KM" mark.

c1934 6.5in (16.5cm) high

$400-600 SCG

A Keith Murray for Wedgwood moonstone ribbed vase, with "KM" mark.

c1934 5.5in (14cm) high

$700-1,000 SCG

A Keith Murray for Wedgwood moonstone tall vase, 'KM' mark.

This style of mark was introduced in 1934.

c1934   9.5in (24cm) high

$600-900   SCG

A Keith Murray for Wedgwood moonstone ribbed vase, with signature mark.

This style of mark was introduced from 1932.

c1932   6.5in (16.5cm) high

$800-1,200   SCG

A Keith Murray for Wedgwood moonstone vase, with signature mark.

c1932   7.5in (19cm) high

$300-400   SCG

A Keith Murray for Wedgwood moonstone vase, with signature mark.

c1932   6.5in (16.5cm) high

$600-900   SCG

A Keith Murray for Wedgwood moonstone tall vase, with signature mark.

c1932   11in (28cm) high

$700-1,000   SCG

A Keith Murray for Wedgwood moonstone tankard, printed mark.

5in (12.5cm) high

$70-100   L&T

A Keith Murray for Wedgwood moonstone tankard, with signature mark.

c1932   4.75in (12cm) high

$50-80   SCG

A Keith Murray for Wedgwood moonstone coffee pot, with platinum-glazed handle and "KM" mark.

c1934

$300-400   SCG

A Keith Murray for Wedgwood moonstone milk jug, with platinum-glazed handle and "KM" mark.

c1934   2.5in (6.5cm) high

$60-90   SCG

A Keith Murray for Wedgwood blue bowl, with "KM" mark.

c1934   *6in (15cm) diam*

$400-600   **SCG**

A Keith Murray for Wedgwood blue fluted bowl, with "KM" mark.

c1934   *10in (25.5cm) diam*

$400-600   **SCG**

A Keith Murray for Wedgwood blue bowl, with "KM" mark.

c1934   *6.5in (16.5cm) diam*

$400-600   **SCG**

A Keith Murray for Wedgwood matt straw, ribbed vase, with "KM" mark.

c1934   *7in (18cm) high*

$600-900   **SCG**

A Keith Murray for Wedgwood straw bowl, with "KM" mark.

c1934   *5.75in (14.5cm) diam*

$400-600   **SCG**

A Keith Murray for Wedgwood straw bowl, with "KM" mark.

c1934 5.75in (14.5cm) diam

$400-600   **SCG**

A Keith Murray for Wedgwood matt straw melon bowl, with signature mark.

c1932   *9.5in (24cm) diam*

$300-400   **SCG**

A Keith Murray for Wedgwood matt straw, fluted vase, "KM" mark.

c1934   *7.5in (19cm) high*

$700-1,000   **SCG**

A Keith Murray for Wedgwood black basalt vase, with ribbed decoration, with signature mark.

4in (10cm) high

$600-900   **Clv**

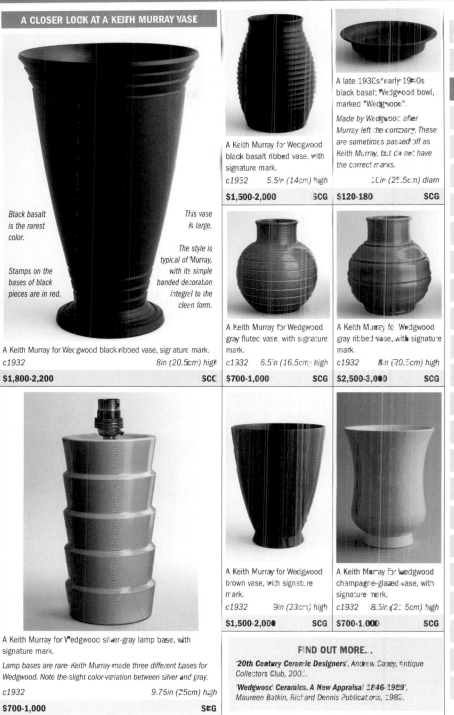

A CLOSER LOOK AT A KEITH MURRAY VASE

Black basalt is the rarest color.

Stamps on the bases of black pieces are in red.

This vase is large.

The style is typical of Murray, with its simple banded decoration integral to the clean form.

A Keith Murray for Wedgwood black ribbed vase, signature mark.

c1932   8in (20.5cm) high

$1,800-2,200   SCG

A Keith Murray for Wedgwood black basalt ribbed vase, with signature mark.

c1932   5.5in (14cm) high

$1,500-2,000   SCG

A late 1930s/early 1940s black basalt Wedgwood bowl, marked "Wedgwood".

Made by Wedgwood after Murray left the company. These are sometimes passed off as Keith Murray, but do not have the correct marks.

10in (25.5cm) diam

$120-180   SCG

A Keith Murray for Wedgwood gray fluted vase, with signature mark.

c1932   6.5in (16.5cm) high

$700-1,000   SCG

A Keith Murray for Wedgwood gray ribbed vase, with signature mark.

c1932   8in (20.5cm) high

$2,500-3,000   SCG

A Keith Murray for Wedgwood silver-gray lamp base, with signature mark.

Lamp bases are rare. Keith Murray made three different bases for Wedgwood. Note the slight color-variation between silver and gray.

c1932   9.75in (25cm) high

$700-1,000   SCG

A Keith Murray for Wedgwood brown vase, with signature mark.

c1932   9in (23cm) high

$1,500-2,000   SCG

A Keith Murray for Wedgwood champagne-glazed vase, with signature mark.

c1932   8.5in (21.5cm) high

$700-1,000   SCG

FIND OUT MORE...

'20th Century Ceramic Designers', Andrew Casey, Antique Collectors Club, 2001.

'Wedgwood Ceramics. A New Appraisal 1846-1959', Maureen Batkin, Richard Dennis Publications, 1982.

A B C D E F G H I J K L M N O P Q R S T U V W XYZ

CERAMICS

Collectors' Notes

- The pottery at Newcomb College, New Orleans was set up in 1896 to teach it's mainly female students a career that would be suitable for young ladies. The male students made the pots by hand, which would be decorated by the women to their own designs.
- This feminine pottery has soft, curved forms with usually floral decoration inspired by native flora which is then covered in a blue or green glaze. Decoration featuring fauna, birds and insects is uncommon and fetches a premium.
- Early pieces have a high gloss finish and are the most sough-after, but by 1910 a waxy glaze was being used. In 1914, the soft matte glaze, which the pottery is generally associated with, was introduced.

An early Newcomb College bud vase, carved by A.R. Urquhart with blue-green leaves on a lighter ground. marked, reglued top.

1905　　*6in (15cm) high*

$1,500-2,000　　**CR**

A Newcomb College bowl, carved by A.F. Simpson, with four protruding 'handles' and decorated with white trumpet vine on a light blue green-ground, marked.

1918　　*8in (20.5cm) diam*

$1,200-1,800　　**CR**

A Newcomb College low bowl, carved by Henrietta Bailey, with trefoils on a medium blue ground, marked.

1923　　*5.75in (14.5cm) diam*

$1,000-1,500　　**CR**

A Newcomb College bulbous vase, carved by Sadie Irvine, with pink roses and yellow centers on a dark blue matte ground, restoration to cracks around rim.

1927　　*8.25in (21cm) high*

$1,500-2,000　　**CR**

A Newcomb College cylindrical bud vase, carved by Sadie Irvine, with tall pines and a full moon, marked, hairlines and repair to rim.

1931　　*6.5in (16.5cm) high*

$1,500-2,000　　**CR**

A Newcomb College bulbous vase, carved by Henrietta Bailey, with a band of white and yellow blossoms on medium blue ground, marked, hairline to rim.

1932　　*6in (15cm) high*

$1,200-1,800　　**CR**

A Newcomb College bulbous vase, carved by Sadie Irvine, with Spanish moss, live oak trees, and full moon, stamp mark, small nick to rim.

1931　　*6.25in (16cm)*

$3,500-4,000　　**CR**

A Newcomb College cabinet vase, covered in a speckled glossy blue to green glaze, marked and dated.

1941　　*3.25in (8.5cm) high*

$450-500　　**CR**

A Newcomb College pitcher, decorated with a band of excised leaves on a speckled indigo glossy ground, stamped mark and paper label.

3.5in (9cm)

$300-350　　**CR**

A Newcomb College low bowl, covered in a purple matte glaze, restoration to chip at rim, "NC/JM/246".

8in (20cm) wide

$280-320　　**R**

Collectors' Notes

- The Noritake pottery was founded in 1904 near Nagoya, Japan by Baron Ichizaemon Morimura. It produced hard paste porcelain tablewares, teawares and figures for export.

- Noritake is often grouped under the group banner 'Nippon' as the American McKinley Tariff Act of 1891 demanded that all Japanese wares imported into the US bear the 'Nippon' mark. This continued until 1921 when the wording was changed to 'Made in Japan' or 'Japan'.

- Most designs were initially copied from late 19thC and early 20thC Western designs, and were decorated with floral, foliage and landscapes in soft pastel tones with gilt detailing.

- During the 1920s and 1930s, the Noritake factory commissioned new patterns from notable designers of the time, such as Frank Lloyd Wright. Today these are highly sought after and valuable. Look for excellent and fine hand-painting and sensitive use of color and form.

A 1920s Noritake cup and saucer, with hand-painted gilt decoration and lakeside scene.

Saucer 5in (12.5cm) wide

$120-180   **BAd**

A Noritake hand-painted plate, with desert scene.

6.75in (19.5cm) wide

$100-150   **BAd**

A 1930s hand-painted Noritake vase, decorated with flowers and birds.

6in (15.5cm) high

$120-180   **BAd**

A Noritake mayonnaise set. c1930 Bowl 5.25in (13.5cm) w

$100-150   **BAd**

A 1930s Noritake ashtray, with hand-painted geometric pattern.

The black and white speckled design simulated the popular Japanese decorative technique of crushed eggshell.

4.5in (11.5cm) wide

$60-90   **BAd**

A blown-out Nippon vase, hand-painted scenic decoration with three eagles sitting on rocks, signed on bottom with green mark.

The large size, excellent condition and exquisite detailing of the hand-painted scenic decoration make this a more valuable piece.

10in (25.5cm) high

$3,000-5,000   **JDJ**

A Nippon large two-handled scenic vase, with gold decoration, lake scene with mountains and trees.

13in (33cm) high

$350-400   **JDJ**

An H. & S.L. Oriental hand-painted dressing table box, with floral and gilt motifs.

3.5in (9cm) wide

$60-90   **BAd**

An L. & Co. Nippon small lidded bowl, with hand-painted floral and gilt details.

3.25in (8cm) high

$60-90   **BAd**

CERAMICS

Collectors' Notes

- In 1910, potter Margaret Cable was hired to run the Ceramics department at the University of North Dakota School of Mines.
- Initially utility ware was produced and early pieces show Art Nouveau influences. By 1913, the School of Mines seal was used on all significant pieces produced.
- Later pieces show Art Deco influences, then local floral and fauna as well as scenes of local life such as native Americans, cowboys on horse back and covered wagons. Decoration is typically carved or sgraffito with some painted pieces.
- Cable taught until 1949 when she retired to California. She died in 1960.
- A number of her students went on to establish potteries of their own.

A North Dakota School of Mines squat vessel, carved by Flora Huckfield, with stylized bales of wheat under an ivory to caramel speckled glaze, circular stamp mark/artist's mark "N.D. Wheat", restoration to top of one bale.

5.5in (14cm) diam

$450-550   **CR**

A North Dakota School of Mines bulbous vessel, covered in rose-to-blue matte glaze, stamped mark.

3.5in (9cm) high

$350-400   **CR**

A North Dakota School of Mines bentonite clay vessel, painted by Phyl Darwin, with birds and leaves on terracotta ground, marked.

3in (7.5cm) high

$450-500   **CR**

A North Dakota School of Mines/WPA Ceramics flaring vase, covered in terracotta speckled semi-matte glaze, ink stamp "WPA CERAMICS N.DAK".

6in (15cm) high

$500-600   **CR**

A North Dakota School of Mines vessel, carved by Renner, with sloping shoulder and decorated with birds in sgraffito against a glossy brown ground, marked. minor fleck to rim.

1952   5.75in (14.5cm) high

$500-600   **CR**

A rare North Dakota School of Mines totemic Sigma Delta Chi trophy, covered in 'burnished' glaze, inscribed "Awarded to the Cavalier Chronicle, Cavalier ND/Best Front Page Make Up", firing line to two sides, restoration to four small areas, small bruise to top.

A North Dakota School of Mines rabbit figurine, by Margaret Cable, with green and brown flowers on a brown ground, marked "MC/105".

4.75in (12cm) high

$600-700   **CR**

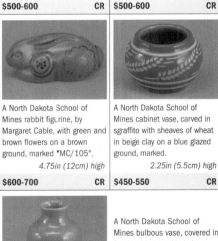

A North Dakota School of Mines cabinet vase, carved in sgraffito with sheaves of wheat in beige clay on a blue glazed ground, marked.

2.25in (5.5cm) high

$450-550   **CR**

Founded at DePauw University in Greencastle, Indiana, on 17th April, 1909, Sigma Delta Chi was an honorary journalistic society. A chapter at the University of North Dakota was established in 1921. Sigma Delta Chi still exists today as the Society of Professional Journalists.

1937   11.5in (29cm) high

$700-800   **CR**

A North Dakota School of Mines bulbous vase, covered in Persian blue crackled glaze, marked.

6.5in (16.5cm) high

$220-280   **CR**

A North Dakota School of Mines squat vessel, carved by Margaret Cable, with a band of blue flowers and green leaves on a light blue ground, circular stamp/artist mark.

5in (12.5cm) diam

$900-1,000   **CR**

A North Dakota School of Mines 'Pasque Flower' flaring vase, by F. Huckfield, in blue on shaded ground, circular stamp/artist's mark.

3.75in (9.5in) high

$500-600   **CR**

A North Dakota School of Mines spherical jardinière, painted by Eleanor Allen, with birds and butterflies, stamped and signed.

1955   8in (20.5cm) diam

$250-300   **CR**

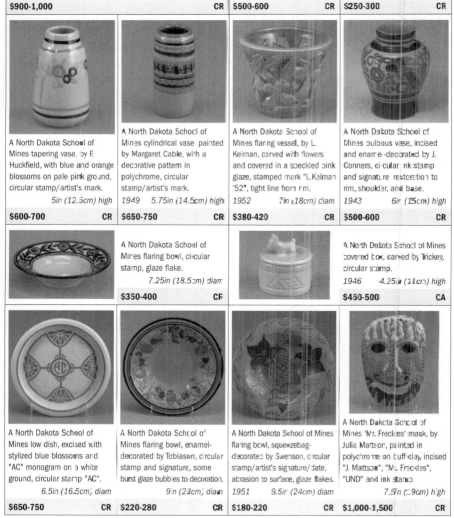

A North Dakota School of Mines tapering vase, by F. Huckfield, with blue and orange blossoms on pale pink ground, circular stamp/artist's mark.

5in (12.5cm) high

$600-700   **CR**

A North Dakota School of Mines cylindrical vase painted by Margaret Cable, with a decorative pattern in polychrome, circular stamp/artist's mark.

1949   5.75in (14.5cm) high

$650-750   **CR**

A North Dakota School of Mines flaring vessel, by L. Kelman, carved with flowers and covered in a speckled pink glaze, stamped mark "L.Kelman '52", tight line from rim,

1952   7in (18cm) diam

$380-420   **CR**

A North Dakota School of Mines bulbous vase, incised and enamel-decorated by J. Conners, circular ink stamp and signature, restoration to rim, shoulder, and base.

1943   6in (15cm) high

$500-600   **CR**

A North Dakota School of Mines flaring bowl, circular stamp, glaze flake.

7.25in (18.5cm) diam

$350-400   **CF**

A North Dakota School of Mines covered box, carved by Trickey, circular stamp.

1946   4.25in (11cm) high

$450-500   **CA**

A North Dakota School of Mines low dish, excised with stylized blue blossoms and "AC" monogram on a white ground, circular stamp "AC".

6.5in (16.5cm) diam

$650-750   **CR**

A North Dakota School of Mines flaring bowl, enamel-decorated by Tobiason, circular stamp and signature, some burst glaze bubbles to decoration.

9in (23cm) diam

$220-280   **CR**

A North Dakota School of Mines flaring bowl, squeezebag-decorated by Swenson, circular stamp/artist's signature/date, abrasion to surface, glaze flakes.

1951   9.5in (24cm) diam

$180-220   **CR**

A North Dakota School of Mines 'Mr. Freckles' mask, by Julia Mattson, painted in polychrome on buff clay, incised "J. Mattson", "Mr. Freckles", "UND" and ink stamp.

7.5in (19cm) high

$1,000-1,500   **CR**

A B C D E F G H I J K L M N O P Q R S T U V W XYZ

CERAMICS

Collectors' Notes

- Nursery ware ceramics were produced specifically for children. Initially these consisted of plates, mugs and tableware, and later figurines were added to production.
- They were first produced in the early 19th century and had surfaces decorated with color transfers of moral and educational mottoes and images. Hence, as the child ate, they could still be educated and instructed with a moral code.
- The first few decades of the 20th century saw a move away from such 'serious' themes into more relaxed and whimsical ones. This began with more natural scenes, or scenes including charming animals or relating to children's stories, being produced.

- In 1926, the English book illustrator Mabel Lucie Attwell (1879-1964), who produced a popular series of designs for cards during WWI, released a range of ceramics produced by Shelley. The 'cute' cartoon-like children that feature on these pieces are typically chubby in appearance and involved in colorful activities that aimed to delight a child.
- Attwell's designs became very popular during the 1930s, with sets even being used in the nurseries of Princesses Elizabeth and Margaret, and later of Prince Charles.
- Look for popular images, such as 'Man In The Moon'. Wear to the transfer and chips or cracks caused through use will reduce value and desirability.

A late 19thC child's mug, "A Token of Love" inscribed below the figure of a woman and child, very minor rim chips.

2.25in (5.5cm) high

$400-600   **Daw**

A late 19thC child's mug, inscribed "To Washington the Patriot of America", with eagle and shield motif each side of handle.

2.5in (6.5cm) high

$400-600   **Daw**

A child's mug, "Playing at Marbles", small crack at top of handle; together with a child's mug, "Blind Man's Bluff".

Each 2.5in (6.5cm) high

$220-280 (each)   **Daw**

A pair of mid-19thC 'Our Early Days' children's plates, inscribed with scenes titled "The Pet" and "Little Titty", the rims enameled with flower sprays in green and violet.

6in (15.5cm) diam

$180-220   **DN**

A Dawson 'Hannibal Crossing the Alps' pattern child's plate, the center printed in mulberry with the titled scene, the rim molded with a running strawberry and trellis design enameled in green, black and dark red, impressed "Dawson".

c1835-50   *7in (18cm) diam*

$120-180   **DN**

A child's plate, inscribed "The Pet Lamb", the rim molded with flowers and leaves enameled in green and crimson, the center printed in green with the titled design of a girl playing with a lamb beneath a tree, unmarked.

c1830-60   *5.25in (13.5cm) diam*

$120-180   **DN**

A 1930s Mabel Lucie Attwell for Shelley nursery bowl.

Attwell's elves are usually green-bodied, yellow and brown elves are more sought after.

6in (15cm) diam

$180-220   **SCG**

A 1930s Mabel Lucie Attwell for Shelley 'Plane' nursery bowl.

6in (15cm) diam

$180-220 — **SCG**

A 1930s Mabel Lucie Attwell for Shelley "Good Ned" nursery bowl.

6in (15cm) diam

$150-200 — **SCG**

A 1930s Mabel Lucie Attwell for Shelley 'Man in the Moon' nursery trio set.

Plate 6in (15cm) diam

$500-700 — **SCG**

A 1930s Mabel Lucie Attwell for Shelley 'Man in the Moon' nursery beaker.

This is a sought-after design.

2.75in (7cm) high

$300-350 — **SCG**

A 1930s Mabel Lucie Attwell for Shelley 'Man in a Caravan' nursery beaker.

2.75in (7cm) high

$280-320 — **SCG**

A 1930s Mabel Lucie Attwell for Shelley 'Duck' nursery tea set.

$1,200-1,800 — **Bev**

A Shelley nursery tea set, designed by Mabel Lucie Attwell, comprising teapot and cover, milk-jug and sugar basin, printed factory mark, facsimile signature.

5in (13cm) high

$1,000-1,500 — **WW**

A Royal Doulton 'Bunnykins' pattern child's breakfast service, comprising plate, cereal bowl and mug, all signed by the artist Barbara Vernon.

Plate 7in (18cm) diam

$60-90 — **Daw**

A 1930s Mabel Lucie Attwell for Shelley nursery chamber pot.

The mark shown is the mark found on the base of this pot and all of Attwell's ceramics with Shelley.

$600-900 — **SCG**

A twin-handled nursery bowl, by Elizabeth Mary Watt, painted with toadstools and running rabbits, painted monogram.

6.75in (17cm) diam

$400-600 — **L&T**

CERAMICS

BREININGER POTTERY

- A ninth generation Pennsylvanian German, Lester Breininger, first began producing his historically inspired redware pottery and molded animal forms in the 1970s.
- His decorative style and techniques follow Pennsylvanian German traditions and include slip-trailed and sgraffito decorated pieces, many with moralistic German inscriptions.
- His high quality early pieces are desirable, as are his large and highly 'folky' dishes and chargers.
- As well as the date and location of manufacture, Breininger often inscribes the reverse with charming observations on the weather.
- A bird-shaped Christmas tree decoration made by Breininger was recently displayed on the White House Christmas tree.
- The pottery is still in existence today and Breininger's work, particularly his vintage pieces, is becoming increasingly collectible.

A Breininger Pottery yellow-glazed plate, decorated with a green accent and a sgraffito design of pig and apple, signed "Brein nger Pottery Robesonia PA December 15, 1995".

7in (18cm) diam

$70-100 **AAC**

A Breininger Pottery yellow-glazed dish, decorated with a green accent and a sgraffito design of a chicken, signed "TM Breininger Robesonia 1974 16/17 #1".

8in (20cm) diam

$100-150 **AAC**

A Breininger Pottery yellow-glazed plate, decorated with a green accent and a sgraffito design of a farmer with a sheep, signed "Breininger Pottery Robesonia PA Aug 10, 1990".

7in (18cm) diam

$50-70 **AAC**

A Breininger Pottery yellow-glazed plate, decorated with green splotches and a sgraffito design of three fish and wavy lines, signed "L Breininger Robesonia Dec 1974".

6in (15cm) diam

$20-30 **AAC**

A Breininger Pottery clear and yellow-glazed charger, decorated with green leaves and a sgraffito design of two peacocks and a tulip growing from a heart, signed "TM L & B Breininger Robesonia PA May 3, 1976".

10in (25.5cm) diam

$180-220 **AAC**

A Breininger Pottery clear and yellow-glazed charger, decorated with green leaves and a sgraffito design of two peacocks and a tulip growing from a heart, signed "TM L & B Breininger Robesonia PA May 3, 1976".

10in (25.5cm) diam

$120-180 **AAC**

A Breininger Pottery hand-formed black-glazed cat sculpture, with clear-glazed base, dated "Jan 1991".

Base 5in (12.5cm) wide

$50-70 **AAC**

A Breininger Pottery hand-formed clear-glazed cat, signed "Breininger Pottery Robesonia PA Sept 1991".

3.75in (9.5cm) high

$20-30 **AAC**

A Breininger Pottery hand-formed clear-glazed bird sculpture, on a round base, with yellow and black slip decoration, signed "TM 70".

2.25in (5.5cm) wide

$15-25 **AAC**

SEAGREAVES POTTERY

- The Seagreaves Pottery was founded in Pennsylvania Dutch country by James Christian Seagreaves and his painter wife, Verna. His work shows strong Pennsylvania German influences and is usually signed with his initials 'JCS'.

- A mill worker by trade, Seagreaves' only reputed formal training was from an itinerant Greek potter named George Karris, who stopped by their shop and taught him how to use a potter's wheel.

- Birds, and particularly bird whistles with an opening at one end to blow through, are a signature form.

- Black is the rarest color and was not always successful.

A Seagreaves Pottery redware bird, blue and yellow with black spatter decoration.
8in (20cm) long

$200-300   AAC

A Seagreaves Pottery redware double-faced owl, decorated with pink and black splotches.
5.5in (14cm) high

$220-280   AAC

A Seagreaves Pottery redware bird with black spiked base and black spatter decoration.
8in (20cm) long

$200-300   AAC

A Seagreaves Pottery white clay bird, in brown and black with embossed decoration.
5.75in (14.5cm) long

$180-220   AAC

A Seagreaves Pottery redware plant bird, decorated with black, yellow and green splotches.
6in (15cm) long

$120-180   AAC

A Seagreaves Pottery redware plant bird, decorated with black, yellow and green splotches.
6in (15cm) long

$120-180   AAC

A Seagreaves Pottery redware bowl, yellow with green splotches and a sgraffito design of a bird and a tulip.
10in (25.5cm) diam

$220-280   AAC

A Seagreaves Pottery redware charger, with a sgraffito design of a tulip and German script border.
12in (30.5cm) diam

$300-400   AAC

A Seagreaves Pottery redware bowl, with everted rim and decorated with black splotches, flakes on edge.
6.25in (16cm) diam

$10-15   AAC

A Seagreaves Pottery redware plate, the clear glaze with yellow dots.
6in (15cm) diam

$30-40   AAC

A Seagreaves Pottery redware candlestick, with handle and pie-crust edge, the clear glaze with black splotches.
6.5in (16.5cm) wide

$60-90   AAC

A Seagreaves Pottery redware tile, decorated with black splotches and a raised hex sign.
4.25in (11cm) wide

$15-25   AAC

STAHL POTTERY

- Production of redware in a traditional Pennsylvania German style began under Charles Stahl in 1850 and continued until his death in 1896.
- His sons Thomas and Isaac took over the pottery until 1902 when competition from mass production forced them out of business.
- After seeing prices for their father's work rise and wishing to continue the tradition, the pottery was reopened by the brothers in 1934, producing household and custom-made pieces in the same traditional style.
- Thomas died in December 1942 but the pottery continued until 1943 when a shortage of materials halted production, until the Fall of 1945 when it was resumed until Isaac's death in 1948.
- Isaac's son Russell continued the business until 1956 when the kiln was fired for the last time. The Stahl family's work, particularly that produced by Charles, is becoming more desirable and collectible. Not all pieces are signed, although Thomas and Isaac usually signed their work. Look for examples that demonstrate traditional decorative techniques, such as sgraffito, where the colored surface is scratched away to reveal the underlying clay.

A Stahl Pottery bean pot, with brown-glazed interior and rolled rim, marked "28", otherwise unsigned, small chip on rim.

4in (10cm) wide

$10-20   **AAC**

A Stahl Pottery brown-glazed flowerpot, with attached saucer, unsigned, much loss to glaze.

6.75in (17cm) diam

$5-10   **AAC**

A Stahl Pottery vase, with two-rib decoration in black, unsigned, base repaired.

3.25in (8.5cm) wide

$12-18   **AAC**

A Stahl Pottery vase, of ribbed design with applied flower decoration and wavy top, unsigned, handles missing.

8in (20cm) high

$80-120   **AAC**

A Stahl Pottery brown-green glazed bowl, with pie-crust edge and coggled decoration, signed "Made by I.S. Stahl Sep 4 1939", minor flakes.

6.25in (16cm) diam

$50-80   **AAC**

A Stahl Pottery mottled brown-glazed bowl, with coggled outside rim, signed "By Stahl 1953".

6.25in (16cm) diam

$30-50   **AAC**

A Stahl Pottery yellow-glazed bowl, decorated with a sgraffito design of tulips, the border with German inscription, signed "Made by I.S. Stahl Aug 5th 1941", chip on rim.

8.5in (21.5cm) diam

$100-150   **AAC**

Collectors' Notes

- 'Pendelfin' was started in Burnley, Lancashire, UK in 1953 by Jeannie Todd and Jean Walmsley Heap, who began making figures at home as gifts. Figures included witches, pixies and other mythical creatures.

- Production soon expanded and became commercial. In 1955, their first rabbit, 'Father Dungaree Rabbit' was made and outsold all previous models. A highly successful family of rabbits followed, although other animal figure ranges were released briefly. Rabbits are the only animals figures made today.

- Many different figures have been in continual production since the 1960s, with Pendelfin still producing today. Some are released specially for the collectors' society – the Pendelfin Family Circle.

- Figures that are out of production or have variations in features will usually hold higher values.

- Collectors prize figurines and other pieces that are not rabbits. Examples include squirrels, witches, gnomes 'Pixi-Bods' elves and wall plaques. These usually fetch high prices when offered for sale.

- Look for rare figures, such as gray mice, and the ultra-rare 'Pixi-Bod caravan' – reputedly only 14 were produced in 1965. The original Rabbit family of five figures from the 1950s is also highly desirable and hard to find.

- As large numbers of the later models were produced, condition is important with chips or other damage reducing value considerably.

A rare Pendelfin 'Daisy Duck' figure, out of production, slight repair to back and minor wears.

c1958   5.75in (12.5cm) high

$1,000-1,500   PSA

A Pendelfin 'Cyril Squirrel' figure, dressed in pink, out of production, minor wears.

7.5in (12.5cm) high

$600-900   PSA

A Pendelfin 'Mother Rabbit' figure, dressed in blue.

No longer in production Mother Rabbit was the second figure produced by Pendelfin, in 1956.

7.5in (12.5cm) high

$280-320   PSA

A Pendelfin brown 'Mother Mouse' figure, dressed in green, minor wear.

Produced between 1961 and 1966, mice were first released in gray. Despite changing the color to brown, their unpopularity with collectors led to their withdrawal.

1961-66   4in (10cm) high

$300-350   PSA

A Pendelfin 'Kipper Tie Father Rabbit' figure, dressed in lilac, minor wear.

This figure was released in 1960 as a remodeled version of 'Dungaree Father Rabbit', which was the first rabbit figure produced by Pendelfin, in 1955. He can be recognized by his larger size, smaller ears and lack of tie. The first 'Father Rabbit' had ears so large they caused the model to fall over and become damaged.

1960-70 7.5in (12.5cm) high

$180-220   PSA

A Pendelfin 'Robert Satchel' figure, dressed in blue, out of production, minor wear.

5.5in (12.5cm) high

$120-180   PSA

A B C D E F G H I J K L M N O P Q R S T U V W XYZ

Collectors' Notes

- In 1921 the well-established firm of Carter & Co. Pottery in Poole, England, set up a subsidiary called Carter Stabler & Adams, which from an early stage was known as the Poole Pottery.

- Truda Adams (later Truda Carter), wife of Managing Director John Adams, became a leading designer. With a background in embroidery design, she worked with stylized floral, foliate and geometrical patterns in Art Deco styles and bright colors. Her work was innovative and highly popular and was included in many exhibitions.

- Red-bodied ware was produced from 1922-1934. Painted marks identify the decorator, rather than the designer.

- When the war started, production dropped but began to grow again after 1946, still producing or adapting some of Carter's designs. She retired in 1950.

- Look for pieces that exemplify the style of the period – a combination of bright colors, stylized, flatly rendered, often large, flowers and geometrical designs. Some of Carter's designs are still produced as tribute pieces today because her work remains so popular with collectors.

A 1930s Poole Pottery Art Deco oviform vase, designed by Truda Carter and painted by Myrtle Bond.

9.75in (25cm) high

$1,000-1,500   **DN**

A 1930s Poole Pottery slender oviform vase, an unusual pattern probably designed by Truda Carter from the 'G' series and probably painted by Rene Hayes (Harvey).

8.25in (21cm) high

$280-320   **DN**

A 1930s Poole Pottery broad oviform vase, designed by Truda Carter and possibly painted by Vera Wills.

9.75in (25cm) high

$350-400   **DN**

A large 1930s Poole Pottery red earthenware oviform vase, designed by Truda Carter and painted by Truda Rivers.

14.25in (36cm) high

$1,200-1,800   **DN**

A rare 1930s Poole Pottery vase, designed by Truda Carter and painted by Ruth Pavely, impressed "Poole England" painter's mark and "203/KN".

8in (20cm) high

$1,000-1,500   **DN**

A 1930s Poole Pottery ogee-shaped vase, impressed and painted marks.

4.75in (12cm) high

$120-180   **LFA**

A large 1930s Poole Pottery red earthenware dish, designed by Truda Carter and painted by Truda Rivers.

15.25in (39cm) diam

$700-1,000   **DN**

An unusual 1930s Poole Pottery red earthenware dish, designed by Truda Carter and painted by Ann Hatchard, in European faïence manner.

12in (30.5cm) diam

$500-700   **DN**

A large 1930s Poole Pottery red earthenware dish, designed by Truda Carter and painted by Ann Hatchard.

14.75in (37.5cm) diam

$400-600   **DN**

Collectors' Notes

- After the war, Poole Pottery realized the need for a creative and free thinking designer to revive their flagging fortunes. Lamp designer Alfred Burgess Read was chosen and became highly influential during the 1950s.
- His most important contribution was the innovative, stylish 'Contemporary' range, which placed Poole at the forefront of British design again. This range was typified by colored bands or columns, often over-painted with geometric shapes, stylized leaf motifs and crossing strands.
- Read worked closely with senior thrower Guy Sydenham on shapes and with decorator Ruth Pavely on designs. All pieces were hand-thrown and hand-painted. Pavely adapted designs to shapes and trained paintresses.
- Designs appear very similar to Swedish ones, particularly the organic forms used at the same time by Stig Lindberg at the Gustavsberg Pottery.
- The 'freeform' range was introduced c1956 and included the 'Tadpole', 'Ravioli' and 'Stars' patterns. Read resigned in 1957 but the range was produced until 1962.
- Large pieces in popular and typical patterns such as 'PKT', 'PLC', 'PRP' tend to hold higher values. As 1930s Poole pieces have become highly popular and valuable, collectors have begun to look at later periods, resulting in a growth in values of 1950s Poole Pottery.

A Poole Pottery 'PRP' pattern vase, designed by Alfred Read, painted by Iris Downton.
c1953   7.75in (19.5cm) high

$300-400   **GGrt**

A Poole Pottery 'PRP' pattern vase, designed by Alfred Read, painted by Diane Holloway.
c1953   6in (15cm) high

$280-320   **GGrt**

A Poole Pottery 'PRP' pattern vase, designed by Alfred Read, painted by Diane Holloway.
c1953   5in (12.5cm) high

$220-280   **GGrt**

A Poole Pottery 'PRP' pattern charger, designed by Alfred Read, painted by Diane Holloway.
c1953   12.75in (32.5cm) diam

$600-900   **GGrt**

A Poole Pottery 'PRP' pattern charger, designed by Alfred Read, painted by Gwen Haskins.
c1953   9.75in (24.5cm) diam

$350-400   **GGrt**

A Poole Pottery 'PKT' Peanut vase, designed by Alfred Read, painted by Gwen Haskins.
c1953   10.5in (26.5cm) high

$700-1,000   **GGrt**

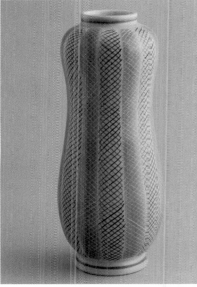

A Poole Pottery 'PKT' pattern Peanut vase, designed by Alfred Read, painted by Gwen Haskins.
c1953   13.5in (34cm) high

$1,200-1,800   **GGrt**

A Poole Pottery 'PKT' pattern vase, designed by Alfred Read, painted by Gwen Haskins.
c1953   10.5in (27cm) high

$400-600   **GGrt**

A Poole Pottery 'PKT' pattern vase, designed by Alfred Read, painted by Diane Holloway.
c1953   5.75in (14.5cm) high

$300-350   **GGrt**

Collectors' Notes

- In 1960, Susan Williams-Ellis, daughter of Sir Clough Williams-Ellis, creator of the famous village of Portmeirion in Wales, bought historic pottery decorating company A.E. Gray Ltd. She used the company to decorate items to be sold in the Portmeirion gift shop she ran.

- In 1961, Susan and her husband bought the Kirkhams Ltd. pottery. This move enabled her to design and make pieces as well as decorate them. The company is still producing Portmeirion today.

- Many of Williams-Ellis' patterns show close links to textile design and also the influence of Henry Moore and Graham Sutherland, her teachers at Chelsea Polytechnic, London.

- Look out for the 'Dolphin' pattern, with a yellow background, which is one of Portmeirion's first patterns. The green 'Malachite' pattern is also rare and much sought after, as it was very expensive to produce so was not available for long.

- Examine all pieces carefully, particularly for chips to

A Portmeirion Pottery 'Talisman' pattern vegetable dish, designed by Susan Williams-Ellis.

c1962   6.5in (16.5cm) wide

$280-320   **GGrt**

A 1970s Portmeirion Pottery 'Talisman' pattern lidded jar, designed by Susan Williams-Ellis.

7.5in (19cm) high

$50-80   **L**

A Portmeirion Pottery 'Talisman' pattern jug, in blue and green, designed by Susan Williams-Ellis.

c1962   6.75in (17cm) high

$120-180   **GGrt**

A pair of Portmeirion Pottery 'Talisman' pattern oil and vinegar bottles, designed by Susan Williams-Ellis, in green and blue, some staining.

c1962   8.75in (22.5cm) high

$80-120   **GGrt**

A Portmeirion Pottery 'Tivoli' pattern, Seraph shape, coffee set, designed by Susan Williams-Ellis, including six cups and six saucers and a coffee pot.

c1964   12.5in (31.5cm) high

$500-700   **GGrt**

A Portmeirion Pottery 'Tivoli' pattern medium store jar, in blue and green, designed by Susan Williams-Ellis.

'Tivoli' was first produced in 1964, following her visit to the Tivoli Gardens in Copenhagen.

c1964   6in (15.5cm) high

$80-120   **GGrt**

A Portmeirion 'Magic Garden' pattern coffee set, designed by Susan Williams-Ellis, including six cups, six saucers and a coffee pot, of cylindrical shape.

c1970   13.25in (33.5cm) high

$500-700 (set)   **GGrt**

A pair of Portmeirion Pottery 'Monte Sol' pattern oil and vinegar bottles, designed by Susan Williams-Ellis.

c1965   9in (23cm) high

$150-200   **GGrt**

A Portmeirion Pottery 'Variations' pattern medium store, designed by Susan Williams-Ellis.

c1964   6in (15.5cm) high

$100-150   **GGrt**

A 1970s Portmeirion Pottery 'Totem' pattern teapot, designed by Susan Williams-Ellis.

6in (15cm) high

$30-50   **L**

FIND OUT MORE...

'Portmeirion Pottery', by Stephen McKay & Steven Jenkins, published by Richard Dennis, 2000.

Collectors' Notes

- The Rookwood Pottery was established by Maria Longworth Nichols (1849-1932) in Cincinnati in 1880.
- In 1883, William Watts Tyler, joined the company as manager and in 1890, when his friend Mrs Nichols remarried and moved abroad, he took control.
- The success of the pottery can be largely credited to Tyler as he standardized the production of existing lines and encouraged new and unusual designs and glazes.
- The company closed 1961 and the rights and molds were bought by the Mississippi Clock Company who continued production until 1965.
- The current owner releases a small production run from the original molds each year.

An early Rookwood Standard Glaze Dark lidded jar, painted by A.R Valentien, with a turtle amidst blossoms, stamped "ROOKWOOD 1885 A.R.V. 47A".

1885   9.5in (24cm) high

$500-600   CR

A Rookwood Standard Glaze Light small pitcher, painted by Emma Foertmeyer with roses, marked.

1890   2.75in (7cm) high

$280-320   CR

A Rookwood Standard Glaze Light bulbous vase, painted by Harriet Strafer, with apple blossoms, marked, short tight line from rim, lines around handle.

1891   7in (18cm) high

$500-600   CR

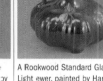

A Rookwood Standard Glaze Light ewer, painted by Harriet Strafer, with clover blossoms, marked.

1892   6in (15cm) high

$380-420   CR

A Rookwood Standard Glaze jug, painted by unidentified artist, with silver stopper, decorated with corn, flame mark, the stopper engraved "JTK".

1896   7in (18cm) high

$800-900   CR

A CLOSER LOOK AT A STANDARD GLAZE VASE

Standard Glaze pieces are usually decorated with floral designs, making this portrait rare and desirable.

The Standard Glaze was introduced in 1884 and became the standard finish until c1909.

William Purcell McDonald worked for Rookwood from 1882 until 1931.

The 'pillow' vase shape is unusual and adds to the value.

A rare Rookwood Standard Glaze pillow vase, painted by William P. McDonald, with woman's portrait, flame mark "707B/W/WPMD".

1894   5.5in (14cm) high

$1,000-1,500   CR

A Rookwood Standard Glaze pitcher, painted by E. Lincoln with pansies, marked.

1898   6.25in (16cm) high

$450-550   CR

A Rookwood Standard Glaze chocolate pot, painted by Caroline Steinle, with orange and brown nasturtium, flame mark "772/CS".

1899   9in (23cm) high

$900-1,000   CR

A Rookwood Standard Glaze bulbous pitcher, painted by Leona Van Briggle, with maple leaves, marked.

1899   4.75in (12cm) high

$500-600   CR

A Rookwood Standard Glaze faceted vase, painted by S. Coyne, with brown maple leaves, marked.

1903   8.25in (21cm) high

$400-500   CR

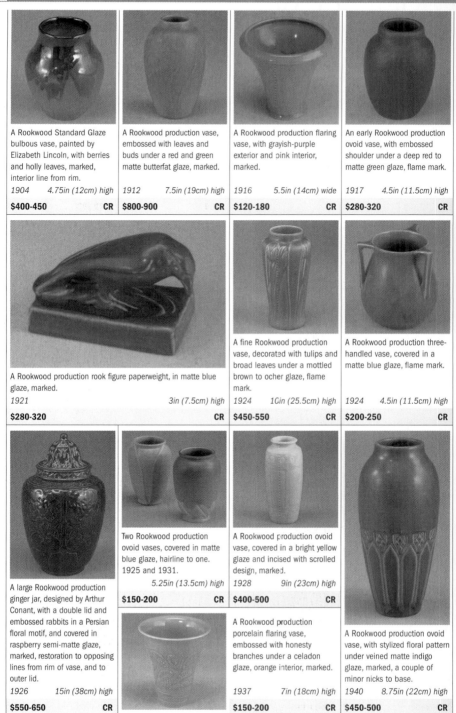

A Rookwood Standard Glaze bulbous vase, painted by Elizabeth Lincoln, with berries and holly leaves, marked, interior line from rim.

1904   *4.75in (12cm) high*

$400-450   **CR**

A Rookwood production vase, embossed with leaves and buds under a red and green matte butterfat glaze, marked.

1912   *7.5in (19cm) high*

$800-900   **CR**

A Rookwood production flaring vase, with grayish-purple exterior and pink interior, marked.

1916   *5.5in (14cm) wide*

$120-180   **CR**

An early Rookwood production ovoid vase, with embossed shoulder under a deep red to matte green glaze, flame mark.

1917   *4.5in (11.5cm) high*

$280-320   **CR**

A Rookwood production rook figure paperweight, in matte blue glaze, marked.

1921   *3in (7.5cm) high*

$280-320   **CR**

A fine Rookwood production vase, decorated with tulips and broad leaves under a mottled brown to ocher glaze, flame mark.

1924   *10in (25.5cm) high*

$450-550   **CR**

A Rookwood production three-handled vase, covered in a matte blue glaze, flame mark.

1924   *4.5in (11.5cm) high*

$200-250   **CR**

A large Rookwood production ginger jar, designed by Arthur Conant, with a double lid and embossed rabbits in a Persian floral motif, and covered in raspberry semi-matte glaze, marked, restoration to opposing lines from rim of vase, and to outer lid.

1926   *15in (38cm) high*

$550-650   **CR**

Two Rookwood production ovoid vases, covered in matte blue glaze, hairline to one. 1925 and 1931.

    5.25in (13.5cm) high

$150-200   **CR**

A Rookwood production ovoid vase, covered in a bright yellow glaze and incised with scrolled design, marked.

1928   *9in (23cm) high*

$400-500   **CR**

A Rookwood production porcelain flaring vase, embossed with honesty branches under a celadon glaze, orange interior, marked.

1937   *7in (18cm) high*

$150-200   **CR**

A Rookwood production ovoid vase, with stylized floral pattern under veined matte indigo glaze, marked, a couple of minor nicks to base.

1940   *8.75in (22cm) high*

$450-500   **CR**

A Rookwood aqua matte glazed vase, painted by A.R. Valentien, with dogwood in aqua matte, signed and stamped with Rookwood mark and "#906C".

6.5in (16.5cm) high

$1,200-1,800 **Daw**

A Rookwood Wax Matt squat vessel, painted by Albert Pons, with an abstract pattern in green and purple on a blue ground, marked.

1907 8.5in (21.5cm) wide

$600-700 **CR**

A Rookwood green matte glazed vase, by Cecil A. Duell, # 1120, stamped Rookwood mark, initialed "C.A.D".

5.25in (13.5cm) high

$500-600 **Daw**

A Rookwood painted matte cylindrical vase, painted by Elizabeth Noonan, with blue and blue-green rooks in flight, flame mark "VIII/952E/V/E.N".

1908 7.5in (19cm) high

$1,800-2,200 **CR**

A Rookwood four-sided vase, decorated by unknown artist, with tulips under a pink and green mottled matte glaze, marked.

1910 11.25in (28.5cm) high

$700-800 **CR**

A Rookwood paperweight of a crouching monkey, in matte green glaze, marked.

1930 4in (10cm) high

$350-400 **CR**

A Rookwood Jewel Porcelain bulbous vase, painted by Elizabeth McDermott, flame mark "XVIII/1278F/EPM".

1918 7.25in (18.5cm) high

$1,500-2,000 **CR**

A Rookwood Jewel Porcelain bud vase, painted by Charles J. McLaughlin, with pink apple blossoms on ivory and indigo ground, flame mark "XIX/2308/CJM".

1919 6.5in (16.5cm) high

$750-850 **CR**

A Rookwood Jewel Porcelain spherical vase, painted by A. Conant, with chrysanthemums in polychrome, marked, several cracks.

1919 5.5in (14cm) high

$500-600 **CR**

A Rookwood Jewel Porcelain coupé-shaped vase, painted by Lorinda Epply, flame mark "XXXI/2254E/LE".

1931 5.5in (15cm) diam

$1,000-1,500 **CR**

A Rookwood porcelain scalloped bowl, painted with a bluebird on bamboo branches.

1946   8.5in (21.5cm) diam

$400–500   **CR**

A Rookwood Iris Glaze mug, painted by A. Bookprinter, with yellow blossoms and green leaves, marked.

1904   4.5in (11.5cm) high

$600–700   **CR**

The Iris Glaze was developed from the Cameo range and was officially launched in 1894

Floral is the most common decoration followed by fauna and lastly landscapes and seascapes, which attract a premium.

Due to the high clarity of this glaze, crazing has a dramatic negative affect on value.

Note the gradually darkening of the glaze from top to bottom, which is typical of this range.

A Rookwood Iris Glaze vase, painted by Irene Bishop, with a branch of purple wisteria, flame mark "V/950D/IV/W".

1905   8.25 (21cm) high

$2,200–2,800   **CR**

A Rookwood Vellum bulbous vase, painted by Carl Schmidt, with polychrome peacock feathers on blue-gray ground, marked, X'ed for light clouding on shoulder.

1904   5.25in (13.5cm) high

$650–750   **CR**

A Rookwood Vellum vase, painted by Sally Coyne, with pink poppies on a gray ground, fine overall crazing, marked.

1908   2.75in (7cm) high

$600–700   **CR**

An early Rookwood jug, enamel-decorated in the Aesthetic Movement style with celadon and brown flowers on ivory and red ground, incised mark, stamped date.

1885   4.5in (11.5cm) high

$500–600   **CR**

A Rookwood vase, of tapering shouldered form, with cylindrical rim, painted with a spray of holly on a graduated amber ground, impressed mark, incised initials "C. A. B.".

7.75in (19.5cm) high

£250–300   **L&T**

A large Rookwood pottery vase-form lamp base, covered in a pale blue and buff flambé glaze, paper label and impressed marks "No. 2372".

1920   16.5in (42cm) high

$700–800   **SI**

A Rookwood Cameo Glaze pitcher, finely painted by unidentified artist, with white clover blossoms, marked.

1889   5in (12.5cm) wide

$200–250   **CR**

Collectors' Notes

■ The Swedish factory Gustavsberg, founded in 1825, is one of the most important Scandinavian ceramics factories. Led by two key designers, Wilhelm Kage and his pupil and successor Stig Lindberg (1916–1982), they produced highly innovative tin glazed earthenware (faience) ranges designed by Lindberg from 1942 onward.

■ Lindberg's shapes were clean, simple and often 'freeform', inspired either by organic forms or by the 'New Look' style of the 1950s. Patterns were brightly colored and proto-abstract in style, with geometric or wavy rhythmic designs that anticipated trends such as Op Art by nearly a decade.

■ Kage and Lindberg were highly influential, inspiring potteries in other countries such as the Rye and Poole Potteries in England. Lindberg is also known for brightly colored whimsical pattern designs.

■ In Finland, Arabia (founded 1932) was the dominant factory, led by Kaj Franck and employing designers such as Ulla Procopé. They became very well known for their tableware ranges. All their work is clearly marked.

■ All factories helped to define the comfortable but innovative modernity that Scandinavian design has become known for, and that the mid-20th century public desired. Look for pieces by major factories such as Gustavsberg and designers that sum up key themes. As many were produced and used day-to-day, look for those examples in the best condition.

A Gustavsberg dish, by Stig Lindberg.

c1940-50   10in (25cm) wide

$320-380   GGrt

A Gustavsberg oblong platter, by Stig Lindberg, with original trade labels.

c1940-50   13in (33cm) wide

$400-600   GGrt

A Gustavsberg dish, by Stig Lindberg.

c1940-50 10.25in (26cm) wide

$300-500   GGrt

A Gustavsberg oblong platter, by Stig Lindberg.

c1940-50 12.5in (31.5cm) wide

$600-900   GGrt

A Gustavsberg freeform bowl, by Stig Lindberg, blue and white stripes, original trade labels.

c1940-50   10.5in (26.5cm) wide

$350-400   GGrt

A Gustavsberg dish, by Stig Lindberg.

c1940-50   8in (20.5cm) wide

$220-280   GGrt

A Gustavsberg vase, by Stig Lindberg, painted on the inside of the mouth with wild flowers.

c1942   11.75in (30cm) high

$280-320   GGrt

A Gustavsberg vase, by Stig Lindberg, of melon shape, with pink stripes and scalloped collar.

c1940-50 8.5in (21.5cm) high

$400-600   GGrt

An Arabia white-glazed earthenware shell-shaped dish, by Kaj Franck, from the ARA series.

1947-53

$50-80   MHT

Two Arabia porcelain matt-glazed teapots, by Ulla Procopé, with cane handles.

c1953

$60-90 (each)   MHT

An Arabia porcelain bowl, by Friedl Holzer-Kjellberg, with pierced "rice" design, signed "Arabia F H KJ made in Finland".

c1955   3.25in (8.5cm) high

$180-220   MHT

A 1950s Arabia ginger jar, by Francesca Mascitti-Lindhl, with pitted oxblood over green glaze.

$120-180   MHT

An Arabia 'Ruska' stoneware bowl, by Ulla Procopé, with mottled brown glaze.

c1960   8in (20cm) diam

$50-80   MHT

A Rorstrand 'Delikat' printed and handpainted vase, by Marianne Westmann.

Many Scandinavian ceramics produced at this time had patterns that were interchangeable, so people could mix and match ranges and colorways.

1954

$50-80   MHT

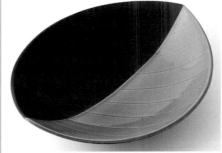

A 1960s Rorstrand leaf dish, stamped to base "Rorstrand".

11in (28cm) wide

$120-180   MHT

A Rorstrand Studio/Atelje bowl, with molded textured decoration, painted marks to base.

c1965   5in (12.5cm) high

$150-200   MHT

A Soholm ceramic panel, modeled with bust of a girl, covered in a green-brown glaze, stamped "SOHOLM STENTOJ BORNHOLM DENMARK".

17in (43cm) high

$220-280   FRE

A Soholm Pottery pitted stoneware vase, impressed marks to base "Solholm Bornholm Denmark Stentoj. handmade".

Made on the Danish island of Bornholm.

$100-150   MHT

A pair of Hoganas stoneware barrel-shaped jars.

c1970

$60-90   MHT

A 1950s Nymolle 'Masquerade' vase, by Bjørn Wiinblad, with red decoration, signed to base.

6.5in (16.5cm) high

$80-120   MHT

A Norwegian earthenware dish, unknown maker, highly decorated with abstract foliage, painted marks to base "806/414e handmade in Norway".

c1960

$100-150   MHT

An American blue spatterware toddy plate, with red, yellow and teal peafowl.

5in (12.5cm) diam

$450-500 **Pook**

An American blue spatterware paneled plate, with berry wreath pattern.

9.25in (23.5cm) diam

$100-150 **Pook**

An American yellow spatterware paneled plate, with red cockscomb.

9.5in (24cm) diam

$2,000-2,500 **Pook**

An American red and green rainbow spatterware bull's-eye cup plate.

4.25in (11cm) diam

$250-300 **Pook**

An American purple spatterware paneled plate, with berry wreath pattern.

7.25in (18.5cm) diam

$350-400 **Pook**

An American green and blue rainbow spatterware cup plate, with bull's-eye and scalloped rim.

3.25in (8.5cm) diam

$550-650 **Pook**

An American red spatterware cup and saucer with blueberry decoration.

$4,000-4,500 **Pook**

A spatterware cup and saucer, slight wear to the rims.

Saucer 5.75 (14.5cm) d

$200-300 **AAC**

A spatterware plate, with green sponge decoration, centered with red house motif.

8.5in (21.5cm) diam

$700-800 **Daw**

An American rainbow spatterware drape creamer

3.25in (8.5cm) diam

$2,500-3,000 **Pook**

An unusual American small blue spatterware paneled pitcher, with rose.

4in (10cm) high

$1,000-1,500 **Pook**

A purple spatterware tea pot with rose decoration.

6.25in (15.75cm) high

$300-400 **AAC**

CERAMICS

Collectors' Notes

- Figures were made in the 'Five Towns' of the Staffordshire Potteries in England – Stoke, Burslem, Hanley, Longton and Tunstall – from the 18thC and throughout the 19thC.

- Early Staffordshire figures are usually made from pearlware and can be identified by their round or square plinth bases and the use of bocage: bushes or branches issuing from tree trunks.

- In the late 1830s, production began on a range of figures called 'flatbacks', which were made specifically to stand on shelves, mantelpieces or against walls. They were easier and cheaper to produce. They were usually formed from a press-molded front and back, with a concave base. Flatbacks are sought after by collectors today. Many were imported into the US.

- Pieces made during the mid-19thC show multicolored, detailed decoration, while later pieces have much less color and detail.

- Staffordshire figures often represent famous figures or events of the day. The Royal Family and military and naval heroes were particularly popular, as were foreign royalty and politicians, actors and even infamous criminals and well-known animal characters. The early figures often bear little resemblance to the personality, as likenesses were not readily available. Later examples used publications such as 'The Illustrated London News' as a reference.

A mid-19thC small Staffordshire figure of a sailor, partially colored.
4in (11cm) high

$120-180   **DN**

A mid-19thC Staffordshire figure of a sailor, partially colored and gilded, one hand restored.
7in (18cm) high

$150-200   **DN**

A mid-19thC Staffordshire model of a sailor, leaning on a capstan, partially colored and gilded, restored.
7.75in (20cm) high

$100-150   **DN**

A Staffordshire figure of a British sailor, the base with gilt inscription "ENGLAND", sparsely colored and gilded.
c1854   9in (23cm) high

$180-220   **DN**

A mid-19thC Staffordshire group of the 'Sailor's Return', partially colored and gilded, on a titled rectangular base, hat overpainted.
12.5in (31.5cm) high

$180-220   **DN**

A late 19thC Staffordshire group of a sailor and companion, partially colored and gilded, some enamel flaking.

$50-80   **DN**

A Staffordshire figure of the 'Soldier's Dream', partially colored and gilded, some areas of enamel flaking.
c1854   9in (23cm) high

$100-150   **DN**

A Staffordshire figure of Prince Albert, modeled standing in ceremonial uniform, partially colored and gilded.
c1845   2.75in (28cm) high

$180-220   **DN**

A pair of Staffordshire figures of a sailor and companion, partially colored and gilded, woman's hand restored.
c1854   7.25in (19cm) high

$300-400   **DN**

A mid-19thC Staffordshire pair of equestrian figures, probably Prince Albert and Queen Victoria, partially colored and gilded

Largest 8in (20.5cm) high

$320-380 DN

A mid-19thC Staffordshire figure of Admiral Lord Nelson, partially colored and gilded, restored tip of hat.

7.75in (20cm) high

$220-280 DN

A Staffordshire flat-back figure of Emperor Napoleon.

15.75in (40cm) high

$180-220 LC

A Staffordshire figure of Guiseppe Garibaldi, modeled standing holding a flag titled "LIBERTE", partially colored and gilded, slight wear.

c1864   10.25in (26cm) high

$180-220 DN

A mid-19thC Staffordshire theatrical figure of John Kemble as Hamlet, partially colored and gilded, on a shaped gilt-line base, some hairline cracks, restored neck.

7.75in (20cm) high

$220-280 DN

A mid-19thC Staffordshire theatrical group, modeled with a couple arm in arm, wearing Jacobean dress, fully colored and gilded, restored.

9in (25cm) high

$280-320 DN

A 19thC Staffordshire figure of a girl, seated on a rock and holding a bird's nest.

6in (15cm) high

$50-80 Clv

A mid-19thC Staffordshire group of a faggot gatherer and her companion, mostly colored and gilded.

12.5in (32cm) high

$150-200 DN

Animals

A pair of 19thC Staffordshire spill vases.

5in (13cm) high

$350-400 Clv

A pair of 19thC Staffordshire penholders, formed as greyhounds.

$70-100 Clv

A 19thC white-glazed Staffordshire 'Willow' pattern cow creamer, the base with a molded leaf.

5in (13cm) high

$60-90 Clv

An American pottery two-handled jug, brown glazed ovoid vertical ribbed body, centrally applied inverted trumpet form spout.

14in (35.5cm) high

$250-300　　　**SI**

A brown stoneware jug, impressed mark "Lewis Jones, Pittston, PA.".

10in (25.5cm) high

$80-120　　　**SI**

A blue and gray stoneware glazed crock, marked "R.J.Miller & Co. Wholesale/King Street, Alexandria VA".

9.5in (24cm) high

$280-320　　　**SI**

A Pennsylvania 12 gallon salt-glaze stoneware preserving jar, by Thomas F. Reppert, of ovoid form with lug handles and a flattened rolled collar, stenciled and freehand decorated in cobalt, marked "T.F. REPPERT./GREENSBORO. PA", brown slip-glazed lining.

Thomas F. Reppert of Greensboro was active between 1880-1893.

22in (56cm) high

$1,200-1,800　　　**SI**

A cobalt-decorated salt-glazed stoneware two-gallon jar, by Hugh C. Smith, the lug handles decorated with feathered vine and flowers at front and leafy devices at back, impressed "H C Smith Alex & DC".

Hugh Smith of Alexandra, Virginia and District of Columbia was active between 1825-1842.

12in (30.5cm) high

$1,000-1,500　　　**SI**

Three American salt-glaze stoneware vessels, one by Wilkinson and Fleming, one by Robert T. Williams and one unmarked.

Largest 17in (43cm) high

$650-750　　　**SI**

Three salt-glaze stoneware crocks, the first impressed "Miller and Alex" and decorated with cobalt flowers, the second stenciled in cobalt "E.J.Miller & Son & Co., Dealers in China and Glass Ware Alexandria, VA", the third, of one gallon size, impressed "F.J.Miller". 1856-1867

Largest: 9.75in (25cm) high

$1,000-1,500　　　**SI**

Two Pennsylvania salt-glaze stoneware vessels, by Thomas F. Reppert, both of ovoid form with lug handles, incised at shoulders.

Largest: 16in (40.6cm) high

$800-1,200　　　**SI**

A redware pottery storage jar, probably Connecticut, iron oxide glaze, manganese splotches.

A Pennsylvania redware peg lamp, of petticoat form.

This is a very rare form of Betty lamp.

A miniature redware jug, made in Maine.

c1810　　　*3.5in (9cm) high*

$620-700　　　**RAA**

c1820　　　*3in (7.5cm) high*

$1,750-1,950　　　**RAA**

c1830　　　*10.5in (26.5cm) high*

$570-650　　　**RAA**

Collectors' Notes

- Lawyer William Day Gates established a pottery in Terra Cotta, Illinois in 1881.
- The Teco line was introduced in 1902 with the matte green color the most common glaze. Gates was strongly influenced by architecture and many of his pieces show this influence with buttressed handles and geometric shapes.
- Teco's organic designs combine Art Nouveau and Prairie School styling with long sinuous lines and flowing, tendril like handles. Green is again the most common glaze and examples in other colors are less sought-after.

A tall Teco wallpocket, embossed with full-height leaves under a smooth charcoaled matte green glaze, stamped "TECO", minute fleck to one hole.

17in (43cm) high

$2,200-2,800   **CR**

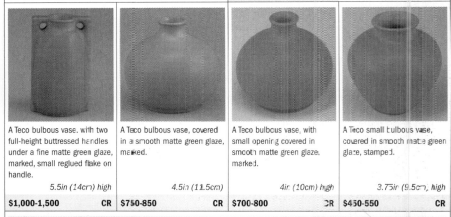

A Teco bulbous vase, with two full-height buttressed handles under a fine matte green glaze, marked, small reglued flake on handle.

5.5in (14cm) high

$1,000-1,500   **CR**

A Teco bulbous vase, covered in a smooth matte green glaze, marked.

4.5in (11.5cm)

$750-850   **CR**

A Teco bulbous vase, with small opening covered in smooth matte green glaze, marked.

4in (10cm) high

$700-800   **CR**

A Teco small bulbous vase, covered in smooth matte green glaze, stamped.

3.75in (9.5cm) high

$450-550   **CR**

Saturday Evening Girls

Collectors' Notes

- The Saturday Evening Girls Club was initially established to offer Boston's immigrant girls an alternative career to factory work or unemployment.
- Started by Mrs. James Storrow in 1899, the club moved to new premises in 1908 and changed it's name to the Paul Revere Pottery. Until the outbreak of WWI, the pottery's main production was vases, tableware, lamp bases and tea-sets, with a brief and unsuccessful period of manufacturing doll's heads during the war.
- The pottery closed in 1942.

A Saturday Evening Girls goblet, with band of gray rabbits on a yellow and gray ground, marked, hairlines and chip.

3.75in (9.5cm)

$220-280   **CR**

A Saturday Evening Girls serving bowl in yellow with white wax-resist rim, marked, several hairlines.

1922   8.5in (21.5cm) diam

$150-200   **CR**

A Paul Revere/Saturday Evening Girls milk pitcher, 'David His Jug', with a polychrome medallion of white goose in landscape on a yellow ground, circular stamp.

4.25in (11cm) high

$750-850   **CR**

CERAMICS

Collectors' Notes

- Artus Van Briggle started working for the Rookwood Pottery in 1887 after studying at the Cincinnati Art School. While studying in Paris he became fascinated by the dead matte glazes of the Chinese Ming Dynasty.
- Van Briggle returned to Cincinnati in 1896 and began researching the glaze. That same year he started his own studio while still working part time at Rookwood. A bout of tuberculosis forced him to Colorado Springs in 1899. Once recovered his experimentation continued, and by 1900 he was exhibiting his matte glaze at the Paris Exposition Universalle under the Rookwood banner. Within the year he had established his own pottery in Colorado Springs.
- Following his death in 1904, his wife Anne continued production using her husbands molds. Pieces made during Van Briggle's lifetime are the most sought-after. As they are becoming more scarce, collectors are now looking for pieces produced after his death.

A Van Briggle bulbous vase, embossed with full-height leaves under a fine frothy sheer blue-green glaze, marked "AA VAN BRIGGLE COLO.SPGS 797", restoration to base and rim.

1908-11   9in (23cm) high

$750-850   **CR**

A Van Briggle bulbous vase, embossed with swirling leaves under a frothy pearl-gray glaze, marked "AA VAN BRIGGLE COLO SPGS 357".

1908-11   4.5in (11.5cm) high

$1,000-1,500   **CR**

A Van Briggle bulbous vessel, covered in matte turquoise glaze, marked, small hairline from rim.

1905   4.25in (11cm) high

$400-500   **CR**

A Van Briggle small bulbous vase, embossed with a band of leaves and covered in indigo and rose speckled matte glaze, incised "AA/Van Briggle/?9", tight interior line from burst bubble, minute fleck to rim.

4in (10cm) high

$80-120   **CR**

A Van Briggle bulbous vessel, covered in a speckled blue-over-rose matte glaze, incised "AA/1915/414".

1915   4in (10cm) high

$280-320   **CR**

A Van Briggle cabinet vase, embossed with trefoils under a mottled green to purple glaze, marked "AA VAN BRIGGLE COLO SPGS 190".

1908-11   3in (7.5cm) high

$500-600   **CR**

A Van Briggle tear-shaped cabinet vase, embossed with daisies under a frothy dark blue-green glaze, marked "AA VAN BRIGGLE COLO SPGS 682".

1908-11   4in (10cm) high

$600-700   **CR**

An unusual Van Briggle cabinet vessel, embossed with berries and leaves under a frothy pink glaze, marked.

1908-11 3.75in (9.5cm) wide

$350-450   **CR**

A Van Briggle cabinet vase, embossed with pasqueflowers under a rich ultramarine frothy glaze, marked.

1908-11   2.5in (6.5cm) high

$350-400   **CR**

A Van Briggle cabinet vase, embossed with trefoils under ultramarine matte glaze, signed and dated.

1914   3.5in (9cm) diam

$350-400   **CR**

A 1930s Van Briggle cabinet vase, incised and embossed with trefoils in peacock feathers and covered in an experimental teal blue frothy sheer glaze, marked "AA VanBriggle/Colo.Spgs.", ink mark "12", #310.

3.25in (8.5cm) high

$350-400   **CR**

A Van Briggle bulbous cabinet vase, embossed with butterflies and covered in a pink and pale blue frothy glaze, incised mark "684", #684.

1907-12   3.5in (9cm) diam

$300-400   CR

A Van Briggle spherical cabinet vase, embossed with crocuses under a chartreuse-to-sky blue matte glaze, marked, small piece of oval glaze missing.

1907-11   2.5in (6.5cm) high

$220-280   CR

A Van Briggle squat vessel, embossed with leaves under an active matte mustard glaze, mark partially obscured by glaze, some burst glaze bubbles to surface

c1905   6.25in (16cm) diam

$450-550   CR

A Van Briggle squat vessel, embossed with leaves, covered in red, green, and blue feathered matte glaze, mark covered by glaze, tight line to rim.

1908-11   5in (12.5cm) diam

$350-400   CR

A Van Briggle squat vessel, embossed with Celtic knots under a sheer frothy light green glaze, marked.

1908-11   6in (15cm) diam

$550-650   CR

A Van Briggle 75th Anniversary limited edition squat vessel, embossed with pine boughs under matte blue and turquoise glaze, complete with 75th Anniversary pamphlet.

1975   9in (23cm) wide

$300-400   CR

A Van Briggle squat vessel, embossed with mistletoe covered in a light-green glaze, marked, large stilt-pull or bottom, tight line stemming from this, very short line to rim.

1906   4.5in (11.5cm) diam

$400-500   CR

A Van Briggle squat vessel, covered in a superior frothy blue-gray matte glaze over red clay, marked "#209".

1906   5.5in (14cm) diam

$500-600   CR

A Van Briggle squat vessel, embossed with dragonflies and covered in mottled blue matte glaze, incised "AA/Van Briggle/20", Y-shaped crack from rim.

$150-200   CR

A Van Briggle bowl, embossed with leaves under a fine feathered grape-purple glaze, marked "#578".

1908-11 5.25in (13.5cm) wide

$750-850   CR

A Van Briggle vase embossed with daffodils over a fine frothy pink glaze, very short tight line to rim, restoration to base, mark obscured by glaze.

A Van Briggle pitcher, covered in a fine feathered light yellow glaze, the red clay showing through, marked "AA VAN BRIGGLE COLO SPRINGS 1906".

1906   6in (15cm) diam

$550-650   CR

c1907   6.5in (16.5cm) high

$700-800   CR

A Van Briggle corseted vase, embossed with tryllium under a chartreuse and turquoise sheer glaze, mark partially obscured by glaze.

c1907   7.25in (18.5cm) high

$800-900   **CR**

A Van Briggle vase, with sloping shoulder embossed with leaves and covered in matte blue-green glaze, marked "#454".

1908-11   5.5in (14cm) high

$600-700   **CR**

A Van Briggle ovoid vase, covered in smooth matte yellow glaze, incised "AA/Van Brigg e/Colo. Spgs./269".

1907-12   7.5in (19cm) high

$650-750   **CR**

A Van Briggle tall urn, embossed with leaves under a frothy light green matte glaze, hairline to handle and small still-pull, marked "AA VAN BRIGGLE CCLD. SPCS."

1908-11 13.25in (33.5cm) high

$900-1,200   **CR**

A Van Briggle gourd-shaped vase, covered in smooth speckled green and blue glaze, marked "AA VAN BRIGGLE 1905 319".

1905   *5.25in (13.5cm) high*

$1,200-1,800   **CR**

A 1930s Van Briggle large urn, with ribbed body, covered in turquoise and blue matte glaze, illegible mark.

12.5in (32cm) diam

$220-280   **CR**

A 1930s Van Briggle Indian vase, embossed with three different Indian chief heads under a deep red and green matte glaze, incised "AA/Van Briggle/COLO. SPGS", bruise to one chin.

11in (28cm) high

$650-750   **CR**

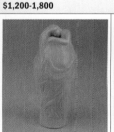

A Van Briggle 'Lorelei' vase, covered in a turquoise matte glaze, incised "AA/Colo.Spgs./J".

The 'Lorelei' vase was one of Van Briggle's first designs and became his signature piece. Early examples made during his lifetime fetch a premium.

11.5in (29cm) high

$280-320   **CR**

A Van Briggle Indian vase, embossed with three different Native American heads under green and brown matte glaze, marked.

c1928 11.25in (28.5cm) high

$700-800   **CR**

An early 20thC Van Briggle flower bowl and flower holder, the oval bowl with irregular rim, molded at one end with a young maiden kneeling on a rock, the conforming flower-holder modeled as a turtle atop a rock, both glazed in turquoise-blue, incised conjoined "A"s within a rectangle and signed "Van Eriggle/Colo. Spgs."

14in (36cm) diam

$800-1,200   **SI**

A Van Briggle incense burner, with a gnome crouching in a crescent, covered in purple and indigo glaze, unmarked.

4.5in (11.5cm) high

$350-400   **CR**

CERAMICS

A miniature Goldscheider wall mask.
c1925-8   4.5in (11.5cm) high
$400-600   **SCG**

A Goldscheider wall mask.
1925-8   11in (28cm) high
$1,200-1,800   **SCG**

A Goldscheider wall mask.
c1925-8   10in (25.5cm) long
$1,200-1,800   **SCG**

A Goldscheider 'Tagedy' wall mask.
c1925-8   (34.5cm) long
$1,200-1,800   **SCG**

A miniature Goldscheider wall mask.
c1925-8   4.5in (11.5cm) high
$400-600   **SCG**

A C. & Co. wall mask, by Copes.
c1934   8in (20cm) high
$180-220   **PC**

A C. & Co. wall mask, by Copes.
c1934   7in (18cm) high
$150-200   **Bev**

A Beswick wall mask.

12in (30.5cm) high
$400-600   **Bev**

A C. & Co. wall mask, by Copes.
c1934
6.5in (16.5cm) high
$150-200   **Bev**

An Austrian Goebel wall mask.
1928-34   8in (20cm) high
$220-280   **Bev**

A 1940s Leonardi wall mask.
20in (51cm) high
$220-280   **Bev**

A pair of Royal Worcester jugs, each printed with floral sprays on an ivory ground, gilt loop handles, puce printed mark, shape number 1094.

c1890   *4.75in (12cm) high*

$220-280   **PH**

A pair of Royal Worcester porcelain trees, by Dorothy Doughty, entitled "Crabapple and Butterfly", with delicate blossoms and blue butterflies, shape number 5-66550.

9.5in (24cm) high

$220-280   **JDJ**

A Royal Worcester porcelain bulbous-shaped jug, with gilted reeded handle, painted foliate decoration, No. 1094.

The printed number in the box on the base of the jug is known as a 'registered design number'. These were applied for and taken out as a form of protection for an innovative design. Until 1883, they used a complicated diamond motif, where each letter and number referred to a different aspect, such as the day and month of registration. From 1884, these were replaced by a number.

4.75in (12cm) high

$150-200   **Clv**

A Royal Worcester porcelain urn-shaped two-handled vase, with painted foliate decoration, no. 2209.

5.25in (13.5cm) high

$220-280   **Clv**

A Royal Worcester porcelain ovoid vase, with painted foliate decoration, no. 302.

5in (13cm) high

$180-220   **Clv**

A Royal Worcester porcelain miniature three-handled loving cup, with painted foliate decoration.

1.5in (4cm) high

$80-120   **Clv**

A Royal Worcester platter, designed by Scottie Wilson, printed with stylized birds and plant forms, printed factory marks.

Scottie Wilson (1888-1972) was a self-taught artist who grew up in Scotland before moving to Canada in the 1920s, where he took up drawing. Returning to England in 1945, he was included in the "Surrealist Diversity" exhibition at the at the Arcade Gallery in London and went on to meet Picasso and Jean Dubuffet, a leader in the field of 'Outsider Art'. In the 1960s he was commissioned by Royal Worcester to design a series of dinnerwares, which was produced until 1965.

13in (33cm) wide

$150-200   **L&T**

A Royal Worcester porcelain figure, 'Summer Regatta, High Society'.

9.5in (24cm) high

$60-90   **Clv**

A Royal Worcester cobalt and gold-decorated porcelain vase, losses.

11.5in (29cm) high

$70-100   **Daw**

A large Amphora vase with two arched, buttressed handles and scalloped base, embossed with stylized cherries and leaves under a smooth matte green glaze, minor nick to one handle, bruise to base, Amphora mark/Austria.

17in (43cm) high

$900-1,000 **CR**

A Baudin three-sided vase, embossed with chestnut leaves under a turquoise, green and black vellum flambé glaze, glaze flake to rim, script mark.

c1910 *6in (15cm) high*

$380-420 **CR**

A Bennington Rockingham Toby jug, with restoration.

Established by James Norton in 1793, the pottery became the largest manufacturer of pottery in US during the 19thC until its closure in 1894.

$60-80 **TA**

A mid-to-late 19thC molded Bennington USA Rockingham glazed spittoon, and a molded flint enamel spittoon, some imperfections.

$220-280 **SI**

A Broadmoor baluster vase, by J.B. Hunt, covered in gunmetal black glaze, signed "Broadmoor Pottery, Denver Colo., J.B.Hunt".

7in (18cm) high

$250-300 **CR**

A Bennington-type jug, some chips.

$45-55 **TA**

A Burley Winter bulbous vase, with ring handles covered in a Famille Rose glaze, incised "53".

6.5in (16.5cm) high

$80-120 **CR**

A Royal Doulton cabinet vase covered in a fine burgundy crystalline glaze, circular stamp mark.

4in (10cm) high

$200-250 **CR**

A Clewell bud vase, covered in a fine bronze and verdigris patina, incised mark and number.

6.25in (16cm) high

$400-450 **CR**

A Clifton matte green bulbous cabinet vase, marked.

After leaving the Weller Pottery in 1905, W.A. Long set up the Clifton Pottery in Newark, NJ. His low-relief Art Nouveau designs were inspired by Van Briggle.

1905 *3.25in (8.5cm) high*

$200-250 **CR**

An Auguste Delaherche tapered ribbed vase, covered in red and green mottled semi-matte glaze, small bruise to rim, stamped "Auguste Delaherche".

4.25in (11cm)

$450-550 **CR**

A rare Denver White bulbous vase, cameo-decorated with white trees on blue-gray clay, incised "Denver W", firing line to inner rim.

5.5in (14cm) high

$450-550 **CR**

A rare Denver White baluster vase, of green, blue, and sand marbleized clay, incised "Denver W".

5.25in (13.5cm) high

$450-550 CR

A Galloway planter, with curled rim covered in turquoise and amber crystalline glaze, stamped "Galloway", tight line from rim and a few chips to feet.

6.5in (16 5cm) high

$150-200 CR

A Gouda two-handled vase, with squat base and tall neck, painted with pink and purple flowers with green leaves against a beige and indigo ground, painted house mark/Zuid Holland.

9.5in (24cm) high

$500-600 CR

A Grueby small bulbous vase, with vertical ribs under a fine curdled matte green glaze, circular stamp.

4.75in (14.5cm) high

$1,200-1,800 CR

A Goldscheider portrait plaque, "Mater Purisima".

The factory was founded by Friedrich Goldscheider in Vienna in 1885 and continued by his family until its closure in 1954. The factory is best known for its decorative Art Nouveau figures and Art Deco figures and masks.

c1895

17in (43cm) high

$220-280 TA

A Haeger 'Early American' vase with luster drip glaze on matte black, marked.

6in (15cm) high

$80-120 TA

A Jugtown pear-shaped vase, covered in Chinese blue glaze with red flashes. circular stamp.

6in (15cm) high

$1,200-1,800 CR

A Kenton Hills coupé-shaped vase, by R. Dickman, painted with ferns in pink and purple on a crackled ivory ground, faint impressed mark, signed "R. Dickman/Unica", long hairline from rim.

5.25in (13.5cm)

$250-350 CR

A fine Lauder, Royal Barum bulbous vase, with three applied handles, excised with birds on blooming branches and covered in forest green, amber, and mahogany glaze, incised "Lauder Barum/March 1910".

1910   8.75in (22cm) high

$450-550 CR

A fine Lauder, Royal Barum tapering vase, with scrolled handles and ruffled rim, excised with fish and sea plants in green and blue on a glossy ivory ground, small glaze flakes, incised "Lauder, Barum".

9in (23cm) high

$220-280 CR

A Leach Pottery stoneware pitcher, possibly lacking a lid, signed "Leach", and stamped with lizard and wheel.

Benard Leach established the St Ives Pottery in Cornwall. He had developed an interest in Japanese and Korean pottery while teaching in Japan. He produced Oriental influenced pieces as well others inspired by English slipware.

10in (25.5cm) wide

$200-250 CR

A Richard Lind large bulbous vessel, with carved band above shoulder, covered in a glossy black glaze, signed "Lind".

11.75in (30cm) wide

$200-250 CR

Two J. & J.G. Low tiles, molded with profiles of a Classical man and woman, covered in sheer olive green glaze, stamped "J. & J.G. LOW/Patent/Art Tile Works".

6in (15cm) wide

$200-250 CR

A Delphin Massier two-handled bulbous porcelain vase, painted with a fall scene of birch trees by a creek, under a vellum finish, artist-signed "JN/JH", and "Delphin Massier/Vallurais".

5.25in (13.5cm) high

$500-600 CR

A Natzler asymmetrically-folded bowl, covered in mottled beige semi-matte glaze, short and tight nick to rim, signed "Natzler", in ink.

2.5in (6cm) high

$600-700 DRA

A New Orleans Art Pottery small vessel, covered in mottled matte purple glaze, chipping of glaze to interior bottom, and small flake at rim, incised New Orleans.

4.25in (11cm) wide

$150-250 CR

A Niloak 'Mission Ware' corseted vase, stamped "Niloak".

9.25in (23.5cm) high

$180-220 CR

A George Ohr flaring vase, with closed-in rim, covered in gunmetal brown-speckled light green glaze, stamped "G.E.OHR BILOXI", a couple of minor glaze flakes to rim.

4in (10cm) wide

$2,000-2,500 CR

A George Ohr red bisque clay vessel, with rounded neck and protruding shoulder, stamped "G.E. OHR/Biloxi, Miss.", grinding chips around base, a couple of flecks to rim.

Ohr (1857-1918) produced studio pottery from his Biloxi Pottery in Mississippi, which are typifed by thinly potted vessels of irregular form.

3.75in (9.5cm) wide

$1,200-1,800 CR

A planter, probably executed by an Overbeck student, incised with a band of squares, and covered in a matte café-au-lait glaze, incised "EW".

$180-220 CR

A rare Overbeck flower frog, with applied and reticulated five-petal flowers in yellow, purple, and blue, one reglued petal, chip to another, marked "OBK".

5in (12.5cm) high

$200-250 CR

An Overbeck figurine of a cello player, with pink leaf hat, marked "OBK".

3.5in (9cm) high

$400-500 CR

An Overbeck figurine of a Victorian lady, in white, blue, and pink patterned hoop dress, stamped "OBK".

4.25in (11cm) high

$350-450 CR

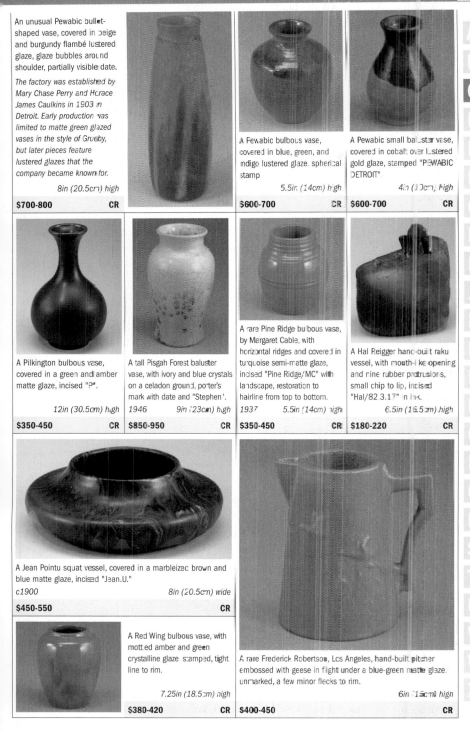

An unusual Pewabic bullet-shaped vase, covered in beige and burgundy flambé lustered glaze, glaze bubbles around shoulder, partially visible date.

The factory was established by Mary Chase Perry and Horace James Caulkins in 1903 in Detroit. Early production was limited to matte green glazed vases in the style of Grueby, but later pieces feature lustered glazes that the company became known for.

8in (20.5cm) high

$700-800   CR

A Pewabic bulbous vase, covered in blue, green, and indigo lustered glaze. spherical stamp

5.5in (14cm) high

$600-700   CR

A Pewabic small baluster vase, covered in cobalt over lustered gold glaze, stamped "PEWABIC DETROIT".

4in (10cm) high

$600-700   CR

A Pilkington bulbous vase, covered in a green and amber matte glaze, incised "P".

12in (30.5cm) high

$350-450   CR

A tall Pisgah Forest baluster vase, with ivory and blue crystals on a celadon ground, potter's mark with date and "Stephen".

1946   9in (23cm) high

$850-950   CR

A rare Pine Ridge bulbous vase, by Margaret Cable, with horizontal ridges and covered in turquoise semi-matte glaze, incised "Pine Ridge/MC" with landscape, restoration to hairline from top to bottom.

1937   5.5in (14cm) high

$350-450   CR

A Hal Reigger hand-built raku vessel, with mouth-like opening and nine rubber protrusions, small chip to lip, incised "Hal/82 3.17" in ink.

6.5in (16.5cm) high

$180-220   CR

A Jean Pointu squat vessel, covered in a marbleized brown and blue matte glaze, incised "Jean.U."

c1900   8in (20.5cm) wide

$450-550   CR

A Red Wing bulbous vase, with mottled amber and green crystalline glaze, stamped, tight line to rim.

7.25in (18.5cm) high

$380-420   CR

A rare Frederick Robertson, Los Angeles, hand-built pitcher embossed with geese in flight under a blue-green matte glaze, unmarked, a few minor flecks to rim.

6in (15cm) high

$400-450   CR

A Rockingham pitcher, with hound handle, dog and hunter with gun motif on one side, pheasant in a tree motif on other side.

7in (18cm) high

$120-180 **Daw**

A Roseville green Baneda squat vase, tight line to rim, black foil label.

Founded in Roseville, Ohio in 1890 by George F. Young, the pottery moved to Zaneville, Ohio in 1910. Wares produced between 1900 and 1920 are the most sought-after and include the 'Rozane' range.

4in (10cm) high

$400-500 **CR**

A pair of Roseville double-handled pottery vases, marked "#986-9", losses.

9.5in (24cm) high

$250-300 **Daw**

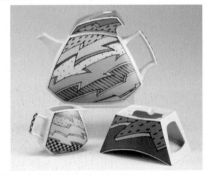

A Rosenthal 'Flash' lidded teapot, with burner and creamer, unmarked.

Teapot 7.75in (19.5cm) high

$350-400 **CR**

A Watchee lion figure, covered in brown matte glaze some firing lines, incised mark.

17in (43cm) long

$180-220 **CR**

A Shearwater ribbed tapering vase, covered in matte turquoise and gunmetal glaze, stamped mark, two hairlines from rim.

7.75in (19.5cm) high

$100-150 **CR**

A rare Walrich chamberstick, embossed with pine cones under a speckled brown glaze, stamped mark, repair to spout.

4.25in (11cm) diam

$80-120 **CR**

A Weller La Sa bullet-shaped vase, decorated with pine trees in front of a mountain lake, tight line to rim, unmarked.

6in (15cm) high

$300-350 **CR**

An unmarked pottery vase, possibly unmarked Weller, raised leaf motif, blue matte glaze.

8in (20cm) high

$45-55 **Daw**

A Weller Woodland jardinieré, tight hairline to bottom.

6in (15cm) high

$120-180 **TA**

An American spongeware spittoon.

c1880 7.25in (18.5cm) diam

$100-150 **BCAC**

A early 20thC American yellow ware bowl.

8.5in (21.5cm) diam

$70-100 **BCAC**

A late 19thC spill holder attributed to the Bell Pottery.

3.25in (8.5cm) high

$300-400 **Pook**

An American tin-glazed pottery frog mug, with lizard handle and blue glaze, monogrammed "M.B.C.", losses.

6in (15cm) high

$250-300 **Daw**

A late 19thC ceramic barbers shop patriotic shaving mug for 'Roby Buck', made in Germany.

3.25in (8cm) high

$150-200 **BCAC**

A George North Morris redware dish, with female mask decoration, bears paper label from Cape Cod Clay, George North Morris, Hyannis, Massachusets, losses.

10in (25.5cm) wide

$80-120 **Daw**

A large Austrian vase, with three buttressed handles, covered in blue and green glazes, fleck to two handles, and to base, stamped "Austria", with tower and "JBD".

13.25in (33.5cm) high

$280-320 **CR**

A European vase, covered in a rich purple, gold and blue lustered glaze, with applied branch of apples in matte red and green, some repairs and losses to leaves, illegible stamp mark.

9in (23cm) high

$220-280 **CR**

A tall redware pitcher, with applied wreath and blossoms in green and with on a banded ground, chips to spout.

10in (25.5cm)

$150-200 **TA**

An American redware chamber pot.

$180-220 **TA**

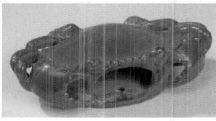

An unusual stoneware wall pocket of crab shape, hand modeled with olive green glaze, unmarked.

8in (20cm) wide

$120-180 **TA**

A B C D E F G H I J K L M N O P Q R S T U V W XYZ

An Angelo Garzio stoneware pitcher, decorated with fish in dark brown wax-resist on a gray and amber ground, signed and dated.

1985   8.75in (22cm) high

$120-180   **CR**

A rare Keramos elephant figure, covered in cherry red crackled glaze, stamped "Keramos/Made in Austria".

5.5in (14cm) wide

$400-450   **CR**

A B.B. Craig double face two-handled jug of brown, white, and gray marbleized clay with indigo glaze, signed.

11.75in (30cm) high

$600-700   **CR**

Two David MacDonald stoneware pieces, a corseted covered jar and a pitcher, both with incised unglazed ribs in abstract pattern on chocolate brown semi-matte ground, signed and dated.

1985   12.5in (32cm) high

$120-180   **CR**

A McCoy mantel vase, in the form of leaves.

c1935   11.75in (30cm) wide

$60-80   **TAB**

A rare John Marresh pottery humidor, in the shape of a wooden barrel with a dog coming out of the top, impressed on bottom "J M 167", some wear to coloring on barrel bands, slight char mark to one side of barrel and small open bubble.

7.5in (19cm) high

$400-500   **JDJ**

A 1940s McCoy 'peach' jar.

8.75in (22cm) high

$50-70   **TAB**

A Marco Zanini for Memphis/Ceramic Falvia 'Colorado' porcelain teapot, comprised of stacked and buttressed forms in polychrome glaze, superficial crazing line to overglaze on spout, Memphis stamp mark.

Marco Zanini (b1954) graduated in architecture in 1978 and was a founding member of Memphis. He collaborated with Ettore Sottsass and was a principal member of Sottsass Associati. Zanini continues to design and works on mechanical, electronic, furniture, interior and architectural projects.

11.5in (29.25cm) high

$450-550   **DRA**

A Nathalie Du Pasquier for Memphis 'Carrot' porcelain vase, of corseted form, in teal blue glaze with spotted and striped mid-sections in polychrome, Memphis label.

The Memphis Group was founded in Milan in 1981 by a group of designers and architects and was the brain child of Ettore Sottsass. Their work combines elements of Art Deco, Pop Art, 1950s kitsch and futurism.

12in (30.5cm) high

$350-400   **DRA**

A Bernard Moore rabbit, with red flambé and spotted blue glaze, glass eyes, "BM" painted signature, minute glaze pop to mouth.

3in (7.5cm) high

$900-1,000 **FRE**

An important 1960s Daniel Rhodes large stoneware sculptural vase, with bulbous top and four-sided base linked with 'draped fabric' and covered in ultramarine, green and amber dead-matte glaze, unmarked.

22.5in (57cm) high

$1,500-2,000 **CR**

An Ann Smith double-gourd shaped porcelain vase, with striped pattern in cobalt and white glossy glaze alternating with random patches of gray-green and amber on an ivory matte ground, signed "Smith/91" on the bottom.

1991   *13.25in (33.5cm) high*

$180-220 **DRA**

An Ettore Sottsass for Memphis 'Euphrates' porcelain vase, comprising stacked and spouted forms in black, yellow, and white glazes, "E. Sottsass for Memphis" label.

1983   *15.75in (40cm) high*

$600-700 **DRA**

An Ettore Sottsass for Memphis 'Tigris' porcelain vase, comprised of stacked spouted and coiled forms covered in powder blue, white and black glaze, "E. Sottsass for Memphis" label

1983   *15.5in (39.25cm) high*

$450-500 **DRA**

A Carl Walters for Stonelain faïence rooster vase, with red and black decoration on an ivory ground, marked.

11in (28cm) high

$220-280 **CR**

An Italian faïence cat figure, covered in bright polychrome glaze, unmarked.

14in (35.5cm) wide

$50-70 **CR**

A B C D E F G H I J K L M N O P Q R S T U V W XYZ

An Arts and Crafts oak table clock, attributed to L. and J.G. Stickley, with circular face in a pagoda-shaped frame, unmarked.

9in (23cm) wide

$350-400　　　　**CR**

An early 20thC Art Nouveau eight-day balloon clock, the mahogany case with boxwood decoration and shell inlay.

8.75in (22cm) high

$700-1,000　　　　**Pen**

A Chase advertising electric wall clock, manufactured by Pan Clock Co. (New York), with company slogan and logo, numerals and hands in red and black against a white ground, mounted in a brass frame.

Chase Brass & Copper Company (founded 1876) are a famous American manufacturer making metal household goods from 1930 onward, working in a Modernist, almost 'Art Deco' style, with clean surfaces and lines. They primarily used copper, brass and chromed metal and employed noted designers including Walter von Nessen and Russell Wright. They saw their 'golden age' during the 1930s, with production ceasing after World War II.

15.25in (38.5cm)high

$400-600　　　　**DRA**

A French Art Deco brown marble and black onyx mantel clock, with stepped top and base and square enameled face in red and black with brass hands and trim, face stamped "MADE IN FRANCE".

9.75in (25cm) high

$800-1,200　　　　**DRA**

A Moon Crest digital clock, in copper casing, working condition, foil label.

8.75in (22cm) long

$70-100　　　　**DRA**

An unusual Vitascope clock, with wood effect Bakelite case and electric mechanism lighting and moving the ship on the waves.

When connected to an electricity supply, the clock works and the internal marine scene is lit up, with the ship gently rocking in the waves. The finish on this example is very unusual, it is more commonly found with a plain cream, black or brown Bakelite casing.

c1940

$600-900　　　　**ET**

A Herman Miller 'Asterisk' clock, by George Nelson, re-enameled, Herman Miller label.

George Nelson (1908-1986) was an important Modernist designer who worked in interior, industrial and exhibition design. In 1945 he began a long association with the Herman Miller Furniture Company of Zeeland, Michigan, where as head designer he developed an innovative line of furniture and commissioned new designs from others, including Charles Eames.

10in (25.5cm) diam

$280-320　　　　**DRA**

A Clayton Bailey robot alarm clock, aluminum with red LCD, in working condition, operating instructions on bottom, signed Clayton.

Clayton Bailey (b1939) is a noted artist living on the West Coast of the US whose art combines humor with his interest in science and chemistry. He has been making a series of robot sculptures from 'found objects' and other components since 1976, one of which is owned by Bill Gates.

1984　　　12.5in (32cm) high

$800-1,200　　　　**DRA**

"Captain America", No. 135, Mar. 1971, published by Marvel Comics.

$10-15 MC

"Captain America", No. 137, May 1971, published by Marvel Comics.

$8-12 MC

"Captain America", No. 163, July 1973, published by Marvel Comics.

$7-10 MC

"Daredevil", No. 13, July 1966, published by Marvel Comics.

$50-80 MC

Daredevil", No. 19, Aug, 1966, published by Marvel Comics.

$80-120 MC

"Daredevil", No. 22, Nov. 1966, published by Marvel Comics.

$15-25 MC

Collectors' Notes

- Comics cover a wide range of genres including cartoon characters, such as Mickey Mouse and Bugs Bunny, Westerns, Horror, War, Romance and, of course, Superheroes. Comic book history is divided into three eras:

- **Golden Age (1938-c1955)**

  This period starts with the introduction of Superman in "Action Comics" No.1 published by Detective Comics (DC). The character proved to be hugely popular and by 1939 Superman had his own comic book. Other Superheroes born to the DC Comics stable include Bob Kane's Batman, first appearing in Detective Comics No. 27 in May 1939, Wonder Woman, Green Lantern and The Flash.

- **Silver Age (c1956-c1969)**

  Interest in Superhero comics had dwindled towards the end of the Golden Age but this new era saw the rebirth and modernization of many of the old superheroes as well as the arrival of new ones. This was in part due to Marvel Comics and its creative director, Stan Lee, whose characters include the Amazing Spider-man the Fantastic Four, The Incredible Hulk and the Uncanny X-Men. This revitalization lead to comic book collecting becoming a more serious hobby.

- **Bronze Age (c1970-c1979) and later**

  By the 1970s collecting had become an established hobby. Popular characters continued to evolve and new characters were added, including those aimed at more adult markets. The release of a number of films at the end of the 20thC which finally captured the essence of the superheroes met with the fans' approval and encouraged a new interest in collecting.

- One of the most important factors in valuing a comic is its condition. Early comics were made of low quality paper and were not intended to be kept and as a result can be very difficult to find in good condition. Rips, tears, missing pages and covers will all reduce a comic's desirability, as will notations by previous owners.

"Fantastic Four", No. 29, Aug. 1965 published by Marvel Comics.

$30-50 MC

"Fantastic Four", No. 33, Dec. 1965, published by Marvel Comics.

$80-120 MC

"Fantastic Four", No. 34, Jan. 1965, published by Marvel Comics.

$50-80 MC

"Fantastic Four", No. 37, Apr 1965, published by Marvel Comics.

$70-100 MC

COMICS

"Fantastic Four", No. 40, July 1965, published by Marvel Comics.

$60-90   MC

"Fantastic Four", No. 43, Oct. 1965, published by Marvel Comics.

$15-25   MC

"The Incredible Hulk", No. 106, Aug. 1968 published by Marvel Comics.

$70-100   MC

"The Incredible Hulk", No. 107, Sept. 1968, published by Marvel Comics.

$80-120   MC

"The Incredible Hulk", No. 105, July 1968, published by Marvel Comics.

$50-80   MC

"The Incredible Hulk", No. 115, May 1969, published by Marvel Comics.

$40-60   MC

"The Amazing Spiderman", No. 10, Mar. 1964, published by Marvel Comics.

$500-700   MC

"The Incredible Hulk", No. 121, Nov. 1969, published by Marvel Comics.

$10-15   MC

"The Incredible Hulk", No. 123, Jan. 1970, published by Marvel Comics.

$8-12   MC

"The Amazing Spiderman", No. 18, Nov. 1964, published by Marvel Comics.

$120-180   MC

"The Amazing Spiderman", No. 22, Mar. 1965, published by Marvel Comics.

$150-200   MC

"The Amazing Spiderman", No. 24, May 1965, published by Marvel Comics.

$60-90   MC

"The Amazing Spiderman", No. 26, July 1965, published by Marvel Comics.

$320-380   MC

"The Amazing Spiderman", No. 28, Sept. 1965, published by Marvel Comics.

$500-700   MC

"The Amazing Spiderman", No. 29, Oct. 1965, published by Marvel Comics.

$150-200   MC

"X-Men", No. 106, Aug. 1977, published by Marvel Comics.

$30-50   MC

"X-Men", No. 109, Feb. 1978, published by Marvel Comics.

$20-30   MC

"X-Men", No. 115, Nov. 1978, published by Marvel Comics.

$30-50   MC

"X-Men", No. 121, May 1979, published by Marvel Comics.

$60-90   MC

"X-Men", No. 45, June 1968, published by Marvel Comics.

$20-30   MC

"X-Men", No. 48, Apr. 1975, published by Marvel Comics.

$40-60   MC

"X-Men", No. 64, Jan. 1970, published by Marvel Comics.

$30-50   MC

A
B
C
D
E
F
G
H
I
J
K
L
M
N
O
P
Q
R
S
T
U
V
W
XYZ

"Action Comics", No. 230, July 1957, published by DC Comics.

$30-40   MC

"Action Comics", No. 358, Jan. 1968, published by DC Comics.

$3-5   MC

"Adventure Comics", No. 262, July 1959, published by DC Comics.

$12-18   MC

"Adventure Comics", No. 263, Aug. 1959, published by DC Comics.

$12-18   MC

"The Atom", No. 5, Mar. 1963, published by DC Comics.

$12-18   MC

"The Atom", No. 6, May 1963, published by DC Comics.

$8-12   MC

"Batman", No. 131, Apr. 1960, published by DC Comics.

$15-25   MC

"Batman", No. 143, Oct. 1961, published by DC Comics.

$15-25   MC

"Batman", No. 155, May 1963, published by DC Comics.

$50-80   MC

"Batman", No. 165, Aug. 1964, published by DC Comics.

$15-25   MC

"Batman", Nc. 178, Feb. 1966, published by DC Comics.

$6-9   MC

"Batman", No. 200, Mar. 1968, published by DC Comics.

$15-25   MC

"Detective Comics", No. 263, Jan. 1959, published by DC Comics.

$15-25   MC

"Detective Comics", No. 270, Aug. 1959, published by DC Comics.

$15-25   MC

"The Flash", No. 198, June 1980, published by DC Comics.

$3-5   MC

"Green Lantern", No. 22, July 1963, published by DC Comics.

$8-12   MC

"Green Lantern", No. 24, Oct. 1963, published by DC Comics.

$8-12   MC

"Hawkman", No. 4, Nov. 1964, published by DC Comics.

$12-18   MC

"Justice League of America", No. 27, May 1964, published by DC Comics.

$100-150   MC

"Justice League of America", No. 29, Aug. 1964 published by DC Comics.

$50-80   MC

"Justice League of America", No. 32, Dec. 1964, published by DC Comics.

$40-60   MC

"Justice League of America", No. 34, Mar. 1965 published by DC Comics.

$50-80   MC

"Justice League of America", No. 35, May 1965, published by DC Comics.

$30-50   MC

"Justice League of America" No. 36, June 1965, published by DC Comics.

$20-30   MC

A B C D E F G H I J K L M N O P Q R S T U V W XYZ

"Superman", No. 125, Nov. 1958, published by DC Comics.

$20-30   MC

"Superman", No. 129, May 1959, published by DC Comics.

$15-25   MC

"Superman", No. 134, Jan. 1960, published by DC Comics.

$15-25   MC

"Superman", No. 153, May 1962, published by DC Comics.

$7-10   MC

"Superman", No. 157, Nov. 1962, published by DC Comics.

$6-9   MC

"Action Comics", No. 291, Aug. 1962, published by DC Comics.

$2-3   MC

"The New Wonder Woman", No. 172, Sept. 1967, published by DC Comics.

$120-180   MC

"The New Wonder Woman", No. 174, Feb. 1968, published by DC Comics.

$10-15   MC

"The New Wonder Woman", No. 182, June 1969, published by DC Comics.

$6-9   MC

"The New Wonder Woman", No. 185, Dec. 1969, published by DC Comics.

$6-9   MC

"The New Wonder Woman", No. 186, Feb. 1970, published by DC Comics.

$7-10   MC

"The New Wonder Woman", No. 190, Oct. 1970, published by DC Comics.

$6-9   MC

"Bugs Bunny", No. 203, Dec. 1978, published by Whitman.

$1-2   MC

"Looney Tunes", No. 192, Oct. 1957, published by Dell.

$3-4   MC

"Tom and Jerry", No. 230, June 1966, published by Dell.

$2-3   MC

"Tweety & Sylvester", No. 1, published by Warner Bros. Pictures Inc.
1963

$3-4   MC

"Walt Disney's Mickey Mouse", No. 65, May 1959, published by Dell.

$2-3   MC

"Walt Disney's Comics and Stories", No. 240, Sept. 1960, published by Gold Key.

$3-4   MC

"Walt Disney's Super Goof - The Thief of Zanzibar", No. 1, published by Gold Key.
1965

$3-4   MC

"Walt Disney's Mickey Mouse", No. 191, Jan. 1979, published by Whitman.

$2-3   MC

"Fightin' Army", No. 55, Nov. 1963, published by Charlton.

$2-3   MC

"Fightin' Army", No. 69, July 1966, published by Charlton.

$2-3   MC

"Our Fighting Forces", No. 107, Jun. 1967, published by DC Comics.

$2-3   MC

"Our Fighting Forces" No. 73, Apr 1963, published by DC Comics.

$6-9   MC

"Army War Heroes", No. 12, Jan. 1966, published by Charlton.

$2-3   MC

"Army War Heroes", No. 2, Feb. 1964, published by Charlton.

£2-3   MC

"Fightin' Marines", No. 61, Dec. 1964, published by Charlton.

$2-3   MC

"Fightin' Marines", No. 75, July 1967, published by Charlton.

$2-3   MC

"The Horse Soldiers", No. 1048, published by Dell. *1959*

$12-18   MC

"The Lone Ranger", No. 128, July 1959, published by Dell.

$6-9   MC

"Rawhide Kid", No. 30, Oct. 1962, published by Atlas.

$8-12   MC

"Six-Gun Western", No. 4, July 1957, published by Atlas.

$7-10   MC

"Tomahawk", No. 62, June 1959, published by DC Comics.

$4-6   MC

"Two-Gun Kid", No. 45, Dec. 1959, published by Marvel Comics.

$6-9   MC

"Western Comics", No. 71, Oct. 1968, published by DC Comics.

$8-12   MC

"Wyatt Earp", No. 4, May 1956, published by Atlas.

$7-10   MC

FIND OUT MORE...

Robert M. Overstreet, '**The Official Overstreet Comic Book Price Guide**', Gemstone Publishing, 33rd edition, 2003.

Collectors' Notes

- The advent of transfer printing in the late 18thC, and the improved manufacturing and distribution methods of the 19thC, led to an ever-increasing number of commemorative items, especially from the reign of Queen Victoria onward.

- This growth has continued during the 20thC, leading to a huge variety of commemorative items available to collect. Consequently most collectors focus on a particular personality, subject area or time period.

- A highly popular collectible area is royalty, including the short-lived reign of Edward VIII, and HM Queen Elizabeth II and her family. Due to her long current reign, Elizabeth II's reign has thousands of items associated with it.

- Collectors should look for items of good quality or by noted factories or designers. The mugs designed by Eric Ravilious are a good example, as are those designed by Charlotte Rhead. Popular national figures or personalities, such as Sir Winston Churchill, are also popular as interest crosses collecting fields.

- Humor is a desirable element and many of the anti-Hitler pieces are popular for this reason, as much as for their illustration of the sentiments of the period.

- As most items were produced in large numbers, condition is vital, with worn or damaged pieces usually being less valuable. Also look for unusual variations, for example in color, and items produced in smaller limited editions of a few hundred pieces.

Royal

A Wedgwood 1953 coronation mug, designed by Eric Ravilious, of cylindrical form, printed and painted in colors, printed and painted marks.

4in (10cm) high

$400-600   **L&T**

A Wedgwood 1953 coronation mug, designed by Richard Guyatt, of cylindrical form, with printed and painted marks.

c1953   4in (10cm) high

$150-200   **L&T**

A Holkham Pottery mug, made to commemorate the coronation of Queen Elizabeth II.

c1953   3in (8.5cm) high

$50-80   **H&G**

An Arthur Wood earthenware lion-handled mug, made to commemorate the coronation of Queen Elizabeth II.

c1953   4.75in (12cm) high

$70-100   **H&G**

A small Arthur Bowker lion-handled bone china mug, made to commemorate the coronation of Queen Elizabeth II.

c1953   3.25in (8.5cm) high

$50-80   **H&G**

A Wedgwood earthenware mug, made to commemorate the coronation of Queen Elizabeth II, with the Duke of Edinburgh on the reverse.

c1953   4.25in (10.5cm) high

$60-90   **H&G**

A Paragon bone china dish, made to commemorate the coronation Queen Elizabeth II.

c1953   4.25in (10.5cm) diam

$50-80   **H&G**

A Paragon 'Coronation' china plate, printed and over-enameled with the Royal Coat of Arms, within a cobalt blue border inscribed in gilt, printed marks.

10.5in (26.5cm) diam

$120-180   **HamG**

A Fortostile earthenware plaque, made to commemorate the coronation of Queen Elizabeth II.

c1953   6in (15cm) high

$60-90   **H&G**

A Royal Crown Derby bone china pin tray, made to commemorate the coronation of Queen Elizabeth II.

c1953   *4.25in (10.5cm) long*

$50-80   **H&G**

A silver commemorative letter knife, commemorating the coronation of Queen Elizabeth II, with a Sheffield hallmark.

c1952   *8.5in (21.5cm) long*

$60-90   **TAB**

A Paragon bone china tazza, commemorating the visit of Queen Elizabeth II to Canada to open the St Lawrence Seaway.

c1959   *2.75in (7cm) high*

$7-10   **TAB**

A Spode bone china tankard, made to commemorate the Silver Jubilee of Queen Elizabeth II.

c1977   *4in (10cm) high*

$60-90   **H&G**

A Masons earthenware mug, made to commemorate the Silver Jubilee of Queen Elizabeth II.

c1977   *5in (13cm) high*

$300-400   **H&G**

A Copeland Spode earthenware mug, made to commemorate the coronation of King George VI and family, portrait by Marcus Adams.

c1937   *3.25in (8.5cm) high*

$120-180   **H&G**

A Coalport blue and gold bone china mug, made to commemorate the coronation of King George VI and Elizabeth.

c1937   *3.25in (8.5cm) high*

$180-220   **H&G**

A Wedgwood commemorative mug, designed by Eric Ravilious, to commemorate the coronation of King George VI.

c1937

$700-1,000   **REN**

A one-handled vase, designed by Charlotte Rhead for Crown Ducal, made for the coronation of King George VI and Elizabeth.

c1937   *7.25in (18.5cm) high*

$350-400   **H&G**

A Copeland Spode large earthenware mug, made to commemorate the coronation of King George VI and Elizabeth.

c1937   *5.5in (14cm) high*

$180-220   **H&G**

A Beswick earthenware mug, made to commemorate the coronation of King George VI and Elizabeth.

c1937   *3.5in (8.5cm) high*

$60-90   **H&G**

A Royal Doulton small bone china beaker, made to commemorate the coronation of King George VI and Elizabeth.

c1937   *3.5in (9cm) high*

$60-90   **H&G**

A Royal Doulton bone china ivory enameled beaker, made to commemorate the coronation of George VI and Elizabeth.

c1937   3.75in (9.5cm) high

$500-700   **H&G**

A Wedgwood earthenware beaker, made to commemorate the coronation of George VI and Elizabeth.

c1937   4.5in (11.5cm) high

$80-120   **H&G**

A Paragon 'Coronation' china plate, for George VI, printed and over-enameled with the Royal Coat of Arms, and an inscribed border, printed marks.

10.5in (26.5cm) diam

$70-100   **HamG**

A molded glass plate, to commemorate George VI's coronation.

9.75in (24.5cm) diam

$50-80   **OACC**

A Royal Doulton earthenware loving cup, made to commemorate the coronation of George VI.

c1937   4in (10.5cm) high

$700-1,000   **H&G**

A General Household Utilities earthenware teapot, shaped as a crown, made to commemorate the coronation of King George VI and Elizabeth.

c1937   5in (12.5cm) high

$320-380   **H&G**

A Copeland Spode earthenware bowl, produced as a gift from the Cloth Workers' Company, made to commemorate the coronation of King George VI and Elizabeth.

c1937   8.5in (22cm) diam

$300-400   **H&G**

A Grimwades earthenware plate, made to commemorate the visit of Edward, Prince of Wales, to South Africa.

A similar and less rare plate was made for his visit to Canada.

c1924   8.75in (25cm) diam

$180-220   **H&G**

A Paragon china plate for the proposed coronation of Edward VIII, printed and over-enameled with the Royal Coat of Arms, within an inscribed border, printed marks.

10.5in (25.5cm) diam

$70-100   **HamG**

An earthenware mug, designed by Dame Laura Knight, with certification of authenticity, made to commemorate the proposed coronation of Edward VIII.

c1936-1937   *Mug 3.25in (8cm) high*

$80-120   **H&G**

A Copeland for Thomas Goode earthenware mug, made to commemorate the coronation of King Edward VIII.

c1936-1937 3.25in (8.5cm) h

$80-120   **H&G**

A Royal Doulton earthenware mug, made to commemorate the proposed coronation of Edward VIII.

c1936-1937 4in (10cm) high

$60-90   **H&G**

A Royal Stafford bone china teapot, made to commemorate the proposed coronation of Edward VIII.

The delicate and decorative handle on this teapot is prone to damage which would reduce the value.

c1936-1937   *6in (15cm) high*

$350-400   **H&G**

A Copeland Spode earthenware jug, made to commemorate the proposed coronation of Edward VIII.

c1936-1937 3in (7.5cm) high

$100-150   **H&G**

A Melba China bone china globe, made to commemorate the proposed coronation of Edward VIII, inscribed "The empire on which the sun never sets".

1936-1937 3.75in (9.5cm) h

$220-280   **H&G**

A Bretby pottery earthenware jug, made to commemorate the proposed coronation of Edward VIII.

This jug plays 'God Save the King'.

c1936-1937 8.25in (21cm) h

$220-280   **H&G**

A Royal Doulton beaker, commemorating the coronation of King Edward VIII.

1937   *4in (10cm) high*

$30-50   **TAB**

A Coalport bone china plate, made to commemorate the death of the Duke of Windsor, a limited edition of 1,000.

Edward was king for less than a year in 1936. He abdicated in December, allowing his marriage to Wallis Simpson, and took the title of Duke of Windsor. After his death, his body was taken from his Paris home in the Bois de Bolougne to be interred at Frogmore, Windsor.

c1972   *10.5in (27cm) diam*

$150-200   **H&G**

A pair of J. & J. May bone china mugs, made to commemorate the betrothal, on left, and wedding, on right, of Prince Charles and Lady Diana Spencer.

c1981   3.75in (9.5cm) high

$70-100 (each)   **H&G**

A Crown Staffordshire bone china loving cup, made to commemorate the wedding of Prince Charles and Lady Diana Spencer.

1981   3.25in (8cm) high

$50-80   **H&G**

A large Paragon bone china lion-handled loving cup, made to commemorate the marriage of the Prince of Wales and Lady Diana, limited edition of 750.

c1981   5in (13cm) high

$350-400   **H&G**

A Royal Doulton bone china beaker, made to commemorate the wedding of the Prince of Wales and Lady Diana Spencer.

Only six examples of this beaker were made in blue as specimens. As such they are extremely rare and highly sought after. The beaker was released publicly in brown sepia and is worth $50-80 in that color.

c1981   3.75in (9.5cm) high

$600-900   **H&G**

A J. & J. May bone china mug, made to commemorate the birth of Prince William.

c1982   3.5in (9cm) high

$80-120   **H&G**

A pair of Royal Crown Derby bone china miniature loving cups, made to commemorate the births of Prince William and Prince Harry respectively.

c1982-1984

$70-100 (each)   **H&G**

A Caverswall bone china beaker, Prince Charles' 40th birthday, limited edition 250.

1988   4.5in (11.5cm) high

$70-100   **H&G**

A Royal Doulton miniature bone china loving cup, made to commemorate the 50th birthday of Prince Charles, limited edition of 950.

1998   1.5in (4cm) high

$50-80   **H&G**

Two views of a plate commemorating Queen Victoria's Diamond Jubilee.

c1897

$400-600   **BS**

A Royal Doulton beaker, made to commemorate Queen Victoria's Golden Jubilee.

1887

$30-50   **PSA**

A Doulton bone china mug, made to commemorate the marriage of Princess May and George, Duke of York.

1893   *3in (8cm) high*

$150-200   **H&G**

A French earthenware soup dish, showing Tsar Nicholas II and the Tsarina, printed in green and brown with their portraits, to mark their state visit to Paris in 1896, with printed and impressed marks.

1896   *10.5in (26.5cm) diam*

$300-400   **HamG**

A Rosenthal porcelain plaque, of Kaiser Wilhelm II, molded with his profile in saxe blue within a border molded with the Kaiser's titles, printed green mark.

1907-1910 8.75in (22.5cm) diam

$70-100   **HamG**

A Clokie and Company earthenware mug, made to commemorate the visit of Princess Viscountess Lascelles to Castleford.

1925   *3.25in (8.5cm) high*

$180-220   **H&G**

A WWI Princess Mary's gift tin, with one complete packet of cigarettes; and a clay pipe, the bowl with the Victoria crown, castle, Inniskillings, Sphinx and Egypt all within shamrocks, the stem marked "Derry Castle", in good condition.

The contents of the tin must be complete and all pieces must be intact and in excellent condition to hold such a value. As many were made and they were given out to be used, there are many empty tins available on the market which are usually worth 5-15% of this value, depending on condition.

An earthenware egg cup, showing Princess Margaret Rose.

c1937   *2.5in (6cm) high*

$60-90   **H&G**

$150-200   **W&W**

Political Commemoratives

A blue and white 'Abolition of Slavery' plate, entitled "Freedom First of August 1838", depicting freed slaves standing before a hut bearing the word 'Liberty', within a florette border, hair crack.

9.25in (23.5cm) diam

$280-320   **HamG**

A Wallis Gimson and Co. plate, with portrait of Gladstone, "rd No. 4050" mark.

1884   *9.75in (24.5cm) diam*

$50-80   **HamG**

An octagonal earthenware plate, printed with the portrait of Charles Stuart Parnell, MP, by Wallis Gimson and Co., slight chip.

Parnell (1846-1891) is a leading figure in Irish history, and strongly advocated Home Rule and land ownership for Irish farmers. His legendary lengthy speeches in Parliament as MP for Meath aimed to draw attention to his policies by disrupting the smooth running of Parliament.

9.75in (24.5cm) wide

$300-400   **HamG**

A flower-shaped earthenware plate, printed in black with a portrait of Lord Randolph Churchill against a rose, thistle and shamrock background, marked "rd No.49184", maker's mark "F.W.G".

11.5in (29.5cm) wide

$180-220   **HamG**

A 19thC Conservative Club bone china plate, decorated with a central device and a border of roses, inscribed "Conservative Club"

8.75in (22.5cm) diam

$30-50   **WW**

A European bone china bowl, commemorating the union between Austria and Germany, depicting Wilhelm II and Franz Josef.

c1914-1915 9in (23cm) diam

$180-220   **H&G**

A rare Doulton earthenware jardinière, made to commemorate the Australian Federation.

1901   4.75in (12cm) high

$1,000-1,500   **H&G**

A late 19thC to early 20thC Musterschutz porcelain tankard, modeled as an elderly gentleman with drooping full moustache, possibly commemorating or celebrating Bismarck, the pewter mounted hinged lid modeled as a turnip top.

6.75in (17cm) high

$80-120   **Chef**

A Neville Chamberlain figure, made to commemorate his period in parliament from 1913 to 1939.

c1939   11in (28cm) high

$70-100   **H&G**

A plaster bust of Neville Chamberlain.

c1940   6.75in (17cm) high

$120-180   **H&G**

A small Lancaster's earthenware character jug, of Neville Chamberlain.

3in (7.5cm) high

$60-90   **H&G**

A Ridgways earthenware mug, made to commemorate Neville Chamberlain.

c1938   4.75in (12cm) high

$150-200   **H&G**

A Drostdy ware mug, made to commemorate Rhodesian Independence and showing Ian Douglas Smith.

1965   4.25in (11cm) high

$70-100   **H&G**

A Mercian China earthenware mug, showing Sir Alec Douglas Home and President Idi Amin, commemorating the immigration of Ugandan refugees to Britain.

1972   5in (13cm) high

$70-100   **H&G**

An Edward Heath plate, commissioned by the Commemorative Collectors' Society.

1975   10.5in (27cm) diam

$70-100   **H&G**

An English Fielding's novelty miniature chamber pot ashtray, commemorating the Nazi invasion of Poland in 1939, the bottom of the interior with a caricature of Adolf Hitler.

1.5in (3.5cm) high

$300-350   **AOY**

A Chown bone china mug, made to commemorate New Labour's election victory.

1997   3.25in (8.5cm) high

$20-30   **H&G**

Sir Winston Churchill

A composite bust of Winston Churchill, by B. Clemens, on a wooden base.

c1944   11.5in (29cm) high

$320-380   **H&G**

A Winston Churchill cigar/cigarette lighter, by Tallent.

Portrayals of Churchill with his familiar trademarks, such as his cigar, are very popular amongst collectors.

c1940-1944 8.25in (21cm) h

$150-200   **H&G**

An earthenware toby jug of Winston Churchill, produced by J. & G. Meakin.

c1941   6.25in (16cm) high

$180-220   **H&G**

A small Cooper Clayton earthenware character jug, depicting Winston Churchill.

c1951-1952 3.25in (8cm) h

$60-90   **H&G**

A Spode Winston Churchill 'in memoriam' plate, from a limited edition of 5,000.

c1965   10.5in (27cm) diam

$150-200   **H&G**

Collectors' Notes

- The New York World's Fair was held in Flushing Meadow in Queens at the end of the Depression. The theme was the world of tomorrow and the Fair put trust in science and technology to allow personal freedom and create a prosperous and harmonious world.

- Two buildings are icons of the exhibition and of the Machine Age – the spike shaped Trylon and spherical Perisphere. Although in reality they were painted white, most memorabilia incorporating the buildings is often in orange and/or blue - the colors of the exhibition

- The Perisphere contained the 'Democracity' - an enormous model of an ideal city with pleasant suburbs for families. The Trylon was 700ft high and was connected to the Perisphere by a giant ramp, called the Helicline.

- TV was also introduced to the American public, with the first programme being launched during the fair by RCA.

- Look for memorabilia that includes the recognizable buildings or represents the key themes strongly.

A commemorative ceramic tankard, for the World's Fair, the bottom stamped "KKS892".

c1939   5in (12.5cm) high

$80-120   **TM**

A commemorative ceramic novelty watering can, for the World's Fair, with luster finish, the base marked "MADE IN JAPAN".

c1939   4in (10cm) high

$60-90   **TM**

A commemorative glass, for World's Fair, showing the Medicine and Public Health Buildings.

c1939

$30-50   **AIS**

A World's Fair plastic "One Piece Salt & Pepper Shaker", marked "Emeloid Co. of Arlington N".

Orange and blue were the official colors of the New York World's Fair.

c1939   3.5in (9cm) long

$40-60   **CEC**

A commemorative silver-plated ladle, for the World's Fair.

c1939   5.75in (14.5cm) long

$30-50   **AIS**

A card envelope containing 20 photographs of the World's Fair.

c1939 Photos 2.25in (6cm) w

$30-40   **TM**

A World's Fair map and guide, with stamp for tour guide company.

c1939   8.75in (22.5cm) high

$15-20   **AIS**

A very rare commemorative Pathegrams Inc. Ciné Vue Bakelite viewer, for the World's Fair, together with two boxes of movie views.

c1939 Box 7.25in (18.5cm) w

$120-180   **TM**

A commemorative metal bracelet, for the World's Fair.

c1939   2.25in (6cm) long

$30-40   **AIS**

Collectors' Notes

- During the first decades of the 20th century, fashion was dictated by haute couture, clothing tailor-made for individuals by leading designers, most often in Paris.

- A move towards comfort and ease of movement, necessitated by war, began c1914 and carried on into the 1920s and 1930s when shapes were looser, without corsetry and had flowing skirts and lines. Detailing was often very intricate, using opulent materials. 'Flapper' clothes, such as the tunic dresses of the 1920s and 1930s, are an excellent example and are often found with intricate sequin, gold thread or beadwork patterns.

- The austerity and 'utility' ware of the WWII period was changed by the 'New Look' of the late 1940s and 1950s. The 1950s and 1960s offer excellent opportunities for the costume collector as there are a great many comparatively inexpensive, and often wearable, items of clothing readily available on the market due to mass production in these decades.

- From the 1950s onwards, clothing became increasingly colorful and jaunty as mass production allowed styles and tastes to change more often, leading to more ephemerally fashionable garments.

- Look for clothes that epitomize the period in terms of shape, color and patterning, or are indicative of important movements such as 'street fashion' in the 1960s or 'Punk' in the 1970s. The work of key designers, for example Emilio Pucci in the 1960s and Vivienne Westwood from the 1970s onwards, is very collectible and often expensive. Many are worn as well as being collected and go through periods of extremely high popularity.

- Condition is vital. For example, beadwork on a Flapper dress can be nearly impossible to repair, especially if the fabric is torn. Tears, stains and sweat marks will reduce value. Pay attention to labels as these will affect value. For example, a Dior or Chanel haute couture labeled dress will fetch more than a boutique labeled dress by the same designer.

A mauve floral printed lawn dress, with vertical stripes, mock pin tucks with full sleeves and ruched applique on the bodice.

c1880

$30-50　　　　**AAC**

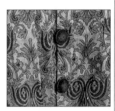

An American printed wool challis, in tan and brown on a blue/gray ground, trimmed at the collar, cuffs and pockets with brown velvet and tan cotton bodice lining.

c1880

$200-300　　　　**AAC**

An American black velvet cape, with black satin appliqué and embroidery of dull glass black beads, fully lined with black silk damask, elaborately beaded.

c1890

$70-100　　　　**AAC**

An American black and white silk printed visiting dress, trimmed at the bodice and hem with black silk satin, with black satin-covered buttons and lace yoke and cuffs.

c1900

$120-180　　　　**AAC**

An American printed silk visiting dress, with peach silk detailing, lace yoke and cuffs and faceted glass buttons and double-breasted effect.

c1900

$60-80　　　　**AAC**

A black silk velvet vest, with lace applique, elaborately embroidered with steel beads, small silver sequins and turquoise glass beads, lined with plain cotton weave, with considerable hand stitching.

c1900

$60-80　　　　**AAC**

An American white lawn lingerie dress, with lace insertions and elaborate pin tucks, buttoning up at the back, with mother-of-pearl buttons.

c1905

$100-150　　　　**AAC**

An American white lawn lingerie dress, with embroidered netting on the bodice, tucks, ball fringe and smocking at the waistline, lace insertion at hem.

c1910

$60-80 | **AAC**

An American pale green embroidered silk chiffon gown, with train in a cream satin floral pattern, lace yoke, cream chenille fringes and glass beaded bodice.

c1910

$70-100 | **AAC**

An American black silk and wool dress, with gored skirt, cream lace yoke, trimmed with rose silk bows and a large collar with rose silk piping.

c1910

$80-120 | **AAC**

An American pale avocado green silk chiffon wrapper or jacket, with long sleeves and handkerchief hem and fabric-covered buttons.

c1920

$150-200 | **AAC**

An American black silk chiffon and black lace gown, with handkerchief hem and black silk satin-covered button trim.

c1920

$70-100 | **AAC**

A rose silk velvet sleeveless gown, with dropped waistline, trimmed with gold sequins and gold metallic fabric inside the deep v-neckline.

c1920

$200-300 | **AAC**

An American black silk satin cloak, with fabric-covered button closures at the neckline and yoke, with Marabou feather trimming at the cuffs and hem, fully lined with black crepe.

c1920

$80-120 | **AAC**

An American white lawn sleeveless chemise, with a dropped waistline and lace insertion of eyelet lace, net and hidden buttons up the back.

c1920

$200-300 | **AAC**

An American gown, with green lace bodice, long sleeves, velvet floral appliqué to one shoulder and a skirt of green silk chiffon and lace, underpinnings of green taffeta.

c1925

$50-70 | **AAC**

A pink silk sleeveless dress with a tie at the neckline and a dropped waist with flounces at the hem.

c1925

$30-40 | **AAC**

An American gown, of black Chantilly lace over peach silk crepe with a hem of peach silk chiffon, dropped waistline with black velvet sash.

c1925

$220-280 | **AAC**

A B C D E F G H I J K L M N O P Q R S T U V W XYZ

A pair of 1920s American black corduroy spats, trimmed with black fur, with label for "Motor Boots Spats, Designed and Made By Cambridge Rubber Co".

9.75in (25cm) wide

$20-30 AAC

The 'New Look' was launched by Christian Dior as his first collection in 1947 and influenced styles into the 1950s.

'New Look' skirts are typically longer and fuller. The waist is cinched, often with a corset, presenting a feminine, curving hourglass shape.

Shoulders are rounded, not padded, and more opulent materials were used. The style is softer and longer in length.

The 'New Look' broke away from the privations of war and was shockingly unlike styles of the previous decades.

A late 1940s/50s 'New Look' black dress, size 12.

$70-100 VV

An American green wool/crepe dress, with pin-tuck belt appliqué with iridescent green glass beaded buckle, long cuffed sleeves and open neckline and draped skirt.

c1940

$20-40 AAC

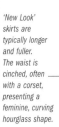

An American black velvet full-length gown, with quilted collar and a panel of satin floral embroidery up the front, cuffs also embroidered.

c1945

$50-80 AAC

A pale tangerine brocade gown, trimmed with a large flat bow on the bodice and eyelash fringe all over, camisole top and fitted full-length skirt.

c1955

$20-40 AAC

A 1950s green rayon taffeta ball gown, with gold sequins, size 12.

$30-50 VV

A 1950s green and red floral dress, with red bodice.

Size 10/12

$50-70 VV

A 1950s printed cotton dress, by Montana Fashions, with orange band and decorated with poppies.

$50-80 CCL

A 1950s blue felt skirt, with applied poodle motif.

$40-60 CCL

A 1950s full circle printed cotton skirt, with musician motifs.

$80-120 CCL

An American ivory quilted circular skirt, with gold metallic threads and elaborate floral applique in pink velvet with green and tan stems and leaves, with further rhinestone detailing.

c1955

$60-90 AAC

A hand-painted Mexican full circle skirt, with altered waist band.

$80-120 CCL

A 1950s Tailored Junior red jacket, with black velvet trim, size "S".

$70-100 CCL

A 1950s Italian Dolphin Royal 'Domino' pattern bikini.

$60-90 SM

A 1950s Sea Sprite polka dot bikini, size 33

$50-80 SM

A 1950s printed toweling beach robe.

$30-40 CCL

A 1960s red/orange wool coat, by Lilli Ann, with black-beaded collar.

$180-220 CCL

A silk jersey full-length gown, with long, fitted sleeves and wrap style straight skirt, labelled "Bessie, Firenze, Italia, 100% Pure Silk, made in Italy Expressly for Elizabeth Arden".

c1960   Size 6-8

$20-30 AAC

A 1960s Mary Quant-style mini dress.

$20-30 CCL

A CLOSER LOOK AT A 1960s DRESS

The design is by Andy Warhol, and features his famous 'Pop Art' Campbell's Soup can motif, representing mass production.

The shape and cut of the dress is typically 1960s, with modern and simple lines.

They are comparatively fragile and cannot be cleaned easily. They were marketed in quantity but were not popular so were discontinued. Today, they are rare.

Feeling and looking like paper, it is made from 80% cellulose and 20% cotton and was a statement on throwaway aspects of 'Popular culture.

An Andy Warhol design 'The Souper Dress', with original label two tears and a few stains.

c1960   38in (96.5cm) long

$1,400-2,000 FRE

A sheath dress, embroidered with iridescent lilac sequins on a knitted wool base, trimmed with pearls, rhinestones, silver and white glass beads, labelled "Vic & Vic Haute Couture made in British Crown Colony", size 6-8.

c1960

$20-30 AAC

An American seafoam green silk chiffon gown, embroidered all over with iridescent green/silver sequins and a cascading fringe of silver glass bugle beads, with underdress of seafoam green crepe, labelled "Adele Simpson".

c1960

$70-100 AAC

A B C D E F G H I J K L M N O P Q R S T U V W XYZ

A Pucci silk jersey suit, the dress is printed with a signature in jewel tone shades of green, purple and blue, with a folded notched collar, long cuffed sleeves, empire waist and a mid-length A-line skirt, labeled Emilio Pucci, retailed exclusively by Saks Fifth Avenue, size 12.

$800-1,200 **RTC**

A Jackie O-style white ribbon jacket.

$80-120 **CCL**

An American evening top of sheer white silk chiffon, embroidered all over with iridescent cream/mauve sequins and clusters of blue glass looped beads, unworn. *c1960*

$40-60 **AAC**

A 1970s patterned dress.

$60-80 **S&T**

A 1970s full length dress, decorated with flowers.

$70-100 **CCL**

A 1970s camel wool coat, by Eastex, with faux fur trim, size 14.

$70-100 **CCL**

A 1970s red gingham shirt, with applied felt flowers and diamanté.

$50-70 **CCL**

A 1970s wrap-around skirt, size 32.

$30-50 **CCL**

A Chanel evening dress, of black and navy net with finely pleated body and short skirt, having a see-through bodice terminating in twisted net straps and voluminous net train from the back waist applied with sequins, Chanel label "71580".

$450-550 **KBon**

A Vivienne Westwood ensemble, of stone and gray-colored silk georgette, printed with a pattern of child-like portraitures, with Vivienne Westwood fabric label and signature, British size 10.

$300-400 **KBon**

Collectors' Notes

■ A general and growing interest in vintage clothing and accessories has led to vintage purses becoming not only hotly collected and widely used today as accessories, but also copied by modern purse designers.

■ Look for bags that show the popular styles of the day, as well as for novelty-shaped purses. Plastic purses from the 1950s, often made from Lucite, and those with colorful plastic fittings, are very popular. The work of many modern and contemporary designers, such as Judith Leiber, has also become collectible.

■ As purses are practical items, the condition of vintage bags is very important, whether the buyer's intention is to use the purse or to add it to a collection. Torn linings, wear through daily use and other damage will affect values detrimentally. Purses in mint condition will command a premium.

A late 19thC American light tan linen reticule or pouch, with embroidered floral design, lacks drawstring.

10.25in (26cm) long

$6-9　　　　AAC

A 1910s American pouch-style linen purse, with embroidered blue peacock design and drawstring top.

14.25in (36cm) long

$30-40　　　　AAC

A 1900s metallic and satin embroidered reticule or pouch, lined with red cotton.

10in (25cm) long

$30-50　　　　AAC

A tooled and colored leather clutch bag, lined with beige moiré.

c1920　　　　*9in (23cm) wide*

$30-50　　　　AAC

An enameled mesh purse, with an Art Nouveau design metal clasp.

c1920　　　*7in (18cm) long*

$100-150　　　　AAC

An early 1950s silk 'duffle' purse, probably American, of striped pattern with embroidered flowers and an ivorine frame, with a carved ivorine clasp of an oriental figure.

8in (20.5cm) wide

$400-600　　　　CRIS

An American green wicker and floral print cotton purse, with drawstring top.

c1935　　　*6in (15cm) high*

$30-40　　　　AAC

A silk purse, with a plastic clasp and handle.

c1930

$40-60　　　　PC

A early 1930s French purse, black suede with white and beige glass bead paisley trim and small enamel cameo.

13.25in (34cm) wide

$400-600　　　　CRIS

A 1940s American purse, with voile body and butterscotch Bakelite frame.

8in (20.5cm) wide

$150-200   **CRIS**

A 1940s black leather purse.

$30-50   **PC**

A 1940s python-skin purse.

$40-60   **PC**

An American gold mesh purse, with brass frame, chain handle and rhinestone decorated clasp, labeled "Whiting & Davis Co Mesh Bags".

c1940

$30-50   **AAC**

A 1940s Ann Marie telephone purse, black buckskin with gilt frame.

This example was made as a V.I.P gift for residents of The Ritz, Paris.

8.25in (21cm) high

$1,800-2,200   **CRIS**

A 1940s Ann Marie playing cards purse, black buckskin with gold club, spade, heart and diamond motifs and ivory dice clasp.

11.5in (29cm) wide

$700-1,000   **CRIS**

A 1940s Ann Marie champagne bucket purse, black buckskin with clear Lucite top and handle, and gold-plated trim.

This bag was made as a Christmas gift for V.I.P. residents of The Ritz, Paris.

7.5in (19cm) wide

$2,200-2,800   **CRIS**

A 1950s rigid purse, with velvet-covered exterior, brass strips and plastic lid.

11.5in (29cm) high

$70-100   **AAC**

A 1950s American purse, with brass frame and clasp and black Lucite body, inset with abstract brass motifs.

12in (30cm) high

$150-200   **CRIS**

A 1950s American purse, with brass frame and clasp and black Lucite body, inset with abstract brass motifs.

12in (30cm) high

$150-200   **CRIS**

A 1950s American cornflower motif purse, by Source-Bag, New York, with brass frame, black plastic handle and body, one side with white cloth, fine yellow beads and amber cabochon cornflowers.

10.5in (27cm) high

$150-200   **CRIS**

A 1950s American 'beehive' purse, with pearlized plastic body and handle, and clear plastic lid inset with brass bee motifs.

7in (18cm) wide

$220-280   **CRIS**

A 1950s American 'beehive' purse, the body of ribbed and pearlized white Lucite, the top of clear Lucite with inset gold-plated bee motifs.

Rigid plasic purses were first made at the end of the 1940s, mostly in New York, and they are highly desirable. Beehive-shaped bags such as this one are very popular. Look out for cracks or crazing as this shows the material is deteriorating. The interior of the bag may also smell, which is another sign.

5.5in (14cm) high

$400-600　　　　　　　　　　**CRIS**

A 1950s American purse, with nacreous Bakelite body and handle, and gold-plated fittings.

8.5in (22m) wide

$150-200　　　　　　　　　　**CRIS**

A 1950s American 'casket' purse, with black Lucite body with abstract pattern 'gold p n' decoration, and carved clear Lucite lid.

6.75in (17cm) long

$220-280　　　　　　　　　　**CRIS**

A 1960s white wickerwork purse, made in Hong Kong, one side with felt and fine bead decoration, depicting a mermaid, fish and shell, and with white plastic handle.

12.25in (31cm) wide

$220-280　　　　　　　　　　**CRIS**

A 1950s/1960s white wickerwork purse, made in Hong Kong, one side with felt and fine bead flower and leaf decoration, and with gold-plated rope handle.

15in (38cm) wide

$220-280　　　　　　　　　　**CRIS**

A 1960s Japanese purse, the white raffia body decorated with coral, pink, yellow, white and green velvet vegetables, with faux pearl highlights.

12in (30cm) wide

$150-200　　　　　　　　　　**CRIS**

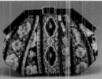

A Judith Leiber black satin and polychrome embroidery clutch evening purse, set with Swarovski crystals, in the original box, with brass bag.

9in (23cm) wide

$700-1,000　　　　　　　　　　**DRA**

Collectors' Notes

- Beadwork bags are decorated with a form of embroidery where tiny glass beads are threaded onto silk thread before being stitched to a light silk or other fabric ground.
- Beadwork was popular during the 19thC, but saw its heyday in the 1920s and 1930s and was produced until the 1950s. Belgium, Germany, Czechoslovakia and France were prolific producers and exporters of beaded purses.
- As the beads are made of glass or sometimes cut-steel, the color usually remains bright even after long periods of time.
- Beware of damage such as tears and loss of beads as repair of the lining fabric and the beads can be extremely difficult. Lining fabrics also have a tendency to become brittle and disintegrate through age, making them extremely delicate.

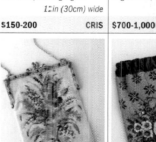

A 1870s beaded purse, possibly French, with jeweled clasp

9in (23cm) long

$150-200　　　　　　　　　　**BCAC**

A pale blue beadwork reticule or pouch, with cream cotton lining and navy blue silk top and drawstring.

c190C　　　9.5in (24cm) long

$50-80　　　　　　　　　　**AAC**

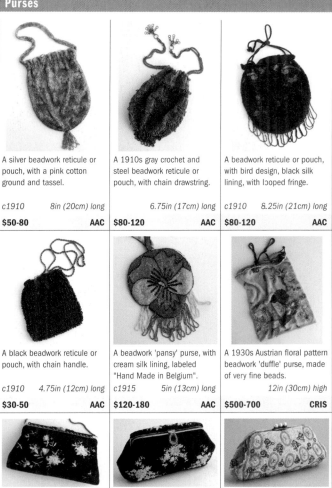

A silver beadwork reticule or pouch, with a pink cotton ground and tassel.

c1910   8in (20cm) long

$50-80   AAC

A 1910s gray crochet and steel beadwork reticule or pouch, with chain drawstring.

6.75in (17cm) long

$80-120   AAC

A beadwork reticule or pouch, with bird design, black silk lining, with looped fringe.

c1910   8.25in (21cm) long

$80-120   AAC

A beadwork purse, with floral design, lined with purple faille, with label reading "MADE IN BELGIUM".

c1910   9.75in (25cm) long

$120-180   AAC

A black beadwork reticule or pouch, with chain handle.

c1910   4.75in (12cm) long

$30-50   AAC

A beadwork 'pansy' purse, with cream silk lining, labeled "Hand Made in Belgium".

c1915   5in (13cm) long

$120-180   AAC

A 1930s Austrian floral pattern beadwork 'duffle' purse, made of very fine beads.

12in (30cm) high

$500-700   CRIS

A small early 20thC unlined beadwork purse.

4in (10cm) long

$12-18   AAC

A 1940s French or Belgian beadwork purse, with glass bead background, embroidered with gold-plated frame.

8.5in (22cm) wide

$220-280   CRIS

A 1940s French or Belgian beadwork purse, with glass bead background, embroidered with a gold-plated frame.

8.5in (22cm) wide

$220-280   CRIS

A 1940s French embroidered beadwork purse, made of white, gold, pink and gray fine glass beads.

13.25in (34cm) wide

$400-600   CRIS

A small 1940s French embroidered beadwork purse, with fine polychrome beads.

7in (18cm) wide

$400-600   CRIS

A late 1940s French beadwork purse, with fine black glass beads and brass frame and chain handle.

8in (20.5cm) wide

$150-200   CRIS

An early 1950s French or Belgian beadwork purse, with fine silvered glass beads.

8.5in (22cm) wide

$220-280   CRIS

A beadwork purse, lined with white satin and with a label reading "MADE IN FRANCE".

c1950   9in (23cm) wide

$20-30   AAC

A 1950s French or Belgian beadwork purse, with fine red glass beads, brass chain handle and brass catch with rhinestone finial.

8in (20cm) wide

$300-400   CRIS

An American early 19thC hand-stitched avocado green silk bonnet, with cape-like back, lined with polished cotton.

13.5in (34cm) long

$12-18   **AAC**

An early 19thC American white figured cotton cap, with lace and ties.

9.5in (24cm) long

$5-8   **AAC**

A late 19thC American green cotton bonnet with rushing, fabric bows, a back cape, padding with white cotton lining and lace inside the brim, trimmed with light brown and tan fur.

11in (28cm) high

$6-9   **AAC**

A late 19thC American black cotton mourning sun bonnet, with gathered crown, black cape and ties.

18.5in (47cm) long

$15-25   **AAC**

An American cream colored crocheted bonnet, with gold and satin detailing.

c1900   *8.75in (22cm) long*

$10-15   **AAC**

An early 20thC lady's and a child's floral printed cotton caps, both lined with tan cotton or linen, probably Scandinavian.

Largest 9in (23cm) wide

$8-12   **AAC**

An American wide brimmed black horsehair fashion hat, on a wire frame, black silk lining and trim with rhinestone clip.

c1910   *15.25in (39cm) wide*

$30-50   **AAC**

A black woven horsehair asymmetrical 'Helmet' hat, with grosgrain ribbon and applied linen gardenia flower.

$150-200   **LH**

An unlabeled silk-lined black velvet hat, with ostrich plumes and silk poppy.

c1905

$180-220   **LH**

A 1920s woven straw cloche hat, with green velvet band and silk poppy flowers.

The very small size – 6.25in (16cm) wide – of this hat indicates that it may have been made for a young girl or child.

6in (15cm) high

$60-90   **LH**

A 1920s violet woven straw cloche hat, with applied fabric flowers.

7.5in (19cm) high

$60-90   **LH**

An American black straw fashion hat, with ostrich plume and black silk grosgrain ribbon band and bow.

c1930   *11.75in (30cm) wide*

$15-25   **AAC**

A
B
C
D
E
F
G
H
I
J
K
L
M
N
O
P
Q
R
S
T
U
V
W
XYZ

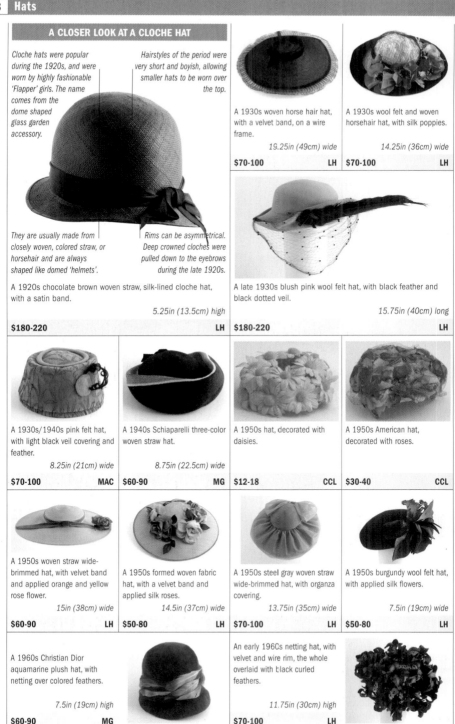

A CLOSER LOOK AT A CLOCHE HAT

Cloche hats were popular during the 1920s, and were worn by highly fashionable 'Flapper' girls. The name comes from the dome shaped glass garden accessory.

Hairstyles of the period were very short and boyish, allowing smaller hats to be worn over the top.

They are usually made from closely woven, colored straw, or horsehair and are always shaped like domed 'helmets'.

Rims can be asymmetrical. Deep crowned cloches were pulled down to the eyebrows during the late 1920s.

A 1920s chocolate brown woven straw, silk-lined cloche hat, with a satin band.

5.25in (13.5cm) high

$180-220   **LH**

A 1930s woven horse hair hat, with a velvet band, on a wire frame.

19.25in (49cm) wide

$70-100   **LH**

A 1930s wool felt and woven horsehair hat, with silk poppies.

14.25in (36cm) wide

$70-100   **LH**

A late 1930s blush pink wool felt hat, with black feather and black dotted veil.

15.75in (40cm) long

$180-220   **LH**

A 1930s/1940s pink felt hat, with light black veil covering and feather.

8.25in (21cm) wide

$70-100   **MAC**

A 1940s Schiaparelli three-color woven straw hat.

8.75in (22.5cm) wide

$60-90   **MG**

A 1950s hat, decorated with daisies.

$12-18   **CCL**

A 1950s American hat, decorated with roses.

$30-40   **CCL**

A 1950s woven straw wide-brimmed hat, with applied orange and yellow rose flower.

15in (38cm) wide

$60-90   **LH**

A 1950s formed woven fabric hat, with a velvet band and applied silk roses.

14.5in (37cm) wide

$50-80   **LH**

A 1950s steel gray woven straw wide-brimmed hat, with organza covering.

13.75in (35cm) wide

$70-100   **LH**

A 1950s burgundy wool felt hat, with applied silk flowers.

7.5in (19cm) wide

$50-80   **LH**

A 1960s Christian Dior aquamarine plush hat, with netting over colored feathers.

7.5in (19cm) high

$60-90   **MG**

An early 1960s netting hat, with velvet and wire rim, the whole overlaid with black curled feathers.

11.75in (30cm) high

$70-100   **LH**

A mid- to late 1960s two-color woven straw hat, by Bellini, with orange trim and grosgrain band.

Although this hat is small it was made to sit on top of the head, rather than lower down. The cowboy hat and style has most recently and popularly been revived by Madonna for her 'Music' album.

11.5in (29cm) wide

$150-200   **LH**

A 1970s blue straw hat, with applied faux pearl plastic stars, squares and rectangles shapes and faux pearl plastic hat pin, by Adolfo of New York and Paris.

12.25in (31cm) wide

$60-90   **MAC**

A pair of American early 19thC black kid and velvet silk embroidered lace-up shoes with stacked heels.

9in (23cm) long

$70-100   **AAC**

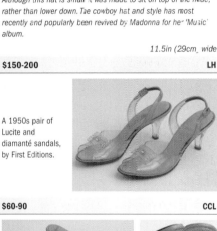

A 1950s pair of Lucite and diamanté sandals, by First Editions.

$60-90   **CCL**

A 1940s pair of hollow heel shoes, made in the Philippines, hand-embroidered and decorated with roses.

$120-180   **CCL**

A 1950s pair of Lucite and diamanté stiletto sandals, by Style Pride, with Spring-o-lators.

$70-100   **CCL**

A pair of slingback stiletto sandals, by Guildmark, with clear plastic, faux leather and faux pearl.

$30-50   **CCL**

A 1950s pair of straw mules decorated with beadwork.

$60-90   **CCL**

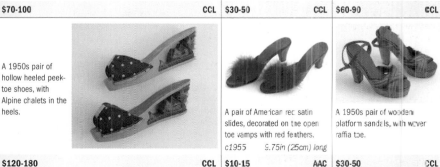

A 1950s pair of hollow heeled peek-toe shoes, with Alpine chalets in the heels.

$120-180   **CCL**

A pair of American red satin slides, decorated on the open toe vamps with red feathers.

c1955   9.75in (25cm) long

$10-15   **AAC**

A 1950s pair of wooden platform sandals, with woven raffia toe.

$30-50   **CCL**

A 1960s pair of clear plastic and pink velvet wedge heeled sandals, by Fashion Stride, decorated with pink velvet flowers.

$30-50   **CCL**

A pair of hand-painted and embroidered stiletto sandals, made in Singapore.

$150-200   **CCL**

A 1960s pair of cross-over wedge heeled sandals, by Jodi-Ann Inc., decorated with embroidered beads and faux pearls.

$30-50   **CCL**

A 1970s pair of wooden platform sandals, with plastic toes decorated with cherries.

$70-100   **CCL**

A 1970s pair of Clarks Intrigue Skyline brown lace court shoes.

$50-80   **CCL**

A vintage pair of red 'The Clyde' Puma trainers, size 11 1/2, in original box with Clyde Frazier on the side spinning a ball on his finger.

$60-90   **HA**

A 1950s pair of peach-colored plastic sunglasses, made in the US.

$20-30   **CCL**

A 1950s pair of bronze plastic sunglasses, made in the US, with spotted decoration.

$20-30   **CCL**

A 1960s pair of clear plastic spectacles, with reflective metallic green stripes.

5.25in (13.5cm) wide

$30-50   **BB**

A 1960s pair of plastic spectacles, with checkerboard design, made by KONO of US.

5.5in (14cm) wide

$30-50   **BB**

A 1960s pair of multi-colored laminated plastic spectacles, by Carezza of Italy.

6in (15cm) wide

$50-80   **BB**

A very rare pair of white plastic Courreges sunglasses, with slits, marked "FRANCE".

A pair of children's 'The Flintstones' novelty spectacles, with original packaging.

c1976   *4.25in (10.5cm) wide*

$30-50   **BB**

Outer space and the 'Future' were popular themes during the 1960s, the decade that witnessed Barbarella's galactic exploits in 1968 and man's first visit to the moon in 1969. André Courreges summed up and influenced this fascination with his clothing designs. These included the influential 'Moon Girl' collection in 1964, with its ultra-modern lines and white and silver colors, nongender specific outfits and 'futuristic' materials. These sunglasses are typical of that style and are today very desirable amongst collectors.

6in (15cm) wide

$300-500   **MAC**

A 1960s pair of aluminum and gold filled spectacles.

This style of spectacles is currently extremely popular, mainly due to the popularity of the film "Malcolm X" which featured this style of glasses. As a result, many designers are copying this style.

$30-50   BB

A 1980s pair of folding novelty 'Michael Jackson' sunglasses, with original case

5.5in (14cm) wide

$30-50   BB

An early 20thC purple, green and yellow silk scarf.

24in (61cm) wide

$7-10   AAC

A WWI 'sweetheart' cotton handkerchief.

These hankies would have been given to soldiers by their wives or sweethearts as a token before they went off to war.

c1914   13in (33cm) wide

$30-50   DH

A 1940s Echo 'Life With Mother' pattern silk scarf.

30.5in (77.5cm) wide

$50-80   Ren

A 1950s printed cotton handkerchief, decorated with poodles.

11in (28cm) wide

$6-9   CCL

A 1950s printed cotton scarf, decorated with poodles.

18in (46cm) wide

$12-18   CCL

A Rennies silk scarf, designed by Trickett & Webb with illustration by Jeff Fisher, produced in a limited edition of 400.

1996   30.5in (77.5cm) wide

$50-80   Ren

A 1930s Pucci silk scarf.

With his extremely brightly colored geometric or wavy patterns, the designs of Italian nobleman Emilio Pucci (1914-1992) became iconic during the 1960s. His instantly recognizable clothes are also immensely fashionable and wearable today and go through periods of popularity every few years. As with many popular designs, there were copies, both contemporary and modern. Look closely at the pattern which should include a printed 'Emilio' signature, denoting it is an authentic Pucci piece.

A 1950s pair of white gloves, with faux pearl detail.

$5-8   CCL

$120-180   CCL

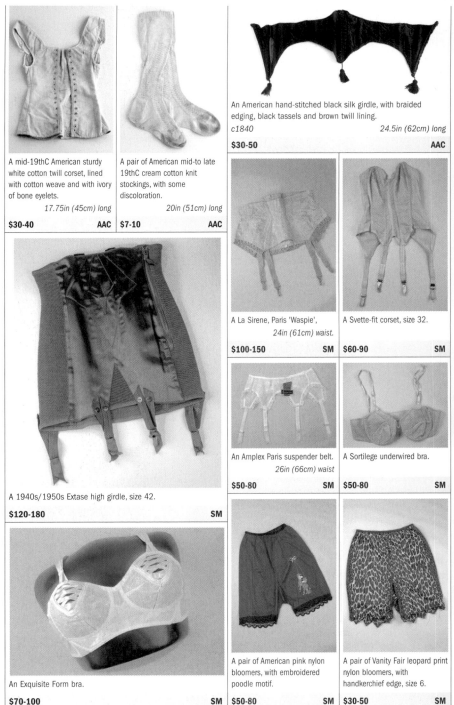

A mid-19thC American sturdy white cotton twill corset, lined with cotton weave and with ivory of bone eyelets.

17.75in (45cm) long

$30-40 AAC

A pair of American mid-to late 19thC cream cotton knit stockings, with some discoloration.

20in (51cm) long

$7-10 AAC

An American hand-stitched black silk girdle, with braided edging, black tassels and brown twill lining.

c1840 *24.5in (62cm) long*

$30-50 AAC

A La Sirene, Paris 'Waspie',

24in (61cm) waist.

$100-150 SM

A Svette-fit corset, size 32.

$60-90 SM

A 1940s/1950s Extase high girdle, size 42.

$120-180 SM

An Amplex Paris suspender belt.

26in (66cm) waist

$50-80 SM

A Sortilege underwired bra.

$50-80 SM

An Exquisite Form bra.

$70-100 SM

A pair of American pink nylon bloomers, with embroidered poodle motif.

$50-80 SM

A pair of Vanity Fair leopard print nylon bloomers, with handkerchief edge, size 6.

$30-50 SM

A 1950s paper nylon slip, with pink ribbon.

$30-50 CCL

A box of Postscript nylons, containing two pairs.

Box 9.5in (24.5cm) high

$50-80 SM

A pair of Camp seamfree nylons.

$15-20 SM

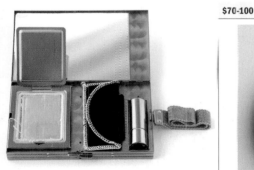

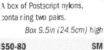

A 1950s Pilcher circular gold-plated compact, with polished horse design on lid, mint condition.

3.75in (9.5cm) diam

$70-100 MAC

A 1940s/50s Schick Mfg. Co. mother-of-pearl covered 'Standard Carry All' compact, with gold link chain for carrying, the other side with space for cigarettes, mint condition.

It is hard to find compacts – like this example – complete with all the accessories and in mint condition. Compacts were very fashionable and useful in their day and often show signs of use. If this had been used and showed signs of wear, its value would be around half the value of this example.

c1949

$150-200 BBG

A 1930s/1940s early plastic Art Deco fingernail buffer, with revolving center, the back marked "POL".

The user would place their fingers into the device and around the central shape and revolve it, polishing their nails against the padded lining.

4in (10.5cm) high

$120-180 AOY

A 1940s painted silk tie, with purple ground and glitter details, decorated with a hula girl on the beach.

$180-220 CVS

A 1940s handpainted silk tie, by Cravate Triomphe, with starfish design.

$50-80 CVS

A 1940s painted silk tie, decorated with a dancing couple and a drummer, with motto "Dance Pretty Lady".

$120-180 CVS

A 1970s plain black silk 'peek-a-boo' tie, printed to the interior with a strawberry blonde bathing beauty.

Peek-a-boo ties are being copied by contemporary designers such as Paul Smith.

$120-180 CVS

A 1970s painted silk tie, decorated with a Neanderthal caveman dragging a woman, with the motto "Friendly Persuasion".

$70-100 CVS

A 1940s handpainted silk tie, titled "The Canary Blues".

$80-120 CVS

A 1940s handpainted acetate, rayon and nylon tie, by Diane, decorated with a scene of a log cabin amongst palm trees.

$60-90 CVS

A 1950s printed silk tie, by Herb J. Hawthorns Inc, Houston, Texas, titled "Doodle Bugger, 1951".

This was an oil rigger's club tie.

$60-90 CVS

A 1940s handpainted silk tie, by Regal of California, with colored abstract pattern.

$30-40 CVS

Collectors' Notes

- The Titanic, along with her sister ship, the Olympic, was owned and run by the White Star Line, one of the world's largest shipping companies. Of huge size and with an opulent interior, she was advertised as unsinkable due to her double-lined bottom and hull divided into 16 watertight compartments.

- Work began in Harland & Wolff's shipyards in Ireland in 1899 and she set sail for New York from Southampton on April 10, 1912.

- At 11.40pm on April 14, she struck an iceberg and began to take on water, sinking some time after 2am on the 15th with a loss of 1,500 lives. She was one of the first ships in history to send the S.O.S. (Save Our Souls) distress signal. Artefacts and memorabilia

related to her have become immensely popular and valuable, partly due to the Hollywood blockbuster film, but also to the proximity of the centenary.

- The Mauretania was also originally advertised as unsinkable and was owned by the Cunard Line, White Star Line's competitor. Similarly luxurious and dubbed a 'floating palace', she made her first trans-Atlantic cruise in 1906. She was also known for her speed.

- During the war she served as a hospital ship, but by the 1930s and the Depression, she was sailing to unfamiliar ports such as Nassau with ten day cruises costing only $140. In 1934, Cunard and White Star merged and work on a new range of luxury liners began, and the ship was broken up in 1935.

A pair of postcards of the RMS Titanic, both captioned "White Star triple-screw steamer Titanic, 45,000 tons", one with subtitle "This & the sister ship Olympic 45,000 are the two largest vessels in the world", the other an identical view but issued after the disaster in the Spithead Series with subtitle "which sank on April 15th 1912, with 1635 people".

$180-220   **DN**

Two postcards of the RMS Titanic one pre-disaster by Reginald Silk of Portsmouth captioned "RMS Titanic on her maiden voyage, 10th April 1912, Silk 2 stern view", showing the vessels "Among the icebergs" with caption detailing the event and further information on the back.

$400-600   **DN**

An RMS Titanic postcard, published by W. & T. Gaines Leeds posted April 30, 1912, part message reads "How distressing to read the account ...", good condition slight wear to corners.

Along with original artefacts, any contemporary memorabilia related to the Titanic disaster is much sought after and usually fetches high prices. Whilst postcards and images of the luxury liner are not usually very valuable, if they specifically mention the Titanic as this example sent 15 days after the ship sunk does the value is much higher. Letters or postcards sent from the Titanic when it left Southampton or docked at Cherbourg and Queenstown, Ireland, are all even higher value.

$1,000-1,500   **W&W**

A large sepia photograph of the RMS Titanic, presumably leaving Southampton on her maiden (and only) voyage, April 1912, from an original negative.

21.5in (54.5cm) wide

$60-90   **W&W**

Harrison, Leslie, 'A Titanic Myth - A Californian Incident', published by W. Kimber & Co.

Tells the story of the captain of the Californian, which was 19 miles away when the Titanic sunk and was blamed by many for the loss of 1,500 lives.

1992   9.5in (24cm) high

$15-25   **COB**

A program of events for the RMS Mauretania.

1947   6in (15cm) high

$4-6   **COB**

An RMS Mauretania brochure.

1955/6

$30-50   **COB**

A 1:48 scale model of an RMS Titanic 30ft standard lifeboat.

Base 9.5in (24cm) wide

$100-150   **COB**

A pull-out deck plan of the RMS Mauretania.

1939   10.25in (26cm) high

$80-120   **COB**

Collectors' Notes

- The development of the steam engine influenced ships even more than trains. It led to an explosion in ship building in the mid-19th century, when ships were mainly used for transporting mail.

- By the turn of the century large, often opulent, cruise liners were being built by vast shipping companies such as the Cunard Line and its competitor, the White Star Line, owned from 1902 by J. Pierpont Morgan's International Mercantile Marine company. Ships included the Olympic, Titanic, Lusitania and Mauretania.

- Another surge occurred after the 1920s and 1930s, when the Normandie, Queen Mary and Queen Elizabeth were built. Used as hospitals during wartime, they played host to many of the wealthy and famous during peacetime.

- The increase in inexpensive air flights and an attitude towards modernity and away from established practices during the 1960s and 1970s began a decline in cruising, and very few cruise liners survived, but a large amount of memorabilia from holidays, immigrations and emigrations had already been generated.

- Look for artefacts or memorabilia related to notable ships or lines. Many document the glamor and luxury on these ships, as well as the grandeur of these floating palaces and of sea travel. Items directly from ships are usually more valuable and desirable than commemorative pieces. Posters, particularly in Art Deco styles with strong graphic design, are currently very popular and valuable. The market is still young, but has shown strong growth recently.

An RMS Queen Mary souvenir cup and saucer, made by Aynsley, commemorating her maiden voyage on May 27, 1936.

The RMS Queen Mary was launched in 1934 and passengers included celebrities and stars such as Greta Garbo and Clark Gable. During the war she carried over 80,000 troops and played a notable role in the Allied campaign. Now, she is moored in Long Beach, California as a hotel and tourist attraction.

Saucer 5.5in (14cm) diam

$150-200   COB

A hand-painted RMS Queen Mary commemorative water jug, by Suzanne Handcrafts.

1936   4.5in (11.5cm) high

$40-60   COB

A Morning Post supplement from the RMS Queen Mary, dated May, 1936.

16in (40.5cm) high

$30-50   COB

An RMS Queen Mary souvenir jigsaw puzzle.

1936   Box 9.5in (24cm) wide

$40-60   COB

An RMS Queen Elizabeth dinner menu, for Sunday, October 20, 1968.

This was used during the liner's last voyage.

10.5in (26.5cm) high

$15-25   COB

A course book for the RMS Queen Elizabeth.

1964   11.75in (30cm) wide

$50-80   COB

A 1960s RMS Queen Elizabeth souvenir pencil.

7in (18cm) long

$12-18   COB

A BI Education Cruises 1983 brochure.

11.5in (29cm) high

$8-12   COB

A Canberra souvenir key ring.

2in (5cm) wide

$6-9   COB

Two Canadian Pacific Steamships Limited luggage labels.

6.5in (16.5cm) wide

$6-9 (each)   COB

A Canadian Pacific Triangle Route menu.
1932   8.75in (22cm) high
$15-25   **COB**

A blank radiogram form from the Cunard Steamship Co. Ltd.
10.25in (26cm) high
$7-10   **COB**

A Cunard West Indies Cruise in Mauretania pamphlet.
1965   9in (23cm) high
$8-12   **COB**

A 1960s French Line brochure for the mailsteamer Antilles.
11.75in (30cm) high
$60-90   **COB**

A pack of Greek Line souvenir playing cards.
3.75in (9.5cm) wide
$10-15   **COB**

A Hamburg-Amerika Line souvenir brochure.
c1937   11.75in (30cm) high
$60-90   **COB**

A KMP Line sailing schedule for 1938.
9.75in (25cm) high
$15-25   **COB**

A 1930s deck plan for the Normandie.
12.75in (32.5cm) high
$120-180   **COB**

A double pack of 'Orient Line to Australia' patience cards, by John Waddington, London, in padded turquoise box.
4in (10cm) wide
$15-25   **LG**

A late 1950s/early 1960s Orient Line pennant for the SS Orsova.
14.5in (37cm) wide
$15-25   **COB**

A 1930s Mores 'Sneezy' tooth brush holder.

3.75in (9.5cm) high

$150-200   **Bev**

A 1930s Mores 'Bashful' tooth brush holder.

3.75in (9.5cm) high

$150-200   **Bev**

A 1930s Mores 'Doc' tooth brush holder.

3.75in (9.5cm) high

$150-200   **Bev**

A Steiff Mickey Mouse doll, with chest tag, perfect ear tag and button, brightly colored open mouth and strong rubber stamping on foot, area of sewing repair on neck, pants faded, missing tail.

12in (30.5cm) high

$5,000-7,000   **NB**

A Funny Flex Mickey and Minnie, Minnie in polka dot skirt, wood-jointed with original decals.

5in (12.5cm) high

$300-400   **NB**

A pair of Schmidt limited-edition ceramic musical 'Mickey and Minnie Mouse' figures.

14in (36cm) high

$120-180   **F**

A rare Charbens Salco series die-cast model No. 3 'Mickey and Minnie's Barrel Organ', in original box.

$300-350   **F**

An Ideal Pinocchio fully jointed painted wood and composition doll, with original oil cloth collar and felt bow tie, light paint wear and crazing on head.

7.5in (19cm) high

$120-180   **NB**

An American Ideal Ferdinand doll, painted composition with jointed legs, original flower and tail, crack underneath near rear leg joint.

8.25in (21cm) high

$120-180   **NB**

A painted composition Donald Duck bank, serious wear.

6.5in (16.5cm) wide

$30-50 NB

A Chein Donald Duck lithographed tin mechanical bank.

6.5in (16.5cm) wide

$70-100 NB

A Walt Disney Productions Mickey Mouse musical money box.

6in (15cm) high

$20-30 DH

A Swiss Walt Disney Productions Mickey Mouse biscuit tin.

c1932   8.25in (21cm) wide

$600-900 DH

A 1930s European Mickey Mouse tin.

6in (15cm) wide

$300-400 DH

A 1930s 'Official Mickey Mouse Store' badge, marked "Walt Disney 1937", made by Kay Kamen Ltd of New York and London.

1.25in (3cm) wide

$20-30 HGS

A yellow Catalin Disney Donald Duck pencil sharpener.

1.5in (3.5cm) wide

$70-100 BCAC

An early Hallmark Cards Disney Mickey Mouse 'Happy Birthday' card.

4.25in (11cm) high

$15-25 BCAC

An early 20thC baby's rattle, the brass ring suspending painted celluloid figures of Snow White and the Seven Dwarfs.

$60-90 F

A rare autographed sketch of Jack Skellington, by Tim Burton from his film "The Nightmare Before Christmas".

$300-500 MSC

A B C D E F G H I J K L M N O P Q R S T U V W XYZ

DOLLS

Collectors' Notes

■ Impressed or incised marks on the back of a bisque doll's head often gives a mold number which will help to identify a doll maker. Some dolls can be recognized by their facial shapes and characteristics.

■ Large dolls and those made by certain renowned manufacturers will fetch higher prices. A pleasing 'appeal', a lifelike appearance and fine quality molded and painted detailing are also factors that command higher values.

■ A doll should be complete with its original body, as replaced parts usually devalue a doll. A head is worth roughly 50 percent of the value of a whole doll. Look for original clothing, especially if it shows the fashions of the period. This is rare, so appropriate clothing is acceptable.

■ Examine the head for cracks and other damage. Shining a strong light into a head will reveal hard to spot cracks, but always ask permission before removing a wig. Bisque should be smooth and clean.

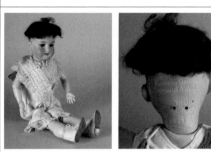

An Armand Marseille bisque head doll, modeled as a young girl with brown glass eyes and partly open mouth revealing four upper front teeth, brown hair wig, on a jointed composition body impressed marks and numbered "390N", some damage.

20in (51cm) high

$220-280 F

An Armand Marseille bisque shoulder-plate doll, modeled as a young girl with a long brown wig, weighted blue glass eyes and partly open mouth with teeth, on a kid leather body, impressed marks, some damage.

22.5in (57cm) high

$300-400 F

An Armand Marseille bisque head doll, modeled as a young girl with weighted blue glass eyes and open mouth revealing two upper front teeth and moving tongue, brown hair wig, on a five-piece composition body, impressed marks and numbered "996".

16in (40.5cm) high

$280-320 F

An Armand Marseille bisque head child doll, sleeping eyes, open mouth, molded composition, limbs and body, impressed "A14M".

Armand Marseille, of Thuringia, Germany, is one of the most prolific bisque doll makers, with production beginning in 1885 and peaking in the first three decades of the 20thC. Their dolls bear the letters 'AM' as part of the incised markings. Look for dolls with finely painted, less simplistic features.

24in (61cm) high

$400-600 LC

An Armand Marseille bisque head doll, with weighted blue glass eyes, closed mouth, on a rag body, impressed marks and "341".

10in (25.5cm) high

$180-220 F

An Armand Marseille bisque head 'Dream Baby', with blue glass eyes, closed mouth, composition body and limbs, impressed mark "341/6".

6.75in (17.5cm) high

$300-400 LC

A bisque socket head doll, jointed composition body, human hair wig, impressed "HC 16" and "Duchess A156M Made in Germany".

34in (86.5cm) high

$700-1,000 WHA

An Armand Marseille 'Floradora' bisque shoulder head doll, stationary glass eyes, mohair wig, replaced pate, new cloth body, impressed "Flora Dora AM Made in Germany'.

13in (33cm) high

$150-200 WHA

A Heubach-Koppelsdorf bisque head child doll, sleeping blue eyes and open mouth, with four teeth, composition molded body and limbs, impressed mark "250.16 Germany".

7in (18cm) high

$300-400 LC

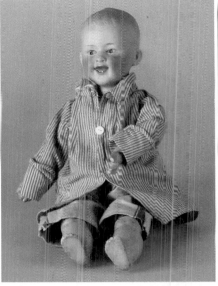

A Gebrüder Heubach bisque head 'Laughing Boy' doll, with tinted, molded hair and intaglio eyes, his open mouth molded with teeth, on jointed composition body, impressed and printed marks.

Gebrüder Heubach of Thuringia, Germany, were active between 1840 and c1945. As well as for all-bisque 'Piano' babies they were known for their notable character dolls, such as this one. Typically, they have exaggerated, characterful expressions often with rosy cheeks and eyes highlighted with a white dot. Bodies are usually crudely modeled from composition or cloth

13in (33cm) high

$400-600 F

A Heubach doll, with wardrobe, in wicker basket, all original.

7in (17.5cm) high

$1,200-1,800 DE

A Heubach Koppelsdorf bisque head black baby doll, with sleeping eyes, No. 350 12/0.

10.75in (27cm) high

$280-320 ClW

A Heubach Koppelsdorf painted bisque socket head doll, five-piece jointed composition body, painted shoes, some damage and replaced wig, impressed "Heubach Koppelsdorf 250/15/0 German".

8in (20cm) high

$70-100 WHA

A Gebrüder Heubach 'Piano Baby', the tinted bisque baby with molded hair and intaglio eyes, sat in a seated pose with outstretched arms and crossed legs, impressed rising sun mark.

11in (28cm) high

$700-1,000 F

A Kestner bisque shoulder head doll, sleeping eyes, open mouth, kid body with bisque lower arms, rivets at hips and gussets at knees, mohair wig, plaster pate, old diagonal hairline across forehead, impressed "dep Kestner 1441".

12.5in (32cm) high

$150-200 WHA

A Kestner shoulder head doll, sleeping eyes, original eyelashes, open mouth, later mohair wig, cloth body, jointed with rivets at hips and knees, tiny chip back shoulder plate, impressed "147" and "Made in Germany".

13in (33cm) high

$150-200 WHA

A Kestner bisque shoulder head doll, static eyes, open mouth, cracked and mended shoulder plate, V-shaped piece out of crown, kid body mended, cloth legs.

18in (46cm) high

$70-100 — **WHA**

A Kestner bisque socket head doll, sleeping eyes, open mouth, human hair wig, remnants of plaster pate, jointed composition body, original finish, with undergarments, boots and socks, red stamp "Excelsior", marked "Made in Germany 171".

Kestner & Co. was founded in 1816 in the Thuringia area, which was renowned for doll production. Their dolls were exported to and were very popular in the US, but not as popular in the UK. Dolls with gray eyes or chubby limbs and well defined digits are sought after and more valuable. They merged with Kammer & Reinhardt in 1930.

19in (48cm) high

$400-600 — **WHA**

A Kestner bisque turned head doll, sleeping eyes, closed mouth, kid body, mohair wig, plaster pate, updated costume, impressed "H".

17in (43cm) high

$400-600 — **WHA**

A Simon & Halbig bisque socket head doll, pierced ears, sleeping eyes, original pate, wig, open mouth, shoes, earrings, necklace, locket and metal purse, joint composition body, replaced body parts, impressed "SH 1009".

18in (46cm) high

$400-600 — **WHA**

A Simon & Halbig bisque socket head doll, sleeping eyes, open mouth, one tooth chipped, pierced ears with earrings, modern synthetic wig, jointed composition body, original finish, original undergarments, impressed "SH 1079 DEP 7 Germany".

16in (40.5cm) high

$300-500 — **WHA**

A Simon & Halbig bisque shoulder head doll, sleeping eyes, open mouth, replaced mohair wig, kid body with gussets, bisque lower arms, four fingers, chipped right hand, original undergarments, impressed "S&H 1010 DEP".

20in (51cm) high

$120-180 — **WHA**

A very large Simon & Halbig for Kammer & Reinhardt bisque-head doll, with sleeping brown eyes, open mouth with four teeth, brown hair and ball-jointed straight limb 'toddler' body, wearing a broderie anglaise blouse, blue skirt, lace-trimmed apron, and flower-trimmed hat with lace veil, the head marked "K * R / SIMON & HALBIG / 100", hands repaired.

The German company Simon & Halbig was active between c1869 and 1930 and was highly prolific, producing heads for other doll companies such as Kammer & Reinhardt and Jumeau. Early dolls have closed mouths, later ones open mouths. Incised markings include the "SH" letters. Mold numbers usually identify their date of production. The company closed in 1930.

39.75in (101cm) high

$2,000-3,000 — **DN**

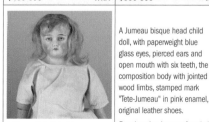

A Simon & Halbig bisque shoulder-plate doll, on a cloth body with bisque lower arms, impressed marks to head "1250 Germany No. 3", some damage.

13in (33cm) high

$180-220 — **F**

A Jumeau bisque head child doll, with paperweight blue glass eyes, pierced ears and open mouth with six teeth, the composition body with jointed wood limbs, stamped mark "Tete-Jumeau" in pink enamel, original leather shoes.

French maker Jumeau, founded in 1842, was responsible for releasing the first bébé in 1885, a doll shaped like a chubby young girl and not a slim lady. Its dolls were popular, but competition from inexpensive German imports from Thuringia led to the company's decline and closure in 1899. The dolls' heads are clearly marked with the factory name.

17.5in (44cm) high

$3,200-3,800 — **LC**

A Jumeau/Limoges bisque-head doll, with long brown hair, fixed blue eyes, open mouth with four teeth and fully jointed composition body marked with a label "BEBE JUMEAU / Diplome d'Honneur" on the back, the head marked "Limoges , FRANCE", wearing a simple blue dress and white shift.

14.25in (36cm) high

$300-400 **DN**

A Jumeau/SFBJ bisque-head doll, with long brown hair, sleeping eyes, open mouth with four teeth, and fully jointed composition body marked with a label "BEBE JUMEAU / Diplome d'Honneur" on the back, the head marked "SFBJ / 60 / PARIS / -0-".

14.25in (36cm) high

$300-500 **DN**

An Alt, Beck & Gottschalk shoulder head doll, impressed "639 5", with paperweight eyes, closed mouth, forehead damage, kid body with gussets, mended, replaced wig.

13in (33cm) high

$150-200 **WHA**

A Porzellanfabrik-Burggrab bisque head child doll, sleeping eyes, open mouth, composition molded body and limbs, impressed "Porzellanfabrik-Burggrab 169/2 Germany".

16.25in (41cm) high

$320-380 **LC**

A Cuno & Otto Dressel bisque-headed doll, modeled as a young girl with weighted brown glass eyes and partly open mouth revealing four upper front teeth, brown hair wig on a jointed composition body, impressed marks.

14in (35.5cm) high

$300-400 **F**

An Einco bisque-headed doll, modeled as a young girl with weighted brown glass eyes and party open mouth revealing upper front teeth, brown hair wig, on a jointed composition body, printed and impressed marks.

Einco also produced googly eye dolls.

18in (46cm) high

$300-500 **F**

A Goebel bisque shoulder head child doll, inset glass eyes, open mouth new mohair wig, kid body with rivet joints at hips and knees, replaced new forearms, impressed "521".

13in (33cm) high

$120-180 **WHA**

A Heinrich Handwerck bisque socket head doll, minor wig pulls, pierced ears, sleeping eyes, original pate and mohair wig, joint composition body, original finish, impressed "109-11, Germany, Handwerck".

20in (51cm) high

$400-500 **WHA**

A German piano baby ensemble in dome, probably by Hertwig.

Gebrüder Heubach were the primary producers of the all-bisque decorative 'Piano' babies that look like this example.

c1890

$1,000-1,500 **BEJ**

A Minerva metal shoulder head doll, molded blonde hair, painted eyes, embossed "Minerva" or front shoulder plate and "Germany" on back shoulder plate, missing arms, legs replaced, old cape and undergarments.

15in (38cm) high

$70-100 **WHA**

A Walther & Sohn bisque head shoulder doll, blonde wig, blue eyes and open mouth of five teeth, fabric body, impressed mark "241/14".

A Franz Schmidt bisque head baby doll, the domed head with painted hair, on a composition body, marked "F. S. & Co. 1272/35", some damage.

c1910

$400-600 ATK

An SFBJ model number 60 bisque headed doll, with composite body and ball joints, some clothing, blue glass eyes, open mouth and four upper teeth.

22.75in (58cm) high

$300-400 WHP

9in (23cm) high

$120-180 LC

An 1890s German shoulder head doll, on kid body, unmarked.

17in (43cm) high

$400-600 BEJ

A German all bisque doll, with one-piece head and torso, wire strung one-piece limbs, orange flat boots, white socks with blue trim, painted black eyes, closed mouth, crocheted outfit, impressed "6248 3/0".

4in (10cm) high

$60-90 WHA

A German all bisque doll, with one-piece head and torso, blue glass set eyes, mohair wig, wire strung one-piece limbs, chip left upper arm, blue flat shoes, white socks with green trim, impressed with indistinct marking, possibly "5020", on head.

3.25in (8.25cm) high

$120-180 WHA

A German all bisque one-piece head and torso doll, with blue glass sleeping eyes, closed mouth, impressed with indistinct mark "5??/2" on head, mohair wig, one-piece limbs with hidden stringing loops.

4.5in (11.5cm) high

$280-320 WHA

A German bisque socket head doll, new paperweight eyes, open mouth, pierced ears, multi-articulated composition body, original finish, new wig, impressed "DEP".

c1895 *22in (56cm) high*

$400-600 WHA

A German all bisque doll, with one-piece head and torso, blue glass set eyes, closed mouth, original mohair wig with tiny cardboard pate, back impressed "161", wire strung one-piece limbs.

4in (10cm) high

$280-320 WHA

Two German all bisque dolls, with rigid necks, wire strung one-piece arms and legs, molded blonde hair with blue bows, painted blue eyes, closed pursed mouths, brown one-strap shoes, white stockings with blue bands, impressed "P-15".

5in (13cm) high

$120-180 WHA

Two German bisque shoulder head dolls, both with long blonde hair and bows, painted blue eyes, pursed mouths, brown cloth bodies, bisque lower arms and knees with molded ruffles at bodice, blue shoes and white socks, one with chipped shoulderplate, impressed "Germany".

5in (13cm) high

$150-200 WHA

A bisque shoulder head doll, inset glass eyes, open mouth, new mohair wig, new cloth body, old bisque hands, tag on petticoat: "This doll head came from Uncle Bob in Newport, RI, I made the body. EWJ", impressed horseshoe mark "W&G 1C/0".

14in (35.5cm) high

$60-90   **WHA**

A bisque doll, in the manner of Kling, modeled as an 'American Schoolboy', with brown flock wig, open blue glass eyes and closed mouth with painted lips, on a kid leather body with bisque arms.

15in (38cm) high

$600-900   **F**

c1920

$320-380

A pair of bisque head adult dolls, with painted blue eyes with red lid line, closed mouth, lambswool wigs, cloth bodies, bisque lower legs, original costumes, label under stand "350, Rue Saint-Honoré (Pres la Place Vendôme), Old Curiosity Shop Paris".

8in (20cm) high

WHA

A large 1930s French bisque doll, with red lips.

29.5in (75cm) high

$800-1,200   **HB**

A Japanese Nippon child doll.

c1915   *28in (71cm) high*

$400-600   **DE**

A set of bisque triplets, with molded blonde hair and pink ribbon, one-piece head, torso and legs, painted features, strung arms and legs, embossed "Made in Japan".

5.5in (14cm) high

$60-90   **WHA**

A bisque shoulder head doll, with cardboard pate, horseshoe mark, stationary eyes, open mouth, mohair wig, new cloth body.

12in (30.5cm) high

$70-100   **WHA**

A bisque socket head doll, blue glass set eyes, closed mouth, original long mohair wig, five-piece paper-mâché body, peg strung, impressed "5".

6in (15cm) high

$300-400   **WHA**

A French fashion bisque socket head replica Bru doll, cloth body with bisque forearms, impressed "S. Antoon 1993".

16in (40.5cm) high

$300-400   **WHA**

A Googley Kewpie-type doll.

9in (23cm) high

$1,000-1,500   **DE**

Two bisque bald head dolls, each with white dome, peg strung in center, flange neck, unmarked set eyes, closed mouth, mohair wig, five-piece peg strung wood and composition body, black painted boots with heels.

10in (25.5cm) high

$400-600   **WHA**

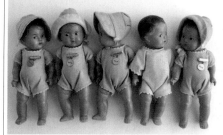

A composition Louis Amberg 'Little Amby' boy doll.

8.25in (21cm) high

$100-150   DE

A composition Louis Amberg 'Little Amby' girl doll.

8.25in (21cm) high

$80-120   DE

A rare set of five composition Madame Alexander 'Dionne Quints' toddlers, one redressed, with badges reading "Cecile", "Marie", "Emelie", "Annette" and "Yvonne".

The value of this set would have been higher if they were all in original clothing. This set was produced to commemorate the birth of the Dionne identical quintuplets in Ontario, Canada, in 1934. Their birth captured popular and media interest at the time, partly due to the efforts of the doctor who delivered them. Over 3 million people visited their home, set up by Ontario's government. Interestingly, the chances of identical quints being born is 57 million to one. Today, only three of the quintuplets survive.

Each 7.5in (19cm) high

$1,000-1,500   DE

A composition Madame Alexander 'Dr Allen Defoe' doll.

This doll is rare, in fine condition clothing and with original rubber gloves. Dr Defoe delivered the Dionne quintuplets and publicized their story.

1937-1939   15in (38cm) high

$1,500-2,000   DE

A 1940s Vogue 'Toddles' composition doll.

7in (18cm) high

$100-150   DE

A Vogue composition Indian 'Toddles' doll, with original clothing and sticker.

From 1937 to c1948, all Vogue dolls were made from the more inexpensive and robust composition. During the war years, when supplies of materials were low, Vogue used an 8in doll from the (R&B) Effanbee Company, early examples are marked "R&B", later ones "Vogue". After 1948, plastic was used.

1937-1948   7.5in (19cm) high

$220-280   DE

A composition doll, with blonde wig, opening blue glass eyes and partly open mouth with teeth, on a five-piece composition body fitted with a walking mechanism, in original box.

24in (61cm) high

$60-90   F

A pair of rare Munich art dolls, by Marion Kaulitz, each with painted composition head, closed painted mouth and rosy cheeks, the little boy with dark blue eyes, short brown mohair wig, and on a fully jointed composition body, wearing original red and white striped pants with braces and shirt, the girl with light blue eyes, longer red hair and fully jointed composition body, wearing a navy flannel tunic, ocher blouse, tartan underskirt, head band and underclothes.

These are amongst the earliest character dolls, and were sold in Hermann Tietz, a Munich department store, from 1908. They are typically dressed in provincial clothing.

c1911   13in (33cm) high

$1,800-2,200   BonC

Collectors' Notes

- After making and selling dolls as a hobby, Barbara Annalee Thorndike began to produce dolls professionally during the early 1950s. She was supported by her husband Chip who developed the internal wire frame that allowed their felt dolls to be posed - leading to them becoming known as 'mobilitee' dolls.

- The first catalog was produced c1954 and their business expanded greatly during the 1960s, when dolls were sold in over 40 states. 1964 saw the opening of their first factory, although many workers continued to make dolls from their homes.

- The 1970s saw further expansion and in 1983 a museum and collectors' society were founded. Despite Annalee's death on April 7, 2002, dolls are still being designed and made.

- Mice are popular animals, as are other animals and people, often dressed in bright costumes. Many are part of themed ranges, such as Thanksgiving, Halloween and Christmas.

- Dolls are usually part of a limited edition – the size of the run can affect the value. Desirable dolls from a short production run will be popular.

- Early dolls from 1950s are much sought after, as are unique dolls or those signed by Annalee herself. These usually command a premium.

- Keep the dolls out of strong sunlight, which can fade the bright colors and beware of attack from pests such as moths.

Mice

An Annalee 'Dartboard Mouse' doll.
2001
$30-40   MSC

An Annalee 'Naturalist Mouse' doll, from an edition of 436.
1972   7in (18cm) high
$70-100   MSC

An Annalee 'Railroad Mouse' doll.
2001
$30-40   MSC

An early 1950s Annalee doll.
$200-250   MSC

A 1990s pair of Annalee 'Policeman Mouse' and 'Jailhouse Mouse' dolls.

$30-40 (each)   MSC

A 1990s Annalee 'Nurse Mouse' doll.
3in (7.5cm) high
$15-20   MSC

A 1990s Annalee 'Teacher Mouse' doll.
3in (7.5cm) high
$15-20   MSC

A 1990s Annalee 'Get Well Soon' doll.
3in (7.5cm) high
$15-20   MSC

A 1990s Annalee 'Midnight Snack Mouse' ornament.
3in (7.5cm) high
$15-20   MSC

An Annalee 'Robin Hood Mouse' doll, from an edition of 6838.
1990   7in (13cm)
$30-40   MSC

An Annalee 'Maid Marion Mouse' doll.
1990   7in (18cm)
$30-40   MSC

An Annalee 'Friar Tuck Mouse' doll.
1990   7in (18cm)
$30-40   MSC

An Annalee 'Indian Girl Mouse' doll, from an edition of 4,492 and an 'Indian Boy Mouse' doll, from an edition of 3,246.

1986

$70-100 (pair)   **MSC**

An Annalee 'Country Cousin Boy Mouse' doll.

1967   *18in (45.5cm) high*

$500-800   **MSC**

An Annalee 'Country Cousin Boy Mouse' doll.

1967   *7in (18cm) high*

$200-250   **MSC**

An Annalee 'Country Cousin Boy Mouse' doll.

1967   *12in (30.5cm) high*

$300-500   **MSC**

An Annalee 'Mr Miggie' The Mexican Tailess Mouse doll.

1967   *7in (18cm) high*

$150-200   **MSC**

Two Annalee dolls, 'Retired Grandma Mouse' and 'Retired Grandpa Mouse', from an edition of 1,104.

1974   *12in (30.5cm) high*

$180-220 (each)   **MSC**

Other Animals

A 1980s Annalee 'Just In Time Bunny' doll.

     10in (25.5cm) high

$300-350   **MSC**

A 1960s Annalee 'Bride and Groom Frogs' doll.

     10in (25.5cm) high

$300-350   **MSC**

A pair of Annalee 'Victorian Bunny' dolls.

1998   *12in (30.5cm) high*

$80-100   **MSC**

A CLOSER LOOK AT ANNALEE DOLLS

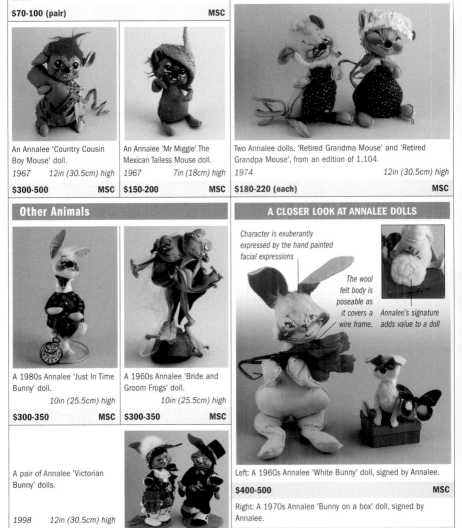

Character is exuberantly expressed by the hand painted facial expressions

The wool felt body is poseable as it covers a wire frame.

Annalee's signature adds value to a doll

Left: A 1960s Annalee 'White Bunny' doll, signed by Annalee.

$400-500   **MSC**

Right: A 1970s Annalee 'Bunny on a box' doll, signed by Annalee.

$220-280   **MSC**

An Annalee 'Laura May Cat' doll.
1967   12in (30.5cm) high
$500-700   MSC

An Annalee 'Tubby Elephant' doll.
1969   8in (20cm) high
$300-350   MSC

A one-of-a-kind Annalee 'Bee' doll.
$400-600   MSC

A one-of-a-kind Annalee 'Blue Bird' doll.
$400-600   MSC

An Annalee 'Hot Pink Monkey' doll from an edition of 70, signed.
1970   22in (56cm) high
$800-1,200   MSC

Left: An Annalee 'Lamb' doll, from an edition of 487.
1975   5in (12.5cm) high
$80-120   MSC

Right: An Annalee 'Lamb' doll, from an edition of 234.
1975   8in (20cm) high
$200-250   MSC

Elves and People

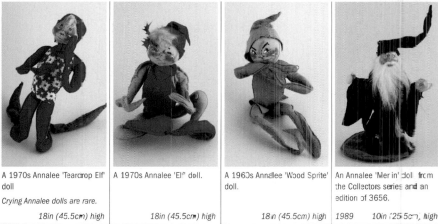

A 1970s Annalee 'Teardrop Elf' doll
Crying Annalee dolls are rare.
18in (45.5cm) high
$180-220   MSC

A 1970s Annalee 'Elf' doll.
18in (45.5cm) high
$220-280   MSC

A 1960s Annalee 'Wood Sprite' doll.
18in (45.5cm) high
$400-600   MSC

An Annalee 'Merlin' doll from the Collectors series and an edition of 3656.
1989   10in (25.5cm) high
$80-120   MSC

DOLLS

A 1970s Annalee 'Cyrano de Bergerac' doll.

10in (25.5cm) high

$1,000-1,500　　　**MSC**

A 1960s Annalee 'Skier' doll, the skis signed by Annalee.

10in (25.5cm) high

$800-1,200　　　**MSC**

An Annalee 'Painter with Ladder' doll.

1965　　14in (35.5cm) high

$1,500-2,000　　　**MSC**

A pair of 1960s Annalee 'Go-Go Boy & Girl' dolls.

10in (25.5cm) high

$400-600　　　**MSC**

A 1970s Annalee 'Boy in Basket' doll.

$200-250　　　**MSC**

Halloween

An Annalee 'Flower Kid' doll, from the 'Trick or Treat' series.

The first Halloween mouse appeared in 1978, but it was not not until 1985 that other mice and dolls were pulled together to form a Halloween range.

2000　　　　　7in (18cm)

$30-50　　　**MSC**

An Annalee 'Pumpkin Kid' doll, from the 'Trick or Treat' series and an edition of 1897.

2000　　　　　7in (18cm)

$40-50　　　**MSC**

An Annalee 'Tiger Kid' doll, from the 'Trick or Treat' series.

2000　　　　　7in (18cm)

$30-40　　　**MSC**

An Annalee 'Devil Kid' doll, from the 'Trick or Treat' series and from an edition of 2610.

1994   12in (30.5cm)

$50-80   MSC

An Annalee 'Frankenstein Kid' doll, from the 'Trick or Treat' series.

2000   7in (18cm)

$40-60   MSC

An Annalee 'Dragon Kid' doll, from the 'Trick or Treat' series.

1990   18in (45.5cm)

$80-120   MSC

Two Annalee dolls, 'Tags' and 'Tatlers', from the 'Trick or Treat' series.

1997   7in (17.5cm)

$50-80 (each)   MSC

Christmas and Valentine

A 1960s Annalee 'Tinsel Elf' doll.

18in (45.5cm) high

$300-500   MSC

A 1960s Annalee 'Workshop Elf' doll.

18in (45.5cm) high

$350-400   MSC

A unique Annalee artist's proof 'Haunted Tree' doll, from the 'Halloween' series, signed "Annalee '95".

1995   14.5in (37cm) high

$700-1,000   MSC

An Annalee 'Patriotic Santa' doll, made in China.

2001   15in (38cm) high

$50-80   MSC

A 1990s Annalee 'Irish' Santa' doll, made exclusively for Filene's department store.

$30-120   MSC

Three 1970s Annalee 'Choir Boys' and 'Choir Girls' dolls.

10in (25.5cm) high

$80-120 (each)   **MSC**

A pair of 1960s Annalee 'Christmas Morning Kids' dolls.

10in (25.5cm) high

$1,500-2,000   **MSC**

A 1960s Annalee 'Christmas Baby' doll.

12in (30.5cm) high

$400-600   **MSC**

An Annalee 'Ski Mouse' doll, with Santa outfit.

2001

$50-80   **MSC**

An Annalee 'Christmas Giraffe', with elf rider, from an edition of 488.

1985   *Giraffe 22in (56cm) high*

$400-600   **MSC**

Left: An Annalee 'Valentine' girl doll.

1957   *10in (25.5cm) high*

$800-1,200   **MSC**

Right: An Annalee 'Valentine' girl doll, from an edition of 6271.

The doll on the right was made as a tribute to the one of the left.

1986   *7in (18cm) high*

$120-180   **MSC**

Four Annalee 'Valentine Panda' dolls, from an edition of 1940.

These four dolls all have different facial expressions.

1986   *10in (25.5cm) high*

$80-120 (set)   **MSC**

FIND OUT MORE...

The Annalee Doll Museum, Reservoir Road, Meredith, New Hampshire, U.S.A..

www.annalee.com - the home of Annalee dolls online, with guidance for researching retired and vintage dolls.

A composition Googly doll, with cloth body, wooden shoes and original dress.

The value would have been higher if her hair was intact.

16.5in (42cm) high

$70-100 DE

A Biscaloid 'Black Mammy' doll, with cloth body and original clothing.

c1910   13.5in (34cm) high

$120-180 DE

An early Chad Valley cloth doll, modeled as an Eastern lady, with painted and molded corduroy face, her skirt formed as a hand-warmer.

18in (46cm) high

$60-90 F

An early Chad Valley cloth doll, with a painted and molded felt face, dressed as Cinderella, with a label to the underside of the foot "Emile Littler's Cinderella".

12.5in (32cm) high

$120-180 F

An early Deans cloth sailor doll, with blue velvet suit, composite head with 'Nevada' tassled head band.

9in (23cm) high

$80-120 W&W

A 1930s British cloth child doll, probably Deans.

17in (43cm) high

$220-280 BEJ

A German Käthe Kruse No. 7534 cloth child doll, with painted hazel eyes, brown hair on a cloth body and wearing a flannel tartar skirt with matching red shirt, in card box, together with a red check-lined coat with hood, knitted sweater, hats, dress, various under-clothes and two pairs of shoes, marked on foot, some clothes added.

Käthe Kruse made a small variety of cloth-bodied dolls between 1911 and 1956. Early dolls with three hand-stitched seams on their heads fetch a premium. Clean fabric and intact paint are also important considerations for value.

c1930   20in (51cm) high

$1,200-1,800 BonC

A Lenci felt doll, with pressed felt head, painted features and curled hair, dressed in green shorts and Alpine-style jacket and hat, all in felt.

20in (51cm) high

$100-150 DN

A 1930s Italian Lenci series 300 pressed felt boy doll with painted eyes, mouth and eyebrows, signed on left foot, some paint peeling from eyes.

17in (43cm) high

$700-1,000 BonC

A Norah Wellings brown velvet black doll, with fixed brown glass eyes, painted mouth, wearing integral green velvet dungarees, label to foot.

11.5in (29cm) high

$70-100 DN

A 1930s/1940s pair of German Black Forest fabric dolls, with tag reading "Gordon Germany".

13.75in (35cm) high

$280-320 DE

DOLLS

Collectors' Notes

- Although mid-18thC records refer to 'pincushion dolls', it was during the 19thC and early 20thC that half dolls became popular. Popularity dwindled after the 1930s and by the end of the 1940s, production had all but ceased.

- Half dolls are typically waist high with a head and arms. Acting as a decorative accessory, they would be attached to a cloth 'skirt' which would cover household objects from teapots to powder boxes. The skirt could also be stuffed and used as a pincushion. They were bought and used by adults, rather than played with as children's toys.

- The majority are made from porcelain or bisque, but examples in wood and wax are known. Examples from the 1920s and 1930s often display fashions of the time. Naked or bald half dolls would have been dressed and fitted with a wig.

- Look at the form to discern the value of vintage examples. The least expensive are from one mold and have arms molded to the body. The middle price versions have gaps between the arms and body and the most expensive versions have outstretched arms, sometimes with accessories, which were made by attaching parts from several molds.

- German factories such as Dressel & Kister, Heubach, Goebel and Kestner were the most prolific makers, and makers' marks or mold numbers often appear on the taper of the doll.

- Look for high quality painting and smooth bisque. Damage reduces value. Large sizes are very desirable as are original skirts. Reproductions do exist, often from the Far East – these are obviously not as desirable, or as valuable, and are usually of poorer quality.

A porcelain half doll, modeled as a young girl, incised marks.

c1925   4.25in (11cm) high

$50-80   F

A porcelain half doll, modeled as a young lady, incised marks "14652".

c1925   3.5in (9cm) high

$50-80   F

A porcelain half doll, modeled as a lady, incised marks "13753".

c1925   3.75in (9.5cm) high

$20-30   F

A porcelain half doll, modeled as an attractive young female, incised marks "16365".

c1925   3.75in (9.5cm) high

$30-50   F

A porcelain half doll, modeled as a pretty young lady, incised marks "13215".

c1925   4in (10cm) high

$50-80   F

A porcelain half doll, modeled as a pretty young lady, incised marks "13704".

c1925   4in (10cm) high

$50-80   F

A ceramic half doll, modeled as a young lady in winter dress, with painted decoration, incised marks.

c1935   4in (10cm) high

$50-80   F

A porcelain half doll, modeled as a pretty young girl, incised marks.

c1925   2 .5in (6.5cm) high

$70-100   F

A porcelain half doll, modeled as a lady, incised marks "Germany 19008".

c1925 3.25in (8cm) high

$50-80 F

A porcelain half doll, modeled as a lady, incised mark.

c1925 3.25in (8.5cm) high

$30-50 F

A porcelain half doll, modeled as a young lady.

c1910 5in (12.5cm) high

$30-50 F

A German porcelain half doll, modeled as a lady, impressed '484".

c1910 3.5in (9cm) high

$60-90 F

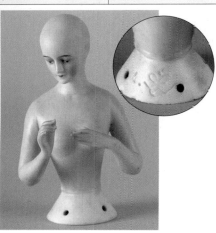

An early 20thC Goebel ceramic half doll, modeled as a naked female, her face with delicate, molded, painted features, marked "BT442 4", some damage.

5in (12.75cm) high

$100-150 F

A German porcelain half doll, modeled as a naked young lady, in tinted bisque finish, impressed marks.

c1925 5.5in (14cm) high

$60-90 F

A porcelain half doll, modeled as a pretty young female, incised marks, "15147".

c1925 4.25in (11cm) high

$30-50 F

A porcelain half doll, modeled as a naked lady.

c1910 4in (10cm) high

$100-150 F

A porcelain half doll, modeled as an attractive lady, incised marks "1193".

c1925 4in (10cm) high

$30-50 F

A CLOSER LOOK AT A HALF DOLL

This is a very well-modeled doll.

Her features are delicately portrayed and painted.

Her hand is outstretched and holds a rose, both features that require skill from the modeler.

The outstretched arm and rose are susceptible to damage, intact examples are desirable.

A porcelain half doll, modeled as a naked young lady with well modeled and painted facial features, holding a single red rose in her hand, some damage.

3in (7.5cm) high

$220-280 F

A porcelain half doll, modeled as an attractive female.

c1910   *2.25in (5.5cm) high*

$80-120   **F**

A porcelain half doll, modeled as a naked young female, incised marks "4884".

c1910   *2.75in (7cm) high*

$50-80   **F**

A porcelain half doll, modeled as a pretty young lady, incised marks "15460".

c1925   *4.75in (12cm) high*

$30-50   **F**

A porcelain half doll, modeled as a lady holding a small bouquet of flowers, some damage.

c1925   *4in (10cm) high*

$30-50   **F**

A porcelain half doll, modeled as a young lady wearing a Tam o' Shanter and shawl, incised marks "14901".

c1925   *3.25in (8.5cm) high*

$50-80   **F**

A porcelain half doll, modeled as an attractive female, incised marks "14208".

c1925   *3.75in (9.5cm) high*

$60-90   **F**

A porcelain half doll, modeled as an attractive young lady, incised marks "11206".

c1925   *3.75in (9.5cm) high*

$50-80   **F**

A porcelain half doll, modeled as a lady.

c1925   *2.5in (6.5cm) high*

$20-30   **F**

A porcelain half doll, modeled as a lady holding a string of beads.

c1925   *2.5in (6.5cm) high*

$50-80   **F**

A porcelain half doll, modeled as a lady, incised marks "5942".

c1925   *2.75in (7cm) high*

$60-90   **F**

A porcelain half doll, modeled as a lady in Art Deco dress, incised marks "10039".

With her stylized hair, brightly colored and geometrically designed coat and her 'sans souci' gaze, this elegant lady-about-town epitomizes the 1930s, a period when half dolls were very popular.

c1925   *3.25in (8.5cm) high*

$300-400   **F**

A pair of porcelain half dolls, the Dutch boy holding a yellow painted pipe, the Dutch girl holding a rose.

c1925   *1.75in (4.5cm) high*

$30-50 (each)   **F**

A ceramic half doll, modeled as an attractive young female, mounted on an upholstered fabric skirt base.

c1935   5.5in (14cm) high

$50-80   **F**

A porcelain half doll, modeled as a lady mounted on an upholstered fabric skirt base, with separate attached cast porcelain legs.

c1925   3in (7.5cm) high

$50-80   **F**

A bisque porcelain half doll, modeled as an attractive naked female with brown painted molded hair, painted molded facial features and jointed arms.

c1925   2in (5cm) high

$50-80   **F**

An early 20thC porcelain half doll, modeled as a lady wearing a luster-glazed hat and dress, mounted on an upholstered fabric skirt base, with separate attached cast porcelain legs.

3.5in (9cm) high

$70-100   **F**

A porcelain half doll, modeled as a lady wearing a white dress, mounted on an upholstered fabric skirt base, with separate attached cast porcelain legs.

c1925   4.25in (11cm) high

$50-80   **F**

A porcelain half doll, modeled as an attractive lady with painted molded features and applied hair wig, her ears with painted earrings, holding an orchid in her hand.

c1925   6in (15cm) high

$70-100   **F**

A porcelain half doll, modeled as a young lady, mounted on an upholstered fabric skirt base, with separate attached cast porcelain legs.

c1935   5.25in (13cm) high

$50-80   **F**

A porcelain half doll, modeled as a Dutch girl holding a basket of tulips, on padded shaped base.

c1935   6in (15cm) high

$50-80   **F**

A porcelain half doll, modeled as a young lady, mounted on a metal frame and dressed in a green fabric, forming a lampshade.

c1925   11in (28cm) high

$70-100   **F**

FIND OUT MORE...

'Collector's Encyclopaedia of Half Dolls', by Frieda Marion, published by Crown Publications, 1988.

DOLLS

Collectors' Notes

- Barbie was introduced at the American Toy Fair in New York City in 1959 by Ruth and Elliot Handler, founders of Mattel Toys. She was inspired by a 'Lilli' doll bought by Ruth Handler in Switzerland. Ruth thought that as her daughter grew, she would need a three-dimensional doll to replace the paper fashion dolls popular at the time.

- Barbie received mixed reviews at first, as she was so unlike any other dolls produced before. However, the public grew to love her and, from 1960, her popularity became assured.

- Barbies produced after 1972 are considered 'modern' and are of limited interest to most collectors. Those produced before 1972 are deemed 'vintage' and are more desirable. Looking at the features of a doll help to date it. For example, if she has 'bubble cut' hair, she dates from 1961-1967.

- Barbies with 'pony tail' hairstyles were produced between 1959 and 1964 and are highly sought after with around six different types available. Beware, as this hairstyle was reproduced by Mattel during the 1990s, so look at other features including eyes, skin tone and style of head.

- Barbie's earliest eye color was white, then blue. Barbie is marked on her bottom, with the marks helping to date and identify her. The date shown is not the date she was made, but the patent date, meaning she was made sometime after the date shown.

- As many Barbies were sold, condition and completeness are vitally important aspects. Dolls that have not been played with, complete examples with boxes and accessories will all be worth more. Most collectors look for examples that show very light signs of wear from play, but are complete – if the condition is better, the value usually rises.

- The metal in earrings can cause a greening of the ears on 1960s dolls, if left in place for a long time. Although this will usually reduce a doll's value, it can often be removed – consult a professional restorer.

A CLOSER LOOK AT BARBIE

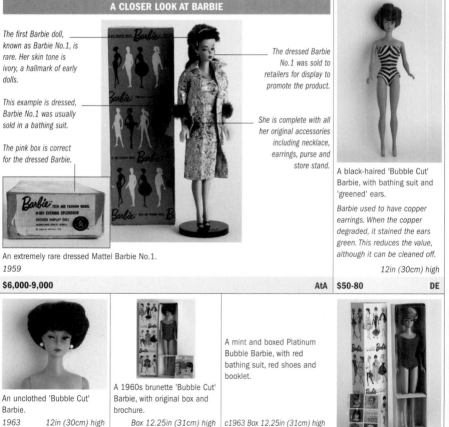

The first Barbie doll, known as Barbie No.1, is rare. Her skin tone is ivory, a hallmark of early dolls.

This example is dressed, Barbie No.1 was usually sold in a bathing suit.

The pink box is correct for the dressed Barbie.

The dressed Barbie No.1 was sold to retailers for display to promote the product.

She is complete with all her original accessories including necklace, earrings, purse and store stand.

An extremely rare dressed Mattel Barbie No.1.
1959

$6,000-9,000   AtA

A black-haired 'Bubble Cut' Barbie, with bathing suit and 'greened' ears.

Barbie used to have copper earrings. When the copper degraded, it stained the ears green. This reduces the value, although it can be cleaned off.

12in (30cm) high

$50-80   DE

An unclothed 'Bubble Cut' Barbie.
1963   12in (30cm) high

$60-90   DE

A 1960s brunette 'Bubble Cut' Barbie, with original box and brochure.
Box 12.25in (31cm) high

$150-200   DE

A mint and boxed Platinum Bubble Barbie, with red bathing suit, red shoes and booklet.

c1963 Box 12.25in (31cm) high

$300-350   AtA

A 'Titian Bubble Cut' Barbie with bathing suit.

'Titian' was the name given to this color of Barbie's hair.

12in (30cm) high

$120-180   DE

An early Mattel Inc. 'Barbie' doll, dressed as Guinevere, in original box.

11.5in (29cm) high

$320-380   F

A TNT Barbie.

11.5in (29cm) high

$60-90   DE

A 'Miss America' Barbie, with clicking legs.

12in (30cm) high

$60-90   DE

A Mattel 'Hawaiian' TNT Barbie, in original box.

TNT stands for 'Twist N' Turn', a waist feature that was first seen in the mid-1960s.

c1975 Box 12.5in (31.5cm) high

$60-90   DE

A boxed Supersize Barbie, with 'Super Hair'.

c1978   18.5in (47cm) high

$120-180   DE

A Malibu Barbie.

12in (30cm) high

$20-30   DE

A flock-hair Ken doll, with outfit.

Ken, Barbie's boyfriend, was first introduced in 1961 with blond flock hair and beach clothing and towel.

12.25in (31cm) high

$30-40   DE

A flock-hair Ken, with outfit, rubbed hair.

12.25in (31cm) high

$20-30   DE

A 'Talking Ken', with clothing, mute.

12.25in (31cm) high

$20-30   DE

A TNT brunette 'Flip Francie'.

Francie was Barbie's modern cousin' and was produced from 1966-76.

11in (28cm) high

$180-220   DE

A Mattel Francie with bent legs.

11.25in (28.5cm) high

$120-180   DE

A Mattel 'Skipper'.

1964-1970 9in (23cm) h

$20-30   DE

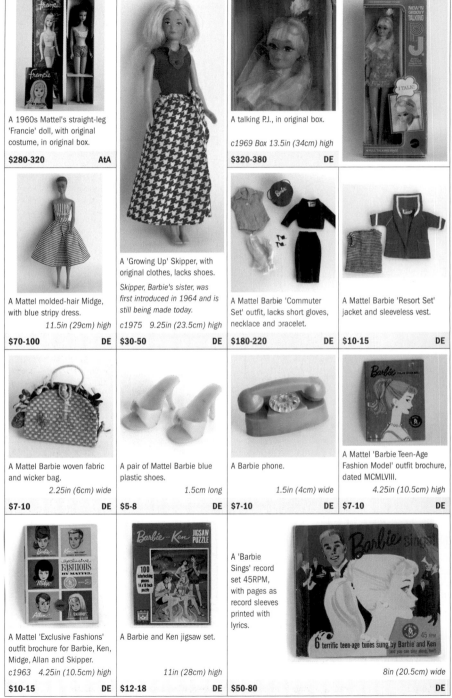

A 1960s Mattel's straight-leg 'Francie' doll, with original costume, in original box.

$280-320   **AtA**

A talking P.J., in original box.

c1969 Box 13.5in (34cm) high

$320-380   **DE**

A 'Growing Up' Skipper, with original clothes, lacks shoes.

Skipper, Barbie's sister, was first introduced in 1964 and is still being made today.

c1975 9.25in (23.5cm) high

$30-50   **DE**

A Mattel molded-hair Midge, with blue stripy dress.

11.5in (29cm) high

$70-100   **DE**

A Mattel Barbie 'Commuter Set' outfit, lacks short gloves, necklace and bracelet.

$180-220   **DE**

A Mattel Barbie 'Resort Set' jacket and sleeveless vest.

$10-15   **DE**

A Mattel Barbie woven fabric and wicker bag.

2.25in (6cm) wide

$7-10   **DE**

A pair of Mattel Barbie blue plastic shoes.

1.5cm long

$5-8   **DE**

A Barbie phone.

1.5in (4cm) wide

$7-10   **DE**

A Mattel 'Barbie Teen-Age Fashion Model' outfit brochure, dated MCMLVIII.

4.25in (10.5cm) high

$7-10   **DE**

A Mattel 'Exclusive Fashions' outfit brochure for Barbie, Ken, Midge, Allan and Skipper.

c1963 4.25in (10.5cm) high

$10-15   **DE**

A Barbie and Ken jigsaw set.

11in (28cm) high

$12-18   **DE**

A 'Barbie Sings' record set 45RPM, with pages as record sleeves printed with lyrics.

8in (20.5cm) wide

$50-80   **DE**

Collectors' Notes

- Due to the large number produced and sold, the condition of plastic dolls is especially important. Bodies and faces should be fresh and clean and clothes unfaded. Hair must be set in its original style as children tended to brush it into other styles.

- Look for rare or unusual examples by leading manufacturers. Boxed plastic dolls that are also 'box fresh' will command a sizeable premium. Important names to look for are Mattel's 'Barbie', Vogue's 'Ginny' and 'Madame Alexander'.

A Madame Alexander '1st Argentina Girl' plastic doll, #771.

1973-1976   8in (20cm) high

$30-50   DE

A Madame Alexander 'Morocco' bent knee doll, with original clothing and tag.

The doll and her clothing are in mint condition with bright colors, which adds to her desirability and value as they are usually faded, stained or even lost.

8in (20cm) high

$300-400   DE

A Madame Alexander 'Scottish' bent knee doll, with original clothing and tag.

8in (20cm) high

$100-150   DE

A CLOSER LOOK AT A PLASTIC DOLL

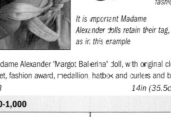

This doll has its original box, which is also in excellent condition.

Not only is the hair set in its original style, it also retains the delicate hairnet and curlers.

She still retains her original accessories including hatbox and fashion award.

It is important Madame Alexander dolls retain their tag, as in this example

A Madame Alexander 'Margot Ballerina' doll, with original clothing, hairnet, fashion award, medallion, hatbox and curlers and box.

1953   14in (35.5cm) high

$700-1,000   DE

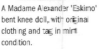

An Alexander-Kins 'Beth' doll, on original plastic Madame Alexander stand, with original clothing and label.

8in (20cm) high

$320-380   DE

A 'Ginny' hard plastic bent knee walker doll.

8in (20cm) high

$150-200   DE

A Madame Alexander 'Priscilla' plastic doll, with bent, jointed knees and original clothing and tag.

8in (20cm) high

$220-280   DE

A Madame Alexander 'Eskimo' bent knee doll, with original clothing and tag, in mint condition.

1967-1969   8in (20cm) high

$280-320   DE

A 'Ginny' bent knee walker doll, with original clothing and box, with headband, glasses and instruction booklets.

8in (20cm) high

$300-400   DE

A 1960s W. Goebel plastic boy doll.

10.75in (27cm) high

$120-180   **DE**

A 1970s Mary Quant 'Bubbles' plastic doll.

$30-50   **TH**

A Revlon plastic doll, by Ideal, with original clothing, necklace and label.

This doll has rare red hair, which adds to her desirability and value. The color is usually brown. She is also in mint condition.

18in (46cm) high

$400-600   **DE**

A Pedigree hard plastic walking doll, with brown hair and opening blue plastic eyes.

21in (53.5cm) high

$70-100   **F**

A 'LuAnn Simms' hard plastic doll, by Roberta, Horsmann & Valentine.

1953   *18in (46cm) high*

$150-200   **DE**

A 1980s 'Tiny Tears' plastic doll.

The Tiny Tears doll by American Character Doll was 'fed' water in a bottle through the mouth allowing her to wet herself and shed tears. The first version hit the shelves c1950 and her subsequent popularity ensured she went through a number of updates over the following decades. Early examples have solid heads, often with molded hair, and jointed rubber bodies. Later examples are deemed less attractive by collectors.

12in (30cm) high

$100-150   **DE**

A German celluloid doll, with a turtle mark.

c1920-30

$100-150   **HB**

A 1950s German celluloid boy doll, with original box.

8in (20cm) high

$60-90   **DE**

A china headed doll, with deep shoulder plate, high brow, black molded hair with vertical curls, finely painted features, blue eyes, red lid liner, original body and limbs, low heel black boots with blue decoration, body repaired, hard stuffed, impressed "0".

12in (30.5cm) high

$120-180 WHA

A china shoulder head doll, black molded hair with white center parting and vertical curls, deep shoulder plate, painted blue eyes with red lid liner, black dot on end of nose, contemporary body, with leather arms and china hands.

22in (56cm) high

$300-500 WHA

Two china dolls, both with painted black hair, the smaller on new cloth body with parian limbs, wearing a petticoat and the larger with blue painted eyes with red lip liner, slightly smiling, cracked and mended shoulder, new cloth body.

Larger 21in (54cm) high

$120-180 WHA

A china head doll, black molded hair, high brow, blue eyes with red lid line, smiling mouth, deep shoulder plate with original china arms, old mended twill body, dressed.

12in (30.5cm) high

$180-220 WHA

A china doll, with black molded hair, low brow, shallow shoulder plate, blue painted eyes, old body with original arms and legs mended, undergarments, brown moulded boots and heels.

13in (33cm) high

$120-180 WHA

Two china shoulder head dolls; the smaller with blonde curly hair, cloth body, repaired, the larger with repainted paper-mâché shoulder head, with molded blonde curls, paper label "GL 2020", old cloth body, lower arms missing.

Larger 25in (63cm) high

$180-220 WHA

A late 19thC/early 20thC Parian doll, original clothes.

$700-1,000 DE

A parian shoulder-head blonde doll's house doll, molded blonde hair with center parting, original limbs, black painted boots with heels, antique petticoat and crocheted hat.

5in (12.5cm) high

$120-180 WHA

A 1930s German china doll, with jointed head, replaced lace skirt.

$400-600 Gats

A 1930s German ceramic lady doll, with original lace.

As well as the fact that she is dressed in her original lace costume, the style of this doll's pose, hair and dress epitomize the 1930s, hence her higher value.

$700-1,000 Gats

An early china luster shoulder head doll, short black hair with brush marks around face, painted blue eyes with red lid line, deep shoulder plate.

2.5in (6.5cm) high

$400-600 WHA

A Grenier-type paper-mâché shoulder head doll, with original paint, paper label on back, no lettering, black hair with ears exposed, curls to nape of neck, detached and mended lower leather arms, original cloth body and undergarments, appropriate replaced dress, replaced homemade shoes, straw bonnet.

18in (45.75cm) high

$180-220　　　　　**WHA**

A CLOSER LOOK AT PAPER-MÂCHÉ DOLLS

The heads are made from painted paper-mâché, which is prone to wear and damage. These are in excellent condition, with no repainting.

The shoulders have paper labels bearing Greiner's name and one of two patent dates, 1858 and 1872.

They were made by Ludwig Greiner of Philadelphia, who was granted the first US patent to manufacture doll's heads. He was active between 1858 and 1883.

Dolls' clothes were usually home made. These are contemporary and in fine condition, with a 19thC paper label detailing the dolls' histories attached to the skirts.

Left: A Greiner paper-mâché shoulder head male doll, black molded hair, painted blue eyes, all cloth body, with patent sticker labeled "1858".

16.5in (42cm) high

$4,000-6,000　　　　　**Ber**

Right: A Greiner paper-mâché shoulder head woman doll, black molded hair, painted blue eyes, cloth body with kid leather arms, hand written history attached to petticoats, new kid arms covering original arms beneath, wears red cotton sprigged dress, undergarments, silk shoes and silk patchwork bonnet, with patent sticker labeled "1858".

Large dolls, measuring 35in high and more, are usually worth twice the value of smaller dolls.

16in (40.5cm) high

$2,800-3,200　　　　　**Ber**

A paper-mâché shoulder head doll, completely repainted shoulder head, original old body with undergarments and leather boots, appropriate later dress, label on back shoulder plate "M&S Superior 2015".

21in (53cm) high

$60-90　　　　　**WHA**

A paper-mâché shoulder head doll, bald with remnants of mohair wig, painted blue eyes and lower lashes, cloth body sawdust stuffed, with original paper-mâché limbs, orange boots.

17in (43cm) high

$180-220　　　　　**WHA**

A Victorian Pierotti-type poured wax head and shoulder plate doll, with fabric body, kid lower arms and hands, wearing a wool gown and bonnet with cape, later repairs.

17.25in (44cm) high

$150-200　　　　　**DN**

A Victorian wax-over-composition head and shoulder plate "Christmas Fairy" doll, pale glass eyes, blonde wig and fabric body with composition lower arms and legs, silk and lace dress.

11.5in (29cm) high

$100-150　　　　　**DN**

A late 19thC poured-wax head and shoulder plate doll with fixed blue glass eyes, fabric body, wax lower arms and hands, and wax lower legs and feet, possibly representing Queen Victoria.

23.25in (59cm) high

| $220-280 | WHA |

A Schoenhut farmer doll, original paint.

| $300-500 | DE |

A Schoenhut "Jigs" doll.

Albert Schoenhut & Co of Philadelphia, US, were founded in 1872. Its dolls are typically made from wood, with sprung joints and bear incised marks that include Schoenhut's name, making them easy to identify. Schoenhut also produced a number of other wooden toys and games, becoming the major American producer of wooden toys.

| $400-600 | DE |

A Gofun head Japanese doll, all original, with miniature Art Nouveau bench and accessories, including a tiny doll and cased mirror.

Gofun headed dolls have heads coated in a paste made from crushed oyster shells. Other materials used on the doll include wood, wire and straw. Large sized, fine examples in excellent condition and dressed in unfaded, brightly colored original silk clothing and with contemporary accessories such as this one fetch high values.

c1890 *24in (61cm) high*

| $3,000-4,000 | BEJ |

Ten early 19thC German peg-jointed wooden dolls, all with painted features, black hair and in original dresses, some with limbs missing, together with a glazed china 'Frozen Charlotte' in original christening gown.

First 3.5in (9cm) high

| $1,500-2,000 | BonC |

A composition shoulder head Chinese child doll, bald head with "Q" mark, painted features, jointed cloth body with composition hands, also marked "Five Finger Ching".

1921 *10in (25.5cm) high*

| $220-280 | WHA |

An Ichimatsu Japanese baby doll, mold line separation right side of head, original clothes, non-functioning voice box.

13in (33cm) high

| $150-200 | WHA |

An English 'Dollie Daisie Dimple' paper doll, cardboard trunk containing lithographed doll on stand, seven brightly colored dresses, apron, underclothes, hats and tennis racket, with original instructions and "The Birthday' story book.

c1915 *Trunk 7in (18in) long*

| $120-180 | BonC |

Collectors' Notes

- Gebrüder Heubach were founded c1820 and most active between 1840 and c1945. They were based in Lichte in the Thuringia area of Germany, known for its porcelain which was used to make dolls as well as ornaments and household wears.
- Heubach initially produced doll heads and later complete dolls, but they are also known for their all bisque figurines, aimed at children and adults alike. They also produced fairings. Pieces by Heubach are marked with a rising sun or with a square.
- One of their best-known ranges was the 'Piano' babies, small, cute, all-bisque models made to sit on top of a household piano. Many figurines are made from a thin bisque which is very easy to chip and crack, so care must be taken not to buy a damaged example, or to damage a mint example.

A Heubach farm boy figure, mint condition.

c1910-1920

$300-400   **DE**

A Heubach 'Lobster Boy' figure, mint condition, signed inside.

c1910-1920

$300-500   **DE**

A Heubach figure, signed, thumb tip repaired.

c1910-1920

$120-180   **DE**

A Heubach 'Thinker' bisque figure, the seated nude baby with painted features, hair and molded quiff, finger in mouth and curled up toe, marked on base.

c1910   *5in (13cm) tall*

$70-100   **BonC**

A Heubach bisque 'Fantasy' piece.

c1910-1920

$400-600   **DE**

A black Heubach figure, signed, one finger repaired.

This figure is more valuable than others as the children are black, which is a very rare feature.

c1910-1920

$500-700   **DE**

A Heubach 'Little Character' doll, the bisque subject seated in a green glazed bowl as a wash tub, impressed rising sun mark.

4.75in (12cm) high

$300-500   **LC**

A Heubach 'Little Character' doll, a child seated in a green-glazed wash tub bowl, rising sun impressed mark.

4in (10cm) high

$300-500   **LC**

A fine model dressing table, maker unknown.

Age, quality of manufacture and detailing and size are important factors when considering values for doll's furniture or doll's house furniture. This Victorian piece is finely modeled from good quality wood, with a good shape and fine detailing.

c1890   9in (23cm) high

$400-600   **BEJ**

A French doll's armoire unmarked.

c1890   16in (41.5cm) high

$400-600   **BEJ**

A German doll's toy wooden piano.

c1900   13.5in (35.5cm) high

$300-400   **BEJ**

A French wrought iron doll's bed.

c1890   16in (40.5cm) high

$300-500   **BEJ**

An early doll's bed, quilts and ladder back doll chair.

$300-500   **WHA**

A doll's wicker and rye straw chair.

c1890   8.5in (22cm) high

$120-180   **RAA**

A miniature 1852 engraving of Ely, by Spink, in an ebony and silver frame and made for a doll's house.

$40-60   **SF**

A 1930s doll's miniature wicker three-piece suite, comprising: two armchairs; a two-seater settee; and a circular-topped occasional table.

$15-25   **F**

A collection of doll's house china.

$80-120   **WHA**

A selection of dolls' clothing and accessories, including hats, shoes and a purse.

$300-400   **WHA**

An American doll's dress, in sheer blue wool twill with a lace collar and appliqué.

c1900 Skirt 9.5in (24cm) long

$40-60   **AAC**

A 19thC doll's trunk, with compartments filled with doll garments, costumes and socks.

$300-500   **WHA**

A French miniature Gladstone bag, the brown leather bag with metal clasp, top opens to blue silk-lined compartment, lifts to reveal section for sewing utensils, including gilt scissors, ivory thimble, pin holder, reel and cotton thread.

c1880   *2in (5cm) high*

$300-500   **BonC**

An English painted wooden doll's house, the façade front and sides in yellow sand stone with brick lines, pitch roof having attic and round glazed etched window, a further five glazed etched windows and paneled front door, opens to the front in tow wings, with brass knobs and catches, to four rooms on two levels.

c1860   *28in (71cm) high*

$700-1,000   **BonC**

A selection of doll's house furniture, comprising tin accessories, canopy bed, chairs and washboard.

$320-380   **WHA**

A Tri-ang doll's house, half-timbered with double gable front, cream painted on a green base, fitted for electricity, in need of some restoration.

$220-280   **Chef**

An English painted wooden dolls house, black pitched roof with molded gables and twin chimneys, front garden with turned white fencing, two central and six bay windows, central front door with molded portico, front hallway and two landing with staircase, on three levels, each room having tinplate or carved wooden fireplace, papered walls.

c1870   *54in (137cm) high*

$3,200-3,800   **BonC**

A doll's house, in the form of an Elizabethan timber framed manor house, the pitched roof with brick chimneys hinged to one side, the front with porch and removable stepped glazed window bay, the rear with removable panels, on a baize covered plinth.

     54.25in (138cm) wide

$2,800-3,200   **L&T**

A miniature toy grocery shop, with wooden case, 'wallpaper', wooden cabinet with 12 drawers, embossed tin signs and a quantity of produce.

Early Victorian examples with large amounts of detailing are very valuable. Look for desirable scenes such as kitchens, shops and school rooms, with a number of original characters and accessories.

c1890   *25.25in (64cm) wide*

$1,000-1,500   **ATK**

A chalet-style wooden doll's-house, of pine construction, with a quantity of furniture.

     27.5in (70cm) long

$180-220   **DN**

A miniature toy grocery shop, with wooden case, 'wallpaper', wooden cabinet with 12 drawers, embossed tin signs and a quantity of produce.

c1890   *28.5in (72cm) wide*

$800-1,200   **ATK**

A pressed metal bathroom miniature diorama, with bath, water closet and sink, originally with working running water and illuminating light, together with a miniature bisque doll.

$60-90   **F**

Collectors' Notes

- At the end of the 1980s, interest in 'retro' styles from the 1950s onward began to grow. Previously, these had been largely ignored, partly because they were still too recent in the public mind to be of interest. However, collecting interest is increasing in pieces from the 1970s, which are very affordable today.

- Today the movement is so strong that people actively seek to find 'retro' objects to decorate their home, summoning up the decades that witnessed the modern 'New Look', 'Flower Power' and 'Free Love'.

- Look for pieces that are evocative of the period you wish to collect, in terms of shape, color, use and surface design. Key themes are: modernity with its clean lines and forms that are different from work of previous decades; bright colors moving from a postwar freshness to drug-induced psychedelia; and an eye for the future, with themes from outer space and science fiction as well as futuristic technology and design providing convenience at home.

- This period also witnessed the birth of popular culture, many of the most prolific musical movements that survive today, and the teenager as a social and economic force. After WWII the Fifties saw a return to glamor, often using motifs of scantily clad ladies allied with images from gambling and drinking.

- A consumer 'throwaway' society was also born. Many pieces that fell out of style were discarded and as a result select pieces can be rare. Look for undamaged objects as many were mass-produced, inexpensive and heavily used. Those in less than excellent condition will not be as attractive to collectors and will fetch lower prices.

A 1950s Vacwonder 'Olympia' vacuum flask, with scenes of various field sports.

10.25in (26cm) high

$60-90   MA

An English 14-piece coffee service, comprising six cups and saucers, coffee pot and sugar bowl decorated with a poodle eyeing a tree, marked "British Anchor".

1958   Pot 7.75in (20cm) high

$180-220 (set)   MA

A Japanese 15-piece tea service, by Lucky, comprising six cups and saucers, teapot, sugar and milk jug, decorated with stylized orange and black leaves, with wreath and crown backstamp.

$120-180 (set)   MA

A Carlton ware-style coffee pot, unmarked, with vegetable decoration.

11.5in (29cm) wide

$15-25   MA

A Kosy Kraft 'Ever-Hot' three-piece tea service, chrome over pink ceramic, mint and boxed.

This is one of at least five colorways. Without the original box this set would be worth under $50.

Teapot 5in (13cm) high

$70-100   MA

A 1950s Czechoslovakian or German porcelain cup and saucer.

Saucer 4.5in (11.5cm) wide

$30-40   AOY

An unmarked English plate, with dancing couple motif.

9.5in (24.5cm) diam

$20-30   MA

A Royal Tudor 'Fiesta' pattern plate, by Barker Bros.

6.5in (16.5cm) diam

$6-9   L

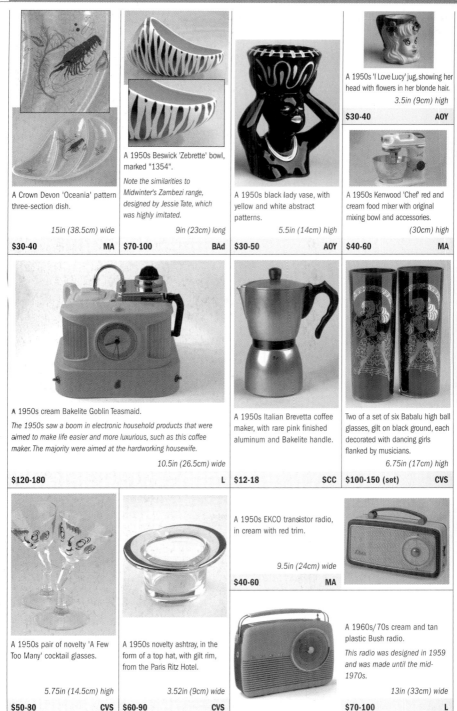

A Crown Devon 'Oceania' pattern three-section dish.

15in (38.5cm) wide

$30-40 MA

A 1950s Beswick 'Zebrette' bowl, marked "1354".

Note the similarities to Midwinter's Zambezi range, designed by Jessie Tate, which was highly imitated.

9in (23cm) long

$70-100 BAd

A 1950s black lady vase, with yellow and white abstract patterns.

5.5in (14cm) high

$30-50 AOY

A 1950s 'I Love Lucy' jug, showing her head with flowers in her blonde hair.

3.5in (9cm) high

$30-40 AOY

A 1950s Kenwood 'Chef' red and cream food mixer with original mixing bowl and accessories.

(30cm) high

$40-60 MA

A 1950s cream Bakelite Goblin Teasmaid.

The 1950s saw a boom in electronic household products that were aimed to make life easier and more luxurious, such as this coffee maker. The majority were aimed at the hardworking housewife.

10.5in (26.5cm) wide

$120-180 L

A 1950s Italian Brevetta coffee maker, with rare pink finished aluminum and Bakelite handle.

$12-18 SCC

Two of a set of six Babalu high ball glasses, gilt on black ground, each decorated with dancing girls flanked by musicians.

6.75in (17cm) high

$100-150 (set) CVS

A 1950s pair of novelty 'A Few Too Many' cocktail glasses.

5.75in (14.5cm) high

$50-80 CVS

A 1950s novelty ashtray, in the form of a top hat, with gilt rim, from the Paris Ritz Hotel.

3.52in (9cm) wide

$60-90 CVS

A 1950s EKCO transistor radio, in cream with red trim.

9.5in (24cm) wide

$40-60 MA

A 1960s/70s cream and tan plastic Bush radio.

This radio was designed in 1959 and was made until the mid-1970s.

13in (33cm) wide

$70-100 L

A 1950s Decca Dansette record player, decorated with nursery rhyme scenes after Dora Roderick.

The 1950s saw the emergence of both the 'Rock and Roll' and 'Pop' music scenes. The teenager who began to have a small amount of disposable income due to part-time evening and weekend jobs, was also born. Music and records became an essential part of life and were played on Dansettes, which although expensive in their day, were in every teenager's bedroom, often having been bought through 'hire purchase'. Between 1950 and 1970, when more inexpensive Japanese imports flooded the market, over one million Dansettes were sold.

13.5in (34.5cm) wide

$120-180   **MA**

A late 1950s four-tier occasional table, with central column supporting four tiers on four turned legs.

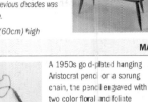

Both the shape of the tiers and the colors used are highly evocative of the 1950s when such modern but affordable furniture quite unlike that of previous decades was extremely fashionable.

23.75in (60cm) high

$120-180   **MA**

A 1950s gold-plated hanging Aristocrat pencil on a sprung chain, the pencil engraved with two color floral and foliate design, in original box.

Pencil 4in (10cm) high

$60-90   **TAB**

A late 1950s lipstick vending machine, by Priscilla Alden Cosmetics Inc, Clifton New Jersey, retains original lipsticks to interior, with the exception of "Coral Twist".

14in (36.5cm) wide

$300-400   **MA**

A 1958 Ballyhoo Calendar Company calendar, with painted pin-ups.

1958   11in (28cm) high

$150-200   **CVS**

A 1959 Playboy 'Playmate' calendar, including Jane Mansfield as Miss July.

Hugh Heffner launched Playboy magazine in December 1953, the first issue having a nude centerfold of Marilyn Monroe. Retailing at 50cts, over 54,000 copies were sold. The desirability and values of early magazines and items such as this calendar are usually discerned from the subject of the cover and centerfold, any other content relating to notable names and the condition.

1959   12.5in (32cm) high

$120-180   **CVS**

Sixties

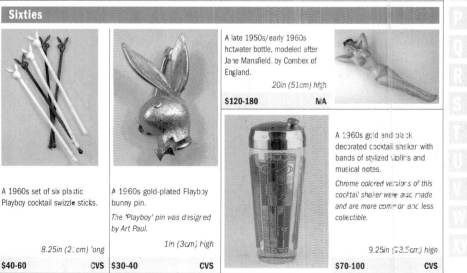

A 1960s set of six plastic Playboy cocktail swizzle sticks.

8.25in (21cm) long

$40-60   **CVS**

A 1960s gold-plated Playboy bunny pin.

The 'Playboy' pin was designed by Art Paul.

1in (3cm) high

$30-40   **CVS**

A late 1950s/early 1960s hotwater bottle, modeled after Jane Mansfield, by Combex of England.

20in (51cm) high

$120-180   **MA**

A 1960s gold and black decorated cocktail shaker with bands of stylized violins and musical notes.

Chrome colored versions of this cocktail shaker were also made and are more common and less collectible.

9.25in (23.5cm) high

$70-100   **CVS**

A 1960s novelty cigarette holder, in the form of a globe on stand, with telescopic top above fitted interior.

6.25in (16cm) high

$120-180   **CVS**

A 1960s German ceramic bowl.

4in (10cm) high

$15-25   **L**

A 1960s German vase, marked "249/30".

12in (30.5cm) high

$70-100   **L**

A 1960s ITHO floor heater.

Looking either like an invading space craft from a galaxy far, far away or something Mr Jetson might buy for Mrs Jetson, the shape of this heater perfectly shows the public fascination with science fiction and outer space during the 1960s.

13.75in (35cm) diam

$70-100   **L**

A piece of 1960s 'Sea Holly' fabric, by David Whitehead.

David Whitehead Fabrics were manufactured in Lancashire, UK during the 1950s and 1960s. The company employed many leading artists and designers including Terence Conran, John Piper, Henry Moore and Eduardo Paolozzi.

$20-30 (per meter)   **L**

Seventies

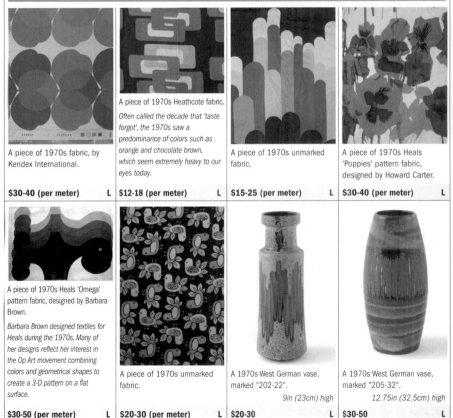

A piece of 1970s fabric, by Kendex International.

$30-40 (per meter)   **L**

A piece of 1970s Heathcote fabric.

Often called the decade that 'taste forgot', the 1970s saw a predominance of colors such as orange and chocolate brown, which seem extremely heavy to our eyes today.

$12-18 (per meter)   **L**

A piece of 1970s unmarked fabric.

$15-25 (per meter)   **L**

A piece of 1970s Heals 'Poppies' pattern fabric, designed by Howard Carter.

$30-40 (per meter)   **L**

A piece of 1970s Heals 'Omega' pattern fabric, designed by Barbara Brown.

Barbara Brown designed textiles for Heals during the 1970s. Many of her designs reflect her interest in the Op Art movement combining colors and geometrical shapes to create a 3-D pattern on a flat surface.

$30-50 (per meter)   **L**

A piece of 1970s unmarked fabric.

$20-30 (per meter)   **L**

A 1970s West German vase, marked "202-22".

9in (23cm) high

$20-30   **L**

A 1970s West German vase, marked "205-32".

12.75in (32.5cm) high

$30-50   **L**

A 1970s West German vase, marked "205-26".

10.5in (26.5cm) high

$30-40   **L**

A 1970s matt brown glazed German vase, with incised decoration.

8.5in (21.5cm) high

$30-50   **L**

A 1970s matt white porcelain Bavarian vase.

7.5in (19cm) high

$60-90   **L**

A 1970s Carlton ware guardsman moneybank.

5.5in (14cm) high

$50-80   **L**

A 1970s Carlton ware owl moneybank.

5.5in (14cm) wide

$70-100   **L**

A 1970s Carlton ware coffee set, comprising coffee pot, milk jug and sugar.

Pot 12.5in (31.5cm) high

$70-100   **L**

A 1960s/70s Pac-A-Pic picnic set for four people, the four trays complete with beakers and cutlery, with registered design mark.

14in (36cm) wide

$60-90   **CVS**

A 1970s Heinz ice bucket, made by Insulex-Isslex.

7.75in (20cm) high

$15-25   **MA**

A 1970s Pifco Warmasphere floor heater.

12.75in (32.5cm) diam

$40-60   **L**

A 1970s cream plastic Braun AG desk fan.

6in (15cm) high

$70-100   **L**

A 1970s Italian 'Penny' 45rpm 'handbag' record player.

$100-150   **MA**

A 1970s Peerless Transistor Six globe radio.

8.5in (21.5cm) high

$120-180   **L**

A 1976 Butlins Butlinland Skegness souvenir plate by Royal Falconware, Weatherby, Hanley.

Holiday camps around England provided many families with enjoyable holidays from the 1950s onward, with Butlins being one of the most successful. The introduction of increasingly inexpensive aeroplane flights meant affordable holidays abroad soon affected their popularity and attendance dropped seriously.

4in (10.5cm) diam

$5-8   **MA**

Collectors' Notes

- One of the most important things to consider when collecting film and television props and memorabilia is the provenance. Reputable dealers and auction houses should be able to provide you with a letter of provenance or certificate of authenticity.

- As the market for screen-used props has grown, studios often release props after production or give them away at premieres and these should come with a certificate. If not, ask the dealer or auction house how the item was obtained.

- Props that are used in key scenes or are pivotal to the plot are most sought after, although you should be aware that more than one example was often made, as a backup or with different stages of distress or use.

- Look out for pieces used in, or memorabilia relating to popular or blockbuster films such as "Titanic", "Gladiator" and the Harry Potter series, as well as classics like "James Bond" or "Star Wars" as they are more likely to retain their popularity and value.

- Condition should also be considered, although it is common for props to be damaged or worn from heavy use during filming. Items that are only seen in the background or from a distance are often of poor quality or only roughly finished.

An original piece of concept artwork for the space shuttle from "Armageddon", signed by Vehicle Designer Harald Belker, dated '97 and numbered 1/28 mounted together with a color still of the cast signed by Will Patton, Bruce Willis, Ben Affleck, Michael Clarke and Owen Wilson.

c1998   *27in (69cm) high*

$280-320   **CO**

A silver painted special effects pike head from "Braveheart", mounted on a custom-made background in Perspex case.

1995   *24in (61cm) high*

$180-220   **CO**

A checkered hessian English Knight's tunic from "Braveheart".

1995

$120-180   **CO**

Two black-and-white sketches from "101 Dalmatians", used as set dressing from Cruella De Vil's apartment, featuring models wearing clothes made from animal skins, mounted, framed and glazed

1996   *38.5in (98cm) high*

$180-220   **CO**

A 'Dr. Alex Durant (Anthony Perkins) model from "The Black Hole", in a blue Palomino Company uniform.

This item was sold with a certificate of authenticity from the current owner explaining that the figure was obtained from the Walt Disney Studios.

c1979   *20in (51cm) high*

$500-700   **CO**

An original 'Revisec Final Draft' script from "Alien", used by Rob Dickinson of the Video/Electronics Dept, with an invitation for a Special Screening at the Odeon, Leicester Square and a facsimile 20th Century Fox contract and termination of employment letter signed by the film's Production Manager, Garth Thomas.

c1979

$320-380   **CO**

An 'alien face hugger' stasis tube from "Alien", comprising a clear Perspex container, similar to those visible in the first film in the "Alien" series.

c1979   34.5 in (88 cm) high.

$400-500   **CO**

A full 'Scottish Warrior' costume from "Braveheart", comprising a large tartan kilt which wraps over to form a shawl, green cotton padded breast plate, light brown colored heavy woollen tunic, leg wraps, a pair of knee-high brown suede boots and a black long haired wig, as worn by an extra in the film.

1995

$400-600   **CO**

A pre-production scale model of 'Rocky' from "Chicken Run", mounted on aeroboard together with a tiny paper outhouse, mounted over a custom-made background with digital stills and descriptive text, in a perspex display case.

2000	*11in (28cm) high*

$80-120   **CO**

A white envelope from "Drowning Mona", addressed to Miss Riley, with a lipstick kiss mark, made by Neve Campbell in the film, matted with an image of Ellen Rash (Campbell) kissing the wedding invitation, framed and glazed.

2000	*18in (46cm) high*

$280-320   **CO**

A 'Taelon' bridge costume from 'Gene Roddenberry's Earth Final Conflict", the all-in-one nylon suit, with painted on body markings.

c1997

$180-220   **CO**

An original script from the pilot episode of the Warner Bros. TV series "The Flash", together with storyboards for scene 65, involving a bike chase.

1990

$100-150   **CO**

A black MA2 crew jacket from "Event Horizon", with fur collar with "Event Horizon Crew '97" embroidered on the left breast in silver with the Event Horizon logo on the back.

1997

$180-220   **CO**

Pair of prop arrows from 'Gladiator', two special effects flaming arrows from the film starring Russell Crowe.

32in (81cm) long

$80-120   **CO**

A large rubber prop Barbarian axe from "Gladiator", painted to simulate wood and steel, with a plate on the axe head which was used to strap the weapon to a victim.

2000	*46in (117cm) long*

$180-220   **CO**

A wooden prop Roman sword and scabbard from "Gladiator", painted to simulate steel, with a wooden handle ornately carved with the figure of a head, in leather scabbard with brass detail, used in the arena battle scenes in the film.

2000	*34in (86cm) long*

$280-320   **CO**

A Roman Infantry shield from "Gladiator", a rectangular brown canvas shield with wooden handle used by an extra in battle sequences in the film.

2000	*44in (112cm) high*

$300-500   **CO**

A green crew T-shirt from "Harry Potter and the Philosopher's Stone".

These T-shirts were given to cast and crew as a Christmas gift during filming.

2001

$80-120   **CO**

A pilot's khaki-colored flight suit from "James Bond - Die Another Day" with badges on left arm.

2002

$280-320   **CO**

A B C D E F G H I J K L M N O P Q R S T U V W XYZ

An American football used and signed by Bruce Willis in "The Last Boy Scout".

1991

$220-280   **G**

A pair of "Carmen Miranda" platform shoes worn by Lucille Ball during an episode of "I Love Lucy".

$1,000-1,500   **G**

A 'Damian Falco's' khaki colored name tag from "James Bond - Die Another Day", embroidered in blue with "Falco" (Michael Madsen) mounted with a digital still from the film with the Die Another Day logo.

2002   *16in (41cm) high*

$70-100   **CO**

A prop resin 'Ice' panel from "James Bond - Die Another Day", used on the exterior of the Ice Palace, matted with a copy of an artist's production drawing/design of the palace.

2002   *26in (66cm) high*

$100-150   **CO**

A wooden prop harpoon from "Moby Dick", with a base metal spike.

1956   *58in (150cm) long*

$180-220   **CO**

A band uniform worn by Robert Preston in "The Music Man".

1962

$1,000-1,500   **G**

A baseball jacket worn by Robert Redford in "The Natural", signed.

1984

$2,200-2,800   **G**

A prop scorpion from "The Mummy Returns".

This prop was used in the crypt scene, together with live scorpions when Rick (Brendan Fraser) and Evie (Rachel Weisz) first find the Scorpion King's amulet.

2001

$180-220   **CO**

A prop paper napkin from "Monkeybone", used as set dressing and printed in fluorescent green with the 'Coma Bar' insignia, mounted with digital stills featuring the bar and a descriptive plaque, framed and glazed.

2001   *15in (38cm) wide*

$60-90   **CO**

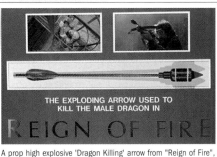

A prop high explosive 'Dragon Killing' arrow from "Reign of Fire", mounted, framed and glazed within a display showing two scenes from the film in which an arrow can be seen.

2002   *26in (66cm) wide*

$380-420   **CO**

A hard rubber gun-metal colored prop Commando revolver from "Resident Evil", marked "Taurus-Brasil", box framed.

2002   *14in (36cm) long*

$280-320   **CO**

A black hard rubber prop Commando hand gun from "Resident Evil", marked "Walther P99 014545", box framed.
2002   14in (36cm) long
$280-320   CO

A prop US army helmet worn by Tom Hanks in "Saving Private Ryan", the interior of the outershell bearing label reading "Miller", signed on the front in silver pen by Tom Hanks.
1998
$3,000-5,000   CO

A prop wood and steel M1 Carbine rifle from "Saving Private Ryan".
1998   44in (112cm) long
$280-320   CO

Two prop severed limbs from "Saving Private Ryan", from the Normandy landing scenes.
1998
$220-280   CO

Two prop canisters from "Star Wars: Episode - The Phantom Menace", used as set dressing in the film.
1999   12in (30.5cm) high
$280-320   CO

A replica white metal "White Star Line" dinner knife from "Titanic", used as set dressing, mounted with a dining scene from the film, box framed.
1997   13in (33cm) long
$180-220   CO

A pair of geologist's pick axes from "Superman", one lightweight prop wooden pick axe, painted to resemble the other real pick axe, manufactured by Stanley, both used in the film.
1978   13.5in (34cm) long
$180-220   CO

A Western-style hat worn by Robert Conrad in the TV series "Wild Wild West".
1965-70
$1,000-1,500   G

A green velvet hat with large plume worn on screen by Greta Garbo.
$1,000-1,500   G

A Pathé Pictures Inc. typed single page contract letter to Judy Garland, addressed "Miss Judy Garland, 129 South Rockingham Avenue, West Los Angeles, California", and "Re: Pathé and Kingsrow Distribution Agreement", signed twice by Judy Garland at the bottom, on behalf of Kingsrow Enterprises Inc., once in her capacity of President, matted with a black and white image of Garland as Dorothy.
12.5in (32cm) high
$700-1,000   CO

Dean Martin's tan leatherette-covered glass flask, printed with a humorous poem and slogan.
Legendary drinker Martin sent this to Joe Franklin from California, informing Franklin that he had used this flask as a prop during a television show and it had only ever been filled with water.
$220-280   G

West, Mae, "Goodness Had Nothing To Do With It - The Autobiography of Mae West", signed on the front cover 'Mae West", in blue ink.
$220-280   CO

Collectors' Notes

■ Classic cult TV programs and films are becoming increasingly popular as they re-run on cable channels and are released on video and DVD and, as a result, the demand for vintage toys and merchandise is growing.

■ Look for pieces made at the beginning of a show's run, as these were often made in smaller numbers, as well as those that are connected to popular seasons or periods such as Tom Baker's fourth 'Dr Who'. Condition is important, as is the original packaging, including instructions and certificates.

■ A number of popular TV series including 'The X-Files' and 'Buffy the Vampire Slayer' have come to an end and classic programs like 'Battlestar Galactica', 'Wonder Woman' and 'Thunderbirds' are being remade at present, which could bring increased demand for vintage memorabilia.

■ Quintessentially British, 'Dr Who' has a huge following across the globe and even though no new episodes have been recorded since Paul McGann's eighth Doctor's unpopular TV film outing in 1990, the series is regularly voted most popular sci-fi series by fans.

■ Toys and games from the 1960s and 70s are hard to find, especially in good condition, and attract a premium. However, at the end of 2003, the BBC is withdrawing all licenses for manufacturers to produce new 'Dr Who' memorabilia, which will make all items increasingly desirable.

■ As much as 'Dr Who' is British, so 'Star Trek' is American. Now in it's fifth incarnation, the franchise is still going strong. The Hamilton Collection produces a popular range of plates but has recently lost their license so these could be ones to watch in the future. Plates should be in mint condition, with their boxes and certificate of authenticity. Look for examples that had short production runs.

A set of six 'Doctor Who' Premier trading cards, by Cornerstone.

The set forms a picture of William Hartnell on the reverse.

1994   *3.5in (9cm) high*

$30-50 (each card)   TP

A set of 50 'Doctor Who and the Daleks' trading cards, for Cadet Sweets.

This series was re-issued in 1983 with "Goodies" replacing "Cadet Sweets" on the reverse. Unusually, a complete re-issue set is worth more than the original at approximately $150-200.

1964   *Cards 2.5in (6.5cm) wide*

$100-150   TP

A 'Doctor Who Adventures' trading card, by Cornerstone, signed by Louise Jamison (Leela).

1995   *3.5in (9cm) wide*

$10-15   TP

A 'Doctor Who Adventures' trading card, by Cornerstone, signed by Tom Baker (4th Doctor) on reverse.

1995   *3.5in (9cm) wide*

$12-18   TP

A 'Doctor Who Adventures' trading card, by Cornerstone, signed by Nicola Bryant (Peri).

1995   *3.5in (9cm) wide*

$10-15   TP

A 'Doctor Who Companions' trading card, by Cornerstone, signed by Wendy Padbury (Zoe Heriot).

1995   *3.5in (9cm) wide*

$10-15   TP

A 'Doctor Who The Doctors' trading card, by Cornerstone, signed by Colin Baker (6th Doctor).

1995   *3.5in (9cm) wide*

$12-18   TP

A 'Doctor Who An Unearthly Child' BT phone card, by Jonder International Promotions, with factsheet.

1994-7 Card 3.5in (9cm) wide

$15-20 TP

A 'Doctor Who The Daleks' BT phone card, by Jonder International Promotions, with factsheet.

1994-7 Card 3.5in (9cm) wide

$15-20 TP

A limited edition 'Doctor Who The Trial of a Time Lord' video box set, by the BBC.

1993 8.5in (21.5cm) high

$60-90 TP

A limited edition 'Doctor Who Daleks' video box set, by the BBC.

1993 8.5in (21.5cm) wide

$60-90 TP

A 'Doctor Who The Five Doctors' video, by the BBC.

1985 8in (20.5cm) high

$30-50 TP

A 'Doctor Who Revenge of the Cybermen' video, by the BBC.

1985 8.5in (21.5cm) high

$20-30 TP

A rare 'Doctor Who The Five Doctors' video gift pack, issued by Dapol for Boots, with Dalek figure.

1990 10in (25.5cm) wide

$70-100 TP

A 'Doctor Who The Missing Stories - The Evil of the Daleks' audio cassette, by the BBC.

1992 5.5in (14cm) wide

$25-35 TP

A 'Doctor Who The Missing Stories - The Power of the Daleks' audio cassette, by the BBC.

1993 5.5in (14cm) wide

$25-35 TP

A limited edition "Dalekmania" box set, by Lumiere.

1995 16.75in (42.5cm) wide

$60-90 TP

Lydecker, John, "Doctor Who and Warriors' Gate", published by Target.

1982 7in (18cm) high

$25-35 TP

Baker, Pip and Jane, "Doctor Who - The Mark of the Rani", published by Target.

1986 7in (18cm) high

$30-50 TP

Baker, Pip and Jane, "Dr Who - The Terror of the Vervoids", published by Target.

1988   *7in (18cm) high*

$25-35   **TP**

Davis, Gerry, and Bingeman, Alison, "Doctor Who - The Celestial Toymaker", published by Target.

1986   *7in (18cm) high*

$25-35   **TP**

A "Dr Who 1974" annual, published by World Distributors.

1974   *11.5in (29cm) high*

$12-18   **TP**

A "Dr Who 1977" annual, published by World Distributors.

1977   *11.5in (29cm) high*

$12-18   **TP**

A "Dr Who 1978" annual, published by World Distributors.

1978   *11.5in (29cm) high*

$10-15   **TP**

A "Doctor Who 1981" annual, published by World Distributors.

1981   *11.5in (29cm) high*

$10-15   **TP**

A "Doctor Who 1984" annual, published by World Distributors.

1984   *11.5in (29cm) high*

$8-12   **TP**

A "Doctor Who 1992" year book, published by Marvel.

1992   *11.5in (29cm) high*

$8-12   **TP**

A "Doctor Who 1994" year book, published by Marvel.

1994   *11.5in (29cm) high*

$8-12   **TP**

A "Doctor Who 1995" year book, published by Marvel.

1995   *11.5in (29cm) high*

$8-12   **TP**

A "Doctor Who The Monsters" book, published by Virgin Publishing.

1992   *11.5in (29cm) high*

$10-15   **TP**

A "Doctor Who Cybermen" book, published by Virgin Publishing.

1995   *11.5in (29cm) high*

$10-15   **TP**

A "Doctor Who 1996" year book, published by Marvel.

1996   *11.5in (29cm) high*

$8-12   **TP**

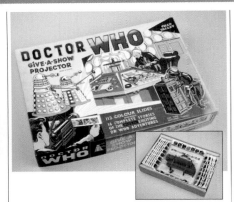

A rare 'Doctor Who Give-A-Show Projector', by Chad Valley.
c1965

$220-280   TH

A 'Doctor Who Linx' figure, by Classic Moments.
c2002   6in (15cm) high

$30-40   TP

A 'Doctor Who Draconian' figure, by Classic Moments
c2002   7in (18cm) high

$30-40   TP

A 'Doctor Who Sensorite' figure, by Classic Moments.
c2002   7in (18cm) high

$30-40   TP

A red and gold 'Doctor Who Dalek' figure, by Dapol.
c2002 Figure 4in (10cm) high

$6-9   TP

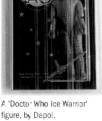

A 'Doctor Who Ice Warrior' figure, by Dapol.
c2002 Figure 4.5in (11.5cm) h

$6-9   TP

A 'Doctor Who Silurian figure, by Dapol.
c2002 Figure 4.25in (11cm) h

$6-9   TP

A set of three 'Doctor Who Dalek Roll-A-Matics' by Product Enterprises Ltd.
c2002 Daleks 2.5in (6.5cm) h

$15-25   TP

A 'Doctor Who Mark I Dalek' figure, by Media Collectables.
c2002 Figure 1.75in (4.5cm) w

$8-12   TP

A 'Doctor Who Cyberman Attacking' figure, by Media Collectables.
c2002 Figure 2in (5cm) high

$8-12   TP

A 'Doctor Who Battle for the Universe' boardgame, by The Games Team Ltd.
c1989 Box 15.5in (39.5cm) w

$15-25   TP

A 'Star Trek 25th Anniversary' commemorative plate, by the Hamilton Collection, designed by Thomas Blackshear.

Production of this, and other plates in the 25th Anniversary series, was limited to 14 days' firing.

1991   8.25in (21cm) diam

$150-200   **TP**

A 'Star Trek 25th Anniversary Scotty' commemorative plate, by the Hamilton Collection, designed by Jack Martin.

1991   8.25in (21cm) diam

$40-60   **TP**

A 'Star Trek 25th Anniversary Uhura' commemorative plate, by the Hamilton Collection, designed by Jack Martin.

1991   8.25in (21cm) diam

$40-60   **TP**

A 'Star Trek 25th Anniversary Sulu' commemorative plate, by the Hamilton Collection, designed by Jack Martin.

1991   8.25in (21cm) diam

$40-60   **TP**

A 'Star Trek 25th Anniversary Chekov' commemorative plate, by the Hamilton Collection, designed by Jack Martin.

1991   8.25in (21cm) diam

$40-60   **TP**

A 'Star Trek: The Next Generation Lt. Worf' commemorative plate, by the Hamilton Collection, designed by Thomas Blackshear.

1993   8.25in (21cm) diam

$40-60   **TP**

A 'Star Trek: The Next Generation Lt. Cmdr. LaForge' commemorative plate, by the Hamilton Collection, designed by Thomas Blackshear.

1993   8.25in (21cm) diam

$40-60   **TP**

A 'Star Trek: Voyagers U.S.S. Enterprise NCC-1701' commemorative plate, by the Hamilton Collection, designed by Keith Birdsong.

1993   8.25in (21cm) diam

$40-60   **TP**

A 'Star Trek: Voyagers Klingon Battlecruiser' commemorative plate, by the Hamilton Collection, designed by Keith Birdsong.

1993   8.25in (21cm) diam

$40-60   **TP**

A 'Star Trek Captain's Tribute' commemorative plate, from the 30 Years series, by the Hamilton Collection, designed by Todd Treadway.

Production of this plate was limited to 28 days' firing.

1997   8.25in (21cm) diam

$70-100   **TP**

A Japanese shuttle, based on the film "2001".

c1975

$100-150 | **TH**

An "A-Team" M-16 rifle by Daisy Toy.

c1983

$25-35 | **TH**

A rare "Airwolf" die-cast gift set, by ERTL.

These gift sets are rarely found complete.

c1984

$60-90 | **TH**

A "The Addams Family The Thing" money bank.

c1964

$60-90 | **TH**

An "Aliens vs Corp. Hicks" limited edition set of figures, by Kenner, from an edition of 25,000 made exclusively for Kaybee Toys.

c2000

$40-60 | **TD**

A 1960s "Avengers Stead's Sword Stick" display card, by Lone Star.

With the sword stick, this would be worth approximately $400-600.

$80-120 | **TH**

A box of 1966-style "Batman" trading cards, by Topps.

c1989

$60-90 | **TH**

A pair of Batman and Robin figures, by Warner Bros., from the Golden Age Collection.

2000

$60-90 | **TH**

A "Battlestar Galactica" Ovion figure, by Mattel.

The Sci-Fi Channel is currently working on a mini-series 're-imagining' Battlestar Galactica due to air in December 2003 and includes a female 'Starbuck'!

c1978

$40-60 | **TH**

A "Battlestar Galactica" story book, by Brown Watson.

1978

$3-4 | **TH**

A "Battlestar Galactica" story book, by Grandreams.

1978

$4-6 | **TH**

A "The Bionic Woman Bionic Beauty Salon", by Kenner.

US Cable Entertainment are developing a re-make of this classic 1970s show.

c1976

$40-60 | **TH**

A "Bionic Woman Designer Budget" outfit, by Denys Fisher.

c1973

$15-25 TH

A "Bionic Woman Designer Budget Fashions" outfit, by Denys Fisher.

c1973

$15-25 TH

A "Bionic Woman Designer Budget Fashions" outfit, by Denys Fisher.

c1973

$15-25 TH

A "Bionic Woman" annual, by Brown Watson.

1978

$8-12 TH

A "Buck Rogers in the 25th Century Laserscope Fighter", by Mega Corp.

c1979

$40-60 TH

A "Charlie's Angels" large piece puzzle.

c1972

$7-10 TH

A "Blade Runner Android 001" limited edition figure, by Time Wave Zero, from an edition of 500.

2002

$150-200 TH

A Universal Picture "Dracula" assembly kit, by Aurora.

c1964

$300-400 TH

A "Dukes of Hazzard" Hazzard County Sheriff car, by Ideal.

c1981

$20-30 TH

An "Escape from New York" board game, by TSR Hobbies, Inc.

c1981

$30-40 TH

A "The Real Ghost Busters Ghost Zapper", by Kenner.

'The Real Ghostbusters' animated series ran from 1986 to 1991 and chronicled the on-going adventures of the original 'Ghost Busters'.

1984

$15-25 TH

A 1970s "The Fonz" badge, made in the US.

1in (2.5cm) diam

$10-15 CVS

A "Raiders of the Lost Ark Indiana Jones action figure", by Kenner.
c1981

$220-280 TH

A "Jurassic Park" official annual, by Grandreams.
1992

$2-3 TH

A "Logan's Run" annual.
The TV series 'Logan's Run' was based on the 1976 film of the same name and ran from 1977-78.
1979

$4-6 TH

A "Knight Rider" die-cast Knight 2000, by ERTL.
c1982

$60-90 TH

A "Knight Rider" racetrack game, by Darda Toys.
c1982

$100-120 TH

A Robot YM-3, by Masudaya.
This robot was produced in Japan to commemorate the 20th anniversary of the airing of the first "Lost in Space" episode on September 15, 1965.
1985

$25-35 TH

A late 1960s "The Monkees" bubble gum card display box by A & BC.
With its original lid, this display box would be worth approximately $220.

$60-90 TH

A Japanese "Nightmare Before Christmas' Jack Skellington figure.
c2000

$40-60 TH

A "The Six Million Dollar Man" Back Pack Radio, by Kerner.
c1973

$20-30 TH

A "Nightmare on Elm Street" Freddy Krueger figure. by Matchbox.

A whole range of these changeable dolls was planned, but only the character of Freddy was ever produced.

c1989

$40-60　　TH

A Secret Sam weapon case, by De Luxe Toys.

Many toy companies produced generic spy toys to cash in on the popularity of 1960s spy themed programs such as 'The Man from U.N.C.L.E.', and the 'James Bond' film franchise.

c1969

$150-200　　TH

A "For mash get Smash" robot.

c1974

$40-60　　TH

A "Space 1999" annual, by World Distributors.

1977

$6-9　　TH

A Spider-Man License plate, with full packaging.

1967

$40-60　　HC

A "Starsky & Hutch" Target Range game, by Arco.

1977

$60-90　　TH

A "Stingray" action submarine, by Matchbox.

c1993

$30-50　　TH

An original 'Spitting Image' puppet head of Paul Newman, from the satirical UK TV series, comprising a painted foam and latex caricature of the actor, with steel cable attachments for moving the eyes and making the forehead frown, inscribed "Newman" on the nape of the neck, on a separate wooden stand.

This item was sold with a letter of authenticity, explaining that the puppet was originally obtained at Roger Law's (co-creator of the program) sale, held at Sothebys.

17in (43cm) high

$1,200-1,800　　CO

A "Street Hawk" motorcycle with Jesse Mach rider, by Kenner.

c1984

$25-35　　TH

A "Superman vs Doomsday" pair of figures.

c1995

$8-12　　TH

A sealed box of "Terminator 2 - Judgement Day" stickers, by Toppes.

c1991

$15-25　　　　**TH**

A "Terminator 2 - Judgement Day Cyberdyne T-800 Endo Skeleton" kit, by Tsukuda.

c1991

$30-40　　　　**TH**

A "Tarzan" with the White Hunter holster, by Lone Star.

c1966

$40-60　　　　**TH**

A "Terrahawks Action Zeroid" figure, by Bandai.

c1983

$60-90　　　　**TH**

A "Thunderbirds Lady Penelope" painting book.

c1971

$15-25　　　　**TH**

A "Thunderbirds Lady Penelope" annual, by Jarrold & Sons Ltd.

1966

$12-18　　　　**TH**

A "Tron" glow in the dark yo-yo, by Duncan.

c1982

$30-40　　　　**TH**

A "The Uncanny X-Men Magneto" figure, by Toy Biz.

c1991

$8-12　　　　**TH**

A rare "Wanted Dead or Alive" Josh Randall/Steve McQueen figure, by Toys McCoy.

c1997

$300-500　　　　**TH**

Collectors' Notes

■ Amberina glass fades from a strong ruby red down to light amber. Usually the ruby red is at the top of the piece and the amber at the base. When the ruby is at the base, it is known as 'reverse Amberina'.

■ The coloring is produced by using heat sensitive glass containing colloidal gold, a part of which is reheated before letting it cool, changing the amber color to a ruby red color. The technique was patented by Joseph Locke of the New England Glass Co. in Cambridge, Massachusetts in 1883.

■ It was very successful and made by a number of companies, including Mount Washington who called it 'Rose Amber'. Amberina is accasionally signed by individual companies, such as Libbey, and a few have a paper label, which adds to their value.

In general, look for examples that show a full and strong range of color tones.

■ Also look for variations, including 'plated' Amberina, which has an internal casing of creamy white glass making the colors appear very differently. It is scarce and very valuable and desirable to collectors. Ribbed pieces were only made by the New England Glass Co. and are similarly sought after.

■ Collectors use certain terms to describe the surface patterning, including 'I.T.P.' for 'inverted thumb print' which described the thumb-shaped indentations, and 'D.Q.' for 'diamond quilted', which again describes the all-over pattern of gently impressed diamond shapes.

An Amberina four corner vase, deep coloring with four ruffled corners.

4in (10cm) diam

$220-280　　　**JDJ**

An Amberina ladies cuspidor, fuschia shading to amber with flaring top to bowl.

5.25in (13.5cm) diam

$300-350　　　**JDJ**

An Amberina diamond quilted pattern bowl, with nice coloring.

4.25in (11cm) diam

$80-120　　　**JDJ**

An Amberina diamond quilted pattern bowl, with nice coloring.

4.25in (11cm) diam

$80-120　　　**JDJ**

An Amberina finger bowl, deep coloring with inverted scalloped rim.

5in (12.5cm) diam

$180-220　　　**JDJ**

An Amberina thumbprint pattern pitcher.

9in (23cm) high

$180-220　　　**JDJ**

A reverse Amberina inverted thumbprint small pitcher, with clear applied ribbed handle.

6in (15cm) high

$250-300　　　**JDJ**

An Amberina square top pitcher, with inverted thumbprint decoration and amber reeded applied handle, scratches around center of pitcher as well as tool marks, otherwise very good.

7in (18cm) high

$150-200　　　**JDJ**

A 1930s small crackle finish Amberina-color glass jug.

3.5in (9cm) high

$5-7　　　**TAB**

An Amberina ribbed pitcher, with applied amber reeded handle.

8in (20cm) tall

$200-250　　　**JDJ**

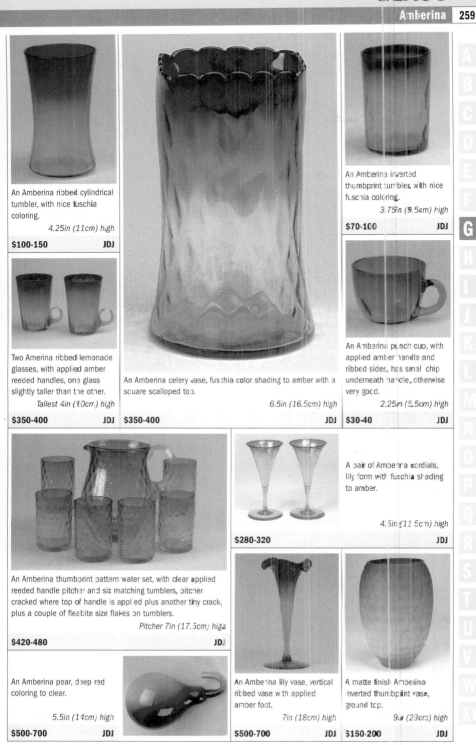

An Amberina ribbed cylindrical tumbler, with nice fuschia coloring.

4.25in (11cm) high

$100-150 JDJ

Two Amerina ribbed lemonade glasses, with applied amber reeded handles, one glass slightly taller than the other.

Tallest 4in (10cm) high

$350-400 JDJ

An Amberina celery vase, fuschia color shading to amber with a square scalloped top.

6.5in (16.5cm) high

$350-400 JDJ

An Amberina inverted thumbprint tumbler, with nice fuschia coloring.

3.75in (9.5cm) high

$70-100 JDJ

An Amberina punch cup, with applied amber handle and ribbed sides, has small chip underneath handle, otherwise very good.

2.25in (5.5cm) high

$30-40 JDJ

An Amberina thumbprint pattern water set, with clear applied reeded handle pitcher and six matching tumblers, pitcher cracked where top of handle is applied plus another tiny crack, plus a couple of fleabite size flakes on tumblers.

Pitcher 7in (17.5cm) high

$420-480 JDJ

A pair of Amberina cordials, lily form with fuschia shading to amber.

4.5in (11.5cm) high

$280-320 JDJ

An Amberina pear, deep red coloring to clear.

5.5in (14cm) high

$500-700 JDJ

An Amberina lily vase, vertical ribbed vase with applied amber foot.

7in (18cm) high

$500-700 JDJ

A matte finish Amberina inverted thumbprint vase, ground top.

9in (23cm) high

$150-200 JDJ

Collectors' Notes

- Burmese glass is a type of satin finish art glass that shades from yellow to pink. It was patented by glassmaker Mount Washington in 1885 and was used to make small ornamental vases, tableware and dressing table items.

- It was licensed to Thomas Webb & Sons of England from 1886, where it became as popular as it was in the US. English Burmese glass is often called 'Queen's Burmese' after its popularity with Queen Victoria.

- Fakes are known, and can be recognized by a heavier weight, unusual shapes that were never used in authentic Burmese and more garish colors. Handle as much original Burmese as possible as this will help you identify fakes.

- Look out for pieces that are decorated with enameling as these command a premium if in excellent condition. Again, beware of fakes as many undecorated pieces were decorated in the 1950s and 1960s, so examine the decoration and compare it to others.

A small Burmese pitcher with applied handle.

3.5in (7.5cm) high

$600-900   **JDJ**

A small Burmese creamer with applied handle.

3.5in (9cm) high

$350-400   **JDJ**

A ribbed Burmese vase, with flared base and alternating pink and yellow scalloped top.

5.25in (13.5cm) high

$300-500   **JDJ**

A tall Burmese tricorn lily vase.

10.5in (26.5cm) high

$220-280   **JDJ**

A Burmese twisted vase, ending in tricorn ruffled top.

6.25in (16cm) high

$220-280   **JDJ**

A Burmese sugar bowl, with pink to yellow shading.

3.75in (9.5cm) diam

$220-280   **JDJ**

A Burmese vase, with flaring and ruffled rim, fading from pink to yellow.

6in (15cm) high

$220-280   **JDJ**

A decorated Burmese squat-footed jar, with hand-painted floral decoration and gold highlights around base and rim, with cover, although probably not original.

4in (10cm) high 6in (15cm) diam

$1,200-1,800   **JDJ**

A Burmese small fairy lamp, deep pink to yellow coloring with pressed glass base, base signed "S. Clarke Fairy Pyramid".

4in (10cm) high

$220-280   **JDJ**

A Burmese small shallow plate.

5.25in (13.5cm) diam

$100-150   **JDJ**

Emile Gallé (1846-1904)

- The Gallé factory was founded by Charles Gallé in Nancy, France, in the 1840s. His son, Emile, studied glassmaking and was inspired by other French glass masters such as Rousseau and began making colored, cameo glass from the late 1880s.

- His cameo pieces had up to seven layers of colored glass cut back by carving and acid. Some were also enameled or had gilt detailing. He became a major influence in the developing Art Nouveau movement and built his own factory in 1894 producing three ranges: one-off pieces, high-priced limited editions and more numerous, less expensive standard pieces.

- He won the 'Grand Prix' in 1900 at the Paris Exhibition and died in 1904, with his wife carrying on with production. All production between 1904 and 1914, when the factory closed due to WWI, is marked with a star.

- When the factory reopened in 1919, production restarted, but fewer layers and less sophisticated designs were used and colors were typically paler. The factory is still in production today.

A Gallé cameo vase, decorated with leaves and berries in green, orange and brown, signed on side of vase, base appears to have been ground down.

7in (18cm) high

$600-900   JDJ

An Emile Gallé bulbous cameo vase, decorated with purple pansies on a blue ground, small nick to rim, signed "Gallé".

6.5in (16.5cm) high

$400-600   CR

A Gallé cameo pin dish, decorated with amethyst flower blossoms over green and clear frosted glass, signed on side of dish "Gallé".

The signature on a piece of cameo glass is not meant to be shown at the front, but should be hidden by turning the piece around.

4.25in (11cm) diam

$300-500   JDJ

A Gallé cameo covered box, decorated with green ferns, the cover decorated with green butterflies on a frosted green and white background, signed on the side "Gallé" with a star, has large crack.

7in (18cm) high

$500-700   JDJ

A Gallé cameo cabinet vase, decorated with flower blossoms and leaves in amethyst on a frosted green background, signed on side of vase "Gallé".

3.5in (9cm) high

$400-600   JDJ

A Gallé bottle shaped vase, transparent green glass with cameo decoration of grapes and leaves, signed "Gallé" on side of bottle.

12in (30.5cm) high

$300-500   JDJ

Daum

- Jean Daum took over a glass factory as a result of a bad debt in 1878 and soon was joined by his sons Auguste and Antonin. Inspired by the work of Emile Gallé, during the 1890s, the two brothers began to produce the art and cameo glass for which the firm became renowned.

- Led by Antonin Daum, forms, color and decoration are typically Art Nouveau in style, with organic motifs taken from nature such as flowers, leaves and trailing vines. In 1909, Auguste's son Paul took over and, seeing the decline of the Art Nouveau taste, began to produce clear vases. The Daum factory later became a major influence on Art Deco glass.

- The factory still exists today, producing colored and high quality clear 'crystal' glass.

A miniature Daum cameo vase, of flattened tapering form and rectangular shaped neck, the green tinted gray ground overlaid with mauve colored flowers and leaves on a round foot, signed in relief "Daum Nancy".

3.75in (9.5cm) high

$400-600   DN

A Daum Frères 'Feuilles de rosier' pattern four-handled vase, decorated with rose bush branches, hairline crack, engraved and originally rubbed with gold "DAUM NANCY", Lorraine cross.

c1901 8.75in (21.8cm) high

$700-1,000   FIS

A Daum cranberry glass vase, with cameo decoration of leaves and berries with white and enameling highlights, signed "Daum Nancy" in gold lettering on base.

5in (12.5cm) high

$400-600   **JDJ**

A Daum cameo bowl, with cameo and enameled decoration of holly leaves and berries on a chipped ice background, signed on base "Daum Nancy France", minor wear to gold paint on the rim otherwise excellent condition.

3.25in (8.5cm) high

$300-500   **JDJ**

An Arsall cameo vase, with overlay colors of green and pink over clear frosted glass with a cameo decoration of flower blossoms, leaves and stem, signed within the design "Arsall".

11.75in (30cm) high

$500-700   **JDJ**

A d'Argental cameo vase, decorated with morning glories and leaves in amethyst color on a frosted yellow background, signed on side.

7in (18cm) high

$500-700   **JDJ**

A d'Argyl cameo vase, decorated with flowers, branches and leaves, signed on side of vase "D'Argyl".

9in (23cm) high

$400-600   **JDJ**

A d'Argental cameo vase, decorated with blossoms, stems and leaves in blue on yellow, signed decoration on side of vase "d'Argental".

6in (15cm) high

$700-1,000   **JDJ**

A de Vez cameo vase, decorated with cherries and leaves against a cream background and background decoration of farm buildings, trees, lake and mountains, signed in cameo "de Vez", some minor roughness at lip, probably from manufacture.

The cameo technique can be seen very clearly on this vase, even though it is relatively unsophisticated, using only two layers. Here the dark glass layer that cases the cream body has been cut back to both reveal the contrasting color and also to form the leaves and lake. The thickness of the cutback dark glass varies giving different levels of translucency, adding to the visual interest.

6.25in (16cm) high

$300-400   **JDJ**

A de Vez miniature cameo vase, decorated with blue trees, water and islands against a green background, signed in cameo "de Vez".

3.5in (9cm)

$400-600   **JDJ**

A de Vez cameo vase, decorated with a tropical scene of palm trees and mountains in blue and cranberry on an amber background, signed "De Vez".

7.5in (19cm) high

$800-1,200   **JDJ**

A Gouvenin cameo vase, decorated with thistles in green and amethyst and clear, signed on side "Gouvenin".

10in (25.5cm) high

$600-900   **JDJ**

A Legras cameo vase, decorated with flower blossoms and leaves in rust, brown, gray and yellow on an opaque cream colored background, signed "Legras" on the side, some cracks.

7.25in (18.5cm) high

$60-80   **JDJ**

A Legras cameo oval bowl, decorated with a winter scene, signed.

10in (25.5cm) wide

$280-320   **TA**

A signed Mont Joy cameo vase, decorated with yellow and gold flower blossoms with green leaves on a brown 'chipped ice' background, signed on base.

7.5in (19cm)

$500-700   **JDJ**

A Pantin cameo vase, decorated with fuchsia blossoms and leaves in turquoise over amber glass, signed on base "Cristallerie de Pantin".

6in (15cm) high

$700-1,000   **JDJ**

A Weis miniature cameo vase, decorated with a purple iris against a cream background, signed on the side in cameo "Weis".

1.75in (4.5cm) high

$120-180   **JDJ**

An unsigned cameo vase, decorated with green shamrocks against a frosted background the background decorated with acid-cut flowers, stems and leaves.

6in (15cm) high

$300-400   **JDJ**

A Moda cameo vase, decorated with brown and white flowers on a frosted background, signed "Moda" on side.

11.25in (28.5cm) high

$300-500   **JDJ**

A Muller cameo biscuit jar, decorated in cameo and enamel with flower blossoms, leaves and stems on a 'chipped ice' background, original metal hardware, signed on the underside of base, "Muller Croismare".

7in (18cm) high

$500-700   **JDJ**

A Muller cameo vase, decorated with a lakeside scene in amethyst, orange and yellow, signed "Muller Freres Luneville".

4.25in (11cm) high

$500-700   **JDJ**

A Richard cameo atomizer, decorated with flower blossoms, stems and leaves in amethyst over pink glass, signed on the side.

7in (18cm) high

$400-600   **JDJ**

A French cameo tumbler, decorated with oak leaves and stems and a stylized bubble border in red cameo cut against a bright yellow background, illegible signature engraved on the side, tiny hairline at the lip.

3.5in (9cm) high

$60-90   **JDJ**

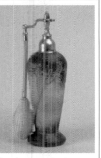

A French cameo atomizer, decorated with a scene of trees and a pond in green over clear frosted glass, unsigned.

8.25in (21cm) high

$400-600   **JDJ**

FIND OUT MORE...

'Cameo Glass: Masterpieces from 2000 Years of Making', published by The Corning Museum of Glass, 1982.

'French Cameo Glass', by Bernice & Henry Blount, published by Wallace-Homestead Book Co. 1982.

Collectors' Notes

- This inexpensive and vividly colored iridescent glass gained its unusual name in the 1960s when collecting interest and a revival began. It is possible it was given away as prizes at fairs - hence its name. It is also known as 'poor man's Tiffany' and was sold inexpensively to those who wanted the look of fashionable Tiffany glass without paying the high prices.

- It was popular from the 1900s until the 1930s and was made from pressed glass made in molds that was then sprayed with metallic powders to obtain the iridescent effect. It mimicked the far more expensive and popular art glass produced by factories such as Tiffany and Loetz.

- Major makers were based in the US and included Northwood (1888-1925) who became Dugan & Diamond after 1913, Imperial Glass Co. (est. 1902) and Fenton Art Glass Co (est.1904), who produced and popularized carnival glass from 1907.

- Despite mass-producing and exporting large quantities, the American industry faded during the 1920s and Europe and other countries such as Mexico took over. In England, Sowerby was a major producer from the 1920s until c1939, often using 19th century molds not originally used for making carnival glass.

- Prices have risen as numbers of collectors have grown. However, as it was made in large quantities, more common pieces can still be collected affordably. Collectors search for rare shapes and colors, and undamaged pieces. When identifying color, hold a piece to the light - do not rely on looking 'past' the iridescence in normal light.

- Plates are a popular collecting area, but as they are hard to make, they are rarer and usually more valuable. Look for variations in pattern and rare shapes in unusual colors. Also look for black and red pieces, which are rare colors for carnival glass.

A 'Magpie' pattern dark amethyst carnival glass bowl.

Edges on these dishes can be serrated or smooth. The bird is probably a New Zealand Parson bird, not a magpie.

5.5in (14cm) diam

$80-120　　　　**BA**

A 'Kingfisher' pattern deep amethyst carnival glass bowl.

This pattern was first made in 1923.

9.5in (24cm) wide

$150-200　　　　**BA**

A Northwood 'Good Luck' pattern amethyst carnival glass bowl.

8.5in (21.5cm) diam

$220-280　　　　　　**BA**

A Dugan Diamond 'Grape Delight' pattern amethyst carnival glass bowl.

7in (18cm) diam

$60-90　　　　**BA**

A pair of Northwood 'Acorn Burrs' amethyst carnival glass bowls.

c1911　　4.75in (12cm) high

$80-120 (pair)　　**BA**

A Fenton 'Wild Blackberry' pattern amethyst carnival glass bowl.

6.5in (16.5cm) diam

$80-120　　　　**BA**

A Northwood 'Three Fruits' pattern amethyst carnival glass bowl.

8.75in (22cm) diam

$70-100　　　　**BA**

A 'Windmill' pattern amethyst carnival glass bowl.

7.25in (18.5cm) diam

$120-180　　　　**BA**

An Imperial 'Heavy Grape' pattern amethyst carnival glass nappy.

A nappy is a shallow bowl or dish.

5.25in (13.5cm) diam

$80-120　　　　**BA**

A pair of Northwood 'Peacocks on a Fence' pattern amethyst carnival glass bowls.

This pattern was produced in large numbers in many different colors.

9in (23cm) diam

$600-900   **BA**

A 'Lotus and Dragon' pattern amethyst carnival glass bowl.

8.5in (21.5cm) wide

$70-100   **BA**

A Fenton 'Peacock and Grape' pattern amethyst carnival glass bowl.

8.75in (22cm) diam

$70-100   **BA**

A 'Peacock's Tail' pattern amethyst carnival glass bowl.

5.5in (14cm) diam

$50-80   **BA**

A Dugan Diamond 'Question Marks' pattern amethyst carnival glass two-handled compote.

1910-1920 6.5in (16.5cm) wide

$60-90   **BA**

An Imperial 'Ripple' pattern amethyst carnival glass vase.

10.5in (26.5cm) high

$120-180   **BA**

An Imperial 'Pansy' pattern amethyst carnival glass nappy.

6.5in (16.5cm) diam

$80-120   **BA**

An Imperial 'Diamond Rings' pattern amethyst carnival glass punch cup.

2.5in (6.5cm) high

$60-90   **BA**

A Diamond 'Stork and Rushes' pattern amethyst carnival glass punch cup.

2.75in (7cm) high

$40-60   **BA**

An Imperial 'Windmil' pattern amethyst carnival glass bowl.

8in (20cm) diam

$80-120   **BA**

A pair of Fenton 'April Showers' pattern carnival glass vases.

14in (35.5cm) high

$400-600   **AOY**

GLASS

A Fenton 'Horses' Head Medallion' pattern marigold carnival glass bowl.

c1912   *7.5in (19cm) diam*

$70-100   **BA**

A Northwood 'Wishbone' pattern marigold carnival glass bowl.

7.5in (19cm) diam

$70-100   **BA**

A rare Fenton 'Little Fishes' pattern marigold carnival glass bowl, model no. 1607.

c1914-1918 6in (15cm) diam

$100-150   **BA**

A 'Kangaroo' pattern marigold carnival glass bowl.

c1924   *5in (12.5cm) diam*

$80-120   **BA**

A rare Fenton 'Panther' pattern marigold carnival glass bowl.

5in (12.5cm) diam

$100-150   **BA**

A Diamond Glass 'Pony' pattern marigold carnival glass bowl.

8.25in (21cm) diam

$60-90   **BA**

A 'Swan' pattern marigold carnival glass bowl.

9in (23cm) diam

$120-180   **BA**

A 'Hobnail and Button' pattern marigold carnival glass bowl.

6.5in (16.5cm) diam

$60-90   **BA**

A 'Flower Block' pattern marigold carnival glass rose bowl.

This piece would have been made to imitate and contend with more expensive cut glass examples. The metal flower holder lid is often missing, reducing the value greatly.

6in (15cm) diam

$220-280   **BA**

A rare 1920s 'Golden Harvest' pattern marigold carnival glass decanter, possibly by the Diamond Glass Company.

These decanters, often accompanied by sets of goblets, were less expensive than similar cut glass examples and were sold at a time when bright colors and iridescent finishes were very popular.

12in (30.5cm) high

$80-120   **BA**

A pair of Brockwitz 'Triands' pattern marigold carnival glass vases.

Brockwitz of Germany was opened in 1903 and was the largest European carnival glass producer by the late 1920s.

c1930   *8in (20cm) high*

$50-80   **BA**

A Northwood 'Butterfly' pattern green carnival glass two-handled compote.

This pattern can have a plain or 'threaded' exterior.

7.5in (19cm) wide

$70-100 BA

A Fenton 'Butterflies' pattern green carnival glass two-handled compote.

Note the difference in the pattern on this example, despite the similarity in names to the previous example. This pattern has eight butterflies on the rim and one in the center.

7in (18cm) diam

$70-100 BA

A Fenton 'Stag and Holly' pattern green carnival glass bowl. c1912

8.5in (21.5cm) diam

$120-180 BA

A Northwood 'Good Luck' green carnival glass bowl.

Green is a comparatively rare color.

8.25in (21cm) diam

$150-200 BA

An Imperial 'Lustre Rose' pattern Helios carnival glass bowl.

7.75in (20cm) diam

$70-100 CA

A Northwood 'Wild Rose' pattern green carnival glass bowl.

7.5in (19cm) diam

$80-120 BA

A Fenton 'Wild Blackberry' pattern green carnival glass footed compote.

6.25in (16cm) diam

$70-80 BA

A Northwood 'Singing Bird' pattern green carnival glass beaker.

4in (10cm) high

$80-120 BA

An Imperial 'Ripple' pattern green carnival glass vase.

9in (23cm) high

$50-80 BA

A Fenton 'Dragon and Lotus' pattern blue carnival glass bowl.

Plates in this pattern are rare.

8.5in (21.5cm) diam

$120-180 BA

A Northwood 'Grape and Cable' pattern green carnival glass milk jug.

This was one of Northwood's most prolific patterns, being produced in over 40 different shapes from 1910 onward. There are also a number of variations to the pattern.

3in (7.5cm) high

$70-100 BA

FIND OUT MORE...

'The Standard Encyclopedia of carnival Glass', by Bill Edwards and Mike Carwile, published by Collector Books, 8th Edition, 2002.

'The Pocket Guide to carnival Glass' by Monica Lynn Clements and Patricia Rosser Clements, published by Schiffer Publishing. 2001.

A B C D E F G H I J K L M N O P Q R S T U V W XYZ

A John Brekke contemporary art glass vase, with impressionistic faces and figures on the exterior in brown and clear glass, the interior completely covered with letters and words in cameo, entitled "2 Germany One Snake", signed on side "J B".

Brekke was born in Chicago in 1955 and studied glass at the Art Institute of Chicago and then a general arts degree at the University of Wisconsin. He moved to New York where he set up as a glass maker, expressing ideas and referencing historical events in glass, making 'pictures of time'. The title and date of this work perhaps suggest a link to the fall of the Berlin Wall in 1989. In 1999 he went to Australia, where he recorded the trip in a journal, making a body of work from his memories and recordings upon his return.

1990-91

$3,500-4,000   **JDJ**

A contemporary Donald Carlson art glass vase, in cardinal red with applied black foot, with long spindled neck and flaring top, signed on base "CARLSON 9675".

12.5in (32cm) high

$180-220   **JDJ**

A David Goldhagen studio glass vase, blown glass, engraved "David Goldhagen 2/82".

15.75in (40cm) high

$550-650   **FRE**

A contemporary art glass sculpture, with rich purple glass pipe in horseshoe fashion encircled by coils of blue and white striated glass, signed on bottom "T BURSHAW II 1991".

8.5in (21.5cm) high

$220-280   **JDJ**

A Chris Heilman large paperweight vase, decorated with wisteria and gardens, signed and dated.

2000   8.5in (21.5cm) high

$850-950   **JDJ**

A Lisa and Peter Ridabock vase, multi-colored from Ocean Wave Series 3, with lines of color swirling like wave, the interior of vase is cased in turquoise blue, signed on foot "RIDABOCK '94".

9in (23cm) high

$550-650   **JDJ**

A Duncan McClellan art glass vase, entitled "Seeing All Sides of the Issue", signed "DUNCAN MCCLELLAN".

McClellan went to work with John Brekke at the New York Experimental Glass Workshop. He uses overlay, cutting and graal techniques and finishes pieces with acid etching, grinding and polishing. These processes allow him to include imagery on both the outside and inside.

11.5in (29cm) high

$1,800-2,200   **JDJ**

A Michael Pavlik blown and cased studio glass vase, engraved "Michael Pavlik 1979 #1393".

Pavlik graduated from Prague College of Arts & Crafts in 1963, and worked as a graphic artist. Escaping the Eastern Block in 1967 with a diamond pin hidden in a sandwich, he went to Paris and then the US. His work is in many collections, including the Corning Museum of Glass.

5in (24cm) high

$1,200-1,800   **FRE**

A Lisabeth Sterling cameo 'Whisper' vase, depicting fantasy faces whispering to each other, signed "(WHISPER) LISABETH STERLING '95".

Sterling studied glass at the Pennsylvania Academy of Fine Arts. Using a diamond-tipped tool, she engraves complex patterns on glass. Her designs have narrative aspects and she says of her work, "Images in my engravings are much like lucid dreams on glass."

12in (30.5cm) high

$2,800-3,200   **JDJ**

A Milon Townsend paperweight, with lamp-worked three dimensional dragon sitting on a glass paperweight obelisk, signed and dated.

1998   5.5in (14cm) high

$800-900   **JDJ**

Collectors' Notes

■ Depression glass is inexpensive, mass-produced, colored or clear glassware, produced during the Great Depression of the 1920s and 1930s. It was made using a tank-molding process, where ingredients were heated in a tank and forced through pipes into molds.

■ Around six companies produced most of the glass available today. Of these, popular companies amongst collectors include: Anchor Hocking, Jeanette, Indiana Glass Co. and Hazel Atlas. Depression glass pieces were usually used as promotional giveaways in gas stations, cereal boxes or movie theaters, and it was very cheap to buy.

■ Colors are typically bright, to counteract the drabness of the Great Depression. Green is one of the most typical colors, and much of it was produced by the Anchor Hocking Glass Co. Pink is as popular today as it was during the 1920s. During the mid-1930s, tastes began to revert to clear glass, and crystal was often used. These pieces are heavier in weight.

■ Most collectors collect by pattern, which were named after festive, historical, geographic or natural themes, amongst others. Examine patterns carefully and learn how to recognize them, as patterns usually identify the manufacturer. 'Jubilee' is a highly sought-after pattern, but other patterns are very similar and are often mistaken for it.

■ Examine glass closely before buying it to look for damage – try to examine it clean. Some wear through use, shown by light criss-crossing lines, is acceptable, but chips and cracks are not. Bubbles and ripples give pieces character and are also acceptable.

■ Reproductions do exist, so look carefully at color and pattern. Reproduction colors are usually paler or look very different – reproduced pink is more orange than the original. Certain patterns were not produced in some colors. The pattern on reproductions is not usually as fine as the original or it is unusually sharp, with no signs of age.

A 'Cameo' Depression glass green cup and saucer.
Saucer 6in (15.5cm) diam

$15-25 CamA

A 'Princess' Depression glass cup and saucer.
Saucer 5.75in (15cm) diam

$15-25 CamA

A 'Lovebird' Depression glass green creamer.
3in (8cm) high

$8-12 CamA

A 'Colonial Block' Depression glass goblet.
5.75in (15cm)

$8-12 CamA

A 'Doric' Depression glass green tumbler.
4in (10.5cm) high

$70-100 CamA

A 'Tearoom' Depression glass tumbler.
6in (15.5cm) high

$50-80 CamA

A green 'Tearoom' Depression glass vase.

The Art Deco 'Tearoom' pattern, made by the Indiana Glass Company, is an early, heavily pressed pattern that was made for restaurants and soda fountains. It is prone to chipping.

6.75in (17.5cm) high

$70-100 CamA

An 'American Pioneer' Depression glass lamp.
8in (20.5cm) high

$100-150 CamA

A 1930s green Depression glass sandwich plate, with a flower and foliate etched pattern.

This pattern is often mistaken for 'Jubilee'.

9.75in (24.5cm) diam

$30-40 TAB

A green 'Tearoom' Depression glass banana split dish.

The banana split dish in this design is a popular piece, both with collectors and for nostalgic reasons, therefore the high price.

7.5in (19cm) long

$70-100   **CamA**

A 1930s clear Depression glass dish.

10.75in (27cm) diam

$20-30   **TAB**

A 1930s large, clear Depression glass bowl, with a scalloped rim.

11.5in (29.5cm) diam

$30-40   **TAB**

A 1930s round, clear Depression glass platter, with hexagonal 'Hobnail' and 'Sunburst' patterns.

12.5in (32cm) diam

$20-30   **TAB**

A 1930s square, clear Depression glass platter, with dotted design.

11in (28cm) wide

$30-40   **TAB**

A 'Colony' Depression glass pitcher.

8.25in (21cm) high

$150-200   **CamA**

A 1930s clear Depression glass milk jug.

4in (10cm) high

$6-9   **TAB**

A 1930s clear Depression glass sugar bowl, with lid.

5.25in (13.5cm) high

$6-9   **TAB**

A 'Crisscross' Depression glass sugar bowl and cover.

Sugar bowls were popular Depression glass pieces and many were produced.

5.5in (17.5cm) wide

$30-50   **CamA**

A 1930s clear Depression glass sugar bowl, with heavy line design.

4.5in (11.5cm) wide

$3-5   **TAB**

An 'English Hobnail' Depression glass iced tea glass.

6.25in (17cm) high

$3-5   **CamA**

A pair of 'Chintz' Depression glass candlesticks.

Candlesticks are highly desirable, especially in pairs. During the 1930s, they added a touch of glamor to the table.

5.25in (12cm) high

$50-80   **CamA**

A 'Chintz' Depression glass juice glass.

4.75in (13cm) high

$20-30   **CamA**

A 'Candlewick' Depression glass serving plate.

_4in (35.5cm) wide

$70-100 CamA

A 'Candlewick' Depression glass celery dish.

13.5in (34.5cm) diam

$40-60 CamA

A 'Candlewick' Depression glass serving tray.

$70-100 CamA

A 'Candlewick' Depression glass etched dish, with sterling base.

5.5in (14cm) diam

$50-80 CamA

A 'Candlewick' Depression glass fancy box, with three interior dividers.

'Candlewick' is prone to damage around the protruding edges, particularly on desirable lidded pieces such as this.

7.5in (19cm) diam

$300-400 CamA

A 'Candlewick' Depression glass mallard-cut cigarette box.

5.25in (13.5cm) wide

$120-180 CamA

A 'Candlewick' Depression glass covered butter-dish.

7in (18cm) long

$50-80 CamA

A pair of 'Candlewick' Depression glass candlesticks.

5.5in (14cm) diam

$100-150 CamA

A pair of 'Candlewick' Depression glass candlesticks.

5 5in (14cm) diam

$50-80 CamA

A 'Candlewick' Depression glass sauce boat and stand.

8.25in (21cm) wide

$180-220 CamA

A 'Candlewick' Depression glass 80oz pitcher.

9in (23cm) high

$180-220 CamA

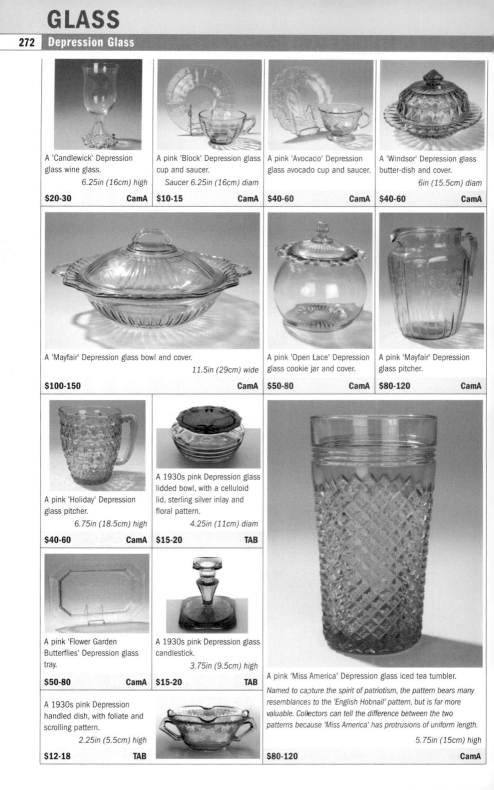

A 'Candlewick' Depression glass wine glass.
6.25in (16cm) high
$20-30   **CamA**

A pink 'Block' Depression glass cup and saucer.
Saucer 6.25in (16cm) diam
$10-15   **CamA**

A pink 'Avocado' Depression glass avocado cup and saucer.
$40-60   **CamA**

A 'Windsor' Depression glass butter-dish and cover.
6in (15.5cm) diam
$40-60   **CamA**

A 'Mayfair' Depression glass bowl and cover.
11.5in (29cm) wide
$100-150   **CamA**

A pink 'Open Lace' Depression glass cookie jar and cover.
$50-80   **CamA**

A pink 'Mayfair' Depression glass pitcher.
$80-120   **CamA**

A pink 'Holiday' Depression glass pitcher.
6.75in (18.5cm) high
$40-60   **CamA**

A 1930s pink Depression glass lidded bowl, with a celluloid lid, sterling silver inlay and floral pattern.
4.25in (11cm) diam
$15-20   **TAB**

A pink 'Flower Garden Butterflies' Depression glass tray.
$50-80   **CamA**

A 1930s pink Depression glass candlestick.
3.75in (9.5cm) high
$15-20   **TAB**

A pink 'Miss America' Depression glass iced tea tumbler.

Named to capture the spirit of patriotism, the pattern bears many resemblances to the 'English Hobnail' pattern, but is far more valuable. Collectors can tell the difference between the two patterns because 'Miss America' has protrusions of uniform length.
5.75in (15cm) high
$80-120   **CamA**

A 1930s pink Depression handled dish, with foliate and scrolling pattern.
2.25in (5.5cm) high
$12-18   **TAB**

A 'Sharon' Depression glass pitcher.
9in (23cm) high
$100-150   **CamA**

A yellow 'Normandy' Depression glass pitcher.
8in (20.5cm) high
$120-180   **CamA**

A yellow Depression glass measuring cup, with reamer.
6in (15.5cm) high
$320-380   **CamA**

A 'Sharon' Depression glass sherbet.
3.5in (9cm) diam
$8-12   **CamA**

A 1930s yellow Depression glass footed dish.
3in (7.5cm) high
$15-18   **TAB**

A yellow 'Sharon' Depression glass soup cup.
6.25in (16cm) wide
$20-30   **CamA**

A 'Horseshoe' Depression glass bowl.
9.5in (24cm) diam
$30-50   **CamA**

A 'Florentine' Depression glass relish dish.
10in (25.5cm) long
$20-30   **CamA**

A yellow 'Hermitage' Depression glass tumbler.
4in (10cm) high
$7-10   **CamA**

A 1930s cobalt blue Depression glass plate.

Cobalt blue is a highly desirable color today and was only produced in limited quantities.

8.75in (22.5cm) wide
$30-40   **TAB**

A blue 'Caprice' Depression glass bowl.
13in (33cm) diam
$50-80   **CamA**

A blue 'Royal Lace' Depression glass vegetable bowl.
11in (28cm) wide
$50-80   **CamA**

A blue 'Modern Tone' Depression glass cup and saucer.

Saucer 5.5in (14cm) diam

$15-20   **CamA**

A 'Caprice' Depression glass creamer and sugar bowl.

3in (8cm) high

$30-50   **CamA**

A 'Moondrops' Depression glass tumbler.

4.75in (12cm) high

$15-20   **CamA**

An Indiana red 'Sandwich' Depression glass goblet.

5.5in (14cm) high

$30-50   **CamA**

An Indiana red 'Sandwich' Depression glass cup and saucer.

6in (15.5cm) diam

$30-40   **CamA**

A 'Jenny Ware' Depression glass mixing bowl.

6in (15.5cm) diam

$50-80   **CamA**

A 'Swirl' Depression glass tumbler.

5in (13cm) high

$80-120   **CamA**

A 'Moondrops' Depression glass creamer and sugar bowl.

Creamer 13.5in (34.5cm) high

$15-25   **CamA**

A 1930s black Depression glass dish, with a silver overlay.

Black, introduced in the 1930s by the L.E. Smith Company, is an unusual and desirable color for Depression glass, as it was produced in comparatively small quantities despite its popularity. Highlights can be found in silver, gold, white or pink.

2.75in (7cm) high

$20-30   **TAB**

An amethyst-colored 'Royal Lace' Depression glass toddy set, with nine pieces.

$180-220 (set)   **CamA**

Collectors' Notes

- Rene Lalique (1860-1945) was born near Rheims, France and began by making jewelry in the Art Nouveau style, which became highly popular.

- During the 1890s, he began to experiment with glass, jewelry and small perfume bottles. He later sold these in his shop in Paris, which opened in 1905. By 1910 he stopped making jewelry to concentrate on glass, and won a contract from perfumier François Coty to make perfume bottles.

- By the 1920s, he had three factories making an ever-growing range of pressed and molded glass items, including vases, bowls, ashtrays and chandeliers. They typically used frosted, opalescent, milky and clear glass. Glass was also often gently stained with color to highlight select molded elements.

- Throughout the 1920s and 1930s, Lalique himself designed all pieces that went into production. Most of his designs were modern and clean, with repeated decorative motifs, often geometric or inspired by nature, many with friezes of animals or figures.

- Marks can be etched or molded and can help to date a piece. Pieces made after 1927 have 'France' added to his initial and surname.

- After his death in 1945, no further pieces were marked with his initial 'R' before his surname. Pieces with a small 'registered mark' of an 'E' in a circle were manufactured recently.

- Lalique is also considered the 'king of the car mascot', with prices for his consistently inventive and impressive mascots rising considerably over the past decade.

- The majority are figural or in the form of animals, posed to suggest speed, power or strength. Highly successful in their day, many copies were made in France, England and Czechoslovakia, so consider the detailing and size and examine the base for correct marks to ensure authenticity. As with imitations of his other ranges, many still have a high value, especially if by a noted maker such as Red Ashay.

A Lalique 'Moissac' pattern frosted and clear amber glass vase of tapered and cylindrical form, molded with leaves, wheel etched mark "R. Lalique, France", etched mark 'No. 992".

5in (13cm) high

$400-600   **L&T**

A Lalique 'Moissac' pattern clear and frosted glass vase, of tapering cylindrical form, molded in relief with leaves molded mark "R. Lalique".

5in (13cm) high

$220-280   **L&T**

A Lalique clear glass vase, with floral decoration, signed on base in block letters "R. Lalique", three chips to the rim.

6.75in (17cm) diam

$1,000-1,500   **JDJ**

A Lalique clear glass vase, with holly pattern and green staining, signed in block letters on underside "R. Lalique".

7.5in (19cm) high

$1,000-1,500   **JDJ**

A modern Lalique 'Ondines' pattern clear and frosted glass vase, engraved "Lalique France".

23cm (9in) high

$700-1,000   **DRA**

A CLOSER LOOK AT A LALIQUE VASE

This piece is large, impressive and in excellent condition, showing hallmarks of Lalique's styling during this period.

Lalique was known for his frosted glass effects, often juxtaposed against glass of great clarity.

The lines of this vase, made c1931, show Art Deco styling, being architectural, angular and clean.

Lalique often incorporated interconnected friezes of animals as decorative elements, like the birds used here.

A Lalique 'Mesanges' clear and frosted glass vase, etched "R. LALIQUE FRANCE".

c1931   *13in (33cm) high*

$3,000-4,000   **DRA**

A Lalique 'Lys' pattern clear, frosted and opalescent glass bowl, of circular form with three feet molded as flower-heads, molded mark "R. Lalique".

9.5in (24cm) high

$700-1,000 **L&T**

A Lalique clear and frosted glass bowl, molded with radiating dandelion leaves, molded and etched marks, "R. Lalique France No 3215".

9.5in (24cm) high

$220-280 **L&T**

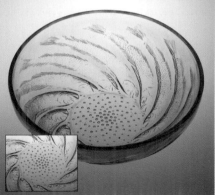

A Lalique clear and opalescent glass bowl, of circular form molded with a band of fish, molded mark.

9.25in (23.5cm) diam

$400-600 **L&T**

A modern Lalique 'Floride' pattern clear and green glass bowl, with black enamel details, engraved "Lalique France".

7.25in (18.5cm) diam

$300-500 **DRA**

Six Lalique molded glass side plates, each acid-stamped "LALIQUE".

5.75in (14.5cm) diam

$180-220 **FRE**

A Lalique 'Pissenlit No. 1' pattern clear and frosted glass serving plate, with gray patina, wheel-cut "R. LALIQUE FRANCE".

11.5in (29.5cm) diam

$400-600 **DRA**

A Lalique 'Epis' pattern clear and frosted glass serving plate, with green patina, etched "R. LALIQUE FRANCE".

11.5in (29.5cm) diam

$400-600 **DRA**

A set of five Lalique molded crystal dishes, each acid-stamped "Lalique", one with chip.

6.25in (16cm) long

$150-200 **FRE**

A Lalique 'Fauvettes' pattern opalescent glass ashtray, with blue patina, etched "LALIQUE FRANCE".

c1924 *7in (17.5cm) diam*

$320-380 **DRA**

A Lalique black glass serving plate, border patterned with waves, engraved "Lalique France".

Black is a very unusual color for Lalique glass.

27.5cm (11in) long

$400-600 **DRA**

A set of four Lalique 'Hagueneau' pattern clear and frosted glass white wine glasses, etched "R. Lalique France".

$300-500 **DRA**

FAKES AND REPRODUCTIONS

- Lalique's immense success led to the growth of a number of imitators who produced glass in the style of Lalique. These included French makers Sabino, Etling and Genet and British makers Jobling and Bagley. These often beautiful pieces have values in their own right as period imitations.

- Although they are not fakes, as they were not marked with Lalique's name and sold as Lalique, collectors should examine all pieces carefully as some pieces have had the original maker's name ground away at a later date and replaced with a Lalique mark.

- Similarly, some later pieces of Lalique – produced after 1945 – have pre-1945 marks added to them to raise value. Molded marks use a blocky 'sans serif' font only, with engraved marks usually only appearing on mold-blown, not pressed, examples.

- Pieces marked with the words 'Paris', 'Rene' and 'Made in France' should be viewed with suspicion, although the latter is used on some very modern pieces. Other hallmarks of fakes include too evenly demarked color, thinner rims, a lighter weight and less refined detailing when compared to authentic Lalique.

A set of six Lalique 'Carnes' pattern Bordeaux wine glass, etched "R. Lalique France".

8in (20cm) high

$700-1,000 — DRA

A Lalique 'William' pattern clear and frosted glass cocktail glass, with blue enameled details, engraved "R. Lalique France".

6.75in (17cm) high

$400-600 — DRA

A set of six Lalique 'Enfants' pattern clear and frosted glass liqueur glasses, with sepia patina, etched "LALIQUE CRYSTAL FRANCE", one repaired.

1.5in (4cm) high

$700-1,000 — DRA

A Lalique molded crystal cruet set, engraved "Lalique France" to base.

5.5in (14cm) high

$400-500 — FRE

A set of three Lalique molded crystal glasses, each acid-stamped "R. Lalique".

Tallest 4.5in (11.5cm) high

$150-200 (set) — FRE

A set of six Lalique 'Nippon' pattern clear glass knife rests, etched "R. Lalique".

3.5in (9cm) long

$400-600 — DRA

A Lalique for D'Orsay 'Le Lys' pattern clear and frosted glass powder box, with sepia patina, molded "R LALIQUE FRANCE".

3.25in (8.5cm) diam

$300-400 — DRA

A Lalique 'Fontainbleau' pattern clear and frosted glass box, with gray patina, molded 'R. Lalique'.

3.25in (8.5cm) diam

$500-700 — DRA

A B C D E F G H I J K L M N O P Q R S T U V W XYZ

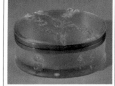

A Lalique 'Copellia' pattern clear and frosted glass box, the hinged cover with gilt metal mounts, engraved "Lalique, France".

6.75in (17cm) long

$400-500   **DRA**

A Lalique 'Hirondelles' pattern clear and frosted glass cigarette box.

4in (10cm) wide

$600-900   **DRA**

A Lalique 'Sirenes' pattern frosted glass perfume burner, of cylindrical form molded with a frieze of mermaids, lacking stopper, molded mark "R. Lalique".

9in (22.5cm) high

$400-600   **L&T**

A Lalique 'Corday' pattern molded glass perfume bottle, with original paper labels, molded "BOTTLES MADE IN FRANCE R. LALIQUE."

4.25in (11cm) high

$280-320   **FRE**

A modern Lalique cigarette lighter, holder and ashtray, with heavy lion bosses, "Lalique France" inscribed in script.

$500-700   **CW**

A modern Lalique 'Tête D'Aigle' clear and frosted glass car mascot, engraved "Lalique France".

4in (10cm) high

$280-320   **DRA**

A Lalique 'Sainte-Christophe' pattern clear and frosted glass car mascot, with amethyst tint, molded "R. LALIQUE FRANCE".

5in (13cm) high

$700-1,000   **DRA**

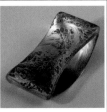

A Lalique 'Feuilles D'Artichaut' pattern clear and frosted glass rocker blotter, with sepia patina, original metal, molded "R. Lalique".

6.25in (16cm) long

$1,000-1,500   **DRA**

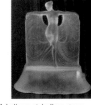

A Lalique-style lime green frosted glass night light, in the form of a nude with feather shawl, original electrification, two small surface mold lines.

11in (28cm) high

$700-1,000   **JDJ**

A Lalique 'Louis Pasteur' clear and frosted glass commemorative portrait medallion, molded marks.

4in (10cm) high

$300-500   **DRA**

MONART

- Monart was an art glass range produced in the Moncrieff Glassworks, Perth, Scotland from 1924, by the Spanish glassmaker Salvador Ysart and his sons, under the patronage of Isobel Moncrieff. Production never topped 10% of the entire factory's output, peaking c1936 and ceasing in 1961.

- Colors are strong, typically greens and pinks, with mottling, marbling and the addition of gold aventurine. This layer is cased with a layer of clear glass. Shapes are free blown, with many based on forms of oriental ceramics.

- Useful identifying features can be found on the base of pieces. The pontil mark is polished and the rim is often polished flat. A paper label is highly desirable.

A Monart glass vase, the mottled body with bubble inclusions.

6.75in (17cm) high

$300-400   L&T

A Monart glass vase, the mottled body with band of multicolored swirls, pale mottled band to the rim.

7.75in (20cm) high

$180-220   L&T

A Monart glass vase, the mottled body with amethyst and aventurine inclusions to the rim, and a similar Monart glass vase.

Larger 7.75in (20cm) high

L $100-150 R $130-220 L&T

A Monart glass vase, the mottled body with green mottling and pulled threads from shoulders to rim, small internal bruise.

10.5in (27cm) high

$220-280   DN

A Monart glass vase, the mottled body with amethyst and aventurine inclusions to the rim.

9in (23cm) high

$150-200   L&T

A Vasart glass vase, the green body with amethyst and aventurine inclusions to the rim; and another Vasart glass vase, the pink body with a blue swirling band, pale green to the rim, etched mark.

7.75in (20cm) high

$60-90 (each)   L&T

A near pair of Monart vases, the mottled bodies with amethyst inclusions to the rim.

9in (23cm) high

$600-900   L&T

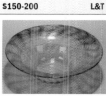

A Monart flared glass bowl, 'UB' shape, with horizontal webbing in milky-orange tones, shading through amethyst to black with areas further decorated with aventurine.

13in (33cm) diam

$150-200   DN

A Vasart glass vase, the green body with amethyst inclusions to the rim; and another Vasart vase, the pale blue body with turquoise rim, etched mark.

7.75in (20cm) high

$70-100 (each)   L&T

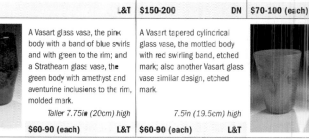

A Vasart glass vase, the pink body with a band of blue swirls and with green to the rim; and a Strathearn glass vase, the green body with amethyst and aventurine inclusions to the rim, molded mark.

Taller 7.75in (20cm) high

$60-90 (each)   L&T

A Vasart tapered cylindrical glass vase, the mottled body with red swirling band, etched mark; also another Vasart glass vase similar design, etched mark.

7.5in (19.5cm) high

$60-90 (each)   L&T

A Vasart vase, the base of the rim decorated with swirled inclusions, pontil mark to base.

7.25in (18.5cm) high

$120-180 | **AOY**

A Vasart glass posy basket, mottled glass, with pontil mark and signature to base.

4in (10cm) high

$50-80 | **AOY**

A Vasart glass table lamp, with pale mottled blue glass and mottled rust glass to the rim, etched mark.

$500-700 | **L&T**

A Vasart glass bowl, the mottled body with orange inclusions to the rim and allover swirl design, etched mark.

8.75in (22cm) diam

$100-150 | **L&T**

A Vasart hat-shaped bowl, with mottled base and rim, pontil mark and signed on base.

2.25in (6cm) high

$50-80 | **AOY**

VASART & STRATHEARN

■ In 1947, three of Ysart's sons left Moncreiff's and founded 'Ysart Bros' in Perth, Scotland. It produced 'Vasart' glass until a buyout by Teacher's Whisky in 1965 when it was renamed 'Strathearn'. Colored glass was discontinued in the late 1970s.

■ Colors are usually paler than Monart, being mainly from a pastel palette. Bands of S-shaped swirls, known as 'Paisley Shawl', where the enamels were pulled and twisted, are common.

■ Vasart bases tend to be rounded rather than flat and most often bear the company name etched around the underside of the base base. The pontil marks on Strathearn pieces are impressed with a small, boldy designed leaping salmon.

A Strathearn glass vase, the mottled body with swirling inclusions and molded marks; and another Strathearn glass vase with aventurine inclusions and molded marks.

10in (25cm) high

$70-100 (each) | **L&T**

A green Monart vase; and a Strathearn glass vase, the mottled red body with amethyst and aventurine inclusions to the rim, molded mark.

Larger 7.5in (19cm) high

$50-80 (each) | **L&T**

A Strathearn glass vase, with ring of colored swirls to waist, the pontil mark impressed with the leaping salmon motif.

8.25in (21cm) high

$80-120 | **AOY**

Collectors' Notes

- Mount Washington was founded by Deming Jarves of the Boston & Sandwich Glass Co in 1836. In 1866 it was bought out by Libbey and moved to New Bedford, MA three years later.
- Libbey sold the company to Pairpoint in 1870 and in 1894 it became part of Pairpoint Mfg Co, who eclipsed it by the turn of the century, but continued to make many of its ranges into the 20th century.
- It was a popular and prolific producer, making a huge variety of highly decorated utilitarian art glass. It also made the popular Amberina glass and patented Burmese glass.
- A further, high quality range was the porcelain-like Crown Milano which used opal-white colored glass decorated with intricate hand-painted enamel decoration. However, it only took half as long as porcelain to make.
- Much Mount Washington is easily damaged. Examine the enameling carefully for signs of wear as this is often very susceptible and being a particular characteristic of this type of Mount Washington, wear affects value seriously.

A Mount Washington rosebowl, beige to off-white with floral and leaf decoration and an inverted pinched rim.

3.5in (9cm) high

$300-500 JDJ

A Mount Washington cracker jar, unfired Burmese glass with enamel and hand-painted floral and leaf decoration, engraved silver-plated lid, not original, some wear.

7in (18cm) high

$60-90 JDJ

A Mount Washington fig-shaped shaker, decorated with leaves and flowers.

2.5in (6.5cm) high

$220-280 JDJ

A Mount Washington Crown Milano vase, melon-ribbed with long neck and folded down tricorn top, decorated with tulips with gold enameled scrolls and leaves, signed with purple "CM" crown mark.

13.25in (33.5cm) high

$4,000-6,000 JDJ

A Mount Washington Crown Milano bride's bowl, unfired Burmese glass with ruffled top and a decoration of gold leaves, flower blossoms, stems and pink traceries, marked on underneath with purple 'crown', the signed silver-plated holder with a bird figure, some wear.

Many metal fittings were manufactured by Pairpoint, who owned Mount Washington from 1894, and bear the mark 'Pairpoint Mfg. Co.'

12.5in (31.5cm) high

$2,000-3,000 JDJ

A Mount Washington Crown Milano vase, of bulbous shape with long neck, Persian pattern with gold scrolls gold, pink, brown and blue beading with gold tracery, unsigned, minor loss to beading.

11.25in (28.5cm) high

$1,500-2,000 JDJ

A CLOSER LOOK AT A MOUNT WASHINGTON VASE

Royal Flemish, patented in 1894, is considered the most important and finest glass produced by Mt Washington.

It typically used transparent, colorless and frosted glass as a base.

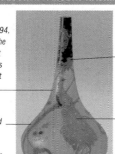

The use of gilt enameling is also typical of Royal Flemish.

The enameled details are beautifully hand-painted with animals being desirable motifs, particularly exotic ones like the peacock.

A Mount Washington Royal Flemish peacock vase, decorated with a gold peacock with beads, gold leaves, scrolls and panels, the neck has purple coloring with gold asterisks, signed with Royal Flemish mark and '594".

13in (33cm) high

$7,000-10,000 JDJ

A Mount Washington Burmese tankard water pitcher, decorated with green and brown ivy with gray tracery and applied gold enameling on the rim and handle.

9in (23cm) high

$4,000-6,000 JDJ

Collectors' Notes

- The island of Murano in Venice, Italy, has been associated with glass manufacture for centuries. It is the center of Venetian glassmaking and the location for many factories and designers.
- The postwar years saw an explosion in manufacture, with a variety of modern designs in bright colors being produced across a full spectrum of price ranges. Key factories which led this 'rebirth' included Barovier & Toso and Venini. Designers were also instrumental, and the work of Fulvio Bianconi (1915-1996), Gio Ponti (1891-1979), Carlo Scarpa (1906-1978) and Dino Martens (1894-1970) in particular is highly sought after and valuable.
- Many companies copied or were inspired by each other and so precise identification of a maker can be problematic. To identify unmarked pieces, compare them with as many named pieces as possible at dealers, auction houses and in reference books so you can recognize glassmakers' shapes and styles.
- The proliferation of Murano glassmakers also means that there is a huge range of less expensive, non-designer pieces in similar modern styles to collect.
- The work of contemporary glassmakers is also worth considering. Massimiliano Pagnin, Massimiliano Schiavon and Vittorio Ferro use traditional techniques such as 'murrine'.

A Venini honey-colored glass bowl, by Vittorio Zecchin.

c1925   5.75in (21.5cm) high

$500-700   **Qu**

A Venini flaring pillow vase, with bubbles and gold foil on a red sommerso ground, unmarked.

6.75in (17cm) wide

$320-380   **DRA**

A Venini marqueterie turtle figure, with amber head, legs and tail with amber shell and marqueterie inlay of turquoise blue iridescent squares, signed on the bottom "VENINI ITALIA".

5in (12.5cm) long

$600-900   **JDJ**

A 1950s A.V.E.M. Murano glass toothpick holder, with red interior and red foil sticker.

2.5in (6.5cm) high

$50-80   **MHC**

A 1950s A.V.E.M. Murano oval glass dish, with red base.

A.V.E.M. stands for 'Arte Vetreria Muranese', a company which was founded c1932 and flourished during the 1950s under the guidance of Giorgio Ferro in the early 1950s and Ansolo Fuga from 1955-1968.

12.75in (32.5cm) wide

$180-220   **TGM**

A Cenedese charcoal smoked glass bull figure, unmarked.

Founded in 1946, the Gino Cenedese factory employed the renowned Alfredo Barbini as artistic director between 1947-50.

7.5in (19cm) high

$300-500   **DRA**

A Barbini oversized flaring ribbed bowl, the exterior of clear purple glass lined in lattimo, with Barbiri label.

18in (45.5cm) diam

$280-320   **CR**

A Cenedese block form aquarium glass sculpture, with a yellow and brown fish and green plants, a few scratches and a nick to one corner, unmarked.

5.5in (14cm) wide

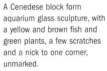

$180-220   **DRA**

A Venini & Co. glass bottle vase, marked "Venini Murano ITALIA", of cylindrical form with thin pulled-in neck, dark green with white and dark red overlay, etched on three lines lacks stopper.

1946-50   11.5in (29cm) high

$300-500   HERR

A CLOSER LOOK AT VENINI GLASS

This vase was made by Venini & Co., founded in 1925 and one of Murano's most innovative factories.

It was designed by Fulvio Bianconi (1915-1996). A leader in Post Modernist Italian style, his work is highly sought after.

It is very modernist in style, with bright colors that are typical of the period.

The bands of patterning recall Dino Marten's more valuable patchwerk 'pezzato' vases, and have a similar effect on the transparent bottle.

A Venini glass bottle vase, by Fulvio Bianconi, of tall cylindrical form with dark green overlay and one light blue and two red melted-on glass stripes, the spherical stopper with partial overlay in cornflower blue marked "Venini Murano ITALIA", etched on three lines.

c1951-5   16.25in (41cm) high

$1,000-1,500   HERR

A Venini glass bottle vase, by Fulvio Bianconi, the slender oviform vessel with tall cylindrical neck, in deep emerald green with primrose-yellow band around the lower section, the drop-in ovoid stopper also in primrose-yellow, indistinct marks on base.

14.25in (36cm) high

$280-320   DN

A Venini bottle vase by Paolo Venini, of hexagonal form, smoke-colored, decorated with red spiral threads, the colorless glass stopper with red overlay, marked "Venini Murano Italia" etched on three lines.

8.5in (21.5cm) high

$800-1,200   HERR

A Venini tessuto vase, of heavily bulbous form with thick, vertically melted-on glass bands in white, yellow and purple, etched mark "Venini Italia 81" and two labels.

1981   12.75in (32.5cm) high

$700-1,000   HERR

A Venini ruby red handkerchief vase, etched "Venini/Murano/Italia".

The handkerchief vase, or 'fazzoletto', is one of Paolo Venini's most characteristic designs it was widely copied by other makers, but these pieces are worth less. Look for pieces bearing an inscription to secure authenticity.

8.5in (21.5cm) high

$600-900   DRA

A Venini cased handkerchief vase, with red exterior and white interior, acid etched mark.

7.75in (19.5cm) high

$400-600   DN

A small Venini handkerchief vase, internally decorated with alternating bands of lemon and amethyst latticino threading.

2.75in (7cm) high

$120-180   DN

A 1950s Venini fazzoletto vase, of octagonal form, with 'Zanfirico' decoration, with opaque white melted-on threads, marked "Venini Murano ITALIA".

7.5in (19cm) high

$300-400   HERR

A 1960s Fratelli Ferro opaline glass vase, with foil labels.

8.25in (21cm) high

$40-60   **MHC**

A Seguso Vetri d'Arte sommerso vase, by Flavio Poli, tear-drop shaped with cased amber glass.

c1955   10.5in (26cm) high

$400-600   **Qu**

FIND OUT MORE

'Venetian Glass 1890-1990' by Rosa Barovier Mentasti, published by Arsenale Editrice, 1992.

The Corning Museum of Glass, One Museum Way, Corning, New York, 14830. www.cmog.org

The Glass Museum, Oratorio di San Sebastiano, Piazza San Sebastiano, 17041 Altare, Italy. www.isvav.it/italiana.htm

A Seguso for Oggetti tall cylindrical vase, with orange and black stripes on clear glass, etched "Seguso A.V. por Oggetti".

Oggetti is a luxury retailer of decorative home accessories founded in 1975 by Robert & Nancy Frehling. Originally, all their items were selected from Italian makers, but since the 1980s they have looked further afield. The word 'oggetti' is Italian for 'objects'.

15.75in (40cm) high

$220-280   **CR**

A Seguso Vetri d'Arte sommerso vase, by Flavio Poli, of funnel form with clear cased cobalt blue body and green base.

c1958   9.75in (24cm) high

$1,000-1,500   **Qu**

A 1950s Seguso Vetri D'Arte Archimede opaline glass vase, the body sprinkled in pink with gold foil overlay, unmarked.

6.75in (17cm) high

$320-380   **HERR**

A Fratelli Toso murrine two-handled vase.

Murrines are small, flat squares cut from a rod of glass. They are laid on a flat surface and heated. A near molten clear glass body is then rolled on top. The squares stick to the glass body and then appear like the tesserae of a mosaic covering the entire body of the piece.

c1910   4in (10cm) high

$400-600   **Qu**

A 1960s Murano sommerso navy blue geometric vase.

5.75in (14.5cm) high

$60-90   **TGM**

A 1960s Murano sommerso red geometric vase.

5.75in (14.5cm) high

$60-90   **TGM**

A 1960s Murano sommerso yellow geometric vase, with partial foil label for L. Nason.

4.5in (11.5cm) high

$40-60   **TGM**

A 1960s Murano sommerso yellow geometric vase.

6.25in (16cm) high

$50-80   **TGM**

A 1960s Murano sommerso gray geometric vase.

6.5in (16.5cm) high

$50-80   **TGM**

A 1950s Murano sommerso glass vase, triple cased green, amber and red, in the form of an owl.

10.5in (27cm) high

$80-120 **TGM**

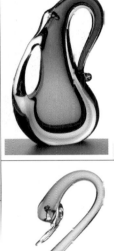

A 1950s Murano triple cased sommerso freeform vase.

Glass using techniques such as 'sommerso' is popular and remains surprisingly inexpensive.

11in (28cm) high

$180-220 **PC**

A 1950s Murano triple cased sommerso freeform vase.

6.75in (24.5cm) high

$120-180 **PC**

A 1950s Murano triple cased sommerso freeform vase.

8.5in (21.5cm) high

$80-120 **PC**

A 1950s Murano triple cased sommerso swan figure, in clear green and amber.

The sommerso technique involves encasing strongly colored glass in a layer of contrasting colored glass before the whole is encased in a heavy layer of clear glass. The clear glass exterior casing can be carved with strong facets, or pulled into extended shapes, creating interesting and complex optical effects.

14.5in (37cm) high

$180-220 **PC**

A 1950s Murano triple cased sommerso duck figure, with green foil sticker with curling edges.

6.25in (16cm) high

$40-60 **TGM**

A Murano tall frosted yellow glass vase, with clear frosted foot.

17.5in (44.5cm) high

$70-100 **GC**

A Murano tall frosted green glass vase, with clear frosted foot.

14.25in (36cm) high

$50-80 **GC**

A Murano tall red glass vase, with clear foot.

14.25in (36cm) high

$70-100 **GC**

A Murano tall blue glass vase, with clear foot.

16in (40.5cm) high

$60-90 **GC**

A latticino glass bowl and underplate, in Venetian latticino design.

Plate 7.25in (18.5cm) diam

$180-220　　　**JDJ**

A large Murano glass figural candelabra, in the style of Barovier, with two floriform holders and blackamoor in red and white period dress with gold foil and applied details on a circular base, some chips, unmarked.

16.75in (42.5cm) high

$400-600　　　**DRA**

A Murano handkerchief vase, internally decorated with vertical bands of latticini, alternately colored pink and turquoise.

4in (10cm) high

$70-100　　　**DN**

A Pair of Murano sommerso glass pheasants, in green and amber, with Murano glass labels.

Largest 13.75in (35cm) high

$80-120　　　**CR**

A fine Murano glass stoppered vessel, with controlled bubbles and gold foil against an orange ground, with some small chips and gold foil Murano label.

9.5in (24cm) high

$280-320　　　**DRA**

A 1980s VeArt Murano honey-colored glass vase, with company label, boxed.

18in (46cm) high

$300-400　　　**HERR**

A 1960s Murano glass bowl, with random red spots, and gold aventurine, with an outer layer of white glass to the base.

8.25in (21cm) wide

$40-60　　　**AOY**

A contemporary glass piece 'Fussvogel', by R Z Sperl.

13.5in (34cm) high

$1,800-2,200　　　**FM**

A contemporary Italian glass sculpture, by Silvio Vigliaturo.

16.5in (42cm) high

$1,000-1,500　　　**FM**

A contemporary glass piece, by Zanfiriro.

21.5in (55cm) high

$1,500-2,000　　　**FM**

An Aureliano Tosc glass fish, by Dino Martens, of clear glass with white trails with pierced bubbles and azure blue, cobalt blue, dark violet and orange/yellow powder enamel.

c1960　　　*9.75in (24.5cm) long*

$700-1,000　　　**Qu**

Collectors' Notes

- The interest in and popularity of 'peachblow' glass was caused by the sale of a Chinese vase from the collection of Mary Morgan, in 1886. The vase fetched the vast sum of $18,000 and was decorated with an 18th century 'peach bloom' glaze derived from copper.

- Peachblow glass aimed to imitate the 'peach bloom' coloring of this vase, with replicas first being produced by Hobbs, Brockunier & Co, of Wheeling, West Virginia, whose 'Wheeling Peachblow' has an opaque white glass interior casing and shades from red to amber/yellow.

- It was extremely popular and other makers followed with their own versions, including Mount Washington and The New England Glass Company, who called it 'Wild Rose'.

- Look for pieces that have coloring that is as close to the original ceramic glaze as possible, such as the double gourd vase illustrated. Mount Washington 'peachblow' is also highly collectible and desirable.

A peachblow small, footed, tricorn vase, in pink shading to off-white.

5in (12.5cm) high

$100-150   JDJ

A peachblow spooner, deep pink shading to off-white with square crimped rim.

4.5in (11.5cm) high

$500-800   JDJ

A small peachblow tricorn vase, of bulbous shape with deep ruffles, pink shading to white, slight damage.

3.25in (8cm) high

$700-1,000   JDJ

A peachblow fingerbowl, with ruffled top, deep pink shading to off-white.

5.5in (14cm) diam

$500-800   JDJ

A large peachblow bowl, with ruffled top and deep coloring, damage to the rim.

9.25in (23.5cm) diam

$300-500   JDJ

A peachblow bowl, deep pink shading to yellow with a folded ruffled top.

5.5in (14cm) diam

$150-200   JDJ

A Mount Washington peachblow tricorn bowl, pink shading to pale blue, with a ground pontil.

3in (7.5cm) wide

$700-1,000   JDJ

A pair of Wheeling peachblow salt and pepper pots, colored deep pink fading to off-white.

4in (10cm) high

$220-280   JDJ

A Wheeling peachblow double gourd vase, fuchsia shading to amber with a creamy-white interior lining.

The exceptionally fine coloring of this vase and its shape make it highly desirable. It was manufactured by Hobbs, Brockunier & Co. of Wheeling, West Virginia, the leading maker of peachblow glass.

7.5in (19cm) high

$2,800-3,200   JDJ

A peachblow gourd vase, deep pink shading to off-white with creamy white lining.

10in (25.5cm) high

$180-220   JDJ

A Wheeling peachblow cruet, of bulbous form with fuchsia to amber coloring, applied reeded amber handle with creamy-white lining, stopper not original.

5.5in (14cm) high

$800-1,200   JDJ

A Royal Bohemia graduated red, orange and yellow glass vase.

c1968   *13.5in (34cm) high*

$70-100   **GC**

A Royal Bohemia amber glass vase, with geometric patterns.

1970-72   *7in (17.5cm) high*

$40-60   **GC**

A Royal Bohemia cylindrical clear glass vase, with geometric pattern.

1970-72   *9.75in (25cm) high*

$30-50   **GC**

A Royal Bohemia lined and graduated red, orange and yellow glass vase.

c1968   *6.25in (16cm) high*

$40-60   **GC**

A Royal Bohemia small orange glass vase, with hobnail-like circular pattern.

1970-1972 5in (12.5cm) high

$30-50   **GC**

A Royal Bohemia large clear glass vase, with raised geometric pattern, designed by Jiri Repasek for the Podebrady branch of the Bohemia Glassworks.

This pattern is also found on wider vases and ashtrays. Other colors used included a delicate light blue.

1970-72   *9.75in (25cm) high*

$40-60   **GC**

A Royal Bohemia blue glass vase, with raised hobnail-like circular design.

1970-1972 7in (17.5cm) high

$40-60   **GC**

A Royal Bohemia clear glass vase, with vertical textured wavy pattern.

1970-72   *9in (23cm) high*

$40-60   **GC**

Collectors' Notes

- The Bohemian Glassworks National Corporation was formed by the merger of five established Czech glass factories in 1965, with the factory at Podebrady being one of the most notable. Production continues today.
- From the 1950s, Podebrady in particular turned increasingly to modern design. Thick, press-molded glass with abstract, deep relief designs are typical of production from the 1950s to the 1980s.
- Much of the glass can be easily identified, although it is not marked, by the raised and machine-cut square bases. In its time, it was plentiful and affordable and collectors are just beginning to pay attention to it. Beware of scratches which will detract from the color and pattern as well as the value.

A Royal Bohemia green glass vase, with two raised hobnail-like circular patterns.

1970-72   *9in (23cm) high*

$40-60   **GC**

A Royal Bohemia small clear glass vase, designed by Jiri Repasek, with raised geometric pattern.

1970-72   *8in (20cm) high*

$30-40   **GC**

A Royal Bohemia clear glass vase, with conical prunts.

1970-72   *10in (25.5cm) high*

$40-60   **GC**

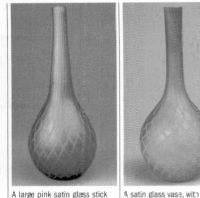

A large pink satin glass stick vase, with diamond quilted pattern, slight bruising.

12in (30.5cm) high

$80-120 JDJ

A satin glass vase, with diamond quilted pattern dark blue shading to light blue, miror damage

10in (25.5cm) high

$60-90 JDJ

An English satin glass zipper vase, shading from a brown to white with interior pink lining, vertical ribbing.

The satin-like, matte surface effect is gained by treating the glass with acid after its manufacture. It was very popular in the US, England and Europe in the late 19thC and is most often found with molded surface decoration in striped or dotted patterns, ruffled edges or combined with metal mounts.

9in (23cm) high

$1,200-1,800 JDJ

A large lavender satin glass vase, with diamond quilted pattern.

12.5in (31.5cm) high

$500-800 JDJ

A large mother-of-pearl satin glass vase, light blue ribbed, with ruffled top.

15.5in (39.5cm) high

$100-150 JDJ

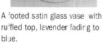

A footed satin glass vase with ruffled top, lavender fading to blue.

8in (20.5cm) high

$70-100 JDJ

A two-handled satin glass vase, with square top, diamond quilted pattern, blue to white shading and frosted applied handles, small chip to handle.

7.5in (19cm) high

$200-300 JDJ

A satin glass vase, pink to off-white shading with tricorn ruffled rim.

11in (28cm) high

$80-120 JDJ

A decorated tricorn ruffle satin glass vase, with diamond quilted pattern and pink to white shading, decorated with gold highlights and coralene.

9.5in (24cm) high

$100-150 JDJ

A satin glass vase in silver-plated holder, the square ruffled top vase with diamond quilted pattern and orange to opalescent shading, the engraved holder with flowers leaves cherries and birds.

7.5in (19cm) high

$600-900 JDJ

GLASS

Riihimäki Glassworks

- Riihimäki was founded in Finland in 1910 and changed its name to Riihimaën Lasi Oy in 1937. It produced container, window and domestic glass. Domestic designs tended to be traditional, including cut lead crystal table ware and mold-blown pieces.
- Through the 1930s and 1940s, design competitions were held, which resulted in talented new designers joining the glassworks. Nanny Still joined in 1946, and Timo Sarpaneva, Helena Tynell and Tamara Aladin joined in 1949.

- Most pieces produced during the 1950s and 1960s were mold-blown in strong, jewel-like colors. Clean-lined geometric forms and textured surfaces were the leading aesthetics of the period.
- Artist-signed pieces are usually more valuable, most are unsigned or only bear the factory name or a small polar bear mark. Look for pieces that show either of the two main stylistic characteristics and are unscratched, as scratches detract from the purity of the glass, and its texture.

A Riihimaën Lasi Oy Fossil range aqua blue glass vase, by Helena Tynell.

The 'Fossil' range has become harder to find over the past few years, and as a result prices have risen.

6.25in (16cm) high

$100-150   **GC**

A Riihimaën Lasi Oy olive green Fossil range glass vase, by Helena Tynell.

8.75in (22.5cm) high

$70-100   **GC**

A Riihimaën Lasi Oy 'Pironki' vase, by Helena Tynell.

c1975   8.25 (21cm) high

$180-220   **MHT**

A Riihimaën Lasi Oy 'Emma' vase, by Helena Tynell.

c1975   8.25 (21cm) high

$180-220   **MHT**

A Riihimaën Lasi Oy mold-blown 'Venturi' vase, by Helena Tynell.

c1975   8.25'n (21cm) high

$180-220   **MHT**

A Riihimaën Lasi Oy large 'Pompadour' vase, by Nanny Still, with export label for "Finncristal".

c1970   11in (28cm) high

$180-220   **MHT**

A Riihimaën Lasi Oy small 'Pompadour' vase, by Nanny Still.

c1968   8.75in (22cm) high

$120-180   **MHT**

Two Riihimaën Lasi Oy 'Pompadour' vases, with turned rims, by Nanny Still.

c1968   Tallest 11in (28cm) high

S $180-220 L $200-250 MHT

Three Riihimaën Lasi Oy vases, by Nanny Still.

1969-70 Tallest 12in (30cm) h

$60-90 (each)   **GC**

Three Riihimaën Lasi Oy vases, by Tamara Aladin.

1969-70 Tallest 11in (28cm) h

$60-90 (each)   **GC**

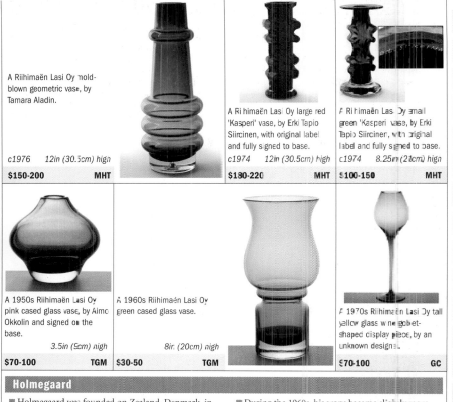

A Riihimaën Lasi Oy mold-blown geometric vase, by Tamara Aladin.

c1976   *12in (30.5cm) high*

$150-200   **MHT**

A Riihimaën Lasi Oy large red 'Kasperi' vase, by Erki Tapio Siircinen, with original label and fully signed to base.

c1974   *12in (30.5cm) high*

$180-220   **MHT**

A Riihimaën Lasi Oy small green 'Kasperi' vase, by Erki Tapio Siircinen, with original label and fully signed to base.

c1974   *8.25in (21cm) high*

$100-150   **MHT**

A 1950s Riihimaën Lasi Oy pink cased glass vase, by Aimo Okkolin and signed on the base.

3.5in (9cm) high

$70-100   **TGM**

A 1960s Riihimaën Lasi Oy green cased glass vase.

8in (20cm) high

$30-50   **TGM**

A 1970s Riihimaën Lasi Oy tall yellow glass wine goblet-shaped display piece, by an unknown designer.

$70-100   **GC**

Holmegaard

- Holmegaard was founded on Zealand, Denmark, in 1825 and from the 1830s produced bottles and pressed glass including tableware. In 1941, Per Lütken joined as designer.
- During the 1940s and 1950s Lütken's designs focused on the plasticity of glass and used organic forms, such as buds and teardrops, as inspiration. Coloring is typically cool and subtle such as 'smoke' (gray) and aqua (pale blue) but bright colors are known.
- During the 1960s, his work became slightly more geometric. Lütken also pioneered more robust drinking glasses, many having his characteristic everted rims.
- Many of his pieces are signed with his initials and dated. His glass is exceptionally pure and clear, so condition is important. Rim chips, even if ground down, will be visible and will reduce value.

A Holmegaard blue tinged vase, by Per Lütken, signed and dated on the base "HOLMEGAARD PL 1958".

1958   *3.25in (8.5cm) high*

$50-80   **TGM**

A Holmegaard small heart-shaped gray vase, designed by Per Lütken, signed and dated on the base "HOLMEGAARD PL 1959".

1959   *2in (5cm) high*

$30-50   **TGM**

A Holmegaard vase, by Per Lütken.

1959-1960   *6.25in (16cm) high*

$80-120   **GC**

A Holmegaard vase, designed by Per Lütken, signed and dated on the base "HOLMEGAARD PL 1960".

1960   *5.25in (13.5cm) high*

$60-90   **TGM**

A B C D E F G H I J K L M N O P Q R S T U V W XYZ

GLASS

A Holmegaard vase, designed by Per Lütken, signed and dated on the base "HOLMEGAARD PL 1961".

1961   *4.25in (10.5cm) high*

$60-90   **TGM**

A Holmegaard brown glass tapering vase, by Per Lütken, signed with his monogram on the base.

8.75in (22cm) high

$50-80   **GC**

A Holmegaard green vase, by Per Lütken.

1959-60   *11.5in (29cm) high*

$150-200   **GC**

A Holmegaard cylindrical blue glass vase, by Per Lütken, signed with his monogram on the base.

12in (30.5cm) high

$80-120   **GC**

A Holmegaard purple tri-form section vase, by Per Lütken, dated and inscribed "HOLMEGAARD" on the base.

1955   *10.25in (26cm) high*

$150-200   **GC**

A Holmegaard white bowl, by Michael Bang, from the Atlantis range.

c1980   *3in (7.5cm) high*

$30-50   **MHT**

A large, bulbous purple glass bottle.

The maker of this unsigned piece is not confirmed. It was previously thought to have been by Whitefriars, but is now thought to be by Holmegaard.

14.25in (36cm) high

$300-350   **GC**

Kosta & Boda

- Boda was founded in Sweden in 1864, producing bottles and pressed glass. By 1946 it had been bought by Eric Afors, who injected new impetus, including bringing in the talented Eric Hoglund as designer.
- Kosta was founded in 1742 and like most factories, began to concentrate on design in the 1920s. Employing outside designers but always beaten by rival Orrefors, a new era began in 1950 when the talented Vicke Lindstrand left Orrefors for Kosta. His designs were varied and highly successful with engraved figural or abstract designs and optical effects with internal threading.
- Kosta, Boda and Afors merged in 1964 and in 1976 the group became known as Kosta Boda. In 1997, Orrefors was added, enlarging the company which is still producing decorative and functional glass today.

A Boda large bottle vase, by Eric Hoglund.

Hoglund's designs are characterized by thickly rendered glass, often in orange, blue and ruby glass, with impressed or molded primitively formed figures or animals as decoration.

c1965   *14.5in (37cm) high*

$180-220   **MHT**

A 1930s Kosta large, internally ribbed, optic blue vase, by Ellis Berg, signed to base "B473".

10.5in (26.5cm) high

$150-200   **MHT**

A Kosta oviform vase, by Vicke Lindstrand, marked "Lindstrand Kosta" and signed "LH 1260".

2.75in (7cm) high

$120-180   **DN**

A Kosta blown and cut crystal glass vase, by Monica Morales Schildt, engraved "Kosta Mona Schildt 0-29", bruises to body, designed 1967.

Morales Schildt worked at Kosta between 1958 and 1970. She had trained with the prestigious Italian glass factory Venini so many of her designs have a strong resemblance to typical Murano production.

9in (23cm) high

$220-280   **FRE**

A Kosta heavy clear glass cased over brown glass bowl, by Vicke Lindstrand, with smoky moonshine effect.

c1955   7.25in (18.5cm) wide

$220-280   **MHT**

A pair of Kosta Boda candlesticks, with yellow caning to stem, with an etched mark.

6in (15cm) high

$320-380   **DRA**

A Kosta Boda large bottle vase, by Bertil Vallien, with all-over texture and applied print to front.

10.75in (37.5cm) high

$180-220   **MHT**

A 1980s Kosta Boda purple vase, marked "Handmade".

8in (20cm) high

$80-120   **JH**

Orrefors

A 1930s Orrefors glass vase, the decoration designed by Vicke Lindstrand, the flared clear glass vessel engraved with a naked male swimmer swimming towards the base, signed "Orrefors Lindstrand1049.A2 KR"?, also "Orrefors lM 108", small chip on foot.

These vases with engraved divers and rippling 'water' effect sides were very popular in the 1930s. There is an example of this vase in the glass collection of the Victoria & Albert Museum, London.

8.75in (22cm) high

$300-350   **DN**

An Orrefors glass vase, designed by Vicke Lindstrand, engraved with an exotic bird in flight, on a solid black glass foot, signed "Orrefors L. 1253.A2" and "f Gu 66".

7in (18cm) high

$120-180   **DN**

A 1960s Orrefors opaline glass vase, with wavy rim, signed on the base "Orrefors Tal 3090/1'.

2.5in (6cm) high

$40-60   **TGM**

A mid-20thC Orrefors engraved glass vase, engraved with a young satyr playing reed pipes, inscribed "Orrefors. F2468.bb.9.5".

$50-60   **SI**

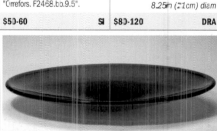

A Orrefors large 'Expo' blown-glass charger, by Sven Palmqvist, engraved "Orrefors Expo PM 243-62 Sven Palmqvist".

20.5in (52cm) diam

$500-700   **FRE**

An Orrefors glass bowl, with block-cut decoration, minor damage, with an etched mark.

8.25in (21cm) diam

$80-120   **DRA**

A Nuutajärvi Notsjö chestnut dish, by Kaj Franck, signed "Nuutajärvi Notsjö".

Kaj Franck worked for Nuutajärvi Notsjö between 1950 and 1976.

2.5in (6.5cm) wide

$60-90　　　　**MHT**

A Nuutajärvi Notsjö glass vase, by Gunnel Nyman, the slender oviform having an internal cavity of 'rose' color, cased in clear glass and surrounded by a web of bubbles, signed on base "G.Nyman", "Notsjö" and dated "1947".

12.5in (31.5cm) high

$280-320　　　　**DN**

A Nuutajärvi Notsjö bowl, model no. kf233, by Kaj Franck, signed "Kaj Franck Nuutajärvi Notsjö 62".

1962　　　3.5in (9cm) wide

$100-150　　　　**MHT**

A Nuutajärvi Notsjö bowl, model no. kf245, by Kaj Franck, signed "K Franck Nuutajärvi Notsjö 64".

1964　　　7in (18cm) wide

$120-180　　　　**MHT**

A Nuutajärvi Notsjö candlestick, by Oiva Toikka, signed "Nuutajärvi Notsjö".

9in (23cm) high

$150-200　　　　**MHT**

An Afors glass vase, by Ernest Gordon, of flattened oviform, internally decorated with a ruby-colored cavity and applied with an extra clear glass 'skin' set at an angle on the lower part of the vessel, signed on base "Afors", "GH391" and "Ernest Gordon".

8in (20cm) high

$120-180　　　　**DN**

A Flygfors low green glass vase, by Paul Kedlef.

3.5in (9cm) high

$60-90　　　　**GC**

A Hadeland vase, by Willy Johansson, signed "Hadeland 60 WJ".

1960　　　6.5in (16.5cm) high

$120-180　　　　**MHT**

A CLOSER LOOK AT A TIMO SARPANEVA VASE

The mold interior is rough wood, giving the texture to the glass. This idea was used later by Baxter at Whitefriars.

Each time the mold is used, the molten glass burns it, changing it, and making each piece effectively unique.

Nature often inspired Scandinavian glass designers, here, the inspiration is tree bark.

The designer Timo Sarpaneva has signed the base of this vase.

A tall pop art vase, cased red glass over white, attributed to Bengt Orup for Johansfors.

15.75in (40cm) high

$70-100　　　　**MHT**

A Kastrup tall tapering vase, by E. Bang, with 'knop' form.

17.75in (45cm) high

$80-120　　　　**GC**

A Iittala bark pattern 'Finlandia' vase, by Timo Sarpaneva, signed 'TIMO SARPANEVA 3331' on the base.

Designed in 1965, 'Finlandia' was a key range.

c1965　　　6.75in (17cm) high

$150-200　　　　**TGM**

A Ruda abstract molded vase, with textured decoration to all sides.

c1965   7in (18cm) high

$70-100   **MHT**

A Ruda glass vase, with textured decoration featuring a Viking warrior and maiden, one to each side.

c1965   8.5in (21.5cm) high

$80-120   **MHT**

A Skruf cylindrical internally decorated vase, with flaring rim.

c1980   9in (23cm) high

$80-120   **MHT**

A 1960s Stenhytta opaline glass vase, with blue stripes, signed "STENHYTTA WW."

5in (13cm) high

$60-90   **TGM**

A Strömbergshyttan glass vase, by Edvard Strömberg, imported by E fverson.

Gerda and Edvard Strömberg began their careers designing for the Swedish factory Eda. In 1933, they left to set up their own factory, Strömbergshyttan. This vase is typical of their work, which also included carved and faceted pieces, all in simple, austere styles.

10.5in (27cm) high

$220-280   **GC**

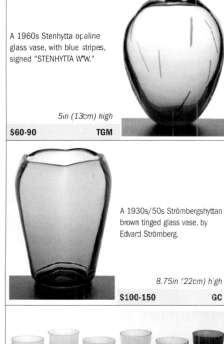

A 1930s/50s Strömbergshyttan brown tinged glass vase, by Edvard Strömberg.

8.75in (22cm) high

$100-150   **GC**

A Swedish tall necked fruit-shaped vase, in cerulean blue and white-cased glass.

A J. Wuidart & Co. set of six 'Harlequin' tumblers, by Strömberg.

c1950   3.5in (9cm) high

$70-100   **MHT**

19.75in (50cm) high

$100-150   **GC**

GLASS

Collectors' Notes

- Steuben Glassworks was founded in Steuben County, New York, in 1903 by T.J. Hawkes and Frederick Carder. Initially, the factory supplied blanks to Hawkes' factory, but Carder soon began experimenting with art glass, inspired by his experiences at Stevens & Williams in England.

- In 1904, he patented a formula for an iridescent colored glass that was very similar to Tiffany's 'favrile'. After fighting off a court case from Tiffany, he produced the range from 1905 onward in a variety of colors.

- The talented Carder built the Steuben Glass Co. factory solidly, acquiring new furnaces, hiring more staff and designing all the products himself. He 'ruled with an iron rod', ensuring quality was always extremely high.

- After being bought by the Corning Glass Works in 1918, Steuben released a variety of designs during the 1920s and went from strength to strength.

- In 1933, Arthur Amoury Houghton Jr. took over as President due to dwindling profits caused by the Depression. He swiftly replaced Carder and, in response to the popularity of carved, clear Scandinavian glass, oversaw the development of a 'G10M', a lead crystal glass of amazing clarity that could also be carved.

- The company was re-launched in 1935, using this glass and employing a range of noted designers such as Walter Dorwin Teague. The 1970s saw a trend for simple, stylized animal figurines. Since then, the tradition of employing outside designers has continued, ensuring simplicity and strength of design. As a result, pieces have become highly collectible, although many vintage crystal pieces are still affordable and commonly available.

A Steuben bulbous cabinet vase, of lustered blue glass, etched "2048" with triangular paper label.

2.5in (6.5cm) high

$350-400 CR

A Steuben gold Aurene blown-glass vase, etched "Steuben".

8in (20cm) high

$1,000-1,500 FRE

A Steuben blue Aurene blown glass vase, etched "STEUBEN", scratch to lip.

8in (20cm) high

$1,200-1,800 FRE

An iridescent art glass bowl, possibly Steuben, in blown amethyst glass.

3.5in (9cm) high

$280-320 FRE

A Steuben gold Aurene on calcite on compote, with applied pedestal foot, unsigned.

6in (15cm) diam

$280-320 JDJ

A Steuben verre de soie vase, iridescent frosted glass with applied cranberry threading, unsigned, very good condition.

6in (15cm) high

$180-220 JDJ

A large Steuben glass centerbowl, with iridescent blue-green interior and white exterior, some short scratches to center, unmarked.

14.75in (37.5cm)

$500-700 CR

A Steuben blue Aurene darner, iridescent blue finish, unsigned, one small chip to base of handle.

6.5in (16.5cm) high

$500-700 JDJ

A large Steuben blown-glass 'Cluthra' vase, with fleur-de-lis acid stamp "STEUBEN", large heat crack.

Cluthra glass was made using large particles of powdered enamels on clear glass which also included bubbles.

11.75in (30cm) high

$400-600 FRE

A Steuben rosaline glass cornucopia vase, with an alabaster foot, signed on foot in block letters, minor interior surface scratches.

8in (20.5cm) high

$300-500 JDJ

A Steuben grotesque bowl, amethyst shading to clear, signed on base, scratches to interior of bowl.

11.5in (29cm) wide

$380-420 JDJ

Nine Steuben green blown-glass plates, at least one acid-stamped "STEUBEN".

8.75in (22cm) diam

$380-420 FRE

A Steuben blown-crystal snail, engraved "Steuben".

4in (10cm) high

$180-220 FRE

A Steuben blown-crystal pelican, engraved "Steuben".

$80-120 FRE

A Steuben blown-crystal compote, engraved "1701" on foot, scratch to rim.

10in (25.5cm) diam

$280-320 FRE

A Steuben blown-crystal fruit bowl, engraved "Steuben".

9.75in (25cm) high

$380-420 FRE

A Steuben blown and cut crystal owl, engraved "Steuben".

5in (12.5cm) high

$280-320 FRE

A rare Steuben blown and engraved crystal bicentennial goblet, engraved "Steuben 159-200", from an edition of 200, boxed with accompanying certificate.

8in (20cm) high

$800-1,200 FRE

A pair of Steuben blown crystal candlesticks, engraved "Steuben" to base.

9.25in (23.5cm) high

$450-500 FRE

Two Steuben etched-crystal zodiac pyramids, depicting Pisces and Scorpo, each engraved "Steuben".

2.5in (6.5cm) high

$150-200 FRE

FIND OUT MORE...

'The Glass of Frederick Carder', by Paul Gardner, published by Crown Publishers, 2002 (Gardner was Carder's long-time colleague and associate).

'Frederick Carder & Steuben Glass', by Thomas Dimitroff, published by Schiffer Publishing, 1998.

'Steuben Glass: An American Tradition in Crystal', by Mary Jean Madigan, published by Harry N. Abrams, 1982.

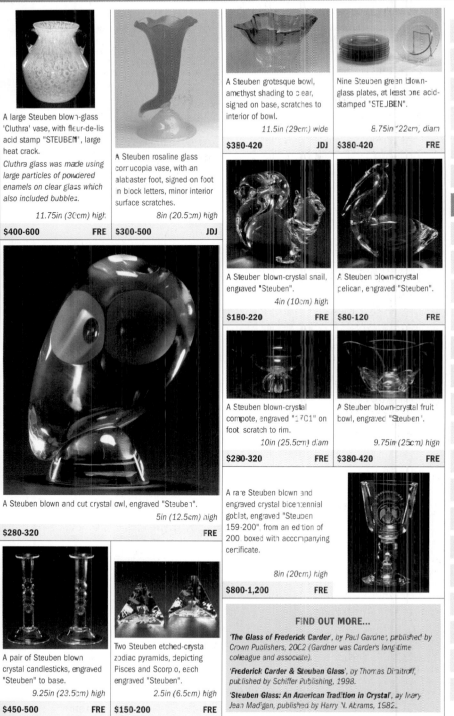

Collectors' Notes

■ The son of an American jeweler, Louis Comfort Tiffany (1848-1933) traveled widely in his youth, experiencing many different decorative styles. He founded the 'Tiffany Glass Company' in 1885 and began making lamps in 1890.

■ In 1894, he patented a technique to create an iridescent glass inspired by excavated Roman glass and called it 'Favrile'. It was treated with metal oxides and with acidic fumes to create a deeply lustrous iridescence. Tiffany made this glass in several colors, gold being the most popular and therefore the most commonly found today.

■ In 1924, Tiffany dissolved the glass company and it was bought by A.D. Nash, his employee and colleague. The resulting A. Douglas Nash Corporation continued to make glass in his styles, but without the Tiffany name. This company closed in 1931.

■ During the late 1960s, Tiffany's work was re-evaluated and collecting began. Fakes have appeared as prices have risen. Look at as much authentic Tiffany as possible and consult books to learn shapes, and which marks were used on different types of objects.

■ Small pieces of Tiffany are still affordable to the collector and there is enough variety to build up a satisfying collection. Quality was closely controlled at Tiffany so even these pieces are finely made.

A Tiffany iridescent gold bowl, with vertical ribbing and scalloped top, signed "LCT Favrile 1253", crack to base.

5in (12.5cm) diam

$200-250 JDJ

A Tiffany iridescent gold bowl, with blue and purple highlights, scalloped top, signed on base "LCT".

9in (23cm) diam

$500-700 JDJ

A Tiffany iridescent gold plate, coloring with vertical ribs and scalloped edge signed "LCT Favrile 3085", minor interior scratches.

7.25in (18.5cm) diam

$250-300 JDJ

A Tiffany iridescent gold finger bowl, with ten twists around the side, signed "LCT Favrile".

4.75in (12cm) diam

$500-700 JDJ

A Tiffany iridescent gold open salt bowl, with four feet and flaring rim, signed "LCT", one foot chipped.

2.25in (5.5cm) diam

$180-220 JDJ

A small Tiffany small iridescent gold vase, with blue highlights, signed on base "LCT M1438".

3in (7.5cm) high

$500-700 JDJ

A Tiffany small iridescent gold vase, with blue and amethyst highlights with eight applied rattails, signed on the base "LCT M5649", one small chip to one of the rattails.

4in (10cm) high

$500-700 JDJ

A Tiffany Favrile iridescent glass bowl, with incurved meandering rim, and exhibiting a mauve-golden sheen, signed "L.C.T." on base.

4in (10cm) high

$120-180 DN

A Tiffany blue Favrile glass jar, signed and with label, losses.

2.5in (6.5cm) high

$400-600 Daw

A Tiffany pastel bowl, with clear center and pastel green border at lip, signed on rim "LCT Favrile V998", some minor scratches to interior and evidence of grinding to the edge and underside of one place on lip.

7.75in (19.5cm) diam

$250-350 JDJ

Collectors' Notes

- Whitefriars, founded in the 17th century, was acquired by James Powell in 1834 and was renamed 'Powell & Sons'. It reverted to its original name in 1962.
- Powell & Sons became known for its fashionable art glass in the early 20th century, producing subtly colored and clear glass decorated with internal streaks or waves and applied external 'trails' of glass.
- Scandinavian glass, with its organic forms and subtle colors, was a strong influence. In 1954 the talented designer Geoffrey Baxter was employed, taking this aesthetic further and introducing new colors, casings, pulled lips and more fluid forms.
- Textured glass was highly fashionable during the 1960s and 1970s and Whitefriars, like Scandinavian factories, was at the forefront of this style with Baxter's 'Textured' range being designed in 1966 and released in 1967.

- The glass was blown into wooden molds with highly textured interiors, often with added internal protrusions such as wire or nail heads, that gave the exterior of the glass a strong texture.
- The 'Textured' range was diverse and immensely popular, with highly fashionable shapes such as the 'Banjo'. Despite this popularity, difficulties with the British economy took their toll on Whitefriars, which closed in 1980.
- Collecting interest has been strong for the past ten years and prices have risen. However, they still look set to rise further for rare, large and characteristic pieces. With textured examples, look for a good and varied range of texture on the exterior, as each time the mold was used it was burnt, affecting the interior texture. Pieces made in heavily used molds have little variation in the texture and are less desirable.

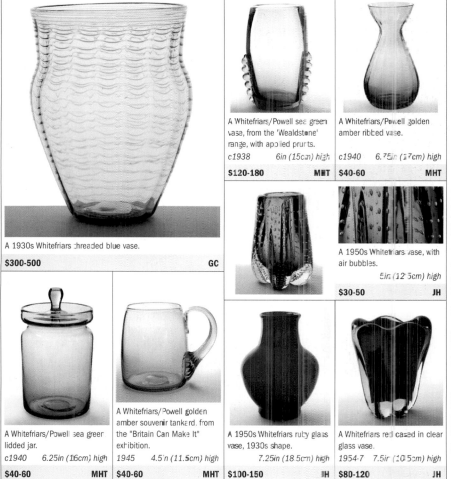

A 1930s Whitefriars threaded blue vase.

$300-500   **GC**

A Whitefriars/Powell sea green vase, from the 'Wealdstone' range, with applied prunts.
c1938   6in (15cm) high

$120-180   **MHT**

A Whitefriars/Powell golden amber ribbed vase.
c1940   6.75in (17cm) high

$40-60   **MHT**

A 1950s Whitefriars vase, with air bubbles.
5in (12.5cm) high

$30-50   **JH**

A Whitefriars/Powell sea green lidded jar.
c1940   6.25in (16cm) high

$40-60   **MHT**

A Whitefriars/Powell golden amber souvenir tankard, from the "Britain Can Make It" exhibition.
1945   4.5in (11.5cm) high

$40-60   **MHT**

A 1950s Whitefriars ruby glass vase, 1930s shape.
7.25in (18.5cm) high

$100-150   **JH**

A Whitefriars red cased in clear glass vase.
1954-7   7.5in (10.5cm) high

$80-120   **JH**

A Whitefriars 'Cow Parsley' vase, by Geoffrey Baxter.

c1955   *8.75in (22cm) high*

$400-600   **GC**

A Whitefriars 'Ocean Blue' glass vase, by Geoffrey Baxter.

This range appeared in the 1957 catalogue.

c1957   *6in (15.5cm) high*

$30-50   **GC**

Two Whitefriars 'Bat Wing' vases, by Geoffrey Baxter.

c1957   *9.5in (24.5cm) high*

$300-400   **GC**

A rare Whitefriars 'Aquamarine' vase, by Geoffrey Baxter.

This vase is made from two different colored glasses – blue and green. They were incompatible in the furnace and always broke down leading to the work being discarded. Only around five successful examples have ever been found by collectors.

c1957   *3.75in (9.5cm) high*

$1,200-1,800   **GC**

A rare Whitefriars 'Evening Sky' vase, by Geoffrey Baxter.

Like 'Aquamarine', this vase is made from two different colored glasses – blue and pink. Again, they were incompatible in the furnace. These were the only two colorways to have such problems. Only around ten successful examples are known of this technique.

c1957   *10in (25.5cm) high*

$1,200-1,800   **GC**

Two Whitefriars 'Beak' vases, by Geoffrey Baxter.

c1957   *12.25in (31cm) high*

$1,200-1,800   **GC**

A Whitefriars special commission large red dish, by Geoffrey Baxter.

c1958

$180-220   **MHT**

A large Whitefriars clear glass duck, with applied beak and foot and internal repeated rings of bubbles decoration.

6.5in (16.5cm) high

$40-60   **GC**

A late 1960s Whitefriars vase.

6.25in (16cm) high

$30-50   **JH**

A Whitefriars 'Shadow Green' waisted vase, by Geoffrey Baxter, from the Blown Soda range.

This range appeared in the 1962 catalogue.

c1962   *8in (20cm) high*

$20-30   **GC**

A Whitefriars cinnamon vase, by Geoffrey Baxter.

c1962   9.5in (24.5cm) high

$300-500   **GC**

A CLOSER LOOK AT A WHITEFRIARS VASE

A glassmaker making this vase lost control by accident one day and elongated the case, hence the name 'Swungout'.

It was produced in four colors; willow, cinnamon, indigo and later the rare pewter color.

Baxter liked the organic shape so much he put it into production.

Other names include the 'Mutton' or 'Lamb chop' vase and the 'Long John' vase.

A Whitefriars 'Swungout' willow colored glass vase, by Geoffrey Baxter.

c1962   15.75in (40cm) high

$800-1,200   **GC**

A 1960s Whitefriars vase, in cased glass.

6.25in (16cm) high

$30-50   **JH**

A 1960s Whitefriars sea green wave ribbed bowl, by Geoffrey Baxter.

12in (30.5cm) high

$70-100   **MHT**

A 1960s Whitefriars Sea Green vase, by Geoffrey Baxter.

7.75in (19.5cm) high

$100-150   **MHT**

A 1960s Whitefriars green optical ribbed bowl, by Geoffrey Baxter.

9.5in (24cm) wide

$70-100   **MHT**

A 1960s Whitefriars three-sided ruby glass vase, by Geoffrey Baxter.

9.5in (24cm) high

$30-50   **MHT**

A late 1960s Whitefriars clear and sage green swirl vase.

9.5in (24cm) high

$40-60   **JH**

A Whitefriars sage green color vase, by Geoffrey Baxter, from the Knobbly range.

7.5in (19cm) high

$40-60   **GC**

A Whitefriars sky blue full-lead crystal glass bud vase, by Geoffrey Baxter.

8.5in (21.5cm) high

$20-30   **GC**

A B C D E F G H I J K L M N O P Q R S T U V W XYZ

A Whitefriars 'Streaky Green' glass vase, by Geoffrey Baxter.

The Streaky range came in two colorways, Streaky Green and Streaky Purple.

c1972   *7in (17.5cm) high*

$80-120   **GC**

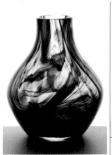

A Whitefriars 'Streaky Purple' glass vase, by Geoffrey Baxter.

c1972   *7in (18cm) high*

$120-180   **GC**

A Whitefriars 'New Studio' range ruby color glass vase, by Geoffrey Baxter, with applied silver chloride decoration.

The addition of silver chloride gives the glass this particular colored and streaked effect.

c1974   *7in (18cm) high*

$300-500   **GC**

A Whitefriars tangerine 'Stitched Square' glass vase, by Geoffrey Baxter.

The value of this vase is lower as there are a number of bubbles on the right hand side, that distract from the design and quality of glass.

6in (15cm) high

$100-150   **GC**

A Whitefriars aubergine color 'Stitched Square' glass vase, by Geoffrey Baxter.

6in (15cm) high

$280-320   **GC**

A Whitefriars 'Banjo' vase, by Geoffrey Baxter.

c1967   *12.5in (32cm) high*

$2,200-2,800   **GC**

A Whitefriars 'Rocket' vase, by Geoffrey Baxter.

c1967   *11.75in (30cm) high*

$1,500-2,000   **GC**

A Whitefriars cinnamon color 'Totem Pole' glass vase, by Geoffrey Baxter.

The pattern was made by nailing a curled thick wire to the inside of the mold. The nail head shapes can be seen at some of the corners. From the Textured range designed in 1966 and sold from 1967.

10.25in (26cm) high

$280-320   **GC**

A Whitefriars Ruby Red 'Late Textured' range vase, by Geoffrey Baxter.

c1972   *8in (20cm) high*

$80-120   **GC**

A Whitefriars tangerine color 'Basketweave' glass vase, by Geoffrey Baxter, from the 'Original Textured' range.

c1967   *10.75in (27cm) high*

$600-900   **GC**

A Whitefriars pewter color 'Pineapple' glass bottle, by Geoffrey Baxter, from the 'Late Textured' range.

c1972   *8in (20.5cm) high*

$120-180   **GC**

A Whitefriars tangerine color 'Pineapple' glass vase, by Geoffrey Baxter, from the 'Late Textured' range.

c1972   *7in (17.5cm) high*

$120-180   **GC**

A Whitefriars orange TV vase, designed in 1966.

c1967-73 6.75in (17cm) high

$150-200   **JH**

A Blenko tall Amberina glass vase, model 6223.

Blenko was founded by William Blenko, a British glassmaker, in 1922 in Milton, West Virginia. Blenko was a superb color maker and the factory also made stained glass. It was extremely successful and employed many designers from the mid-1940s, the most notable being ceramicist Winslow Anderson, Wayne Husted and, from 1964, Joel Philip Myers. Look for one-off hand-blown pieces by Myers. Colors are always bright and strong and the company still exists, producing domestic and decorative glass and stained glass.

c1962   11.5in (29cm) high

$100-150   **MHT**

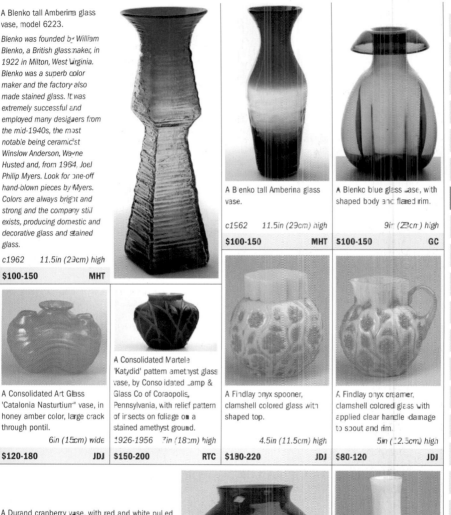

A Blenko tall Amberina glass vase.

c1962   11.5in (29cm) high

$100-150   **MHT**

A Blenko blue glass vase, with shaped body and flared rim.

9in (23cm) high

$100-150   **GC**

A Consolidated Art Glass 'Catalonia Nasturtium' vase, in honey amber color, large crack through pontil.

6in (15cm) wide

$120-180   **JDJ**

A Consolidated Martele 'Katydid' pattern amethyst glass vase, by Consolidated Lamp & Glass Co of Coraopolis, Pennsylvania, with relief pattern of insects on foliage on a stained amethyst ground.

1926-1956   7in (18cm) high

$150-200   **RTC**

A Findlay onyx spooner, clamshell colored glass with shaped top.

4.5in (11.5cm) high

$180-220   **JDJ**

A Findlay onyx creamer, clamshell colored glass with applied clear handle, damage to spout and rim.

5in (12.5cm) high

$80-120   **JDJ**

A Durand cranberry vase, with red and white pulled feather decoration and five wheel cut rosettes and leaves, unsigned, top has been ground, interior staining.

Durand glass was made at the Vineland Flint Glass Works, in Vineland New Jersey, and was founded in the late 19thC. After WWI, Victor Durand Jr. took over in 1924 and brought in designers and workers from the recently closed Quezal glassworks. A new art glass department was thus formed and was successful. However, when Durand died unexpectedly in 1931, the factory lost its way and was sold to the Kimball Glass Company in 1932.

8in (20.5cm) high

$400-500   **JDJ**

A Findlay onyx vase, clamshell colored glass with raised silver decoration, some small chipping to rim and base has crack along bottom and sides.

9in (23cm) high

$800-900   **JDJ**

A signed Kelva decorated box, raised scalloped edging around lid and base with hand painted floral decoration to the top of lid, good condition.

8in (20.5cm) diam

$120-180 JDJ

A Phoenix Glass goose vase, large oval-shaped blue vase with three raised white geese in flight decoration on each side and original paper label on bottom, two tiny fleabite flakes on top of rim.

9.5in (24cm) high

$300-400 JDJ

Three Pairpoint 'Vintage' pattern cobalt blue items, large footed centerpiece bowl engraved, two covered vases, bowl has internal surface scratches.

The Pairpoint Company was founded in New Bedford, Massachusetts, in 1880, initially making metal items. In 1894, they merged with Mount Washington to produce art glass, some combined with Pairpoint metal mounts. These strongly colored cobalt blue pieces in the 'Vintage' pattern are very popular and desirable, hence their high price. Pairpoint is also well known for its mold blown, glass-shaded lamps, which are much sought after.

12in (30.5cm) high

$2,200-2,800 JDJ

A Rubina Verde vase, swirl cranberry opalescent clear ruffled rim, small flake to top of rim.

4.75 (12cm) wide

$40-50 JDJ

A Smith Bros sweetmeat jar, melon ribbed with floral decorations and gold highlights on a faded yellow background, with a decorated silver-plated cover and rope twisted handle, signed on bottom.

5.5in (14cm) high

$200-400 JDJ

A Smith Bros creamer and sugar, decorated with blue pansies on a cream background, each is mounted with silver-plated hardware, dark tarnish to silver plate otherwise very good to excellent condition.

Creamer 3.75in (9.5cm) high

$300-500 JDJ

A signed Smith Bros. decorated vase, beige background vase with a vibrant decoration of a hummingbird and flowers, some wear to gold highlights, minor roughness to rim, otherwise good condition.

8in (20.5cm) high

$200-300 JDJ

A Smith Bros vase on stand, beige colored vase with floral decoration resting in a three-legged silver-plated stand with three perched birds, small flake to vase rim, plus minor roughness to rim.

11in (28cm) high

$150-300 JDJ

A Walter Dorwin Teague clear glass footed vase etched with circles and intersecting lines, some scratches to foot, unmarked.

Walter Dorwin Teague (1883-1960) was a leading American industrial designer who worked in many media including glass, plastic and metal and was a noted interior designer. His modern, often streamlined, designs are much sought after.

12in (30.5cm) high

$300-500 DRA

A Vasa Murrina vase, stretched green coloring with silver-plated rim cap, bruise to side of vase at widest point, otherwise very good condition.

9.25in (23.5cm) high

$100-200   **JDJ**

A signed Wave Crest powder jar, decorated milk glass covered powder jar, hinge broken, liner missing otherwise good condition.

5in (12.5cm) wide

$100-200   **JDJ**

A Wave Crest ferner, opalescent with gold and floral decoration, metal rim cap, metal feet, each foot having a lion's face.

Wave Crest was made by C.F. Monroe of Meriden, Connecticut. It is made from milk glass which is richly decorated, making it a form of art glass. Many pieces have brass mountings. Early pieces have a black mark, whilst later pieces bear a red mark or a paper label. Monroe also made the similar Kelva range.

7in (18cm) diam

$300-400   **JDJ**

A 1930s milk glass vase, with tear drop and dot pattern.

7in (18cm) high

$5-10   **TAB**

A 1930s milk glass bud vase, with rounded stepped base.

6in (15cm) high

$5-7   **TAB**

A 1930s milk glass fluted vase.

5.5in (14cm) high

$4-8   **TAB**

A 1930s milk glass powder puff container.

5in (12.5cm) wide

$4-8   **TAB**

A 1930s milk glass hobnail table lamp.

Milk glass, also known as 'opal' glass, is a translucent glass most familiarly produced in white, but also found in blue, yellow, and even black. Makers included McKee, Kemple and Westworeland Glass Co. It was primarily pressed or mold blown and was inexpensive, being used for commemorative pieces and tableware or in florists or as table vases in diners. The higher quality pieces and animal-shaped covered dishes are much sought after by collectors, many of the latter having been made by McKee. Modern reproductions are common but they are easily recognisable from the poorer quality molding and detailing.

14.25in (36cm) high

$20-30   **TAB**

A 1940s Tiffin opal glass beehive shaped vase, with flared rim.

8.75in (22cm) high

$30-40   **GC**

A B C D E F G H I J K L M N O P Q R S T U V W XYZ

A 1940s Tiffin opal glass banded vase.

6.5in (16.5cm) high

$30-40 GC

A large iridescent gold vase, with green heart and vine decoration, unsigned, large crack to base.

11.5in (29cm) high

$280-320 JDJ

An iridescent art glass vase, the gold base with red heart and vine decoration, button pontil, unsigned, crack to base.

Although unsigned, the attractive contrasting red 'Art Nouveau' leaf and tendril inspired design and the quality of the gold iridescent surface make this a desirable and valuable piece, despite its damage.

11.25in (28.5cm) high

$450-500 JDJ

An iridescent art glass vase, the gold coloring with green dot pattern, ruffled top, unsigned, vase has a large crack.

4.25in (11cm) diam

$60-80 JDJ

A decorated shaker, handpainted leaves on a yellow fading to white background.

3in (7.5cm) high

$30-50 JDJ

An egg-shaped shaker, blue fading to yellow with handpainted floral decoration.

2.5in (6.5cm) high

$30-50 JDJ

A swirled glass vase, melon shaped four-cornered ruffled top cranberry to opalescent vase, chip to top ruffle.

6.5in (16.5cm) wide

$60-80 JDJ

A cranberry opal stripe basket, with four corner ruffled top and applied twisted handle, crack where one side of handle is applied.

7.5in (19cm) high

$120-180 JDJ

A pink pitcher, with applied handle and flower, light to dark pink shading, amber colored applied ruffle rim and feet and applied flower.

10.5in (26.5cm) high

$200-250 JDJ

A daisy and button amber-colored pitcher, with applied reeded handle.

5in (12.5cm) high

$12-18 JDJ

A CLOSER LOOK AT A PAIR OF AGATA TUMBLERS

Agata was patented by the New England Glass Company in 1886 and was derived by Joseph Locke from their 'Wild Rose' peachblow range.

The more marked and numerous the splotches, the more desirable and valuable a piece is, with the most desirable having an all-over pattern.

It is made from one layer of glass, the outer surface of which is decorated with random 'splotches'.

The colors on these examples are very strong and have good tonal variation. This glass is virtually never signed.

A pair of Agata tumblers, rich color and nice shading with only moderate staining.

3.75in (9.5cm) high

$300-400 JDJ

Collectors' Notes

■ The major Western holidays, including Christmas and Halloween, have been celebrated for centuries, but it was not until the early 20th century that items associated with them began to be made on a larger scale. Over the past decade, collecting memorabilia has mushroomed.

■ Santa Claus is perhaps the most popular character. Many credit artist Haddon Sundblom and his series of advertisements for Coca-Cola with popularizing the now-familiar appearance of Santa.

■ Santa figures produced during and before the 1930s are scarce and very desirable. Along with decorations and ornaments, the vast majority were made in Germany until WWII. From the 1930s onward, Japan became an increasingly prolific producer, making many items from celluloid. The US also began to produce pieces from the 1920s.

■ The tradition of using a Christmas tree as a room centerpiece is reputed to have been brought to the UK from Germany by Queen Victoria's husband Prince Albert. They were not commonly used in the US until the 1920s. Early trees made from colored 'goose feather' are highly desirable today. By the 1960s, plastic had overtaken tin and glass as the material for ornaments and the 'golden age' of collectible holiday memorabilia had all but ended.

■ Halloween, the ancient pagan festival celebrated the day before the Christian festival All Saints Day, began to take off as a public celebration in the US in the 1890s. By the 1930s it had become a commercial event. 'Trick or treating', where children are 'bribed' with sweets to prevent them causing mischief has been popular in the US ever since. As a result much of the memorabilia associated with this festival relates to sweets. Characterful jack-o-lanterns, which were produced in quantity, are becoming scarcer and highly collectible.

A German Christmas 'Belsnickle', sweet container, white with red trim and with original feather tree branch.

It is unusual to find a Belsnickle (or Nicholas in fur) with a colored trim, making this example more desirable.

c1910   8in (20cm) high

$1,000-1,500   SotT

A 1930s Japanese Christmas sweet bag, with celluloid Santa face.

7in (18cm) high

$70-100   SotT

▲ 1920s/1930s American papier-mâché Christmas roly-poly, by Schoenhut.

5in (12.5cm) high

$250-300   SotT

▲ 1930s German Christmas sweet container, in the form of a Santa which separates at the waist, with rabbit fur beard, felt jacket, composition pants and boots and feather tree branch.

8in (20cm) high

$400-600   SotT

A 1930s Occupied Japan Santa Claus on skis figure, with papier-mâché face and felt face.

The skis are usually missing from these figures.

$60-90   SotT

A 1940s Japanese composition and felt Santa Claus figure.

5.5in (14cm) high

$100-150   SotT

A 1950s American plaster coated Santa Claus figure.

7in (18cm) high

$60-90   SotT

A 1940s German plaster-coated pressed card Christmas sweet container, in the form of a snowman, with "Venetian" glass coating.

5in (14cm) high

$120-180   SotT

F 1950s American plastic Christmas lolly holder in the form of a snowman on skis.

5in (12.5cm) high

$30-50   SotT

A 1920s German Christmas feather tree, made from a green-dyed goose feather.

These trees came in a number of sizes, and the larger versions are usually more collectible. Colored trees such as blue or burgundy are also more sought-after.

8.5in (21.5cm) high

$70-100 SotT

Halloween Memorabilia

German pressed card Halloween black cat lantern, with original candle insert and face.

This is the second largest of six sizes.

3.5in (9cm) high

$400-600 SotT

An early American small Christmas tree, laden with assorted Christmas decorations and ornaments.

$500-700 BCAC

A 1930s German Halloween sweet container, in the form of a black cat on a jack o'lantern.

4.5in (11.5cm) high

$180-220 SotT

A 1920s German card Halloween jack o'lantern rattle, with paper lithographed decoration and metal feet.

$220-280 SotT

A Santa Christmas cake decoration.

1.5in (3.5cm) high

$20-30 LG

A standing ceramic Snowbaby.

Snowbabies were first made in Germany in the early 20thC, and may have been inspired by marzipan cake decorations. Condition and size are important aspects of value, with larger sizes fetching much higher prices. These larger-sized babies are also usually more detailed and more finely modeled. Beware as many Far Eastern reproductions have been made since the 1960s, which have noticeably less fine painting and modeling, especially around the face.

1.5in (3.5cm) high

$30-50 LG

A Christmas cake decoration, of a boy in a red outfit with teddy.

1.75in (4.5cm) high

$30-50 LG

A 1930s German Halloween sweet container, in the form of a witch.

4.25in (11cm) high

$220-280 SotT

A 1930s German wooden Halloween ratchet, with papier-mâché witch face.

4.25in (11cm) wide

$200-400 SotT

A 1920s/30s German Halloween sweet container, in the form of a vegetable man on a base.

3in (7.5cm) high

$220-280   SotT

A 1930s German Halloween sweet container, in the form of a bale of hay with a face.

2in (5cm) high

$220-280   SctT

A 1930s German plester-coated Halloween jack o'lantern, with original insert face.

3.5in (9cm) high

$220-280   SotT

A rare 1940s double-sided papier mâché Hallowe'en lantern.

$150-200   JPA

A 1950s American pressed pulp Halloween jack o'lantern with two-tone and original insert face.

Two-tone faces are rare and desirable.

4.75in (12cm) high

$120-180   SotT

A 1950s American pressed pulp jack o'lantern, with green top and original insert face.

4.5in (11.5cm) high

$100-150   SotT

A 1950s American pressed pulp Halloween party cup, with original base.

$60-90   SotT

A 1950s plastic Halloween lolly holder, decorated with a black cat and jack o'lantern.

2.75in (7cm) high

$20-30   SotT

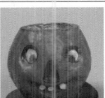

A 1950s plastic Halloween lolly holder on wheels, in the shape of a jack o'lantern, with a witch and cat.

3in (7.5cm) high

$60-90   SotT

A 1950s tin Halloween no semaker, by US Metal, with wooden handle.

5in (12.5cm) long

$40-60   SotT

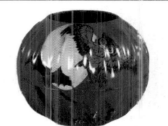

A US Metal Toy Mfg. Co. 'Trick or Treat' Pumpkin, good condition.

6in (15cm) diam

$12-18   SAS

Collectors' Notes

- Thanksgiving, a festival celebrating and thanking God for blessings received that year, was first celebrated in 1619 and then in 1621. It continued sporadically across America and in 1789 George Washington proclaimed November 26th as a day of national thanksgiving. In 1941, after two small date changes, Congress set the date as being the fourth Thursday of November.

- The most desirable and valuable pieces of holiday memorabilia date from the first few decades of the 20thC. 19thC items are very rare and can be very valuable. Items focus around the traditional icon of thanksgiving, the turkey.

- Easter is the Christian festival which commemorates the resurrection of Christ. It is held on the Sunday after the first full moon following the spring Equinox (March 21). The word is thought to come from 'Eostre', the name of the pagan goddess of Spring.

- The traditional Easter egg symbolizes the central theme of new life and rebirth. The Easter bunny is often said to have begun as a hare, which was the earthly form taken by Eostre. The Germans began the Easter tradition of making and giving candy and cakes. Emigration spread it to the US, where the tradition was taken up and developed.

- Items from Germany are highly collectible. Look for early pieces, such as candy containers, and particularly examples marked 'Germany' which generally date from before 1918. Those marked 'German Republic' date from c1918-1933. Japanese pieces, usually in composition or celluloid, date from the late 1940s onward.

A 1940s German papier-mâché Thanksgiving turkey hen candy container, opening at the neck.

3.75in (9.5cm) high

$100-150 | **SotT**

A 1940s American composition Thanksgiving turkey candy container.

6.5in (16.5cm) high

$200-300 | **SotT**

A 1950s Japanese composition Thanksgiving turkey candy container.

4in (10cm) high

$40-60 | **SotT**

A 1950s Japanese plaster-coated Thanksgiving candy container, in the form of a turkey on spring legs.

4in (10cm) high

$50-80 | **SotT**

A 1920s German Easter dressed female rabbit candy container, with flocked head and glass eyes.

6in (15cm) high

$300-350 | **SotT**

A 1950s Japanese composition Thanksgiving turkey table favor.

3.5in (9cm) high

$120-180 | **SotT**

A 1930 German pressed hard board Easter crouching rabbit candy container.

5.5in (14cm) high

$100-150 | **SotT**

A 1940s German plaster-coated Easter bunny candy container, with spring ears and glass eyes.

4.5in (11.5cm) high

$100-150 | **SotT**

A 1940s German gold plaster-coated papier-mâché Easter bunny candy container.

5.25in (13.5cm) high

$80-120 | **SotT**

A Georgian gold-framed panel brooch, with glazed hair locket center, the rectangular frame of naturalistic form.

1in (2.5cm) wide

$150-200 F

A late 19thC gold-filled mourning pin, containing hair.

Mourning jewelry is the collective name for jewelry commemorating a deceased person. The person is remembered by an inscription, photograph or with a 'relic', such as a locks of hair which are sometimes woven into a pattern. It was very popular in the Victorian period, but originated centuries before.

2in (5cm) high

$50-80 TAB

A late 19thC gold-filled mourning pin, with hair in the form of a wheatsheaf.

2.25in (5.5cm) high

$30-50 TAB

A Victorian gold mourning brooch, with an overlaid quatrefoil design, set with seed pearls with blue enamel and ropework, photo locket reverse.

$180-220 F

A Victorian gold-foiled garnet and quartz brooch, of quatrefoil pattern with closed back collet mounts, new pin to reverse.

After the death of Prince Albert, Queen Victoria went into mourning, wearing the traditional mourning color of black. Mourning became a national obsession and even dictated jewelry taste, with dark and black jewelry being more popular than bright, sparkling pieces.

$320-380 F

A Victorian gold locket brooch, with wire and bead decoration, rock crystal front panel, glazed reverse and containing a Russian gentleman's portrait, painted on ivory, slight damage to frame.

1.75in (4.5cm) high

$280-320 F

A Victorian brooch, the central oval-cut amethyst within a seed pearl surround.

1.25in (3cm) wide

$280-320 F

A Victorian 15ct gold panel brooch, of oval design with bead and wirework decoration and glazed locket reverse.

1.5in (4cm) wide

$60-90 F

1.75in (4.5cm) diam

A 15ct gold decorative bar brooch, set with a single old-cut diamond.

$60-90 F

A Victorian gold gem-set brooch, of circular form, with foiled aquamarine center stones in leaf and buckle panels, the frame with applied wirework detail.

1.75in (4.5cm) diam

$280-320 F

A Victorian gold wreath brooch, set with pearls and demantoid garnets in between delicately enameled leaves of white and green.

$350-400 F

A Victorian diamond and enamel circular locket, the central brilliant cut diamond within a single-cut diamond surround, to a deep blue enamel ground, with locket reverse, later mounted on a 9ct gold bar brooch.

2in (5cm) wide

$180-220   **F**

An Edwardian 14ct gold seed pearl brooch, designed as two shamrocks each set to the center with a seed pearl.

1in (2.5cm) wide

$120-180   **F**

An Edwardian 15ct gold openwork brooch, set with amethyst and seed pearls.

$400-600   **F**

An Edwardian 9ct gold insect brooch, modeled as a spider with a circular-cut amethyst thorax and oval-cut abdomen.

2in (5cm) long

$150-200   **F**

An early 20thC 15ct gold diamond bar brooch, collet set to the center with an old brilliant-cut diamond.

$180-220   **F**

An Art Deco 15ct white gold, sapphire and diamond bar brooch, set to the center with a rectangular-cut sapphire between two pairs of single-cut diamonds.

2.25in (5.5cm) long

$280-320   **F**

A white metal pin in the form of an aeroplane viewed from the front, the 'body' and 'engines' of the plane set with rose-cut diamonds.

Possibly made to commemorate or commissioned by a WWII fighter pilot.

c1940   *2.25in (5.5cm) long*

$150-200   **F**

A CLOSER LOOK AT A GEORG JENSEN PIN

Georg Jensen (1866-1935) is a highly popular maker. He opened his design, jewelry and silverware company in Copenhagen, Denmark in 1904.

His designs were most often inspired by nature.

This is typical of his work, where simple, elegant forms were combined with ornamentation.

Although the workshop is still active today, vintage pieces such as this are hotly sought after.

A Georg Jensen pin, in the form of a grazing deer in woods, reverse stamped "298".

2.25in (5.5cm) wide

$500-700   **TAB**

An oval brooch of two halves, set with graduated cultured pearls and diamonds to the center, mounted in white metal, originally a double clip.

$320-380   **F**

A 14ct white gold spray brooch, set with ten cultured pearls and having baguette and eight-cut diamonds to the stem and leaves.

$350-400   **F**

An 18ct white gold diamond set dog-shaped brooch/pendant, with textured finish and yellow gold collar set with eight brilliant-cut diamonds.

1in (2.5cm) wide

$120-180   **F**

An Art Deco 18ct white gold and platinum single stone diamond ring, in box setting with stepped design to the shoulders.

The use of platinum and geometric shapes, which even extend to the stones, are hallmarks of Art Deco jewelry.

$600-900   **F**

An Art Deco style graduated five stone emerald-cut diamond half hoop ring, flanked to either side by a small baguette diamond.

$500-700   **F**

A platinum mounted Art Deco style cocktail ring, with a central circular jade panel in a diamond-set head, with a marquise black onyx set to either side.

$400-600   **F**

A platinum mounted two stone old-cut diamond crossover ring.

$500-700   **F**

A Victorian gold ring, set with five turquoise stones, with plain tapering band.

$100-150   **F**

An Edwardian 18ct gold gentleman's ring, set with a central cushion shape old-cut diamond, flanked to either side by pear shape old-cut diamonds, Birmingham hallmarks.

1908

$700-1,000   **F**

A circular aquamarine and diamond cluster ring, with millegrain edging and a single diamond to either shoulder.

$400-600   **F**

An 18ct gold diamond cluster ring.

$500-700   **F**

A graduated five stone old-cut diamond half hoop ring.

$1,000-1,500   **F**

A tinted yellow old-cut diamond single stone ring, with clawset mount, stamped "18ct".

$400-600   **F**

An 18ct gold oval carved coral cameo ring, depicting the face of a Classical female, with a small diamond set to either shoulder

$300-400   **F**

A 9ct gold dress ring, in the form of a hand with opal and garnet set cuff and ring to finger set with garnet.

$100-150   **F**

A B C D E F G H I J K L M N O P Q R S T U V W XYZ

A Victorian gold, black enamel and seed pearl pendant, set to the center with three seed pearls to an engraved and enameled scroll shaped surround, suspended from a hexagonal bar, with belcher chain.

$220-280   **F**

A Victorian oval coral, diamond and enamel locket/pendant, set to the center with an oval coral bead, within a black enamel border, star set with rose-cut diamonds, with locket reverse and snake link chain.

1.5in (3.5cm) long

$400-600   **F**

A Victorian gold-mounted agate and split pearl locket-back pendant, with a high domed red agate center in pearl surround with bow surmount, glazed back missing.

1.25in (3cm) diam

$320-380   **F**

An Edwardian gold, ruby and seed pearl pendant, in the form of a lady's gloved hand, set with two circular-cut rubies and a seed pearl in a shamrock motif, with an 18ct gold belcher link chain.

1.5in (4cm) long

$150-200   **F**

An Edwardian 15ct gold amethyst and seed pearl set openwork pendant.

$500-700   **F**

An Art Nouveau pendant, set with pink tourmaline, seed pearls and peridot.

The almost organic, plant-like curves, as well as the overall design, identify this as being in the Art Nouveau style.

$600-900   **F**

A citrine and agate pendant, of wirework scroll form, collet set with seven circular-cut citrines, with central pansy carved agate, with belcher link chain.

Pendant 3.25in (8cm) long

$280-320   **F**

An early 20thC 18ct gold, platinum and diamond treble clef pendant, claw set with two brilliant-cut diamonds.

1.5in (4cm) long

$300-500   **F**

A European gold pendant of Art Nouveau design, set with an old-cut diamond and two pearls, with a further pearl drop.

$600-900   **F**

A Wedgwood jasperware oval pendant/brooch, decorated with a Classical figure, with scroll surmount.

2in (5cm) long

$80-120   **F**

A 1950s red coral necklace and pin.

Pin 2in (5cm) high

$50-80   **TAB**

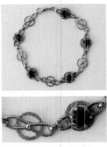

A Victorian turquoise fancy link bracelet, the central scroll-shaped panel collet set with five circular turquoise cabochons, with locket back, to an articulated chain with engraved waisted hexagonal spacers.

Turquoise stones were typically used as ornamentation from the 1840s to the 1880s, although they are found on later pieces.

$300-500   **F**

An early 20thC 9ct gold and turquoise gate link bracelet, composed of seven three-bar links, each collet set to the center with a circular turquoise cabochon, with brick link spacers and snap fastening.

$300-350   **F**

An 18ct gold jade bracelet, with five pierced and carved octagonal jade pendants between belcher links, with octagonal snap fastening cast with a Chinese character.

$280-320   **F**

A 9ct gold bracelet, claw set with five hessonite garnets interspaced by oval and circular links.

$150-200   **F**

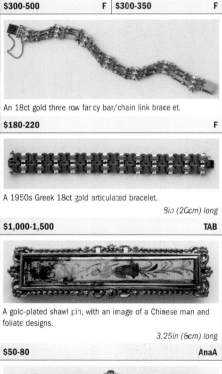

An 18ct gold three row fancy bar/chain link bracelet.

$180-220   **F**

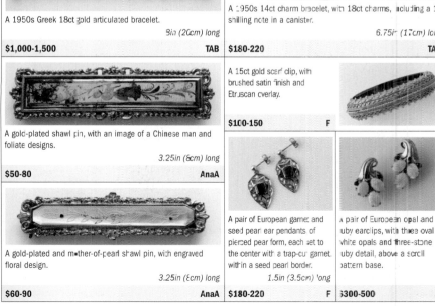

A 1950s 14ct charm bracelet, with 18ct charms, including a 10 shilling note in a canister.

6.75in (17cm) long

$180-220   **TAB**

A 1950s Greek 18ct gold articulated bracelet.

8in (20cm) long

$1,000-1,500   **TAB**

A 15ct gold scarf clip, with brushed satin finish and Etruscan overlay.

$100-150   **F**

A gold-plated shawl pin, with an image of a Chinese man and foliate designs.

3.25in (8cm) long

$50-80   **AnaA**

A pair of European garnet and seed pearl ear pendants of pierced pear form, each set to the center with a trap-cut garnet within a seed pearl border.

1.5in (3.5cm) long

$180-220   **F**

A pair of European opal and ruby earclips, with three oval white opals and three-stone ruby detail, above a scroll pattern base.

$300-500   **F**

A gold-plated and mother-of-pearl shawl pin, with engraved floral design.

3.25in (8cm) long

$60-90   **AnaA**

A B C D E F G H I J K L M N O P Q R S T U V W XYZ

A pair of American silver cuff links, the pointed oval faces connected by one large link and engraved "H" on one side and "C" on the other, unmarked, scratches and dents.

It is unusual to find such early cufflinks.

c1770   0.75in (2cm) long

$300-400   **FRE**

A pair of American lady's enameled and pressed metal cuff links.

0.75in (2cm) high

$30-40   **AnaA**

A pair of chain link panel cuff links, each decorated with a flower and set with a single gem including diamond, emerald, sapphire and ruby.

$150-200   **F**

An early 20thC pair of American onyx inlaid pressed brass cuff links.

1in (2.5cm) diam

$20-30   **AnaA**

An early 20thC pair of 18ct gold, platinum, onyx and seed pearl cuff links, of hexagonal form, each millegrain collet set to the center with a seed pearl to an onyx ground.

$180-220   **F**

A 1920-30s pair of enamel double-sided cuff links.

$100-150   **CVS**

A pair of oval gold-plated base metal cuff links, with initials.

0.5in (1.5cm) wide

$15-25   **AnaA**

A pair of 1950s novelty horse's head gold-plated cuff links.

0.5in (1.5cm) wide

$20-30   **AnaA**

A pair of 1930s American enameled cuff links, in the form of clock faces.

0.75in (2cm) diam

$50-80   **AnaA**

A pair of base metal oval cuff links, decorated with ocean liners, with belcher links, possibly a souvenir of the HMS Queen Mary.

Base metal cuff links such as these can be found with a variety of images, including sporting, drinking and animal themes, usually fetching around the same value as this example unless the image is rare or can be traced to a notable event or person.

$40-60   **F**

A 1960s set of gold and diamanté wraparounds and matching shirt studs, made in the US.

3.5in (9cm) wide

$100-150   **SM**

A pair of silver gilt cuff links, enameled in red, blue and green in a harlequin design, with belcher link connections, Birmingham hallmarks.

1998

$70-100   **F**

Lea Stein

- Paris-based designer Lea Stein (b. 1931) started her design company in 1957 and by 1965 was making buttons from rhodoid, a form of cellulose acetate used to make spectacle frames.

- By the end of the 1960s Stein had started to design jewelry from the same material using a lamination process she had invented which allowed her to create the layers of color, texture and pattern for which she has become famous. Consequently, no two Lea Stein pieces are identical. They are all signed.

- Lea Stein's vintage period lasted from 1969 to 1981. During this period the company grew to employ more than 50, but competition from Asia forced it to close. An American dealer bought a large number of pieces and began selling them and making them popular with collectors.

- Vintage pieces include Rabbit, Rhino, Panther, Crocodile, Choupette (basset hound), Poodle, Tomcat, Felix, Carmen (Joan Crawford), Ballerina (Scarlett O'Hara), Skateboard Boy, Tennis Woman and stretch bracelets.

- Stein returned to designing in 1988, making one or two new pieces a year as well as recreating vintage designs. For example, the fox, her most popular piece, is a vintage piece still made today. Collectors should be aware that it is very hard to tell new and vintage pieces apart and they are all signed in the same way: 'Lea Stein – Paris' on the pin backing.

- New designs include Buba (owl), Bacchus, Gomina (sleeping cat), Atila (standing cat), Tortoise and Ric (dog). Mrs Ladybug was introduced in 1988, Porcupine and Gompil (fox's head) in 2000, Penguin and Cicada in 2001 and 2002 saw a new cat, Sacha.

A late 1970s Lea Stein Gomina 'Sleeping Cat' pin, made of laminated rhodoid.

3in (7.5cm) wide

$70-100　　　　**Cris**

A late 1980s Lea Stein 'Black Cat with Ball' pin, made of laminated rhodoid.

2.75in (7cm) wide

$70-100　　　　**Cris**

Two early 1990s Lea Stein Bacchus 'Cat's Head' pins, made of laminated rhodoid.

2.5in (6cm) wide

$60-90 (each)　　**Cris**

An early 1990s Lea Stein 'Tortoise' or 'Turtle' pin made of laminated rhodoid.

3in (8cm) long

$60-90　　　　**Cris**

A 1980s Lea Stein 'Felix Brothers' cat pin made of laminated rhodoid.

3.25in (8.5cm) high

$100-150　　　　**Cris**

An early 1990s Lea Stein 'Little Tortoise' pin, made of laminated rhodoid.

2.5in (6cm) wide

$50-80　　　　**Cris**

A Lea Stein 'Porcupine' pin, made of laminated rhodoid.

2000-2001 3in (7.5cm) wide

$60-90　　　　**Cris**

A late 1980s Lea Stein 'Hippo' pin, made of laminated rhodoid.

1.5in (4cm) wide

$60-90　　　　**Cris**

A late 1980s Lea Stein 'Owl' pin, made of laminated rhodoid.

1.5in (3.5cm) high

$60-90　　　　**Cris**

A late 1980s Lea Stein 'Elephant' pin, made of laminated rhodoid.

2.5in (6cm) wide

$70-100 Cris

A late 1980s Lea Stein 'Ric' dog pin, made of laminated rhodoid.

3.5in (9cm) long

$60-90 Cris

A Lea Stein 'Penguin' pin, made of laminated rhodoid.

2001-2002 3.5in (9cm) high

$100-150 Cris

A late 1980s Lea Stein 'Rooster' pin, made of laminated rhodoid.

2.5in (6.5cm) wide

$60-90 Cris

An early 1980s Lea Stein 'Buba' owl pin, made of laminated rhodoid.

2.5in (6cm) high

$60-90 Cris

An early 1980s Lea Stein 'Half-Colorette' pin, made of laminated rhodoid.

2in (5.5cm) diam

$70-100 Cris

An early 1980s Lea Stein 'Indian' pin, made of laminated rhodoid.

2in (5.5cm) high

$100-150 Cris

A late 1980s Lea Stein 'Edelweiss' flower pin, made of laminated rhodoid.

3.5in (8.5cm) high

$100-150 Cris

A 1980s Lea Stein 'Ballerina' pin, also known as a 'Scarlett O'Hara' pin, made of laminated rhodoid.

2.5in (6.5cm) high

$100-150 Cris

Two late 1990s Lea Stein 'Cravat-tie' pins, made of laminated rhodoid, the left with gold inclusions.

3.5in (9cm) long

$70-100 (each) Cris

A 1980s Lea Stein square 'Rainbow Umbrella' pin, made from laminated rhodoid.

1.5in (4cm) wide

$80-120 Cris

A late 1970s Lea Stein 'Egyptian Eye' pin, made of laminated rhodoid.

3in (8cm) wide

$70-100 Cris

Trifari

A 1930s Trifari gold-plated pin.
3in (8cm) long

$300-350 | Rox

A 1950s Trifari faux pearl pin.
3in (7.5cm) wide

$70-100 | Cris

A 1950s Trifari turquoise and ruby 'Bow', on gold-plated casting.
3in (8cm) long

$180-220 | Cris

A 1950s Trifari 'Maltese Cross' pin, gold-plated with blue cabochons, blue enamel and clear crystal rhinestones.
2.5in (6.5cm) diam

$70-100 | Cris

A mid-1950s Trifari 'Maple Leaf' pin, gold-plated with coral cabochons.
The maple leaf is the national symbol of Canada.
3in (8cm) long

$80-120 | Cris

A 1930s Trifari citrine belly 'Fish' pin, by Alfred Philippe.
2.25in (6cm) long

$220-280 | Rox

A late 1950s Trifari silver alloy 'Tulip' pin.
3.25in (8.5cm) long

$40-60 | Cris

A 1950s Trifari stylized 'Fruit' brooch, with gilt chain tassels.
6.75in (17cm) long

$80-120 | Cris

A 1950s Trifari pink and white 'Flower' necklace.
Flowers 0.5in (1cm) diam

$300-400 | Rox

A 1950s Trifari 'Floral' motif necklace and earrings, with faux pearls and small black crystal rhinestones on gold-plated castings.
Necklace 15in (38cm) long

$700-1,000 | Cris

A 1960s Trifari pink pin, with pairs of clip and dropper earrings.
Pin 2.25in (6cm) long

$70-100 | Rox

Marcel Boucher

- French-born Marcel Boucher was apprenticed to Cartier in Paris. In 1925 he moved to America and continued to work for the firm until the 1930s, when he moved to Mazer Bros in New York where he designed shoe buckles.
- His first collection of costume jewelry consisted of twelve bird brooches which were bought by Saks Fifth Avenue and became an extraordinary commercial success.
- The company was active from 1937 to 1971. Boucher's designs are renowned for the way they mixed traditional and imaginative designs, especially a fusion of naturalistic and geometric forms.
- Pieces popular with collectors include enamel figural brooches from the 1930s, brooch and earring sets from the 1950s and 1960s, and parures from the same era.

A 1950s Marcel Boucher necklace, bracelet and earrings, twisted-rope design, alternating between gilded strand and pavé crystal strand.

Pavé setting is a technique used to mount stones in a side-by-side formation, so that the setting is barely visible in between.

Earrings 1in (2.5cm) diam

$400-600 — Cris

A 1940s Marcel Boucher necklace and earrings, rhodium-plated with clear crystal rhinestones.

Necklace 15in (38cm) diam

$400-600 — Cris

A 1950s Marcel Boucher 'Leaf' motif necklace, silver-plated.

16.5in (42cm) long

$80-120 — Cris

A 1950s Marcel Boucher circular 'Floral and Bow' motifs pin and earrings, with sapphire blue and clear crystal rhinestones on a rhodium-plated frame.

Pin 2in (5cm) diam

$80-120 — Cris

A 1950s Marcel Boucher fold-over necklace with movable clasp, in heavy gold plate and claw-set clear set crystals, with two pendant faux pearl drops.

24in (61cm) long

$300-400 — Cris

A 1950s Marcel Boucher 'Leaves' pin and earrings, gold-plated with clear crystal rhinestone highlights.

Pin 4in (10cm) high

$80-120 — Cris

A 1950s Marcel Boucher 'Fruit Tree' pin, with a ladder and basket, the tree, basket and ladder rhodium-plated, the fruits of faux pearl and faux turquoise.

1.5in (4cm) high

$60-90 — Cris

A 1940s Marcel Boucher retro-style bow pin, sterling silver and gold-plated with faux sapphires and rhinestones, with a Marcel Boucher logo and marked "sterling".

3in (7.5cm) long

$280-320 — RG

A 1950s Marcel Boucher 'Rooster' pin, gold-plated with a faux pearl.

1.5in (4cm) high

$40-60 — Cris

A late 1940s pair of Marcel Boucher retro-style 'Fan' motif earrings, gold-plated.

1in (2.5cm) long

$20-30 — Cris

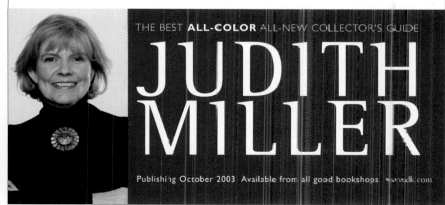
A
B
C
D
E
F
G
H
I
J
K
L
M
N
O
P
Q
R
S
T
U
V
W
XYZ

JEWELRY

NAPIER

- Napier was founded in 1875 in North Attleboro, Massachusetts, and originally named Whitney & Rice. It manufactured chatelaines, watch chains and silver plated matchboxes.

- The company changed its name to Carpenter & Bliss in 1882 and nine years later moved to Meridien, Connecticut. By this time it was a pioneer of the new fashion for costume jewelry.

- It became The Napier Company in 1922 and success was assured in the 1950s when it received a number of publicity coups, including photographs of Miss America with a box overflowing with Napier jewelry.

- By the 1960s it had more than 1,200 designs and today it is the largest costume jewelry manufacturer in the US.

- It is known for its striking yet sober designs featuring clean lines and basic shapes: triangles, squares and circles are frequently used.

A Napier necklace, bracelet and earrings demi-parure, gold-plated with clear crystal rhinestones.

Necklace 16in (41cm) long

$120-180   **Cris**

A late 1950s Napier 'Fruit' motif charm bracelet, with silver alloy fruits and chain.

8in (20cm) long

$100-150   **Cris**

A mid-1950s Napier 'Leaf' pin and earrings, gold-plated.

Pin 2in (5cm) high

$50-80   **Cris**

A mid-1950s Napier 'Elephant' pin, with blue and red crystal rhinestones and faux pearl drops on a gold-plated casting.

1.5in (3.5cm) high

$60-90   **Cris**

A mid-1950s Napier charm bracelet, gold-plated with green, turquoise, rose-pink and amethyst crystal rhinestones, green and dark- and light-blue glass beads and a faux pearl.

7in (18cm) long

$120-180   **Cris**

VENDÔME

- Vendôme was established as a subsidiary of Coro in 1944 when the mark was first used on charm bracelets and pieces of faux pearl jewelry. The Vendôme line became successful in the 1960s when Helen Marion began designing for the line.

- Vendôme's combination of good design and superior materials led it to supersede Corocraft as Coro's top line.

- The Vendôme mark was last used in 1979.

- Look for good quality rhinestones and faceted crystal beads.

A mid-1950s Vendôme floral pin and earrings, with blue and white lucite flowers and green lucite leaves, with clear crystal rhinestone highlights.

Pin 2in (5cm) wide

$150-200   **Cris**

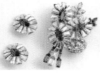

A mid-1950s Vendôme 'Floral' motif pin and earrings, with blue crystal rhinestones and faux pearls, hand-wired to filigree gold-plated frames.

Pin 2in (5cm) diam

$100-150 Cris

A late 1950s Vendôme bangle and earrings, silver-plated with powder-blue cabochons and sapphire crystal rhinestones.

Earrings 1.5in (4cm) diam

$300-350 Cris

A 1950s Vendôme brooch, in the shape of a bouquet of flowers, set with aurora borealis and clear stones in keystone settings.

3.25in (8.5cm) long

$280-320 Cris

A mid-1950s Vendôme floral pin and earrings with silver filigree, green and blue crystal rhinestones and faux pearls.

Pin 2in (5cm) high

$100-150 Cris

A 1960s Vendôme necklace and earrings, gold-plated and set with paste baguettes.

This necklace can be extended which is a sign of quality.

18.75in (48cm) long

$220-280 Wain

A mid-1950s Vendôme necklace and earrings, with peridot, topaz, citrine and lines of aurora borealis stones, all handset on gunmetal-plated settings.

Gunmetal is a gray, bronze-like alloy usually used in the manufacturing of gun barrels. Aurora borealis stones are named after the blue and green northern lights seen in skies between November and May.

$220-280 Cris

A Vendôme pin, 'After George Braque', one from a series of six, gold-plated with blue enamel, clear crystal rhinestones, a faux pearl and an amethyst glass cabochon.

A complete set of six pins is very rare and would be worth approximately $3,000.

2.25in (5.5cm) high

$300-350 Cris

1.5in (3.5cm) diam

Matisse & Renoir

A Matisse 'Maple Leaf' pin and earrings, in white and yellow-ocher enamel on copper.

Pin 2.5in (6.5cm) long

$100-150 Cris

A mid-1950s Matisse 'Maple Leaf' pin and earrings, blue and blue-black enamel on copper, with copper berry highlights.

Pin 2.5in (6.5cm) long

$100-150 Cris

A mid-1950s Matisse 'Maple Leaf' pin, in red enamel on copper with copper berry highlights.

2in (5cm) long

$70-100 Cris

A Matisse 'Artist's Palette' pin, in blue, yellow and brown enamel on copper.

2.75in (7cm) long

$70-100 Cris

A mid-1950s Matisse 'Twin-leaf' pin copper with white and gun-metal grey enamel highlights.

3in (8cm) long

$50-80 Cris

A late 1940s Renoir copper bangle, with 'Swiss Cheese' decoration.

1.5in (4cm) wide

$100-150 Cris

A
B
C
D
E
F
G
H
I
J
K
L
M
N
O
P
Q
R
S
T
U
V
W
XYZ

A mid-1950s Renoir copper bangle, with hooped wired decoration and rope molding borders.

1in (2.5cm) wide

$80-120 | **Cris**

A mid-1950s Matisse necklace and earrings, gold-plated with pastel pink enamel.

Necklace 18in (46cm) long

$120-180 | **Cris**

Regency

A 1950s Regency necklace, bracelet and earrings demi-parure, gold-plated with blue and green glass stones.

Necklace 15.25in (39cm) long

$300-350 | **Cris**

A 1950s Regency bracelet and earrings, with multicolored crystal rhinestones.

Bracelet 6.25in (16cm) long

$150-200 | **Cris**

A 1950s Regency necklace and earrings, gold-plated with prong-set aurora borealis and green cabochons and tear drops.

Necklace 17.25in (44cm) long

$180-220 | **Cris**

A mid-1950s Regency 'Leaf' motif pin and earrings, gold-plated with aurora borealis and lime green crystals.

Pin 2.25in (5.5cm) long

$150-200 | **Cris**

A 1950s Regency 'Scrolling Leaf' motif pin and earrings, gold-plated with prong-set pale blue and amethyst glass stones.

Pin 2in (5cm) long

$80-120 | **Cris**

A 1960s Regency 'Floral' motif pin, gunmetal-plated with red cabochons, some mirror-backed, and aurora borealis centers.

2in (5cm) diam

$70-100 | **Cris**

A mid-1950s Regency 'Butterfly' pin, gold-plated with prong-set jonquil and aurora borealis rhinestones.

2.25in (5.5cm) wide

$80-120 | **Cris**

A 1950s J.J. biblical figure entwined with snake pin, antiqued goldtone casting, with ruby and aurora borealis rhinestone highlights.

3.5in (9cm) long

$50-90   **JJ**

A late 1970s/early 1980s JJ 'Safe' pin, of gilt- and bronze-finish base metal, the door opens to reveal a bag of coins.

1.5in (4cm) wide

$30-40   **JJ**

A 1990s AJC 'Cat in Washing Machine' pin, of faux gilt and white enameled base metal with faux pearl soap bubbles.

2.5in (6.5cm) long

$40-60   **Abij**

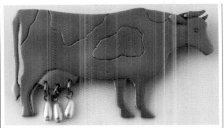

A late 1970s/early 1980s JJ 'Cow' pin, of white metal with faux pear udders.

The Jonette Jewelry Co. (JJ) has been operating in East Providence, Rhode Island, since 1935. Originally called The Providence Jewelry Company, it was renamed after its founders, John and Etta Lisker, when it reopened after World War II. It remains a family-run business. It has been making novelty jewelry since the 1970s, inspired by the success of its earlier ballerina pins and mother-of-pearl figurals. Pieces originally cost one dollar but are of above average quality. JJ also makes Christmas tree pins.

1.5in (3.75cm) wide

$30-40   **JJ**

A late 1980s/early 1990s JJ 'Cat and Fishbowl' pin, the cat of pewter-finish base metal and the bowl in glass.

2.5in (6.5cm) wide

$40-60   **Abij**

A late 1980s/early 1990s JJ 'Puppy in front of Mirror' pin, in faux gilt base metal and mirror glass.

2in (5cm) wide

$40-60   **Abij**

A 1990s AJC 'Gumball Machine' pin, of faux gilt base metal with red and green enameling.

The American Jewelry Chain Company has been making jewelry since 1927. It is based in Providence, Rhode Island.

2.5in (6.5cm) long

$40-60   **Abij**

A 1960s Art 'Apple' pin and earrings, in colored paste.

Art jewelry often resembles Victorian and Renaissance revival pieces. It is good quality and features fine filigree or stamped metalwork and colored rhinestones.

$70-100   **Wain**

A mid-1950s Art fruit pin and earrings, with blue, green and aurora borealis crystal rhinestones on gunmetal-plated castings.

Pin 1.75in (4.5cm) long

$120-180 **Cris**

A mid-1950s Art 'Bouquet-of-flowers' pin and earrings, with pastel pink, yellow, amber and green lucite, and clear crystal rhinestones, on gold-plated castings.

Pin 2in (5cm) long

$70-100 **Cris**

A mid-1950s Art necklace, bracelet and earrings demi-parure, with red cabochons and aurora borealis crystal rhinestones on a gold-plated frame.

Necklace 15.25in (39cm) long

$150-200 **Cris**

A late 1950s Art pear pin, of yellow and green enamel on a gold-plated casting.

1.5in (3.5cm) long

$50-80 **Cris**

A late 1980s Butler and Wilson tartan 'Butterfly' pin, with red, blue and green enamel on a gold-plated casting.

2.5in (6cm) wide

$40-60 **Cris**

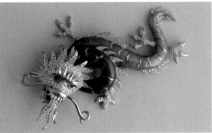

A mid-1990s Butler and Wilson 'Oriental Dragon' pin, with blue and green enamel, clear crystal rhinestones and red cabochon eyes, on a gold-plated casting.

4.25in (11cm) long

$120-180 **Cris**

A mid-1950s Hattie Carnegie 'Flower' pin, gold-plated with clear crystal rhinestones.

4in (10cm) long

$150-200 **Cris**

A 1950s Hattie Carnegie stylized 'Goat's Head' pin, made from blue and orange lucite, lapis glass beads and clear crystal rhinestones.

3.75in (9.5cm) long

$180-220 **Cris**

A 1950s Hattie Carnegie 'Mask' pin, with faux pearls and clear crystal rhinestones on a gold-plated casting.

2.5in (6.5cm) high

$300-350 **Cris**

A 1960s Ciner 'Flower' pin.

$70-100 **Wain**

A 1950s Ciner necklace and bracelet, with crystal cabochons on gold plate.

Bracelet 7.5in (19cm) long

$220-280 **Cris**

A 1950s Ciner 'Cow' and 'Dog' pin, gold-plated casting decorated with imitation turquoise and ruby.

Each 1.5in (3.5cm) long

$150-200 (both) Cris

A mid-1940s Corocraft pin, gold-plated over sterling silver with ruby red and clear crystal rhinestones.

3.25in (8.5cm) wide

$120-180 Cris

Two Henkel and Grosse for Christian Dior plastic coral bracelets.

Henkel and Grosse are a German firm, based in Pforzheim, who still make jewelry today.

c1965 *9in (23cm) long*

$150-200 (each) Wain

A late 1950s Eugéne necklace, with twin strands of hand-wired faux pearls and rose montées.

15.75in (40cm) long

$150-200 Cris

A late 1980s Stanley Hagler 'Pearls and Flowers' necklace and earrings, with turquoise and amethyst glass beads, hand-wired with gold-plated wire.

Necklace 22in (56cm) long

$400-600 Cris

A late 1980s Stanley Hagler 'Butterfly' pin, with champagne and yellow glass beads hand-wired to a filigree gold-plated frame.

3.75in (9.5cm) wide

$280-320 Cris

A late 1970s Stanley Hagler flower pin, with turquoise glass petals and powder-blue beads, hand-wired to a filigree gold-plated frame.

3in (8cm) diam

$150-200 Cris

A 1950s Miriam Haskell pin and earrings.

Earrings 1.5in (4cm) long

$150-200 Rox

A Iomaz gold-plated and enameled bracelet, pin and earrings.

Pin 1.5in (4cm) long

$1,000-1,500 (set) TR

A late 1960s Kenneth Jay Lane (KJL) 'Dragon' pin, with black and cream enamel, green cabochons and clear crystal rhinestones, on a gold-plated casting.

2.5in (6.5cm) wide

$120-180 Cris

A 1950s Joseff of Hollywood 'Crown' pin, Russian gold-plated with clear crystal rhinestone finial, signed "Joan Castle".

Joan Castle is Joseff's wife. She designed this piece for the T.V. programme 'Queen For A Day'.

2in (5cm) wide

$300-400 Cris

A late 1950s Lisner 'Hearts' motif necklace, pin, bracelet and earrings parure, silver-plated with pink, mauve, blue and white lucite hearts.

Necklace 14in (36cm) long

$220-280 Cris

A Lisner necklace, bracelet and earrings demi-parure, with pastel-colored lucite cabochons and crystal rhinestones.

Necklace 15.35in (39cm) long

$150-200   **Cris**

A late 1950s Lisner 'Leaf' motif necklace, bracelet and earrings demi-parure, made of brown and amber lucite and crystal rhinestone highlights.

Necklace 16.5in (42cm) long

$180-220   **Cris**

A late 1950s Lisner C-scroll pin, gilt-framed with green lava stones and aurora borealis crystal rhinestones.

2in (5cm) wide

$70-100   **Cris**

A 1950s pair of Mazer Bros. earrings, gold-plated with large pale blue octagon crystal stones, small clear crystal rhinestones and faux pearls.

1in (2.5cm) long

$70-100   **Cris**

A mid-1950s pair of Mazer Bros. 'Caterpillar' earrings, rose gold-plated with large amethyst glass stones and small, clear crystal rhinestones.

1.25in (3cm) long

$70-100   **Cris**

A late 1950s pair of Mazer Bros. 'Leaf and Berry' motif earrings, gold-plated with turquoise cabochons and diamanté.

2in (5cm) long

$150-200   **Cris**

A 1950s pair of Elsa Schiaparelli 'Leaf' motif earrings, gunmetal-plated with olivine and amber lucite leaves.

2.2in (5.5cm) long

$100-150   **Cris**

A 1950s set of Mazer Bros. bangle and earrings, gold-plated with large green glass stones and small amethyst rhinestones.

Earrings 1in (2.5cm) diam

$300-350   **Cris**

A late 1990s Herve van der Straeten gold-plated 'Flower' pin and earrings, with faux pearl centers.

Pin 2.75in (7cm) long

$150-200   **Cris**

A Mazer Bros. 'King and Queen' crown pin, sterling silver with amethyst cabochons and red, blue, green and clear crystal rhinestones.

2.5in (6.5cm) high

$300-350   **Cris**

A late 1990s Herve van der Straeten gold-plated 'Bow' pin and earrings.

Pin 4in (10cm) long

$150-200 | **Cris**

A late 1990s Herve van der Straeten necklace, with gold-plated and clear lucite lozenge-shaped links.

19in (48cm) long

$220-280 | **Cris**

A late 1990s Herve van der Straeten pendant necklace and earrings, with gold-plated and clear lucite lozenge-shaped links and drops.

Necklace 20in (51cm) long

$220-280 | **Cris**

An early 1950s Made in Austria 'Fruits and Leaves' pin, silver alloy with red glass.

2.5in (6cm) long

$100-150 | **Cris**

An Austrian necklace and earrings, with aurora borealis pear-shaped cabochons handset in claw settings.

Earring 1in (2.5cm) long

$220-280 | **Cris**

A necklace with a French faux turquoise cluster and diamanté multiple link cluster chain.

c 920   19.75in (50cm) long

$300-400 | **Cris**

A late 1940s Made in Austria 'Fruits and Leaves' pin gold-plated with red, amber and green glass and a rose pink crystal rhinestone highlight.

2in (5cm) long

$100-150 | **Cris**

An early 1950s Made in Austria 'Fruits and Leaves' pin, gold-plated with topaz and amber glass and a rose pink crystal rhinestone highlight.

2.25in (5.5cm) long

$100-150 | **Cris**

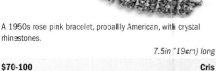

A 1950s rose pink bracelet, probably American, with crystal rhinestones.

7.5in (19cm) long

$70-100 | **Cris**

A late 1940s pair of Made in Austria 'Fruits and Leaves' earrings, gold-plated with green, pink and red glass.

1.5in (3.5cm) long

$100-150 | **Cris**

A 1940s set of aquamarine, ruby and jonquil earrings and pin.

Pin 3.5in (9cm) long

$150-200 | **Cris**

FIND OUT MORE...

'Costume Jewellery', by Judith Miller, published by Dorling Kindersley, 2003.

Collectors' Notes

- Although Christmas tree pins have existed since the 1940s, they did not become widely popular until the Korean war when, over the 1950 Christmas period, worried mothers wore these cheerful pins and sent them to their sons fighting overseas.

- They are typically in the festive colors of green, red and blue, but examples in other colors recalling icy days and snow can be found. Materials include enamel, crystals and beads.

- From the 1950s, their popularity grew and many of the leading costume jewelry manufacturers made examples, such as Stanley Hagler, Hobé, Trifari and Eisenberg. As a result there is a diverse range to collect from and Christmas tree pins have become a collecting area of their own.

A Stanley Hagler Christmas tree pin, set with molded opaque glass f owers, crystal rhinestones and jadeite beads.

1980s   *2.75in (7cm) high*

$80-120   **Cris**

A Stanley Hagler Christmas tree pin, set with opaque white glass beads and blue crystal rhinestones.

1980s   *3in (7.5cm) high*

$100-150   **Cris**

A Stanley Hagler Christmas tree pin, set with frosted glass leaves, aurora borealis disks, pearls and crystal rhinestones.

1980s   *2.75in (7cm) high*

$120-180   **Cris**

A Stanley Hagler Christmas tree pin, set with molded glass flowers and leaves set with crystal rhinestones.

1980s   *3.5in (9cm) high*

$120-180   **Cris**

A Stanley Hagler Christmas tree pin, set wih molded and painted glass stones, glass beads and crystal rhinestones.

1980s   *3in (7.5cm) high*

$80-120   **Cris**

A Stanley Hagler Christmas tree pin, set with hand-wired green glass beads, a red glass flower and crystal rhinestones.

1980s   *2.25in (6cm) high*

$120-180   **Cris**

A CLOSER LOOK AT A CHRISTMAS TREE PIN

These beads are hand-wired which is typical of Stanley Hagler who learnt this technique whilst working for Miriam Haskell.

Green glass beads are hand-wired on to the gold-plated filigree backing. This is a further typical feature of Hagler.

The beads are made from colored glass, meaning the strong colors will not fade.

The flower is raised, giving a three dimensional effect.

A Stanley Hagler Christmas tree pin, set with green glass beads, red glass flowers, red, green and yellow crystal rhinestones.

1980s   *3.5in (9cm) high*

$120-180   **Cris**

A limited edition Stanley Hagler Christmas tree pin, set with heart-shaped green glass stones, mother of pearl cabochons and bell flowers, simulated seed pearls and crystal rhinestones.

1980s   *3.75in (9.5cm) high*

$120-180   **Cris**

A Stanley Hagler Christmas tree pin, set with hand-carved red and green glass petals and red crystal rhinestones.

1980s   *2.5in (6.5cm) high*

$80-120   Cris

A Stanley Hagler Christmas tree pin, set with glass and jadeite beads, rh nestones, bell flowers and glass flowers.

c1990   *4in (10cm) high*

£120-180   Cris

An Eisenberg Ice Christmas tree pin, textured gold tone metal set with green enamel clear crystal rhinestones.

1950s   *2.25in (6cm) high*

$30-50   Cris

An Eisenberg Ice Christmas tree pin, textured gold tone metal set with green, red and clear crystal rhinestones.

1980s   *2.75in (7cm) high*

$50-80   Cris

An Eisenberg Ice Christmas tree pin, gold-tone textured metal set with aurora borealis and clear crystal rhinestones.

1980s   *2.5in (6.5cm) high*

$30-50   Cris

F Eisenberg Ice Christmas tree pin, yellow tone textured metal set with green enamel and multi-colored crystal rhinestones.

1980s   *1.75in (4.5cm) high*

£30-50   Cris

A Cristobal Christmas tree pin, set with crystal rhinestones.

Fifty of each of 6 colorways were made, totaling 300 pins.

1999   *4in (10cm) high*

$70-100   Cris

A Cristobal Christmas tree pin, set with red, amber and pale and dark green crystal rhinestones.

1999   *4in (10cm) high*

$70-100   Cris

A Cristobal Christmas tree pin, set with diamanté, glass cabochons and baguettes.

1999   *4.25in (11cm) high*

$120-180   Cris

F Cristobal Christmas pin, set with red and green enamel and clear crystal rhinestones.

1999   *4.25in (10.5cm) high*

£120-180   Cris

$150-200   Cris

An Original by Robert Christmas pin, with enamel, glass beads and a rhinestone.

Two versions of this tree were made: one with red glass beads, the other with simulated pearls. This version is the more desirable. This example is in good condition. Those with missing beads or badly rubbed enamel can be worth up to a third less.

2.5in (6.5cm) high

FIND OUT MORE...

'Collector's Guide: Costume Jewellery', by Judith Miller, published by Dorling Kindersley, 2003.

A
B
C
D
E
F
G
H
I
J
K
L
M
N
O
P
Q
R
S
T
U
V
W
XYZ

Collectors' Notes

- The jazz age of the 1920s and 1930s, with its bright and exhilarating fashions, led to a boom in the 'new' and highly colorful materials of cast phenolics and Bakelite being used in jewelry design. Although nearly all plastic jewelry from this period is known as 'Bakelite jewelry', it is important to remember that this is an umbrella term that covers many different early plastics such as Lucite and phenolic, and includes Bakelite.

- Plastics were cheap to produce and could be molded or carved in a huge variety of ways. Early designs from the 1920s were plainer and simpler than later examples. Geometric and floral patterns typical of Art Deco styling were popular.

- During its heyday in the 1930s, Bakelite jewelry was stocked by the most prestigious stores, such as Saks, Harrods and Macy's, who dedicated a shop window display to it in 1935. Its comparatively affordable price was ideal for ladies hit by the financial hardships of the Great Depression.

- Deeply or intricately and boldly carved pieces in bright colors tend to be the most valuable. Look also for the desirable 'apple juice' plastic, particularly those pieces carved and decorated from the reverse. Novelty subjects and figural shapes are also highly desirable.

- As new, more inexpensive, plastics were introduced from the late 1940s and 1950s onwards, quality began to decline. Unless by a notable designer or of fine quality, pieces produced from this period onwards are less desirable to collectors.

- Beware of cracks or deep scratches which will devalue a piece and cannot be repaired satisfactorily.

A carved 'apple juice' Bakelite heavy bangle, with three large and one small flowerhead-carved sections, evenly spaced with painted accents.	A reverse-carved 'apple juice' Bakelite bangle, with eight different floral and foliate-carved lobed sections.	A reverse-carved 'apple' juice Bakelite bangle, with fine cross-hatched pattern.	A 1930s 'apple juice' Lucite hinged bangle, with reverse-carved and colored flowers and foliage.
0.75in (2cm) wide	*1.25in (3cm) wide*	*1in (2.5cm) wide*	*2.75in (7cm) wide*
$400-600 Daw	**$200-300** Daw	**$180-220** Daw	**$400-600** BY

A carved butterscotch Bakelite bangle, with four ribs with alternating ribs centering three floral-carved reserves.	A heavily carved butterscotch Bakelite bangle, two clusters of three flowerheads with two single flowerheads and foliage.	
1.5in (4cm) wide	*1in (2.5cm) wide*	
$180-220 Daw	**$500-800** Daw	A butterscotch and black hinged bangle, with foliate carving all over.
A carved butterscotch Bakelite bangle, deep-carved floral and foliate carving.	A two-tone Bakelite and metal bangle, joined with four green bars banded by metal.	
	1.5in (4cm) wide	*1.5in (4cm) wide*
$300-400 Daw	**$280-320** Daw	**$800-1,200** Daw

South Street Antiques Market

an Antiquarians Delight.....

20 DEALER-ATTENDED SHOPS ON 2 FLOORS

Featuring: Furniture, Vintage Clothing and accessories,
Watches, China, Lighting, Hats,
Artwork, Glass, Costume and Fine Jewelery,
Pop-Culture, Christmas, Eyewear, Kitsch, Kitchen,
Coins, Upholsterer on premises and much more.
Fresh merchandise daily

Open Year round

615 S. 6th Street Philadelphia, PA 19147 USA 1/2 BLK from South Street 215 592 0256	Wednesday 12-7pm Thursday 12-7pm Friday 12-8pm Saturday 12-8pm Sunday 12-7pm Closed Monday and Tuesday

Center City Philadelphia's <u>Only</u>
INDOOR COLLECTABLES' MARKETPLACE

est. 1986

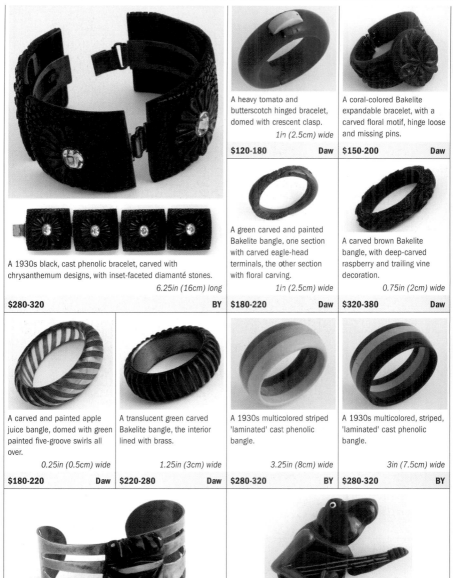

A heavy tomato and butterscotch hinged bracelet, domed with crescent clasp.

1in (2.5cm) wide

$120-180   **Daw**

A coral-colored Bakelite expandable bracelet, with a carved floral motif, hinge loose and missing pins.

$150-200   **Daw**

A 1930s black, cast phenolic bracelet, carved with chrysanthemum designs, with inset-faceted diamanté stones.

6.25in (16cm) long

$280-320   **BY**

A green carved and painted Bakelite bangle, one section with carved eagle-head terminals, the other section with floral carving.

1in (2.5cm) wide

$180-220   **Daw**

A carved brown Bakelite bangle, with deep-carved raspberry and trailing vine decoration.

0.75in (2cm) wide

$320-380   **Daw**

A carved and painted apple juice bangle, domed with green painted five-groove swirls all over.

0.25in (0.5cm) wide

$180-220   **Daw**

A translucent green carved Bakelite bangle, the interior lined with brass.

1.25in (3cm) wide

$220-280   **Daw**

A 1930s multicolored striped 'laminated' cast phenolic bangle.

3.25in (8cm) wide

$280-320   **BY**

A 1930s multicolored, striped, 'laminated' cast phenolic bangle.

3in (7.5cm) wide

$280-320   **BY**

A 1920s brass bangle with an applied, carved cast phenolic scarab, with gold-painted and inset steel faux-jewel finish.

Scarab 2in (5cm) high

$220-280   **BY**

A 1930s green carved cast phenolic banjo-playing frog pin, the arm moving to 'play' the banjo.

2.75in (7cm) high

$2,200-2,800   **BY**

A 1930s carved green cast phenolic pin, of a man playing a pipe.

2.25in (6cm) high

$150-200 **BB**

A 1930s Bakelite and Catalin novelty 'Black Porter and Case' pin, with gold-plated bow pin.

3.25in (8cm) high

$400-600 **TM**

A WWII Bakelite 'Patriotic Drum' pin, with wooden drumsticks missing clip.

$70-100 **Daw**

An apple green plastic and parcel giltwood pineapple pin.

2in (5cm) high

$30-50 **Daw**

A laminated three-color Bakelite pin, of domed octagonal shape, centering a small disc in green, maroon and gold, with a diamond star motif.

1.25in (3cm) diam

$180-220 **Daw**

A CLOSER LOOK AT BAKELITE JEWELRY

This patriotic pin was specially commissioned by Lord & Taylor to commemorate the coronation of Edward VII in 1936. The pin soon sold out.

When George became king after Edward's abdication in December 1936, the remainder of the block was used for a second edition.

Rods of differently colored phenolic would be cast or laminated together lengthwise to create a Union Jack pattern at each end. Slices would then be cut off across the block to make each flat pin.

Lord & Taylor, founded in 1827, is the oldest speciality department store in the USA.

A rare 'laminated' Union Jack red, white and blue Bakelite pin, inset in a wooden frame.

c1935 *2.25in (5.5cm) wide*

$300-400 **Daw**

A 'Star Dust' Bakelite pin, of rounded rectangular shape with rounded sides, slightly scalloped top, clasp broken.

2in (5cm) wide

$40-60 **Daw**

A 1930s cast phenolic and Catalin geometric necklace.

Pendant 2.25in (6cm) high

$120-180 **BB**

A 1930s cellulcid cream chain link and tan disk necklace and bracelet.

Necklace 15.75in (40cm) long

$300-400 **MAC**

A 1939-40 New York World's Fair necklace, worked in polychrome plastic, wood and hand-wrought copper, in lieu of the original precious stones and metal.

This is the last of 50 necklaces commissioned by the Tibetans and made by Rodrigo Moure for the Tibetan Exhibit.

26.75in (68cm) long

$350-400 **Daw**

A 1930s pair of green cast phenolic bird earrings.

1.5in (3.5cm) wide

$100-150 **BB**

Collectors' Notes

■ Although jelly has been made since medieval times when it was primarily savory, it was not until the late 18thC and the Victorian period when it grew in popularity as cookery books began to include jelly recipes. Molds became more varied in style and were easier to produce thanks to the potteries making a number of technical break-throughs.

■ Major makers of pottery molds were Shelley, Copeland and Minton, who produced cream and white wares from the mid-19thC to the early 20thC.

■ From the early 20thC onwards, comparatively inexpensive enameled metal molds dominated, many with the clean, architectural lines of the developing Art Deco period. By the 1940s, jelly was beginning to decline in popularity. Molds were now made from aluminium and became less inventive in form.

■ Animals, flora and fauna are popular and highly collected subjects. They probably originated with the 'sotelties' of the Tudor Court, where jellies were molded into amusing or pastoral shapes for the entertainment of the Court.

■ Look for early pottery molds, particularly in novelty shapes, and strongly Art Deco styled molds indicative of the period. Condition is important, with dents to metal molds and cracks or chips to pottery molds reducing value. Molds by known makers are very popular.

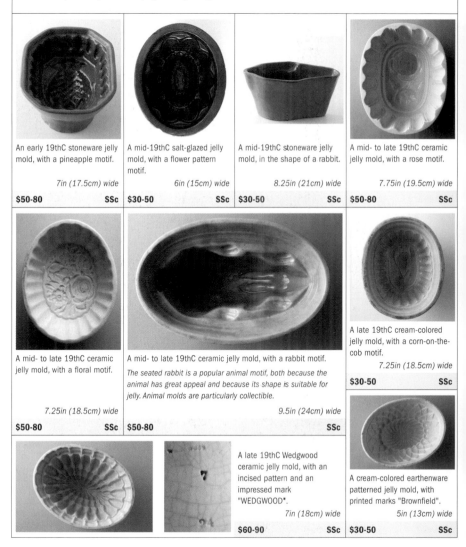

An early 19thC stoneware jelly mold, with a pineapple motif.

7in (17.5cm) wide

$50-80   **SSc**

A mid-19thC salt-glazed jelly mold, with a flower pattern motif.

6in (15cm) wide

$30-50   **SSc**

A mid-19thC stoneware jelly mold, in the shape of a rabbit.

8.25in (21cm) wide

$30-50   **SSc**

A mid- to late 19thC ceramic jelly mold, with a rose motif.

7.75in (19.5cm) wide

$50-80   **SSc**

A mid- to late 19thC ceramic jelly mold, with a floral motif.

7.25in (18.5cm) wide

$50-80   **SSc**

A mid- to late 19thC ceramic jelly mold, with a rabbit motif.

The seated rabbit is a popular animal motif, both because the animal has great appeal and because its shape is suitable for jelly. Animal molds are particularly collectible.

9.5in (24cm) wide

$50-80   **SSc**

A late 19thC cream-colored jelly mold, with a corn-on-the-cob motif.

7.25in (18.5cm) wide

$30-50   **SSc**

A late 19thC Wedgwood ceramic jelly mold, with an incised pattern and an impressed mark "WEDGWOOD".

7in (18cm) wide

$60-90   **SSc**

A cream-colored earthenware patterned jelly mold, with printed marks "Brownfield".

5in (13cm) wide

$30-50   **SSc**

A ceramic jelly mold, with a fruit motif.

6in (15.5cm) wide

$30-50 SSc

A French ceramic jelly mold, with printed marks for "Mehan Depost France".

The protruding cone would have left a 'well' in the jelly into which cream would be poured.

5.75in (14.5cm) diam

$20-30 SSc

A French ceramic jelly mold, with printed marks for "Mehan C P & Co France".

5.5in (14cm) diam

$20-30 SSc

A Booth's ceramic jelly mold, with bird motif, with "Booths" printed and impressed marks.

1891-1906   *6in (15.5cm) wide*

$50-80 SSc

A pair of Cetem ware individual jelly molds, with flower motif.

3.5in (8.5cm) wide

$50-80 SSc

A Copeland ceramic jelly mold, with a strawberry motif, with an impressed mark.

7in (18cm) wide

$50-80 SSc

Three Shelley 'Star' design jelly molds.

1912-25   *Largest 5.75in (14.5cm) diam*

$60-90 (each) SSc

A copper jelly mold.

2in (5.5cm) high

$50-80 OACC

An individual copper jelly mold.

3in (8cm) wide

$60-90 SSc

A 1920s/30s enamel patty pan.

3.5in (9cm) diam

$10-15 SSc

Two 1920s/30s enamel jelly molds.

6.75in (17cm) wide

$15-20 SSc

A pair of early 20thC sycamore children's butter pats.

5.75in (14.5cm) long

$20-30 SSc

An unusual late 19thC pair of sycamore butter-working floats.

8.25in (21cm) long

$30-50 SSc

A late 19th/early 20thC sycamore butter knife.

10.5in (26.5cm) long

$20-30 SSc

Two butter working spoons.

Largest 8.75in (22.5cm) long

$30-50 (each) SSc

A late 19th/early 20thC Welsh butter scoop.

9in (23cm) long

$60-90 SSc

An early 20thC sycamore butter working table.

27.5in (69cm) long

$120-180 SSc

An early 20thC sycamore dairy bowl.

13.75in (35cm) diam

$300-400 SSc

A late 19th/early 20thC milking stool.

9.75in (25cm) high

$80-120 SSc

An early to mid-19thC milking stool.

10.25in (26cm) high

$100-150 SSc

A late 19thC West Country sycamore butterstamp.

5in (13cm) long

$60-90 SSc

A late 19th/early 20thC wooden milk pail, with one pint milk measure.

$60-90 SSc

A mid- to late 19thC sycamore butter mold, with flower motif.

8.75in (22cm) long

$60-90 SSc

A Danish iron, brass body with iron posts.

c1750   5.5in (14cm) long

$480-520   ATK

A flat iron, from Saarland, Germany, cast iron with brass inlaid top together with a brass 'cathedral' trivet.

c1920 Iron 6.5in (17cm) long

$250-300   ATK

A Westphalian ox-tounge iron, polished cast iron body with Art Nouveau iron trivet.

c1890 Iron 8in (20cm) long

$80-120   ATK

A Saunders 'Silver Streak' Pyrex iron, with clear glass, red enameled metal dial and black knob, fraying to one end of original cord, marked.

9in (23cm) long

$1,000-1,500   DRA

A Nuremberg style iron, brass body with turned wooden handle.

5.5in (14cm) long

$320-380   ATK

A steel iron, with turned wooden handle.

6.25in (16cm) long

$200-250   ATK

A European charcoal iron, with replacement handle and lion's head catch

$20-30   D

A porcelain toaster, by the Porcelier Mfg. Co., Greensburg, Pennsylvania, with basket-weave design and floral decoration lacks porcelain handle.

c1928

$800-1,200   ATK

An American porcelain toaster, by the Pan Electric Mfg. Co., Cleveland, Ohio, decorated with the 'Blue Willow' pattern, in working order.

c1928

$1,500-2,000   ATK

A food chopper.

This form is more common than the one on the right.

c1790   6.75in (17cm) long

$55-65   RAA

A food chopper design hand forged by a blacksmith

c1790   7.5in (19cm) long

$350-395   RAA

A black-finished tin 'potato picker'.

Often mistaken for a thimble, one of these would be worn on each finger and the picker would plunge his hands into the soil to pull potatoes.

1.5in (3.5cm) high

$15-25   **CBe**

An early tin egg scale.

12.5in (32cm) long

$40-50   **BCAC**

An iron egg coddler.

2.25in (6cm) high

$25-35   **BCAC**

Two 19thC earthenware cake molds, in the shape of sheep, excellent condition.

This is an unusually large size for a cake mold.

15in (38cm) long

$150-200   **BCAC**

A metal tray-form chocolate mold, producing 24 separate candies, in forms including bronco busting cowboy, Native American warrior on horseback, Native American Chief with bow stallion and covered wagon.

13.25in (33.5cm) high

$50-70   **TWC**

A milk glass hanging salt cellar, with a blue painted wooden lid.

4.25in (11cm) high

$180-220   **BCAC**

A late 19thC pine and iron coffee mill, maker unknown, original finish.

12in (30.5cm) high

$80-120   **TWC**

A copper teapot, side handle, 'half' form teapot.

6in (15.25cm) high

$150-200   **AAC**

A late 19thC brass trivet stand, pierced top, on claw-and-ball feet, with stamped registered design mark.

10in (25.5cm) wide

$15-25   **KG**

A fruit wood olive spoon, central bowl scoop.

17in (43cm) long

$12-18   **D**

A 19thC brass kitchen ladle, stamped "3".

17in (43cm) long

$30-35   **KG**

A late 19thC brass hearth brush, the brush with sliding floral relief cylinder.

20in (51cm) long

$12-18 KG

A cast iron match safe.

c1860 7in (17.5cm) long

$150-200 RAA

A brass match safe shovel and bucket design.

c1880 9.25in (23.5cm) long

$180-220 RAA

An uncommon double goffering iron, the base with high relief floral pattern.

hot solid metal cylinders heated in a hearth were inserted into the long cone, over which fabric was shaped before being set by the heat. They were used for shaping sleeves and collars. They are not commonly found with such decorative bases and with double irons.

13.75in (35cm) high

$300-400 ET

A pair of early 19thC brass ejector candlesticks, each of plain column form on square swept foot, repairs.

7.5in (19cm) high

$60-90 KG

An enameled metal graniteware candle stick.

5.5in (14cm) wide

$80-120 BCAC

An 18thC half-skein pine wood niddy-noddy, a rare size. *Niddy-noddies were used for winding wool.*

11in (28cm) long

$180-220 RAA

An early black painted candle mold, for six candles.

10.25in (26cm) long

$30-40 BCAC

A turned mahogany kitchen 'cat' or all-purpose stand.

9.5in (24cm) high

$120-180 ET

An Electrolux cannister vacuum cleaner, designed by Lurelle Guild, with chrome and aluminum housing on a 'sled' base, with original power cord.

22.5in (57cm) long

$280-320 DRA

A 1940s tin lunch box, with red plastic handle

10.25in (26cm) long

$40-60 BCAC

A pair of 1930s chrome Art Deco 'face' lamps, by the Revere Company.

These lamps were possibly designed by Helen Dreyfuss, wife of designer Henry Dreyfuss. Chrome was a very popular material during the Art Deco period. With their extreme simplicity, these lamps recall tribal masks or the work of the painter Modigliani, which was in turn inspired by tribal art.

10in (25.5cm) high

$400-600 DEtc

A 1930s Art Deco chrome and black enameled metal table lamp, with original shade and chroming.

18in (46cm) high

$600-900 DEtc

A 1930s pair of Art Deco table lamps, with frosted glass stepped shades, chromed gazelles and black vitrolite glass bases.

The stepped bases, figures and frosted shades that mimic the work of Rene Lalique are typical hallmarks of the Art Deco period.

8.75in (22cm) high

$400-600 DEtc

A 1930s pair of tiered copper Art Deco tabletop torchères, with wooden bases.

10.25in (26cm) high

$500-700 DEtc

A 1930s copper and chrome 'Machine Age' pivoting desk lamp.

The shade swivels and pivots.

13.75in (35cm) high

$300-400 DEtc

A pair of 1930s Art Deco frosted glass boudoir lamps, with female figures gazing, birds and palms, by Tiffin.

Each 8.25in (21cm) high

$500-700 DEtc

A 1940s painted plaster, wood and brass 'carousel horse' table lamp, with original fabric shade.

27.5in (70cm) high

$220-280 DEtc

A 1930s Art Deco painted wood table lamp, with original paint.

15.25in (29cm) high

$220-280 DEtc

A rare 1930s enameled metal penguin night light, the catalin beak being the switch.

10.25in (26cm) high

$400-600 DEtc

A 1930s copper and base metal patriotic 'Statue of Liberty' lamp and smoker's compendium, with ashtrays, lighter and storage, the top with cast images of Presidents and political buildings.

27.25in (69cm) high

$500-700 DEtc

A 1930s hollow painted metal 'elephant' boudoir lamp, bookend and ashtray set, by Jennings Brothers, Brooklyn, NY.

It is hard to find a complete set as they were often split up.

13in (33cm) high

$300-500 DEtc

A frosted glass 'Saturn' lamp, with internally painted stars and planets.

These lamps were produced to commemorate the 1939 New York World's Fair, which celebrated technology and the future. This theme is shown in the 'planet' shaped shade with stars and planets on i.

c1939   12.25in (31cm) high

$300-500   DEtc

A Walter Dorwin Teague for Polaroid Corp. executive desk lamp, with brown Bakelite base and hooded shade, on a conical brushed aluminum shaft, unmarked.

Designer and typographer Walter Dorwin Teague (1883-1960) was influenced by Le Corbusier after visiting Paris. On his return to New York, he founded one of the first industrial design consultancies and designed cameras for Kodak, pens for Scripto and glass for Steuben, as well as others. His streamlined and functional designs arose from his interest in symmetry and proportion.

c1939   12.75in (88.5cm) high

$700-1,000   DRA

A pair of 1950s Modernist speckled black and gold painted plaster table lamps, with original shades.

Where possible, collectors should look for lamps that have original, period shades as they are as much a part of the lamp as the base.

24in (61cm) high

$300-400   DEtc

A rare brown Bakelite, wood and chrome 'airplane' lamp with clock, by Sessions.

Later versions have rubber, not wooden wheels. The propellers on this example are replaced - they were originally chrome.

c1948   20.5in (52cm) wide

$400-600   DEtc

A pair of 1930s painted plaster 'fairy' lamps, with original shades.

33.75in (86cm) high

$700-1,000   DEtc

A pair of painted plaster and glass 'goldfish' table lamps, by Reglor of California, with period shades.

c1952   32in (81cm) high

$500-700   DEtc

A pair of 1950s Modernist painted and textured plaster table lamps, with original parchment shades.

32.75in (83cm) high

$300-500   DEtc

A very rare 1950s painted chalk and fabric lady dancer table lamp, the dress as a shade.

37in (94cm) high

$1,000-1,500   DEtc

A 1950s brass-colored glazed ceramic parrot table lamp, the parrot illuminates.

17in (43cm) high

$220-280   DEtc

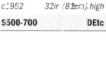

A 1950s painted plaster leaping fish backlit TV lamp, the light shining through two panels under the fish.

These lamps were designed to be placed on top of a television.

17.75in (45cm) wide

$100-150   DEtc

LUNCH BOXES

Collectors' Notes

- The first collectible character lunch box was produced in 1950 and the last c1985 when the golden age of the collectible metal lunch box ended. Their demise was apparently due to ongoing pressure from parents, initially in Florida, who were concerned that they were being used as weapons in the playground. Although plastic and steel were used nearly equally from 1972 to 1987, plastic is cheaper to produce and more durable.

- Since production ceased, lunch boxes have become popular and highly collectible, partly due to childhood nostalgia and partly due to their colorful artwork, which represents many aspects of popular culture. There is also cross-market interest, for example, 'Star Wars' lunch boxes appeal to fans of 'Star Wars' as well as to lunch box collectors.

- Desirable makes include Thermos (also known as King Seeley Thermos before 1960), Aladdin, Adco-Liberty and Ohio Art.

- All boxes came with Thermos bottles that fitted into lid of dome-top boxes or vertically into the box itself. This must be present for the box to hold the highest value. Bottles also have a value all of their own and are often collected to complete a box set.

- Condition is vital, as boxes were made to be used and are often worn. Wear, such as scratches, dents and loss of the decal, lower the value considerably, with only examples in mint or excellent condition being desirable, unless very rare. Look carefully to check whether the bottle and box are not original and have been married – the condition of each may be different.

- Some collectors focus solely on dome-topped lunch boxes, which were based on the shape of the traditional worker's lunch box.

A near mint metal 'Hoppalong Cassidy' lunchbox with Thermos bottle, by Aladdin Industries of Nashville, Tennessee.

Hoppalong Cassidy was the first 'character' to feature on a metal lunch box, in 1950. The earlier version has a shaped character decal, not a rectangular decal as this example, dating from 1952. Both versions were also available in blue which carry a similar value. Chicago industrial designer Robert Burton was responsible for the artwork, and went on to produce most of Aladdin's lunch boxes during the 1950s.

c1950   Lunchbox 8in (20.5cm) wide

$500-700   **STC**

An Adco-Liberty 'The Lone Ranger' lunch box and Thermos bottle.

c1955   8.75in (22cm) wide

$500-800   STC

An Aladdin 'Zorro' lunch box and thermos bottle.

c1960   8in (20.5cm) wide

$350-400   STC

An Aladdin 'Jetsons' lunch box and Thermos bottle.

c1965   9in (22.5cm) wide

$2,000-2,500   STC

A Thermos 'Central Station' bottle and two views of a 'Firehouse' dome-topped lunch box.

Note the side view of the shaped lid, which is a characteristic of Thermos lunch boxes and does not appear with Aladdin dome-topped lunch boxes. The bottom of this finely decorated box lists fire safety practices.

c1960   9in (22.5cm) wide

$400-600   STC

A Thermos 'Fireball XL5' lunch box and Thermos bottle.

The artwork for this box was created by Wally Wood, a top artist for DC Comics in the 1950s and beyond.

c1965   8.75in (22cm) wide

$280-320   STC

An Aladdin Enterprises 'U.S. Mail' lunch box and Thermos bottle.

c1970   9in (22.5cm) wide

$120-180   STC

A Thermos 'Chitty Chitty Bang Bang' lunch box.

This example with the missing Thermos bottle would be worth $70-90 more.

c1970   8.75in (22cm) wide

$150-200   STC

A Thermos 'Beatles Yellow Submarine' bottle and two views of a metal lunch box.

c1970   8.75in (22cm) wide

$1,000-1,500   STC

A Thermos 'Star Wars' lunch box and Thermos bottle.

c1930   8.75in (22cm) wide

$200-300   STC

An Aladdin Industries 'Peter Pan' lunch box and Thermos bottle.

c1970   8.75in (22cm) wide

$180-220   STC

A Thermos 'Snoopy' dome-topped metal lunch box and Thermos bottle.

c1970   9in (22.5cm) wide

$220-280   STC

An Aladdin Industries Charlie's Angels' lunch box and Thermos bottle.

c1980   8in (20cm) wide

$200-250   STC

A Thermos 'Star Wars Empire Strikes Back' lunch box and bottle.

c1980   8.75in (22cm) wide

$100-150   STC

A Thermos 'Rambo' lunch box with plastic Thermos bottle.

'Rambo' was the last metal lunch box produced, which is ironic considering the issue during the 1970s concerned children using lunch boxes as playground weapons.

c1985   8.75in (22cm) wide

$80-120   STC

An Aladdin Industries 'Popeye' lunch box and Thermos bottle, with embossed detailing.

c1980   8in (20.5cm) wide

$70-100   STC

FIND OUT MORE...

The Illustrated Encyclopaedia of Metal Lunch Boxes, by Allen Woodall and Sean Brickell, published by Schiffer Publishing, 1999

The Fifties and Sixties Lunchbox, by Scott Bruce, published by Chronicle Books, 1988.

MARBLES

Collectors' Notes

- Collectible marbles can be divided into three types, by age: German handmade marbles produced from c1860-c1920; American machine-made marbles produced from c1905 onward; and contemporary marbles, produced mainly in the US.

- German handmades are usually the most desirable and often the most valuable. The majority were produced from the 19th century, until the outbreak of WWI led to exports ending and a decline in the industry. These examples can be identified by a smoothed down, but slightly rough area or pontil mark where the marble was removed from the rod.

- There are many different types and sub-types, particularly with Swirls. Look for complex designs and symmetry. Bright, intricate multicolored marbles and large marbles are usually very popular. The majority are categorized by the elements they contain and the style of the elements. Certain colors such as blue and red are rare.

- American machine-made marbles are rapidly growing in popularity, as yesterday's children become today's collectors and the limited supply of handmades dries up. Leading factories included Akro Agate Company, Peltier Glass Company and Christensen Agate Company, who are said to have made the most colorful American marbles.

- Contemporary marbles are usually identified and priced as such. There are a number of artists, such as Mark Matthews, still producing colorful designs today and their work is often ardently collected.

- Condition is very important with American machine-made and contemporary marbles, but less so with German handmades. However, examine a marble closely to look for scratches, 'hit' marks and even tiny, shallow chips as these will devalue a marble by a half or more. All the marbles shown here are in excellent to near mint condition.

- A final factor determining value is 'eye appeal'. Look for bright color, complexity and symmetry, but factors that appeal to one collector may not to another.

A German Latticinio Core Swirl marble, in near mint condition.

c1860-1920 1in (2.5cm) diam

$60-90   **AB**

A rare orange core strand German Latticinio Core Swirl marble, in near mint condition.

c1860-1920 1.5in (4cm) diam

$400-600   **AB**

A German Solid Core Swirl, in near mint condition.

Examples with a colored core only, without an outer layer are known as 'Naked Solid Core Swirls'.

1in (2.5cm) diam

$60-90   **AB**

A German right twist, two layer white Latticinio Core Swirl in colored glass marble, in near mint condition.

This marble began as a transparent green glass rod that was rolled twice in rods of white glass between casings to create two 'layers' of latticinio under a final layer of green glass. In Swirls, the colored base glass is much rarer than clear base glass. This factor, and the complex production, make this marble valuable.

c1860-1920   *1in (2.5cm) diam*

$1,500-2,000   **AB**

A German Divided Core Swirl marble, in near mint condition.

c1860-1920 1.25in (3cm) d

$70-100   **AB**

A German 'End-of-Day' Onionskin marble, with sprinkled mica chips.

c1860-1920 1in (2.5cm) diam

$300-500   **AB**

A German Ribbon Core Swirl marble, in near mint condition.

The twist on this example is exceptional, with superb symmetry and even width. Less symmetrical and even swirls are worth half the value of this marble.

c1860-1920 1in (2.5cm) diam

$300-350   **AB**

A German 'End-of-Day' Onionskin marble, in near mint condition.

This is the most typical Onionskin with a subsurface layer of opaque white covered with panels of stretched pink and blue glass.

c1860-1920 1in (2.5cm) diam

$300-350 AB

A German 'End-of-Day' Onionskin marble.

Unusually, 'End-of-Day' relates to constructing the marble, rather than the traditional meaning of using waste glass at the end of the day to make an object. 'End-of-Day' marbles use stretched flecks of colored glass rather than the rods found in Swirls.

c1860-1920 1.25in (3cm) diam

$1,200-1,800 AB

A German 'End-of-Day' Joseph's Coat marble, in near mint condition.

A 'Joseph's Coat is constructed with a layer of tightly packed colored strands or bands beneath the surface.

c1860-1920 1.25in (3cm) diam

$500-700 AB

A German 'End-of-Day' Cloud marble.

Clouds differ from Onionskins in that the flecks of glass are not stretched, but remain as flecks. This example has a clear base and a slight left-hand twist to the flecks which is less common than a right-hand twist.

c1860-1920 1.75in (4.5cm) d

$400-600 AB

A German or American 'End-of-Day' type Banded Opaque marble, made with stretched flecks of glass.

c1860-1920 1in (2.5cm) diam

$120-180 AB

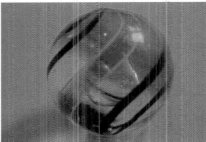

A German Banded Lutz marble.

The name Lutz relates to Nicholas Lutz, of the American manufacturer Sandwich Glass, who used ground copper flakes suspended in glass to give the impression of gold, as in the twists of this marble. Later research has shown that marbles were never made at Sandwich Glass, but the name has survived.

c1860-1920 1in (2.5cm) diam

$300-400 AB

A German Ribbon Lutz marble.

There are a number of different constructions for Ribbon Lutz marbles. This example has two core ribbons in orange and blue. The core is edged by two Lutz bands edged with white strands.

c1860-1920 1in (2.5cm) diam

$300-500 AB

A German Onionskin Lutz marble, in near mint condition.

An Onionskin Lutz has an Onionskin core covered with Lutz which is then cased in clear glass. Here, the Lutz is in splotches and the core is a Cloud, as the glass flecks have not been stretched.

c1860-1920

$800-1,200 AB

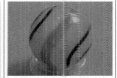

A Banded Lutz marble in near mint condition.

Colored base banded Lutz marbles are rarer than clear Banded Lutz marbles. Opaque white base example, are rarer than transparent bases.

c1860-1920 0.75in (2cm) diam

$300-500 AB

A Banded Lutz marble, in near mint condition.

Colored base Banded Lutzes are rarer than clear Banded Lutzes. Opaque bases, like this opaque black base example, are rarer than transparent bases.

c1860-1920 0.75in (2cm) diam

$300-500 **AB**

A German 'Indian' Lutz marble.

There are two types of Indian Lutz, this is the rarer variety and has a black base with between two and four Lutz bands edged with colored strands. The more common variety has a clear glass casing.

c1860-1920 *0.75in (2cm) diam*

$700-1,000 **AB**

A German 'Indian' marble, in near mint condition.

An 'Indian' has an opaque black base with two bands of colored Swirl type strands, as in this example, or two bands of stretched color.

c1860-1920 0.75in (2cm) diam

$70-100 **AB**

A rare four band German 'Indian' marble, in excellent condition.

c1860-1920 0.75in (2cm) d

$70-100 **AB**

A German or American 'Clambroth' marble, with opaque white base and colored strands.

c1860-1920 0.75in (2cm) diam

$300-350 **AB**

A German 'Peppermint Swirl' marble, with rare mica additions to the blue bands, in near mint condition.

c1860-1920 0.75in (2cm) diam

$300-350 **AB**

A German or American 'Clambroth' marble.

'Clambroth' marbles have an opaque base with equally spaced strands in various colors on the surface. This example has an opaque black base which is rare.

c1860-1920 0.75in (2cm) diam

$300-500 **AB**

A CLOSER LOOK AT A GERMAN MARBLE

A 'Lightning Strike' is a very rare type of German marble. A couple of dozen are known to exist.

Most 'Lightning Strikes' have the same colored lightning strikes on each side.

This is the only example known to collectors with two differently colored 'Lightning Strikes'.

It is opalescent on a semi-opaque white base.

Two views of an extremely rare German 'Lightning Strike' marble.

c1900-1920

$4,000-6,000 **AB**

A German or American 'Sulphide' marble, with a figure of a dog.

c1860-1920 *1.75in (4.5cm) d*

$120-180 **AB**

Collectors' Notes

- A molded figure made of a white porcelain-like material known as a 'sulphide' is inserted into a glass casing and formed into a sphere. A high level of skill and craftsmanship was required to make these marbles.
- The figure had to be heated to the same temperature as the molten glass otherwise the marble would crack. Skill was also required to avoid air bubbles when placing the figure in the marble.
- Sulphides are hotly collected and often fetch high prices. Look for human figures, mythical characters and inanimate objects, which are rare. Farmyard and domestic animals are more common. Handpainted sulphides and those with colored glass casings are much sought after.

A German or American 'Sulphide' marble, with a handpainted figure of a reclining cow with green grass, black ears, nostrils, eyes and mouth and spots, cased in clear glass.

Handpainted figures are rare and desirable, requiring a great deal of skill to create.

c1860-1920   1.75in (4.5cm) diam

$2,200-2,800   AB

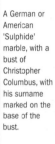

A German or American 'Sulphide' marble, with a bust of Christopher Columbus, with his surname marked on the base of the bust.

This example is rare twice over as it is cased in clear blue glass and has a human figure as its subject.

c1860-1920   1.75in (4.5cm) diam

$3,000-4,000   AB

A German or American 'Sulphide' marble, with figure of children's author and illustrator Kate Greenaway, in near mint condition.

c1860-1920   1.75in (4.5cm) d

$300-500   AB

A German 'Paperweight' marble, in near mint condition.

There are two types of 'Paperweight' marbles. One looks like a millefiori paperweight and the other has a scattering of translucent flecks of color, which are also known as 'Confetti' marbles. They always have one pontil.

c1880-1920 0.75in (2cm) diam

$100-150   AB

A German 'Cornhusk Swirl' marble, in near mint condition.

A 'Cornhusk Swirl' is a transparent color base swirl with a subsurface wide band of opaque white. They are almost always found in a transparent light brown color.

2.5in (6.5cm) diam

$50-80   AB

A German or American 'Mica' glass marble.

'Mica' marbles are simple to make. A rod of glass is rolled in mica chips and then coated in another layer of glass. Clear is common; red, yellow and purple are rarer.

c1860-1920 0.75in (2cm) diam

$50-80   AB

A German or American 'Handmade Opaque', in near mint condition.

This is the simplest marble to make, being cut off a single colored rod. Rose is a rare color, they are usually white, green or blue.

c1860-1915 0.75in (2cm) diam

$50-80   AB

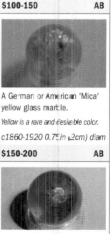

A German or American 'Mica' yellow glass marble.

Yellow is a rare and desirable color.

c1860-1920 0.75in (2cm) diam

$150-200   AB

A rare red German or American 'Handmade Opaque' marble.

c1860-1915   0.75in (2cm) d

$30-50   AB

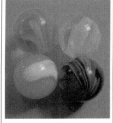

Four American Christensen Agate Company 'Slag' marbles, in near mint condition.

Christensen Agate Company's 'Slag' marbles can be identified by having one or two 'cut-off', truncated lines and by their bright colors.

c1925 Largest 0.75in (2cm) d

$15-25 (each)　　　　　**AB**

Two American Christensen Agate Company 'Guinea' marbles.

The 'Guinea' is one of the Holy Grails for marble collectors. They have a transparent blue, brown or clear base with flecks of bright colors covering 20-100 percent of the surface and one or two seams. As with many highly desirable objects, there are many reproductions and replicas, including some by Vacor de Mexico.

c1925-1929　　　　　　Largest 0.75in (2cm) diam

$300-350 (each)　　　　　**AB**

Two American Christensen Agate Company 'Striped Opaque' marbles, in 'electric' colors.

'Striped Opaques' have bands of color brushed onto the surface of the opaque marble and one or two cut-off lines.

c1927-1929 0.75in (2cm) diam

$150-200 (each)　　　　　**AB**

An American Akro Agate Co. 'Popeye Corkscrew' near mint condition.

Popeye Corkscrews have an internal spiral of white and clear colors. The name comes from the boxes in which they were sold, which had 'Popeye' on the cover. Those with more than one white and clear spiral are called 'hybrids'.

c1927-35　　　　　0.75in (2cm) diam

$300-350　　　　　**AB**

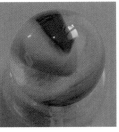

An American Akro Agate Company 'Sparkler', with clear base and bands of white and other colors.

1930-1935 0.75in (2cm) diam

$50-80　　　　　**AB**

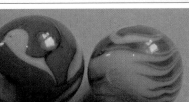

Left: An American Christensen Agate Company 'Turkey Head' Swirl marble.

c1927-1929　　　　　0.75in (2cm) diam

$60-90　　　　　**AB**

Right: An American Christensen Agate Company 'Flame' Swirl marble.

This is so-called as the pattern resembles the flames seen on 'hot rod' or 'boy racer' cars.

c1927-1929　　　　　0.5in (1.5cm) diam

$220-280　　　　　**AB**

Four American Akro Agate Company 'Slag' marbles, in near mint condition.

Akro Agate Slags are the simplest in design and the least colorful. There are also many more Slags made by Akro Agate on the market than by other manufacturers.

1920-1935 0.75in (2cm) diam

$5-8 (each)　　　　　**AB**

An American Peltier Glass Company 'Slag' marble.

Slag marbles are single stream as opposed to variegated stream marbles. They are opaque white mixed into a transparent color. Four companies made them; M.F. Christensen & Son Company, Christensen Agate Company, Akro Agate Company and Peltier Glass Company. Peltier's are identified by very tightly spaced white layers.

c1925-1935 0.75in (2cm) diam

$10-15　　　　　**AB**

Four German or American clay marbles.

Clay marbles were made in Germany and the US between 1800 and 1920, and are still made in France today. They are considered unattractive and of little value to collectors.

0.5in (1.5cm) diam

$1-1.50 (for four) **AB**

Four 20thC Far Eastern 'Cat's-eye' marbles.

All companies have made cat's-eye marbles since c1948. They are common and have minimal value to marble collectors.

$1-1.50 (for four) **AB**

An American Jody Fine 'Banded Swirl' marble.

Jody Fine has been producing handmade contemporary marbles longer than any other producer.

c1980-1995 1.5in (4cm) diam

$15-25 **AB**

An American North River Glass murrine marble.

This small studio produced marbles for around five years during the 1980s.

c1985 1.5in (4cm) diam

$50-80 **AB**

An American Boyer Glassworks flower design marble

c1990-2000 1.25in (3cm) diam

$50-80 **AB**

An American Salazar Art Glass 'Aquarium' marble.

David Salazar is a well-known American maker of paperweights who also makes marbles. The 'Aquarium' design is a trademark of his.

c1995 1.75in (4.5cm) diam

$70-100 **AB**

Mark Matthews is one of the top marble makers in the US and two examples of his work are in the Victoria & Albert Museum, London.

Matthews uses the 'Graal' technique developed at the Scandinavian glass factory Orrefors during the 1920s to achieve the effect.

This marble is from his 'Animal Skin' range, copying patterns on animal skins in the Smithsonian Institute.

There are fourteen different animal skins in the series and all are proportionately sized to the actual animal.

An American Matthews Art Glass 'Jaguar' marble, from the 'Animal Skin' range.

c2000 1.75in (4.5cm) diam

$600-900 **AB**

An American Rolf and Genie Wald 'Joseph's Coat with Lutz' marble.

c2002 1.75in (4.5cm) diam

$150-200 **AB**

An American Josh Simpson 'Planet' marble.

Simpson has produced his Planet marbles since the early 1980s, each is a unique design of an 'alien' planet.

c1995 1.5in (4cm) diam

$60-90 **AB**

An American Fritz Glass 'Ribbon Core Swirl' marble

Fritz Lauenstein is considered to be one of the top American marble artists working today.

c2000 1.5in (4cm) diam

$20-30 **AB**

FIND OUT MORE...

'Marbles – Identification & Price Guide', by Robert Block, published by Schiffer Publishing, 1999.

An early 20thC ship in a bottle, the five-masted wooden ship with paper name label 'S.Maria', fabric flags and waxed paper sails.

11.75in (30cm) long

$50-70   ET

An early 20thC ship in a bottle, the wooden ship with four wooden masts, paper sails and flags and string rigging sailing past a wooden lighthouse, with painted sky and sea.

9.75in (25cm) long

$60-90   ET

An early 20thC ship in a bottle, the three-masted wooden ship sailing past a coastal scene with wooden lighthouse.

11.75in (30cm) long

$70-100   ET

An early 20thC ship in a bottle, the four-masted wooden ship with wooden masts and string rigging, sailing past a lighthouse.

The good level of background painting, with a small lighthouse on the 'headland', and the good detailing of the ship itself make this a more desirable bottle. The bottle is also corked with a decorative cork and stopper.

11.75in (30cm) long

$80-120   ET

A cased waterline model of the three-masted sailing clipper 'Sarah', fully rigged, no sails and with four ship's boats on deck.

Ship 26in (66cm) long

$400-600   DN

A pair of 19thC pink lusterware plaques, one decorated with a war ship inscribed "La Bretagne - 140 guns", the other with a ship and inscribed "May Peace & Plenty on our Nation Smile and Trade with Commerce Bless the British Isle".

9.25in (23.5cm) wide

$400-600   WW

A 19thC glass ship's decanter, with ribbed neck.

9in (23cm) high

$220-280   ET

A Liverpool creamware baluster jug, transfer-printed with a three-masted gunship in full sail in black monochrome, the obverse with "An East View of Liverpool Light House and Signals on Bidston Hill", indexed and enameled, pouring lip repaired, base cracked.

7.25in (18.5cm) diam

$800-1,200   GorL

An American scrimshawed tooth, the front showing a gunship firing cannons, the reverse with portrait of Commodore W. Bainbridge, with a burgundy colored rope twist border.

4in (10cm) high

$1,200-1,800   ET

A CLOSER LOOK AT A SCRIMSHAW

Scrimshaw refers to the art of scratching a design onto bone, tusks or teeth. It was primarily practiced in the 19thC by whalers and seamen during voyages.

The 'Great Harry' was commissioned by King Henry VIII in 1512 and was huge in size, with 1,000 guns. She was accidentally burnt in 1533.

Fakes made from resin are numerous. Red hot pins or gentle rubbing with an emery board and smelling the dust will indicate if it is resin.

Fakes also usually have uniform lines on their base made by a cutting machine smoothing the base. The interior is also 'smooth' and does not have the tooth root.

A 19thC scrimshawed tooth, engraved with the gunship 'The Great Harry' on the front and a portrait of Henry VIII on the reverse.

3.5in (9cm) high

$400-600   **ET**

A 19thC handmade sailor art wooden anchor, signed " Athos, Mass."

8.75in (22cm) high

$70-100   **BCAC**

An enameled silver cigarette case, by Mappin & Webb, painted with naval signals and engraved "Presented to Alice Brounlie as a souvenir of Kittie the winner of the Coronation cup 1904", Chester hallmarks.

1904   3.5in (9cm) high

$700-1,000   **Tag**

Three South Pole exploration photographic cards, by Rotary, featuring Captain Scott: an "In Memoriam" card and two copies of the ship 'Terra Nova' with inset portrait.

$60-90   **DN**

A 'Faithful Freddie' binnacle compass, taken from a submarine.

When used on cast iron ships or iron submarines, which have their own magnetism, correctors have to be fitted to the compass housing. These are spheres of iron that are placed on either side of the case and are usually painted green or red.

c1930   18in (45.5cm) high

$1,200-1,800   **BA**

A British Lifeboat compass, by E. Esdaile & Sons, Sydney, dated 15.2.1951, with petroleum lamp and burner on side.

c1951   8.75in (22cm) high

$280-320   **ATK**

A brass compass, marked "The Boston".

14in (9.5in) wide

$220-280   **BA**

A brass sextant, by J.J. Wilson & Son, Sunderland.

10in (25.5cm) wide

$400-600   **BA**

A rosewood and brass-bound cased two day marine chronometer, by Whyte, Thomson & Co , Glasgow, the silvered dial with subsidiary seconds and up/down dials, in three tier case with ivorine roundels to the front, inscribed "Whyte, Thomson & Co.. Maker to the Admiralty, 144 Broomie aw. Glasgow, No 4492" and with "Highest Award and Silver Medal Awards for 1886".

7.45in (19cm) high

$2,800-3,200   **L&T**

Collectors' Notes

■ Gramophones were developed by Emile Berliner in 1887 and became popular around the turn of the century. They use a needle and soundbox to pick up sound from grooves in the record, which is amplified through a horn.

■ Decorative horn gramophones are the most popular, particularly those by Berliner and HMV. Beware of later reproductions, mainly marked HMV, which have flooded the market recently. They can be often identified by the yellow brass horn.

An Apollo table-model horn gramophone, in mahogany case with transferred label, fitted with Apollo "Grand Prix Milan 1906" soundbox and mahogany seven-leaf horn, the case with supplier's plaque for "Alphonse Cary / Gramophone Agent / Newbury".

$400-600   **DN**

A Columbia Phonograph Co. Graphophone Imperial (BJ), in mahogany case with sound box and nickel-plated 11-leaf horn and double spring motor.
c1905   23.75in (59cm) long

$1,200-1,800   **ATK**

A Parlophon gramophone, in mahogany case with fluted horn decorated with stylized peacock feathers, marked "Parlophon Rekord".

$600-900   **ATK**

A rare Victor Talking Machine Co. "Victor Monarch Special (Rigid Arm)" gramophone, oak case with nickeled brass horn on rigid arm and original soundbox.
c1902

$3,000-5,000   **ATK**

A Gramophone Company Star No. 6 gramophone, with oak case with deluxe rope twist detailing, brass horn, wooden record box and fitted mahogany carrying case with gray felt storm cover.

As well as being a rare model made by the renowned Gramophone Company, the high value can be attributed to the excellent condition and complete array of accessories.

$3,000-4,000   **ET**

A children's tinplate Pigmyphone, by Bing of Nuremburg, with original soundbox and key, in working order.
c1930

$220-280   **ATK**

A tinplate children's nursery gramophone, with integral tinplate horn and reflecta Gem soundbox.
c1910

$600-900   **AOY**

A "Recordon" disc recording machine, by Thermionic Products Ltd., in a brown Bakelite case.
11.75in (30cm) wide

$70-100   **DN**

Musical Boxes

■ Music boxes enchanted many Victorian children and adults, being popular from the 1850s until the late 1880s. Protruding pins on a clockwork and gear-driven revolving cylinder strike 'teeth' on a metal comb to produce the sound. The depth of the tone depends on the length of the 'tooth'.

■ Makers to look for include Nicole Frères, B.A. Bremond and Paillard. The maker, condition and decorative detailing of the case as well as the condition of the mechanism will affect value. Look carefully at the comb to see if any teeth are broken or have been replaced. Beware of winding tired or stalled mechanisms as this can cause severe damage.

A 19thC Swiss cylinder musical box, playing twenty airs, faux rosewood and stenciled case.

24in (61cm) wide

$1,200-1,800   **LC**

A 19thC Swiss cylinder musical box, rosewood-cased with marqueterie inlays, bells in sight, playing eight airs.

The 'Bells in Sight' feature is desirable to collectors. During the tune, small hammers strike the bells producing a sound.

16.25in (41cm) wide

$700-1,000 LC

A 19thC rosewood-cased cylinder musical box with bells and drum in sight, marqueterie inlay decoration.

16.5in (42cm) wide

$1,200-1,800 LC

A Swiss marqueterie rosewood cylinder music box.

The poor and faded condition of the case of this musical box has devalued it, even though it could be restored. An example in good condition would be worth around $700-1,000.

c1885   16in (40.5cm) long

$600-900 SI

A small tortoiseshell cylinder musical box, with segmented comb and key-wound mechanism.

The comb is unusual as each tooth is made from a separate sheet of metal, rather than the whole comb being made from a single sheet.

c1820   3.75in (9.5cm) wide

$800-1,200 ET

A Polyphon No.23S disc music box, playing 6.5 in discs, with 31-tooth comb, with 5 discs.

Usually, larger discs and boxes are more valuable.

c1900

$400-600 ATK

A Polyphon Nr. 103 coin-operated disc music box, playing 15.75in discs, in walnut case with 78-teeth double comb, together with three discs.

These vertical disc musical boxes were often set up in public areas, such as shops, to vide audio entertainment and are often found with slots on the side onto which a coin was inserted to make the mechanism play a tune.

1900   32.25in (82cm)

$2,200-2,800 ATK

A Heinrich Zimmerman "Adler" disc music box, playing 10.5in discs, with 61-teeth comb, together with 11 discs, restored.

c1900

$1,200-1,800 ATK

An American automatic juke-box for 20 records, with colorful lighted plastic décor and richly grained wood, chromium trim and blue mirrored panels, good working condition, including keys, records of contemporary hits, service manuals and a framed lobby card for 'Bus Stop' enclosed.

This juke box became very popular after featuring in the Marilyn Monroe movie 'Bus Stop'.

c1946   57in (144.5cm) high

$4,000-6,000 ATK

A 'Rock-Ola' model 1426 juke-box, with 20 record selections, with 5, 10, 25 cent chutes, colorful front, excellent working condition.

c1947   58in (147.5cm) high

$4,000-6,000 ATK

A German songbird automaton.

c1930   9in (23cm) high

$400-600 BEJ

A tortoiseshell hearing aid.

5.75in (14.5cm) high

$220-280   **BA**

An English ear trumpet.

9.25in (23.5cm) high

$180-220   **BA**

A pair of faience cylindrical drug jars and covers, with pointed knops, one knop a wooden replacement.

c1820   *10in (25.5cm) high*

$280-320   **LFA**

An early 19thC molded tortoiseshell ear trumpet, formed of two pieces.

11in (28cm) long

$120-180   **ET**

A nickel-plated steel monaural stethoscope.

6.5in (16.5cm) high

$15-25   **ET**

A turned wooden stethoscope.

7in (18cm) high

$80-120   **BA**

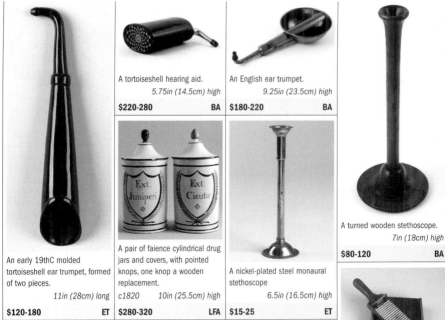

A set of eight mid-19thC blue chemist's bottles and stoppers, of shouldered cylindrical form, one applied with a paper label, the remainder with gilt-band labels; some wear to labels, some small chips and some stoppers probably matched.

As well as being of interest to collectors of medical instruments, colored bottles and those with ornate labels have recently attracted considerable decorative interest.

9.5in (24cm) high

$1,200-1,800   **DN**

A 19thC mahogany and brass pillmaker, complete with fruitwood dish and metal pill mold.

Although commonly seen, they are very rarely complete, especially with the small wooden dish. Incomplete, the main board is worth under $70.

12.5in (31.5cm) long

$200-300   **ET**

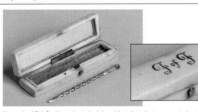

An early 19thC silver dental pick, with twisted stem, contained in a gold and ivory case with "F of F" inscription to lid and mirror to lid interior.

Case 2.5in (6.5cm) long

$300-350   **ET**

A set of dental instruments, by H. Neville & Co., Sheffield and Gray and Selby, Nottingham, in original cloth roll.

c1900

$150-200   **ATK**

An unusually large 19thC veterinary fleam, with three blades.

Fleams were used for bloodletting.

4in (10cm) long

$60-90   **ET**

A rare Victorian Kent Artillery Militia officer's leather helmet, with silver-plated front peak binding, ear rosettes with Royal Crest, silver-plated crowned escutcheon and wreath, helmet plate with gilt grenade over crossed cannon.
c1853-55

$1,000-1,500   **W&W**

A Victorian Royal Midlothian Yeomanry Cavalry officer's black leather helmet, with large ornamental helmet plate in gilt and white metal wreath of thistles, "VR" within Scottish badge, Garter belt, and motto, lion head ear bosses, leather headband, light marks to skull.

$1,200-1,800   **W&W**

A Black Watch officer's feather bonnet, with four tails, red, white and blue diced wool headband and black silk tassels, gilt Sphinx over "Egypt" badge on rosette, scarlet feather plume, leather and silk lining, in cardboard box with label of "J & R Glen, Edinburgh".

$1,800-2,200   **W&W**

A good Scots Guards Highland piper's feather bonnet, diced red, white and blue wool headband, four tails, silk tassels, silver-plated badge on rosette, blue-over-red feather plume, leather and silk lining, patent leather chinstrap, good condition.

$400-600   **W&W**

A French Napoleonic Light Infantry Regiment shako, felt body with leather crown and peak, silver band trim, copper chainscales on ear bosses, brass badge.

$1,200-1,800   **W&W**

A French cavalry trooper's steel helmet, brass binding to peaks, ear-to-ear plate bearing white metal French horn and ornamental embossed comb with Medusa head finial, plume socket on left, hair plume with plaited center section, maker's name "Siraudin Paris".

$800-1,200   **W&W**

A Prussian Infantry Other Ranks Pickelhaub, black leather skull with brass fittings and gilt plate, leather chinstrap and nine segment lining, painted cockades, Berlin maker's stamp inside crown, and inside stamped "J R 152 1907 2B", some wear and losses.

$300-500   **W&W**

A rare Shanghai Rangers officer's blue pill box hat, with scarlet headband, piping and braiding, small gilt Shanghai Volunteer Corps button in the center, patent leather chinstrap, leather and silk lining inscribed "Shanghai Rangers, August 1880".

$300-500   **W&W**

A rare Imperial Russian Grenadier's miter cap, large brass plate in front with die-struck eagle surmounted by crown and motto scrolls, one scroll with inscription including the date "12th Oct 1877", hessian liner with storekeeper's stamp dated "1910", wear and damage.

$3,000-4,000   **W&W**

A vintage American fireman's helmet, from Somers Point, New Jersey, manufactured by Cairns & Bros., New York, losses.
15in (38cm) long

$150-200   **Daw**

A 19thC Indian dagger bichwa, with recurved double-edged blade, swollen diamond section tip, deeply struck with two maker's marks, brass loop shaped hilt, broad knucklebow decorated with geometric ornament, grip with stepped devices, baluster turned button, good condition.

The word 'bichwa' can be literally translated as 'scorpion' alluding to the sharp 'stinging' blade. Bichwa blades are typically double-curved and double-edged, with the wielding hand protected by a curving cover.

Blade 8.5in (21.5cm) long

$280-320 W&W

A large 19thC Indian tulwar hilted kukuri, swollen single-edged blade, chiseled on both sides with flute player and attendants within palmettes and foliage, iron hilt of traditional form silver damascened with geometric designs overall, good condition.

Blade 17.75in (45cm) long

$220-280 W&W

A 19thC Indian gold damascened all-steel dagger jambiya, broad curved heavy double-edged blade, with thickened tip, deeply chiseled and gold damascened with foliage, tigers and deer, iron hilt chiseled overall with foliage and gold damascened, dark patina.

Blade 8.25in (21cm) long

$280-320 W&W

A 19thC Indian all-steel dagger khanjar, broad recurved double-edged blade, chiseled overall with flowering foliage, hilt with raised collar to grip, chiseled overall, some age wear.

Blade 9in (23cm) long

$120-180 W&W

A late 19thC Moroccan silver-mounted dagger jambiya, with curved double-edged blade, silver-mounted wooden hilt and silver sheath engraved and deeply chiseled overall with flowers and foliage, silver suspension rings and upturned finial.

Blade 9in (23cm) long

$180-220 W&W

A 19thC silver-mounted Malayan dagger bade bade, curved single-edged etched pamor blade, silver hilt embossed and chased with foliage, in wooden sheath with horn top, ten narrow silver bands, tip of chape crushed.

Blade 12.25in (31cm) long

$300-500 W&W

A late 19thC Malayan dagger bade bade, faceted blade with false edge, hippopotamus ivory mounts, foliate carved pommel with raised ribs, in wooden sheath with carved mounts, ivory cracked on one side.

11in (28cm) long

$300-500 W&W

An unusual 19thC Burmese dagger dha, heavy broad single-edged blade, silver damascened on both sides with various figures and inscriptions, silver hilt with three figures engraved in silhouette, in nickel sheath.

13.5in (34.5cm) long

$320-380 W&W

A 19thC Indian scissor katar, exterior blades open to reveal inner blade with thickened shallow diamond section tip, twin handlebars open blades when squeezed, traces of silver damascened foliate decoration, some age wear.

16.25in (41.5cm) long

$300-400 W&W

A good Austrian pioneer's sidearm falchion, model 1862, with broad, heavy single-edged fullered blade, steel crosspiece marked "2077", riveted wooden grips, in steel mounted black leather scabbard, good condition.

Blade 18.25in (46.5cm) long

$180-220 W&W

A 1930s-style Hungarian officer's dagger, silvered eagle mounts over brass, with scabbard.

$120-180 LC

A French infantryman's brass-hilted sidearm gladius, with swollen shallow diamond section blade, etched "Chatellerault 1832" with arsenal stamp, one piece regulation brass cruciform hilt, in its brass-mounted leather scabbard, good condition.

Blade 19.25in (49cm) long

$220-280 W&W

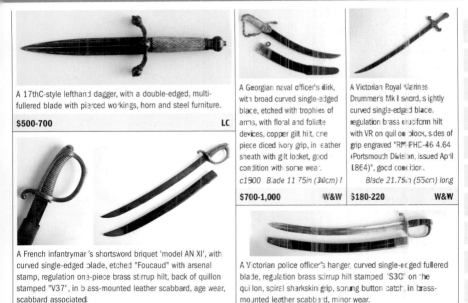

A 17thC-style lefthand dagger, with a double-edged, multi-fullered blade with pierced workings, horn and steel furniture.

$500-700   LC

A Georgian naval officer's dirk, with broad curved single-edged blade, etched with trophies of arms, with floral and foliate devices, copper gilt hilt, one piece diced ivory grip, in leather sheath with gilt locket, good condition with some wear.

c1500   Blade 11.75in (30cm) l

$700-1,000   W&W

A Victorian Royal Marines Drummer's Mk I sword, slightly curved single-edged blade, regulation brass cruciform hilt with VR on quillon block, sides of grip engraved "RM PHD-46 4.64 (Portsmouth Division, issued April 1864)", good condition.

Blade 21.75in (55cm) long

$180-220   W&W

A French infantryman's shortsword briquet 'model AN XI', with curved single-edged blade, etched "Foucaud" with arsenal stamp, regulation one-piece brass stirrup hilt, back of quillon stamped "V37", in brass-mounted leather scabbard, age wear, scabbard associated.

c1802   Blade 23.25in (59cm) wide

$150-200   W&W

A Victorian police officer's hanger, curved single-edged fullered blade, regulation brass stirrup hilt stamped 'S30' on the quillon, spiral sharkskin grip, sprung button catch, in brass-mounted leather scabbard, minor wear.

Blade 24in (61cm) long

$300-400   W&W

A 19thC Dyak headhunter's Mandau sword, swollen single-edged blade, slightly curved with concave side, wooden hilt carved with stylized teeth and leeches, iron wire-bound grip, in wooden scabbard with carved top and woven rattan bindings, good condition, some age wear.

Blade 24.25in (61.5cm) long

$150-200   W&W

A 19thC Dyak parang latok sword, with a swollen broad single-edged blade to octagonal elbow, silver grip embossed and chased with foliage, raised borders, carved bone pommel, good condition.

The Dyak are the indigenous tribes of the island of Borneo. Largely unaffected by modern civilization; their farming and hunter-gatherer based culture is still dominated by shamanistic and animistic religious cults. Intertribal warfare has remained, with headhunting being an important feature.

Blade 18.5in (47cm) long

$700-1,000   W&W

One of a pair of 19thC Chinese river pirates period swords, each with shallow diamond section double-edged blade, inlaid with brass circles, brass mounts, crosspieces in the form of a Makarra's head pommels cast with dragons in clouds, fluted horn grips, in sanded sharkskin-covered scabbard with brass mounts and pommel, hanging bands with additional pictogram and dragon, good condition.

Blades 18in (45.5cm) long

$600-900   W&W

A 19thC Indian axe, silver damascened steel head with edge and square-shaped peen, on copper haft engraved with a floral diaper pattern, pommel unscrews to reveal stiletto, some wear and damage.

21in (53.5cm) long

$700-1,000   W&W

An unusual 19thC Indian axe, crescent-shaped steel head with silver damascened foliage, on ebony shaft with brass mounts, one ring missing.

27.75in (70.5cm) long

$180-220   W&W

A Meissonier print, depicting a cavalry officer reading a report before two Hussars in a room, inscribed "Achille Jacquet" and dated, framed, minor damage to borders.

1860   13.5in (34.5cm) high

$180-220   **W&W**

A colored print, after R. Hillingford, depicting the Duke of Wellington "Summoned to Waterloo-Brussels, dawn of June 16th 1815", framed.

$150-200   **W&W**

An Ackerman print, "7th Royal Fusilliers", showing two officers in full dress and another in undress, after the original by H. Martens, No. 8 in the series "R. Ackerman's Costumes of the British Army", dated, mounted and framed, good condition.

1855   12in (30.5cm) high

$60-90   **W&W**

A large black and white print, "Bonaparte, General en Chef de L'Armee d'Italie", after the original by Janet Lange, mounted and framed in gilt, few small chips to frame.

19in (48.5cm) wide

$120-180   **W&W**

A watercolor of mounted Polish Lancers, signed "Trinakonsky"(?), depicting a corporal carrying a carbine and others with lances, all wear foul-weather lance caps, framed.

14in (35.5cm) wide

$600-900   **W&W**

A watercolor of the Thames at Greenwich, general view with three decker first rate ship of the line, paddle steamer and various smaller boats, naval base towers in the background, gilt frame, unsigned, two foxing spots.

c1850   10.5in (26.5cm) wide

$700-1,000   **W&W**

An original artwork for London Illustrated News, or a contemporary paper, depicting the departure from an Italian quayside of a figure to the accompaniment of the band, as he embarks on a British tender, initialed "FD", framed.

11.5in (29cm) high

$60-90   **W&W**

A WWI war loan poster, "Pay 5 shillings for this, and help crush the Germans-apply at the nearest Post Office", framed, good condition.

28in (71cm) high

$150-200   **W&W**

An oil on canvas painting, "Original Dug-Out 1914, "Zero" Hour", depicting a Tommy in tin helmet with rifle silhouetted against a white cug out wall, a candle burns on the right, on wooden stretcher, old repairs to back.

42in (106.5cm) high

$220-280   **W&W**

A carved marble bust of the Duke of Wellington, wearing full dress uniform with decorations, including black stone plinth, good condition.

13in (33cm) high

$1,200-1,800   **W&W**

Collectors' Notes

- Mobile and cellular phones use radio frequencies transmitted between many base stations that divide any area into cells. Calls are transferred from base station to base station as the user travels between them. The basic concept began in 1947, but the technology could not be developed.

- Although Bell Laboratories in the US developed the cellular communications technology earlier, Dr Martin Cooper is credited with inventing the first truly portable handset at Motorola in 1973.

- The American Federal Communications Commission at first limited amounts of radio frequencies allowing only 23 conversations by radio in any given area. This limited any developments until 1968, with cellular phones being approved finally in 1982.

- From then a number of analogue based systems were developed, including ETACS (Total Access Communication System), but these were found to be insecure. Partly due to this and a proliferation of different systems in many countries, European countries worked together from 1982 to produce a

- secure, digital global standard, GSM (Global System for Mobile Communications).

- Early cellular phones were expensive, large and cumbersome with heavy batteries. Talk and standby time were short. By the early 1990s, technical innovations allowed them to become smaller and truly portable. Soon they became inexpensive and almost 'disposable,' with people renewing them regularly and throwing away older models.

- Look for large early phones from the 1980s and early 1990s, landmark models that were the first to use certain technologies, or those that captured public imagination such as the 'Mars Bar' phone. As they were made in large quantities to be used and carried around, many were worn or damaged. Look for those in the best condition.

- There is little or no literature available to the collector beyond original magazine reviews and instructions. This market is still extremely young, with very few collectors, but will undoubtedly change and adapt over the coming years.

A Bosch 509e dual band GSM cellular phone, with transparent orange fascia.

c1999   6.25in (16cm) long

$15-25   **GC**

A Swedish Ericsson EH97 Hotline ETACS cellular phone, with flip up aerial.

This phone was a direct copy of the popular English Orbitel and was Ericsson's first handheld portable phone.

1992-1993 7in (17.5cm) long

$15-25   **GC**

A black Motorola 850CX ETACS phone.

This phone cost between $350 and $450 when released in the late 1980s.

c1987   7.75in (19.5cm) long

$100-150   **GC**

A grey Motorola 'Personal Phone' ETACS cellular phone.

This phone cost $350 when released and is unusual in that it has no LCD or digital display.

c1992   6.25in (16cm) long

$40-60   **GC**

A Motorola 8800X ETACS cellular phone, with Motorola fitted leather case with sleeve for spare battery.

1990-1991

8in (20cm) long

$120-180   **GC**

A grey Motorola MicroTac Duo ETACS cellular phone, with flip and extending aerial.

c1992   6.5in (16.5cm) long

$30-50   **GC**

A black Motorola MR1 flip-phone PCM cellular phone, with extending aerial.

c1994   6in (15.5cm) long

$40-60   **GC**

A black Motorola Startac GSM cellular phone.

c1998 3.75in (9.5cm) long

$70-100 GC

A British NEC 22a ETACS cellular phone, lacks aerial.

When released, this model was sold for $600.

c1993 7in (18cm) long

$20-30 GC

A black angular NEC P4 ETACS cellular phone, for Mercury Communications, with retractable aerial.

Costing $600 new, this phone had eight hours of standby time.

1992-1993 7in (17.5cm) long

$30-40 GC

A navy blue Nokia 101 ETACS cellular phone, for Peoples Phone, with extending aerial.

1992-1993 6.75in (17cm) l

$30-50 GC

A black Nokia 100 analogue cellular phone, with extending aerial, for Vodafone.

c1993 6.75in (17cm) l

$40-60 GC

A walnut Nokia 2110 cellular phone.

c1994 6.5in (17cm) l

$50-80 GC

A British Orbitel 902 GSM cellular phone, with extending aerial.

c1994 7.5in (19cm) l

$70-100 GC

A Philips TCD308 Diga GSM cellular phone, with sliding microphone cover, for Cellnet.

c1997 6.75in (17cm) l

$20-30 GC

A Pioneer PCC730 analogue cellular phone, with flip cover and extending aerial.

c1993 6.5in (16.5cm) l

$40-60 GC

A Japanese pink Peoples Phone CTN7000 ETACS cellular phone.

This model was also available in fluorescent green.

c1995 6.75in (17cm) long

$30-40 GC

A black Siemens S6 Classic GSM cellular phone.

This phone had a Hi-Fi loudspeaker earpiece.

1996-1997 7.5in (19cm) long

$30-50 GC

A Siemens C10 PCN cellular phone, for Vodafone.

c1998 6.25in (16cm) long

$20-30 GC

A Sony CM-DX1000 GSM cellular phone, with sliding earpiece and extending aerial.

This was also known colloquially as the 'Mars Bar' phone, due to its similarity in shape to the Mars Bar.

c1995 7in (17.5cm) long

$120-180 GC

One of the six hand-painted heraldic silk panels created to adorn the black velvet pall which covered the coffin of Horatio Nelson, Viscount, Victor of Trafalgar (1758-1805), portraying two escutcheons displayed accollée and bearing the impaled arms of Lord and Lady Nelson, surmounted by a coronet and famed within a gilt border, pinned into a glazed frame for display.

The panel adorned Nelson's coffin during its journey up the River Thames, it was then placed on the 'Grand Funeral Car', which bore his body in procession from the Admiralty to St. Paul's Cathedral for burial on January 9, 1806. Provenance: Formerly the property of the Rev. Dr. Scott, Lord Nelson's Chaplain, and thence by direct descent.

c1806   23in (60cm) high

$50,000-60,000   **DN**

A double-page letter from Horatio Nelson, Viscount, Victor of Trafalgar, with integral blank leaf, 4vo, signed "Horatio Nelson" to "His Royal Majesty Prince William Henry", sent from Exmouth, dated April 22, "I arrived here a few days ago and purpose no accident", small portion of upper right-hand side torn away with obvious modern repair.

9in (23cm) high

$4,000-6,000   **DN**

A single page letter from Horatio Nelson, Viscount, Victor of Trafalgar, with integral blank leaf, 4vo, signed "Nelson & Bronte" to Philip Langmead, Mayor of Plymouth, dated 22nd January 1801, in his secretary's hand, with Nelson's signature at the end, discussing "the honor which the corporation of Plymouth intend to confer upon me", with an envelope bearing a red seal.

9in (23cm) high

£1,500-2,000   **DN**

An early 19thC English twin-handled sauce tureen, cover and stand, decorated with a pair of enclosed armorials of Vice Admiral Horatio, Viscount Nelson of the Nile K B.

10.25in (26cm) wide

$3,000-5,000   **L&T**

An early 19thC white marble commemorative wall-tablet, carved and inscribed with a verse in praise of Horatio Nelson, in a later oak frame with plain pediment.

c1805   20in (51cm) wide

$2,200-2,800   **DN**

A Georgian hand-painted paper wallet for skeins of winders, exterior with floral painted and gilt lined borders, front with an oval label reading 'A Token of friendship', the reverse with a painted panel showing musical instruments and a musical score titled 'Nelson's Victory August 1st 1798', edges bound in ribbon.

4in (10cm) wide

$400-600   **KBon**

An English Delft bowl, with a bust portrait of Nelson.

c1905   9.75in (25cm) diam

$220-280   **3onS**

A 1940s EPNS souvenir spoon for the HMS Victory, by Sampson Mordan & Co.

4in (10cm) high

$8-12   **COB**

A Prattware commemorative naval jug, one side molded with Captain Berry, the reverse with Admiral Nelson, each between ships and titled, a few small rim chips and a faint short hairline.

c1800   6in (15.5cm) high

$400-600   **WW**

A 1970s European silver model of the HMS Victory.

6.25in (15cm) wide

$400-600   **COB**

A Lantern Riche magic lantern, some parts repainted but retains original burner.

This is the tallest of a series of nine magic lanterns.

c1880   15in (41cm) high

$320-380   **ATK**

A Carrée magic lantern, by Lapierre, Paris, lacks burner.

c1880   10in (25.5cm) high

$280-320   **ATK**

A Salon magic lantern, by Lapierre, Paris, for 2in slides, repainted.

Magic lanterns are an early form of projector, pre-dating the cinematic moving image. Colored printed or hand-painted glass slides were placed behind a lens, illuminated by gas flames (later electricity) and projected onto a wall or screen. A story, often moralistic, was told through a number of slides. Large mahogany lanterns with multiple lenses, or small tin examples decorated in bright colors like this one, are very desirable. If the lantern is in a novelty shape, such as an Eiffel Tower, or by a well known name such as Lapierre, its value will be higher. The colors should be bright and the finish original and intact. Plain, black lanterns are less popular and less valuable.

c1880   11in (28cm) high

$220-280   **ATK**

A magic lantern, by Lapierre, Paris, with original box, 11 glass slides and burner.

c1910

$120-180   **ATK**

A Faust magic lantern, by Gebrüder Bing, together with twelve 3in slides, electrified.

Contained in a fitted box with small glass slides of children's stories, these lanterns were popular toys. Look for complete examples in excellent condition.

c1904   14.5in (37cm) high

$220-280   **ATK**

A mahogany and brass magic lantern, by J.H. Dallmeyer, London, with a tinplate top cover and ventilated chimney, brass lens assembly and mechanical slide holder, each side with opening door, light porthole and attached ivorex-type label, converted for electric operation involving a new base.

This would have originally been powered by gas, but has been later converted to electricity.

$280-320   **DN**

A late 19thC hand-painted mahogany and brass 'chromotrope' magic lantern slide.

By turning the handle the colored pattern revolves like a kaleidoscope.

7in (17.5cm) wide

$80-120   **ET**

A late 19thC mahogany and glass mechanical hand-painted chromotrope slide for a magic lantern.

$220-280   **ET**

A Brewster-type stereoviewer, with wooden eyepiece and central focussing, together with 61 stereocards showing scenes of Germany, two by W. England.

Stereography was popular from the mid-19thC until the early 20thC. A camera with two lenses a small distance apart was used to take two slightly different views of the same image. When mounted side-by-side on a card and viewed through a stereoscopic viewer, the images blend into one and this appears three-dimensional. Tourist views, cities, the countryside and historical sights are popular images found on cards.

$300-350   **ATK**

An Art Nouveau-style tin stereoscopic viewer, by P.H. Suchard, with ten stereoview cards.

$280-320   ATK

A 'Taxiphote' table-mounted stereoviewer, by Jules Richard, Paris, with 450 stereocards.

The stereocards are held inside the body on a revolving rack. Light is admitted from either the back or the top.

c1910

$500-700   ATK

A miniature Mutoscope, or 'flicker' machine, by the World Syndicate Co. Inc., New York, NY., patent date 9 September 1919.

Drawings clipped from US newspapers could be gathered in this machine and animated.

c1920

$500-700   ATK

A Kinora viewer by Kinora Ltd., London, with two reels; No. 190 of horse-riding and No. 345 of firemen in horse-drawn carriages.

c1910

$1,000-1,500   ATK

A pair of Georgian silver spectacles, with extending arms terminating with small loops and with hallmark for Birmingham.
1822

$180-220   ET

A 1950s coin-operated marble vending machine, with "View-Master" stereoviewer, probably French.

$300-500   ATK

A German Ernst Plank tinplate camera obscura, with ground glass plate under the lid.

These were used for viewing a scene which was projected through the sliding lens and onto a ground glass plate via a mirror positioned at 45 degrees.

c1890

$400-600   ET

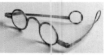

A pair of silver folding spectacles, by F. Hedley, Richmond, in tortoiseshell case.

Case 5in (12.5cm) long

$150-200   BA

A pair of steel 'ring side' spectacles, stamped "5C".

c1770   *4.75in (12cm) wide*

$300-500   ET

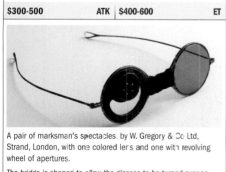

A pair of marksman's spectacles, by W. Gregory & Co Ltd, Strand, London, with one colored lens and one with revolving wheel of apertures.

The bridge is shaped to allow the glasses to be turned over so the revolving wheel of apertures could be worn on either eye.

c1890   *4.75in (12cm) wide*

$120-180   ET

An ivory cased brass pocket telescope.

Cracks in the ivory cases of these telescopes will reduce the value considerably.

$300-500   ET

A brass pocket telescope with acquered exterior, some chips to acquer.

Telescopes often bear the name of the maker around the eyepiece lens or on the first draw tube of the telescope.

$220-280   ET

A Chinese export famille rose flared bowl, decorated with panels of figures and flowers on a scale ground with gilt swag borders.

4.75in (12cm) diam

$120-180   **DN**

A Chinese export famille rose tapering coffee pot and cover, with floral swagged borders and decorated with a European coat-of-arms, together with an English market tea bowl and saucer en suite.

$700-1,000   **DN**

Two Chinese export famille rose coffee cans, together with two coffee cans decorated with flowers.

c1800

$70-100   **DN**

An 18thC Chinese export famille rose ogee lozenge section tea caddy and cover, decorated with a coat-of-arms against a scattered floral ground, Qianlong period.

Famille rose describes the palette of colors used for decoration that centered around pink. Although the pink color was developed by Dutchman Andreas Cassius in the mid-17thC, it was perfected by the Chinese after being brought to them in the 1720s. Large numbers of pieces were made for export to the West during the 18thC, 19thC and early 20thC. Early pieces tend to be finely decorated, but quality declined as production increased to keep up with growing demand. Look closely at the quality of decoration and buy the best you can as these will remain the most desirable. Many 18thC pieces have coats-of-arms as it became common practice for wealthy and noble families to commission Chinese painters to decorate ceramics with their armorial bearing.

5in (12.5cm) high

$1,000-1,500   **DN**

A 1920s/30s small famille rose vase, the ovoid body painted with Wang Xizhi with his two attendants with two geese, with mark of Hongxian.

Later famille rose pieces are marked "CHINA" or "MADE IN CHINA".

8in (20cm) high

$180-220   **DN**

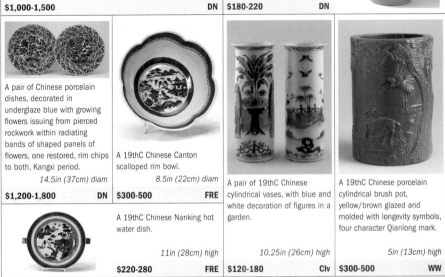

A pair of Chinese porcelain dishes, decorated in underglaze blue with growing flowers issuing from pierced rockwork within radiating bands of shaped panels of flowers, one restored, rim chips to both, Kangxi period.

14.5in (37cm) diam

$1,200-1,800   **DN**

A 19thC Chinese Canton scalloped rim bowl.

8.5in (22cm) diam

$300-500   **FRE**

A 19thC Chinese Nanking hot water dish.

11in (28cm) high

$220-280   **FRE**

A pair of 19thC Chinese cylindrical vases, with blue and white decoration of figures in a garden.

10.25in (26cm) high

$120-180   **Clv**

A 19thC Chinese porcelain cylindrical brush pot, yellow/brown glazed and molded with longevity symbols, four character Qianlong mark.

5in (13cm) high

$300-500   **WW**

A Chinese porcelain brush pot, with stallion decoration and translucent yellow glaze, some losses.

An early 19thC Chinese blanc de Chine model of a buffalo, with a small boy playing a flute.

'Blanc de Chine' pieces are made from a pure, white porcelain with a very smooth glaze and have been made since the 16thC at the Dehua kilns in the Chinese province of Fujian. The most common shapes are small figures of ho-tai (Buddha) and Guanyin, the Chinese goddess of mercy. Early pieces tend to have a warmer, ivory tinge, whilst later pieces are 'colder' white or have a blue tinge.

A Chinese blanc de Chine porcelain figure of a sage.

4.5in (11.5cm) high

6.75in (17cm) high

12.25in (31cm) high

$800-1,200   **Daw**   **$700-1,000**   **WW**   **$80-120**   **Clv**

A pair of Chinese Late Qing dynasty famille rose baluster vases with covers, with floral reserves in the famille rose palette on a blue ground with stylized cloud details and lotus with yellow overglaze lappet foot at base.

A Kangxi vase, raised prunus bird and landscape decoration, riveted restoration to the base.

c1900   23in (58.5cm) high

22.75in (57.5cm) high

$700-1,000   **RTC**   **$1,200-1,800**   **LC**

A 19thC Chinese export celadon glazed garden seat, six-sided form with raised white enamel decoration.

A Chinese porcelain ginger jar, with enamel glaze with wire inlay, turquoise blue ground borders large panels, one with man pulling cart of flowers, other panel depicts moonlight scene with geese flying over landscape.

18.5in (47cm) high

12in (30.5cm) high

$320-380   **LC**   **$280-320**   **AAC**

A CLOSER LOOK AT AN IMARI CHARGER

Look for variations in the decoration, showing hand-painted details. Later, 20thC pieces are printed. Bright, even gold details usually indicate later production.

Large plates made before c1910 have small indentations on the underside from kiln supports. Foot-rims on older pieces are also brown and dirty.

Older Imari has an uneven glaze, reflect light on the surface to check. White areas on older pieces also have a gray tone, more modern pieces are a 'cleaner' white.

Pre-20thC Imari was fired in wood-burning kilns, pits or specks of ash in the surface show it is an older piece.

An Imari charger, decorated with a mountainous landscape and buildings with offset panel of women dancing, in blue, red, green and yellow with gilt accents.

Imari ware was produced in Arita, Japan. It was shipped to other parts of Japan and the West from the port of Imari on the island of Kyushu, hence its name. The highly recognizable Imari palette includes a vivid underglaze blue, gray, red and gold. Green and turquoise are also found. It originated in the late 17thC but matured around the turn of the 19thC and was exported in large numbers. Patterns usually comprise overlapping and geometrical panels with complex decoration of flowers, landscapes or scrolling. Examine bodies carefully for cracks.

24in (70cm) diam

$500-700 **AAC**

An Imari charger, the central panel with cloud design surrounded by wide border of Oriental landscape with birds, in blue, red, green and yellow with gilt accents.

18in (45.75cm) diam

$300-400 **AAC**

A large late 19th/early 20thC Japanese Imari circular charger, painted with a gnarled apple tree and pair of water buffalo, with cloud scroll border, signed, Meiji period.

14.75in (37.5cm) diam

$280-320 **L&T**

A pair of late 19th/early 20thC Japanese Imari baluster vases with covers, painted in gilt and typical Imari colors, Meiji period.

17.5in (44.5cm) high

$400-600 **RTC**

A Japanese Imari koro and pierced cover, with scroll handle and knop and decorated in typical style with growing flowers.

6in (15cm) high

$220-280 **DN**

A Japanese Imari pear-shaped vase, with a tall slim neck, decorated with panels of flowers and foliage, neck restored.

c1700 *8.5in (22cm) high*

$280-320 **WW**

A pair of late 19thC two-handled Kutani vases, the globular-shaped bodies with traditional iron red and gilt decoration.

Kutani ware uses a five-color palette comprising cobalt blue, yellow, green, red and a brownish purple. It was developed by a 17thC alchemist named Goto Saijiro who studied porcelain at the famous town of Arita, where Imari ware is produced.

9.75in (25cm) high

$280-320 **Clv**

A 19thC Japanese Imari fluted jardinière, decorated in typical style with panels of flowers.

11.75in (30cm) high

$300-500 **DN**

A Satsuma slender ovoid vase, decorated with a band of figures in a spring river landscape within brocade lappet borders.

6in (15cm) high

$150-200 DN

A Sumida Gawa vase, decorated with a man on diagonal ledge, with flask at feet, signed.

This vase is typical of Sumida Gawa production with its decoration of high relief figures. Sumida Gawa pieces are usually heavy, and in the form of everyday objects such as teapots and vases. The name derives from the Sumida river near the Asakusa potteries (near Tokyo) where the pottery was made.

5.5in (14cm) high

$300-400 CA

A late 19thC large Japanese enameled porcelain vase, the ovoid body with a tall neck and flared rim, worked in relief with an encircling scaled dragon, enameled overall with blossoming flowers, base broken.

26in (66cm) high

$180-220 FRE

A late 19th/early 20thC Japanese stoneware bottle, with a tapering body, the side molded with a seated figure of Ho Tai.

9.75in (25cm) high

$150-200 WW

A pair of Japanese export vases, baluster two-handled form with flared necks, profusely decorated with raised enameled designs.

24.75in (63cm) high

$280-320 LC

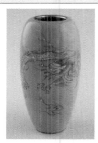

A 20thC Japanese porcelain vase, the ovoid body decorated with a two-tone blue dragon, base with painted iron red mark.

6in (15cm) high

$80-120 Clv

A Japanese porcelain vase, decorated in underglaze blue with a band of irises, with "Makazu Kozan" mark.

7.5in (19cm) diam

$220-280 DN

A Japanese pottery teapot, of rustic design with faux lacquer glaze.

2.75in (7cm) high

$30-50 Clv

Three Japanese porcelain figures of three wise monkeys, each with a carved hardwood stand.

4.75in (12cm) high

$150-200 Clv

Two Chinese carved ivory puzzle balls, the larger carved with flowers, the smaller with writhing dragon decoration, and an open pierced stand decorated with bird and blossom.

Stand 4.25in (11cm) high

$150-200 **L&T**

A late 19thC Japanese carved ivory tusk, depicting a man and a boy on a plinth with an axe, the boy with an eagle on his head, signed on carved hardwood plinth.

12in (31cm) high

$280-320 **L&T**

A 19thC Chinese ivory wrist rest, carved to one side with immortals within cloud scrolls, with a key fret border.

c1850   18in (45.5cm) wide

$400-600 **DN**

A 19thC Chinese ivory wrist rest, finely carved and pierced with ducks swimming beneath lotus, prunus and pine, minor damage.

c1850   9.75in (25cm) wide

$280-320 **DN**

A Japanese carved ivory and lacquered wood figural, probably Daikoku, depicted in a striding pose carrying a full sack, losses.

A 20thC Japanese ivory okimono, carved as a standing man, with a long beard and holding a stick, Showa period.

3in (7.5cm) high

$180-220 **SI**

A 20thC Chinese bronze figure of a duck, stylistically rendered as a crouching figure with one wing raised, incised and raised detailing.

16in (40.5cm) long

$220-280 **FRE**

Figures such as these are called 'okimono'. Often carved in ivory, they were designed to stand in the 'tokonoma' or display alcove in traditional Japanese homes. They often depict gods or mythological personalities. Daikoku is the god of wealth and farmers and one of the seven lucky gods known as the 'Tenbu'. He is usually depicted with a sack of treasure on his shoulder and a lucky mallet which produced riches or grants wishes when tapped. His head and shoulders are often rubbed by people when passing to bring luck.

8.5in (21.5cm) high

$1,500-2,000 **Daw**

A late 19th/early 20thC Japanese bronze figure of a tortoise, depicted walking with head and tail exposed, base signed, tip of tail missing, Meiji period.

7.5in (19cm) long

$700-1,000 **FRE**

A pair of late 19thC Chinese rank badges, one for the front and one for the back, decorated with peacocks sitting amidst a variety of floral branches, with sun in the top right corner of each.

8.5in (21.5cm) high

$300-500 **RTC**

A late 19thC Chinese child's rank badge, of smaller than typical size with a quail surrounded by bats and with sun in the top left corner, on a summer silk gauze ground.

The quail marks the 8th civil rank and bats represent good luck.

9in (23cm) high

$180-220 **RTC**

A Japanese carved and lacquered box, with relief carved genre scene on lid, gilt decoration.

16in (40.5cm) wide

$150-200 AAC

A 19thC Kajikawa School four-case inro, decorated on the roiro ground with a wood pigeon perched on an oak tree in gold, red and black takamakie with details in nashiji, aogai, kirigane, gold foil, mura-nashiji and hiramakie, rich nashiji interior, signed Kajikawa Saku with red pot seal, with a carved lacquer ojime, chip to bottom case, gold foil losses.

An inro is a small rectangular box made up of sections that hung from the 'obi' (sash) of a kimono and held herbs or tobacco. It was fastened with the bead-shaped 'ojime' or with a carved netsuke. They are often richly carved or decorated, like this one, with different high-quality lacquer techniques.

$1,800-2,200 DN

A scarce 1870s Japanese carved wood winding 'chalk line' machine.

The dish held chalk. As the string was unwound it rubbed along the chalk. The string would be tied to an object, pulled taut and tapped to drop chalk dust in a straight line.

7.5in (19cm) long

$100-150 TAB

Four Chinese scholar's objects, comprising a huanghuali brush pot; a jade ink stone; an amber Peking glass brush washer and a carved wood handle brush.

Brush pot 4.5in (11.5cm) diam

$220-280 SI

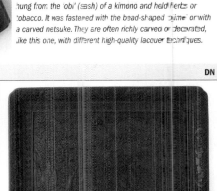

An 18thC Chinese cinnabar lacquer tray, centrally carved with a scholar and boy in a mountainous river landscape within key fret band, the rim paneled with prunus on a cell ground

Cinnabar refers to the red color of the lacquer, which is made by adding mercury to the lacquer, which itself is made from the sap of the Rhus tree. It is often found on carved pieces, as with this example.

16in (41cm) wide

$320-380 DN

A plain 18thC Tibetan ink pot, with original brass stopper.

2.75in (7cm) high

$60-90 TAB

A decorated bronze Tibetan ink pot, with later wooden stopper.

2.75in (7cm) high

$60-90 TAB

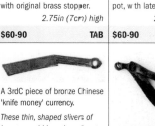

A 3rdC piece of bronze Chinese 'knife money' currency.

These thin, shaped slivers of bronze would have been hung on a belt or chain and pulled off for use.

5.5in (14cm) wide

$180-220 TAB

A late 19thC Tibetan bronze and iron folding blade.

7.75in (19.5cm) wide

$80-120 TAB

A silver alloy Persian lidded tea or coffee cup on stand.

c1900

3.25in (8.5cm) high

$300-400 TAB

A B C D E F G H I J K L M N O P Q R S T U V W XYZ

PAPERWEIGHTS

Collectors' Notes

- Although probably first made in Venice in 1843, glass paperweights became most popular in France, and French factories Baccarat, Clichy and Saint Louis are considered the most important in this field.
- Paperweight diameters are typically 2-4in (5-10cm). Larger weights are known as 'magnums', smaller as 'miniatures'. The base is often comprised of arranged sections of cut glass canes, known as a 'set-up', which create a decorative pattern called 'millefiori'. This is magnified by a dome of clear glass. Other patterns utilize motifs such as animals and flowers.
- The 'golden age' is considered to be the 1840s to mid-1850s. After this, many French glassmakers emigrated to the US to work. British paperweights were produced from 1848 onwards.
- Many weights have been polished to hide damage, so look for flat areas and offset patterns to assess the level of polishing.

Clichy

A Clichy spaced millefiori paperweight, including a pink rose and five green pastry-mold canes.

2.75in (7cm) diam

$600-900 GorL

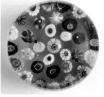

A Clichy spaced concentric millefiori paperweight, with three circles of brightly colored canes about a central turquoise and white set-up.

2.75in (7cm) diam

$300-400 GorL

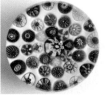

A Clichy 'Sodden Snow' ground, spaced concentric millefiori paperweight, the three circles of canes set on an opaque ground.

3in (7.75cm) diam

$1,000-1,500 GorL

A Clichy scattered millefiori paperweight, with a central pink and green rose, encircled by canes on a clear ground, including one pink and green rose at the outer edge.

3in (7.5cm) diam

$800-1,200 LHS

COLLECTORS' NOTES

- Founded in 1837, Clichy began making paperweights in 1846. They produced very few from 1852 and in 1885, the factory closed down.
- Examples are usually unsigned, but have distinctive characteristics, such as the 'Clichy Rose' – a pink glass cane cut across to resemble an open rose. A cane with the letter 'C' may also be included.
- Other characteristic features of Clichy's work are concentric rings of millefiori, garland patterns on red, blue and green grounds and use of softer colors than other makers.
- Clichy weights are globular in shape with a small, flat, slightly concave base. Most French weights are made from lead glass, but Clichy's are not, so are lighter. When polished, they may show a white line.

A miniature Clichy close-packed millefiori paperweight, including two 'hidden' white roses, a pink and green rose and a complex "C" signature cane, in a white stave basket.

2in (5cm) diam

$4,000-6,000 LHS

A Clichy scrambled millefiori paperweight, with brightly colored whole and partial canes, including a pink and green rose at the outer edge.

3in (7.5cm) diam

$1,000-1,500 LHS

A Clichy close concentric millefiori paperweight, the clear glass set with six rows of millefiori, with a composite crimp cog cane at center, within a basket of opaque red and white staves, crack to base.

3in (7.5cm) diam

$700-1,000 LHS

A Clichy opaque-ground concentric millefiori door handle, with two circles of colored canes, base to handle damaged.

2.5in (6.5cm) diam

$300-350 GorL

A small Clichy concentric millefiori paperweight, with three circles in shades of pink, green and white, above a central pink and white cane.

2in (5cm) diam

$150-200 GorL

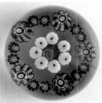

A miniature Clichy patterned concentric millefiori paperweight, the central cane surrounded by white roses, the five green pastry molds alternating with claret canes at the edge.

1.75in (4.5cm) diam

$220-280 GorL

A Clichy faceted concentric millefiori paperweight, with a central pink rose within green and pink canes and an outer ring of dark blue and cream canes, cut with a window and five thumbprints.

2.75in (7cm) diam

$700-1,000 GorL

A Clichy patterned millefiori paperweight, with five clusters of canes about a central pink and white pastry mold, set on an opaque ground.

2.75in (7cm) diam

$700-1,000 GorL

A Clichy C-scroll garlands over 'Sodden Snow' paperweight, with a bouquet of complex millefiori at the center with three tight concentric rings of cane.

Arsenic and antimony were used to secure the soft opaque enamel, which is often known as 'milk' or 'opaque white'.

3in (7.5cm) diam

$2,200-2,800 LHS

A CLOSER LOOK AT A CLICHY PAPERWEIGHT

Clichy produced fewer bouquet paperweights than their competitors, making the Clichy examples rare.

This example maximizes use of three techniques together: the millefiori flowers; the crimped glass leaves; and the lampwork pleated petals.

In 1978, these highly desirable types were exhibited at the famed Corning Museum of Glass.

A Clichy bouquet paperweight, with five millefiori-centered lampwork flowers tied with a pink ribbon, over a clear ground, minor chips.

3in (7.5cm) diam

$7,000-10,000 LHS

A Clichy posy paperweight, with two pink roses and a pink and white cane amongst leaves.

2.25in (6.5cm) diam

$400-600 GorL

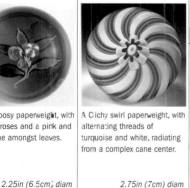

A Clichy swirl paperweight, with alternating threads of turquoise and white, radiating from a complex cane center.

2.75in (7cm) diam

$1,500-2,000 LHS

A Clichy millefiori checker paperweight, with a rose at the center and the edge and with assorted millefiori divided by short segments of atticinio, set on a bed of lace.

This form of ground, made up from white glass strands (atticinio) is often known as 'muslin'.

2.5in (6.5cm) diam

$1,200-1,800 LHS

Collectors' Notes

- Established in 1764 in Lorraine, France, Baccarat produced paperweights from c1845 and is often considered to be the best maker. Examples are found in many different sizes which have less bulging sides than other makers' examples.

- Many weights use millefiori, some of which contain silhouettes of animals, shamrocks (rare) and other motifs. Jean-Baptiste Toussaint, General Manager of Baccarat is credited with introducing animals in 1846 after seeing his nephew Emile Gridel making paper cut-outs of animals.

- Look out for 'signature canes' that use the letter 'B' and the year, 1846 to 1849 inclusive. They are usually marked in red, blue and green on a white cane.

- Examples with dates in the 1850s (1853 and 1859) are probably genuine. However, dates such as 1815 are false and indicate a nongenuine period example, as do centrally placed date canes.

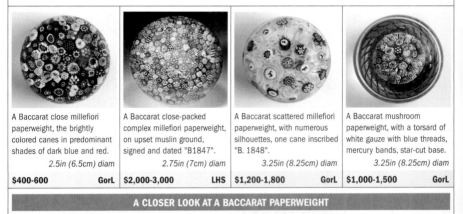

A Baccarat close millefiori paperweight, the brightly colored canes in predominant shades of dark blue and red.

2.5in (6.5cm) diam

$400-600   **GorL**

A Baccarat close-packed complex millefiori paperweight, on upset muslin ground, signed and dated "B1847".

2.75in (7cm) diam

$2,000-3,000   **LHS**

A Baccarat scattered millefiori paperweight, with numerous silhouettes, one cane inscribed "B. 1848".

3.25in (8.25cm) diam

$1,200-1,800   **GorL**

A Baccarat mushroom paperweight, with a torsard of white gauze with blue threads, mercury bands, star-cut base.

3.25in (8.25cm) diam

$1,000-1,500   **GorL**

A CLOSER LOOK AT A BACCARAT PAPERWEIGHT

A very rare Baccarat scattered millefiori paperweight in carpet ground, the numerous silhouette canes include a dog, butterfly or moth, goat and bird, framed within two shamrocks, deer, squirrel, monkey, rooster and pelican, signed/dated "B1848", signed upside down.

2.75in (7cm) diam

$7,000-10,000   **LHS**

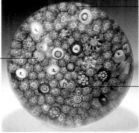

These types, with densely packed canes, are the most prized by collectors and the ground provides the perfect foil for silhouette canes.

Baccarat specialized in complex 'carpet ground' weights, incorporating many bright colors which made visually dramatic weights. This example also includes a date cane.

The variety of silhouette canes demonstrates the creativity and inventiveness of the glassmakers.

A Baccarat trefoil garlands paperweight, with two interlaced complex millefiori garlands, surrounding a ring of complex arrow canes, around a large stardust/star center.

3in (7.5cm) diam

$600-900   **LHS**

A miniature Baccarat white double clematis paperweight, star-cut base, chips towards base.

1.75in (4.5cm) diam

$400-600   **GorL**

A Baccarat Dupont circular garlands paperweight, with six spaced rings of millefiori, each with a complex cane center, around a central garland, with a dark green complex cane center.

2.75in (7cm) diam

$400-600   **LHS**

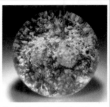

A miniature Baccarat rock paperweight, with green and silver mica.

2in (5cm) diam

$120-180   **LHS**

Collectors' Notes

- The Saint Louis factory was founded in Alsace-Lorraine in France in 1767 and produced paperweights in the mid-19thC.
- Their domes are much higher than their rivals' Some examples have date canes which are usually marked 1848; dates of 1845 and 1849 are known, but rarer.
- The use of single flower designs is common with Saint Louis paperweights, often on a ground of swirling white or pink latticinio.
- Unlike Baccarat, Saint Louis often mixed fruit or flower motifs with usage of millefiori canes and also produced lampworked and sulphide paperweights.

A Saint Louis pelargonium on swirling latticinio paperweight, with a five-petaled red flower, two long green leaves and a curved stem, on double-swirl white latticinio.

2.75in (7cm) diam

$3,000-4,000   LHS

A Saint Louis pompom paperweight, set with a white flower, a complex cane in pink, white, pale blue and yellow is the stamen, on a double-swirl white latticinio cushion, around a thin layer of translucent pink.

2.75in (7cm) diam

$3,000-4,000   LHS

A Saint Louis bouquet of fruit paperweight, with an apple, two pears and three cherries on a bed of green leaves, in a swirling white latticinio basket.

3.25in (8.25cm) diam

$700-1,000   LHS

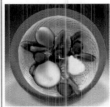

A mid-19thC Saint Louis fruit bouquet paperweight, with a golden apple, two pears, four red cherries and dark green leaves, in a double-swirl white latticinio basket.

2.5in (6.5cm) diam

$1,000-1,500   LHS

A CLOSER LOOK AT A SAINT LOUIS PAPERWEIGHT

The distinctive 'crown' paperweights were a speciality of Saint Louis.

These gather to meet at the apex, where they terminate in a single colored millefiori motif. This almost mirrors the shape of a regal crown, where arms curve up to join at the apex.

Requiring precise and careful work, the globe is hollow with walls lined with alternating twisted filigree twists and colored glass ribbons that arch upwards.

A Saint Louis crown paperweight, with two-color twists, separated by white latticinio twists, comprising 20 spokes drawn down from a complex millefiori of broad cross and floret canes.

2.5in (6.5cm) diam

$1,800-2,200   LHS

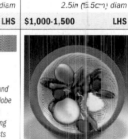

A mid-19thC Saint Louis fruit bouquet paperweight, with a golden apple, two pears, four red cherries and leaves, in a double-swirl white latticinio basket.

2.5in (6.5cm) diam

$1,000-1,500   LHS

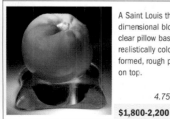

A Saint Louis three-dimensional blown apple on clear pillow base paperweight, realistically colored and formed, rough pontil mark on top.

4.75in (12cm) wide

$1,800-2,200   LHS

A Saint Louis snake on jasper ground paperweight featuring a snake, on an unusual red and white jasper ground, painted with accession number "#1965-464".

2.75in (7cm) diam

$3,000-4,000   LHS

Collectors' Notes

- Distinctive sulphide paperweights comprise a shaped 'cameo' made of white porcelain-like material which is encased in clear glass.
- The technique was developed in France in the early 19th century. This technique was used in the US after 1814 and in the UK after 1819, where it was patented by Apsley Pellatt.
- All three noted manufacturers made sulphide weights, with the best dating from around mid 19th century. Combinations of well-executed techniques, such as elaborate faceting or the inclusion of millefiori, make examples more desirable.

An American New England Glass Company Louis Kossuth sulphide paperweight, with a cameo of the Hungarian freedom fighter, inscribed "Kossuth", the underside of the sulphide inscribed "Ex-Governor of Hungary, Set at Liberty by the People of the United States of America, 1851".

2.75in (7cm) diam

$150-200 | **LHS**

A Saint Louis garlanded sulphide paperweight, of Louis Napoleon Bonaparte, with alternating millefiori on a clear ground.

2.75in (7cm) diam

$600-900 | **LHS**

A Bohemian sulphide paperweight, with a portrait of Kossuth, Governor of Hungary, the reverse with an inscription.

2.75in (7cm) diam

$150-200 | **GorL**

A Bohemian footed Martin Luther sulphide portrait paperweight, with the cameo over a red ground, backed in opaque white glass.

3.75in (9.5cm) diam

$220-280 | **LHS**

A mid-19thC Baccarat King Louis Phillipe sulphide paperweight, on a translucent red ground, with elaborate faceting and star-cut base, wear along the facets.

2.75in (7cm) diam

$600-900 | **LHS**

A faceted sulphide paperweight, with a profile of a military gentleman, cut with a window and on a large star-cut base.

3in (7.75cm) diam

$180-220 | **GorL**

A Baccarat faceted woodsman and dog sulphide paperweight, over translucent cranberry background, slight damage along the facets.

The detailed sulphide was part of a series of hunting images over different grounds, showing elaborate cutting.

3.5in (9cm) diam

$3,500-4,500 | **LHS**

A 19thC faceted and engraved paperweight, probably Bohemian, depicting an amber-colored deer in a woodland setting.

3.25in (8.25cm) diam

$400-600 | **LHS**

A Baccarat faceted sulphide paperweight, showing Joan of Arc surrounded with arcs of laurel sprigs, oak leaves and acorns, on a green flash ground.

3.5in (9cm) diam

$3,500-4,500 | **LHS**

A Whitefriars close concentric millefiori paperweight, with circlets of cog and quatrefoil canes, in a high-profile dome, rough pontil.

English paperweights were produced after c1848.

3.25in (8.25cm) diam

$320-380 LHS

An English footed concentric millefiori paperweight, probably by Richardson, with assorted canes in pink, blue, aqua, red and white, over a clear footed base.

3.75in (9.5cm) diam

$400-600 LHS

A late concentric millefiori weight, the central cane inscribed.

2.25in (5.75cm) diam

$250-300 GorL

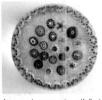

A spaced concentric millefiori paperweight, the two circles of canes about a central silhouette cane with a circle of canes at the edge, the whole set on a tossed muslin ground, perhaps Bohemian, small crack to central cane.

2.75in (7cm) diam

$400-600 GorL

An unusual late 19thC strawberries paperweight, possibly by The Cristallerie de Pantin, near Paris, on a clear ground.

This factory is associated with highly three-dimensional lampwork reptiles, flowers and fruits, as seen here, but made few paperweights. At this time, strawberries were known for their unripe sourness, so the green color seen here would have been correct.

2.75in (7cm) diam

$3,000-4,000 LHS

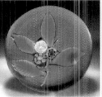

A miniature New England Glass Company nosegay paperweight, with cane flowers and crimped leaves on a thin stem.

2in (5cm) diam

$300-400 LHS

A magnum crimp 'Millville Rose' pedestal paperweight, by Emil Larson for the Millville Glass Factory, over a clear footed base, with an unfinished pontil.

4in (10cm) diam

$2,200-2,800 LHS

A Bohemian-Czechoslovakian high-domed paperweight, with a flower encircled by more, spaced around a multicolored cushion, flat top facets, with geometric facets covering the sides.

3.5in (9cm) diam

$280-320 LHS

A Val St. Lambert millefiori and torsade paperweight, an unusually colored green central cane, held in place by the red, white and blue 'barber-pole' twist, with an encircling filigree torsade.

3.5in (9cm) diam

$400-600 LHS

A late 19thC Chinese black clipper ship paperweight.

Of all early foreign weights, Chinese examples are often well executed, using clean and clear crystal.

2.5in (6.5cm) diam

$300-400 LHS

FIND OUT MORE...

The Corning Museum of Glass, New York, www.cmog.org
Over 1,000 paperweights from the golden age on display.

Bristol City Museum & Art Gallery, Bristol, England,
www.bristol-city.gov.uk The best public collection in the UK.

Lawrence H. Selman, 'All About Paperweights', published by
Paperweight Press, 1992.

Paul Hollister, 'The Encyclopaedia of Glass Paperweights',
published by Paperweight Press, 1986.

A Parker Lucky Curve Duofold Senior, red Permanite button filler with Parker Duofold Pen nib, box and leaflet, excellent condition.

Permanite was the name Parker gave to the plastic it used.

c1927

$350-400   **CO**

A Canadian Parker Lucky Curve Duofold Junior, blue-on-blue Permanite button filler with Canadian Duofold nib, good condition with brassed cap band.

c1927

$150-200   **CO**

A Parker Lucky Curve Junior, mandarin yellow Permanite button filler with Duofold nib, excellent condition.

Junior pens are smaller than standard sized pens, but the same width. Yellow is a rare color for a Duofold.

c1927

$180-220   **CO**

A Canadian Parker Duofold Senior Deluxe, pearl and green veined Permanite button filler with fine 18ct gold Canadian Parker Duofold nib, very good condition with some ambering.

c1930-31

$150-200   **CO**

An oversize Parker Vacumatic, emerald pearl laminated celluloid with later gold Parker arrow nib.

This is is the largest of the Vacumatic pens. Smaller Vacumatics are worth between $60-150 unless a rare variation or with an unusual nib.

c1935

$300-400   **CO**

A Parker Duofold Geometric Standard, green pearl and black celluloid button filler with Parker Pen nib, in near mint condition.

This pen has been nicknamed the 'toothbrush pen' by collectors due to the odd shapes in the plastic that resemble toothbrushes.

c1939

$150-200   **CO**

A 1950s Parker 51 Custom, black plastic aerometric filler, with medium nib, mint condition with original shop chalk marks.

When not in mint condition with chalk marks, the value is usually between $30-50 for a similar pen.

$120-180   **CO**

A Parker 65 Stratus, rolled gold 'Cloud' series cartridge / convertor filler with fine Parker .585 nib, near mint condition.

The surface pattern of this pen wears easily. Worn pens are usually worth less than half the value of this pen.

c1976

$120-180   **CO**

A Waterman's 412 1/2 'Filigree', black hard rubber lever filler with 'three leaf' Sterling filigree and Waterman's Ideal No. 2 nib, very good condition with three engraved initials.

1908-1915

$150-200 CO

A 1920s French Waterman's gold overlaid 52 1/2 'Gothic', black hard rubber lever filler with overlay marked ".750" and with engraved checkered pattern, with Waterman's Ideal No. 1 nib, near mint condition with three engraved initials.

The nib on this pen is too small and should be a larger '2' size. Replaced nibs can affect the value of a pen, more so if the pen is large, or the nib is by another maker and of poor quality.

$150-200 CO

A Waterman's 56, woodgrain effect, black and red mottled hard rubber lever filler with Waterman's Ideal New York No.6 nib, excellent condition.

c1920

$220-280 CO

A 1920s Waterman's 55, cardinal red hard rubber lever filler with Waterman's Manifold No. 5 nib and red feed.

$150-200 CO

A Waterman's 94, blue and yellow rippled hard rubber lever filler with 9ct gold cap band and medium Waterman's No. 4 nib, very good condition.

c1928

$180-220 CO

A Canadian Waterman's 52V, blue and yellow rippled hard rubber lever filler with hallmarked 9ct gold cap band and a later Waterman's nib, boxed, very good condition.

Waterman's used a number and letter code for their pens. Here the '5' denotes a lever filler, the '2' the size of nib and therefore the pen. The 'V' denotes a short pen of standard width.

c1928

$180-220 CO

A Waterman's Lady Patricia, 'Turquoise' blue and gold-bronze marbled celluloid lever filler with fine Waterman's No. 2 nib, very good condition.

c1930

$180-220 CO

A Waterman's 92, brown pearl 'lizardskin' celluloid lever filler, with slightly later English No. 2 nib, very good to excellent condition.

c1935

$150-200 CO

A Montblanc Meisterstück, un-numbered black celluloid push-knob filler with fine oblique 4810 nib, in excellent condition.

Although this pen is un-numbered, it is identical to a 30 size pen. This does not necessarily affect the value.

1931-1934

$280-320 CO

A Montblanc Meisterstück 124 S, hatched black hard rubber piston filler with two color 4810 nib, good condition with signs of wear.

1935-1938

$150-200 CO

A scarce Danish Montblanc K2, coral red button filler with fine Mont Blanc 14C 2 nib.

1937-1946

$80-120 CO

A Danish Montblanc Masterpiece 30, coral red push-knob filler with two-color 4810 Masterpiece nib, very good condition with some wear to gold plating.

1936-1947

$400-600 CO

A very rare 1940s Montblanc button filler, un-numbered black celluloid button filler with brass trim, inset clip and medium oblique Montblanc 3 1/2 tin nib, near mint condition.

This pen is unrecorded in reference books. The style is very unusual for Montblanc, but is similar to French pens, suggesting it was made in France, possibly after WWII.

$120-180 CO

A Montblanc Monte Rosa 042, burgundy red plastic piston filler with wavy cap band and metal Monte Rosa medium nib.

1954-1956

$60-90 CO

A Montblanc Meisterstück 142G, silver pearl striated celluloid piston filler with two-color 4810 ball nib, good condition with some darkening.

1952-1958

$300-500 CO

A rare 1970s Montblanc Carrera, burgundy plastic piston filler with brushed and polished brass cap with "Carrera" script imprint and extra-fine hooded nib.

The holes on the clip were inspired by the holes on the steering wheel crossbars on the 1970s Porsche Carrera. Similar Carrera fountain pens without the brass cap and inscription are worth about half of this value.

$80-120 CO

A late 1920s Conway Stewart Dinkie No. 526 pen and pencil, red casein ringtop lever filler with fine Conway Stewart nib and matching Duro-Point No. 2 pencil, boxed, excellent condition.

Conway Stewart Dinkies were produced during the 1920s in an array of cheerful, bright colors typical of the Roaring 20s. Their small size made them very portable and popular with ladies who could keep them in purses. Some are found contained in small leather wallets with mirrors and other accessories. They were made again in the 1950s, but these models have tapered ends and clips and are usually worth under $60. Collect bright colors, but beware of worn examples or where the plastic has warped with age as value here lies only in unaffected parts.

$180-220   CO

A late 1920s Conway Stewart Dinkie No. 526C pen and Duro-Point pencil, scarlet red celluloid lever filler with very fine Conway Stewart nib and matching propelling pencil, boxed, very good condition with some discoloration to pen barrel.

$100-150   CO

A 1920s Conway Stewart Dinkie No. 526, red and black mottled hard rubber lever filler with medium nib and matching pencil, in leather purse with mirror.

$100-150   CO

A late 1920s Conway Stewart Dinkie No. 540, 'gray jazz' multicolored celluloid ringtop lever filler with broad Conway Stewart nib, boxed, very good condition.

$120-180   CO

A very rare late 1920s Conway Stewart Dinkie No. 540, 'Harlequin' multicolored celluloid lever filler with fine Conway Stewart nib.

$150-200   CO

A 1920s gold-plated Conway Stewart Dinkie, overlaid black hard rubber lever filler with alternating lined and plain decoration, with medium Conway Stewart nib.

Metal overlaid Conway Stewarts are rare, especially if the overlay is marked "Conway Stewart".

$150-200   CO

A 1920s Conway Stewart Dinkie No. 540, emerald green celluloid lever filler with fine Conway Stewart nib, good condition although a little dark.

$50-80   CO

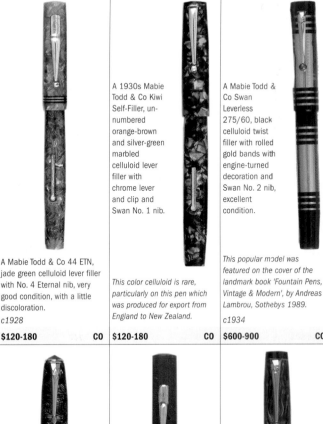

A 1930s Mabie Todd & Co Kiwi Self-Filler, un-numbered orange-brown and silver-green marbled celluloid lever filler with chrome lever and clip and Swan No. 1 nib.

A Mabie Todd & Co Swan Leverless 275/60, black celluloid twist filler with rolled gold bands with engine-turned decoration and Swan No. 2 nib, excellent condition.

A Mabie Todd & Co 44 ETN, jade green celluloid lever filler with No. 4 Eternal nib, very good condition, with a little discoloration.
c1928

This color celluloid is rare, particularly on this pen which was produced for export from England to New Zealand.

This popular model was featured on the cover of the landmark book 'Fountain Pens, Vintage & Modern', by Andreas Lambrou, Sothebys 1989.
c1934

A 1950s Conway Stewart 60, blue and black lined celluloid lever filler with medium Conway Stewart Duro 60 nib, near mint condition.

$120-180 CO | **$120-180** CO | **$600-900** CO | **$100-150** CO

A 1930s Valentine 03, silver pearl and black lined marbled celluloid button filler, with medium Valentine nib, excellent condition.

This pen is very similar to the Parker Duofolds made during this period, this is partly due to the fact that Parker shared a factory with Valentine.

A Conway Stewart 58, green and black line marbled celluloid lever filler with fine Conway Stewart Duro nib, very good condition.
c1949

A 1920s Curzon's Summit, coral red and orange flecked celluloid lever filler with broad Summit 14ct nib, near mint condition.

A 1930s De La Rue 'The De La Rue Pen' 560-85, rare malachite green celluloid lever filler with chrome trim and fine 14ct Warranted De La Rue nib, near mint condition.

$60-90 CO | **$120-180** CO | **$100-150** CO | **$120-180** CO

A limited edition Parker Spanish Treasure Fleet 1715, cartridge /convertor filler with 'grid' pattern and '65' nib, marked "STERLING SILVER", near mint condition, but lacking box and papers.

A limited edition Montblanc Ernest Hemingway ballpoint, from an edition of 30,000, coral red and espresso brown twist-action ballpen, complete with box and papers in mint condition.

1992

$280-320   **CO**

A limited edition Montblanc Oscar Wilde, from an edition of 15,000, pearl and black resin barrel with black cap, vermeil clip and medium 18K Montblanc nib, complete with box and papers, in mint condition.

1992

$600-900   **CO**

A limited edition Montblanc Marcel Proust, from an edition of 22,000, black resin piston filler with octagonal silver barrel overlay, silver trim and two-color medium 4810 nib with hourglass motif, mint condition, complete with box and papers.

1999

$700-1,000   **CO**

This rare pen is made from silver recovered from a Spanish treasure fleet that sunk off the coast of Florida in 1715. 4,821 pens were made, but none are numbered.

1965

$500-700   **CO**

A limited edition Parker R.M.S. Queen Elizabeth, from an edition of 5,000, brass cartridge filler, with medium adjustable nib, mint condition complete with box and papers.

This pen was made from brass recovered from the ship the Queen Elizabeth.

1977

$500-700   **CO**

A 1990s special edition Pelikan M700 Toledo, black plastic piston filler with Toledo metalwork overlay with medium Pelikan nib, complete with box and papers, mint condition.

$220-280   **CO**

A limited edition Visconti Copernicus, from an edition of 999, green hooped celluloid crescent filler with broad 13K Visconti nib, complete with box and papers, mint condition.

The unusual filling system employing a push-down crescent was first used by US company Conklin in the 1920s.

1996

$180-220   **CO**

A special edition Montegrappa cigar pen, tobacco colored mottled brown celluloid cigar-shaped piston filler with white metal clip and medium two-co or nib, complete with humidor-style box and papers, mint condition.

1997

$180-220   **CO**

A brass 'jockey' ink stand.

c1860   5.5in (14cm) high

$400-600   **SS**

A late 19thC Indian engraved brass ink stand, surmounted by a stag, the two wells with hinged elephant covers, on triform base, with three claw-and-ball feet.

5.75in (14.5cm) high

$100-150   **LFA**

A late Victorian Sheffield Plate inkstand, of rectangular form with gadrooned edge, mounted with square pounce and ink bottles in roundel pierced stands, with pen wells, on cabriole feet.

$150-200   **BonS**

A cold-painted bronze inkstand, in the form of a lizard with glass eyes, holding a glass inkwell in its tail.

10.5in (26.5cm) long

$400-600   **DN**

An Edwardian brass desk stand, of rectangular form with a pair of lidded square urn inkwells joined by open balustrade.

14.25in (36cm) wide

$400-600   **L&T**

A WWI French military metal inkwell.

5in (12.5cm) wide

$60-90   **DH**

A Georgian intaglio fob, with swiveling white chalcedony oval panel depicting an 18thC male figure, with flaming comet detail to side, with a gilt frame and steel surmount.

Fob seals were attached to a gentleman's fob chain. These chains also held a pocket watch and other accessories such as pencils or watch keys. The seals were used with wax to sign letters or to seal envelopes. The design or owner's initials engraved on the stone of the seal were stamped into hot wax.

Panel 1in (2.5cm) high

$150-200   **F**

A Georgian gold-mounted citrine intaglio fob seal, with open scroll grip and closed back mount, depicting the coat-of-arms for the Scottish Gordon family, with an inconsistent vine crest, normally used on an Englishman's seal.

c1770-1790

Panel 0.75in (2cm) high

$400-600   **F**

A Georgian 9ct rose gold-mounted intaglio fob seal, with cornelain panel depicting the coat-of-arms for Priestley of Sowerby, Yorkshire, the mount and grip with reeded and spiral decoration.

Panel 0.75in (2cm) high

$300-500   **F**

An early Victorian gold-mounted intaglio cornelian fob seal, depicting the coat-of-arms for Hitchins/Hutchens of Oxfordshire impaling another, with a simple mount and grip.

Panel 0.5in (1.5cm) high

$280-320   **F**

A sterling silver fob seal, with unengraved garnet.

c1900   0.75in (2cm) high

$12-18   **TAB**

A small 19thC gold-plated fob seal, with inset carnelian carved with initials.

0.75in (2cm) high

$30-50   **TAB**

A Victorian 18ct gold-mounted intaglio fob seal, with white chalcedony panel depicting a classical Greek figure possibly Antiochos VIII, with open scroll pattern grip.

Panel 0.75in (2cm) high

$280-320   **F**

A George II "Excise Soap" seal, with rosewood handle.

3.25in (8.5cm) high

$100-150   **Clv**

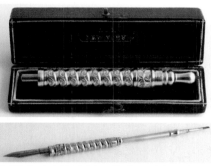

An Aikin Lambert gold-plated combination penholder and pencil, the body finely embossed with curling floral and 'snail' pattern, with pen holder to one end and retracting pencil to other, with rare original box.

c1880

$300-500   **MHC**

A pair of novelty pen and inkwell sets, each in the form of an umbrella concealing a pen, one fitted with a Mentmore 14ct gold nib, and a top hat concealing a screw-capped glass inkwell, the hat is inscribed "A Present from Brighton".

Each 4.25in (11cm) long

$120-180   **DN**

A small pen knife sharpening stone, with wooden handle and card slip cover.

This is an unusually small size. These are mainly found in larger sizes and in burgundy card slip cases

c1840   *4in (10cm)*

$120-180   **MHC**

A late 19thC leather, card and gilt pen nib holder, from the 'Queen & Heroes of India' series, with chromolithographed Baxter print of Prince Napoleon Bonaparte.

2.25in (6cm) high

$70-100   **CBe**

A very rare French Dagron & Cie ink bottle, with moulded pen rest.

French innovator and inventor René Dagron was also responsible for developing the popular Stanhope novelty souvenir.

c1880   *2.5in (6.5cm) high*

$300-500   **JSC**

Collectors' Notes

■ Pez, short for the German word for 'peppermint' (PfeffErminZ), were mint sweets which were first sold in Austria in 1927. It was not until 1948 that the first dispenser appeared. This was shaped like a cigarette lighter and very plain in form, and is referred to as the 'regular' by collectors.

■ In 1952, Pez saw commercial possibilities in the US and opened an office in New York. To capture the lucrative children's market, it decided to make fruit flavoured sweets and add colorful character heads to the tops of its dispensers. The first, produced in the mid-1950s, was Santa Claus. The 'Space Trooper' came shortly afterwards and the first licensed character was 'Popeye'.

■ Many character ranges, including Disney characters, were designed and distributed during the 1970s and 1980s and, in 1987, 'feet' were added to the stems.

Initially molded in thin plastic, they were intended to help the dispenser stand up. Thicker plastic feet were soon introduced, as they were stronger.

■ Patent numbers on the stem of a dispenser will help the collector to work out when the dispenser was made, although the year range is often large as Pez registered only seven patents between 1952 and 2003. There is also a small number on the corner of the stem, which indicates where the dispenser was made.

■ Collectors look for early figural dispensers as well as rarities such as the 1970s 'Sparefroh' elf dispenser, produced for a bank, and the 'Make A Face' Pez with attachable parts, which was withdrawn from sale after fears over children choking on the pieces. Damage such as splits will seriously reduce value and a dispenser must be complete, with the correct parts.

A 1950s white plastic 'regular' Pez dispenser.

3.75in (9.5cm) high

$100-150   **AtA**

A 1970s Walt Disney's 'Goofy B' Pez dispenser, with swinging ears.

4.25in (11cm) high

$30-50   **AtA**

A 1970s Walt Disney's 'Goofy' Pez dispenser, with fixed ears.

The 'Goofy' with fixed ears is usually worth half as much as the 'Goofy B' with swinging ears.

4.25in (11cm) high

$15-25   **AtA**

A 1970s Walt Disney's 'Mickey Mouse' Pez dispenser.

4in (10cm) high

$8-12   **AtA**

A 1970s Walt Disney's 'Porky Pig' Pez dispenser.

4in (10cm) high

$30-40   **AtA**

A 1970s Walt Disney's 'Pinocchio' Pez dispenser.

4in (10cm) high

$180-220   **AtA**

A red plastic 'Space Trooper' robot-shaped Pez dispenser.

The design was probably influenced by the 1950s obsession with science fiction films and outer space. The rocket pack on his back is marked "PEZ".

c1955   *3.75in (9.5cm) high*

$350-400   **AtA**

A Warner Bros 'Daffy Duck' Pez dispenser.

c1978 4.25in (11cm) hi

$15-25   AtA

A 1970s Warners Bros 'Tweety Pie' Pez dispenser.

4.25in (11cm) high

$15-25   AtA

A 1970s 'Popeye' Pez dispenser.

4.25in (11cm) high

$100-150   AtA

A 1960s 'Batman' Pez dispenser, with moving cape.

4.25in (10.5cm) high

$120-180   AtA

A 'Little Orphan Annie' Pez dispense...

c1982 4.25in (11cm) h

$120-180   AtA

A 1990s 'Kermit the Frog' Pez dispenser.

Note the base of this later Pez dispenser, which has thick "feet"

4.25in (11cm) high

$2-3   TAB

A 1970s Larry the Lamb' Pez dispenser.

4.25in (11cm) high

$12-18   AtA

A 1970s 'Elephant' Pez dispenser.

4.25in (11cm) high

$100-150   AtA

A 1970s 'Parrot' Pez dispenser

4in (10cm) high

$50-80   AtA

A 1970s 'Red-beaked Parrot' Pez dispenser.

In these colors, this shape is more valuable than the same shape in yellow and green.

4.25in (10.5cm) high

$70-100   AtA

A rare 1970s French Pez dispenser, with a 'Pif' character head.

4.25in (10.5cm) high

$100-150   AtA

A 1970s 'Cat with Derby Hat' Pez dispenser.

4.25in (11cm) high

$80-120   AtA

A 1970s 'Indian Chief' Pez dispenser, with headdress.

4.25in (11cm) high

$100-150   AtA

A 1970s 'Witch' Pez dispenser

4.25in (11cm) high

$12-18   AtA

A 'Wounded Soldier' Pez dispenser.

4.25in (11cm) high

$150-200   AtA

FIND OUT MORE...

'**Collecting Pez**' by David Welch, published by Bubba Scrubba, 1996.

The Museum of Pez Memorabilia, 214 California Drive, Burlingame, California, 94010, USA. www.burlingamepezmuseum.com

www.pezcentral.com for an online Pez resource and useful links to more sites.

PHOTOGRAPHS

Collectors' Notes

- Photography became popular after Frenchman Louis Daguerre developed the 'daguerrotype' in 1839. This was an image captured and fixed in a light-sensitive layer on a polished metal plate. Daguerrotypes can be recognized by their silver reflection when looked at directly.

- Two other types came later and used different materials. 'Ambrotypes' used a glass plate and 'tintypes', which were the most inexpensive version at the time and were also known as 'ferrotypes', used a base metal plate. Neither of them have the silvery reflectivity seen on daguerrotypes.

- A carte-de-visite, or 'CdV', was an albumen photograph of a person mounted on a single standard-sized card. They were inexpensive to create and could be printed in quantity. Noted personalities such as members of the royal family were widely collected in albums, with images of 'lesser mortals' being given away as mementos to family members and friends.

- When assessing any photograph, firstly consider what type of photograph you have. If the subject matter is a famous sitter or is very unusual or quirky, the value will usually be higher. The photographer may also have a bearing on the value. Condition is also important, with fading, mold, tears, scuffs and other damage reducing value and desirability.

A sixth-plate daguerrotype of a lady, in complete leather-covered case.

3.5in (9cm) high

$50-80   **AnaA**

A sixth-plate daguerrotype of a lady, hand on book, probably a Bible, with hand-tinted tablecloth, in a leather case.

Always look to see what the sitter is holding or doing. 'Trade' subjects, where the sitter is holding a tool, are popular with collectors. Colored hand-tinting, particularly if still strong, is also a desirable feature but not if the tint was added later.

$70-100   **AnaA**

A CLOSER LOOK AT AN EARLY PHOTOGRAPH

The style of costume worn by the sitter usually helps to date early photographs.

The image below is clearly identifiable as a daguerrotype from the reflective silvery appearance when viewed at an angle.

Value is also related to the sitter. This lady is not famous, hence the value is low.

The condition is not mint, with some fading to the edges. Look particularly for sharp images.

An early sixth-plate daguerrotype of a lady, with some fading to the edges in a complete leather-covered case.

$70-100   **AnaA**

A sixth-plate daguerrotype of a seated young man, in partial case.

3.25in (8.5cm) high

$30-50   **AnaA**

A sixth-plate daguerrotype of a seated lady, wearing a lace collar, in a complete leather-covered case.

3.5in (9cm) high

$60-90   **AnaA**

A sixth-plate daguerrotype of a gentleman, in early oval frame and partial leather case.

3.5in (9cm) high

$60-90   **AnaA**

A quarter-plate ambrotype of a husband and wife, in a large snap-shut Union case.

Although most early photographs are held in leather-bound, hinged wooden cases lined with felt and gilt mounts, some are contained in 'Union cases' made from a type of composition. With their finely molded exterior detailing, they are collectible in their own right and usually increase the value of a photograph if undamaged, or of a large size.

Case 5in (12.5cm) high

$180-220   AnaA

A quarter-plate ambrotype of a young man standing, in a red morocco leather case.

5in (13cm) high

$70-100   AnaA

A sixth-plate hand-tinted ambrotype of a child, case lacks lid.

3.5in (9cm) high

$70-100   AnaA

A small tenth-plate tintype of a boy in a hat, in a Union case

2.25in (5.5cm) high

$70-100   AnaA

A quarter-plate ambrotype of gentlemen and ladies, in a partial leather-covered case.

Family views can be popular with collectors, particularly if the image is unusual in some way, such as an image of a family with twins.

4.75in (12cm) wide

$60-90   AnaA

A sixth-plate tintype of a gentleman with two seated ladies, in partial leather-covered case.

3.5in (9cm) high

$50-80   AnaA

A quarter-plate tintype of fighters/boxers, uncased.

c1865   5in (12.5cm) high

$120-180   AAC

A retouched carte-de-visite of Charles Dickens. Featuring Brady/Anthony backmark, minor corner trims.

$100-150   AAC

A carte-de-visite of Samuel Morse, by Gurney, card backmarked "Gurney", trimmed at corners and Morse identification in pencil on image above head of subject.

Morse was the inventor of the famous 'Morse Code' and the 'telegraph' in the late 1830s. In New York in 1838 the telegraph was demonstrated to the public for the first time.

$30-40   AAC

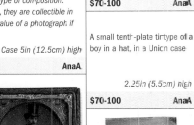

A carte-de-visite of a photographer with camera image backmarked "George Rau's New Photographic Room ~922 Girard Avenue, Philadelphia", subject probably Rau, some surface soiling particularly to reverse with one small dig at upper center away from subject.

$800-1,200   AAC

An American carte-de-visite size tintype of John Wilkes Booth, anonymous, in a Civil War-style cream mount, with a canceled two-cent revenue stamp on verso, probably copied from a paper carte-de-visite, slight surface soil on the mount, faint line extending across the plate from the left and intersecting subject's chin.

$1,500-2,000   CHAA

A photograph of Edward, Prince of Wales, later King Edward VIII, with printed mount "HMS Renown, 1921 - 1922", signed, framed and glazed.

10.25in (25cm) high

$220-280   Clv

Domestic

A 1920s Smiths brown mottled Bakelite mantel clock.

Smiths, England, made a vast range of clocks in colored plastics up until the 1950s.

8in (20cm) high

$50-80   **MHC**

A 1920s multicolored Bakelite electric mantle clock, marked "Ediswan".

7in (18cm) high

$60-90   **JBC**

A 1930s French Bakelite and chrome wind-up clock, marked "JAZ Companie Industrielle de Méchanique Horlogère Paris".

4.25in (11cm) high

$50-80   **JBC**

A pair of 1920s cream urea-formaldehyde candlesticks.

4in (10cm) diam

$20-30   **JBC**

Two brown mottled Bakelite Linsden ware Arts & Crafts-style candlesticks.

These candlesticks were produced in two slightly different colors. A matching pair would command a premium.

$180-220   **MHC**

A 1920s simulated tortoiseshell celluloid vanity set, boxed.

4.75in (12cm) high

$50-80   **JBC**

A CLOSER LOOK AT EARLY PLASTICS

These boxes are part of a larger selection of dressing table accessories including trays, brushes and mirrors.

Here the plastic was made to simulate tortoiseshell, which was an expensive and luxurious product.

The plastic, often marked 'MADE IN ENGLAND', is very thin and delicate. Cracks and damage, such as crazing and a dull surface, affect value greatly.

Two 1920s celluloid simulated tortoiseshell dressing table boxes.

$5-8 (each)   **JBC**

A 1930s Art Deco-style dark brown Bakelite photograph frame.

6.25in (16cm) high

$40-60   **JBC**

A miniature 1920s black Bakelite roulette wheel.

8.25in (21cm) diam

$30-40   **JBC**

A 1940s set of black Bakelite dominoes, in cream urea-formaldehyde box.

Box 6.5in (16.5cm) long

$15-25   **JBC**

A 1940s Gesichts Punkt-Roller massager, with cast phenolic handle.

5in (12.5cm) long

$15-25   **JBC**

Kitchenalia

Three 1930s maroon mottled Bakelite egg cups.

1.75in (4.5cm) diam

$3-5 (each)   JBC

Three 1930s pink mottled Beetleware jelly molds.

2.75in (7cm) diam

$5-8 (each)   MHC

Two 1930s multicolored urea-formaldehyde bowls.

4in (10cm) diam

$7-10 (each)   JBC

A 1920s circular trivet, in brown mottled Bakelite.

5.5in (14cm) diam

$15-25   JBC

A 1920s circular Linsden ware trivet, in dark brown and biscuit Bakelite.

6.25in (16cm) diam

$20-30   JBC

A 1930s copper Art Deco teapot, with Bakelite handle and knob.

6in (15cm) high

$60-90   JBC

A 1940s multi-colored urea-formaldehyde cruet set.

Pepper pot 2in (5cm) high

$20-30   JBC

A 1930s urea-formaldehyde collapsible picnic cup.

2.5in (6.5cm) diam

$15-25   MHC

A 1940s Bel cream maker, in blue urea-formaldehyde and glass, boxed.

This cream maker is common and made in many different colors, but to find one in the original box is rare.

7.75in (19.5cm) high

$40-60   JBC

A 1930s set of four Erinoid napkin rings boxed.

1.75in (4.5cm) diam

$15-25   JBC

A 1930s boxed set of six knives, with dark blue and yellow mottled urea-formaldehyde handles.

Knife 7.25in (13.5cm) long

$30-40   JBC

A 1940s light-brown mottled Bakelite cutlery tray.

12.75in (32cm) long

$30-40   JBC

PLASTICS & BAKELITE

Smoking Accessories

A 1920s pair of brown mottled Bakelite Gadeware ashtrays.

3in (7.5cm) diam

$6-9 (each) JBC

A 1920s brown mottled Bakelite ashtray.

2.5in (6cm) high

$5-8 MHC

A 1930s green mottled Bakelite ashtray, by Stadium.

4in (10cm) diam

$15-25 JBC

A 1930s green mottled Bakelite ashtray, in original box.

3in (7.5cm) wide

$30-40 JBC

A 1930s Bakelite and chrome ashtray, marked "No Fume".

2.75in (7cm) high

$10-12 JBC

A 1920s brown mottled Bakelite cigarette box, marked "WJ Charlesworth, Stechford, Birmingham".

4.75in (12cm) wide

$30-40 JBC

A 1930s urea-formaldehyde and Bakelite 'Parker Pen Cigarette Box'.

Parker is famous for its pens, but it also licensed selected related accessories.

6.5in (16.5cm) wide

$30-40 JBC

A 1930s brown mottled Bakelite 'D.L.I. Flintless' table lighter, by Dorset Light Industries.

4.25in (11cm) high

$20-30 JBC

A 1940s black Bakelite pistol cigarette lighter, marked "JYM Made in France".

4.75in (12cm) long

$30-40 JBC

A 1930s French orange and white marbled phenolic cigarette holder, in original case.

Closed 3.5in (9cm) long

$40-60 JBC

A CLOSER LOOK AT EARLY PLASTICS

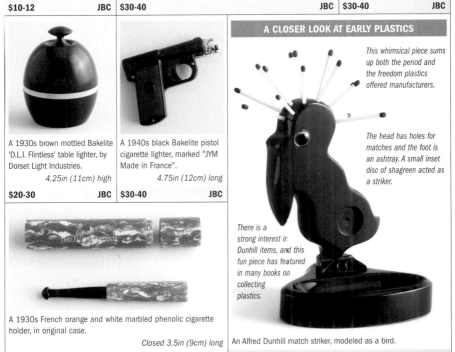

This whimsical piece sums up both the period and the freedom plastics offered manufacturers.

The head has holes for matches and the foot is an ashtray. A small inset disc of shagreen acted as a striker.

There is a strong interest in Dunhill items, and this fun piece has featured in many books on collecting plastics.

An Alfred Dunhill match striker, modeled as a bird.

$400-600 LC

Desk Accessories

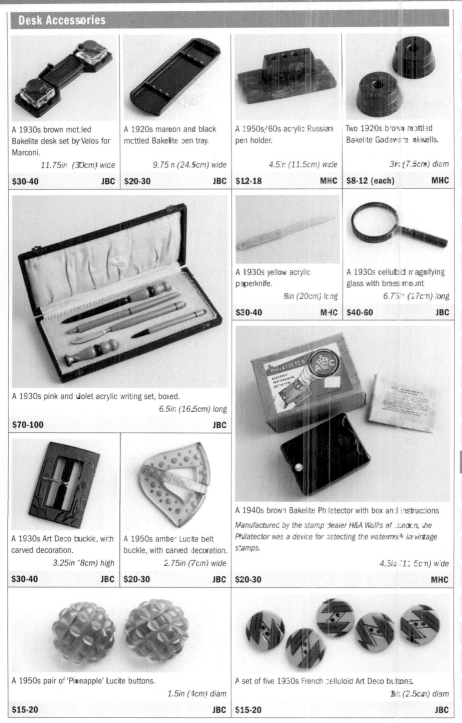

A 1930s brown mottled Bakelite desk set by Velos for Marconi.

11.75in (30cm) wide

$30-40   **JBC**

A 1920s maroon and black mottled Bakelite pen tray.

9.75in (24.5cm) wide

$20-30   **JBC**

A 1950s/60s acrylic Russian pen holder.

4.5in (11.5cm) wide

$12-18   **MHC**

Two 1920s brown mottled Bakelite Gadeware inkwells.

3in (7.5cm) diam

$8-12 (each)   **MHC**

A 1930s pink and violet acrylic writing set, boxed.

6.5in (16.5cm) long

$70-100   **JBC**

A 1930s yellow acrylic paperknife.

8in (20cm) long

$30-40   **MHC**

A 1930s celluloid magnifying glass with brass mount.

6.75in (17cm) long

$40-60   **JBC**

A 1930s Art Deco buckle, with carved decoration.

3.25in (8cm) high

$30-40   **JBC**

A 1950s amber Lucite belt buckle, with carved decoration.

2.75in (7cm) wide

$20-30   **JBC**

A 1940s brown Bakelite Philatector with box and instructions

Manufactured by the stamp dealer H&A Wallis of London, the Philatector was a device for detecting the watermark in vintage stamps.

4.5in (11.5cm) wide

$20-30   **MHC**

A 1950s pair of 'Pineapple' Lucite buttons.

1.5in (4cm) diam

$15-20   **JBC**

A set of five 1930s French celluloid Art Deco buttons.

1in (2.5cm) diam

$15-20   **JBC**

Collectors' Notes

- Film posters from the country of a film's original release are usually the most popular with collectors. Posters for releases in other countries differ in style as well as language – French film posters are known for beautiful images and artwork.

- One sheet film posters (27in x 41in) and British quads (30in x 40in) are the most popular sizes with collectors. Many collectors back posters on to linen to help protect them – this should only be done by a professional.

- The artwork will often play a large part in determining the value of a poster. Look for the work of key artists and striking images or images typical of their period as these will be desirable and fetch high prices. Also look for posters for films that captured the public imagination, or were considered cult hits or classics.

- Condition is very important, as posters were made to be used and were printed on often delicate paper. It is difficult to find a poster from before 1970 in mint condition as most were folded for storage or stored badly. Tears through the image, serious folds and creases should be taken into account when considering a price, but can usually be corrected by professional restorers.

- Beware of color reproductions produced later. These can usually be spotted easily as the image is reproduced photographically on poster paper. Visit an auction or dealer to see originals so you can learn to spot the difference. Re-issue posters are not reproductions but were produced when the film was re-released. Fakes are relatively scarce and can usually be identified by examining the quality of the printing and the paper.

"The Adventures Of Captain Marvel", Argentine poster.

1941   43in (109cm) high

$700-1,000   P

"The Adventures Of Robin Hood", re-release UK quad poster.

c1950s   41in (104cm) high

$3,500-4,500   P

"A.I. Artificial Intelligence", advance US one sheet poster.

This film was preceeded by much interactive prerelease hype on the internet and in other media. The credits on this poster contain hidden marks that relate to a number that could be used interactively.

2001   41in (104cm) high

$100-150   P

"Amélie (Le Fabuleux Destin d'Amélie Poulain)", French, country of origin poster.

2001   63in (160cm) high

$220-280   P

"Apocalypse Now", very rare German A1 poster, with artwork by Robert Peak.

Robert Peak (1928-1992) is considered the 'father' of the contemporary film poster and is known for his striking artwork which departed from the use of film stills and head shots. He also designed posters for "My Fair Lady" and "Superman".

1979   33in (84cm) high

$1,000-1,500   P

"Attack Of The Crab Monsters", US one sheet poster.

1957   41in (104cm) high

$2,500-3,000   P

"Barbarella", rare Argentine poster.

The colorful artwork that is typical of the 1960s makes this a very desirable poster.

1968   43in (109cm) high

$1,800-2,200   P

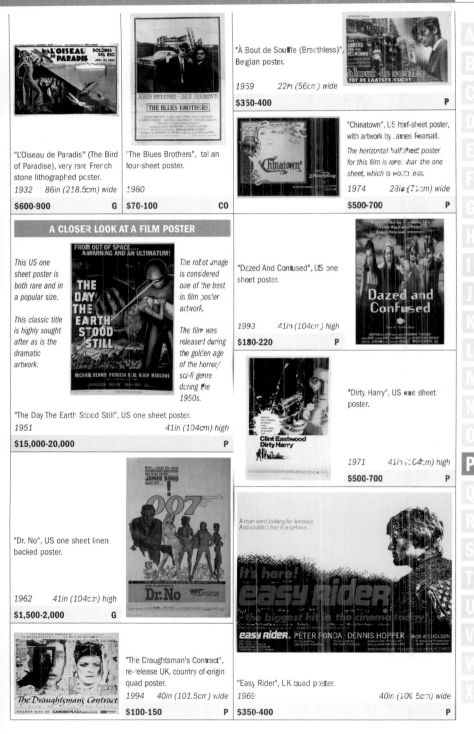

"L'Oiseau de Paradis" (The Bird of Paradise), very rare French stone lithographed poster.
1932   86in (218.5cm) wide
$600-900   G

"The Blues Brothers", tall an four-sheet poster.
1980
$70-100   CO

"À Bout de Souffle (Breathless)", Belgian poster.
1959   22in (56cm) wide
$350-400   P

"Chinatown", US half-sheet poster, with artwork by James Pearsall.

The horizontal half-sheet poster for this film is rarer than the one sheet, which is worth less.
1974   28in (71cm) wide
$500-700   P

A CLOSER LOOK AT A FILM POSTER

This US one sheet poster is both rare and in a popular size.

This classic title is highly sought after as is the dramatic artwork.

The robot image is considered one of the best in film poster artwork.

The film was released during the golden age of the horror/ sci-fi genre during the 1950s.

"The Day The Earth Stood Still", US one sheet poster.
1951   41in (104cm) high
$15,000-20,000   P

"Dazed And Confused", US one sheet poster.
1993   41in (104cm) high
$180-220   P

"Dirty Harry", US one sheet poster.
1971   41in (104cm) high
$500-700   P

"Dr. No", US one sheet linen backed poster.
1962   41in (104cm) high
$1,500-2,000   G

"The Draughtsman's Contract", re-release UK, country of origin quad poster.
1994   40in (101.5cm) wide
$100-150   P

"Easy Rider", UK quad poster.
1969   40in (101.5cm) wide
$350-400   P

"L'Eclipse" (The Eclipse), French grande poster.

1962   63in (160cm) high
$350-400   P

"8½", Italian style B poster.

1963   39in (99cm) high
$700-1,000   P

"Enter The Dragon", US one sheet poster.

1973   41in (104cm) high
$400-600   P

"Gentlemen Prefer Blondes", Australian daybill poster.

Australian posters are recognizable by the appearance of the printing which is akin to a stone-printed lithograph.

1953   30in (76cm) high
$700-1,000   P

"Gigi", re-release US one sheet poster, with art work by Hooks.

1966   41in (104cm) high
$180-220   P

"The Godfather", UK quad poster.

1971   40in (101.5cm) wide
$500-700   P

"Gun Crazy", extremely rare Japanese poster.

1950   29in (73.5cm) high
$2,200-2,800   P

"Guys And Dolls", US one sheet poster.

1955   41in (104cm) high
$600-900   P

"Jailhouse Rock", Argentine stone lithographed poster, with artwork by Giorgio.

1957   43in (109cm) high
$1,000-1,500   P

"High Noon", Argentine poster.

1952   43in (109cm) high
$700-1,000   P

"It's A Wonderful Life", re-release US one sheet poster.

1950s   41in (104cm) high
$3,000-4,000   P

"Kes", rare US half-sheet poster.

1970   28in (71cm) wide
$100-150   P

"Kids", US one sheet poster.

This controversial cult film by an up-and-coming director was highly popular in the US.

1995   41in (104cm) high

$100-150   P

"La Dolce Vita", Argentine store lithographed poster.

1960   43in (109cm) high

$1,000-1,500   P

"Last Tango in Paris", re-release US one sheet poster.

1952   41in (104cm) high

$100-150   P

"Le Mans", Japanese poster.

1971   29in (73.5cm) high

$400-600   P

"Lola", US one sheet poster.

1982   41in (104cm) high

$50-80   P

"The Lord Of The Rings: The Fellowship of the Ring", style A teaser US one sheet poster.

Teaser posters are released before the film's release. Teaser and advance posters are often very similar, but the teaser poster will not carry the film title. The rarer B style poster shows Frodo looking downward at the ring and has a different tagline.

2001   41in (104cm) high

$100-150   P

"The Man Who Wasn't There", US one sheet poster.

The design of the artwork and the title play on Alfred Hitchcock's 1960s classic 'The Man Who Knew Too Much'.

2001   41in (104cm) high

$50-80   P

"Marihuana", Argentine poster, with artwork by Raf.

1950   43in (109cm) high

$500-700   P

"Moby Dick", Italian fotobusta.

1956   27in (76cm) wide

$300-350   P

"Moulin Rouge", style C advance US one sheet poster.

2001   41in (104cm) high

$100-150   P

"My Fair Lady", Italian locandino poster, with artwork by Nistri.

1964   28in (71cm) high

$350-400   P

"My Fair Lady", East German A1 poster, with artwork by Westphal.

1967   32in (81.5cm) high

$350-400   P

"The Night Belongs To Us", Swedish poster, with artwork by Rohman.

1929   *39in (99cm) high*

$1,000-1,500   P

"The Nightmare Before Christmas", US one sheet poster.

1992   *41in (104cm) high*

$150-200   P

"Ocean's Eleven", French stone lithographed petite poster.

1960   *32in (81.5cm) high*

$600-900   P

"The Outlaw Josey Wales", US one sheet poster.

1976   *41in (104cm) high*

$350-400   P

"Planet of the Apes", Japanese one sheet poster.

The Japanese version of this poster is extremely rare, hence a higher value than other countries' versions.

1968   *29in (73.5cm) high*

$1,000-1,500   P

"Planet of the Apes", Belgian poster.

1968   *22in (56cm) high*

$300-400   P

"The Producers", rare style B US one sheet poster.

1967   *41in (104cm) high*

$500-700   P

"Psycho", US one sheet poster.

1960   *41in (104cm) high*

$2,500-3,000   P

"Ran", Japanese poster.

1985   *29in (73.5cm) high*

$400-600   P

"Rear Window", Belgian poster.

1954   *22in (56cm) high*

$600-900   P

"Rebel Without A Cause", US one sheet poster.

1956   *41in (104cm) high*

$3,500-4,500   P

"Rocky", US one sheet poster.

1977   *41in (104cm) high*

$600-900   P

"Rosemary's Baby", US one sheet poster.

1968   *41in (104cm) high*

$350-400   P

"Sabrina", Danish poster, with artwork by Stilling.

1954   *33in (84cm) high*

$700-1,000   P

"The Shining", US insert poster, signed by Jack Nicholson and Stanley Kubrick.

The signatures of lead actor and director of this classic horror film add value to this piece.

1980   *36in (91.5cm) high*

$400-600   G

"The Shining", UK quad poster.

1980　　　　　　*40in (101.5cm) wide*

$300-350　　　　　　　　**P**

"The Silence of the Lambs", advance US one sheet poster.

1990　　　*41in (104cm) high*

$180-220　　　　　　**P**

"Singin' in the Rain", Japanese poster.

1952　　*29in (73.5cm) high*

$1,000-1,500　　　　**P**

"Slacker", rare US one sheet poster.

Despite its comparatively inexpensive value, this was a cult American movie that defined the 'slacker generation'.

1991　　*41in (104cm) high*

$50-80　　　　　　**P**

"Star Wars", re-release style D or 'circus' US one sheet poster, with artwork by Drew Struzan and Charles White III.

The 'D' style was made for summer 1978 re-release and is highly collectible. In 1992 a different-sized fan club reissue was issued rolled – the original was folded.

1978　　*41in (104cm) high*

$400-600　　　　　**P**

"Terror From The Year 5,000", US one sheet poster.

1958　　*41in (104cm) high*

$500-700　　　　　**P**

"A Travers Le Miroir" (Through a Glass Darkly), French language petite poster.

1962　　*32in (81.5cm) high*

$100-150　　　　　**P**

"Trois Couleurs: Bleu", French, country of origin poster.

1992　　*63in (160cm), high*

$150-200　　　　　**P**

"To Kill A Mockingbird", UK quad poster.

1963　　*40in (101.5cm) wide*

$500-700　　　　　**P**

"Vertigo", Argentine one sheet poster, with artwork by Saul Bass.

Designer and animator Bass worked closely with Hitchcock, possibly influencing the Psycho shower scene. He is credited with revolutionizing film credit sequences through use of bizarre, emotional and psychologically disturbing animation techniques. This is classic artwork for a classic film.

1958　　*43in (109cm) high*

$1,200-1,800　　　　**P**

"Yellow Submarine", rare teaser UK quad poster.

1968　　　　*(101.5cm) wide*

$3,000-3,500　　　　**P**

Collectors' Notes

■ Czech film posters are undergoing a continuous and considerable growth in popularity. Under the Communist regime, the Brno Biennal exhibitions were the only major forum for displaying the graphic and artistic achievements of Czech designers and for comparing them to international work.

■ The 1960s saw the start of a golden age, but until the fall of the Communist regime in 1989, they were not highly regarded by experts, nor known widely on the international market.

■ Today they are appreciated for their unique approach to design, which is quite unlike film posters produced in the USA, the UK or other western countries. The use of photography, montage and collage is an important aspect of design, as is the strongly Surrealist and sometimes abstract appearance of the poster. Pop Art is also an influence, as is the manipulation of imagery.

■ Prices are still comparatively low, but have risen over the past years and are still rising. Sizes are also generally much smaller than those produced by other countries, making them easier to display.

■ As with all posters, condition is important. Look for posters with typically Czech and 'unusual' designs and strong imagery for well-known, cult or classic films.

"L'Avventura", Czech poster, designed by Machalek.
1969   *16in (40.5cm) high*
$300-350   P

"The Birds", Czech poster, with artwork by Josef Vyletal.
1970   *33in (84cm) high*
$1,000-1,500   P

"Bonnie and Clyde", Czech poster, with artwork by Josef Vyletal.
1967   *16in (40.5cm) high*
$300-350   P

"Chinatown", Czech poster, designed by M. Hlavacek.
1976   *16in (40.5cm) high*
$220-280   P

"Easy Rider", Czech poster, with artwork by Josef Vyletal.
1969   *16in (40.5cm) high*
$220-280   P

"Gilda", Czech poster.
1946   *33in (84cm) high*
$700-1,000   G

"Giulietta Degli Spiriti", Czech poster, designed by Milan Grygar.
1965   *16in (40.5cm) high*
$300-350   P

"Psycho", Czech poster, designed by Ziegler.
1970   *16in (40.5cm) high*
$400-600   P

"The Seven Year Itch", Czech poster, designed by Kaplan.
1955   *16in (40.5cm) high*
$400-600   P

"The Terminator", Czech poster.
1984   *16in (40.5cm) high*
$220-280   P

FIND OUT MORE...

'Czech Posters of the '60s from the Collections of the Moravian Gallery Brno', published by Moravskaa Galerie v Brnee.

Collectors' Notes

- Over the past two decades, collectors have turned increasingly to psychedelic posters as epitomizing an important part of graphic design from the 1960s.
- The movement began in San Francisco during the late 1960s when artists broke away from the existing styles of commercial concert advertising. They begin promoting them in a new way, revisiting previously used designs but in a new style.
- Forms were often inspired by the Art Nouveau movement, particularly poster designs by Toulouse Lautrec and Alphonse Mucha, with organic, flowing lines. Lettering is typically large and used as a compositional element, often being flowed in to the rest of the design.
- The bright colors and forms epitomize the psychedelic period and its associated use of drugs such as LSD. Reflective materials are also common.
- Look out for posters that typify the style in terms of color and form, and those advertising popular performers such as Jimi Hendrix. Also collectible are examples by noted artists such as Stanley Mouse, Rick Griffin and Victor Moscoso.

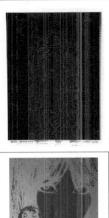

A Sonny & Cher blacklight responsive poster.

This rare poster is one of only two known copies.

1967   23in (58.5cm) high

$1,500-2,000   G

A rare Fantasy Faire and Magic Music Festival poster listing bands including Jefferson Airplane, The Doors, and Country Joe and the Fish.

21in (53.5cm) high

$1,200-1,800   G

An Artist Rights Today poster, signed by Stanley Mouse, Alton Kelley, Victor Moscoso, Wes Wilson, and Rick Griffin created for a fund raising concert in August, 1986.

$1,200-1,800   G

A Donovan "Sunshine Superman" poster, designed by Martin Sharp, metallic finish with black and blue print on a silver ground, framed and glazed.

c1967   32in (81cm) high

$180-220   CO

A Family Dog 'Mist Dance' poster, artwork by Victor Moscoso, photography by Paul Kagan, promoting the Youngbloods, Other Half at the Avalon Ballroom, No. 81-1.

21in (53cm) high

$120-180   CO

A "Welcome Cosmic Visitors The Creator Made The World Come and See It' silkscreen poster, designed by Hapshash & The Coloured Coat.

c1967   30in (76cm) wide

$400-600   CO

$800-1,200   CO

A hand-colored Jimi Hendrix New York/Madrid Feeling Ibiza Rock Conexion poster, hand-colored, titled "New York Rock Conexion Madrid", with further annotation "Rock & Roll Joint Show 1 Ibiza Spain Feeling Ibiza', attributed to Pietro Psaier, mounted, framed and glazed.

34in (86cm) high

A rare concert poster for Jimi Hendrix and The Move at The Albert Hall, Tuesday, November 14, designed by Osiris Visions.

c1967   20in (51cm) high

$800-1,200   CO

A rare Middle Earth 1968 calendar poster, designed by Monk, reading "Truth is Freedom Beauty is Love", designed by Monk.

1968   30in (76cm) high

$300-500   CO

FIND OUT MORE:

'High Art: A History of The Psychedelic Poster', by Ted Owen & Denise Dickson, published by Sanctuary Publishing Ltd, 2001

Collectors' Notes

■ Look for posters advertising races at famous motor racing locations such as Brands Hatch and Goodwood in England and Le Mans in France.

■ Value is usually added if the race was important or if a noted driver was competing, especially if the race marked an important point in their career.

■ The style of the artwork is important. Speeding cars with a good visual sense of movement are desirable. Images of classically styled cars by leading marques or in leading teams are also sought after.

■ Interest in this area is strong, coming from collectors of posters and sporting memorabilia, as well as automobilia collectors.

A 1950s Goodwood Bank Holiday Meeting poster, for Whit-Monday 30th May 1.30 p.m., very tiny piece missing from lower left corner.

30in (76cm) high

$300-500   SAS

A 1950s Goodward International Programme poster, for Saturday., 25th September 2 p.m.

30in (76cm) high

$400-600   SAS

A 1950s 26th R.A.C. Tourist Trophy Race at Goodwood poster, Saturday, 19th August 12 Noon, illustration by MT, three very minor tears.

30in (76.5cm) high

$400-600   SAS

An International Nine-Hour Car Race at Goodwood poster, 20th August, 3 p.m. until Midnight, night-time illustration by Roy Nockolds.

30in (76cm) high

$500-700   SAS

An R.A.C. European Grand Prix at Brands Hatch poster, July 11th 11 a.m., illustration by B.K. Bull, two small tears.

30in (76.5cm) high

$220-280   SAS

A Daily Mail Race of Champions at Brands Hatch poster, Saturday, 13th March 1965 1.30 p.m.

1965   *30in (76cm) high*

$40-60   SAS

A 1966 British Kart Racing Championship at Brands Hatch poster.

1966   *30in (76cm) high*

$40-60   SAS

A 1950s Crystal Palace Motor Racing poster, Saturday 2nd September 2 p.m., illustration by MT.

30in (76cm) high

$220-280   SAS

A mid-1950s Crystal Palace Motor Racing poster, Bank Holiday Monday 6th August 2 p.m, illustration by Raymond Groves, one very minor paper tear.

29.75in (75.5cm) high

$400-600   SAS

A 1950s Crystal Palace Motor Racing poster, Whit Monday 2 p.m., illustration by Raymond Groves, small tear to lower right corner.

30in (76cm) high

$400-600   SAS

A National Six Hour Relay Race for Sports Cars at Silverstone poster, 9th July 1955 1 p.m.

15in (38cm) high

$60-90   SAS

A 'Salon des Cent - Exposition' chromolithographic poster, by Lapierre, signed on plate, also marked "Imp. Charles Verneau, 114 Rue Oberkampf, Paris", framed and glazed.

23.75in (60.5cm) high

$320-380   **DN**

A French 'Foire De Paris' advertising poster, artwork by Azebel.
1918   43in (109cm) high

$500-700   **P**

A French Renault tractors advertising poster, signed "Coulon".

62.75in (159cm) wide

$70-100   **ATK**

An early hand-painted Mutascope poster for "What the Moon Saw".

A Mutascope was an early optical toy found on streets and at seaside and other resorts. A metal box with a viewing aperture contained a reel of photographs. Subject matter was most often erotic. By putting a coin in a slot and turning a handle, the reel revolved at speed and the viewer saw a 'moving' picture.

c1920   21.75in (55cm) high

$280-320   **ATK**

A CLOSER LOOK AT AN ADVERTISING POSTER

Adolpho Hohenstein (1854-1928) began to design posters when working for Ricordi, the Italian music company.

The strongly Art Nouveau curving lines, interlocking 'O's and figures with conflicting perspectives add energy to the design.

He is considered to be the father of Italian poster design, a leader of the Italian Art Nouveau movement and influenced many other poster artists.

Posters from before 1910, when Cinzano's orange and red zebra design was created, are rare.

A 'Cinzano' advertising poster, by Adolpho Hohenstein, Turin.
c1898   66.75in (169.5cm) high

$3,000-3,500   **Swa**

A 'La Houppa' color lithographic advertising poster, by R. Faye, of woman in top hat in bright polychrome, mounted on linen, unframed, some creases and folds, signed upper right in print.
c1930   62in (157.5cm) high

$350-400   **DRA**

A 'Veuve Amiot' color lithographic advertising poster, by Falucci, of a couple drinking champagne, in bright polychrome, mounted on linen, unframed, signed in print upper right.
1936   60in (152cm) high

$180-220   **DRA**

A Belgian 'Maëstro' cigars lithographed advertising poster.

$100-150   **ATK**

A WFA lithographed advertising poster, for skating in New York City Building, Flushing Meadow Park., framed under glass, a few short folds with accompanying loss of ink and some light rippling.
13in (33cm) wide

$280-320   **DRA**

A Berlin Film Festival #1 poster.
1960   32in (81.5cm) high

$300-500   **P**

A black Bakelite EKCO RS2 radio.

Visually, this is the same radio as the M23 released in 1932 and also designed by J.K. White, but a fire destroyed the tooling for the RS2 in late 1931, so a new model was rapidly designed and built with a slightly different speaker configuration. The RS2 is much rarer than the M23.

1931   15.25in (39cm) high

$400-600   LC

A Ferranti-type 145 wireless, AC mains.

c1945   19.5in (50cm) high

$60-90   LC

A Kolster Brandes FB10 AC mains receiver.

This radio is affectionately called the 'Toaster' by collectors and was available in a range of solid and sprayed colors.

c1955

$30-50   LC

An EKCO model AC85 black Bakelite wireless.

This Art Deco styled set was designed by Wells Coates, who also designed the round EKCO radio sets.

c1934   23in (58.5cm) wide

$150-200   LC

A black Philco Type 333 'People's Set' radio, battery powered, lacks back.

c1936

$80-120   LC

A brown Bakelite EKCO Type A22 radio.

c1945   14.5in (37cm) high

$600-900   ATK

Three National Panasonic 'Toot-a-Loop' wrist radios, in red, yellow and green plastic hinged cases.

1970   6in (15cm) long

$70-100 (each)   L&T

An early 1970s radio, by Isis, Hong Kong.

9.75in (25cm) wide

$40-60   MA

Collectors' Notes

■ The most important factor to consider when buying a vintage radio is the case, rather than sound quality. The golden age was from the 1920s until the 1950s, when radios all used valves. After this period, there have been a small number of design classics that interest collectors.

■ Large examples, such as radiograms, are usually less popular partly due to problems displaying and storing them. There are a small number of radios in wooden cases that are collected, but the majority have Bakelite or similar early plastic cases.

■ Black and brown are the most common Bakelite colors. Look out for bright colors in 'catalin', such as orange, blue, green and red which will be more valuable. The shape is also important, with Art Deco, industrially styled or streamlined cases being very desirable.

■ Cracks and chips to the case and missing backs will reduce value. Look for popular makers such as FADA, Emmerson, EKCO (E.K. Cole) and Phillips.

An orange Catalin Fada Radio, model no. 44, with ribbed tuning, volume knobs and square dial, Fada Radio label.

c1941   9in (23cm) wide

$1,800-2,200   DRA

A Bush mottled brown Bakelite DAC 90A radio.

11.5in (29cm) wide

$400-600   LC

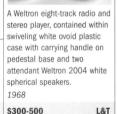

A Weltron eight-track radio and stereo player, contained within swiveling white ovoid plastic case with carrying handle on pedestal base and two attendant Weltron 2004 white spherical speakers.

1968

$300-500   L&T

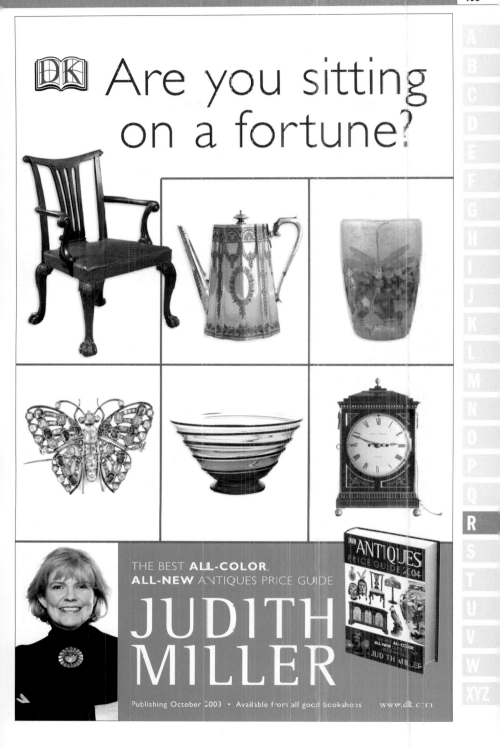
A
B
C
D
E
F
G
H
I
J
K
L
M
N
O
P
Q
R
S
T
U
V
W
XYZ

Collectors' Notes

- Items connected with well-known artists are generally the most sought after and therefore the most valuable. Look for The Beatles, Elvis Presley, Jimi Hendrix and The Doors.

- Ensure that the piece you are buying comes with suitable provenance, which a good dealer or auction house should be able to provide. Provenance may come in the form of research showing an item's history or a letter from the original vendor.

- Autographs have always been a popular collecting area and because of this there are a number of fakes on the market. Huge demand at the time for performers such as The Beatles and Elvis Presley meant that many examples were signed by assistants or family members, or members of the band signed for each other. Autographs with dedications, unless to another famous person, tend to detract from the value. It is also preferable to have groups' signatures on one piece

of paper rather than on many, with signatures in pen rather than in pencil.

- Signed publicity photographs such as those sent out by fan clubs were distributed in huge numbers and the signatures are usually printed.

- The condition of promotional posters is very important. Rips and tears, water stains and missing pieces will reduce the value, as will folds and creases although these can often be restored. As posters were not designed for long term use they were made from low quality material and therefore examples in mint condition are highly sought-after.

- Used and/or signed instruments are very popular, with guitars the most sought after. The prices for these differ, with signed instruments played at significant events commanding high sums. Signed, but unused instruments are the least desirable. Due to their nature, condition does not always affect value.

An original Stuart Sutcliffe ink and watercolor drawing, mounted on card.

This drawing was taken from the sketchbook Sutcliffe submitted for admission to the Royal College of Art, London.

17in (43cm) wide

$700-1,000　　　　CO

An 'EMI Manchester Square' pose promotional display, showing a composite of two famous images of The Beatles leaning over the stairwell of the EMI offices in Manchester Square, London, mounted, framed and glazed.

c1963　　　10in (25.5cm) wide

$100-150　　　　CO

John Lennon's job card from Scarisbrick Water Works.

1959

$10,000-15,000　　　　CO

An 'Introducing The Beatles' press kit, including a biography of the group and a review of their first single "Love Me Do", cover laminated.

1963

$600-900　　　　CO

A handbill from the Odeon, Llandudno, for the week commencing Monday, August 12, 1963, featuring The Beatles among others.

1963　　　10in (25.5cm) high

$700-1,000　　　　CO

A concert program from The Beatles 1963 concert tour of Britain.

This was The Beatles' fourth tour of Britain and ran from November 1 to December 13, 1963 with the main support act of Peter Jay and the Jaywalkers.

1963　　　10.5in (27cm) high

$180-220　　　　CO

A John Lennon autograph, signed in blue ballpoint pen and additionally signed "Paul McCartney", "George Harrison" and "Ringo Starr" by Neil Aspinall, with typed heading "The Beatles Sunderland Empire - Saturday, 30th November 1963", framed with a sepia-colored print of John Lennon with Pete Best in the background.

16in (41cm) high

$3,000-4,000 CO

A handbill for The Beatles at City Hall, Sheffield, Saturday, March 2, 1963, supporting Helen Shapiro, with postal booking form printed at the bottom.

10in (25.5cm) high

$1,200-1,800 CO

A Beatles business card, reading "Sole Direction: A. Williams, Tel. Royal 7943, Bockings. Stanley 1556" printed in black on white card.

Williams was a renowned club-owner/promoter in the Merseyside area who is often credited with being The Beatles' first manager. In reality he merely booked them for a few gigs in the Liverpool area, and later on to perform in Hamburg.

3.5in (9cm) wide

$1,500-2,000 CO

A printer's proof handbill for "Pops Alive!", featuring The Beatles billed for Sunday 31 May, Roy Orbison, Freddie and the Dreamers, Gerry and the Pacemakers and others.

c1964   11in (28cm) high

$400-600 CO

A 'Beatles for Sale' promotional flat, featuring the front cover of the mono album, printed in England.

1964   12.5in (31cm) wide

$180-220 CO

A rare Italian 'I Favolosi Beatles' (With The Beatles) mono LP, No. PMCO 31503, near mint.

1964

$320-380 CO

A complete book of 100 Beatles US stamps, by Hallmark, together with an advertising sticker.

c1964

$80-120 CO

A Performance Return record for Colston Hall, Bristol, dated 10 November 1964, for The Beatles' performance with Mary Wells, together with a tour program.

1964   10in (25.5cm) high

$180-220 CO

An official souvenir program for The Beatles' 1964 Australian tour.

1964

$150-200 CO

A Beatles commemorative coin, minted to commemorate their first visit to the US.

c1964 Display 8in (20cm) high

$60-90 CO

A double-sided promotional flyer for The Beatles' 'A Hard Day's Night', by the Daily Express.

1964   11in (28cm) high

$180-220 CO

A Beatles Fan Club Christmas 45 rpm flexi disc, from December 1964, with original sleeve and newsletter, signed "Best Wishes Anne Collingham"

It appears that Anne Collingham was the fictitious head of The Beatles Fan Club in Great Britain and was an invention of The Beatles' Press Officer Tony Barrow. 'Anne' also wrote a regular column in The Beatles Monthly magazine.

1964

$70-100 CO

A 'Look' magazine poster of Ringo Starr, with photograph by Richard Avedon.

1967   31.5in (80cm) high

$80-120 DRA

A US promotional poster for The Beatles' "White Album", near mint.

1968   *37in (94cm) high*

$300-500   CO

A rare synopsis pamphlet for The Beatles' "Yellow Submarine", produced by United Artists.

1968   *10in (25.5cm) high*

$280-320   CO

A TWA promotional postcard signed and annotated by Paul McCartney, postmarked "Jamaica N.Y".

1968   *5.5in (14cm) wide*

$800-1,200   CO

A Beatles "Let It Be" exhibitors campaign book, the five-page book listing the various promotional and advertising tools available from United Artists.

1970   *12.5in (32cm) high*

$220-280   CO

After John Lennon, "The Hug", limited edition lithograph from an edition of 5,000, chop marked, framed.

c1988   *35.5in (90cm) high*

$300-400   CR

Three John Lennon items, comprising a black and white 'Imagine' poster, a rare calendar commemorating John's 50th birthday in 1991, and a Apple handout featuring John singing.

$80-120   CO

An Apple Corps. John Lennon promotional cloth doll, with a model Rickenbacker signature guitar, marked "The Beatles... Made in China".

1987   *21in (53 cm) high*

$80-120   CO

An unpublished color photograph of Paul and Linda McCartney, photographed with an extra on the set of "Give My Regards to Broad Street" at Silvertown, London Docklands, annotated on the reverse in an unknown hand.

1984   *5in (13cm) high*

$60-90   CO

A Paul McCartney publicity portrait postcard, signed and dedicated "To Tammy Love Paul McCartney X" in blue ballpoint pen, with additional doodled smiley face.

6in (15cm) high

$220-280   CO

An inflatable John Lennon doll, made in Hong Kong, originally part of a set.

c1966   *13in (33cm) high*

$120-180   CO

A signed Paul McCartney promotional postcard.

8in (20cm) high

$280-320   CO

A Paul McCartney doll, molded painted composition shoulder-head with painted features, black real hair wig, cloth body with painted rubber hands, wearing a black velvet suit, white shirt and black felt tie, black leather imitation boots, together with a photograph showing the four Beatles wearing similar suits.

1963-64   *24.5in (62cm) high*

$3,000-4,000   BonC

A rare Paul McCartney and Wings silkscreen concert poster, for Leeds University Union, Saturday, May 19, 1973.

1973   *29in (73cm) high*

$300-500   CO

A set of four Royal Doulton Beatles toby jugs, numbered "D6725", "D6724", "D6727" and "D6726".

1984   *6in (15cm) high*

$700-1,000   CO

A signed flyer for "The Art of Paul McCartney" exhibition, held at the Walker Gallery, Liverpool.

2002

$300-400   CO

A set of Beatles figures, unknown maker, on a homemade stage.

Figures 2in (5cm) high

$120-180   CO

A Beatles merchandising tablecloth, marked "Ulster copyright".

35in (89cm) wide

$220-280   CO

A Beatles 'Sgt Pepper' cloth badge, made to John Lennon's specifications to resemble the Sgt Pepper LP near.

c1967   *3in 7.5cm diam*

$280-320   CO

A Beatles plastic New Sound Guitar, by Selcol.

$180-220   Chef

A Beatles 'Big 6' guitar, manufactured by Selcol (UK), comprising a plastic body with sticker of the group and facsimile autographs on the body, lacks box.

1963-70

$600-900   CO

A complete set of the original "The Beatles Book Monthly" magazines.

This series of magazines began in 1963 and stopped publication when The Beatles split up in 1970. In the mid-1970s they were re-issued with new covers wrapped around original copies. The re-issued magazines have little value.

1963-70

$600-900   CO

'Liverpool Days' and 'Golden Dreams', by Max Scheler and Astrid Kirchherr, limited edition box set featuring photographs of The Beatles in Liverpool during Spring 1964, both signed by the authors.

1994-96

$300-500   CO

A complete The Beatles color picture jigsaw puzzle, in distressed original box.

$150-200   CO

'Fifty Years Adrift', by Derek Taylor, a limited first edition of 2,000, signed on the title page by Derek Taylor and George Harrison, plus ex-Bonzo Dog member Larry Smith, who created the end papers.

This autobiography of Derek Taylor begins with his early days as a journalist and on to his term as The Beatles' publicist, when he became friends with the band. Edited and annotated by George Harrison.

1985

$1,200-1,800   CO

A clipped ticket from the premiere screening of The Beatles' film "Help", at Lowes State Theater Houston, Texas, on Saturday, August 28, 1965, together with a tag reading "I Needed HELP! So Got My Beatles Movie Ticket! Did You?" and an unopened Cured plaster sticking plaster with Beatles HELP! Capitol printed on the reverse, reputedly handed out in the theater.

$150-200   CO

An ABBA album, 'ABBA The Album', signed by all four members, vinyl included.

$280-320   **CO**

An ABBA color laser print, signed by all four members.

$180-220   **CO**

An ABBA publicity postcard, signed by all four members in different colored pens.

6in (15cm) high

$280-320   **CO**

An AC/DC color laser print, signed by the five members of the band in blue marker pen.

$120-180   **CO**

A two-part book plate photograph of The Band, signed by Robbie Robertson, Rick Danko, Levon Helm and Garth Hudson, all in marker pen, together with a inner album sleeve signed "Best Wishes Bob Dylan" next to an image of the singer.

$280-320   **CO**

A Bee Gees 'Saturday Night Fever' soundtrack album sleeve, signed by Robin, Maurice and Robin Gibb, in blue marker pen, vinyl not included.

$280-320   **CO**

An Eric Clapton record sleeve, signed boldly in blue marker pen, vinyl not included.

$70-100   **CO**

A Clash 'Combat Rock' album cover, signed by "Joe Strummer of Clash" and Paul Simonon in blue marker pen and Mick Jones and Topper Headon in black marker pen.

c1982

$180-220   **CO**

A set of four Clash autographs, signed by Mick Jones, Joe Strummer, Paul Simonon and Topper Headon, framed with a photograph of the band.

21in (53cm) high

$180-220   **CO**

A limited edition print titled "Phil Collins ...Hits", from an edition of 350, signed by the artist.

16in (40 cm) high

$280-320   **CO**

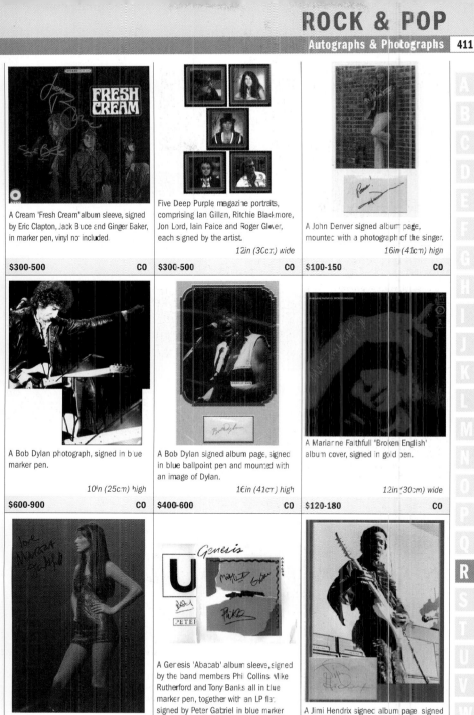

A Cream 'Fresh Cream' album sleeve, signed by Eric Clapton, Jack Bruce and Ginger Baker, in marker pen, vinyl not included.

$300-500   CO

Five Deep Purple magazine portraits, comprising Ian Gillan, Ritchie Blackmore, Jon Lord, Iain Paice and Roger Glover, each signed by the artist.

12in (30cm) wide

$300-500   CO

A John Denver signed album page, mounted with a photograph of the singer.

16in (41cm) high

$100-150   CO

A Bob Dylan photograph, signed in blue marker pen.

10in (25cm) high

$600-900   CO

A Bob Dylan signed album page, signed in blue ballpoint pen and mounted with an image of Dylan.

16in (41cm) high

$400-600   CO

A Marianne Faithfull 'Broken English' album cover, signed in gold pen.

12in (30cm) wide

$120-180   CO

A Marianne Faithfull signed photograph, signed in black marker pen.

10in (25cm) high

$100-150   CO

A Genesis 'Abacab' album sleeve, signed by the band members Phil Collins, Mike Rutherford and Tony Banks all in blue marker pen, together with an LP flat signed by Peter Gabriel in blue marker pen, vinyl not included.

$60-90   CO

A Jimi Hendrix signed album page signed in black pen and mounted with a photograph.

16in (40cm) high

$400-600   CO

A Michael Jackson 'Moonwalker' promotional display, signed in black marker pen.

56in (142cm) high

$100-150   CO

An Elton John 'A Single Man' single sleeve, signed and dedicated "To Roger with love Elton", vinyl included.

$180-220   CO

A Kiss signed LP fold-out sleeve, signed by all four original members, Gene Simmons, Faul Stanley, Peter Criss and Ace Frehley, in marker pen.

24.5in (62cm) wide

$150-200   CO

A Lynyrd Skynyrd Tribute' album sleeve, signed by Allen Collins, Leon Wilkeson, Artimus Pyle, Gary Rossington and Billy Powell in marker pen, vinyl not included. together with a large piece of paper signed by Ronnie Van Zant in blue ballpoint pen.

$400-600   CO

A Madonna signed card, signed in black pen, mounted with a photograph of the singer.

16in (40cm) high

$150-200   CO

A Meatloaf signed photograph, signed in black marker pen.

10in (25cm) wide

$70-100   CO

A Glenn Miller signed pamphlet, signed in black ink.

22in. (56cm) high

$180-220   CO

A Monkees 'More of the Monkees' album sleeve, signed Mike Nesmith, David Jones, Peter Tork and Mike Dolenz, all in marker pen, vinyl not included.

$220-280   CO

A Police signed A&M Records promotional photo, signed by all three band members in blue marker pen.

$80-120   CO

A P.J. Proby Show program, signed on the interior by support acts including The Fourmost, The Chapters, Syd and Eddie, Sandra Barrie, The Artwoods and Brian Freeman.

$60-90   CO

A Queen 'Thank God It's Christmas' single sleeve, signed by Freddie Mercury, Brian May, John Deacon, and Roger Taylor in blue ballpoint pen.

1984

$300-500   CO

A Queen 'News of the World' album flat, signed by Freddie Mercury in black marker pen.

$300-500   CO

A Rolling Stones debut album Decca Mono LK 4605, second pressing sleeve with "Mona" not "I Need You Baby" listing, together with a 1990 London Records promotional Radio Sampler CD and two London Records sales marketing sheets, titled "August 1988 is Rolling Stones Month" with illustrations of 17 Rolling Stones album covers.

$70-100 CO

A Rolling Stones "It's Only Rock 'n' Roll" album sleeve, signed by Mick Jagger, Keith Richards, Bill Wyman, Charlie Watts and Mick Taylor, in blue marker pen, vinyl not included.

$1,000-1,500 CO

A Rolling Stones signed photograph, signed by Keith Richard, Ronnie Wood, Mick Jagger and Charlie Watts, all in blue marker pen, together with a piece of card signed Bill Wyman in black pen.

$300-500 CO

A Rolling Stones 'Beggars' Banquet' album sleeve, signed by Mick Jagger in green ink, vinyl included.

$100-150 CO

A Mick Jagger signed photograph, signed in gold marker pen, framed and glazed

13in (33cm) high

$220-280 CO

A Simon & Garfunkel 'The Concert in Central Park' album sleeve, signed by Paul Simon in blue marker pen and and Art Garfunkel in silver marker, vinyl not included.

$150-200 CO

A U2 'Under a Blood Red Sky' album sleeve, signed by all four band members, vinyl not included.

$220-280 CO

A Van Halen debut album sleeve, signed by David Lee Roth in silver marker, Eddie Van Halen, Alex Van Halen and Michael Anthony all in gold marker pen, vinyl not included.

$280-320 CO

A Wham signed photograph, signed in black marker pen.

$70-100 CO

A Who 'Who Are You' album sleeve, signed by John Entwhistle, Pete Townshend and Roger Daltrey in blue marker pen, vinyl not included.

$220-280 CO

A Neil Young 'Harvest Moon' album sleeve, signed in blue ballpoint pen, vinyl included.

$120-180 CO

A reproduction AC/DC 1995 'Ball Breakers' World Tour poster, with facsimile autographs printed in gold.

24in (61cm) high

$70-100 CO

Five original concert programs for Count Basie, one including Tony Bennett, another featuring Ray Charles and Oscar Peterson, with two ticket stubs for a performance at the Empire, Liverpool.

$120-180 CO

A rare The Doors promotional poster, for their self-titled debut album.

28in (71cm) high

$1,000-1,500 G

An early 1960s Folk Artistes Productions Ltd Champion Jack Dupree concert poster, at the Town Hall, Islington, UK, Saturday, September 17.

27in (69cm) high

$100-150 CO

A giant Frankie Goes to Hollywood German tour poster.

This poster was banned in Germany.

1985   46in (117cm) high

$100-100 CO

An Elton John UK silkscreen concert poster, for gigs at Leeds University Union 10/11 March.

28in (71cm) high

$180-220 CO

A Led Zeppelin 'Tour Over Europe 1980' poster, framed and glazed.

26in (66cm) high

$150-200 CO

A Led Zeppelin poster, promoting a concert at Knebworth Park, UK, headlined by Led Zeppelin on "Saturday August 11th 1979 11am to 11pm", framed and glazed.

26in (66cm) high

$150-200 CO

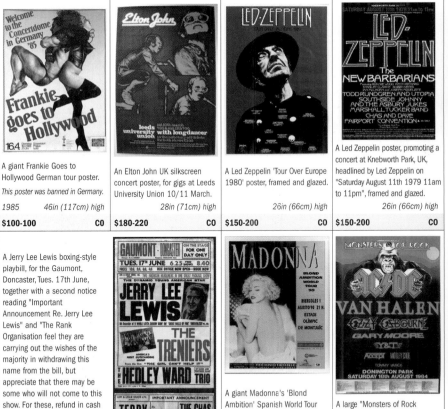

A Jerry Lee Lewis boxing-style playbill, for the Gaumont, Doncaster, Tues. 17th June, together with a second notice reading "Important Announcement Re. Jerry Lee Lewis" and "The Rank Organisation feel they are carrying out the wishes of the majority in withdrawing this name from the bill, but appreciate that there may be some who will not come to this show. For these, refund in cash will be made at the Booking Office in exchange for tickets already purchased".

c1958   Playbill 15in (38cm) high

$1,200-1,200 CO

A giant Madonna's 'Blond Ambition' Spanish World Tour poster, framed and mounted.

1990   54in (137cm) high

$60-90 ATK

A large "Monsters of Rock Festival, Donington" poster, featuring AC/DC, Van Halen, Ozzy Osbourne and Gary Moore.

c1984   59in (150cm) high

$180-220 CO

A Pink Floyd lithographed concert poster, at the Town Hall, Leeds, Friday, May 16th, designed by Hipgnosis.

c1969   29in (74cm) high

$700-1,000   CO

A Rolling Stones' 'Rock and Roll Circus' promotional poster, produced by ABKO, to promote the 1996 release of "Rolling Stones: Rock And Roll Circus December 11 1968" on CD and video, mounted, framed and glazed.

37in (94cm) wide

$150-200   CO

A Pace International poster, featuring Mick Jagger, with its original box.

1971   38in (96.5cm) high

$120-180   CO

A Sex Pistols 'Never Mind the Bollocks' promotional poster signed by Steve Jones, in black felt tip.

32in (81cm) wide

$220-280   CO

A Soft Machine silkscreen concert poster, for the Guildhall, Portsmouth, Thur. 2nd Dec. at 7.30 p.m.

1970-71   30in (76cm) high

$150-200   CO

A Dave Swarbrick concert poster, for the Simon Nichol Malvern Festival Theatre, 10th April 1978.

30in (76cm) high

$100-150   CO

Guitars

A Jefferson Airplane white Fender Squier Stratocaster guitar, signed by Kantner, Balin, Kaukonen, Casady, Slick and Dryden, in blue marker pen.

$1,800-2,200   CO

A B.B. King Epiphone Special Les Paul 'Style' cherry sunburst electric guitar, signed in black marker pen on the body.

$700-1,000   CO

A Led Zeppelin Austin Telecaster 'Style' electric cream finish guitar, signed by Jimmy Page, Robert Plant and John Paul Jones, all in blue marker pen.

$1,000-1,500   CO

A Pink Floyd Fender Telecaster tobacco finish electric guitar, signed by Nick Mason, David Gilmour, Roger Waters and Richard Wright, in blue marker pen.

$1,800-2,200   CO

Collectors' Notes

- Most scientific instruments found today will date from the late 19th or early 20th centuries. Many will be built from lacquered brass, often with fitted cases with a range of accessories. Look for those that have all their accessories as this helps to increase value.
- The name of the maker is important. Although the shape and type of an instrument may be the same, the value will be higher if marked with a renowned maker's name such as Dollond or Beck. Such a name and often the address, if shown, also help to date an instrument.
- Check for condition and quality. Most instruments should be very well engineered. Pieces should 'fit' together very well and work easily. Beware of cleaning brass with abrasive cleaners as this can remove the lacquer, which will devalue the piece.

A rare and early brass microscope, by J. Amadio, London.
c1840
$400-600　　　　**ATK**

A brass microscope, by R. & J. Beck, London, in fitted mahogany case.
1867-94　15.75in (40cm) high
$700-1,000　　　**ATK**

A late 19thC student's lacquered brass compound microscope, with a blackened brass stage.
8in (20cm) high
$100-150　　　　**ET**

A late 19thC lacquered brass drum microscope, with plano-concave revolving mirror.
6in (16cm) high
$50-80　　　　**ET**

An English Cary-type traveling microscope.
These traveling microscopes are also sometimes known as 'botanist's' microscopes. Each part unscrews and is held compactly in the small wooden case that also acts as a stand.
1820-40　12in (30cm) high
$300-500　　　　**ATK**

A 19thC pocket microscope.
2.25in (5.5cm) high
$70-100　　　　**BA**

A small brass bound hand-held 'Stanhope lens' or magnifier.
c1870　1.75in (4.5cm) long
$80-120　　　　**JSC**

A 19th botanist's glass, with case.
2in (5cm) diam
$120-180　　　　**BA**

A large hand-held 'Stanhope lens', with twisted wire handle.
This style of lens is reputed to be very good for examining butterfly wings, and is very useful to botanists. It was invented by the politician Charles, Earl of Stanhope (1753-1816).
c1870　1.25in (3cm) diam
$80-120　　　　**JSC**

An English microscope slide cabinet, containing 100 specimen slides, mostly human, together with an R. & J. Beck pathological list in a leather case.
c1880　14.25in (36cm) high
$400-600　　　　**ATK**

A set of brass apothecary scales, by Paul Altmann, Berlin.

c1910   20in (50.5cm) high

$320-380   **ATK**

A Wheatstone's bridge, by Ruhstrat, Göttingen, together with some early fuses.

c1900   11.75in (30cm) long

$180-220   **ATK**

A scarce Swan lightbulb with wooden base.

c1882   3.5in (9cm) high

$180-220   **ET**

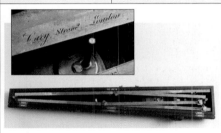

A 19thC pantograph, signed Cary, Strand, London, contained in mahogany case.

A pantograph was used for copying and altering the size of diagrams or maps.

Case 38.5in (98cm) wide

$400-600   **LC**

A Philips terrestrial globe, with brass meridian ring, turned wooden stand and cartouche reading "Philips Educational Terrestrial Globe London Geographical Institute George Philip & Son Ltd 32 Fleet Street".

Globe 6in (15cm) diam

$180-220   **ET**

A 19thC leather-covered printer's rolling pin.

$30-50   **D**

A brass-cased pocket aneroid barometer, by F**E & Sons, Opticians, Edinburgh.

c1900   2in (5cm) wide

$150-200   **ET**

A 19thC unmarked cased pocket aneroid barometer, the red leather-covered case with inset ivory thermometer inside.

2.25in (5.5cm) wide

$300-400   **ET**

A late 18thC red leather-cased pocket thermometer and compass, with mother-of-pearl dial, compass hand missing.

$400-600   **GorL**

An early 19thC mahogany cased dial, with paper label and blued steel needle.

The value would be around 25 percent higher if the lid was not damaged in the left corner.

2.5in (6.5cm) wide

$120-180   **ET**

A late 19thC brass protractor.

6.75in (17cm) wide

$300-400   **BA**

A brass dial, by Stanley, London.

Many instruments marked 'Stanley' are modern reproductions produced in the Far East. These reproductions are made from a very yellow shiny brass, have poor quality detailing and the engraving of numbers lacks the sharpness of authentic pieces.

c1890   5in (12.5cm) diam

$150-200   **BA**

A brass and metal polaris, by Wilson & Gillie, North Shields.

c1890   16in (40.5cm) high

$300-400   **BA**

A 19thC brass alidade level.

12in (30.5cm) long

$300-500   **BA**

A brass level, by Kern, Aarau, Switzerland, with horizontal pitch circle, silver scales.

c1900   14.5in (37cm) wide

$180-220   **ATK**

A brass and gray-painted metal theodolite, by W. F. Stanley & Co., in fitted mahogany case.

c1950   14in (35.5cm) high

$300-400   **ATK**

A 19thC three-draw lacquered brass telescope, with red lacquer finish, signed "Dollond, London" on the first draw.

Beware of instruments signed Dolland (with an 'a') as these are not authentic pieces made by the famous optical instrument maker.

9.25in (23.5cm) long unextended

$300-400   **ET**

A late 19thC pocket sextant, by Geo. Stebbing, Portsmouth, UK.

If a pocket sextant is lacking its telescope, its value is much reduced as it is near impossible to find a replacement that will fit as well as the original.

2.25in (5.75in) wide

$300-500   **BA**

A late 19thC pocket telescope, by Salman & Co, Edinburgh, marked "Reconnoitrer".

Closed 5in (12.5cm) long

$80-120   **BA**

A Vernier's Improved Sight Rule, by Frazer & Son, London.

1901   18in (45.5cm) long

$120-180   **BA**

FIND OUT MORE...

Gerard L'E Turner, '**Scientific Instruments 1500-1900 - An Introduction**', published by Philip Wilson, 1998.

Ronald Pearsall, '**Collecting & Restoring Scientific Instruments**', published by David & Charles, 1974.

SCIENCE & TECHNOLOGY

A Sinclair Cambridge calculator.
This was Sinclair's second calculator.
c1973
$60-90   HLJ

A Sinclair Cambridge Memory calculator.
c1974
$50-80   HLJ

A gold-plated Sinclair Sovereign calculator.
c1977   5.5in (14cm) long
$150-200   HLJ

A stainless steel Sinclair Sovereign calculator, matt finish.
c1977   5.5in (14cm) long
$120-180   HLJ

A Sinclair Enterprise Programmable calculator.
c1979
$60-90   HLJ

A Curta calculator type 1.
c1948
$600-900   ATK

A black Curta calculator type 2, with 11 slides, in black metal canister with instruction leaflet.
$280-320   LC

An early 20thC German Brunsviga adding machine.
15.75in (40cm) wide
$150-200   ET

A long scale calculator by Fowlers.
4.5in (11.5cm) diam
$220-280   BA

A Mark 8 miniature computer, by Jonathan A. Titus, an un-assembled kit-built computer comprising six Mark 8 circuit boards, an Intel 8008 chip, two Signetics 8267 chips, two Signetics 8263 chips, and eight National semiconductor 1101 memory chips.

The Mark 8 preceded the Altair 8800 personal computer by six months as the 'world's first personal home computer. Only the PC boards and plans were supplied by Titus, the rest had to be bought and assembled by the owner. The '8008' was Intel's first 8-bit processor, with a staggering 5mhz speed!

'Sinclair User' magazine, issues 1-4.
c1982   11.75in (30cm) long
$5-8 (each)   HLJ

c1974
$500-800   ATK

SCOTTIE DOG COLLECTIBLES

Collectors' Notes

- Scottie dogs memorabilia dates primarily from the 1920s-1950s, when the motif was used on many jaunty and fashionable items as well as on household objects.

- Many famous personalities owned Scottie dogs, including Shirley Temple and President Roosevelt, whose dog was called 'Fala', the most famous White House dog. Eisenhower's Scottie was called 'Telek' and he was present at the signing of the German surrender in 1945, resting under the table. Continuing the tradition, US President George W. Bush has one too, called Barney.

- Scotties were used heavily in advertising, and helped sell a huge range of products – some collectors concentrate solely on artwork showing Scotties. Look for 'Texaco' and 'Black & White Scottish Whisky' advertising pieces.

- Brightly colored plastic Scottie items from the 1930s are very desirable, as is jewelry featuring Scottie dogs. Lamps tend to hold high values – lamps with glass bases and shades are easily damaged, so complete lamps are rare. Sculptural items such as doorstops, bookends and money banks are also popular with collectors.

A 1930s cast bronze and metal lamp base, with two Scottie dogs looking at a frog, with modern shade.

14.5in (37cm) high

$220-280   **Rox**

A 1930s lamp base, with a chrome-plated metal reclining, long-eared Scottie dog, with modern shade.

14.25in (36cm) high

$180-220   **Rox**

A 1930s American frosted glass Scottie dog table lamp, by Anchor Hocking Glass, with a painted metal Scottie dog to the front.

Another variation of the shade is known, with black and white Scotties and a different border, but the same value.

10in (25.5cm) high

$150-200   **Rox**

A 1930s painted composition Scottie dog bottle opener.

3.5in (9cm) long

$30-50   **DCC**

A 1930s painted composition Scottie dog corkscrew.

5in (12cm) long

$40-60   **Rox**

A 1930s Chase chrome metalware relish dish, with three Catalin Scottie dogs.

9.75in (25cm) wide

$60-90   **Rox**

A 1930s Japanese chrome-plated salt and pepper set, with a Scottie dog and plastic finials.

5.75in (14.5cm) wide

$50-80   **Rox**

An exceptionally rare 1930s Scottie dog novelty light bulb, with the filament modeled as a Scottie dog, with cast iron Art Deco-styled base, base possibly not original.

When plugged in, the Scottie dog and stand glows orange.

7in (18cm) high

$120-180   **DCC**

A 1950s ceramic teapot, modeled as a Scottie dog, with paw raised to form the spout.

6.75in (17cm) high

$50-80   **Rox**

A 1950s set of color-printed metal drinks coasters.

3.25in (8cm) diam

$30-50   **Rox**

A 1930s linen cloth, with woven design showing Scottie dogs outside a barn.

20in (51cm) wide

$15-25   **Rox**

A 1940s yellow Catalin Scottie dog napkin ring, with applied black eyes.

3in (7.5cm) wide

$50-80   **DCC**

A 1930s carved wood seated Scottie dog egg timer, lacks tail.

5in (12cm) high

$60-90   **DCC**

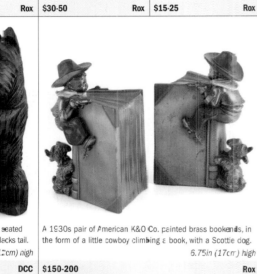

A 1930s pair of American K&O Co. painted brass bookends, in the form of a little cowboy climbing a book, with a Scottie dog.

6.75in (17cm) high

$150-200   **Rox**

A 1930s cast a low metal Scottie dog bookend, marked "COPYRIGHT 1931 No.31 ANDERSON-STARE".

7.75in (19.5cm) high

$60-90   **Rox**

A 1950s Venetian glass Scottie dog, with black glass and aventurine inclusions and original foil label.

9in (23cm) long

$120-180   **Rox**

A 1930s novelty Scottie dog table mirror, possibly a traveling mirror, with gilt metal frame, the reverse inset with a color lithograph of a Scottie.

3.25in (8cm) high

$30-50   **DCC**

A 1950s Swank wall-mounted belt-rack, of carved wood-effect and painted composition.

Swank were an American manufacturer of gentlemen's accessories and are known to have used the Scottie motif regularly.

11in (28cm) wide

$50-80   **Rox**

A German novelty tape measure, the top with a woven fabric Scottie dog design, marked "GERMANY WEST ZONE".

c1950   *2in (5cm) long*

$30-40   **DCC**

A rare 1930s Scottie dog dice, with weighted revolving wooden dice and two metal dogs on a wooden base.

Base 5in (13cm) wide

$120-180   **DCC**

A German, embossed and color-printed wall calendar for 1957, for the American market.

1957   *9in (23cm) high*

$30-50   **DCC**

A 1930s American Art Deco styled Bakelite and painted metal box.

3.5in (9cm) wide

$50-80   **Rox**

A 1930s American Hershey chrome paper knife, mounted with black painted cast Scottie dog.

8.5in (21.5cm) long

$20-30   **Rox**

A 1930s painted cast iron Scottie dog desk magnifier, with movable magnifying glass.

5in (13cm) high

$120-180   **DCC**

A 1930s cast metal and painted 'Flush the Scotty dog' desk pencil holder, with mechanical pencil.

Probably by L.G. Balfour Company, Attleboro, MA.

2in (5cm) high

$20-30   **DCC**

A 1930s wooden Scottie dog desk calendar, with a black dog and wooden holder with paper calendar.

4.5in (11.5cm) high

$40-60   **DCC**

A pressed glass Scottie dog inkwell, with silver-plated mounts. *Becomes black when filled.*

c1900   *3.5in (9cm) high*

$150-200   **DCC**

A 1930s cast and painted metal novelty desk thermometer, with seated Scottie dog.

2.75in (7cm) wide

$30-50   **DCC**

A very rare 1930s bronze McLelland Barclay box, with a Scottie dog on lid.

3.25in (8.5cm) wide

$220-280   **Rox**

A 1930s painted cast metal match holder, formed as a Scottie dog sitting on a book.

2.5in (6.5cm) wide

$70-100   **DCC**

A 1930s carved wood Scottie dog ashtray, with glass liner.

6.25in (16cm) wide

$70-100   **DCC**

A 1930s painted cast metal novelty ashtray, modeled as two Scottie dogs sitting next to a waterlily, lacks glass liner.

4.25in (11cm) wide

$40-60   **DCC**

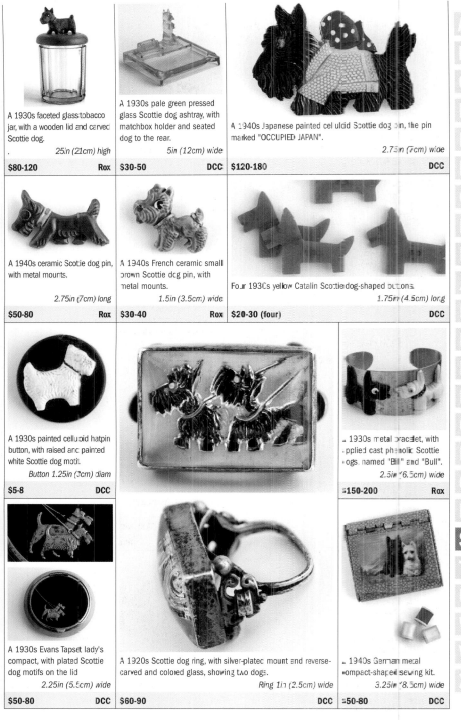

A 1930s faceted glass tobacco jar, with a wooden lid and carved Scottie dog.

25in (21cm) high

$80-120 Rox

A 1930s pale green pressed glass Scottie dog ashtray, with matchbox holder and seated dog to the rear.

5in (12cm) wide

$30-50 DCC

A 1940s Japanese painted celluloid Scottie dog pin, the pin marked "OCCUPIED JAPAN".

2.75in (7cm) wide

$120-180 DCC

A 1940s ceramic Scottie dog pin, with metal mounts.

2.75in (7cm) long

$50-80 Rox

A 1940s French ceramic small brown Scottie dog pin, with metal mounts.

1.5in (3.5cm) wide

$30-40 Rox

Four 1930s yellow Catalin Scottie-dog-shaped buttons.

1.75in (4.5cm) long

$20-30 (four) DCC

A 1930s painted celluloid hatpin button, with raised and painted white Scottie dog motif.

Button 1.25in (3cm) diam

$5-8 DCC

A 1930s metal bracelet, with applied cast phenolic Scottie dogs named "Bill" and "Bull".

2.5in (6.5cm) wide

$150-200 Rox

A 1930s Evans Tapset lady's compact, with plated Scottie dog motifs on the lid

2.25in (5.5cm) wide

$50-80 DCC

A 1920s Scottie dog ring, with silver-plated mount and reverse-carved and colored glass, showing two dogs.

Ring 1in (2.5cm) wide

$60-90 DCC

A 1940s German metal compact-shaped sewing kit.

3.25in (8.5cm) wide

$50-80 DCC

A 1950s Chinese Mr Jonas woven wicker purse, with cut-felt Scottie dogs, with label to the colored fabric interior.

12.25in (31cm) wide

$80-120   **Rox**

A 1930s carved green catalin Scottie dog purse clip.

Catalin is a brightly colored early plastic, popular during the 1930s. For more examples, see the 'Plastics & Bakelite' section.

6.75in (17cm) long

$220-280   **Rox**

A 1950s novelty Scottie dog tie clip, with a reverse-painted dog.

Clip 2.75in (7cm) wide

$50-80   **DCC**

A 1930s novelty tie-rack, with raised plastic Scottie dog motif.

7.75in (20cm) high

$30-50   **Rox**

A 1930s black umbrella, with a carved wood Scottie dog, wearing a catalin hat, handle.

22.75in (58cm) long

$180-220   **Rox**

A 1930s composition white-painted Scottie dog lighter, with lid reading "SOUVENIR OF NEW YORK CITY".

Black version has same value.

3.25in (8cm) wide

$20-30   **Rox**

A 1930s/1940s metal Scottie dog money bank.

3.5in (9cm) high

$70-100   **DCC**

Two views of a 1930s painted metal Scottie dog money bank.

$60-90   **Rox**

A small plush-covered Scottie dog toy.

c1910   *3.25in (8cm) long*

$50-80   **Rox**

A 1940s painted composition Scottie dog pull-along toy, with wooden wheels.

Probably by American manufacturer, Hubley.

4.25in (11cm) wide

$150-200   **Rox**

A 1940s Marx Bros. color lithographed tinplate wind-up 'Wee Scottie' Scottie dog toy, with rubber tail and ears.

5in (13cm) long

$150-200   **DCC**

'Angus and the Ducks', illustrated and written by Marjorie Flack and published by Doubleday & Company, New York.

Angus featured in a series of books by Flack.

c1930   *10in (25.5cm) wide*

$50-80   **Rox**

A 1930s Czechoslovakian 'Angus and the Ducks' blue enameled tin child's mug/pot.

6in (15cm) wide

$70-100   **Rox**

A 1950s painted composition child's dog yard, with model dogs and dog house.

12.25in (31cm) wide

$50-80 Rox

A 1950s Spanish Roldan's 'Klumpie' painted cloth doll, of a traveling lady holding her Scottie dog.

9.75in (25cm) high

$120-180 Rox

A 'Puppy Pansy' limited edition print, by Marion Needham Krupp.

These prints were given to members of the Wee Scots' Collectors Society by the artist, who also illustrated 'Scottie Showcase' by Donna Newton.

c2000 Image 8.25in (21cm) w

$100-150 Rox

Three 1920s Marguerite Kirmse Scottie dog etchings, framed.

Marguerite Kirmse (1885-1924) was a famed British dog artist. She bred and drew Scottish Terriers and was one of the first people to collect Scottie memorabilia. Her work is now desirable amongst Scottie collectors.

14.5in (37cm) wide

$150-200 Rox

A 1950s color lithographed print of 'The Little Ranger', design by George Strauss.

10in (25.5cm) high

$30-40 Rox

A 1930s very rare embossed and varnished copper 'Tramp Art' plaque, by Terry M. Longfellow, depicting a Scottie dog.

19.75in (50cm) wide

$150-200 Rox

A 1950s glass wall hanging plaque, with transfer to reverse showing a lady in period costume, walking a Scottie dog.

5in (12cm) high

$50-80 DCC

A 1930s Canadian Barry Cigar Factory 'Scotty Mild Little Cigars' metal cigar box.

3.25in (8cm) high

$40-60 DCC

A 1930s chromolithographed Happy New Year' novelty card, printed by Gibson, Cincinnati, OH.

4.25in (11cm) wide

$2-3 (each) Rox

FIND OUT MORE...

'Scottie Showcase' by Donna Newton, published by Country Scottie, 1988.

'A Treasury of Scottie Dog Collectables', by Candace Sten Davies & Patricia Baugh, published by Collector Books, 1999.

SCRAPS

Collectors' Notes

- Scraps, also known as 'swaps' and 'die-cuts', were used by children and adults for making greetings cards and collecting in albums. They were also used to decorate screens and small pieces of furniture. This technique is known as 'decoupage' and was popular in the 18thC and 19thC. Scraps depicted typically decorative and sentimental themes and many represented the aesthetics of the period.

- Manufactured scraps probably originated in the early 19thC, and consisted of designs printed on a sheet of paper which were cut out manually. Many of the best early scraps came from Germany, where bakers used them to decorate cakes for celebrations.

- The invention of chromolithography (color printing) in the 1840s meant that scraps became more brightly colored. They began to be sold precut and joined together in a sheet, to be cut or pulled apart. These developments allowed scraps to boom in popularity because they were now less laborious to use and more colorful. They remained popular into the 1930s but, by the 1940s, interest and quality began to decline.

- Look for well-detailed 19thC scraps, which tend to fetch higher prices, particularly if they are large and the colors are still strong. Some scraps were embossed.

- Tears, folds, fading and missing areas will affect value detrimentally. Sought-after subjects include cherubic children, fashionably attired ladies, birds and certain animals.

Animals

A large scrap of a parrot.
4in (10cm) high

$5-8   **AOY**

A large scrap of a parrot.
4in (10cm) high

$3-5   **AOY**

A scrap of a cat seated on a cushion.
3.5in (9cm) wide

$6-9   **AOY**

A scrap of a cat catching a mouse.
3.5in (9cm) wide

$7-10   **AOY**

A scrap of a cat, with raised paw.
2.75in (7cm) high

$5-8   **AOY**

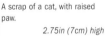

A scrap of a cat's head with blue bow, some wear.
2in (5cm) wide

$2-3   **AOY**

Four joined scraps of cockerels, with decal reading "No.964".

Complete pages of scraps can show the ingenious positioning used by manufacturers to minimize paper wastage.

4.75in (12cm) wide

$30-40   **AOY**

A partly used card of scraps of butterflies.
Card 7.5in (19cm) high

$2-3 (each)   **AOY**

A scrap of a horse and border collie dog.
4.5in (11.5cm) wide

$8-12   **AOY**

Flowers

A large scrap of a red rose.

6in (15cm) wide

$2-3   **AOY**

A large scrap of a yellow rose.

4.75in (12cm) wide

$2-3   **AOY**

A scrap of a red rose.

2.75in (7cm) wide

$6-9   **AOY**

A scrap of a palette and bunch of roses.

1.25in (3cm) high

$2-3   **AOY**

A large scrap of a passion flower.

4.25in (11cm) high

$6-9   **AOY**

A floral scrap of two doves, with motto reading "Life bear for you the sweetest flowers'.

2.75in (7cm) wide

$3-5   **AOY**

A large scrap of a hand and roses.

4.75in (12cm) high

$7-10   **AOY**

A large festive 'Happy New Year' scrap with morning glory flowers.

6.25in (16cm) wide

$10-12   **AOY**

A large scrap of a man's hand bearing snowdrops.

4.75in (12cm) high

$3-5   **AOY**

A scrap of a bunch of flowers.

2.5in (6.5cm) wide

$3-5   **AOY**

Two small scraps of posies.

1.25in (3cm) wide

$2-3 (each)   **AOY**

Three different scraps of flower-filled wheelbarrows.

2in (7.5cm) wide

$2-3 (each)   **AOY**

People

A scrap of a snow baby, with a ball.

3.25in (8.5cm) high

$6-9   AOY

A scrap of a crying toddler, with an apple.

3.5in (9cm) high

$6-9   AOY

A scrap of a chirpy little girl, with two snowballs.

3.25in (8.5cm) high

$6-9   AOY

A scrap of a boy in a blue hat.

3.5in (9cm) high

$2-3   AOY

A charming large scrap of a lady with two roses.

4.75in (12cm) high

$3-5   AOY

A scrap of a Dutch boy holding three fish.

3.25in (8cm) high

$5-8   AOY

A scrap of a Dutch girl holding a basket of flowers.

3.25in (8cm) high

$5-8   AOY

A large scrap of an elegant lady.

Scraps of ladies often conform to stereotypes of Victorian beauty, with flawless, porcelain-like skin, tiny noses, heavy lashed gentle eyes, rosebud mouths and delicate, flower-encrusted gowns.

4in (10cm) high

$10-12   AOY

A scrap of cricketers.

3.25in (8cm) wide

$7-10   AOY

A scrap of a Chinese lady with a fan.

2.25in (6cm) high

$5-8   AOY

Two scraps of Santa Claus with sacks full of toys.

2.75in (7cm) high

$6-9 (each)   AOY

FIND OUT MORE...

The Beryl Peters Collection
www.victorian-imagery.com
A diverse collection of Victorian ephemera and images with over 50,000 items and an online presence.

Collectors' Notes

- The earliest thimbles were made from leather, bronze or iron. Typically, they had domed tops and irregular, hand-punched indentations. Those from the 16thC and earlier are very rare and valuable as so few have survived.
- Machine made steel and brass examples date from the mid-18thC onwards, when shapes became less domed and flatter. The 1750s also saw the invention of the 'nose machine' that allowed regular indentations to be stamped on.
- As needlework became more popular as an art form and social grace throughout the 19thC, the industry mushroomed. Britain and Germany were prolific thimble producers, and Germany made many for export. However, plain machine made steel and brass thimbles are usually of little collectible value as they are so common.
- Early silver thimbles are often not hallmarked as their weight was under the statutory five penny weights. Hallmarking thimbles only became more prevalent after the 1870s.
- Single numbers found on thimbles usually indicate the size of the thimble.
- Due to the huge variety available, many collectors focus on one type of thimble, such as those bearing names, or thimbles by particular makers, such as the prolific British maker, Charles Iles of Birmingham.
- Look for those with scenes, people's names, trade names such as Dorcas, and patent numbers or registered design marks.

A silver Iles thimble, with octagonal sides and punched dot design, with Iles' three thimble trademark and Rd. No. 108544.

As there were no drawings accompanying this, Iles' earliest patent (registered in September 1888) collectors are unsure if the registered design was for the thimble design or Iles' trademark.

$30-50   **CBe**

A base metal Iles 'The Boudoir' thimble, with stamped dot design, and three thimble trademark.

0.75in (2cm) high

$30-50   **CBe**

A base metal Iles "THE 'QUEEN'S RECORD' THIMBLE THE BEST OF ALL'.

This was produced as a souvenir of Queen Victoria's Diamond Jubilee in 1897.

$50-80   **CBe**

An "ILES PATENT VENTILATED" base metal thimble, with ivorine liner.

Produced only by the British company Iles, based in Birmingham, the liner was meant to help ventilate the finger.

c1909

$120-180   **CBe**

An "ILES PATENT" ventilated thimble, with base metal top and ivory liner showing at the rim.

These are not usually found complete as liners were often broken or fell out.

c1900

$120-180   **CBe**

A very rare Iles base metal 'jewel' thimble, stamped "PL PATENT".

The addition of the jewel is for ornamentation only.

c1895

$120-180   **CBe**

A steel-cored 'Dorcas' thimble, by Charles Horner, with plain band and repeated star design.

This variation of the maker's mark indicates it was made after 1905.

$30-50   **CBe**

A steel-cored, silver-plated "DORCAS" thimble, by Charles Horner, with grid and flower design.

Dorcas thimbles are made by taking sheets of silver and steel and laminating them together before die-stamping. Charles Horner was first to patent the steel-core thimble.

$30-50   **CBe**

A floral, silver thimble, 'Princess May' pattern, by Charles Horner, with Chester hallmark, registered number.

Although this pattern may appear to be identical to others, the flowers have straight petals and dot centers, making it unique.

1887

$50-80   **CBe**

A silver thimble, by Charles Horner, with engraved floral pattern, with Chester hallmark.

Steel-cored thimbles were made with steel to last longer.

1857

$30-40   **CBe**

A silver thimble, by Charles Horner, with punched dot design and inset carnelian crown, with Chester hallmark.

$80-120   **CBe**

A gold presentation thimble, by Charles Horner, size seven, with repeated floral motif, inscription reads "M.J. Best-Hill Circle 1945".

1945

$180-220   **CBe**

A silver thimble, by James Fenton, with diamond shapes and punched dots, size 10, with Birmingham hallmark.

1899

$50-80   **CBe**

An unmarked Dorcas steel-cored thimble, with grid pattern, marked "PAT.9", with registered mark.

1887

$30-40   **CBe**

Two views of an extremely rare silver thimble, by James Fenton, showing a bicycle and a bird in foliage, hallmark for Birmingham 1896, with registered number "280564" for July 31st 1896.

Bicycles are a rare decorative motif.

$500-700   **CBe**

A 15ct gold presentation thimble, by James Fenton, with punched dot decoration and inscription to "Mrs T.R. Gillies for services between 1914 and 1918", with hallmark for Birmingham.

1919

$180-220   **CBe**

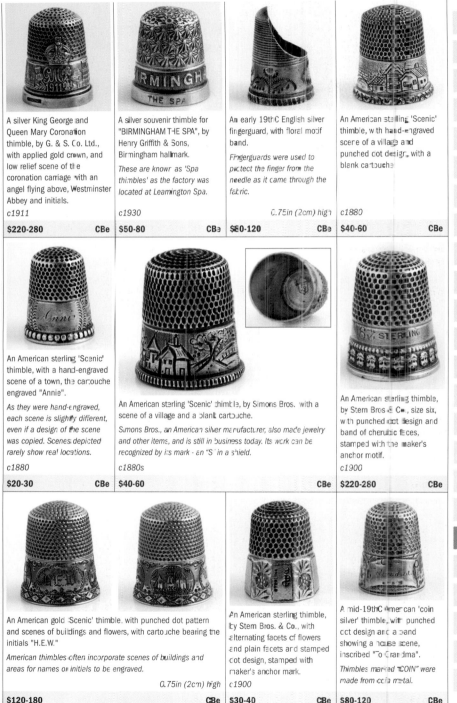

A silver King George and Queen Mary Coronation thimble, by G. & S. Co. Ltd., with applied gold crown, and low relief scene of the coronation carriage with an angel flying above, Westminster Abbey and initials.

c1911

$220-280 CBe

A silver souvenir thimble for "BIRMINGHAM THE SPA", by Henry Griffith & Sons, Birmingham hallmark.

These are known as 'Spa thimbles' as the factory was located at Leamington Spa.

c1930

$50-80 CBe

An early 19thC English silver fingerguard, with floral motif band.

Fingerguards were used to protect the finger from the needle as it came through the fabric.

0.75in (2cm) high

$80-120 CBe

An American sterling 'Scenic' thimble, with hand-engraved scene of a village and punched cot design, with a blank cartouche.

c1880

$40-60 CBe

An American sterling 'Scenic' thimble, with a hand-engraved scene of a town, the cartouche engraved "Annie".

As they were hand-engraved, each scene is slightly different, even if a design of the scene was copied. Scenes depicted rarely show real locations.

c1880

$20-30 CBe

An American sterling 'Scenic' thimble, by Simons Bros. with a scene of a village and a blank cartouche.

Simons Bros., an American silver manufacturer, also made jewelry and other items, and is still in business today. Its work can be recognized by its mark - an "S" in a shield.

c1880s

$40-60 CBe

An American sterling thimble, by Stern Bros & Co, size six, with punched cot design and band of cherubic faces, stamped with the maker's anchor motif.

c1900

$220-280 CBe

An American gold 'Scenic' thimble. with punched dot pattern and scenes of buildings and flowers, with cartouche bearing the initials "H.E.W."

American thimbles often incorporate scenes of buildings and areas for names or initials to be engraved.

0.75in (2cm) high

$120-180 CBe

An American sterling thimble, by Stern Bros. & Co., with alternating facets of flowers and plain facets and stamped cot design, stamped with maker's anchor mark.

c1900

$30-40 CBe

A mid-19thC American 'coin silver' thimble, with punched cot design and a band showing a house scene, inscribed "To Grandma".

Thimbles marked "COIN" were made from coin metal.

$80-120 CBe

An unusual American sterling embroidery thimble, by H. Muhr's Sons, with chased and decorated chevrons.

The pattern on this example is very unusual. The "9" stamping relates to the size of the thimble and the crown motif is the maker's mark for H. Muhr's Sons. Muhrs were in business for a relatively short time, between 1873 and 1894.

c1880

$60-90 CBe

A very rare sterling silver advertising thimble, for "BENEDICT BROTHERS 171 BROADWAY N.Y.", stamped "S" for Shepard Mfg. Co., Mass.

This example is very rare as advertising thimbles were inexpensive giveaways, usually made from cheap materials.

c1920

$30-50 CBe

An American 'ABC Company' brass gadget thimble, with laurel leaf band and with sliding knife for cutting thread, stamped "PAT PEND".

c1900s

$40-60 CBe

An M.T. patented 'gadget' thimble, with sliding mounting with blade to one side, and button sliding up to reveal wire threader.

c1900-1910

$15-25 CBe

A German silver and enamel thimble, with rose motif, the crown inset with blue glass.

This type of thimble was made until the 1970s, but the quality became poorer later.

c1935

$60-90 CBe

An early 20thC German silver thimble, with applied scrolling band inset with turquoise and coral cabochons, stamped "800".

$80-120 CBe

A German World War I iron thimble, with band reading "1914 + 1915 + 1916".

An apocryphal story states that these thimbles were given to people who gave up their metal goods to help the War Effort.

c1916

$80-120 CBe

A 19thC French silver thimble, with a band of scrolling design, punched dot design and shield motif, with French control marks.

Beehive-shaped thimbles are typically French in origin.

0.75in (2cm) high

$80-120 CBe

A French World War I commemorative silver thimble, stamped "FRANCE" and with French control marks, with band reading "N'OUBLIONS JAMAIS! 1914".

c1918

$180-220 CBe

An early 20thC Spanish Toledo-work steel thimble, with Toledo-work band and punched dot design.

0.75in (2cm) high

$40-60 CBe

A European silver thimble, with carnelian crown, with a band reading "ERINDRING" and dual gilt bands.

'Erindring' is a Scandinavian word for remembrance.

c1930

$60-90 CBe

A clear pressed glass shoe-shaped thimble holder, with painted laces and tassles and a silver-plated thimble.

c1870 2.25in (6cm) long

$70-100 JSC

A British blue pressed glass shoe-shaped thimble holder, with silver-plated thimble.

This color and shape are rarer than clear glass examples.

1.75in (4.5cm) high

$150-200 JSC

FIND OUT MORE...

'*A Collector's Guide to Thimbles*', by Bridget McConnel, published by Wellfleet Press, 1990.

'*American Silver Thimbles*', by Gay Ann Rogers, Haggerston, 1989.

'*The Thimble Museum*', Kohlesmünle 6, 97933 Creglingen, Germany, houses a collection of over 3,000 thimbles.

An early to mid-19thC beadwork-on-bone egg-shaped thimble-case, with bone thimble.

1.5in (4cm) high

$120-180 JSC

Collectors' Notes

■ Although sewing tools have been produced for centuries, the late 18thC and particularly the 19thC provide the largest variety available to collectors today due to the huge expansion in production and variety of sewing tools during these periods.

■ Many of the small, finely crafted pieces available today came from the large array of complete, fitted sewing boxes that were available to the late 19thC lady.

■ Mid- to late 19thC tools were made from a variety of materials, including wood, metals such as silver and pressed brass, and even glass. Mother-of-pearl was another very popular material. Mauchlineware and Tartanware items are also commonly found. Silver tools were popular during the early years of the 20thC as the price of silver dropped.

■ Sewing was popular amongst mid- to late 19thC ladies and many 'homemade' items exist. These hand-crafted items have a charm lacking in mass-produced pieces. Items incorporating beadwork, silks, embroidery and commemorative or sentimental themes are typical.

■ Many items commemorated national events such as exhibitions or Royal marriages.

■ As inexpensive sewing machines and better quality factory-made needlework became more available in the early decades of the 20thC, the demand for and production of sewing tools declined sharply.

■ Finely crafted pieces in precious materials will command the highest prices. Sets, most of which are French, should be as complete as possible as missing pieces can be hard to replace exactly.

Needle-cases

A cylindrical Mauchlineware needle-case, with a print of Cambridge Hall, Lord Street, Liverpool.

3.75in (9.5cm) long

$100-150 JSC

A photographic ware needle-case, with an oval photographic image showing "The Summit, Snowdon".

4in (10cm) long

$100-150 JSC

A late 19thC Swiss carved fruitwood fish-shaped needle-case.

4.5in (11.5cm) long

$80-120 JSC

A rare parasol-shaped Mauchlineware needle-case, with a print of Salon de Trouville, the handle pulls out to open.

4.25in (11cm) long

$220-280 JSC

A 19thC Swiss carved pine needle-case.

5in (13cm) long

$70-100 JSC

A 19thC French hand-carved fruitwood souvenir needle-case.

This is unusual as it relates to a single place, the Mer de Glace in Chamonix.

4in (10cm) long

$150-200 JSC

A well-modeled 19thC French carved bone needle-case, in the form of a mackerel.

3.75in (9.5cm) long

$220-280 JSC

An early 19thC French bone needle-case, in the form of a flute, with gold discs for the finger holes.

3.75in (9.5cm) long

$280-320 JSC

A French mid-19thC ivory needle-case, with carved 'brickwork' pattern, the ends carved with flowers.

4in (10cm) long

$120-180 JSC

A vegetable ivory needle-case, with acorn-shaped ends.

c1860 *3in (7.5cm) long*

$80-120 JSC

A vegetable ivory needle-case, of three separate pieces.

Vegetable ivory is carved from the coroso or tagua nut, which is the fruit of a tropical palm. When fresh, it is white but yellows over a period of time. Due to its small size, large pieces are made from more than one nut.

c1870 *3.25in (8.5cm) long*

$120-180 JSC

A geometric patterned beadwork needle-case, over a bone body.

3.5in (9cm) long

$180-220 JSC

A rare boot-shaped beadwork needle-case, on a bone body.

c1850 *3in (7.5cm) long*

$220-280 JSC

An English mid-19thC milk glass needle-case, with painted flowers, "Remember Me" script, gilt bands and paper-lined interior.

3.5in (9cm) long

$220-280 JSC

A mid-19thC milk glass needle-case, overlaid with a latticework of silver and pink glass threads.

3.5in (9cm) long

$180-220 JSC

A mid-19thC straw-work needle-case, with ivory finials.

3.5in (9cm) long

$100-150 JSC

An early 20thC American painted wood 'Sister Susie' thimble holder, with original box and hand-colored card poem.

c1917

$30-50 CBe

An early 20thC American painted wood 'Darby & Joan' needle-case set, with original box and poem on hard-colored card.

c1917   Each 3in (7.5cm) high

$50-80   **CBe**

A mid-19thC German silver swaddled baby figural needle case, the base marked "800"

It was believed that if a child were swaddled tightly for its first three months, it would grow up with stronger bones and help prevent infantile rickets.

2.5in (6.5cm) high

$600-900   **JSC**

A 19thC tapering pressed brass needle-case, by W. Avery & Son, Redditch

4.25in (10.5cm) long

$50-80   **CBe**

A French needle-case, painted to resemble lacquer and with ornate piqué inlay and silver Greek-key band, containing a gold stiletto and bodkin.

c1820   5in (12.5cm) long

$300-400   **JSC**

A 1830s French mother-of-pearl needle-case, with acanthus leaf ends and gilt metal bands.

3.25in (8cm) long

$220-280   **JSC**

AVERYS

■ Averys are pressed brass needle cases made to hold different sized needles. The first, the 'Quadruple Golden Casket', was produced by William Avery of Redditch, Worcestershire, in 1868, but competitors soon followed and now the term has been extended to all brass needlecases.

■ Most Averys date from the 1870s when there was a huge explosion in production. The needles are held in rows that move, or in slots that hold packets.

■ There are three types of Averys – flats, quadruples and figurals. Figurals are the most desirable and valuable, with many shapes inspired by nature.

A pressed brass needle-case, by W. Avery & Son, made for and bearing the name of the retailer "G.H.Y. & Son".

c1870   2.75in (7cm) high

$150-200   **JSC**

'The Unique' needle-case and pin case, made by the jeweler William Lewis of Birmingham.

c1869   3.75in (9.5cm) high

$300-400   **JSC**

A commemorative nickel-plated needle-case, by W. Avery & Son, with impressed design showing the Liverpool Exhibition in 1886.

c1886

$220-280   **JSC**

A gilt metal 'The Quadruple Golden Casket' needle-case, by W. Avery & Son, with leaf and butterfly designs, for needle sizes 6, 7, 8 and 9.

The sliding nodule at the bottom of the box moves the rows of needles up and down to allow selection and easy access.

c1870   2.75in (7cm) high

$220-280   **JSC**

An impressed brass 'The Louise Folding Needle Case, by Hayes, Crossley & Co Patentees', of envelope form with motifs of roses, thistles and miniature beehives.

c1871   3.5in (9cm) wide

$300-500   **JSC**

SEWING COLLECTIBLES

A pressed brass needle packet holder, by W. Avery & Son, Redditch, in shield form, with a repoussé portrait of Princess Alexandra within a laurel wreath, with Rd. Mark diamond.

3.5in (9cm) high

$300-400   **CBe**

A pressed brass needle packet case, by W. Avery & Son, Redditch, in the form of an artist's easel displaying a painting of Queen Victoria's "Diamond Jubilee 1837-1897".

c1897   *4.5in (11.5cm) high*

$400-600   **CBe**

'The Bee Case' needle-case, by W. Avery & Son, the interior of the wings holding different sizes of needle packets, with registered mark.

c1872   *3.5in (9cm) long*

$500-700   **JSC**

Packet Cases

A mid-late 19thC reverse-painted glass needle-case and packet holder, showing Osborne House, with mirror on reverse.

2.25in (6cm) wide

$180-220   **JSC**

A reverse-painted glass needle-case and needle packet holder, showing Shakespeare's birthplace, with silver and gilt highlights and mirror on reverse.

2.25in (6cm) wide

$180-220   **JSC**

A French carved ivory-covered pin case, the covers with pierced design depicting a house under a tree, with silk interior.

2in (5cm) wide

$150-200   **JSC**

A mother-of-pearl covered book-form needle-case, engraved with a foliate motif, with pink silk bow and lining.

The boards would have been bought from a shop and made up into cases by ladies.

c1850   *2.5in (6.5cm) high*

$150-200   **JSC**

A late 19thC card needle box, Baxter lithograph print of The Princess Royal, Princess F.W. of Prussia, from 'Queen Mary' set.

2.25in (6cm) high

$30-50   **CBe**

A late 19thC French card needle-case, with four leaves fanning out to hold sizes 6, 7, 8 and 9 needles.

2.25in (5.5cm) high

$70-100   **CBe**

A chromolithographed card needle packet holder, in book-form, with pull-out drawer.

2in (5cm) high

$70-100   **JSC**

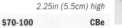

An English 19thC printed and embossed card 'The Victoria Needle Case' needle packet holder box, the lids with blue silk and lithographed pin-cushions, interiors with mirrors and concertina panels to hold different needle packets.

Box 3.25in (8.5cm) wide

$60-90 CBe

A late 19th/early 20thC gilded base metal table-top etui, formed as a Swiss chalet, the hinged cover revealing a fitted interior and standing on a square alabaster foot.

$100-150 Clv

A 19thC "Brown, Davies & Hase Needle Preserver" card needle packet holder, with four card tubes of needles in sizes 6, 7, 8 and 9.

This set is rare as it is complete and unopened.

2in (5cm) high

$70-100 JSC

A hand-assembled silk and ivory parasol-shaped needle holder.

5in (13cm) long

$70-100 JSC

Compendia

A 19thC leather-covered sewing kit, the interior with embroidered pin-cushion, thread winders, scissors, thimble, needle-case and other accessories, case with gilt tooled leather exterior.

Case 7.75in (19.5cm) wide

$300-400 CBe

A French nécessaire, with white metal bodkin, stiletto, thimble, needle-case and scissors, each with French control marks.

Case 5in (12.5cm) wide

$300-400 JSC

A 19thC leather case, containing scissors with gilt metal handles and a thimble.

$100-150 Clv

A 'Spanish Walnut' sewing compendium, including scissors, needle-case, stiletto, bodkin and educational booklet, contained in a walnut shell.

Although a tiny frivolity, each piece is usable. The walnuts were grown in Spain and sent to Paris to be fitted with accessories. Quality of fittings differ, with precious metal examples commanding higher prices.

c1850 *1.75in (4.5cm) high*

$300-400 JSC

A Mauchlineware egg-shaped sewing compendium.

2.25in (5.5cm) high

$100-150 JSC

SEWING COLLECTIBLES

A CLOSER LOOK AT A SEWING COMPENDIUM

The top has intricately carved fretwork and unscrews allowing storage.

This is an early example, with fine quality carving in a luxury material.

Threads could be stored by winding them around the grooves.

The grooves also held a thick wax disc that the thread was rubbed through to prevent breaking.

The interior of the column was used to store needles.

An early 19thC carved ivory sewing compendium.

c1810   6in (15cm) high

$700-1,000   **JSC**

A mid-19thC French kingwood and fruitwood thimble and needle-case compendium, with gilt bands, containing an ivory and gold thimble.

Examples are also known with ivory and ebony bodies. The handle pulls off to store needles and the top unscrews to store the thimble.

3.25in (8cm) high

$300-400   **JSC**

Tape Measures

A souvenir tape measure for the Crystal Palace, showing George and Mary, reverse with advertisement for Branson's Coffee.

c1910   1.5in (3.5cm) wide

$60-90   **CBe**

An 1860s commemorative tape measure for Prince Albert, with a reproduction of a photograph of Albert on one side and posthumous dedication on the other.

1.5in (3.5cm) wide

$60-90   **CBe**

A commemorative tape measure for the 1933 Chicago 'Century of Progress' exhibition, with ivorine sides.

1.5in (3.5cm) wide

$30-50   **CBe**

A celluloid commemorative souvenir tape measure for the 1901 Buffalo N.Y. 'Pan-American Exposition', made by Whitehead & Hoag Co. of Newark NJ.

c1901   1.5in (4cm) wide

$50-80   **CBe**

An early 20thC novelty tape measure, in the shape of Edward VIII.

2.25in (6cm) high

$150-200   **JSC**

An early 20thC novelty tape measure, in the form of a seated Chinaman.

1.75in (4.5cm) high

$100-150   **JSC**

A celluloid novelty tape measure, in the form of Columbus' ship, the 'Santa Maria', with painted highlights.

2.25in (5.5cm) high

$100-150   **JSC**

A vegetable ivory tape measure, in the form of a pineapple, with hand-marked silk tape, bone winder finial.

c1860   1.75in (4.5cm) high

$100-150   **JSC**

An early 20thC novelty tape measure, in the form of a chess table.

Due to the delicate and brittle plastic, two pieces are missing from the board, the value would have been higher, at around $220-280, if they had been retained.

2.25in (6cm) high

$120-180　　　　　**JSC**

A 19thC English turned bone tape measure, with blue silk tape.

1.5in (4cm) high

$120-180　　　　　**JSC**

Miscellaneous

A 19thC blue velvet pin cushion, commemorating Queen Victoria's Jubilee.

2.25in (6cm) wide

$30-50　　　　　**CBe**

A woven silk and lace pin-cushion, commemorating Queen Victoria, by J.A.V. Cash.

c1901　　5.5in (8cm) wide

$70-100　　　　　**CBe**

A 19thC Queen Victoria's coronation commemorative pin-cushion, in red velvet with gold braiding and tassels and metal crown.

2.75in (7cm) wide

$50-80　　　　　**CBe**

A triangular brown velvet pin-cushion, commemorating Queen Victoria's Jubilee.

c1887　　5in (13cm) high

$50-80　　　　　**CBe**

A beadwork pincushion, with gadrooned fringe border.

The small beads and the intricately woven diamond pattern indicate very fine quality and early beadwork.

4.5in (11.5cm) wide

$70-100　　　　　**JSC**

A pair of European porcelain pin-cushion figures, modeled as Dutch child subjects.

3.25in (8cm) high

$60-90　　　　　**LC**

A Mauchl neware 'Burns pin-cushion, the base with two drawers and two Burns-related scenes.

3.75in (9.5cm) high

$180-220　　　　　**KBon**

A vegetable ivory reel holder, with umbrella-shaped top.

c1880　　1.75in (4.5cm) high

$60-90　　　　　**JSC**

A mid-19thC mother-of-pearl thread reel holder, with flower-shaped top and ivory base.

1.25in (3cm) high

$100-150　　　　　**JSC**

A turned ivory thread barrel, with winding finial.

These pieces often came from workboxes which had been broken up.

c1830　　1.5in (4cm) high

$120-180　　　　　**JSC**

A rare set of six Mauchlineware cotton barrels on a stand, each barrel with an ivory aperture and a scene of Glasgow.

6.25in (13cm) high

$800-1,200　　　　　**KBon**

A 19thC Scottish Tartanware cotton dispenser for Clark & Co. of Paisley, lid with a lithograph of the Prince and Princess of Wales, side with holes for different cottons.

4in (10cm) wide

$320-380　　　　　　　　　　　　　　　**CBe**

A Mauchlineware cotton box for J. & P. Coats, lid with transfer of the American eagle and motto, the base stamped "Made in Scotland".

4in (10cm) wide

$60-90　　　　　　　　　　　　　　　**CBe**

A scarce floral Mauchlineware thread-ball container.

c1900　　*3.25in (8cm) high*

$220-280　　　　　　　　**JSC**

An extremely rare commemorative sewing cotton box, in the form of the royal carriage, commemorating the "The Royal Jubilee 1887 Accession of Queen Victoria 1837", with wooden wheels, for Clark & Co. Anchor Sewing Cottons.

c1887　　　　　*10in (25.5cm) long*

$500-700　　　　　　　　**CBe**

An early 20thC American silk embroidered pouch, containing silk threads.

24in (61cm) long

$30-50　　　　　　　**AAC**

An early 19thC carved mother-of-pearl thread winder.

Probably previously part of a workbox.

1.5in (4cm) wide

$60-90　　　　　　　**JSC**

An English hand-cut bone star-shaped thread winder.

1.25in (3cm) wide

$50-80　　　　　　　**JSC**

A late 18thC French mother-of-pearl knotting shuttle, with incised floral and dotted decoration.

3.5in (9cm) long

$300-500　　　　　　　**JSC**

A Tartanware tatting shuttle, with "McBeth" label.

A tatting shuttle was used for making handmade lace, known as 'tatting'.

2.75in (7cm) long

$150-200　　　　　　　**JSC**

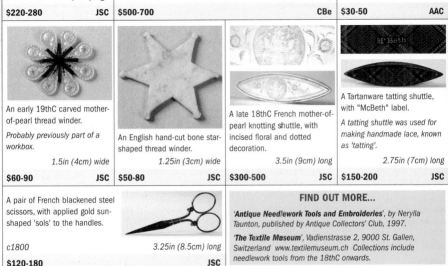

A pair of French blackened steel scissors, with applied gold sun-shaped 'sols' to the handles.

c1800　　　　*3.25in (8.5cm) long*

$120-180　　　　　　　**JSC**

FIND OUT MORE...

'Antique Needlework Tools and Embroideries', by Nerylla Taunton, published by Antique Collectors' Club, 1997.

'The Textile Museum', Vadienstrasse 2, 9000 St. Gallen, Switzerland www.textilemuseum.ch Collections include needlework tools from the 18thC onwards.

SILVER & PLATED WARES

Collectors' Notes

- Vinaigrettes were used from the late 18th century until the late 19th century. They held sponges soaked in aromatic vinegar which were used to ward off offensive smells.

- Under the hinged lid, a carved grille held the sponge in place. Interiors are gilt lined as the gold prevented the vinegar from eating into the metal.

- Early examples are small and plain, later ones are larger and have more intricate grilles and lids. Look out for castle scenes or commemorative inscriptions on lids, fine quality workmanship and hallmarks of leading makers, all of which add to the value.

A silver vinaigrette, by Joseph Taylor, with a swirling foliate pattern, Birmingham hallmarks.

1790

$300-500   **GS**

A silver vinaigrette, by Cocks & Betteridge, with engraved decoration, Birmingham hallmarks.

1807   1.5in (4cm) wide

$400-600   **GS**

A silver vinaigrette, by John Betteridge, with a high relief foliate and scrolling border around a barley panel, Birmingham hallmarks.

1827

$300-500   **GS**

A silver gilt vinaigrette, by Nathaniel Mills, with fine barley patterned sides surrounded by heavy scrolling design borders, the interior panel with scrolling fretwork and clover leaf motif, Birmingham hallmarks.

Nathaniel Mills is a noted silversmith, famed for his vinaigrettes. They are usually of very fine quality with excellent and intricate levels of detailing and are highly desirable to collectors

1824

$500-700   **GS**

A silver vinaigrette, with engraved checkered, tartan pattern, with two initials and silver gilt interior, with maker's mark "JJ" and Birmingham hallmarks.

1838

$300-500   **GS**

A silver vinaigrette, by John Betteridge, with alternating wavy lines and barley patterns, reeded sides and an un-engraved cartouche, Birmingham hallmarks.

1834   1.75in (4.5cm) wide

$320-380   **GS**

A CLOSER LOOK AT A VINAIGRETTE

This was made by Sampson Mordan & Co, renowned and innovative silversmiths, who were well known for their novelty shaped Victorian pencils and other accessories. It also bears an unusual stamp for 'Storr & Mordan', relating to Paul Storr.

The hinged lid fits snugly over the grille, ensuring the scented vinegar does not evaporate.

The horn of plenty or cornucopia shape is unusual and so is desirable to collectors.

The plain finish is unblemished by dents despite the fact that it would have been carried around and the curving metal cone is prone to damage.

A rare and unusual Storr & Mordan silver cornucopia vinaigrette, with London hallmarks.

1871   4in (10cm) long

$400-600   **GS**

A silver vinaigrette, with shaped sides and two ornate initials on the cartouche with maker's mark "D. & F" and Birmingham hallmarks.

1897   2in (5cm) wide

$300-500   **GS**

A silver vinaigrette, by E. Smith, with engraved foliate design and gilt interior, Birmingham hallmark.

1868   1.5in (4cm) wide

$400-600   **GS**

A small Dutch silver vesta case, modeled as a basket with a palmate motif band, with striker to top of lid.

1.5in (4cm) high

$180-220   **GS**

A plain silver vesta case, with striker to base, with maker's mark "MJ" and Birmingham hallmarks.

1893   *2in (5cm) high*

$70-100   **GS**

Collectors' Notes

- Early vesta cases or 'matchsafes' were used around the home but it was not until the 1830s when the 'safety' match was developed that it was possible for matches to be carried around.
- Vesta cases can be recognized by their small size and milled, rough or ridged band, used for striking the match. The majority are in silver and gold. Most date from the mid-19th century onward until the early 20th century, when the matchbook was introduced and the pocket cigarette lighter was developed.
- Look for examples with enameled or intricate engraved decoration, or with witty puns, as well as those by leading makers such as Sampson Mordan. Novelty shapes are also highly collectible, as most were rectangular.

A silver vesta case, with striker to base and engraved foliate pattern and three ornate initials, Birmingham hallmarks.

1903

$60-90   **GS**

A silver vesta case, with a curved back, a swirling foliate pattern and striker to base, Birmingham hallmark.

1903   *1.5in (4cm) wide*

$60-90   **GS**

A silver vesta/match case, in the form of Mr Punch's dog Toby, wearing a feather in his hat and a ruff, with maker's mark "S.M.L.", Birmingham hallmarks.

c1890   *2.25in (6cm) high*

$1,000-1,500   **DN**

A European silver and polychrome enameled vesta/match case, possibly French, in the form of a yellow and white variegated pansy, of shaped outline with two indistinct marks, chip.

2in (5cm) high

$1,200-1,800   **DN**

An Art Nouveau-style silver card case, with repoussé decoration and moiré silk interior, with integral pencil and pockets, Birmingham hallmarks.

1902

$320-380   **GS**

A silver card case, with engraved scrolling pattern and scalloped edges, with two initials in the circular cartouche, Birmingham hallmarks.

1901

$300-400   **GS**

A silver card case, with engraved design, with maker's mark "HM" and Birmingham hallmarks.

1902

$120-180   **GS**

A silver and enameled pillbox, by Norman Grant, of circular form inset with abstract flower head enamel decoration, Edinburgh hallmarks.

1973-74   *2in (5cm) diam*

$100-150   **L&T**

A novelty envelope-shaped stamp box, with maker's mark for "A. & L. Ltd" and Birmingham hallmarks.

1906

$70-100   **GS**

A plated metal toast rack, in the manner of Christopher Dresser, formed by rods of graduating length, linked by small spheres, supported on four pad feet, marked "B&A" and numbered "G8020".

$180-220   **DN**

A silver toast rack, of square form with ball feet, with maker's mark for "M.H. & Co. Ltd" and Sheffield hallmarks.

1919   2.75in (7cm) long

$60-90   **GS**

A silver triangular toast rack, with makers mark for "M.H. & Co. Ltd" and Sheffield hallmarks.

1925   2.75in (7cm) long

$100-150   **GS**

A silver geometrically shaped toast rack, Birmingham hallmarks.

1926   2.25in (5.5cm) long

$60-90   **GS**

A small silver cream jug, with stem and an embossed line of dots to the rims of the foot and the jug, London hallmark.

1773   4in (10cm) high

$600-900   **GS**

A silver cream jug, with line of dots to rim and swags and garland patterns, London hallmarks.

1795   6in (15cm) high

$400-600   **GS**

A cream jug, with plain and reeded finish, London hallmark.

1805   4in (10cm) high

$300-500   **GS**

A silver cream jug, with plain finish and two heavy embossed bands, with maker's mark for "WH" and London hallmarks.

1808   3.5in (9cm) high

$400-600   **GS**

An 'curling' sporting themed silver cruet set, the base in the form of curling sticks, the post as curling stones, for "FBs LTD of Sorley", Sheffield hallmarks.

The sport of curling is popular in Scotland. However it is unusual to find items associated with it, such as this very high quality cruet set.

1902   2in (5cm) long

$500-800   **GS**

A silver tankard-shaped mustard pot, for Reid & Son Ltc of Newcastle upon Tyne, Sheffield hallmark.

1936   2.5in (6.5cm) high

$400-600   **GS**

A silver salt, with lion head bosses and claw feet, with spoon and blue glass liner, maker's mark for "T.D. Ltd", Birmingham hallmarks.

1847   3.75in (9.5cm) wide

$120-180   **GS**

A silver cruet set, with plain finish and curved claw feet, maker's mark for "H C D", Birmingham hallmarks.

1956

$300-400   **GS**

A B C D E F G H I J K L M N O P Q R S T U V W XYZ

A pair of novelty dog-shaped silver salt and pepper shakers, by Mr Hill of William Whitehill Ltd, wearing gilt caps, London hallmarks.

1990   *3.5in (9cm) high*

$700-1,000   **GS**

A pair of silver begging mice salt and pepper shakers by Mr Hill of William Whitehill Ltd, millennium London hallmarks.

2000   *2.5in (6cm) high*

$700-1,000   **GS**

An Edwardian novelty pepper-pot, in the form of a goose, maker's mark rubbed, Birmingham hallmarks.

c1904   *3in (7.5cm) high*

$300-500   **BonS**

A pair of silver cutlery racks, with dolphin head feet, London hallmark.

1840   *2.75in (7cm) long*

$300-400   **GS**

A pair of silver cutlery racks, with plinth bases, Birmingham hallmark.

1898   *3.5in (9cm) long*

$120-180   **GS**

A pair of George III silver scissor snuffers, by Wilkes and John Booth, with gadrooning and monogrammed "CH", London hallmarks.

1811   *7in (18cm) long*

$300-500   **SI**

A pair of silver grape scissors, with low relief floral pattern, maker's mark for "J.W. & R.C.W.", London hallmarks.

1890   *6.5in (16.5cm) long*

$500-700   **GS**

A pair of silver grape scissors, with scallop shell design, maker's mark for "W.G.J.L." Sheffield hallmarks.

1898

$500-700   **GS**

A pair of novelty 'hunting' theme place card holders, in the form of a fox's head within a horseshoe, London hallmark.

1906   *1in (2.5cm) high*

$120-180   **GS**

A pair of Edwardian silver candlesticks, in the form of Composite columns, maker's mark for "W.B. Ltd", Birmingham hallmarks.

1905   *6.5in (16.5cm) high*

$1,000-1,500   **GS**

A silver and ivory mounted biscuit barrel and cover, the ivory lid with serrated and turned handle on cylindrical body with ivory base, Birmingham hallmarks.

c1911   *6in (15cm) high*

$500-800   **L&T**

A Birmingham Guild of Handicrafts Ltd. silver clasp, with a central stylized floral plaque flanked by two fleur-de-lis motifs, maker's mark for Birmingham.

c1900   6.5in (16.5cm) wide

$320-380   **DN**

An Arts and Crafts silver two-piece buckle, each of shaped outline enclosing simplified foliage and stems, maker's mark for Charles Edwards, London.

c1900   5.5in (14.5cm) wide

$150-200   **DN**

A silver two-piece buckle, solidly cast with a foliate outline, bulrushes against rococo shell-motif and where the two pieces link, with a stream of water issuing from a mask into a shell, maker's mark "C.D" possibly for Charles Dumesnil, London.

1902   3.25in (8.5cm) wide

$220-280   **DN**

A Williams Comyns silver two-piece buckle, with two panels of interwoven fine stems and flowers, maker's mark for London.

1901   3.75in (9.75cm) wide

$220-280   **DN**

A W.H. Haeler silver two-piece buckle, with two almost heart-shape panels enclosing highly-stylized florets, marked "W.H.H" for Birmingham.

1902   3.75in (9.5cm) wide

$150-200   **DN**

A silver two-piece buckle, cast with an openwork design of two swallows in flight amid scrolling flowers and foliage, maker's mark possibly for H. Matthews, Birmingham.

c1900   3in (7.5cm) wide

$150-200   **DN**

An Art Nouveau silver two-piece silver buckle, of almost kidney shape, each piece enclosing a dove resting on swirling stems of water-lilies and foliage, maker's mark for Samuel Jacob.

1901   4.5in (11cm) wide

$220-280   **DN**

An Art Nouveau silver two-piece buckle, embellished with scrolling bands interspersed with flowers, maker's mark "S. E&S Ld" for S. Blanckensee & Son, Birmingham.

1906

$120-180   **DN**

A Liberty & Co. 'Celtic' silver two-piece buckle, each of almost heart shape enclosing stylized beasts, their tails forming interwoven celtic-knots, marked "L&Co." for Birmingham.

1906   4.5in (11cm) wide

$180-220   **DN**

A silver two-piece buckle, each piece of scrolling outline and enclosing daisy-like flowers, maker's mark for Synyer & Beddoes, Birmingham.

1899   4in (10cm) wide

$120-180   **DN**

A William Hutton & Sons silver two-piece buckle, of shaped outline embossed with plain slightly lobed panels flanked by stylized lilies, maker's mark for London.

1902   3.5in (8.5cm) wide

$280-320   **DN**

A B C D E F G H I J K L M N O P Q R S T U V W XYZ

Collectors' Notes

- Tobacco has been smoked since the mid-16thC, first in pipes, with cigars following in the early 1800s. Cigarettes began their rise in popularity in the late 19thC, but really overtook other methods of smoking after World War I, when cigarettes were given out to millions of troops.

- Smoking remained very popular and fashionable from the 1920s to the 1950s when the first public health reports began to filter through to the public consciousness. Now it is becoming less popular due to growing health concerns and cities around the world are banning smoking in certain public places. As a result, demand for and production of accessories has fallen.

- The ashtray is a vital prerequisite for the smoker, with the majority of collectible ashtrays found today dating from the late 19thC onwards. The 1920s to the 1950s is a particularly popular period with prolific production. Due to the huge variety available, collectors often choose to collect by category, such as automobile-related or advertising ashtrays.

- The designs and themes often provide a window into the social and economic atmosphere of the time, particularly with war-related or advertising examples. Look for examples that exemplify the styles and fashions of the period or commemorate an important event.

- Collectors should also look for colorful, ceramic novelty ashtrays from the 1930s, as well as those that cross collecting fields, such as airline ashtrays or propaganda ashtrays from the major wars of the 20thC. Ashtrays connected to famous personalities, particularly if they were known as smokers, will usually be very desirable.

- As the majority were mass-produced and were used, condition is important - always buy the best you can.

Films & Personalities

A 1970s Royal Doulton British Airways ashtray, with border made up of flying Concordes, owned and used by Bette Davis, with certificate of authenticity.

3in (7.5cm) diam

$100-150   **CW**

A 1950s ceramic lady head vase-style ashtray, from Lana Turner's dressing room at Universal Studios, with a certificate of authenticity.

5.75in (14.5cm) wide

$300-400   **CW**

A Wallace China ashtray, showing the 10th Pacific Coast Regional Restaurant Convention, owned and used by Roy Rogers, with a certificate of authenticity.

Rogers owned a chain of restaurants in the US, so would probably have attended or sent an employee to the convention.

c1949   5.25in (13.5cm) wide

$400-600   **CW**

A glass and sterling silver ashtray with a wild boar's horn handle, owned and used by Orson Welles, with cigarette or cigar rest and matchbox holder.

Judging from the large size of this ashtray, Welles must have enjoyed smoking!

$400-600   **CW**

A 1960s glass ashtray showing the Lyndon B. Johnson Ranch.

This ashtray is one of two given by Lyndon B. Johnson to his Secret Service guard as a sign of his gratefulness for protecting him after Kennedy had been assassinated. Johnson was the Vice President of the US at the time. The guard subsequently died of a smoking-related cancer.

5.25in (13.5cm) wide

$400-600   **CW**

A faux marble ashtray and pipe, used by Russell Crowe in 'A Beautiful Mind', with certificate of authenticity.

The ashtray is in the shape of a pentagon. This is significant as Crowe's character believed he worked for the American government.

2002   6.75in (17.5cm) wide

$400-600   **CW**

A 1970s Wedgwood ashtray, commemorating the film '2001: A Space Odyssey' by Stanley Kubrick.

6.75in (17.5cm) wide

$60-90   **CW**

A 1950s Made in Japan luster ceramic ashtray, of Little Orphan Annie and a dog.

3.25in (8cm) wide

$100-150   **CW**

A 1960s ceramic ashtray commemorating John F. Kennedy's visit to Berlin.

5.5in (14cm) wide

$120-180   **CW**

Erotic

A 1950s French red tin advertising ashtray, with sultry seminude lady.

The desirability and value of these advertising ashtrays rests on the appearance of the naked lady. Naked and shapely blondes in revealing, teasing poses are particularly sought after! This ashtray is a good example.

4.75in (12cm) wide

$60-90   **CW**

A 1950s American advertising ashtray, with naked lady wearing a chef's hat.

4.75in (12cm) wide

$20-30   **CW**

A 1950s tin advertising ashtray, showing a naked lady by a roaring fire.

4.25in (10.5cm) wide

$20-30   **CW**

A 1950s Made in Japan erotic dancer ceramic ashtray.

3.75in (9.5cm) wide

$20-30   **CW**

A 1950s German ceramic Du-Co Kunst erotic lady ashtray.

5.5in (14cm) wide

$50-80   **CW**

A 1960s ceramic lady ashtray, with moving legs.

The cigarette would be placed under the legs in the well and the heat would cause the legs to move. The red fan she holds is a match striker.

5.5in (14cm) wide

$150-200   **CW**

A 1950s Made in Japan ceramic naked lady double-sided ashtray, a souvenir from Florida.

6.25in (16cm) high

$40-60   **CW**

A 1960s ceramic lady ashtray, with moving legs.

5.25in (13.5cm) wide

$100-150   **CW**

A 1960s ceramic lady in a bathtub ashtray, "Cool Your Butt In My Old Tub".

5.25in (13.5cm) high

$60-90   **CW**

A 1960s ceramic ashtray, with a seated lady on the side.

6in (15.5cm) wide

$50-80   **CW**

Airline

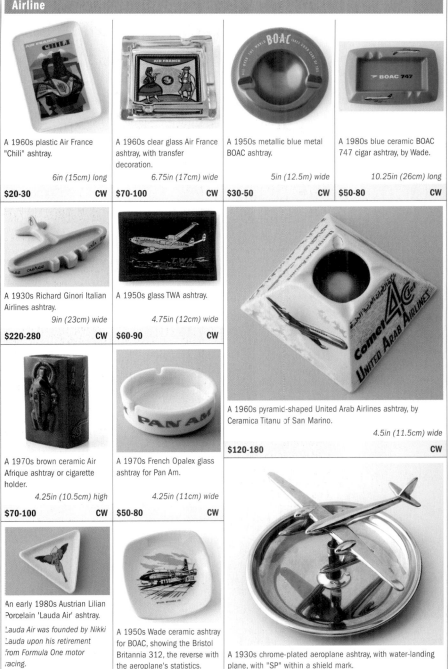

A 1960s plastic Air France "Chili" ashtray.

6in (15cm) long

$20-30 CW

A 1960s clear glass Air France ashtray, with transfer decoration.

6.75in (17cm) wide

$70-100 CW

A 1950s metallic blue metal BOAC ashtray.

5in (12.5m) wide

$30-50 CW

A 1980s blue ceramic BOAC 747 cigar ashtray, by Wade.

10.25in (26cm) long

$50-80 CW

A 1930s Richard Ginori Italian Airlines ashtray.

9in (23cm) wide

$220-280 CW

A 1950s glass TWA ashtray.

4.75in (12cm) wide

$60-90 CW

A 1960s pyramid-shaped United Arab Airlines ashtray, by Ceramica Titanu of San Marino.

4.5in (11.5cm) wide

$120-180 CW

A 1970s brown ceramic Air Afrique ashtray or cigarette holder.

4.25in (10.5cm) high

$70-100 CW

A 1970s French Opalex glass ashtray for Pan Am.

4.25in (11cm) wide

$50-80 CW

An early 1980s Austrian Lilian Porcelain 'Lauda Air' ashtray.

Lauda Air was founded by Nikki Lauda upon his retirement from Formula One motor racing.

3.75in (9.5cm) wide

$50-80 CW

A 1950s Wade ceramic ashtray for BOAC, showing the Bristol Britannia 312, the reverse with the aeroplane's statistics.

4.25in (11cm) wide

$70-100 CW

A 1930s chrome-plated aeroplane ashtray, with water-landing plane, with "SP" within a shield mark.

6in (15cm) high

$180-220 CW

War & Military

A German KPM ceramic WWI Iron Cross ashtray.

c1914   4.75in (12cm) wide

$100-150   CW

A German ceramic ashtray commemorating WWI, with motto reading "God is with Us" and with the Iron Cross.

c1914   3in (7.5cm) high

$70-100   CW

A 1930s German Jimenau porcelain ashtray from Camp Siegfried.

Camp Siegfried was a holiday camp set up by American Jews in Long Island, USA, promoting the Nazi belief system and collecting money for Hitler's Winter Help Fund. However, when war broke out and anti-semitism was revealed, the camp was disbanded, broken up and hastily erased from the national consciousness.

6in (15cm) wide

$220-280   CW

A Copenhagen 'Carlsberg' lager ceramic ashtray, with a Swastika symbol.

The Swastika here may have two meanings. Firstly, it has long been a Nordic symbol of good luck and secondly, it may have been made for Carlsberg retailers in Nazi Germany during the 1930s.

7in (18cm) long

$180-220   CW

A CLOSER LOOK AT AN ASHTRAY

The cast bronze is extremely well modeled and finely detailed.

In August 1939, Hitler went to Obersalzberg and made a speech about invading Poland. This ashtray may have been a commemorative piece or gift to a high-ranking SSD member.

The inscription underneath relates to the 'building site of Hitler's supporters at Obersalzberg', where Hitler's house at Berchtesgaden was located.

The RSD (Reichssicherheitsdienst) was the regiment that protected Hitler and important Third Reich leaders.

A cast bronze and marble ashtray, showing a German soldier's helmet, pack and rifle, with plaque reading "RSD 1939", the base stamped "Baustelle Führergeleit Obersalzberg".

1939   9in (23cm) long

$700-1,000   CW

A 1940s glass World War II propaganda ashtray showing Emperor Hirohito of Japan as a rodent.

This is from a set of three ashtrays, the other two showing Hitler and Mussolini also as rodents.

4.5in (11.5cm) wide

$220-280   CW

A tricorn Longwy Ceramics WWII Allied commemorative ashtray, with American, British and French flags, dated 1944.

4.75in (12cm) wide

$70-100   CW

A WWII onyx and metal ashtray, with a plane on top of a chrome-plated sphere.

8.25in (21cm) long

$180-220   CW

A 1960s House Art glass 'Get Well Soon Your Doctor Just Got Drafted' ashtray from the Vietnam War.

4.75in (12cm) long

$50-80   CW

Novelty

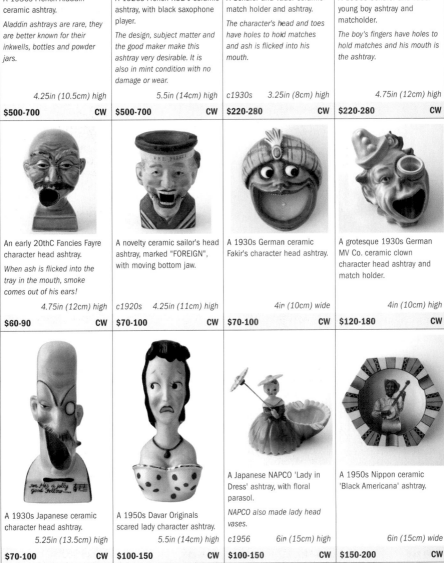

A 1930s French Aladdin ceramic ashtray.

Aladdin ashtrays are rare, they are better known for their inkwells, bottles and powder jars.

4.25in (10.5cm) high

$500-700   **CW**

A 1920s French ROB J ceramic ashtray, with black saxophone player.

The design, subject matter and the good maker make this ashtray very desirable. It is also in mint condition with no damage or wear.

5.5in (14cm) high

$500-700   **CW**

A Schafer and Vader ceramic match holder and ashtray.

The character's head and toes have holes to hold matches and ash is flicked into his mouth.

c1930s   3.25in (8cm) high

$220-280   **CW**

A 1930s Schafer and Vader young boy ashtray and matcholder.

The boy's fingers have holes to hold matches and his mouth is the ashtray.

4.75in (12cm) high

$220-280   **CW**

An early 20thC Fancies Fayre character head ashtray.

When ash is flicked into the tray in the mouth, smoke comes out of his ears!

4.75in (12cm) high

$60-90   **CW**

A novelty ceramic sailor's head ashtray, marked "FOREIGN", with moving bottom jaw.

c1920s   4.25in (11cm) high

$70-100   **CW**

A 1930s German ceramic Fakir's character head ashtray.

4in (10cm) wide

$70-100   **CW**

A grotesque 1930s German MV Co. ceramic clown character head ashtray and match holder.

4in (10cm) high

$120-180   **CW**

A 1930s Japanese ceramic character head ashtray.

5.25in (13.5cm) high

$70-100   **CW**

A 1950s Davar Originals scared lady character ashtray.

5.5in (14cm) high

$100-150   **CW**

A Japanese NAPCO 'Lady in Dress' ashtray, with floral parasol.

NAPCO also made lady head vases.

c1956   6in (15cm) high

$100-150   **CW**

A 1950s Nippon ceramic 'Black Americana' ashtray.

6in (15cm) wide

$150-200   **CW**

Collectors' Notes

- Lighters can be subdivided into pocket lighters, table lighters and compact lighters with cases.
- Dunhill is the most popular and desirable name for collectors. Their first lighter was released in the early 1920s and they are still producing today. Look especially for inset watches or concealed features such as compacts.
- Look for petrol rather than gas lighters, as these will be earlier in date. Gas replaced fluid in the 1950s. Lighters made from precious materials, often by jewelers, or those in novelty shapes such as aeroplanes and animals are popular.
- Wear to plating or loss of parts of covering will affect value detrimentally, as will dents or splits. Replaced parts will also affect value.

A 1940s Swiss silver-plated Dunhill 'Standard' pocket lighter.

2.5in (6cm) high

$120-180 LC

A 1950s silver-plated Dunhill 'Giant' table lighter, with engine-turned decoration.

4.5in (11cm) high

$180-220 LC

A CLOSER LOOK AT A DUNHILL LIGHTER

The panels are made from Perspex carved and painted on the inside.

Fish designs are more commonly found and less valuable than bird designs which are extremely rare and desirable.

Lighters with fish are known as 'Aquarium' lighters, and those with birds are 'Aviary' lighters.

'Aquarium' lighters were made throughout the 1950s, and 'Aviary' lighters only c1951, making them rarer.

A Dunhill 'Budgies' petrol table lighter, of 'fish tank' form, decorated in reverse with budgies perched on branches and trees and enclosing the brass mechanism, the hinged wick cover signed.

c1951   4in (10cm) long

$3,000-4,000 DN

A scarce 1950s American Dunhill 'tinder pistol' lighter.

6in (15cm) long

$700-1,000 GS

An American Magic 'spinner' semi-automatic petrol pocket lighter.

c1897   2.25in (5.5cm)

$300-350 RBL

An English Striker manual petrol pocket lighter, with 9ct gold outer case marked "H&A", Birmingham hallmarks.

1918   2.5in (6cm) high

$180-220 RBL

A 1930s French Flamidor manual petrol pocket lighter, with silver body.

2.25in (5.5cm) high

$180-220 RBL

A 1930s German Triumph manual petrol pocket lighter, silver-cased with auto tank, and windshield.

2in (5cm) high

$150-200 RBL

A 1940s American Evans trigger manual petrol pocket lighter, with lacquer decoration.

2in (5cm) high

$60-90 RBL

A 1940s French Atomy manual petrol pocket lighter, aluminum with unusual fuel and flint access system.

2in (5cm) high

$100-150 RBL

A 1940s Austrian Imco automatic petrol pocket lighter, brass with snuffer release.

2.25in (5.5cm) high

$150-200 RBL

A late 1940s English Rose manual petrol pocket lighter and cigarette case set, silver with gold overlaid decoration.

Case 5in (12.5cm) wide

$400-600 RBL

A Pierre Cardin gas cigarette lighter, probably Italian, with gold sleeve decorated with horizontal waved lines, marked "750", signed on the base.

2.25in (6cm) long

$400-600 DN

A Trench art manual petrol table lighter, brass and copper in the form of a cannon, on a wooden base.

c1914   *4in (10cm) long*

$70-100 RBL

An Asprey table cigar lighter, with flame finial and handle terminating with a bird's head, hallmark for A&Co Ltd, Birmingham.

1933   *5in (13cm) wide*

$300-400 GS

A Hukin & Heath Christopher Dresser-style silver-plated combined cigar lighter and cutter, made to resemble a chamber candlestick with square tray, the central column holding a reservoir with a wick and the handle incorporating the cutter, marked "H&H" and numbered "11467".

5.5in (14cm) high

$350-400 DN

A 1930s painted cast iron Boston terrier electric table lighter.

Press the area between his legs, place a cigarette into his bottom and he lights the cigarette.

5.5in (14cm) wide

$300-350 DEtc

A 1950s Ronson/Minton Floral automatic petrol table lighter.

3.25in (8cm) high

$120-180 RBL

FIND OUT MORE...

*Stephano Bisconcini, '**Lighters**', published by Edizioni san Gottardo, 1984.*

A sterling fob cigar cutter, with Art Nouveau styled lady motif
1.75in (4.5cm) long
$150-200   CAC

A sterling fob cigar cutter, with impressed American eagle motif
1.5in (4cm) long
$180-220   CAC

A sterling fob cigar cutter, with griffin fighting a snake motif.
1.5in (4cm) long
$150-200   CAC

A gold-plated fob cigar cutter, engraved with initials.
1.5in (3.5cm) wide
$60-90   AnaA

A folding gold-plated fob scissor-action cigar cutter, with scrolling foliate design.
This cutter folds flat to be carried.
1.5in (4cm) long
$100-150   CAC

A pocket retractable-scissor-action cigar cutter, with gold leaf and garnet decoration.
1.5in (3.5cm) long closed
$120-180   CAC

A sterling woman with bustle novelty fob cigar cutter.
Figural cutters are very desirable and usually fetch higher prices. This example shows excellent detailing and modeling making it of higher value.
2in (5cm) high
$300-350   CAC

A brass 'boy on potty' pocket cigar cutter.
1.5in (3.5cm) high
$150-200   CAC

A 19thC brass cigar cutter, in the form of a shoe, with match striker on the sole.
2.25in (6cm) long
$70-100   ET

An ebony and metal Champagne Duval fob cigar cutter.
Fob cigar cutters are typically very small and were attached to a fob chain, along with other items such as pencils.
2.25in (5.5cm) high
$100-150   CAC

A B C D E F G H I J K L M N O P Q R S T U V W XYZ

Five French character clay pipe bowls, three representing grotesques.

$500-700   **BAR**

Five 19thC French character clay pipe bowls, from the Gambier factory.

$300-400   **BAR**

Five French polychrome clay pipes, representing the Arab world and the moon.

Largest 5.5in (14cm) long

$300-400   **BAR**

Five African pottery pipe bowls, various regions including Ashanti.

Smallest 2in (5cm) long

$40-60   **BAR**

An African figural clay pipe bowl, together with an African wooden pipe bowl, inlaid with brass and semi-precious stones.

Largest 6.75in (17cm) long

$180-220   **BAR**

Five French polychrome clay pipes, two with character bowls, three with flower motifs.

Largest 8in (20cm) long

$300-400   **BAR**

Four 19thC European meershaum pipes, comprising a 'pressed' pipe with "1788" on the lid, one with primitive bas relief carving of a ram's head, one carved in full relief with a bearded head and one with a plain bowl with silver-colored mounts.

Largest 5.5in (14cm) long

$60-90   **BAR**

A 19thC carved meerschaum cheroot holder, the bowl formed as the head of a cavalier with amber mouthpiece, cased.

Meerschaum pipes are made from magnesium silicate found in rock veins. They are usually intricately carved, most often with the faces of old men. They were popular during the 19thC but had been made from the late 18thC. Look for unusual subjects such as bicycles or erotic subject matter, or those pipes overlaid with precious metal.

$150-200   **Clv**

An early 20thC water pipe with decorative ruby flash glass bow.

Water pipes, also known as 'nargileh' and used in the Middle East and Asia, have a chamber of water through which the smoke passes to cleanse and filter it before inhalation. They are so shaped as the Middle Eastern smoker typically sits on a cushion on the floor, or on a low divan.

$120-180   **BAR**

A 19thC German porcelain pipe, hand-painted with a family musical scene, with wood, horn and woven stem and decorative brass lid and mounts, together with a porcelain pipe bowl, hand-painted with a scene of a horse.

Largest 21.5in (55cm) long

$30-50   **BAR**

A gilt snuffbox, with inlaid Scottish agate plaques, the edges with running hound motif.

c1770   2in (5.5cm) wide

$280-320   **GS**

Left: An 18thC Dutch tobacco box, made of copper and decorated with "before and after marriage" which can be viewed from top or bottom and a coat-of-arms to center.

4.5in (11.5cm) wide

$220-280   **PSA**

Right: A copper snuff box, with hinged lid and "AH" monogram dated.

1793   3in (7.5cm) long

$180-220   **PSA**

A French birch, pressed tortoiseshell-lined snuff box, with carving of "Garibaldi".

c1840   (8.5cm) diam

$220-280   **MB**

A 19thC Russian rectangular silver snuff box, with niello scrolling foliate decoration, probably Moscow, maker's mark "BC".

c1857   2.5in (6.5cm) high

$150-200   **Gorl**

A Scottish 19thC burr walnut box, stamped Geo. Sinclair, Bonnington, of shaped and pointed kidney form with hinged split lid.

9in (23cm) long

$400-600   **L&T**

A Scottish 19thC burr elm snuff mull, of shaped oval form, with split hinged sycamore lid.

5.5in (8cm) long

$300-500   **L&T**

Collectors' Notes

- Snuff-taking became popular at the French court in the late 1500s but did not spread to Britain until the early 1700s. In Scotland, the fashion continued into the late 19th century, long after it had died out elsewhere in Europe and America.

- The late 18th and early 19th centuries saw many intricately decorated silver examples being made, the best by silversmiths such as Nathaniel Mills. Many others were made from a variety of woods, often highly carved. Look for examples with fine decoration in silver or carved or painted wood. Collectors should beware of damaged hinges, ill-fitting lids and poor inscriptions.

A small snuff box, in the shape of a frog with hinged lid.

c1800   2.75in (7cm) long

$500-700   **HD**

An early 19thC silver-mounted rams horn snuffmull engraved to the collar.

$280-320   **L&T**

A Regency wooden snuffbox, with printed and colored cover with three drinking officers, hinge broken.

3.25in (8cm) long

$220-280   **BAR**

A mahogany shoe snuff box, with brass piqué point flower decoration on the toe, pewter toe-cap and heel.

c1830   6.25in (16cm) long

$1,200-1,800   **HD**

An 18thC French ivory snuff rasp, well-carved with a man clutching a sack entitled "L' Avarice" within portico, with fruit and flowers above topped by a shell with shell below, hinge still attached but no iron rasp, cracks.

The use of rasps to grate the compacted tobacco leaves into powder ended in the late 18th century due to the proliferation of ready-ground snuff.

7in (18.5cm) high

$1,200-1,800   **BAR**

A German carved walnut humidor, with carved game bird decoration, with drawer to base.

26in (66cm) high

$320-380 LC

An unusual European enameled silver rectangular cigarette case, simulating the appearance of sharkskin overall, with lozenge-shaped panels picked out in green, beige and white against a coral-colored ground, the ends black-enameled, marked "C&C" with London import marks for 1926, with original leather slipcase.

3.25in (8cm) long

$150-200 DN

A British brass 'Evans Patent Concinnum Machine' cigarette roller.

The user places the paper topped with tobacco inside, closes the lid and turns the side disc to roll the cigarette.

3in (8.5cm) long

$10-20 ET

A pottery tobacco jar, in the form of dog's head wearing a tasseled hat, with pipe in mouth, minor flakes.

6in (15cm) high

$150-200 AAC

A Chase 'Stratosphere' chrome standing ashtray, with spherical top with Bakelite finial on a fluted column shaft and black-enameled base, some scratches and missing trivets to top, stamped mark.

25in (63.5cm) high

$120-180 DRA

A Chase copper standing ashtray, with copper and brass duck with hinged beak on circular tabletop, a few small dents, no visible mark.

24.5in (62cm) high

$300-500 DRA

A Chase 'Lazy Boy' brass smoker's stand, designed by Walter von Nessen, with swiveling composition top on fluted column shaft with curlicue, on circular base, no visible mark.

21.5in (54.5cm) high

$150-200 DRA

A CLOSER LOOK AT A CIGARETTE CASE

This case is by renowned Japanese company Namiki, specialists in 'maki-e' or 'sprinkled picture' lacquerwork. They went into partnership with luxury English retailer Alfred Dunhill in the late 1920s and 1930s.

Most Namiki pieces are signed with an artist's seal or 'kao', and Japanese letters (kanji) stating his name and the Namiki name. Some pieces only bear a 'kao'.

Pieces are usually decorated with motifs from Japanese art, the gold fish is commonly seen, desirable and popular.

This is by leading artist and prize winner Senzan Murata (1901-1976) and the detail would have been painstakingly added layer by layer.

A 1930s Namiki maki-e lacquer cigarette case, decorated by Senzan Murata with a goldfish swimming amongst pond weed and executed in orange, silver and gold hiramaki-e and gold nashiji on a roiro-nuri ground, with a few faint scratches to the background.

$1,200-1,800 CO

Collectors' Notes

- The invention of snowdomes seems to be connected with the development of solid glass paperweights in France in the mid-1800s. These paperweights were expensive and snowdomes may have proved a more affordable alternative.

- At the 1878 Paris Universal Exhibition, Charles Cole, the American Deputy Secretary of the Commission of Glassworks, wrote the first documented report of snowdomes. However, he made no mention of the name or origin of the 'paperweights' he described.

- The first 'souvenir' snowdomes were made to commemorate the construction of the Eiffel Tower for the 1889 Paris Exposition. They proved extremely popular but unfortunately none survive today.

- Production increased during the beginning of the 20thC, predominantly in Europe. Souvenir snowdomes were the most common, particularly of religious sites such as Lourdes and Lisieux, in France.

- The 1940s saw a boom in snowdome production with mass-produced plastic examples taking over from hand-made glass domes. This was aided by Joseph Garaja's patent of 1927, one of the first relating to snowdomes, which enabled them to be assembled underwater and consequently mass-produced, rather than hand-made individually.

- In the 1960s and 1970s Asia began exporting large numbers of domes to the West, but these are often of lower quality and made without copyright.

- The increased interest in collecting means that high quality glass snowdomes are being made once more and are available in a huge range of themes.

- Look out for good quality glass domes, unusual shapes, or those with forms that surround the globe. Examples with see-saws or similar internal moving parts are also desirable.

- The water level can affect value, with empty examples being less popular however some are designed to be refilled. Original boxes are scarce and desirable.

- Snowdomes that cross over to other collecting themes, such as Disney, McDonalds and holiday, tend to be more expensive as they appeal to a wide range of collectors.

A 1970s Acapulco souvenir snowdome, with an octopus.

3in (7.5cm) high

$20-30 NWC

A 1970s souvenir snowdome from Florida, with a dolphin and a see-saw inside.

4in (10cm) high

$20-30 NWC

An early 1980s Hawaii souvenir snowdome, in the form of a treasure chest.

2.75in (7cm) high

$12-18 NWC

An early 1990s Las Vegas souvenir snowdome with dice inside.

2in (5cm) high

$12-18 NWC

An early 1980s New York City souvenir snowdome, with the Twin Towers.

2.75in (7cm) high

$12-18 NWC

A 1970s souvenir snowdome from San Francisco, with a mermaid.

4.5in (11.5cm) high

$20-30 NWC

A late 1950s souvenir Washington, DC 'Water Globe' salt and pepper container, with sliding lid.

2.75in (7cm) high

$20-30 NWC

A 1940s glass and bakelite Niagara Falls souvenir snowdome.

4in (10cm) high

$30-50 NWC

A 1930s glass and bakelite snowdome 'Uncle Alfred - The Hermitage, Tenn', by Pine.

The Hermitage in Nashville was the home of seventh US President Andrew Jackson and Uncle Alfred was his favored house servant.

2.5in (6.5cm) high

$50-80 NWC

SNOWDOMES

A 1940s glass and Bakelite Yellow Stone Park souvenir snowdome.

4in (10cm) high

$40-60 NWC

A 1950s egg-shaped Eiffel Tower souvenir snowdome.

4in (10cm) high

$40-60 NWC

A 1990s Nice souvenir snowdome on a pedestal.

4in (10cm) high

$7-10 NWC

A 1960s London souvenir snowdome, with Horse Guard.

6in (15cm) high

$15-25 NWC

A 1990s Saint Tropez souvenir snowdome.

2in (5cm) high

$7-10 NWC

A 1990s Helsinki, Finland souvenir snowdome.

2in (5cm) high

$7-10 NWC

A 1940s Italian seaside souvenir snowdome, with mermaid.

3in (7.5cm) high

$40-60 NWC

A 1940s Italian seaside souvenir snowdome, with the Virgin Mary on a mirrored base.

4.5in (11.5cm) high

$40-60 NWC

A late 1950s souvenir Sydney Harbor 'Water Globe' salt and pepper container, with sliding lid and original box.

2.75in (7cm) high

$30-40 NWC

A 1990s The Great Wall of China souvenir snowdome.

3in (7.5cm) high

$15-25 NWC

A 1970s/80s Jerusalem souvenir calendar snowdome.

4in (10cm) high

$20-30 NWC

A 1990s Taj Mahal souvenir snowdome.

3in (7.5cm) high

$15-25 NWC

A 1990s Buenos Aires souvenir snowdome.

2in (5cm) high

$10-15 NWC

An early 1970s Walt Disney Productions 'Mickey and Donald' snowdome, with Mickey Mouse and Donald Duck on a see-saw.

3in (7.5cm) high

$30-50 NWC

An early 1970s Walt Disney Productions 'The Wonderful World of Disney' snowdome, with Mickey and Minnie Mouse.

3in (7.5cm) high

$30-50 NWC

An early 1960s Walt Disney Productions Pinocchio snowdome.

This is one from a set of five snowdomes which include Raggedy Anne and Bugs Bunny.

5in (12.5cm) high

$30-120 NWC

An early 1960s Walt Disney Productions Raggedy Anne snowdome.

5in (12.5cm) high

$80-120 NWC

A set of three 1980s McDonalds snowdomes.

This set was given away with Happy Meals in Germany only.

2.25in (5.5cm) each

$20-30 (each) NWC

A set of four McDonalds '101 Dalmatians' snowdomes.

c1996

4.5in (11.5cm) high

$12-18 (each) NWC

Christmas

A 1970s Christmas snowdome, with Santa climbing into a chimney.

5.25in (13.5cm) high

$20-30 NWC

A 1970s Christmas tree snowdome, with Santa Claus.

6in (15cm) high

$30-50 NWC

A late 1960s Snowman snowdome, with see-saw action.

5in (12.5cm) high

$30-40 NWC

A 1970s Snowman snowdome, with Santa inside.

5.75in (14.5cm) high

$30-40 NWC

A fireplace shaped snowdome, with a Christmas choir and Santa Claus and Mrs Claus sitting on top, marked "Brite Star Mfg" and dated.

1976 *5in (12.5cm) high*

$30-40 NWC

An early 1980s Christmas chalet snowdome, with snowman.

3in (7.5cm) high

$20-30 NWC

A 1970s religious illuminated snowdome, with a scene of the Last Supper.

3.5in (9cm) high

$30-40 NWC

A 1970s/80s Lourdes souvenir calendar snowdome.

4in (10cm) high

$20-30 NWC

A 1950s egg-shaped Lourdes souvenir snowdome, by Ets C & Cie.

5in (12.5cm) high

$40-60 NWC

A 1980s/90s bell-shaped religious snowdome.

2in (5cm) high

$10-15 NWC

A 1970s religious souvenir snowdome from Montenero.

5in (12.5cm) high

$30-40 NWC

Others

A rare European glass snowdome, with wax figures of geese on wire tremblers with gold leaf 'snowflakes'.

c1910

$80-120 NWC

A late 1950s 'Salt and Pepper Vegetable Water Globe Set', by Park Smith Corp. NY, with original box.

2in (5cm) high

$30-50 NWC

A rare European glass snowdome, with wax figures of angels on wire tremblers with gold leaf 'snowflakes'.

c1910

$80-120 NWC

An early 1960s set of six Animal Snow Scene snowdomes, by Marx, with rare box.

Each dome is also a game where the aim is to put the hoops over the animals' heads.

2in (5cm) high

$60-90 NWC

A Palitoy 'Snowstorm' snowdome, with a black cat inside, boxed but lacks water.

3.25in (8.5cm) high

$30-50 NWC

A limited edition 'Millennium' snowdome, from an edition of 2,000, numbered and signed by Corbin Bernsen.

Hollywood actor Corbin Bernsen is a snowdome collector and commissioned this snowdome edition to celebrate the new millennium.

3.5in (9cm) high

$30-40 NWC

Collectors' Notes

■ Space memorabilia has become increasingly popular recently, as interest grows for these historically important items. Flight flown items with correct provenances such as clothes and flags are more desirable and valuable as they are rarer, but the large number of commemorative pieces produced are still affordable.

■ Russian pieces are usually more common and less desirable than American pieces. Cosmonauts were allowed to take items home after flights, whereas astronauts were not, or were only allowed a limited number of items.

■ Collectors are also usually unfamiliar with Russian programs and language difficulties make it hard to understand how a piece related to the mission. Americans also landed on the moon first. As a result, American space memorabilia is generally more valuable.

An Alan Shepard signed photograph.
10in (25.5cm) high
$220-280   AGI

A John Glenn signed NASA publicity photo inscribed.
10in (25.5cm) high
$80-120   AGI

A John Young signed NASA publicity lithograph wearing his Gemini spacesuit, inscribed.
10in (25.5cm) high
$300-500   AGI

A signed color lithograph of the earth as seen from the moon, signed by Alan Bean, Frank Borman, Walt Cunningham, Charlie Duke, Dick Gordon & Ed Mitchell.

All of the astronauts have written extensive inscriptions (in mainly gold ink) describing their feelings when looking at the earth from the moon.
10in (25.5cm) high
$700-1,000   AGI

A scarce Buzz Aldrin signed Apollo 11 Beta cloth crew patch, sewn into a gold mylar foil pouch.
7.5in (19cm) wide
$180-220   AGI

A Charles Conrad signed American Space Pioneer patch.
5in (12.5cm) wide
$80-120   AGI

Cortright, Edgar M., "Apollo Expeditions to the Moon", published by NASA, SP-350.

This is still sealed in its original cardboard box.
c1975
$180-220   AGI

Grimwood, James M., Hacker Barton C., "Project Gemini - A Chronology", published by NASA, SP-4002.
1969
$60-90   AGI

A rare NASA press kit, the 91 page document with a number of 'vetting' signatures in the upper right hand corner of the first page, excellent condition.

These documents were distributed mainly to the Press Corps who attended the launch.
$280-320   AGI

A Portmeirion commemorative mug, designed by John Cuffley to commemorate Apollo 11's landing on the moon.

1969   *4in (10cm) high*

$70-100   **H&G**

An Aynsley bone china dish, made to commemorate the first man landing on the moon.

1969   *5.5in (14cm) diam*

$60-90   **H&G**

A rare Robbins commemorative silver medal, commemorating the flight that delivered the US P6 electrical power supply to the International Space Station, from an edition of 141.

Of the 141 medals produced, only 56 were flown. This is an un-flown medal. Gold versions could be purchased by astronauts who flew on that specific flight, silver by any of the astronauts.

c2000

$180-220   **AGI**

David Scott's flown Gemini VIII silver medallion.

1in (2.5cm) diam

$1,500-2,000   **AGI**

A rare Apollo XIII flown Canadian flag, on a yellow bordered presentation certificate, inscribed and signed by James Lovell and Jack Swigert and printed signature of Fred Haise.

6in (15cm) wide

$2,800-3,200   **AGI**

A CLOSER LOOK AT A FLOWN FLAG

This was carried to the International Space Station in August 2001 by STS-105 flight engineer Vladimir Deshurov and returned to earth on board the STS-108.

Deshurov only carried a very few flags as personal mementoes and gifts.

Its rarity is heightened as this is the first U.S. flag from this flight that has been offered for sale.

The blue stamps were made by the on board I.S.S. handstamp, proving it has been there.

A rare flown US silk flag.

2001   *6in (15cm)*

$400-600   **AGI**

A Yuri Gagarin signed photograph, signed in purple ink along the upper left-hand edge of the piece.

$1,200-1,800   **FA**

A rare signed first day cover, dated Sep, 8, 2000, signed by Wilcutt, Altman, Burbank, Lu, Mastracchio, Malenchenko and Morukov.

2000

$80-120   **AGI**

A book of color maxime cards, signed by Gagarin, Titov, Nikolayev, Popovich, Bykovsky, Tereshkova, Komorov, Feoktistov, Belyayev and Leonov.

$400-600   **AGI**

A NASA publicity print of an artist's concept of a lunar base, signed by Dr. Wernher von Braun.

Wernher von Braun (1912-1977) lead the team of German rocket scientists who designed and built the infamous V2 rocket bomb. After the war he went to work for NASA and developed the massive Saturn V rocket that would propel man to the moon.

10in (25.5cm) wide

$400-600   **AGI**

Collectors' Notes

■ Baseballs are a popular format for collecting player's signatures. They are small, making them easy to store or display, and make a tactile alternative to cigarette cards or photographs.

■ Signed baseballs should ideally be official American or National League baseballs and these can be identified by the stamped signature of either the league president before 1999 or Commissioner.

■ Due to the popularity of stars such as Mickey Mantle and Ted Williams fakes are on the market Buy from reputable dealers or auction houses and if in doubt check the signature against an example you know to be authentic.

A Detroit Tigers 1968 baseball, signed by the full team.

$180-220 TA

A Detroit Tigers 1972 baseball, signed by the full team.

$180-220 TA

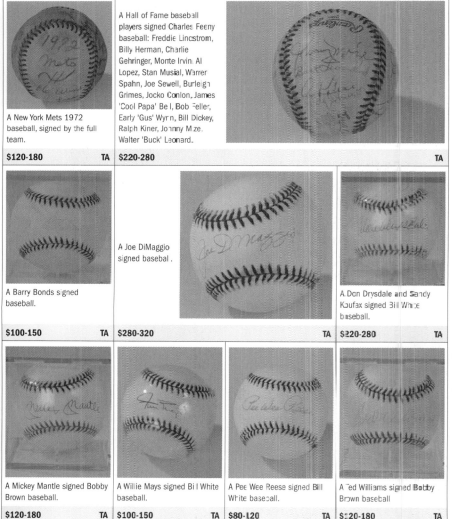

A New York Mets 1972 baseball, signed by the full team.

$120-180 TA

A Hall of Fame baseball players signed Charles Feeny baseball: Freddie Lincstrom, Billy Herman, Charlie Gehringer, Monte Irvin, Al Lopez, Stan Musial, Warren Spahn, Joe Sewell, Burleigh Grimes, Jocko Conlon, James 'Cool Papa' Bell, Bob Feller, Early 'Gus' Wynn, Bill Dickey, Ralph Kiner, Johnny Mize, Walter 'Buck' Leonard.

$220-280 TA

A Barry Bonds signed baseball.

$100-150 TA

A Joe DiMaggio signed baseball.

$280-320 TA

A Don Drysdale and Sandy Koufax signed Bill White baseball.

$220-280 TA

A Mickey Mantle signed Bobby Brown baseball.

$120-180 TA

A Willie Mays signed Bill White baseball.

$100-150 TA

A Pee Wee Reese signed Bill White baseball.

$80-120 TA

A Ted Williams signed Bobby Brown baseball

$120-180 TA

A Louisville Slugger baseball bat, signed by the ten 500 home run hitters: W. Mays, W. McCovey, M. Schmidt, H. Killebrew, T. Williams, F. Robinson, R. Jackson, E. Banks and E. Matthews.

$2,500-3,500   **TA**

A Joe DiMaggio signed Rawlins Slugger baseball bat.

$1,500-2,500   **TA**

A Mickey Mantle and Ted Williams signed Rawlins Slugger baseball bat.

$800-1,200   **TA**

Lefty Grove's 1931 Tour of Japan trunk, by H&M, St. Louis, with several autographed labels on the top, the interior with six drawers on one side and garment area on the opposite, retains original metal tag on top.

On October 15, 1931, sports writer Fred Lieb took an all-star team on a trip to Hawaii and Japan. As well as Groves were Lou Gehrig, Willie Kamm, Al Simmons and Lefty O'Doul.

1931   43in (109cm) high

$4,000-5,000   **HA**

A rare Billy Herman Boston Braves game-worn warm-up jacket, with applied multicolor Indian head Braves logo on reverse, Wilson tag in collar, "Herman" chain stitched on tag inside tail along with "10", typical light to moderate age wear, in unrestored original condition, includes letter of authenticity from Global David Bushing/Dan Knoll/Mike Baker.

Although Herman wore #20 in 1946, his only year with Braves, detailed provenance and several signed photos of Herman with jacket, directly from Herman, confirms that it was his jacket, making it exceptionally rare.

$2,500-3,000   **HA**

A Cleveland Indians home jersey, cream flannel vest-style shirt with #30 on front and back and "Piniella" on back, retains Wilson tag on front of tail along with 1968 chain stitched year tag, restoration includes player lettering and numbers, patch original.

1968

$400-450   **HA**

A Hutch all leather youth-size helmet, together with a pair of red and black leather reach "Young Star" shoulder pads, helmet in excellent condition with good original interior and chin strap.

$80-120   **HA**

Rowe, Col. Wm. H., "Casey Reminiscences", 32 page booklet with lyrical poems regarding the star teams from 1871-1877.

1911

$200-300 HA

A 1913-14 World Tour souvenir book, album of photos taken during the World Tour includes destinations and players, spine has some separation from front cover, book fairly clean.

1913-14

$350-450 HA

Ruth, George Herman, "Babe Ruth's Own Book of Baseball", first edition, signed by Babe Ruth, together with a signed baseball card.

1928

$800-1,200 TA

A Brooklyn Dodgers "Golden Stamp" book complete with unused stamps.

1955

$120-180 HA

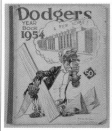

A Brooklyn Dodgers 1954 yearbook, with signatures including Al Campanis, Pee Wee Reese, Duke Snider, Wayne Belardi and Ev Palica.

$250-350 TA

A Brooklyn Dodgers "Golden Stamp" book, including signatures from Pee Wee Reese, Duke Snider, George "Shotgun" Shuba and Carl Erskine and other members of the 1955 team.

$400-600 TA

Durso, Joe, "Yankee Stadium: 50 Years of Drama", first edition, with approximately 190 signatures including Ford, Berra, Koufax, Grim, Dawkins, Kelly, Larsen, O'Connor, Woodling, Hopp, Tittle, Connerly, Hunt, Schofner, and Rizzuto.

1972

$1,200-1,800 TA

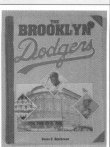

Bjarkman, Peter C., "The Brooklyn Dodgers", first edition, published by St Martin's Press, containing 168 autographs.

1992

$700-1,000 TA

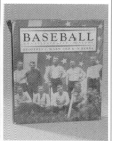

Ward, Geoffrey C., and Burns, Ken, "Baseball, An Illustrated History", first edition, published by Knopf, containing approximately 41 autographs.

1994

$500-700 TA

Chadwick Bill, "The Boston Red Sox", one book in a series of eight, containing 182 autographs including Ted Williams, Carlton Fisk, Pumpsie Green and Dave 'Boo' Ferris.

$800-1,200 TA

A Chicago Cubs World Series full-size pennant, with Cubs holding a bat at left side.

1945

$600-900　　　　　　　　　　HA

A Cleveland Indians felt scroll pennant, with Chief Wahoo and a scrolled list of names on the left, pennant lightly soiled but nice overall appearance.

1952　　　　*29in (73.5cm) long*

$180-220　　　　　　　　　HA

A New York Knicks 1972-73 World Champions beanie hat, together with a New York Knicks pennant.

$20-30　　　　　　　　　　HA

A New York Mets felt pennant, with the 'Mr Met Family', some soiling.

29in (73.5cm) long

$20-30　　　　　　　　　　HA

A New York Mets felt team photo pennant, featuring Y. Berra, T. Seaver, and W. Mays.

1973　　　　*29in (73.5cm) long*

$40-60　　　　　　　　　　HA

A 1940s Philadelphia Stars Negro league pennant, with game scene graphics at left side.

$300-400　　　　　　　　　HA

A 1940s St. Louis Cardinals pennant, with two cardinals sitting on a baseball bat, white background.

29in (73.5cm) long

$30-40　　　　　　　　　　HA

A late 1940s St. Louis Cardinals pennant, with two cardinals sitting on a baseball bat, orange background.

26in (66cm) long

$30-50　　　　　　　　　　HA

A Washington Senators pennant, with the Senator mascot hitting a ball.

27in (68.5cm) long

$80-120　　　　　　　　　HA

A rare 1930s Washington Senators pennant, with U.S. Capitol graphic at left side, very clean overall.

26in (66cm) long

$180-220　　　　　　　　　HA

A 1960s oversized Hall of Fame pennant, with bust shots of all members surrounding an image of the Hall of Fame, tear at tip, lacking tassels.

35in (89cm) long

$50-80　　　　　　　　　　HA

A set of twelve 1970s felt souvenir pennants, including Washington Senators, Yale, Brown, West Virginia Mountaineers, Army and Pitt Panthers.

$40-60 (set)　　　　　　　　SI

A rare Dartmouth vs Harvard baseball game action photograph, taken from a rooftop behind the home plate, on original mount which has two pinholes.

1897   9in (23cm) long

$500-700   **HA**

A Cincinnati Redland Field fold-out postcard display, paper stock mailer with color tinted image of stadium and team on front and advertisement for "The Bismarck Cafe" on reverse, some tape repair to joints on back on a few places.

1912

$180-220   **HA**

Two Baseball Magazine cover photographs of Dave Bancroft and Frank "Pancho" Snyder, by Charles Conlon, each mounted on board with mark up ink on background, each signed by Conlon on back along with Christie's Baseball Magazine collection hologram.

10in (25.5cm) long

$120-180   **HA**

A rare signed Joe DiMaggio photograph, depicting DiMaggio in his New York Yankees uniform reading a scroll presented to him in his rookie year.

c1936   20in (51cm)

$180-220   **TA**

A signed Joe DiMaggio photograph, depicting DiMaggio taking a full swing during an exhibition game.

c1937-1940   14in (35.5cm)

$80-120   **TA**

A photograph of Joe DiMaggio signing his first $100,000 contract, titled "The Yankee Clipper", framed with an autographed card.

c1949   18in (45.5cm)

$120-180   **TA**

An image of Mickey Mantle, pointing to the ball that he hit out of Griffith Stadium, mounted together with a signed magazine cover and a card autographed by Joe DiMaggio.

35in (89cm)

$200-300   **TA**

A rare Negro National League Champions Newark Eagles team photograph, including Doby, Mackey, and Irvin, with some moisture damage at bottom edge.

1946   10in (25.5cm) long

$300-350   **HA**

A 1939 Cincinnati Reds real photo postcard, vignette arrangement picturing team in uniform, a few creases including horizontal across bottom right.

1939

$120-180   **HA**

A signed Milwaukee Braves 1957 World Series photograph, signatures include Bob Buhl, Bobby Malkmus, Red Murff, Johnny Logan, Eddie Mathews, Del Crandall, Gene Conley and Andy Pafco.

14in (35.5cm)

$60-90   **TA**

A signed Mickey Mantle photograph, depicting Mantle racing towards right center during a game against the Washington Senators.

20in (51cm)

$120-180   **TA**

A Willie Mays signed photograph and baseball, in a shadow box frame.

10in (25.5cm)

$180-220   **TA**

A B C D E F G H I J K L M N O P Q R S T U V W XYZ

An early St. Louis vs Detroit program, partially scored in pencil, with some general wear including center fold line and corner chip on cover.
1902

$150-200   HA

A rare July 4, 1907 Chicago Cubs Flag Raising Day program, issued to honor the 1906 World Champion Cubs, some staining and creases.
1907

$500-700   HA

Two Boston Red Sox programs, comprising a 1901 Boston vs Detroit fold-out scorecard and a 1905 Boston vs Washington.
1901/1905

$600-900   HA

A Detroit Tigers program, issued for the game played against Washington, unscored with some period fold lines and a few small abrasions on back cover.
1909

$1,000-1,500   HA

A Pittsburgh vs New York program, with the newly built Forbes Field on front cover, interior is scored in pencil, has vertical fold line.
1909

$400-600   HA

An early Boston vs Brooklyn program, issued for the 1914 Miracle Braves, scored in pencil.

1914

$120-180   HA

A rare April 18, 1923 Yankee Stadium Opening Day program, issued for the first game played between the Yankees and Red Sox in the Yankee Stadium, unscored with some general wear including soiling on cover and restored spine.
1923

$3,000-3,500   HA

A scarce 1929 World Series full ticket and program, issued for Game #1 in Chicago, together with a World Series program at Chicago, very clean and unscored, light fold line.
1929

$1,500-2,000   HA

A rare April 17, 1934 "New" Fenway Park Opening Day program, issued for the first game played in the renovated Fenway Park against the Senators, creasing on back.
1934

$500-800   HA

A signed 1943 World Series program, issued for the 1943 World Series signed by 26 players and coaches of the NL Champion St. Louis Cardinals, some wear.
1943

$700-1,000   HA

Two rare Brooklyn Dodger programs, comprising October 1, 1950 program for Dodgers vs Phillies and October 3, 1946 program for Dodgers vs Cardinals.
1946/1950

$300-350   HA

A New York vs Chicago fold-out scorecard, printed lineups including Ewing, Ward, Welch, Anson, and Clarkson, some age toning.

1885

$500-700 HA

An M.D. Knowlton Co. glove-shaped baseball scorer, by Whitehead & Hoag and advertising paper machinery.

1905   2.5in (6.5cm) high

$120-180 HA

A July 6, 1907 Brooklyn vs Chicago scorecard, with image of Charles Ebbets on the front cover, interior scored in pencil.

1907

$250-300 HA

A 1913 Cleveland vs St. Louis scorecard, scored in pencil with printed lineups including 'Shoeless' Joe Jackson

1913

$350-450 HA

A 1913 World Series ticket stub from Walter Johnson's scrapbook, issued for Game #1 at New York between the Giants and As.

1913

$200-300 HA

A rare 1914 St. Louis Terriers vs Indianapolis Hoosiers Federal League fold-out scorecard, with printed lineups including McKechnie, Kauff, and Roush, scored in pencil, has some general wear including horizontal fold line and some border toning.

1914

$600-900 HA

An unusual Brown vs Harvard cardboard ticket, with ornate decoration including Soldiers Field.

1924   5in (12.5cm) long

$30-40 HA

A Brooklyn Dodgers scorecard, issued for game played against Milwaukee, signed on front cover by ten players.

1957

$50-80 HA

A rare All-Star game ticket stub, issued for game played at Baltimore.

1958

$120-180 HA

A Springfield Republican pocket scorer, with eight dials, front and back advertise The Springfield Republicans sports coverage, very clean.

4in (10cm) long

$50-80 HA

A Keith's Baseball mechanical score counter, by Meeks Co, shaped as a crescent padded catchers mitt and with colorful baseball scene in the center.

2.75in

$120-180 HA

Three ticket stubs, including 1969 World Series Game 3 at Shea Stadium, 1973 World Series at Oakland, and 1956 New York Yankees regular season 7/7/56.

$70-100 HA

A color lithographed baseball decorated fan, titled "The Center of Attraction" at top featuring a vignette of a young woman superimposed over a game scene with two blank scoreboards, the back advertising Minick's Ice Cream Factory in Chambersburg, PA, some creasing.

c1910   13in (33cm) high

$300-400   **HA**

A Yankee Boy pocket tobacco tin, with image of boy in baseball garb on front, very clean with light overall wear.

c1910

$400-600   **HA**

A rare set of three 1930s/40s baseball stuffed animal dolls, with minor age wear.

11in (28cm) high

$280-320   **HA**

A Chicago Cubs schedule fan, with cub mascot on front holding a bat, the back with Cubs home schedule, two small adhesion residue spots on front.

1930

$180-220   **HA**

A 1931 World Series souvenir miniature bat and pennant, advertising Red Goose Shoes and retaining its original attached pennant.

1931   18in (45.5cm) long

$300-400   **HA**

A Brooklyn Dodgers National League Champions souvenir necktie, with printed autographs of players including Campanella, Robinson, Hodges, Furillo, and Walker.

1947

$400-600   **HA**

A wind-up baseball nodder toy, made in Japan, head bounces when wound up, in working order.

$30-40   **HA**

A Jackie Robinson 'Save and Win' lithographed tin dime bank, opens at $5 and features the Brooklyn great on top and his signature printed on the bottom panel, some scratches.

c1950

$200-250   **HA**

A 1950s Ted Williams Cream Root Beer cardboard display sign, with image of Ted in uniform, retains original easel back, some areas of staining on front with a few creases at edges.

30in (76cm) long

$700-1,000   **HA**

A Duke Snider "Baseball Trainer" set, by Wham-O, original box features illustration of Snider batting, some general wear including some staining and a few tears.

c1959

$150-200   **HA**

A 1960s L.A. Dodgers souvenir ladies straw hat, with team name on satin band and five felt player caricatures on brim.

13in (33cm) diam

$100-150   **HA**

A Rocky Marciano signed photograph, with certificate.

Rocky Marciano (1923-69), undefeated world champion between 1952-56.

9.5in (24cm) high

$100-150 TEN

A Muhammad Ali/Cassius Clay signed photograph, depicting the boxer with The Beatles in the 5th Street Gym in Miami, Florida.

1964   20in (51cm) wide

$300-500 TA

A Muhammad Ali/Cassius Clay signed photograph, depicting Ali and Sonny Liston in their second fight.

20in (51cm) wide

$220-280 TA

A Muhammad Ali signed photograph, depicting Ali and Frazier during a fight in Madison Square Garden.

20in (51cm) wide

$220-280 TA

A pair of Muhammad Ali signed boxing shorts, with photograph and certificate.

36in (91.5cm) high

$320-380 TEN

Collectors' Notes

- As with other autographs and memorabilia, the more famous or popular a star, the more sought-after their signature will be and the more likely that fakes are on the market. Many athletes sign contracts with companies and then autograph items exclusively for them. If an athlete charges $70 for a signed photograph then an authentic example is unlikely to be on offer for $30.

- Be wary of items that have multiple signatures from famous boxers, particularly if they are in the same pen and evenly spaced over the item.

- Generally accepted as the greatest boxer of all time, Muhammad Ali's signature is often faked. Ali changed his name from Cassius Clay on March 6, 1964 and the majority of his signatures until the late 1960s include the word "from". Ali's handwriting began to deteriorate from 1982, due to Parkinson's and from this time on, his signatures are smaller.

A Muhammad Ali signed photograph, framed amidst fifteen hologram and collector cards featuring George Foreman, Sugar Ray Leonard, Mills Lane, Mike Tyson and Sonny Liston.

25.5in (65cm)

$400-600 TA

A Riddick Bowe signed photograph.

Riddick Bowe (b.1967), won the World Heavyweight title against Evander Holyfield in 1992 and lost it to him in 1996.

20in (51cm) high

$120-180 TA

A Muhammad Ali signed boxing glove, with certificate.

13in (33cm) long

$180-220 TEN

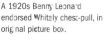

A 1920s Benny Leonard endorsed Whitely chest-pull, in original picture box.

$220-280 HA

FIND OUT MORE:

'Boxing Collectors' News', monthly magazine. BCN, 7511 Raleigh Lane, Jonesboro, GA 30236
http://www.boxingcollectors.com

Collectors' Notes

- Reels are a key area of fishing collectibles as they offer a wide range of designs, dates, technical complexity and price.
- Pre-19thC reels are very simple, but as fishing became more specialized, so did the equipment. A wide range of gadgets were offered, which could be customized to the type of fishing.
- Named reels are generally more popular with collectors than unnamed examples. Names to look out for include Hardy Bros. of England, Allcock and Farlow. Enthusiasts also collect by mechanical type and design, such as 'multiplying', 'half-crank', 'cage' and 'freespool clutch'.
- Condition plays a large part in value and collectors should be aware of any replaced parts or restoration, which should be easy to spot due to the loss of the original patina.

A 1930s Allcock 'Allcock Bell' alloy sea centerpin reel, stamped with 'Stag' regd. trademark, "Allcock Bell" and maker's details.

6in (15cm) diam

$120-180 MM

An Allcock 'Reflex' alloy bait casting reel, backplate stamped with 'Stag' regd. trademark, "Reflex" and details, in good condition.

$180-220 MM

A scarce Hardy half ebonite 'Birmingham' platewind reel, with constant check, the brass handle plate stamped with "Rod in Hand" trademark and bordered oval logo.

c1890   4.5in (11.5cm) diam

$400-600 MM

A C. Farlow & Co. brass platewind reel, with constant check, foot stamped with Farlow's early 'Fish' trademark, back plate scroll engraved "C. Farlow & Co. Makers, 191 The Strand, London", retaining nearly all original bronzing, in original Farlow fitted block leather reel case.

1885-94   2.75in (7cm) diam

$400-500 MM

A scarce C. Farlow & Co. 'Sun' Nottingham mahogany centerpin reel, with brass starback foot stamped "Patent No. 13388/85" (Reuben Heaton), scroll engraved to foot "C. Farlow & Co. Makers, 191 Strand, London."

c1885-94   5in (12.5cm) diam

$150-200 MM

A Hardy Bros 'Perfect' fly reel Dupl. Mark II, ebonite handle, grooved brass foot, drum locking screw.

4.5in (11.5cm) diam

$320-380 Clv

A Hardy 'Perfect' alloy trout fly reel, stamped to reverse of handleplate "J.S." for Jimmy Smith, in Hardy zip leather reel case, restored with highly polished finish to alloy and brass.

3in (7.5cm) diam

$600-900 MM

A very rare Hardy 'Duck's Foot' Altex Mk I fixed spool reel, stamped to back of flyer "Patent Applied For", "Mark I", stamped to interior "D.W." for Denys Ward.

c1932

$400-600 MM

A very rare Hardy 'Match Fishers' alloy turntable centerpin reel, stamped "The Match Fishers' Reel" and marks for Hardy.

1937-39   3.25in (8.5cm) diam

$1,800-2,200 MM

A Hardy Bros brass fly reel, with engraved rod in hand trade mark, bordered oval logo.

4.25in (11cm) diam

$400-500 Clv

SPORTING MEMORABILIA

A scarce Illingworth featherweight trout threadline casting reel, converted from an Illingworth No. 3 Reel with an alloy foot and stem, stamped "Illingworth No. 3 Casting Reel", patent details and "Series J.M. 2 No.6544", in triangular fiberboard box.

$280-320   **MM**

A Hardy Bros metal cast box, with felt liner.

4in (10cm) diam

$30-40   **Clv**

An Ogden Smith Exchequer fly reel, with drum locking screw and brass foot.

3in (7.5cm) diam

$150-200   **Clv**

A very rare D. Slater ebonite combination reel starback stamped "D. Slater's Patent 2887".

c1910   4.75in (13cm) diam

$700-1,000   **MM**

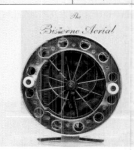

A very rare handmade Paul Witcher 'Bisterne Aerial' alloy centerpin reel, stamped to interior "4/21", stamped to back plate "Witcher", in felt lined leather case.

1996   4in (10cm) diam

$1,500-2,000   **MM**

A Hardy Bros 'Unique' type mahogany brass-mounted fly cabinet, with recessed brass handle, the interior fitted with nine trays with ivorine labels and name plate.

$4,000-5,000   **Clv**

Ten framed salmon flies

$30-50   **TEN**

A Hardy Bros. Practical spring-loaded aluminum line crier, on stand.

$300-500   **Clv**

FIND OUT MORE:

Harold Jellison & Daniel B. Homel, '*Antique & Collectible Fishing Reels: Identification, Evaluation and Maintenance*', published by Forrest Park Publishing, July 1998.

Karl T. White, '*Fishing Tackle – Antiques & Collectibles: Reference & Evaluation*', published by Holli Enterprises, 1995.

The International Fly Fishing Centre and Fly Fishing Museum, 215 East Lewis Street, Livingston, Montana 59047, U.S. www.fedflyfishers.org

The Flyfisher's Club, 69 Brook Street, London W1Y 2ER, holds a vast members-only library devoted to flyfishing with personal copies of books by famed anglers and fishermen.

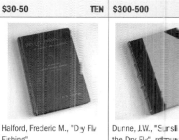

Halford, Frederic M., "Dry Fly Fishing".

1899   9in (23cm) high

$60-90   **TEN**

Dunne, J.W., "Sunshine and the Dry Fly", rebound.

1924   7.5in (19cm) high

$40-60   **TEN**

An Ernie Bonelli Blue & Gray College All-Star leather jacket, some general wear including some surface abrasions, includes letter of authenticity from Ernest Bonelli.

This leather jacket was issued to players for their participation in the 1945 College All-Star game.

1945

$250-300 HA

A Philadelphia Eagles Mark Slater home jersey, white knit jersey with green and silver trim, retaining original "Slater" name on back, Russell Athletic tag on front with chain stitched "78" on front of tail, includes letter of authenticity from Global David Bushing/ Dan Knoll/Mike Baker.

1978

$280-320 HA

A pair of Stall & Dean reeded football shin guards, in unused condition, both with supple leather and flaw ess padding, model #1312.

$150-200 HA

A New York Giants schedule coin, embossed with the home schedule and the reverse advertising "S. D. Childs & Co. Largest Medalists of the World".

1915

$450-500 HA

A rare New York Giants sterling silver season pass, the pennant-shaped pass with blue and white enamelwork commemorating the Giants 1921 World Championship, marked "Lambert Bros., NY", very clean with no enamel chipping.

1922

$1,500-2,000 HA

A San Francisco 49'ers football pennant, with multicolored Goldminer logo on the left side and silver lettering to the right.

29in (73.5cm) long

$30-50 HA

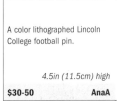

A pair of High School football pennants, for Germantown and Northeast High, both featuring players with open face helmets on the left side.

29in (73.5cm) long

$25-35 HA

A color lithographed Lincoln College football pin.

4.5in (11.5cm) high

$30-50 AnaA

An early 20thC New York Giants souvenir pin, with ribbon and celluloid player.

4.25in (10.5cm) high

$15-25 HGS

A signed Super Bowl XI photograph, with autographs from Pete Banazack, Otis Sisstrunk, Phil Villipiano, Fred Bilitnikoff, Ray Guy and Jack Tatum.

20in (51cm) wide

$250-350 TA

A signed Kenny 'The Snake' Stabler photograph.

20in (51cm) high

$180-220 TA

A signed Tony Dorsett photograph.

Tony Dorsett played for the Dallas Cowboys between 1977 and 1987 and then moved to the Denver Broncos for one year. He won the 1976 Heisman Trophy as the nation's outstanding college player.

20in (51cm) wide

$120-180 TA

Collectors' Notes

■ Golf clubs and balls form the basis of most collections, with collectors often adding pictures, photographs and trophies as decorative elements. Prices have risen over the past decade with high prices being paid for rare 19th century clubs and balls. Despite golf finding its origins between the 15th and 17th century, 18th century and earlier examples are extremely scarce.

■ Clubs found today will usually date from the 19th and 20th centuries. Early versions, which were used with feather-filled balls, were spliced, glued and bound to wooden heads that struck the ball. Handles are typically long and whippy and heads are long.

■ Highly desirable to collectors, they were made from around the 1810s until the 1880s. Look for clubs made by Robert Forgan, Thomas Dunn, Charlie Hunter and Douglas McEwan.

■ When 'gutta percha' balls were introduced, around c1850, club necks became thicker and heads shorter, but were still spliced. This type of club is generally more affordable to collectors. Heads with added brass plates are known as 'brassies' and those with a bulge on the face 'bulgies'. Look for Dunn & Son and Robert Simpson or names of famous players.

■ The forerunners of today's clubs are known as 'socket clubs', where the wooden shaft is inserted into the heads – look for clubs by Robert Simpson, Spalding and others. The late 19th century saw metal headed clubs, known as 'irons', being introduced. Models include 'niblicks', 'putters' and 'mashies'.

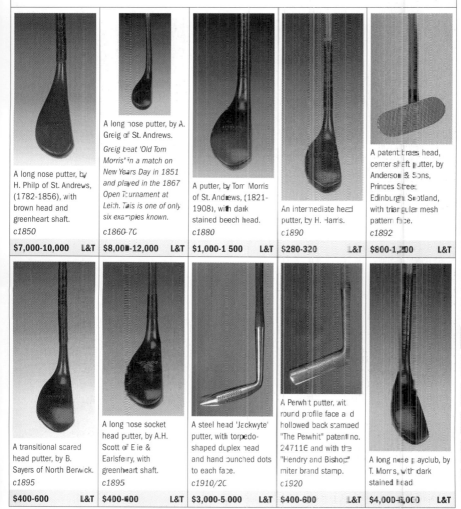

A long nose putter, by H. Philp of St. Andrews, (1782-1856), with brown head and greenheart shaft.
c1850
$7,000-10,000   **L&T**

A long nose putter, by A. Greig of St. Andrews.
Greig beat 'Old Tom Morris' in a match on New Years Day in 1851 and played in the 1867 Open Tournament at Leith. This is one of only six examples known.
c1860-70
$8,000-12,000   **L&T**

A putter, by Tom Morris of St. Andrews, (1821-1908), with dark stained beech head.
c1880
$1,000-1,500   **L&T**

An intermediate head putter, by H. Harris.
c1890
$280-320   **L&T**

A patent brass head, center shaft putter, by Anderson & Sons, Princes Street, Edinburgh, Scotland, with triangular mesh pattern face.
c1892
$800-1,200   **L&T**

A transitional scared head putter, by B. Sayers of North Berwick.
c1895
$400-600   **L&T**

A long nose socket head putter, by A.H. Scott of Elie & Earlsferry, with greenheart shaft.
c1895
$400-600   **L&T**

A steel head 'Jackwyte' putter, with torpedo-shaped duplex head and hand punched dots to each face.
c1910/20
$3,000-5,000   **L&T**

A Perwhit putter, with round profile face and hollowed back stamped "The Perwhit" patent no. 247116 and with the "Hendry and Bishop" miter brand stamp.
c1920
$400-600   **L&T**

A long nose playclub, by T. Morris, with dark stained head
$4,000-6,000   **L&T**

A track or rut iron, with hosel.

The shaft of this rare and early club is unusually constructed from African macassar ebony.

c1820

$5,000-8,000 | **L&T**

A plain face track iron, by F&A Carrick of Musselburgh, Scotland.

c1865/75

$1,800-2,200 | **L&T**

A patent crescent-headed driving iron, by Anderson & Sons of Princes Street, Edinburgh, Scotland.

c1895

$1,800-2,200 | **L&T**

An Urquhart adjustable head iron, no. 2981.

c1895

$1,200-1,800 | **L&T**

A perforated Brown's water iron, by J. Winton of Montrose, Scotland.

c1905

$2,800-3,200 | **L&T**

An iron headed non-skid cleek, by Josh Taylor, patent no. 4601/12, with unusual raised bramble pattern face.

c1913

$2,800-3,200 | **L&T**

A long nose playclub, by R. Forgan of St. Andrews, with a rare large letter stamp.

c1865-70

$3,000-5,000 | **L&T**

A playclub, by Tom Morris of St. Andrews, Scotland, dark stained beach head.

c1875

$2,800-3,200 | **L&T**

A rare one piece playclub, by Dunn & Son of Bournemouth, UK, marked with the patent number 14309.

The whole club is made from a single piece of hickory rather than being spliced, glued and bound, which is extremely rare.

c1895

$3,000-5,000 | **L&T**

A rare aluminum cylindrical headed playclub, the Pambo the 2nd, and stamped "PAMBO", registered 676460 by J.B. Fulford.

This club was designed for all types of shot and is slightly bulged in the center of the head. Fulford only made one other type of club - a putter.

c1895

$3,000-5,000 | **L&T**

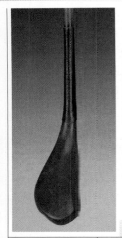

A long nose short spoon, by Hugh Philp of St. Andrews, Scotland, (1786-1856), with thorn head and well lofted face, lemonwood shaft with good patination and owners initials "JWHA".

When the face of the club is described as "well lofted" it means the face is at a good angle to the shaft.

$15,000-20,000   **L&T**

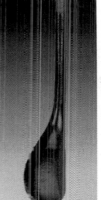

A long nose baffing spoon, by George Daniel Brown of Blackheath and St. Andrews.

Brown represented Blackheath in the first Open in 1860 at Prestwick, finishing 5th. He made hand-hammered balls and his long nose clubs are extremely rare. This club is one of only seven known examples, three of which are in the Royal & Ancient collection at St Andrews, Scotland.

c1850-60

$20,000-30,000   **L&T**

A long nose baffing spoon, by A. Patrick of Leven.
c1865

$4,000-6,000   **L&T**

A long nose brassed niblick, by McEwan of Musselburgh, the head stamped with owners initials "J.M.R".
c1885

$800-1,200   **L&T**

A mammoth niblick, by J. Randall of Ferndown Golf Club, with greenheart shaft.
c1920

$3,200-3,800   **L&T**

A persimmon head Sunday club, with fancy face insert.

$300-500   **L&T**

A Sunday club, in the form of an iron.

$220-280   **L&T**

A Sunday club, in the form of an early golf club.

$150-200   **L&T**

A long nose driver, by R. Simpson of Carnoustie, Scotland.
c1880-35

$1,500-2,000   **L&T**

A long nose driver, by R. Forgan of St. Andrews Prince of Wales stamp.
c1880

$2,000-3,000   **L&T**

A long nose scared head driver, by Tom Morris, with horn insert, lead back weight, later shaft and grip.

$1,500-2,000   **L&T**

A McEwan long nose driver, horn insert, lead back weight, repair at the toe, later shaft and grip.

$1,800-2,200   **L&T**

A B C D E F G H I J K L M N O P Q R S T U V W XYZ

·Collectors' Notes

- Before 1848, golf balls were made from three pieces of thin leather sewn together, turned inside out and stuffed with feathers. The feathers were wet as was the leather. As the ball dried the leather contracted and the feathers expanded, resulting in hardness.

- Due to their stuffing, they were known as 'featheries'. They were then finished with white paint and, in later periods, stamped with the maker's name. Many are still hard today, which is often deemed a sign of authenticity. Look for makers such as Andrew Dickson, Leith and Henry Mills.

- In 1848 a ball made from 'gutta percha', a form of Indian hard rubber, was introduced. They were much cheaper to produce and buy and lasted longer than 'featheries', especially in wet conditions. They had smooth surfaces, but often curved in the air.

- Golfers soon found that scoring or marking the surface ensured a better 'flight' so producers took to patterning the surface, with many diverse surface designs.

- Smooth surfaced 'gutties' are highly sought after today, almost as much as 'featheries'. Look for makers such as Archie Simpson, Alex Patrick and Robert Fogan. Little changed in design until the 1960s, when the one-piece rubber golf ball was developed.

A feathery golf ball, unsigned, distressed condition, clearly showing stuffed interior, numerous hack marks, most paint lacking.

$2,200-2,800   L&T

A J. Gourlay feather ball, stamped "P.S.E"., some hack marks and visible wear, most paint lacking.

$7,000-10,000   L&T

An Allan 29 feathery ball, by Robertson of St. Andrews, Scotland.

$7,000-10,000   L&T

A feathery ball, by T. Morris 27 of St. Andrews.

$12,000-18,000   L&T

A feathery ball, by T. Morris of St. Andrews, indistinctly stamped.

$10,000-15,000   L&T

An Eclipse type gutta ball, with mesh pattern.

$400-600   L&T

An unpainted gutta ball, with mesh pattern, stamped "SPECIAL 27 1/2".

$1,000-1,500   L&T

A Henley gutty ball, some hack marks, paint lacking, 'Union Jack' markings clear, stamped at poles "Henley".

$1,500-2,000   L&T

A line-cut gutta ball, with mesh pattern, stamped "CUNNINGHAM".
c1870

$1,200-1,800   L&T

A Sam Snead Wilson dozen ball display box, with a picture photo of Sam at the top right corner, some light creasing.

9in (23cm) long

$30-50   HA

J. Wilton Adcock, "Reigate Heath Golf Club, Surrey", oil on panel, signed.

c1898

$4,000-6,000 L&T

Frank Watson Wood, "The Sixth Green, Gullane", watercolor, signed and dated.

This is one of a series of paintings of Gullane by Frank Watson Wood. This painting has been owned by the same family since 1850 when it was given to them by the Liberal Club in Edinburgh. This 'freshness to market, the popularity of the series and the subject helped this painting to fetch such a high price.

1934   29in (74cm) wide

$30,000-40,000 L&T

British School, "Harry Vardon, James Braid & John Henry Taylor", St Andrews Open 1910, watercolor, inscribed.

19in (48cm) wide

$1,200-1,800 L&T

British School, "H.R.H., The Prince of Wales, Edward VII", oil on canvas, inscribed.

16.25in (41cm) high

$1,800-2,200 L&T

Crombie, Charles, "The Rules of Golf Illustrated", first edition, published by Perrier, London, with 24 humorous color lithograph plates.

$500-700 L&T

John Blair, "Lundin Links and Largo Law", watercolor, signed and inscribed.

10.5in (26cm) wide

$2,200-2,800 L&T

J** R** Sanders, "Old & Young Tom Putting by the Swilken Burn, St Andrews", oil on board, signed.

27.5in (70cm) high

$500-800 L&T

Frank Watson Wood, "A Panoramic View of the Links at Gullane", watercolor, signed and dated.

1933   29in (74cm) wide

$18,000-22,000 L&T

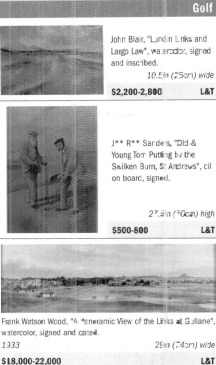

Cecil Aldin, "Westward Ho, 6th Green".

20in (51cm) wide

$6,000-9,000 L&T

W. Heath Robinson, "Sensola, Underwear To Fit All", showing various figures in their underwear under a twilight sky playing golf in a mountainous landscape, watercolor and gouache.

William Heath Robinson (1872-1944) is better known for his illustrations of strange and complicated contraptions and processes which, like this superb image, have a humorous aspect which is only heightened by the sheer determination of the illustrated participants.

28.5in (72cm) high

$6,000-9,000 L&T

Browning, Robert, "A History of Golf, The Royal and Ancient Game", first edition, published by Dent & Sons, London.

1955

$150-200   L&T

A publisher's promotional booklet, for a collection of prints of famous golf links by Cecil Aldin, with six mounted illustrations.

$2,800-3,200   L&T

Farnie, H.B., "The Golfer's Manual", first edition, published by Cupar, Whitehead & Orr.

Farnie was a journalist who was educated at St. Andrews. The first edition was the first book of prose devoted entirely to the game of golf and also the first book of instruction.

1857

$8,000-12,000   L&T

A cased photograph of James Dunn, bearing paper label written in ink "James Dunn crack golfer on Musselburgh in the fifties. Willie and James played against Tom Morris and Allan Robertson on Musselburgh, N.B. and St. Andrews, were eleven up at finish".

Simpson, Sir W.G., "The Art of Golf", first edition, published by Douglas, Edinburgh.

1877

$700-1,000   L&T

$1,800-2,200   L&T

Hutchinson, Horace G., "Golf", first edition, published by Longmans, Green, London.

1890

$1,200-1,800   L&T

Kerr, John, "The Golf-Book of East Lothian, first edition, published by T&A Constable, Edinburgh.

1896

$500-700   L&T

Low, Alexander, "Low's Mixture of Poetry and Prose", first edition, newly bound in half black morocco, signature to frontispiece.

1841

$1,000-1,500   L&T

A Sam Snead signed, framed photograph.

A framed Ben Hogan photograph, together with a signed, typed personal letter.

29.5in (75cm) high

20in (51cm) high

$220-280   TA

$180-220   TA

A framed collage of photographs, relating to the Hardy museum and factory, Alnwick, England.

28in (71cm) wide

$30-50   TEN

A set of six silver golfing coffee spoons, slight dent to one.

4in (10cm) long

$80-120 **TEN**

A set of six silver-plated napkin rings, in the form of half a gutty ball, stamped "H.E.T. & Co. Sheffield".

$300-400 **L&T**

A Royal Doulton Morrisian ware teapot and cover, of almost oval section, transfer printed and painted with Aesthetic golfers on a burgundy ground printed mark.

$1,800-2,200 **L&T**

A collection of 66 silver golfing medal spoons, contained in a fitted oak canteen with lift-out tray.

$700-1,000 **L&T**

A Royal Doulton series ware proverb plate, with golfer "If at first you don't succeed ..".

10.5in (26.5cm) high

$120-180 **TEN**

Three early Dutch Delft golfing tiles, blue designs on a white background, some roughness to edges.

5in (12.5cm) wide

$280-320 **TEN**

An Arthur Wood & Sons biscuit barrel, with ropetwist gilt metal handle and silver lid with opposed panels of two golfers, registered no: 247274 and "B1302" in red.

5.5in (14cm) high

$2,200-2,800 **L&T**

An Osmonds Patent 'The Automation Caddie' canvas bag and leather carrying handles, with brass fixings, canvas golf ball pouch, mounted on a stained wood and metal frame.

$700-1,000 **BW**

A Bussey expert patent caddie, the canvas pencil bag and conforming ball and tee pouch mounted on a mahogany frame with leather strap handles and boxwood legs.

$1,800-2,200 **L&T**

A 1950s "Plus Fours" golf studs box.

2.5in (6.5cm) wide

$8-12 DH

A 1950s Blakeys golf studs box.

2.5in (6.5cm) wide

$8-12 DH

A late 19thC plated and copper golf trophy, with two C-scroll handles, inscribed "Clifton Golf Club Inc. 1898".

5in (14cm) high

$70-100 LFA

A bronze Amateur Golf Championship medal 1899, awarded to J.M. Williamson of Musselburgh, as losing semi finalist, inscribed "Prestwick 1899".

$1,800-2,200 L&T

A white metal trophy of the Scottish Amateur Challenge Shield, Gleneagles 1920, won by Tommy Armour, on an oak mount.

$3,000-5,000 L&T

A hallmarked silver golfer's smoker's stand/companion, presented in 1923.

5in (12.5cm) high

$700-1,000 TEN

Above left: A 9ct gold medal, engraved "Pau Medal, The Hamilton Medal, won by C. Oliphant 1879."

0.75in (2cm) diam

$600-900 BG

Above right: A Bombay Golf Club silver medal, established 1842, with thistle surround and engraved "H.H. Glass Captain".

2in (5cm) diam

$120-180 BG

A spelter Art Deco golfing lady figure, on plinth base.

8in (20.5cm) high

$120-180 TEN

A white metal inkstand, in the form of a golfer at the top of his swing, with a tree stump inkwell, stamped "PT & Co. Sheffield".

$400-600 L&T

An electroplated oval Rococco-style inkstand, with two gutty ball inkwells, with a golfer through his swing and crossed clubs on claw-and-ball feet.

$600-900 L&T

A pewter ashtray, in form of four golf clubs supporting a golf ball.

6in (15cm) high

$60-90 TEN

Collectors' Notes

■ The popularity of European soccer memorabilia continues to grow. Collecting, particularly soccer programs, started in the 1960s, when soccer players such as Bobby Charlton, George Best, Pelé and Bobby Moore began to be admired in the same way as pop or film stars are today.

■ Program collecting is still one of the most popular collecting areas, as prices range dramatically making them accessible to all budgets. Pre-WWI examples, particularly from cup finals, are very sought-after, as are those from important or famous matches.

■ Soccer shirts make up another key collecting area. Shirts fall into three areas: replica shirts issued by the club; shirts worn by players; and shirts worn/signed by players. The last two areas command the highest prices.

A letter on Blackburn Rovers headed paper, together with a telegram, both dated 1907 and relating to Alex Lyle.

$100-150 | **MM**

"The Cup - 50 Years English Cup Finals", first edition with photos and stories of every game.

c1932

$60-90 | **MM**

A Football Association report of the 90th anniversary celebrations on October 21, 1953, in original blue cloth cover with gold lettering and cord, good condition.

$40-60 | **MM**

A menu from Hendon Hall Hotel signed by the 1955/6 England soccer team, including Stanley Matthews and Nat Lofthouse, and another signed by the 1954 Blackpool team.

Hendon Hall Hotel is very close to Wembley Stadium and the England soccer team would stay there before a game.

8in (20.5cm) high

$250-320 | **TEN**

A postcard signed in pencil by Duncan Edwards, Colin Webster, Ray Wood, Liam Whelan, Eddie Colman and Bobby Charlton, plus another card signed by Edwards, Colman, Bill Foulkes and Jackie Blanchflower.

While returning from playing Red Star Belgrade in the European Cup, the aircraft carrying the Manchester United team together with journalists and supporters crashed at Munich airport on February 6, 1958. Among the 23 who died were Edwards, Colman and Whelan; Blanchflower survived but never played again.

$320-380 | **MM**

A World Cup 1966 Final Tie ticket, for the south terrace, priced at £3.15, central fold, otherwise very good condition.

$220-280 | **MM**

A copy of the Football Association "World Cup Report 1966", signed twice by Alf Ramsey, title page is torn and dust wrapper missing, otherwise very good condition.

$120-180 | **MM**

A copy of "Soccer Fanfare" annual, containing more than seventy autographs of footballers including Matt Busby, Jackie Milburn and Nat Lofthouse.

10in (25.5cm) high

$280-320 | **TEN**

A menu from the Football Writer's Association Annual Managers Awards Dinner signed in ink on front cover by Matt Busby, Tom Finney, Jim Armfield and Alan Ball.

1989

$70-100 | **MM**

A set of Pro-Set Football League Collection 1991/2 trade cards, in original binder, 274 individually autographed cards including West Ham and Newcastle, noted names include Cyrille Regis, Dwight Yorke, Tim Flowers.

$150-200 | **MM**

A limited edition print of Eric Cantona 'Phenomenon', from an edition of 350, signed by Cantona and official Manchester United artist E. Stuart Beckett.

34.5in (87.5cm) wide

$320-380 | **TEN**

A "Champions League 2001/2 Official Statistics Handbook", providing full information for all teams including Manchester United, Arsenal, Liverpool and Celtic, past results and other important details.

$80-120 | **MM**

A "Champions League 2001 Final" press pack, Bayern Munich v Valencia, providing full information for the match including background information, stadium and media statistics.

$40-60 | **MM**

A signed limited edition soccer print, "The Boys of '66", with ten autographs of the World Cup winning team, framed.

22in (56cm) high

$300-500 | **TEN**

A 1921 Yorkshire Football Challenge Cup 9ct gold medal, boxed.

Box 3in (7.5cm) long

$320-380 | **TEN**

A silver hallmarked medal, unattributed but acquired in Stoke-on-Trent, complete with suspension ring, engraved on rear "The Football League v The Football League of Ireland at Dublin 19th September 1956", with maker's stamp "Vaughtons and Son".

$280-320 | **MM**

A silver hallmarked Football Association Charity Shield plaque, mounted on an octagonal black Bakelite back plate, engraved "Liverpool v West Ham United Wembley 9th August 1980".

$400-600 | **MM**

A Stirling Albion FC trophy, consisting of a soccer player with ball at feet mounted on a Bakelite stand with plaque which reads "Stirling Albion FC, presented to David Irvine Esq. Director, to mark the winning of the Second Division Championship season".

1957/8 6.5in (16.5cm) high

$120-180 | **MM**

A silver hallmarked trophy, complete with lid engraved to front "Newcastle United Football Club, English Cup Winners 1931-32 Versus Rangers Football Club, Scottish Cup Winners 1931-32 at Ibrox Park Glasgow 14th September 1932".

This match was played as a British Championship decider with each team receiving a trophy.

6in (15cm) high

$280-320 | **MM**

An official Manchester United soccer shirt, bearing 21 team signatures, mounted, framed and glazed with annotation sheet on the reverse.

Overall 37.5in (95cm) high

$1,000-1,500 D

An Arsenal shirt worn by Thierry Henry, in the league game on September 8, 2001 with Premiership flashes, sponsor's logo "Dreamcast" and letter of authenticity.

$1,200-1,800 MM

A Victorian transfer-printed mug, decorated with playing scene.

3.5in (9cm) high

$180-220 TEN

A "Cup Final, 1932 'Regal' Souvenir" Zonaphone record, of the Cup Final, Newcastle v Arsenal, in original paper cover featuring photographs of both teams.

$280-320 MM

Three 8mm films of the 1962 and 1966 World Cup Finals, plus the 1970 Semi-Final, West Germany v Italy, all in original boxes.

$70-100 MM

An early edition of Subbuteo, containing players, goalposts with nets and instructions, boxed.

A pair of size five brown leather boots, with laces, a pair of Skues shin pads, an AGM whistle and a linesman's flag.

$100-150 MM

$80-120 MM

A fine set of six Royal Worcester 'Viceroy' cups and saucers, with the 'three lions' logo to each, plus a matching sugar basin and milk jug, all very good condition.

$80-120 MM

Three Wood Pottery toby jugs, comprising Stanley Matthews in Stoke City kit and Tom Finney in Preston kit, plus another of him in red England kit, plus a ceramic coaster with early soccer scene, good condition.

$80-120 MM

A six-paneled brown and white sportsman's cap, with an interesting gold embossed shield to the front with a motto "Persto et Praesto" below and dated 1930/1 to peak, slight repair to number, otherwise very good condition, complete with a wooden support 's rattle with turned wooden handle in good working order.

$120-180 MM

Three early 1970s Slazenger lawn tennis ball boxes, including a 1971 "Nylon Armoured" box with six matching green 'Panther' balls, good condition; a "Victory" box, hinge split; and "Permascore" box with three matching 'Blue Panther' balls, edges frayed.

$30-50　　　　**MM**

A rare Slazenger "No. 1 Lawn Tennis Racket Gut Reviver" bottle, with original label and cork top in original box as supplied by H. Funston Benson, Sport's Outfitters, Kingston-on-Thames, box lid corners split to one end.

1.5in (4cm) high

$180-220　　　　**MM**

An early leather horseshoe boot, used to protect lawn tennis courts while cutting the grass, complete with leather straps, studded sole and makers patent stamp marks.

$100-150　　　　**MM**

A fine "Kleenball" patent lawn tennis handheld ball cleaner, complete with bristle lining and rarely seen circular handles to each end, good condition.

$600-900　　　　**MM**

Three laminated rackets, comprising a Slazenger 'Victory' with fine color transfer, original leather grip, butt cap and stringing, and two Gray's including a 'Tournament' model with Gray's standard coat of arms, original leather grip and butt cap, and a super 'Coronation' model with "Elizabeth R. 1953" color transfer.

$30-40　　　　**MM**

A glass goblet tennis award, with engraved tennis rackets.

7.5in (19cm) high

$50-80　　　　**TEN**

A mahogany tennis racket press for four rackets, by King and Co., Hull, with leather carrying handle.

15.5in (39.5cm) wide

$120-180　　　　**TEN**

An early 1970s Teddy Tinling lady's cotton tennis dress, retailed by Harrod's, London.

$100-150　　　　**MM**

A framed set of six tennis postcards by E. P. Kinsella.

25in (63.5cm) wide

$150-200　　　　**TEN**

A Wilson tin of three tennis balls, sealed.

c1950　　　*8in (20cm) high*

$60-90　　　　**TEN**

FIND OUT MORE...

Jeanne Cherry, **'Tennis Antiques & Collectibles'***, published by Amaryllis Publishing 1995.*

An official 1928 Amsterdam Olympics program, dated 31st July and providing a full program of events for the day with competitors, results and past Olympic champions, partly completed in ink, fair condition.

1928

$180-220 MM

An official 1912 Stockholm Olympics results program, with Swedish and English text, first page loose, spine frayed and minor tears to the edges of the cover.

$15-25 MM

A Van Melle's commemorative toffee tin, to commemorate the 1928 Olympics, decorated with Olympic scene and other sporting events including track, field, rowing and cycling.

4.75in (12cm) wide

$60-80 MM

An official Olympic Competitor's medal, with colored ribbon and Olympic bar, from the 1932 Olympic Games

$120-180 MM

A scarce 1952 Olympic Games postcard, with a desktop scene depicting all competing nations' flags.

$80-120 MM

A rare 1956 Olympic Games ticket, for the final day on December 8, in the Main Stadium Melbourne Cricket Ground to include the football and closing ceremony, complete with attached perforated stub.

$40-60 MM

A set of three Lalique XVI Winter Olympic medallions, featuring sporting scenes, with original display stands and boxes.

These medallions were made in limited numbers, to the design of the gold, silver and bronze medals presented at the Olympics.

1992

4in (10cm) diam

$700-1,000 DRA

A 'The First Touch' Stevengraph, STG173, with scene of a rugby match, reframed

7.5in (19cm) wide

$600-900 TEN

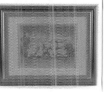

A framed photograph of Somerset County Rugby Football Union team.

1898 20.5in (52cm) wide

$100-150 TEN

A collection of three Cambridge University rugby cloth caps, in cream and red, each with crest to front and two with XI to peak, good.

$80-120 MM

An early Felix Potin, Paris "Polo" biscuit tin, with colored polo scene to lid, rust speckled.

c1900

$50-80   **MM**

A pair of Staffordshire ceramic and enamel hand-painted pillboxes, the lids decorated with hand-painted polo scenes, retailed by Mappin & Webb, the inside of the lids inscribed "The Arco Trophy June 1991" and "1993" respectively.

$100-150   **MM**

A 1980 U.S. hockey team Gold Medal winners signed photograph, signed by each player and coach Herb Brooks.

19.25in (49cm) high

$280-320   **TA**

A Wedgwood for Ralph Lauren bone china dish, with removable lid decorated with color polo match scene.

5.75in (14.5cm) wide

$40-60   **MM**

A limited edition Wedgwood 'Sporting Mug', designed by Richard Guyatt, and decorated with nine major sporting events and venues in white relief against black background, No. 381 from an edition of 500.

The scenes depicted include St.Andrews, Brands Hatch, Twickenham, Wimbledon, The Derby and Wembley.

$50-80   **MM**

A Bobby Orr signed, framed photograph, depicting Orr celebrating scoring the winning goal in the Stanley Cup championship game.

20in (51cm) wide

$280-320   **TA**

A leather gun case, by Linsley Brothers, Leeds, with brass fittings.

33.5in (85cm) long

$300-500   **TEN**

A Stuart clay pigeon trap, standard double with cover, unused.

12in (30.5cm) high

$40-60   **TEN**

A 9ct gold swimming medal.

c1938   *1in (2.5cm) diam*

$50-80   **TEN**

A 1960s Old Hall stainless steel tall 2 pint 'Connaught' coffee pot

6.75in (17.5cm) high

$30-50   **GC**

A 1960s Old Hall stainless steel coffee pot or teapot.

Note the differently shaped finials on some of these tea or coffee pots which may have indicated the contents.

6in (15.5cm) high

$30-50   **GC**

A 1960s Old Hall stainless steel three-quarter pint 'Connaught' teapot.

3.25in (8.5cm) high

$20-30   **GC**

An Old Hall stainless steel sugar sifter.

3in (8cm) high

$25-35   **GC**

An Old Hall stainless steel conical salt and pepper shakers with black plastic bases.

3in (7.5cm) high

$25-35   **GC**

A pair of 1960s Old Hall stainless steel salt and pepper shakers, marked "PAT 607716".

2.75in (7cm) high

$20-30   **GC**

An Old Hall stainless steel toast rack, with rectangular section bars and rivetted base, designed by Robert Welch.

1961   6.5in (16.5cm) long

$30-50   **GC**

Collectors Notes

- Stainless steel was first promoted publicly for domestic use at the 1934 'Ideal Home Exhibition', where Old Hall had the largest stand. Industrial designer Dr Harold Stabler was commissioned to design cutlery and tableware, but they were expensive to manufacture.

- WWII halted production, which resumed in 1945. In 1955, Old Hall appointed Robert Welch (1929-2000) as design consultant. Welch had previously specialized in stainless steel production design at the Royal College of Art and had also trained as a silversmith.

- His designs brought about a renaissance of British metal work designs. During his tenure, his pioneering 'British contemporary' style won three Design Council awards. Designs included a series of hollow ware for P&O's Oriana cruise liner, the Alveston cutlery range and Old Hall candlesticks.

- Many will remember being given Old Hall as wedding presents, such was its popularity and desirability in the 1960s and 1970s. Perhaps due to its proliferation, it has previously been overlooked by collectors. In 1982, Old Hall was sold to Oneida, but a decline in UK stainless steel led to the factory's closure in 1984.

A 1960s Old Hall stainless steel half-pint milk jug.

2.5in (6.5cm) high

$20-30   **GC**

A 1960s Old Hall stainless steel 8oz sugar bowl.

2in (5cm) high

$20-30   **GC**

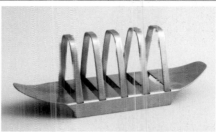

An Old Hall 'Oriana' stainless steel toast rack, designed by Robert Welch.

With its pagoda-esque lines and extreme simplicity, this toast rack won a design award in 1958 and was exhibited at the XII Milan Triennale. It was designed for use on the P&O Oriana cruise liner, hence its name.

c1958   7.25in (18.5cm) long

$30-50   **GC**

A B C D E F G H I J K L M N O P Q R S T U V W XYZ

A 1950s Old Hall stainless steel toast rack.

The finish as well as the shape shows Welch's training as a skilled silversmith working in the modern style. Each upright prong is carefully engineered to fit into the base plate seamlessly, without protruding.

3.5in (9cm) long

$40-60 GC

A pair of 1960s Old Hall stainless steel candlesticks, designed by Robert Welch.

11.75in (30cm) high

$220-280 GC

A pair of Old Hall stainless steel triple candlesticks, with wooden feet, designed by Robert Welch.

9in (23cm) high

$150-200 GC

A 1960s Viners stainless steel and gold-plated wine goblet, designed by Stuart Devlin.

7in (17.5cm) high

$30-50 GC

An Old Hall set of six 'Alveston' tablespoons, designed by Robert Welch, in original box.

c1962

6.n (15cm) long

$120-180 GC

A 1960s set of three Viners stainless steel forks and fish knives, designed by Gerald Benney, in original box.

Box 8in (21cm) long

$70-100 GC

A 1960s set of six Viners stainless steel 'Studio' pattern grapefruit forks, designed by Gerald Benney, in original box.

5.75in (14.5cm) long

$120-180 GC

A 1960s set of seven stainless steel 'Studio' pattern fruit spoons, designed by Gerald Benney, in original box.

Box 9.5in (24cm) high

$120-180 GC

FIND OUT MORE...

'Hand and Machine', by Robert Welch, published by Robert Welch, 1986.

A Viners 'Sable' dessert set, designed by Gerald Benny, with textured handles.

c1970

5in (13cm) high

$40-60 MHT

A Steiff brown mohair teddy bear, straw-filled with black boot button eyes, pointed snout, stitched nose, mouth and claws, swivel head, jointed at shoulders and hips, felt paw pads, button to left ear, nose covered with black felt.

This bear has many of the characteristics of early bears including 'boot button eyes', jointed limbs, long curved arms, a humped back and a shaved muzzle.

A Steiff brown plush 'Teddy Baby'.

8.5in (24cm) high

$700-1,000   **HGS**

c1910   12in (31cm) high

$700-1,000   **BonC**

A small Steiff golden plush teddy bear with fully jointed, center seam body stuffed with wood wool, with hump to back, pointed snout, wooden boot button eyes, and maker's stud in left ear, the body fitted with a tilt growler voice-box, replacement pads sewn on paws.

$700-1,000   **DN**

A Steiff brown teddy bear, dressed in military clothing, some losses.

The addition of a contemporary costume makes this bear attractive to collectors. Steiff bears, made in Germany, are highly desirable and usually have a button in their ear, the style of which can help to date the bear. This button was used from 1920 to 1950, and the shape of the bear suggests it was made in the 1920s or 1930s.

17in (43cm) high

$2,200-2,800   **Daw**

A Chiltern blond mohair teddy bear, with orange glass eyes, brown stitched nose, mouth and claws, shaved muzzle, swivel head and jointed at shoulders and hips, velvet paw pads.

c1930   16in (41cm) high

$320-380   **BonC**

A Chiltern golden mohair teddy bear, straw-filled with orange glass eyes, black stitched nose, mouth and claws, shaved muzzle, swivel head and jointed at shoulders and hips, velvet paw pads.

c1930   20in (51cm) high

$600-900   **BonC**

A Chiltern light brown mohair 'Hugmee' teddy bear, with glass eyes, stitched features, swivel head and jointed at shoulders and hips, velvet paw pads, some wear and damage.

c1930   15in (38cm) high

$100-150   **BonC**

A Chad Valley brown mohair teddy bear, with orange glass eyes, black stitched nose and mouth, swivel head and jointed at shoulders and hips, cloth paw pads, label to foot.

c1930   11in (28cm) high

$280-320   **BonC**

A Hermann articulated teddy bear, fully jointed, with original paper tag, good condition, one thread broken.

13in (33cm) high

$280-320   **SI**

A 1970s Merrythought 'Cheeky' dark gold mohair teddy bear, fully jointed, felt pads, wool-stitched mouth on velvet snout, label reading "Merrythought / Ironbridge, Shropshire" to foot.

15.25in (39cm) high

$400-600   **DN**

A 1920s Schuco 'Yes/No' golden mohair teddy bear, straw-filled with black boot button eyes and tail, mohair worn, paw pads damaged.

A concealed mechanism allows the head to nod or shake by moving the tail. Had he not been so well-loved and worn, the value would have been over $700.

15in (38cm) high

$280-320　　　　**BonC**

A 1920s English golden mohair teddy bear, known as 'Lionel', fully jointed wood wool-stuffed body with a small hump, glass eyes and black wool-stitched snout, inoperative growler.

26.5in (60cm) high

$150-200　　　　**DN**

A 1930s English golden plush teddy bear, possibly by Lines Bros., fully jointed with a small hump, glass eyes and black wool-stitched snout, the rear center seam with an embroidered label reading "Made in England", replacement felt pads.

$180-220　　　　**DN**

A small 1930s English light blond teddy bear, possibly by J.K. Farnell, fully jointed wood wool-stuffed body, with glass eyes and wool-stitched snout.

11.5in (29cm) high

$70-100　　　　**DN**

A small 1930s golden plush teddy bear, fully jointed, wood wool-stuffed body, glass eyes and simple stitched mouth, inoperative growler, one glass eye broken.

9.5in (24cm) high

$60-90　　　　**DN**

Two 1930s/1940s golden plush teddy bears, fully jointed bodies, with glass eyes, black wool-stitched noses and velvet pads, the larger example with detached head.

Larger 22in (56cm) high

$500-700　　　　**DN**

A 1940s English golden plush teddy bear, fully jointed wood wool-stuffed body with a hump and growler, with black wool-stitched snout and velvet pads, the rear center seam with remains of a label, minor damage to snout.

17.75in (45cm) high

$120-180　　　　**DN**

A 1930s German cinnamon-colored mohair teddy bear, possibly by Schuco, fully jointed, with glass eyes and wool-stitched snout.

Provenance: Known as 'Larry', this bear spent some time as a window display in the teddy bear shop in Swanage, UK.

15in (38cm) high

$280-320　　　　**DN**

A German dual-color mohair teddy bear, fully jointed, kapok and wood wool-stuffed body, with glass eyes and wool-stitched snout, replacement felt pads.

14.5in (37cm) high

$70-100　　　　**DN**

An English blue mohair teddy bear, straw-filled, with orange glass eyes, black stitched nose, mouth and claws, swivel head and jointed at shoulders and hips, felt paw pads.

c1950　　　*16in (41cm) high*

$180-220　　　　**BonC**

Two Dean's Rag Book Co. 'Ivy & Brumas' mohair plush polar bears.

A large Austrian light brown mohair teddy bear, with clear glass eyes, shaved muzzle and black stitched nose and mouth, swivel head and jointed at shoulders and hips, plush paw pads.

c1950   24in (61cm) high

$180-220   **BonC**

Dean's Rag Book Co produced these charming mother and cub polar bear toys to celebrate the birth of Brumas, London Zoo's first polar bear cub bred in captivity. It is rare to find the two together as they often became separated.

c1949   Larger 6.5in (16.5cm) high

$300-500   **ET**

A 1950s German mohair Steiff 'Panda Bear', straw-filled, with orange glass eyes, black stitched nose and felt-lined open mouth, swivel head and jointed at shoulders and hips, down-turned felt paw pads and plush feet.

15in (38cm) high

$300-400   **BonC**

Miniature Bears

A Schuco cinnamon plush bear.

3.5in (9cm) high

$180-220   **HGS**

A rare 1950s Schuco golden plush two-faced 'Janus' bear, with knob at base of body to twist head.

3.5in (9cm) high

$600-900   **HGS**

A CLOSER LOOK AT A MINIATURE BEAR

Schuco are very well known for their miniature toys, including bears, monkeys and mice, made between the 1920s and 1970s.

Look for rare colors, such as red and green. Gold is the most common color.

Many of them had novelty uses: this one has a concealed scent bottle.

A Schuco dark brown 'Berliner' teddy bear, with metal crown.

3in (7.5cm) high

$150-200   **HGS**

A Schuco golden plush bear.

c1950   3.5in (9cm) high

$150-200   **HGS**

A Schuco brown mohair 'Scent Bottle' teddy bear, with orange glass eyes, black plastic nose and stitched mouth, swivel head, jointed at shoulders and hips, head lifts off to reveal glass scent bottle in body.

c1950   5.5in (14cm) high

$180-220   **BonC**

A B C D E F G H I J K L M N O P Q R S T U V W XYZ

A 1950s Schuco golden plush bear.

Schuco miniature bears from the 1950s are rounder in form than earlier versions from the 1920s which have thinner limbs and larger, stitched noses.

2.75in (7cm) high

$120-180   **HGS**

A Schuco plush panda bear.

3.25in (8.5cm) high

$180-220   **HGS**

A miniature Steiff golden mohair teddy bear, with black bead eyes, black stitched nose and mouth, swivel head and jointed at shoulders and hips, button to left ear.

c1920   3.5in (9cm) high

$300-400   **BonC**

A miniature Steiff white mohair teddy bear, with black bead eyes, black stitched nose and mouth, swivel head and jointed at shoulders and hips.

c1920   3.5in (9cm) high

$280-320   **BonC**

A miniature Steiff golden mohair teddy bear, with black bead eyes, black stitched nose and mouth, swivel head and jointed at shoulders and hips.

c1920   3.5in (9cm) high

$280-320   **BonC**

An English WWI 'Mascot' golden mohair teddy bear, with clear glass eyes, black felt nose, swivel head and jointed at shoulders and hips.

c1915   3.5in (9cm) high

$300-400   **BonC**

A small gold plush teddy bear.

3.75in (9.5cm) high

$70-100   **LC**

A 1950s Steiff golden plush bear, with original tag.

6in (15cm) high

$600-900   **HGS**

Other Miniatures

A miniature Schuco brown mohair monkey, with painted metal face, felt ears, hands and feet, swivel head and jointed at shoulders and hips.

c1920   3.5in (9cm) high

$120-180   **BonC**

A Schuco plush and tinplate chimp.

2.5in (6cm) high

$80-120   **HGS**

A rare Schuco red plush, felt-dressed monkey.

3.25in. (8.5cm) high

$700-1,000   **HGS**

A rare Schuco orange plush and felt dressed monkey.

3.25in. (8.5cm) high

$700-1,000   **HGS**

A Schuco brown plush and color-lithographed tinplate 'Blecky' monkey.

Turning the plastic pole at the base of his body shakes his head and pushing it makes his tongue stick out.

3.25in. (8.5cm) high

$350-400   **HGS**

A very rare Schuco blue plush, tin and felt monkey pin.

This monkey is rare twice over; it is a pin and it is in blue.

3.25in. (8.5cm) high

$1,800-2,200   **HGS**

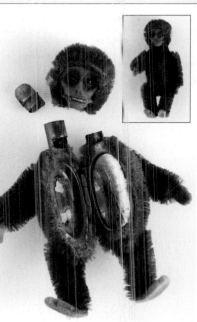

FIND OUT MORE...

'**Bears**' by Sue Pearson, published by De Agostini Editions Ltd., 1995.

'**Teddy Bear Encyclopaedia**', published by Dorling Kindersley, 2001.

Puppenhaus Museum, Steineck-Foundation, Steinenvorstadt 1, 4051 Basle, Switzerland. www.puppenhausmuseum.ch
A collection of over 2,000 teddy bears, most dating from before 1950.

A Schuco mid-brown monkey compact.

The head pulls off to reveal the compact.

3.5in (9cm) high

$300-400   **HGS**

A B C D E F G H I J K L M N O P Q R S T U V W XYZ

A Steiff gray felt elephant on wheels, with black button eyes and white felt tusks, with red felt saddle with gold embroidery, on a metal frame and with wooden wheels, button to left ear.

c1918   *10in (25cm) high*

$300-500   **BonC**

A Steiff elephant, with original ear and neck tags, blanket with bells.

7.5in (19cm) long

$70-100   **NB**

Collectors' Notes

- Margarete Steiff first made animal-shaped pin cushions in the 1890s to give to friends as gifts. Steiff became one of the earliest and most prolific producers of soft toys. As with the company's more famous teddy bears, the button, material and style can help date the toy.
- The 1920s to the 1950s saw the golden age of the soft toy, with Schuco, Chad Valley and others moving into the market. From the 1960s, lesser quality Far Eastern imports flooded the market.
- Look for toys by known makers in fine and clean condition with original labels intact. Large and unusual animals or creatures are popular as are cartoon and character toys.

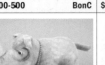

A Steiff rhinoceros, with wood wool stuffed body, felt horn, glass eyes and gray felt pads, with metal tag and yellow label in left ear.

11.5in (29cm) long

$70-100   **DN**

A Steiff white plush lamb, with black boot button eyes, pink stitched nose and mouth, button in left ear.

c1920   *10in (25cm) high*

$50-80   **BonC**

A 1950s Steiff 'Mecki' Hedgehog, with rubber face, rosy cheeks, smile and spiked hair, swivel head to felt body with fur belly, jointed at shoulders and hips, wearing red and white check shirt, gray patched pair of pants held with string, and waist coat, carrying a wooden spoon.

10.52in (27cm) high

$120-180   **BonC**

A Steiff Santa, clown and gnomes, all with rubber heads, Santa wearing red felt outfit and hat, three gnomes wearing felt clothes and hats with large pointed leather shoes.

c1960

$220-280   **BonC**

A miniature ladybird, possibly Steiff, with red bristle coat and black bristle wire legs and antennae.

2.75in (7cm) long

$30-50   **F**

A Schuco Yes/No monkey, with painted metal eyes, plush head and mask face, felt ears, wearing sewn-on bellboy felt clothes of red cap, jacket and boots, black pair of pants, mechanism to tail for Yes/No movement to head.

Moving his rigid tail allows you to make his head nod, or for him to shake his head, hence the 'Yes/No' name. A Yes/No teddy bear was also made, which can be more valuable, depending on condition and size.

c1920   *8in (20cm) high*

$180-220   **BonC**

A Schuco plush and pipe cleaner ladybird.

3.25in (8cm) long

$220-280   **HGS**

A Schuco plush, felt and pipe cleaner duck.

3.5in (9cm) high

$220-280   **HGS**

A 1950s Agnes Brush Winnie The Pooh.

Agnes Brush of Long Island, New York made characters from Winnie The Pooh during the 1940s and 1950s.

13.5in (34cm) high

$300-500   **HGS**

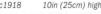

A 1930s black Bakelite 200 series telephone.

These telephones are currently being reproduced in the Far East. One way to tell whether an example is genuine is to run your finger over the numbers on the handset bar. If they are not crisp, it is usually a remolded reproduction.

8in (20cm) wide

$280-320　　L

A CLOSER LOOK AT A TRIMPHONE

The orange color is very rare. Trimphones were originally produced in three two-tone colorways: light gray, green or blue, which are more common and less valuable.

The handset was designed for comfort as well as style and was the first to be placed over the dial rather than at right angles to it. The dial was replaced with buttons c1973.

The design, released in 1964, is modern, minimalist and was highly fashionable in its day. It is now considered by many to be a 20th century design classic.

This was the first telephone without a bell. The 'tone caller' could be altered allowing soft, escalating volume or no tone options.

A rare 1970s orange plastic Trimphone.

8in (20cm) long

$120-180　　L

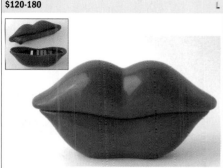

A 1980s red plastic 'Hot Lips' telephone.

8.5in (21.5cm) wide

$40-60　　L

A 1950s black Bakelite 300 series telephone, with original lead.

6in (15cm) wide

$180-220　　L

A 1960s red plastic telephone, by the Reliance Telephone Co.

5in (12.5cm) wide

$60-90　　L

A 1960s red plastic telephone, by the Reliance Telephone Co.

5in (12.5cm) wide

$60-90　　L

A wooden Trub telephone, by Gfeller, designed in the 1970s.

c1994　8.25in (21cm) wide

$100-150　　L

A 1970s cream plastic Ericofon telephone, by Ericsson

The Ericofon was designed in the late 1940s and went into production in 1954. The stylish one-piece design, with the dial in its base, was launched for domestic use in 1956. It came in a multitude of colors. It was discontinued in 1972. Collectors should be aware that modern copies are now on sale.

8.25in (21cm) high

$100-150　　L

A blue plastic 'Cla' T1000GD telephone, by Thomson, designed by Philippe Starck.

11in (28cm) long

$70-100　　L

TELEVISIONS

An American Philco Projection set 48-2500.

1948

$800-1,200   **TVH**

A British Baird 'Everyman' tabletop television.

The front of this television has an applied medallion showing a portrait of John Logie Baird, who died in 1946.

c1949   12in (30.5cm) high

$300-500   **TVH**

Collectors' Notes

■ The world's first domestic television sets were sold to wealthy individuals in London in 1936. As with many early sets, they were beautifully cased in wood. The first daily public service in the US was launched on April 30, 1939 by NBC in New York. Unlike in the UK, the war did not interrupt broadcasting, but few Americans had TV sets, with only around 7,000 sets existing by 1941.

■ Prewar sets are very rare and hard to value. Sizes are typically large and they are usually cased in wood. Examples from the 1950s onward are quite common.

■ Look for landmark examples that exemplify styles of the period, or those that are made from fine materials or are considered design classics, such as the 'Sputnik'. Completeness and condition is important.

A British Pye LV306 television.

c1950

$220-280   **TVH**

A British Pye VT2 television.

c1951

$180-220   **TVH**

A Bush TV62 table television set.

c1956

$120-180   **LC**

An American Philco Preduta television.

c1959

$400-600   **TVH**

A 1970s National Commando 505 portable television.

12in (30.5cm) high

$60-90   **L**

A Keracolor, model B722 television.

This model with a 'teak' appearance finish is extremely scarce.

c1970   33.75in (86cm) high

$700-1,000   **L&T**

An American RCA 'Personal' 8-PT-7030 television, with telescopic aerials.

c1956

$120-180   **TVH**

A 1970s JVC 'Videosphere' television set.

This set was also known as the 'Sputnik' set after the Russian satellites launched in 1957.

12.5in (32cm) high

$300-500   **L&T**

FIND OUT MORE:

Website: www.tvhistory.tv

'TV is King', by Michael Bennett-Levy, by MBL Publications for an exhibition at Sotheby's, 1994.

A Philips 'Discoverer' television set.

c1990   12.5in (32cm) high

$280-320   **L&T**

Collectors' Notes

- Samplers were made by girls and young ladies to practice and demonstrate their needlework skills. Most samplers for sale date from the 19th century, although 17th and 18th century examples can be found, they are expensive.
- Samplers including alphabets, natural themes, such as leaves and flowers, and pastoral scenes are the most common. Colorful, humorous or pictorial examples are sought after as are early versions and those with names, dates and place names.
- Fading, tears and losses will affect value. Look for clean bright and fresh examples. Damage can be caused by unprofessional framing.

An American sampler, by Sarah Evans, completed at 12 years of age, with figures, animals and vine border, surrounding a prayer.

17in (43cm) high

$400-600　　　**AAC**

A needlework sampler, by Sarah Sisson, worked in rows with the alphabet, verses, trees, animals and birds within red fruiting vine border.

1805　17.75 (45cm) high

$700-1,000　　　**Chef**

An early 19thC needlework sampler, by Mary Westoby, with a verse above "Adam" and "Eve" amongst flowers, flanked by orange trees and above reclining stags.

1810　15.75in (40cm) wide

$600-900　　　**Chef**

An early Victorian sampler, worked in colored silks by Mary Ann Bird, aged nine and dated "Aug' 2nd 1839", glazed and framed, some discoloration, foxing and holes to bottom.

15.25in (39cm) high

$700-1,000　　　**KBon**

A late Victorian stitch sampler, by A.G. Stubbs, worked in red wools.

1892　11 5in (29cm) high

$150-200　　　**KBon**

A Victorian needle point embroidery, worked in multi-colored wools and silks depicting a three quarter length portrait of rural girl with a goat beside a tree within a country landscape glazed and framed

18.75in (47.5cm) high

$180-220　　　**KBon**

A beadwork-on-card armorial panel, decorated with a coat-of-arms, in a gilt frame.

Small beads denote an early piece. Beadwork pieces retain their color over long periods as the beads are made from colored glass that does not fade in the light.

c1850-60 16.5in (42cm) wide

$700-1,000　　　**FJA**

A 19thC Chinese panel, worked in colored silks on burgundy silk satin, depicting central mythical dragon, surmounted by a scroll and surrounded by butterflies and mythical birds amidst floral sprays and peonies, mounted, glazed and framed.

32.75in (83cm) wide

$120-180　　　**KBon**

A mid-19thC panel, probably Ottoman, embroidered in silks on linen, with four bands of stylized flowerhead motifs and geometric patterns, with braided edging reserved against a green velvet ground, set within a glazed mahogany fire screen.

23.5in (60cm) high

$280-320 | **KBon**

A 19thC American linen show towel, with red cross-stitched embroidery of flowers, applied woven border and fringe, light staining.

40in (101.5cm) long

$60-90 | **AAC**

An American show towel panel, woven and embroidered with potted flowers and tulip design, with initials "L.K." for Lydia Kriebel, Worcester, Montgomery City, PA.

14.5in (37cm) long

$120-180 | **AAC**

A mid-20thC American white linen pillow case, with drawn work and embroidery.

32.25in (82cm) long

$20-30 | **AAC**

An 1870s European woven wool and silk shawl, with harlequin ends and polychrome fringe detailing, minor faults.

131.5in (334cm) long

$220-280 | **KBon**

An American red, white and blue silk commemorative panel, with eagle, reading "PAX 1901", copyright for Pan American Exposition Co.

c1901   *20.5in (52cm) wide*

$30-50 | **AAC**

Two George Washington Stevengraphs, one by L. Steven of Coventry for the US market; the other by Paterson of New Jersey, with tassel.

Stevengraphs are woven silk pictures invented by Thomas Stevens and were made primarily in England. They were first made as bookmarks c1862, with pictures appearing in 1879, production ceased c1938.

$80-120 | **JDJ**

A late 19thC/early 20thC American log cabin quilt top, in calicos and prints.

38.5in (98cm) wide

$40-60 | **AAC**

An early 20thC American printed cotton handkerchief holder.

11.5in (29cm) wide

$15-25 | **AAC**

A small box of American early printed quilt patches, in calicos, solids and others.

c1900   *2.25in (6cm) wide*

$30-50 | **AAC**

"The Home Art Of Fancy Stitchery", edited by Flora Klickman and published by Frederick A. Stokes & Co., New York, early 1900s.

$15-25 | **AAC**

Garland, Madge, "Fashion - A Picture Guide to its Creators and Creations", published by Penguin, Maryland.

1962

$30-50 | **AAC**

Collectors' Notes

- Corgi toys were first released in 1956 and were often known as 'the ones with the windows' due to their innovation of having plastic windows. They were made by Metoy, founded in the 1930s and based in Wales, UK, as a competitor to Dinky's popular 'Supertoys'.

- By 1959, boots and doors opened and suspension was added, known as 'glidamatic'. Corgi also produced a number of highly successful TV and film tie-in models from the 1960s onward, most notably related to James Bond. Today these are of interest to collectors of film and TV memorabilia as well as Corgi collectors.

- All toys are known by a model number, which helps to date and identify them. However, some numbers were used for more than one model and numbers do not run consecutively in date order.

- Versions and variations add excitement to the hunt and diversity to a collection. Look for rare colors, different interiors or other variations such as cast wheels or 'WhizzWheels', as these can often be more valuable. 'Superdetailing' kits were sold in the 1960s and included window stickers, however, these additions will devalue the toy. Where alternative prices are given, these are for mint models in mint and complete packaging. If the condition is less than mint, then sadly the value will be too.

- Condition must be considered due to the large number of models produced. Many were played with and became worn or damaged. Unless rare, they will not be as desirable to collectors. Scratches and abrasions will devalue a toy, but do not repaint it as this will devalue it further. Boxes are essential, but they must be in excellent condition too.

A Corgi No. 201 Austin Cambridge Saloon, turquoise, flat spun hubs, near mint condition, good condition box.

The green and cream color combination is rarer and is usually 50% more valuable.

1956-61

$120-180 Vec

A Corgi No. 236 Austin A60 Motor School Car, pale blue, spun hubs, mint condition, in good condition box.

A left-hand drive model, with box and leaflet, can double the value.

1964-68

$70-100 Vec

A Corgi No. 224 Bentley Continental Sports Saloon, cream, green, red interior, spun hubs, excellent condition, in excellent condition blue and yellow carded box.

1961-65

$180-220 Vec

A Corgi No. 255 Austin Motor School Car, dark blue, spun hubs, export issue, excellent condition, in good condition blue and yellow carded box.

1964-68

$150-200 Vec

A Corgi No. 475 Citroen Safari "1964 Olympic Winter Sports", white, red skis and sticks, figure, near mint condition, in good but grubby blue and yellow carded box.

1964-65

$150-200 Vec

A Corgi Daktari gift set No. 7, camouflaged open back Land Rover, WhizzWheels, with Dr Marsh Tracy and Paula figures, Judy the Chimp, Clarence to Lion and Tiger, in original packing, with packing bubble, mirror wear.

1968-76

$120-180 W&W

A Corgi No. 246 Chrysler Imperial, red, pale green interior, good condition, in good condition box

The metallic kingfisher blue version, with green interior is worth up to four times the value of this version in excellent condition, with the box.

1965-68

$60-90 Vec

A Corgi No. 233 Heinkel Economy Car, light mauve, spun hubs, near mint condition, in excellent box.

1962-72

$120-180 Vec

A Corgi No. 259 Le Dandy Coupé, blue, white, wire wheels, near mint condition, in excellent condition box.

1966-69

$220-280   **Vec**

A Corgi No. 328 Hillman Imp "Rally Monte Carlo", blue, racing No. 107, spun hubs, mint condition apart from weak rear suspension weak, in good condition blue and yellow box.

If the advertising leaflet is present with this car and the box, add roughly 20% to the value.

1966-67

$100-150   **Vec**

A Corgi No. 335 Jaguar E-type, red, wire wheels, excellent condition including bubble pack, one split to end which has been repaired.

1968-70

$60-90   **Vec**

A Corgi No. 351 Land Rover "RAF", blue, tin rear canopy, flat spun hubs, excellent condition, slight roof mark, in good condition box.

1958-62

$100-150   **Vec**

A Corgi No. 438 Land Rover, metallic green, gray plastic canopy, spun hubs, excellent condition apart from very slight roof marks, in good but grubby blue and yellow carded box.

1963-77

$100-150   **Vec**

A Corgi No. 262 Lincoln Continental Executive Limousine, gold, black, spun hubs, excellent condition, in good condition blister card.

1967-69

$100-150   **Vec**

A Corgi No. 230 Mercedes Benz 220SE Coupé, red, lemon interior, spun hubs, excellent condition, showing slight surface corrosion to base and interior slightly sun faded, in good condition.

1962-64

$70-100   **Vec**

A Corgi No. 230 Mercedes Benz 220SE Coupé, cream, red interior, spun hubs, excellent condition, has been slightly Superdetailed, in good condition box.

1962-64

$60-90   **Vec**

A Corgi No. 253 Mercedes Benz 220SE Coupé, blue, spun hubs, mint condition, couple of casting marks to roof, in good but slightly grubby blue and yellow carded box.

1964-68

$100-150   **Vec**

A Corgi No. 333 Mini Cooper "International Rally", red, white roof, spun hubs, racing No. 21, mint condition, very minor marks, in excellent condition box with flash.

c1966

$280-320   **Vec**

A Corgi No. 226 Morris Mini Minor, dark red, lemon interior, cast hubs, excellent condition, couple of very minor marks to roof, in excellent condition box.

Sky blue or yellow bodies are the rarest colorways and can be worth more than twice the value of the more common red and maroon versions.

1960-68

$120-180   **Vec**

A Corgi Morris Mini Minor, light blue body, red interior, spun hubs, boxed.

$120-180   W&W

A Corgi No. 202 Morris Cowley, gray, flat spun hubs, near mint condition, has been restored, in good condition box.

This example is worth less than the other example as it has been restored, so is not original.

1956-61

$60-90   Vec

A Corgi No. 202 Morris Cowley Saloon, gray, flat spun hubs, near mint condition, in good condition although grubby all-carded blue box.

1956-61

$120-180   Vec

A Corgi No. 205 Riley Pathfinder Saloon, red, flat spun hubs, good condition, in fair but complete all-carded blue box.

1956-62

$70-100   Vec

A Corgi No. 209 Riley Pathfinder Police Car, black, flat spun hubs, aerial, roof box, good condition in good condition all-carded blue box.

1958-61

$120-180   Vec

A Corgi No. 281 Rover 2000TC, purple yellow interior WhizzWheels, near mint condition in excellent condition orange and yellow window box, one end flap slightly marked.

1971-72

$100-150   Vec

A Corgi No. 207 Standard Vanguard Saloon, red over pale green, flat spun hubs, good condition in good condition box.

1957-62

$120-180   Vec

A Corgi No. 352 Standard Vanguard "RAF Staff" Car, blue, flat spun hubs, near mint condition in fair box.

1958-62

$60-90   Vec

A Corgi No. 203 Vauxhall Velox Saloon, flat spun hubs, near mint condition, slightly retouched, in excellent condition.

Also available in red or yellow at the same value range. Early versions came with a leaflet.

1956-61

$120-180   Vec

A Corgi 256 Volkswagen 1200, with East African Safari Trim and rhino, very good condition, boxed.

1965-68

$280-320   Chef

A Corgi No. 228 Volvo P1800, beige, red interior, spun hubs, near mint condition, in good condition box

1962-65

$120-180   Vec

A Corgi No. 258 Volvo P1800 "The Saint's" Car, white, red interior, spun hubs excellent condition, with a very slight hairline crack to front screen and very slight retouching, fair but complete box.

1965-70

$70-100   Vec

A Corgi No. 404 Bedford Dormobile Personnel Carrier, cream, flat spun hubs, near mint condition in good condition box.

Look for the yellow and blue two-tone version. This earlier version is identified by its split windscreen.

1956-62

$120-180   Vec

A Corgi No. 404 Bedford Dormobile Personnel Carrier, cerise, flat spun hubs, good condition has been slightly retouched, in incorrect No. 404M fair but complete all-carded blue box.

$50-80   **Vec**

A Corgi No. 404 Bedford Dormobile Personnel Carrier, yellow, blue roof, spun hubs, excellent condition, slight marks to one side, in good but grubby all-carded blue box.

1956-62

$120-180   **Vec**

A Corgi No. 405 Bedford AFS Tender, green, black ladders, flat spun hubs, near mint condition, very slight Superdetailing, in good condition box.

1956-60

$120-180   **Vec**

A Corgi No. 462 Commer Van "Hammonds", blue, green, white, cast hubs, near mint condition in excellent condition box, damage to one flap.

c1971

$120-180   **Vec**

A Corgi No. 1134 Bedford S "US Army" Fuel Tanker, green, spun hubs, good condition in good condition although grubby around corners blue and yellow carded box.

1965-66

$220-280   **Vec**

A Corgi No. 483 Dodge Kew Fargo Tipper, white, blue, graphite gray chassis, cast hubs, overall excellent condition, apart from bonnet shade is slightly lighter and discoloration to bare metal parts, in good condition blue and yellow carded box.

1968-72

$60-90   **Vec**

A Corgi No. 435 Karrier Bantam Dairy produce van, in light blue with white roof, 'Drive Safely on Milk' decals, boxed, some wear.

1962-63

$50-80   **W&W**

A Corgi 64 Working Conveyor on Forward Control Jeep FC-150, very good condition, boxed.

1965-69

$80-120   **Chef**

A Corgi 150S Vanwall Formula 1 Grand Prix, very good condition, box lacks one end flap.

1961-65

$30-50   **Chef**

A Corgi No. 515a Lotus Mark 11 Le Mans Racing Car, blue, racing No. 3, flat spun hubs, excellent condition, with slight wear to front decal, in good condition blue and yellow carded box, one end flap has been re-Sellotaped.

$120-180   **Vec**

A Corgi No. 313 Ford Cortina GXL "Graham Hill", metallic bronze, black roof, white interior, WhizzWheels, mint condition in orange and yellow window box.

Look for the rare left-hand drive promotional variation with a tan body and a black roof, which can be worth double the value of the standard model.

1970-73

$120-180   **Vec**

A Corgi No. 261 "James Bond" Aston Martin DB5, gold, red interior, silver wire wheels and bumper, in original blue and yellow picture box, with inner pictorial stand, minor wear, complete with secret instructions in opened packet, and self-adhesive unused 007 badge, few minor marks.

1965-69

$150-200   **W&W**

A Corgi No. 261 "James Bond" Aston Martin DB5, with secret instructions, very good condition, boxed.

The difference in price is that this model, the box and accessories are in better condition than the example on the left.

1965-69

$400-600   **Chef**

A Corgi No. 336 "James Bond" Toyota 2000GT, very good condition, boxed.

1967-69

$300-500   **Chef**

A Corgi No. 267 "Batman" Batmobile, black, red wheels, although appear not to be original and fitted at a later date, excellent condition, in good condition slimline blue and yellow window box, missing one inner end flap and secret instruction pack.

1966-77

$220-280   **Vec**

A Corgi No. 269 "James Bond" Lotus Esprit from "The Spy Who Loved Me", white, black, missiles still attached to sprue, mint condition with inner pictorial stand, outer film strip, window box, good condition, although recellophaned.

At the film's premier in 1977, ten gold-plated versions were given out to VIPs.

1977-83

$70-100   **Vec**

A Corgi No. 107 "Batman" Batboat on Trailer, black, orange, gold, mint condition in excellent condition box.

1974-81

$220-280   **Vec**

A Corgi No. 267 "Batman" Batmobile, lacks missiles etc, fair to good condition, box.

$70-100   **Chef**

A Corgi No. 497 "The Man from U.N.C.L.E." Gun Firing Thrush-Buster, lacks ring, overall very good condition, boxed.

1966-69

$180-220   **Chef**

A Corgi No. 497 "The Man From U.N.C.L.E." Thrustbuster, blue, plastic lamps, cast wheels, Waverley ring, mint condition inner pictorial stand excellent.

c1966

$350-400   **Vec**

A Corgi No. 497 "The Man From U.N.C.L.E." Thrushbuster, white, cast wheels and lamps, overall excellent condition retouched in many places, with inner pictorial stand excellent condition, outer picture box good condition.

The white version is rarer than the purplish metallic blue version, hence the higher price.

c1966

$400-600   **Vec**

A scarce Corgi No. 803 Beatles Yellow Submarine, yellow and white body with psychedelic decoration, four periscopes to conning tower, two red hatch covers over four figures, in original box, with green/blue plastic inner.

The version with one red and one white hatch cover can be worth up to 50% more than this version. Unboxed in average condition, these models are relatively common.

1970-71

$500-700   **W&W**

A Corgi No. 266 Chitty Chitty Bang Bang, interior box floor missing, otherwise very good condition, box damaged.

1968-72

$100-150   **Chef**

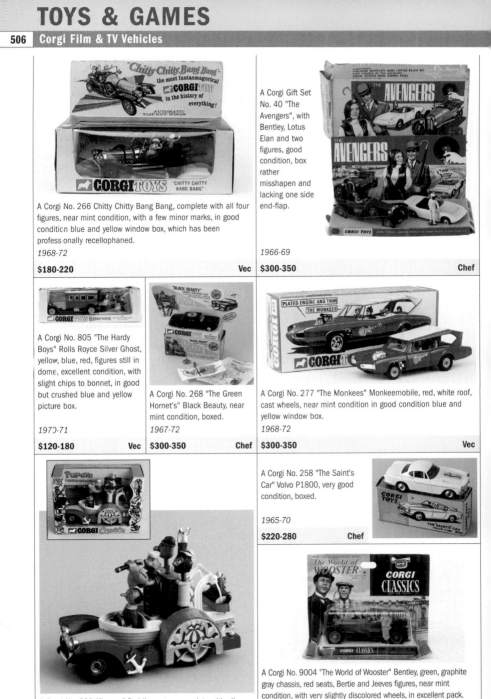

A Corgi No. 266 Chitty Chitty Bang Bang, complete with all four figures, near mint condition, with a few minor marks, in good condition blue and yellow window box, which has been professionally recellophaned.

1968-72

$180-220 Vec

A Corgi Gift Set No. 40 "The Avengers", with Bentley, Lotus Elan and two figures, good condition, box rather misshapen and lacking one side end-flap.

1966-69

$300-350 Chef

A Corgi No. 805 "The Hardy Boys" Rolls Royce Silver Ghost, yellow, blue, red, figures still in dome, excellent condition, with slight chips to bonnet, in good but crushed blue and yellow picture box.

1970-71

$120-180 Vec

A Corgi No. 268 "The Green Hornet's" Black Beauty, near mint condition, boxed.

1967-72

$300-350 Chef

A Corgi No. 277 "The Monkees" Monkeemobile, red, white roof, cast wheels, near mint condition in good condition blue and yellow window box.

1968-72

$300-350 Vec

A Corgi No. 258 "The Saint's Car" Volvo P1800, very good condition, boxed.

1965-70

$220-280 Chef

A Corgi No. 802 "Popeye" Paddle wagon, complete with all original parts and in working order, in a reproduction box, some age wear and chipping.

1969-72

$120-180 W&W

A Corgi No. 9004 "The World of Wooster" Bentley, green, graphite gray chassis, red seats, Bertie and Jeeves figures, near mint condition, with very slightly discolored wheels, in excellent pack.

This was inspired by the adaptation of the popular novels by P.G. Wodehouse, starring Ian Carmichael as the calamitous Bertie Wooster.

1967-69

$150-200 Vec

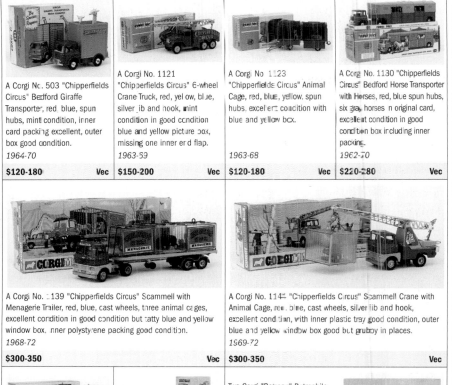

A Corgi No. 503 "Chipperfields Circus" Bedford Giraffe Transporter, red, blue, spun hubs, mint condition, inner card packing excellent, outer box good condition.
1964-70

$120-180 Vec

A Corgi No. 1121 "Chipperfields Circus" 6-wheel Crane Truck, red, yellow, blue, silver jib and hook, mint condition in good condition blue and yellow picture box, missing one inner end flap.
1963-69

$150-200 Vec

A Corgi No. 1123 "Chipperfields Circus" Animal Cage, red, blue, yellow, spun hubs, excellent condition with blue and yellow box.
1963-68

$120-180 Vec

A Corgi No. 1130 "Chipperfields Circus" Bedford Horse Transporter with Horses, red, blue spun hubs, six grey horses in original card, excellent condition in good condition box including inner packing.
1962-70

$220-280 Vec

A Corgi No. 1139 "Chipperfields Circus" Scammell with Menagerie Trailer, red, blue, cast wheels, three animal cages, excellent condition in good condition but tatty blue and yellow window box, inner polystyrene packing good condition.
1968-72

$300-350 Vec

A Corgi No. 1144 "Chipperfields Circus" Scammell Crane with Animal Cage, red, blue, cast wheels, silver jib and hook, excellent condition, with inner plastic tray good condition, outer blue and yellow window box good but grubby in places.
1969-72

$300-350 Vec

A Corgi No. GS19 "Chipperfields Circus" Gift Set, comprising Land Rover with tin canopy and Elephant Cage on Trailer red, blue, spun hubs, good to excellent condition in excellent condition box.
1962-68

$280-320 Vec

Three Corgi Accessories Packs, comprising one "James Bond" Toyota 2000 and two "The Green Hornet", generally good condition.

$180-220 Vec

Two Corgi "Batman" Batmobile Accessory Packs, each containing missiles still attached to sprue, near mint condition, unopened.

$150-200 Vec

Four Corgi advertising signs, comprising a hanging sign; and a smaller hanging sign; a shelf display and a card header stand taken from display stand, fair to excellent condition.

$180-220 (for four) Vec

A small Corgi oval glass display sign.

$280-320 Vec

FIND OUT MORE...

'Ramsey's British Die-Cast Model Toys Catalogue' by John Ramsey, 9th edition, Swapmeet Publications, 2001.

'The Unauthorised Encyclopedia of Corgi Toys', by Bill Manzke, published by Schiffer Publishing, 1997.

Collectors' Notes

- Dinky Toys were first released in 1931 as 'Model Miniatures' accessories to Hornby train sets and were made by Meccano Ltd of Liverpool, UK. Cars were first released in 1934 in the '22' series. They were very popular and competed with the American 'Tootsie Toys' produced at the same time.

- By 1835, there were 200 models to choose from. The 'golden age' of Dinky toys is considered to be between 1931 and 1941, and today, these prewar Dinkys are much sought after and valuable. Production declined during the war. 'Supertoys' were introduced in 1947 and 'Speedwheels' in the 1970s.

- Model numbers help identify a car model and date range. Look out for variations, such as different colors or versions released for certain markets, such as the American or Canadian markets. These can be worth more. Where footnotes give values for alternative variations, these are for mint examples in mint boxes.

- As with all mass-produced items, always consider condition. Prewar Dinkys were made from an unstable alloy which tends to crystallize and fall apart. Condition is important to value. Collectors tend to grade models poor, fair, good, very good, excellent, mint.

- On postwar examples, look carefully for scratches, bruises and other damage which devalues a toy. Boxes should accompany a toy to make it valuable, and these too should be in excellent condition. Models from the 1950-1960s and gift sets are currently very popular.

- By 1979 when the famed Binns Road, Liverpool factory closed, over 1,000 different models had been designed and produced. In 1987, the name was bought by Matchbox and in 1999, the Matchbox brand was bought by Mattel, who make Barbie. Since 2001, the Dinky name has been dormant.

A Dinky No. 30c Daimler, fawn body, black chassis, black ridged hubs, excellent condition, slight mark to roof.
1946-50

$100-150 | Vec

A Dinky No. 30d Vauxhall, olive green, black open chassis, black ridged wheels, good condition.
c1946

$100-150 | Vec

A Dinky No. 30f Ambulance, cream, black chassis, black ridged hubs, good condition.
1947-48

$70-100 | Vec

A Dinky No. 38c Lagonda, green, dark green interior, black ridged hubs, silvered windscreen, excellent condition.
1947-50

$150-200 | Vec

A Dinky Streamlined Fire Engine, red, black ridged hubs, ladder and bell, together with a Streamlined Coach, gray, dark blue mudguards, black ridged wheels, and a Motor Breakdown Truck, red, black ridged wheels, all in good condition.

$150-200 | Vec

Two Dinky cars, a No. 238 Jaguar D type racing car in turquoise, no racing number and a No. 181 Volkswagen Beetle in gray with blue wheels, boxed, minor age wear, minor paint chips.
1951-60

$80-120 | W&W

A Dinky No. 172 Studebaker Land Cruiser, cream lower body, light tan upper body, cream ridged wheels, excellent condition in incorrect box.
1956-58

$100-150 | Vec

A Dinky No. 157 Jaguar XK 120 coupe, two-tone in cerise and duck egg blue, in associated box, some wear to box, minor wear to vehicle.
1957-59

$180-220 | W&W

A Dinky No. 448 Chevrolet Pick-Up and Trailers, good condition.
1963-68

$150-200 | Chef

A Dinky No. 277 Superior Criterion Ambulance, fair condition.

Examples with a 'gold' see-through box are slightly more desirable and valuable than examples with this box

1962-68

$30-50   Chef

A scarce French Dinky Kart No. 512, midget racer with driver, blue cart, silver engine, black wheels, red and gray dressed driver with white helmet, in original box, minor wear.

$180-220   W&W

A Dinky No. 901 Foden Diesel 8-wheel Wagon, second type cab, red cab and chassis, Supertoy wheels, fawn back, small retouch to mudguard, excellent condition in poor box.

1954-57

$150-200   Vec

A Dinky Supertoys No 943 Leyland Octopus Tanker - Esso, fair condition boxed.

1958-64

$120-180   Chef

A Dinky Supertoys No. 563 Crawler Tractor, good condition, boxed.

1948-54

$70-100   Chef

A Dinky Supertoys No. 923 Big Bedford Van 'Heinz', fair to good condition, box worn.

Look out for the variation advertising Heinz Tomato Ketchup, which is much scarcer, having been produced between 1958 and 1959 only, and which can be worth eight times the value of this version in mint condition with mint packaging.

1955-58

$180-220   Chef

A Dinky Supertoys No. 965 Euclid Rear Dump Truck, very good condition, boxed.

1955-61

$120-180   Chef

A scarce prewar Dinky No. 30b Rolls Royce car, with open chassis finished in dark blue with black chassis, white tires, signs of chassis expansion leading to some bowing, minor chips to paint.

1935-40

$180-220   W&W

A scarce prewar Dinky No. 12 Postal Set, comprising Air and GPO Pillar Boxes, Telephone Call Booth in red, additional Call Booth in white, Postman, and No. 34b Royal Mail Van, GR to sides, open windows, all in original blue card box with yellow insert, with original blue string, minor fading to box.

1937-41

$600-900   W&W

A scarce prewar Dinky 33 series No. 33a Mechanical Horse, No. 33d Box Van Trailer with "Hornby Trains", "British Guaranteed" to sides, and No. 33e Dust Wagon Trailer, open wagon, tinplate cover with shutter, and flat truck.

c1935

$320-380   W&W

A scarce prewar Dinky No. 45 Garage, in colorful litho print tinplate, orange tile pattern roof, two opening green doors to front, cream walls, in original card box, minor discoloration and wear.

1935-40

$350-400   W&W

A scarce prewar Dinky No. 48 Gas Station, multi-color finish tinplate and printed garage windows, oil cabinets, in original card box with corrugated card packing piece, together with a T & B petrol pumps Cleveland, Shell, Power and Esso, and a Dinky Pratts motor oil bin, rust to staples, minor fatigue, four spots of rust to underside of base, one hose missing.
1935-41

$400-600 | **W&W**

A Dinky prewar No. 60d Low-Wing Monoplane, red, cream wing tips, silver propeller, good condition, some minor chips around engine housing.
1934-36

$150-200 | **Vec**

A prewar Dinky No. 60s pair of Medium Bombers, with shadow shading camouflage, one with slight fatigue to wings, the other showing no visible signs of fatigue, in good condition box, missing base to box.
1938-40

$300-500 | **Vec**

A Dinky No. 60t Douglas DC3 Airliner, red propellers, gliding pin and hole, PH-ALI, excellent condition, in excellent box.
1938-41

$400-600 | **Vec**

A Dinky No. 60v Armstrong Whitworth Bomber, silver, roundels to wings, gliding pin hole, good condition with no visible signs of fatigue, in good condition box complete with slightly faded instruction leaflet.
1937-41

$280-320 | **Vec**

A Dinky No. 60k Percival Gull "Amy Mollinson", mid-blue, silver, silver propeller, G-A DZO, excellent condition, in good box.
1945-48

$400-600 | **Vec**

A Dinky No. 67a Junkers JU89 Heavy Bomber, black, red propellers, blue lower body, German Cross decals to wing and Swastika decals to rear tail wings, excellent condition, in slightly sun-faded box.
1940-41

$700-1,000 | **Vec**

A Dinky No. 62g Boeing Flying Fortress, silver, red propellers, gliding pin hole, US decals, excellent condition, in good condition box, small split to one side and slightly sun-faded.
1939-41

$300-400 | **Vec**

A Dinky No. 62k The King's Airplane, red, blue, silver, red propellers, G-A EXX, excellent condition with no visible signs of fatigue, in excellent condition box complete with gliding hook and leaflet.
1938-41

$600-900 | **Vec**

A Dinky No. 734 P47 Thunderbolt, silver, black, red plastic propeller, complete with bombs, excellent condition, in blister pack with slightly discolored blister, complete with decal sheet.
1975-78

$180-280 | **Vec**

A French Dinky No. 997 Caravelle SE 210 Airliner, Air France white and silvery livery, F-B GNY registration, boxed, with paperwork, minor wear.
1962-65

$60-90 | **W&W**

A scarce Dinky No. 749 Avro Vulcan Delta Wing Bomber, silver, RAF roundels, excellent condition with slight scratch mark to left-hand side wing.

Only 500 of these planes were made for the Canadian market. There are two versions, one with rounded wing tips, one with pointed.
1955-56

$1,500-2,000 | **Vec**

A Dinky No. 104 "Captain Scarlet" Spectrum Pursuit vehicle, blue, white front bumper, excellent condition including inner pictorial stand and instruction sheet, and outer picture box.

This is the more valuable version of this model, where the seat and the figure are not attached to an opening door.

1968-72

$280-320   Vec

A Dinky No. 104 "Captain Scarlet" Spectrum Pursuit Vehicle. lacks missile good condition, box damaged.

1973-75

$100-150   Chef

A Dinky No. 102 "Joe 90" Joe's Car, green, excellent condition, including inner pictorial stand, outer picture box good condition, but one end flap slightly repaired.

1969-75

$350-400   Vec

A Dinky No. 103 "Captain Scarlet" Spectrum Patrol Car, very good condition, boxed.

1968-75

$180-220   Chef

A Dinky No. 108 "Joe 90" Sam's Car, powder blue, lemon interior, red engine cover, cast wheels, good condition with inner pictorial stand, including instruction sheet, an outer picture box.

1971-75

$180-220   Vec

A Dinky No. 100 "Thunderbirds" Lady Penelope's FAB 1, good condition, box damaged.

1967-75

$150-200   Chef

A Dinky No. 101 "Thunderbirds' 2 and 4, green, yellow legs, red thrusters, excellent condition although showing slight signs of surface corrosion in places, inner pictorial stand good condition, outer picture box fair condition but complete.

1967-73

$400-600   Vec

A Dinky No. 112 "The New Avengers" Purdey's TR7, yellow, black including interior, excellent condition in mint window box.

1978-1980

$70-100   Vec

A Dinky No. 106 "The Prisoner' Mini-Moke, spare wheel cover cracked, otherwise very good condition, boxed.

The most valuable and desirable variation has the axle piercing the spun wheel hubs, so look very closely at the wheels!

1967-70

$280-320   Chef

A Dinky No 109 "The Secret Service" Gabriel Model 'T' Ford, yellow, black, brass screen and grille, discolored, otherwise near mint in good condition box, missing inner packing.

1969-71

$60-90   Vec

A Dinky No. 352 "U.F.O." Ed Straker's Car, yellow, black engine covers. white interior, cast spun hubs, excellent condition in all-carded box.

1971-75

$120-180   Vec

A Tri-ang Spot-On No. 118 BMW Isetta, light blue, cream interior, decals stuck to front and rear, excellent condition, in excellent condition box, complete with leaflet.

The yellow version of this quirky car can be up to 30 percent more valuable.

1960

$100-150   **Vec**

Collectors' Notes

- Die-cast Spot-On models were produced by Tri-ang Toys of Northern Ireland between 1959 and 1967. The company aimed to enter the die-cast toy market dominated by Dinky and Corgi.

- Rather than vary the scaling between models, their models are 'spot-on' at a 1:42 scale, making them appear in-scale when together, and making them more of a 'model' than a toy. To emphasize this, they had extra features such as electric headlamps and 'Flexomatic' suspension. Colors are typically bright and attractive.

- Today, they are highly collectible, with buses, commercial vehicles and gift sets fetching high prices. Color and variation in features such as seats and interiors can make a difference to price, so consult a reference guide. As with all model or toy cars, buy examples in the best condition that you can, preferably with the box.

A Tri-ang Spot-On No. 120 Fiat Multipla, pale blue, red interior, good condition, in fair box.
1960
$60-90   **Vec**

A Tri-ang Spot-On No. 131 Goggomobile, red, cream interior, excellent condition, in fair box, some repairs.
1960
$60-90   **Vec**

A Tri-ang Spot-On No. 131 Goggomobile, red, black roof, cream interior, excellent condition, in excellent condition box.
1960
$100-150   **Vec**

A Tri-ang Spot-On No. 131 Goggomobile, green, cream interior, near mint condition, in good condition box, one end flap Sellotaped down.
1960
$120-180   **Vec**

A Tri-ang Spot-On No. 119 Meadows Frisky, light blue, black roof, cream interior, excellent condition, in near mint box.
1960
$120-180   **Vec**

A Tri-ang Spot-On No. 119 Meadows Frisky, pale blue, gray roof, cream interior, excellent condition, in excellent condition box.
1960
$70-100   **Vec**

A Tri-ang Spot-On No. 154 Austin A40, lilac, black roof, cream interior, near mint condition, in good condition box.
1961
$120-180   **Vec**

A Tri-ang Spot-On No.161 LWB Land Rover, pale gray, white roof, cream interior, good condition, in fair condition box, with some damage to one end.
1961
$120-180   **Vec**

A Tri-ang Spot-On No.166 Renault Floride, red, cream interior, excellent condition, with some chrome loss to bumpers, in fair condition box with Sellotape repair to one end.
1962
$100-150   **Vec**

A Tri-ang No. 184 Austin A60 Cambridge with skis, pale blue white interior roof rack, pole decals fitted to front, in good condition, box slightly crushed.

1963

$70-100 Vec

A Tri-ang Spot-On No. 185 Fiat 500, light gray, cream interior, good condition, in excellent condition box

1963

$100-150 Vec

A Tri-ang Spot-On No.218 Jaguar MK.X, with green, cream interior, driver, with box.

This mid-green is one of the most desirable colors to collectors.

1963

$150-200 Vec

A Tri-ang Spot-On No. 193 NSU Prinz 4, beige, cream interior, driver, excellent condition, including box slight tear mark to one end.

1963

$120-180 Vec

A Tri-ang Spot-On No. 193 NSU Prinz 4, bright green, gray interior, driver, near mint condition, in good condition box, with mark on one end.

1963

$120-180 Vec

A Tri-ang Spot-On No. 157 Rover 3 liter, pale gray, cream interior, rear suspension dropped, excellent condition, in good condition box, some marks from removed label.

This model was produced with and without lights. With lights it is known as the 157SL. A dark blue color is the rarest colorway.

1963

$80-120 Vec

A Tri-ang No 157SL Rover 3 liter with lights, pale gray, cream interior, some chrome loss to plastic parts, good condition, in fair condition box.

1963

$120-180 Vec

A Tri-ang Spot-On No. 289 Morris Minor 1000, pale blue, red interior, excellent condition, in good condition box, slight tear to one corner

1963

$120-180 Vec

A Tri-ang Spot-On No 279 MGPB Midget, red, black mudguards, red interior, excellent condition, in good condition window box, creasing and distortion to cellophane.

1965

$70-100 Vec

A Tri-ang Spot-On No. 266 Bullnose Morris, pale yellow, black mudguards, black plastic roof, red spoked hubs, excellent, in good condition box, some Sellotape repairs and a No.279 MGPB Midget, blue, black mudguards, black interior, excellent condition, in re-cellophaned box.

1965

$30-50 (each) Vec

A Tri-ang Spot-On No. 278 Mercedes 230SL, metallic red, red interior, driver, in window box, slight mark to one surface of cellophane.

1965

$120-180 Vec

FIND OUT MORE

'Ramsay's British Die-cast Model Toys Catalogue', by John Ramsay, 9th edition, Swapmeet Publications, 2001.

A late 1950s Tri-ang Spot-On garage, hardboard and card construction, in a 1930s style with showroom to left-hand side, and petrol forecourt to right-hand side, central opening for access to showroom, workshop, lift to first floor and ramps to first floor and roof top parking, complete and boxed, good condition, minor wear.

19in (48.5cm) long

$300-400 W&W

A Matchbox Series Major Pack M9 Inter-State Double Freighter, with blue tractor unit, unpainted silver trailers with silver doors and orange labels, two wheel variations, one piece double and individual examples, boxed, minor wear.

c1962

$150-200 | **W&W**

A rare Matchbox Superfast No. 32c Leyland Petrol Tanker, in metallic purple with silver tank, NAMC labels, boxed.

Without the NAMC labels, this version is usually worth 30 percent less.

1970-73

$180-220 | **W&W**

A Matchbox No. 56 London Trolley Bus, with black poles and metal wheels, boxed, minor chips, introduced in 1958.

Look out for the variation with gray plastic wheels, which is rarer and more valuable.

$180-220 | **W&W**

A pair of Matchbox Superfast No. 8 Ford Mustang, one red with red interior, the other orangy red, with white interior, both boxed.

1970-71

$280-320 | **W&W**

A Yesteryear Gift Set No. G6, comprising Y1 Allchin Traction engine, Y2 B-type London bus; Y5 Le Mans Bentley, white Y10 Grand Prix Mercedes; and Y13 Santa Fe locomotive, box in good condition, minor wear.

1960

$300-400 | **W&W**

A rare Lesney Moko large scale six-wheel Prime Mover and Six-Wheel Trailer, with two ramp blocks and yellow and red bulldozer load, Prime Mover in orange with green engine covers, No 37 and British Road Services raised casting to doors and back; mid-blue Trailer and blocks, both with gray wheels, bulldozer with green rubber tracks, in original two-part box, minor wear.

An unusual Crescent Toys Model Farm Equipment No. 1815 Hayloader, deck painted in sky blue, red frame and yellow, elevator tines, crankshaft pullies and wheels, complete, minor fatigue.

A Lesney Models of Yesteryear No. 12 Horse Bus, very good condition, boxed.

c1959

$60-90 | **Chef**

c1950

$700-1,000 | **W&W** | **$180-220** | **W&W**

A Penny Series No. 0/100 group of racing cars, including Brabham, Lotus Climax, BRM, Lola Climax and Ferrari, all excellent, in fair box.

$60-90 | **Vec**

A Crescent Toys No. 1276 Scammell Scarab with Esso Tanker, good condition, including box.

1955-59

$150-200 | **Vec**

A Nicky 295 Standard '20' Ambulance, with a 295 box, excellent condition.

$80-120 | **SAS**

A Williams dump truck, painted cast iron, rubber tired metal hubbed wheels, excellent condition.

8in (20cm) long

$250-300　　　　　　　NB

A Hubley fire pumper truck, painted cast iron, cast wheels, integral cast driver, good condition, some rust on wheels.

8in (20cm) long

$120-180　　　　　　NB

An Arcade yellow cab, painted cast iron, original driver, excellent condition, replaced screen grill.

9in (23cm) long

$700-1,000　　　　　NB

A Hubley flame exhaust racer, painted cast iron, rubber tired metal spoked wheels, wheels activate 'flames' going up and down, good condition, some paint loss and light rust on wheels.

11in (28cm) long

$1,000-1,500　　　　　NB

An Arcade Mack ladder truck, painted cast iron with spoked wheels, very good to excellent condition, replaced wheels and one ladder hanger.

18in (45.5cm) long

$600-900　　　　　　NB

A Kenton early style auto dray, painted cast iron, spoked wheels, raised letters on sides, features original driver, some paint loss.

9in (23cm) long

$600-900　　　　　NB

A Friedag double decker bus, painted cast iron, cast metal wheels, half-round passengers and driver.

9in (23cm) long

$600-900　　　　NB

A Cor-Cor Chrysler Airflow, painted pressed steel wind-up with battery operated headlights and European auto dealers tag on bottom, "Lyngby Automobil, Centra Hovedgaden 1, Lyngby, tlf 1030", missing headlights and one bevel, scratching and paint loss, especially on roof

17in (43cm) long

$1,000-1,500　　　　　NB

A Kingsbury pickup truck #359, scarce painted pressed steel with wind-up mechanism, rubber tires and original decals some areas of paint wear.

This version is in the rare blue color and is large in size, making it very valuable. The Kingsbury Manufacturing Co. made steel toys from 1842 until 1942, which were known for their sharper, more authentic detail, allowed by the material and pressing process.

14in (35.5cm) long

$1,000-1,500　　　　　NB

A Kingsbury Roadster, painted pressed steel wind up, with battery operated head lights, some wear, possibly missing a windshield insert.

13in (33cm) long

$350-400　　　　　NB

A Kingsbury Zephyr and camper, painted pressed steel with rubber tires, some wear and discoloration.

23in (58.5cm) long

$250-300　　　　　NB

A Kingsbury dump truck, painted pressed steel wind up, replaced rubber on tires and tailgate.

11in (28cm) long

$350-450　　　　　NB

A Fry's tinplate and card horse-drawn carriage chocolate box, with tinplate horse, card driver and body with tin wheels.

c1900

$600-900   **BonC**

An early 20thC tinplate fire engine, with driver and dappled horses.

10in (25.5cm) long

$800-1,200   **BonC**

A CLOSER LOOK AT A TINPLATE TOY

Although the maker is not known, its very early date and coach shape make it extremely desirable to collectors.

Large tinplate toys are very rare and valuable. This has an opening door and fine detailing, with original lamps.

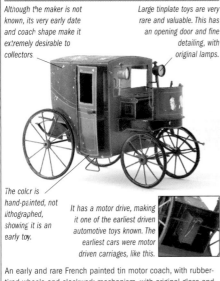

The color is hand-painted, not lithographed, showing it is an early toy.

It has a motor drive, making it one of the earliest driven automotive toys known. The earliest cars were motor driven carriages, like this.

An early and rare French painted tin motor coach, with rubber-tired wheels and clockwork mechanism, with original glass and tufted upholstery on driver's seat and in the coach, two opening doors and finished with fine yellow striping, some paint wear on roof and dashboard exterior.

c1890   *15.5in (39.5cm) long*

$4,000-6,000   **NB**

A battery operated tinplate Porsche "Elektro Matic 7500 FS", by Johann Distler, with two gears, with original packaging.

c1955

$400-600   **ATK**

Collectors' Notes

- Tinplate toys were first produced in the early 19th century and soon replaced wooden toys as they were faster and cheaper to produce and were better suited to more intricate detailing. They were made from a sheet of tin plated steel which was stamped out, bent into shape and decorated.

- Early tinplate is hand-painted, later tinplate was lithographed. Earlier toys tend to show higher levels of detailing, but both are highly collectible. Germany was a key manufacturing country, with factories such as Marklin (founded 1856), Ernst Planck (1866-c1935), Gebrüder Bing (1863-1933) and Lehmann (founded 1881) producing and exporting fine quality toys.

- German tinplate toys were not exported during WWI. In the US, tinplate toys were produced from the 1830s by companies such as Louis Marx (1896-1982) and Ferdinand Strauss (c1914-1942).

- Automotive toys are amongst the most popular with collectors. Look for fine detailing and features such as clockwork or other drives and opening doors. Toys by renowned makers will usually be valuable, and original boxes add value. Size is important, large toys would have been expensive in their day and are usually very valuable now.

- Condition is very important, as although durable, tinplate damages easily. Scratches, rust, dents and splits reduce value, as do broken or missing parts. The surface is difficult to restore and poor restoration also reduces value.

- Tinplate toys were popular until the 1930s, when more inexpensive die-cast toys began to replace them, with plastic replacing them in turn from the mid-20th century. Japan produced tinplate toys from the 1920s onward and many of these are very popular with collectors. The 'golden age' of tin is the late 19th and early 20th century.

A Marx battery operated embossed lithographed tin Coupé, fair to good condition, heavy wear and scratching on roof.

15in (38cm) long

$400-600   **NB**

A Marx clockwork lithographed tin Racer, with checkerboard pattern in grill, excellent condition.

13.5in (34.5cm) long

$300-500   **NB**

A Japanese 'Alps' trademark battery-operated tinplate model Mercedes 230SL, boxed, good condition.

11.5in (29cm) long

$180-220   **Chef**

A Schuco Curvo lithographed tin racer, with spring mechanism.

$220-280   **ATK**

A 1920s Structro clockwork tinplate tractor, worn.

$300-400   **Chef**

A Mettoy tinplate mechanical tractor and trailer, good condition, boxed.

$70-100   **Chef**

A Metoy tinplate mechanical tractor and another larger, good condition.

$70-100 (both)   **Chef**

A Marx Doughboy clockwork lithographed tin tank, with sparking gun action, figure pops up as tank moves, excellent condition, some very minor edge wear.

10in (25.5cm) long

$220-280   **NB**

A late 1950s tinplate battery powered Bristol Bulldog aeroplane, by Straco of Japan, pressed tin radial engine, plastic propeller and rubber wheels, some minor rubbing to finish.

14.5in (37cm) wide

$150-200   **W&W**

A Marx clockwork lithographed tin "Popeye the Champ", with celluloid figures, replaced foot bracket on Brutus, box needs some repair, missing two side flaps and one set of decorated end flaps are detached.

Box 7.5in (19cm) high

$1,500-2,000   **NB**

A battery operated tinplate toy hen, with clucking and egg-laying action, in original packaging.

$70-100   **ATK**

A 1930s German sand pail.

These are hard to find in good condition as they were played with. They often became dented and the sand or earth scratched the attractive scene on the lithographed surface.

7in high

$60-90   **DH**

A 1930s French sand pail.

5.75in (14.5cm) high

$40-60   **DH**

A 1930s Halloween tin toy trumpet, with wooden mouth piece, marked "Foreign".

8in (20cm) high

$20-30   **DH**

A 1920s German tin toy badge.

The googly eyes rotate when the cord is pulled.

2.5in (6.5cm) wide

$120-180   **DH**

FIND OUT MORE...

The Art of The Tin Toy, by David Pressland, published by Schiffer Publishing, 1992.

Tinplate Toys: From Schuco, Bing & Other Companies, by Jürgen Franzke, published by Schiffer Publishing, 1997.

A B C D E F G H I J K L M N O P Q R S T U V W XYZ

Collectors' Notes

- Penny toys are made from thin steel plated with tin and were first made during the 1860s, peaking in popularity around the turn of the 20th century. Surfaces were decorated with brightly colored lithographs and usually embossed, giving added detail. By the 1930s, production ceased in favor of other, die-cast toys.

- They were often copies of larger tin toys and were produced by many of the major tinplate toy manufacturers, particularly around the Nuremburg area of Germany, such as Distler (1900-1962) and Meier. They were also produced in the US and UK.

- They were produced in large quantities and were inexpensive, often being sold by street peddlars.

- Cars, boats and planes are amongst the most frequently found, but novelty and whimsical toys are also popular. Horse drawn vehicles are less so. Many were simply pushed along, but some have a flywheel to drive them along, which adds value.

- Condition is extremely important, unusually, even more so than rarity for some collectors. Many were not looked after as they were inexpensive, and being small and made of thin material, they were easy to damage. Toys with bright, unscratched transfers, no rust and unbroken protruding parts will usually be the most valuable.

A Meier covered lorry penny toy, embossed lithographed tin with drive, with side lamps and headlamps.

The addition of an inertia drive and the excellent detailing makes this a more valuable penny toy. Look out for extra features such as opening doors as this too adds value.

4.5in (11.5cm) long

$600-900 NB

A Fischer large general double-decker bus penny toy, embossed lithographed tin, with driver.

4.5in (11.5cm) long

$400-600 NB

A Meier limousine penny toy, embossed lithographed tin, full-figured driver and cut-out passenger figures, needs a little cleaning.

4.25in (11cm) long

$180-220 NB

A Distler limousine penny toy, embossed lithographed tin, with inertia wheel mechanism and opening door.

3in (7.5cm) long

$320-380 NB

A Meier auto cab and coach penny toy, embossed lithographed tin.

3.25in (8.5cm) long

$300-400 NB

A penny toy garage, with two Kellermann automobiles, embossed lithographed tin, latching garage doors opening to an open car with driver and a sedan both by Kellermann.

As well as being in excellent condition, this toy is complete with two cars and a garage.

Garage 3.5in (9cm) diam

$600-900 NB

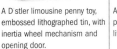

A Fischer hansom carriage penny toy, embossed lithographed tin, with driver.

4.5in (11.5cm)

$150-200 NB

A Meier horse drawn dray penny toy, embossed lithographed tin.

5in (12.5cm) long

$180-220 NB

A Kellermann #227 airplane penny toy, embossed lithographed tin, slight separation near nose of plane, possibly missing prop.

3.25in (8.5cm) long

$150-200 NB

A man with wheelbarrow penny toy, embossed lithographed tin.

3in (7.5cm) long

$180-220 NB

A Fischer porter with trunk penny toy, embossed lithographed tin, trunk opens.

3.5in (9cm) long

$400-600 **NB**

An elephant pulling cart penny toy, lithographed tin, with nodding head action.

5in (12.5cm) long

$300-400 **NB**

A Meier rabbit on platform penny toy, embossed lithographed tin, eccentric axle provides rocking motion, excellent condition.

3in (7.5cm) long

$300-500 **NB**

A Meier jockey on rocking horse penny toy embossed lithographed tin, with riding scenes on runners, some very light bits of surface wear, but strong color.

3.75in (9.5cm) long

$350-400 **NB**

A Distler boy in high chair penny toy embossed lithographed tin, converts from high chair to play table on wheels.

4in (10cm) high

$150-200 **NB**

A Distler goose on platform penny toy, embossed lithographed tin, amusing bobbing head action.

3.5in (9cm) long

$220-280 **NB**

An embossed lithographed tin Victrola penny toy, with crank-operated two-note musical "movement".

3.75in (9.5cm) long

$60-90 **NB**

A Meier embossed lithographed tin sewing machine penny toy.

$60-90 **NB**

A Gelor Einfalt aeronautical penny toy, with "DRGM" patent mark

c1929

$300-350 **CamA**

A Fischer baby carriage penny toy, embossed lithographed tin, some light surface wear on one side of cover.

3.5in (9cm) long

$220-280 **NB**

FIND OUT MORE...

The Museum of London, London Wall, London EC2Y 5HN, www.museumoflondon.co.uk. An outstanding collection of 1,703 penny toys collected by Ernest King.

'Book of Penny Toys', *by David Pressland, published by Pincushion Press, 1999.*

A Schuco Patent clockwork model of a boy violinist, in felt clothes worn.

$120-180   **Chef**

A felt and color-lithographed tinplate wind-up Schuco drummer boy, with original key.

5in (13cm) high

$500-700   **HGS**

A felt and tinplate Schuco wind-up Charlie Chaplin, with original key.

6.5in (16.5cm) high

$700-1,000   **HGS**

A fabric and color-lithographed tinplate Schuco wind-up juggling cowboy, in mint condition, with original box and key.

6in (15.5cm) high

$800-1,200   **HGS**

A plush-covered tinplate and felt Schuco wind-up rabbit.

5.25in (13.5cm) high

$300-350   **HGS**

A felt and color-lithographed wind-up tinplate Schuco monkey on a scooter.

5.75in (14.5cm) high

$1,200-1,800   **HGS**

A color-lithographed tinplate and felt wind-up Schuco tumbling monkey, with original key.

3.25in (8.5cm) high

$220-280   **HGS**

A fabric, plush and plastic Schuco 'Bigo-Fix' dancing mouse, made of plastic-covered wire.

5.25in (13.5cm) high

$120-180   **HGS**

A very rare color-lithographed tinplate and pipe-cleaner Schuco monkey yo-yo.

3.25in (8.5cm) high

$2,200-2,800   **HGS**

A plastic, fabric and plush wind-up Schuco dancing 'Bigo-Fix' mouse, with original box.

6in (15.5cm) high

$350-400   **HGS**

A felt-covered fabric and plastic Schuco 'Bigo-Fix' black boy, with original box.

6in (15cm) high

$400-600   **HGS**

A fabric and felt-covered Schuco wind-up 'Bigo-Fix' clown, with original key and box.

6.25in (16cm) high

$350-400   **HGS**

Collectors' Notes

- Lead figures became popular in the 19th century with their popularity peaking around the early 20th century. Despite a resurgence in popularity in the 1950s in the UK due to the Coronation of Queen Elizabeth II and the introduction of new characters from British children's television programs, use of lead began to wane towards the end of the decade, when plastic, which was cheaper to produce, took over.

- Soldiers are often the most popular type and a large number of numbered sets were produced. Look for complete sets. After WWI, when the country wanted to forget the horrors of war, domestic and pastoral themes dominated, leading to the introduction of farms and zoos.

- Many makers mark their names on the bases, but this is not always the case. Major makers to look for include Britains (founded 1845) who pioneered hollow casting in 1893, which quickly overtook solid

casting, Charbens (1920-1955), John Hill (1898-1960), also often known as Johillco, and Pixyland (c1920-1933).

- Look for fine detailing, original paint and unusual characters or variations. Britains in particular are renowned for their accurate uniforms.

- Look closely at lead figures to see if the figure has been repainted, is missing parts or has had parts replaced through 'customization' or repair. Unusual lumps often indicate a replaced part, and suspiciously fresh, very opaque and differently colored paint can indicate repainting. Handle as many figures as possible to learn how to recognize faults and original features.

- Original boxes will add value, as they were most often thrown away, even more so if the box is in excellent condition. Look for boxes from smaller makers as these are very rare compared to Britain's boxes, which are more common.

A prewar Britains Set 27 Band of the Line, comprising of 11 marching Musicians together with Drum Major, the later Base Drummer and Drummer Boy having garters.

$220-280   Vec

A collection of Britains from Set 35, Royal Marines 1935 version, comprising of 14 marching Marines with rifles at the slope, full pants, together with Officer with a drawn sword, gaiters, one bayonet broken.

$180-220   Vec

A Britains Set 78, Bluejackets comprising of six Running Sailors with Rifles at the Trail, two replacement unpainted arms, petty officer with Drawn Sword, oval bases good, also later version, eight Running Sailors at the Trail together with Petty Officer, slight paint loss overall.

$150-200   Vec

A collection of Britains from Set 104, City Imperial Volunteers, seven mis-matched Infantry Men at the En Guard position, oval dated bases, khaki with slouch hats.

$180-220   Vec

A collection of Britains from Set 147, Zulus, 15 Native Warriors, various paint styles, one base broken, other minor damages only.

$220-280   Vec

Two Britains Set 151, Royal Naval Reserve comprising of seven marching Sailors together with empty-handed Officer.

$80-120   Vec

A Britains Set 187, Arabs, eight marching Arabs with Jezails in their left arms, together with four Arabs running with spear scimitar and jezails from Set 2046.

$180-220   Vec

A collection of Britains from Set 188, Zulu Kraal, comprising of two composition Zulu huts together with eight running Zulus, one spear point missing.

$220-280 Vec

A postwar Britains Set 196 Greek Evzones, eight marching Evzones with rifles at the slope, black jackets.

$120-180 Vec

A Britains Set 212, Royal Scots, four marching at the slope, one bonnet cockade broken, plus Piper, together with five Highlanders at the slope plus piper, seven further Britains pipers, finally, four pipers and two Highlanders by unconfirmed maker.

$180-220 Vec

A collection of Britains from Set 213, Highland Light Infantry, seven marching Highlanders with rifles at the slope, Review dress and red tunics.

$220-280 Vec

A collection of Britains from Set 299, West Point Cadets, eight marching Cadets, rifles at the slope, summer dress, one head loose, together with Set 2033, US Infantry, six marching soldiers at the slope, service dress, steel helmets together with empty-handed officer.

$150-200 Vec

A collection of Britains from Set 1253, U.S. Navy Whitejackets, six marching sailors at the slope together with two empty handed marching officers, one arm damaged, also R.C.M.P., six marching empty-handed Mounties together with a turned in the saddle officer.

$150-200 Vec

A collection of Britains RAF Personnel, from Set 2011, RAF Regiment, seven marching Airmen, slung rifles and a marching officer with baton, together with five aircraftsmen slung rifles, peak caps with officer holding sword scabbard.

$220-280 Vec

A collection of Britains Fusiliers, 16 marching soldiers at the slope, five arms loose, one missing, a marching officer, a 2nd grade guardsman, firing, a guardsman kneeling, firing, unconfirmed maker marching at the slope and a small scale guardsman running at the slope.

$50-80 Vec

Two Greenwood and Ball figures, comprising an 18th Hussars guard and a Royal Scot guard, in original boxes, Hussar badly flaking.

$150-200 SI

A Franklin Mint and Imrie/Risley by Wilson American Revolutionary war figure, sculpted by Imrie/Risley and painted by Wilson depicting a frontiersman, on diorama base.

3in (7.5cm) high

$220-280 SI

A Bombay Field Artillery, comprising of six horse team, three drivers, limber and gun.

$60-90   Vec

A Royal Field Artillery, comprising of six horse team, three drivers, limber, gun and gunners.

$120-180   Vec

A Royal Field Artillery, comprising of recast six horse team with three drivers, limber and 4-7 Naval gun.

$60-90   Vec

A Toy Army Workshop Set No. BS103 six horse 13lb field gun team.

$280-320   Vec

A Britains Set 79, Royal Navy landing party, comprising of Running Petty Officer with drawn sword together with eight mismatched ratings, artillery piece and limber.

$180-220   Vec

A Britains set based on Set 146, R.A.S.C. wagon, repainted to depict a Royal Engineers Unit, comprising of a two horse color harness team, driver and two orderlies in review dress and an open four wheel wagon, gray early finish, together with a similar set light harness green wagon, driver and one orderly converted to Indian soldiers and a British orderly in khaki uniform.

$100-150   Vec

A Royal Engineers pontoon section, four horse team, two drivers, open wagon, wooden pontoon and roadway sections.

$280-320   Vec

A Britains Set 1330, General Service wagon and limber, all repainted and contained in original box with yellow illustrated label.

$220-280   Vec

An R.A.M.C. ambulance, comprising of four horse team, two drivers, wagon with canvas tilt, two orderlies.

$60-90   Vec

A collection of Britains from Set 32 Royal Scots Dragoon guards, later version, all with drawn swords.

$70-100   Vec

A collection of Britains Cavalry from Set 159, two mounted figures with swords, also from Set 94, 21st lancers one mounted lancer and one trumpeter.

$100-150   Vec

A Britains Set 2076, 12th Lancers, four lancers at the carry together with officer on gray horse with drawn sword, one lance tip and one horse's leg broken, minor paint loss.

$70-100   Vec

A Britains Boer cavalry officer, black horse, light brown uniform, holding pistol, good, also two Cossack lancers.

$180-220   Vec

A Britains Set 193 Arabs, three figures on camels, all repainted together with repainted running Arab.

$60-90   Vec

A collection of Britains from Set 33, 16th/5th Lancers, two lancers with lances at the carry together with an officer turned in the saddle, plus from Set 48, Egyptian Camel Corps, three later version camels together with three riders holding rifles.

$220-280   Vec

An Imperial Collectors Figure No. 19 Field Marshall Lord Roberts, 1900, in original box, excellent to mint.

$60-90   SI

A Britains set #1264 4.7 Naval gun, in original box.

$100-150   SI

An Astra Pharos Ltd 12in heavy Howitzer, a few chips, in original, damaged box.

$120-180   SI

A King and Country Waffen SS No. WSS 20.

$120-180   Vec

A Britains set #2175 gun, mounted on a Centurian tank body, a few chips.

6in (15.5cm)

$400-600   SI

A British made lead camouflaged tank, with luster highlights.

6in (15.5cm)

$150-200   SI

A prewar Britains Set 1512 Army Ambulance, square nosed version, dark green, white roundels with red crosses, one rear door has bottom of hinge detached, includes driver only.

$280-320   Vec

A Britains Motorbike Despatch Riders, four late version motorbikers, light khaki on green motorbikes, also one similar model but first fixed wheel version, some possible retouching.

$150-200   Vec

A Richard Courtenay #33 Sir John Beauchamp K.G., mounted with removable helmet, name on base.

$1,200-1,800   Sl

An Alymer figure of Edward Plantagenet, Prince of Wales, Black Prince.

$120-180   Sl

A Bob Horning mounted figure of Eustace D'Ribemont, banner of King of France #17N, signed and dated 1995, with an original box, excellent to mint condition.

$30-50   Sl

An Alymer figure of Jean De Clermont, Marshall of France, mounted, axe bent.

$280-320   Sl

A collection of Britains Knights of Agincourt No.1659, mounted knight with mace, No. 1663 mounted knight with lance broken, two foot knights, one with spear, one with sword.

$180-220   Vec

A Britains Knight of Agincourt, No.1659, mounted knight with mace, in 'stone' type box, no insert.

$220-280   Vec

A Timpo Knights of the Round Table mounted, Sir Mordred, King Arthur Sir Gawaine, Sir Bedevere, some repainting.

$150-200   Vec

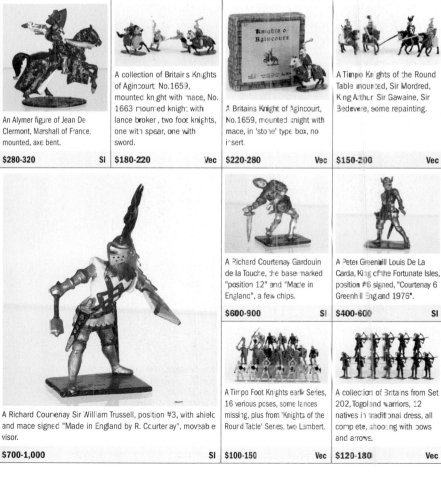

A Richard Courtenay Sir William Trussell, position #3, with shield and mace signed "Made in England by R. Courtenay", moveable visor.

$700-1,000   Sl

A Richard Courtenay Gardouin de la Touche, the base marked "position 12" and "Made in England", a few chips.

$600-900   Sl

A Peter Greenhill Louis De La Carda, King of the Fortunate Isles, position #6 signed, "Courtenay 6 Greenhill England 1976".

$400-600   Sl

A Timpo Foot Knights early Series, 16 various poses, some lances missing, plus from 'Knights of the Round Table' Series, two Lambert.

$100-150   Vec

A collection of Britains from Set 202, Togoland warriors, 12 natives in traditional dress, all complete, shooting with bows and arrows.

$120-180   Vec

A Vertunni figure of Anne D'Autriche #A-20, chip to head.

$60-90 SI

A Vertunni figure of Anne Boelyn.

$120-180 SI

A Vertunni figure of Philippe Le Bon, set #57, excellent to mint.

$280-320 SI

A Vertunni figure of Eleanor of Austria, wife of Frances I, chipped nose.

$60-90 SI

A Vertunni figure of Henry III, Duc De Guise, a few chips base.

$60-90 SI

A Vertunni figure of Henry III, chips to nose and base.

$60-90 SI

A Vertunni figure of Henry VII, chips to leg and hat.

$100-150 SI

A Vertunni figure of Louis XIII, with red cape, excellent to mint.

$70-100 SI

A Vertunni figure of Louis XVI, a few chips.

$150-200 SI

A Vertunni figure of Marie-Antoinette #A-18.

$220-280 SI

A Vertunni figure of the Marquise De Sevigne #A-10.

$70-100 SI

A Minikin Set #5579 or H6 Napoleon, mounted as if crossing the Alps, mace in Occupied Japan, mint.

$80-120 SI

A rare Pixyland Kew Old Mother Hubbard, and a rare nanny holding baby.

$180-220   **Vec**

Three rare Phillip Segal character figures, Little Jack Horner, Woodcutter and Wolfair.

Philip Segal (1938-1950) of Hampshire, England were a short-lived company known for their nonmilitary lead figures and a rare series of soccer players.

$120-180   **Vec**

A very rare figure of 'Just William', winking.

'Just William' is the name of a famous series of children's books by English author Richmal Crompton, focusing on the escapades and exploits of a rather naughty schoolboy.

$120-180   **Vec**

A Morestone Series Enid Blyton's "Big Ears", riding his bicycle yellow and blue clothes with red hat and bicycle, white wheels, in original box, minor paint chips to hat.

$120-180   **W&W**

A Benbros Robin Hood Series, Robin Hood, Mutch, Will Scarlet, Little John, Friar Tuck, Maid Marian, Sheriff of Nottingham and the Bishop.

$180-220   **Vec**

A Timpo Hopalong Cassidy Series, comprising of Lucky, California, Hopalong Cassidy with and without stetson, plus Tim.

$300-350   **Vec**

Four Keymen Soccer Players, Bobby Charlton, Alan Ball, Bobby Moore, Gordon Banks, all excellent, in very good, rare, orange window box.

$180-220   **Vec**

A Sacul T.V. issue Bill and Ben, comprising of Bill and Ben, two original terracotta Flower Pots and Little Weed, Weed head only, some paint loss.

$180-220   **Vec**

A rare Britains Felix the Cat figure, some paint loss.

As well as Felix being a popular cartoon character, this is a rare figure with many protruding parts that are prone to damage.

$600-900   **W&W**

Two Pixyland Felix the Cat figures, smaller figure walking with hands behind his back, larger figure with finger raised and holding his tail.

$180-220   **Vec**

A Luntoy Princess Tai-Lu Siamese Cat figure, in 'TV' type illustrated box.

$220-280   **Vec**

Four Luntoy figures, comprising Ragood, two Tagood, Bobtail, together with an Argosh figure of Peter the Dogood, tail broken but present.

$120-180   **Vec**

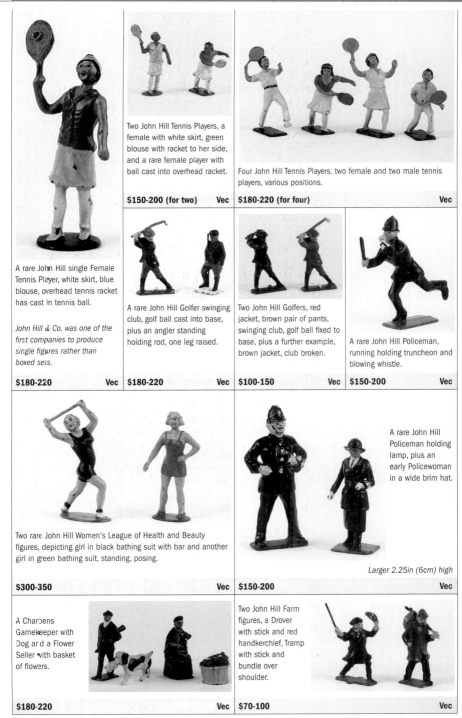

Two John Hill Tennis Players, a female with white skirt, green blouse with racket to her side, and a rare female player with ball cast into overhead racket.

$150-200 (for two)   Vec

Four John Hill Tennis Players, two female and two male tennis players, various positions.

$180-220 (for four)   Vec

A rare John Hill single Female Tennis Player, white skirt, blue blouse, overhead tennis racket has cast in tennis ball.

John Hill & Co. was one of the first companies to produce single figures rather than boxed sets.

$180-220   Vec

A rare John Hill Golfer swinging club, golf ball cast into base, plus an angler standing holding rod, one leg raised.

$180-220   Vec

Two John Hill Golfers, red jacket, brown pair of pants, swinging club, golf ball fixed to base, plus a further example, brown jacket, club broken.

$100-150   Vec

A rare John Hill Policeman, running holding truncheon and blowing whistle.

$150-200   Vec

Two rare John Hill Women's League of Health and Beauty figures, depicting girl in black bathing suit with bar and another girl in green bathing suit, standing, posing.

$300-350   Vec

A rare John Hill Policeman holding lamp, plus an early Policewoman in a wide brim hat.

Larger 2.25in (6cm) high

$150-200   Vec

A Charbens Gamekeeper with Dog and a Flower Seller with basket of flowers.

$180-220   Vec

Two John Hill Farm figures, a Drover with stick and red handkerchief, Tramp with stick and bundle over shoulder.

$70-100   Vec

A Pixyland Kew set, comprising of Huntswoman side-saddle, Huntsman with fox hound, two further mounted Huntsmen, also a Fox and seven running Hounds.

$70-100   Vec

A Charbens Hikers set, with Boy lying down and Girl walking with stick, also Gypsy and Wife with Child from caravan set.

$220-280   Vec

A John Hill Inn Keeper, and rare Market Gardener with tray of vegetables.

$220-280   Vec

A John Hill Wedding Party, comprising of Vicar, Bride, Groom and Bridesmaid.

$120-180   Vec

A Britains Nodding Chinaman, fair condition.

This is an early and rare figure, it was prone to damage and complete examples, even in fair condition are very desirable.

c1878

$220-280   SAS

A rare John Hill figure of Santa Claus.

2.5in (6.5cm) high

$120-180   Vec

A rare John Hill painted Witch with cauldron, plus a rare seated cat and robin.

$180-220   Vec

A Charbens Organ Grinder with organ, donkey and monkey.

$180-220   Vec

A rare F.G. Taylor 1950 model of the State Landau, comprising of brown open landau, four gray horses, two riders, two Postillion riders and seated figure, possibly Queen Mary.

$120-180   Vec

A Pixyland Kew Civilian figures, standing Man with beer tankard, two seated versions of same, one arm loose, a very rare Boy with tray of newspapers, also a very rare 'Boy Blue'.

$220-280   Vec

A rare Crescent set FB/3 Hen Coup, comprising of wooden hen coup, nest, three hens and rabbit, contained in box base only.

$100-150 Vec

A Britains No. 53 Span Roof Greenhouse, dismantled with white door and 'windows', all lugs intact, some paint loss.

$180-220 Vec

A collection of John Hill Garden items, greenhouse, stile, well, water pump, single bridge.

$120-180 Vec

A collection of farm buildings, by various makers, two stable blocks, cottage by A.B. & Co., further small cottage with open shed attached and a small quantity of fencing, all mainly good condition.

$80-120 Vec

A quantity of John Hill Garden items, summer house with tinplate back, rustic table, man with wheelbarrow, closed dovecote, seat, eight bushes and a rare covered seat.

$220-280 Vec

A quantity of John Hill Garden items, open summer house, garden pond, rare prewar see-saw, log, boy waving cap, incorrect girl, no plank, two bushes, four trees, two small trees, hurdle.

$220-280 Vec

Three Pixyland Kew figures of girls on swings.

$280-320 Vec

Four John Hill Haystacks, two square and two round, together with 11 trees by various makers, mainly Hill.

£180-220 Vec

A quantity of Taylor and Barrett F.G.T. figures, comprising two parrots on stand, kennel, beehive, fence section, gate on post, stile, wire fence, water pump, two rustic fences, rare tree with squirrels, three baby chicks.

$120-180 Vec

A Britains dead tree with field gate No.19F, and boy on swing repainted.

$50-80   **Chef**

Seventeen Pixyland Kew Garden items, lawn mower with man, roller, sundial, arbor, six bushes, barrel, two shrubs in drain pots, two bushes in tubs.

$150-200   **Vec**

A quantity of Charbens farm series figures, comprising of cape cart in green with horse, milk cart with horse and milkman, open farm cart yellow with red wheels, orange tractor with driver, rare tree with monkeys in branches, four foot figures.

$150-200   **Vec**

Three Britains large coconut palm trees.

$100-150   **Vec**

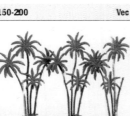

Three Britains three date palm trees, one slightly damaged.

$30-90   **Vec**

A very rare John Hill large pond, cast with detailed cardboard "water", contained in an original red box, taped edges to lid, old marks.

$300-500   **Vec**

Twelve Pixyland Kew Garden items, four fence sections with bushes to top, five trellis sections with climbing flowers, three bush sections.

$180-220   **Vec**

A Britains horse roller with man No.9F, near mint to good, boxed.

$120-180   **Chef**

A Britains General Purpose Plough No.6F, with man and two horses, one repainted, boxed.

$120-180   **Chef**

A two-horse grass mower, with seated man, unknown make, rear mint.

$50-80   **Chef**

A Britains model home farm No.120F, in original trade box, near mint.

$220-280   **Chef**

A Timpo Toys Farm Series boxed set, of 23 pieces including milkmaid, cow, pigs, horses, sheep, trees, fencing, box damaged.

$120-180   **Chef**

A Britains tractor with four Dinky farm vehicles the Fordson Major tractor and driver; the Dinky vehicles comprising 27b Halesowen Farm Trailer, 27c/321 Massey Harris Manure Spreader, 27k Hay Rake and 319 Weeks Tipping Trailer (tailgate missing), unboxed

$220-280   **DN**

Two Britains Circus figures, two walking elephants with clowns holding white hoops, one in gray, one in green, both with yellow facings.

$220-280 Vec

Four Britains Circus tigers, seated on four podia.

$100-150 Vec

Seven Britains Circus figures 450B, comprising three performing elephants, four prancing horses 351B, equestrian balancing on horseback 355b, some paint loss to prancing horses.

$280-320 Vec

Thirteen Crescent Zoo animals, lion, tiger, giraffe, seated camel, crocodile, kangaroo, three ganders, goat, two dogs, goose.

$30-50 Vec

Seven Charbens Circus figures, an elephant with podium, three equestriennes on horseback and three Liberty horses.

Charbens primarily produced nonmilitary figures, its charming 'Circus' range was extremely popular.

$280-320 Vec

Four Pixyland Kew animals, large and small lizards coiled and uncoiled snakes.

$70-100 Vec

Seven Timpo 'My Pet' Series, Pekinese, in illustrated box, St. Bernard, Borzoi, Great Dane, Bulldog, Boston Terrier and one other.

$100-150 Vec

Two rare prewar John Hill Buffalo, both excellent.

$70-100 Vec

A Crescent Matador in full ceremonial dress, holding red cape, together with a charging bull.

$100-150 Vec

A set of twelve Britains Cococubs figures, including Tiny Tusks, Mr & Mrs Pie Porker, Squire Rooster, Peter Pum Poodle, Granny Owl, Monty Monkey, Tubby Bear, Henrietta Fussy Feathers, Nutty Squirrel, Mrs Cracklegoose, Gussie Robin.

Cococubs were given away as free promotions with Cadbury's chocolate. A full set of twelve figures is rare. Condition is important.

$220-280 Vec

Collectors' Notes

- George Lucas changed the way films were merchandized when "Star Wars" was released in 1977. The range of items that were available was astounding and included underwear, bedding, breakfast cereals and, of course, toys.

- At a time when TV shows were considered a more profitable and viable merchandizing source, US company Kenner Toys took a huge risk producing a range for a movie that the film studios had been reluctant to make in the first place.

- Their small size and affordability made them an instant hit with children of the day and in their eight-year run, Kenner produced over 100 figures and a wide range of accessories, vehicles, monsters and playsets allowing fans to recreate their favorite scenes.

- As George Lucas's company Lucasfilm retains the licensing rights to all the Star Wars characters, original props and special effects are very difficult to come by. On the rare occasions that they do come on the market, competition to buy them is very fierce so beware of fakes. The scarcity of props means that the

toys are popular with collectors, as apart from posters, it is very difficult to collect anything else connected to the franchise.

- 'Carded' figures, those still in their original packaging, are worth considerably more than loose figures. Early '12-back' cards showing only the 12 original figures are generally the most sought after. Vehicles and accessories that retain their original boxes and instructions are also more valuable.

- Other licensed manufactures include Palitoy in the UK, Harbert in Italy, Glasslite in Brazil, Takara in Japan, Toltoys in Australia, Lily Ledy in Mexico and Meccano in France. Collectors tend to prefer toys made in their own country, but regional variations did occur and some toys were only available outside America.

- Hasbro produce the figures and toys for the new films and it is difficult to tell how collectible these will prove in the long run, as recent 'Star Wars' films have not been quite as popular with fans.

A Star Wars 'Luke Skywalker' Early Bird action figure.

Overwhelming demand meant that Kenner Toys were unable to produce enough figures leading up to Christmas 1977. Instead, they supplied retailers with 'Early Bird Certificates' which could be later redeemed for toys. This 'Early Bird' Luke figure can be identified as he has a double-extending light saber.

c1978   3.75in (9.5cm) high

$280-320   KF

A Star Wars 'Princess Leia' action figure.
c1978 3.75in (9.5cm) h
$30-50   KF

A Star Wars 'Han Solo' action figure.
c1978 3.75in (9.5cm) h
$15-25   KF

A Star Wars 'Darth Vader' action figure.
c1978 4in (10cm) high
$10-15   KF

A Star Wars 'Ben (Ob-Wan) Kenobi' action figure.
c1978 3.75in (9.5cm) h
$15-25   KF

A Star Wars 'Chewbacca' action figure.
c1978 3.75in (9.5cm) h
$8-12   KF

A Star Wars C-3PO' action figure.
c1978 3.75in (9.5cm) h
$15-25   KF

A Star Wars 'R2-D2' action figure.

c1978 2.25in (5.5cm) h

$30-40 KF

A first issue hard plastic Star Wars 'Stormtrooper' action figure.

c1978 3.75in (9.5cm) h

$15-25 KF

A Star Wars 'Jawa' action figure, with vinyl cape.

This figure was one of the first 12 released, but executives felt that the diminutive figure would seem better value for money with a more 'expensive' looking cloth cape. Beware of fake vinyl capes, the cape should be the same color as the figure.

c1978   2.5in (6.5cm) h

$280-320 KF

A Star Wars 'Jawa' action figure, with cloth cape.

c1978   2.5in (6.5cm) h

$15-25 KF

A Star Wars 'Boba Fett' action figure.

Bounty hunter Boba Fett's first film appearance was in "The Empire Strikes Back", however, he had featured in the poorly received 1978 "Star Wars Holiday Special" TV programme. This figure was released anticipating his role in "The Empire Strikes Back".

c1979 3.75in (9.5cm) h

$20-30 KF

A Star Wars 'Luke Skywalker X-Wing Pilot' action figure.

c1979 3.75in (9.5cm) h

$12-18 KF

A Star Wars - The Empire Strikes Back 'Luke Skywalker (Bespin Fatigues)' action figure, with brown hair.

c1980   4in (10cm) high

$15-20 KF

A Star Wars - The Empire Strikes Back 'Yoda' action figure, with brown snake.

c1980   2in (5cm) high

$30-50 KF

A Star Wars - The Empire Strikes Back 'Lando Calrissian' action figure, with white eyes and teeth showing.

c1980 3.75in (9.5cm) h

$8-12 KF

A Star Wars - The Empire Strikes Back 'Imperial Stormtrooper Soldier (Hoth Battle Gear)' action figure.

c1980 3.75in (9.5cm) h

$12-18 KF

A Star Wars - Return of the Jedi 'Admiral Ackbar' action figure.

c1983 3.75in (9.5cm) h

$8-12 KF

A Star Wars - Return of the Jedi 'Biker Scout' action figure.

c1983 3.75in (9.5cm) h

$12-18 KF

A Star Wars - Return of the Jedi 'Emperor's Royal Guard' action figure.

c1983   4in (10cm) high

$10-15 KF

A Star Wars - Return of the Jedi 'Warok' action figure.

c1985 3in (7.5cm) high

$60-90 KF

An unpainted prototype Star Wars Episode 1 'Boss Nass' action figure, by Hasbro.

c1998   4in (10cm) high

$350-400 KF

A Star Wars Episode 1 'Sith Speeder and Darth Maul' action figure salesman's sample, by Hasbro.

This sample piece has no marking.

c1998 9in (22.5cm) high

$150-200 KF

12in Figures & Carded Figures

A Star Wars 'Chewbacca' large size action figure, by Kenner.

c1978   12in (30.5cm) high

$70-100 KF

A Star Wars 'Han Solo' large size action figure, by Kenner.

c1979   12in (30.5cm) high

$100-150 KF

A Star Wars 'Ben (Obi-Wan) Kenobi' large size action figure, by Kenner.

c1979   12in (30.5cm) high

$70-100 KF

A Star Wars 'Jawa' large action figure, by Kenner.

c1979   8in (20cm) high

$70-100 KF

A Star Wars 'Death Squad Commander' carded action figure, by Palitoy.

These figures were renamed 'Star Destroyer Commander', which are more common.

c1978   9in (22.5cm) high

$400-600 KF

A Star Wars 'Sand Person' carded action figure, by Palitoy.

These figures were originally called 'Tusken Raiders'.

c1978   9in (22.5cm) high

$400-600 KF

A Star Wars 'Greedo' carded action figure, by Kenner.

c1979   9in (22.5cm) high

$280-320 KF

A Star Wars - The Empire Strikes Back 'Han Solo (Bespin Outfit)' carded action figure, by Palitoy.

c1981   9in (22.5cm) high

$180-220 KF

A Star Wars - The Empire Strikes Back 'AT-AT Commander' carded action figure, by Palitoy.

c1982   9in (22.5cm) high

$100-150 KF

A Star Wars - The Empire Strikes Back 'Imperial TIE Fighter Pilot' carded action figure, by Palitoy.

c1982   9in (22.5cm) high

$100-150 KF

A Star Wars - Return of the Jedi 'Gamorrean Guard' carded action figure, by Kenner.

c1983   9in (22.5cm) high

$30-50 FF

A Star Wars - Return of the Jedi 'Princess Leia Organa (Boushh Disguise)' carded action figure, by Palitoy.

c1983   9in (22.5cm) high

$60-90 KF

A Star Wars - Return of the Jedi 'tri-logo' Luke Skywalker (Jedi Knight) carded action figure.

Tri-logo packaging has the logo in English, Spanish and French and was designed to save production costs. Tri-logo figures often have variations from the standard range which makes them sought-after by collectors.

c1983   9in (22.5cm) high

$80-120   **KF**

A Canadian Star Wars - The Power of the Force 'Yak Face' carded action figure, by Kenner.

The 'Power of the Force' range was launched by Kenner in 1985 to revive interest in the waning Star Wars line. A batch of 15 new figures, as well as 22 figures from previous lines, were issued with new packaging and a collectors coin. They did not prove popular but today are highly sought-after. Yak Face is one of the most difficult to find.

c1985   9in (22.5cm) high

$1,800-2,200   **KF**

A Star Wars - The Power of the Force 'Teebo' carded action figure, by Kenner.

c1985   9in (22.5cm) high

$120-180   **KF**

A Star Wars - The Power of the Force 'Han Solo (in Trench Coat)' carded action figure, by Kenner.

c1985   9in (22.5cm) high

$350-400   **KF**

A Canadian Star Wars - Droids 'R2-D2' carded action figure, by Kenner.

This series of 12 figures were based on the cartoon series "Droids: The Adventures of R2-D2 and C3PO" which ran from 1985-6.

c1985   9in (22.5cm) high

$120-180   **KF**

A Star Wars - Episode 1 'Darth Sidious' carded action figure, by Hasbro.

c1998   9in (22.5cm) high

$6-9   **KF**

A Star Wars - Episode 1 'Mace Windu' carded action figure, by Hasbro.

c1998   9in (22.5cm) high

$6-9   **KF**

A Star Wars - Episode 1 'Queen Amidala (Naboo)' carded action figure, by Hasbro.

c1998   9in (22.5cm) high

$6-9   **KF**

A Star Wars - Episode 1 'Darth Maul (Jedi Duel)' carded action figure, by Hasbro.

c1998   9in (22.5cm) high

$4-6   **KF**

A Star Wars - Attack of the Clones 'Boba Fett Kamino Escape' carded action figure, by Hasbro.

c2002   9in (22.5cm) high

$6-9   **KF**

A Star Wars - Attack of the Clones 'Luminara Undali' carded action figure, by Hasbro.

c2002   9in (22.5cm) high

$8-12   **KF**

A Star Wars - Attack of the Clones 'Taun We' carded action figure, by Hasbro.

c2002   9in (22.5cm) high

$8-12   **KF**

A Star Wars 'Imperial TIE Fighter' vehicle, by Kenner, with rare Palitoy sticker.

A normal Kenner version of this ship would be worth about $220.

c1978 Ship 10.5in (26.5cm) w

$280-320 KF

A Star Wars - The Empire Strikes Back 'AT-AT All Terrain Armored Transport', by Palitoy, mint and boxed.

c1980   18in (45.5cm) high

$300-350 KF

A Star Wars Imperial Troop Transporter', by Palitoy.

c1979 Toy 10in (25.5cm) wide

$80-120 KF

A Star Wars - The Empire Strikes Back 'Snowspeeder', by Palitoy.

c1980 Toy 12in (30.5cm) high

$60-90 KF

A Star Wars - The Empire Strikes Back 'Scout Walker' vehicle, by Kenner.

c1980   12in (30.5cm) high

$150-200 KF

A Star Wars - Return of the Jedi 'Slave 1' vehicle, by Palitoy.

c1981 Toy 15.5in (39.5cm) w

$70-100 KF

A Star Wars - Return of the Jedi 'B-Wing Fighter' vehicle, by Kenner.

c1984

$220-280 KF

A Star Wars - The Empire Strikes Back 'Rebel Armored Snowspeeder', by Palitoy.

c1980 Toy 12in (30.5cm) high

$60-90 KF

A Star Wars - The Empire Strikes Back 'MTV-7 Multi-Terrain' vehicle mini-rig, by Kenner.

c1982   9in (22.5cm) wide

$30-40 KF

A Star Wars - Return of the Jedi 'X-Wing Fighter', with "Battle Damaged" look feature, by Palitoy/Meccano.

This vehicle was also released with Empire Strikes Back packaging in 1982, which is harder to find than this example.

c1983   Toy 13in (33cm) long

$60-90 KF

A Star Wars - The Power of the Force 'Tatooine Skiff' vehicle, by Kenner, sealed in the box.

This toy was a late addition to the Kenner range and few were made, they are also quite fragile which makes them hard to find complete or sealed in the box.

c1985   Box 15.5in (39.5cm) high

$600-900 KF

A Star Wars - Return of the Jedi 'AST-5 Armored Sentinel Transport' vehicle mini-rig.

"Mini-rigs" were a range of small vehicles or appliances designed by Kenner Toys and which never appeared on screen.

c1983   3.75in (9.5cm) high

$20-30 KF

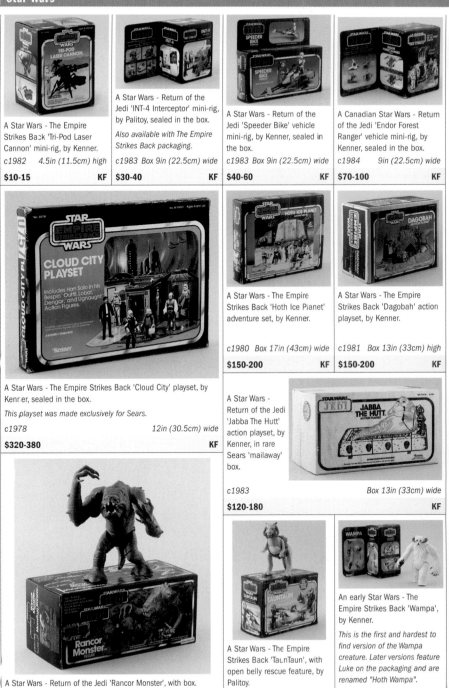

A Star Wars - The Empire Strikes Back 'Tri-Pod Laser Cannon' mini-rig, by Kenner.

c1982   4.5in (11.5cm) high

$10-15   KF

A Star Wars - Return of the Jedi 'INT-4 Interceptor' mini-rig, by Palitoy, sealed in the box.

Also available with The Empire Strikes Back packaging.

c1983 Box 9in (22.5cm) wide

$30-40   KF

A Star Wars - Return of the Jedi 'Speeder Bike' vehicle mini-rig, by Kenner, sealed in the box.

c1983 Box 9in (22.5cm) wide

$40-60   KF

A Canadian Star Wars - Return of the Jedi 'Endor Forest Ranger' vehicle mini-rig, by Kenner, sealed in the box.

c1984   9in (22.5cm) wide

$70-100   KF

A Star Wars - The Empire Strikes Back 'Cloud City' playset, by Kenner, sealed in the box.

This playset was made exclusively for Sears.

c1978   12in (30.5cm) wide

$320-380   KF

A Star Wars - The Empire Strikes Back 'Hoth Ice Planet' adventure set, by Kenner.

c1980 Box 17in (43cm) wide

$150-200   KF

A Star Wars - The Empire Strikes Back 'Dagobah' action playset, by Kenner.

c1981 Box 13in (33cm) high

$150-200   KF

A Star Wars - Return of the Jedi 'Jabba The Hutt' action playset, by Kenner, in rare Sears 'mailaway' box.

c1983   Box 13in (33cm) wide

$120-180   KF

A Star Wars - Return of the Jedi 'Rancor Monster', with box.

c1983   Monster 9in (22.5cm) high

$70-100   KF

A Star Wars - The Empire Strikes Back 'TaunTaun', with open belly rescue feature, by Palitoy.

c1982   Toy 6in (15cm) high

$50-80   KF

An early Star Wars - The Empire Strikes Back 'Wampa', by Kenner.

This is the first and hardest to find version of the Wampa creature. Later versions feature Luke on the packaging and are renamed "Hoth Wampa".

c1982   6in (15cm) high

$100-150   KF

Collectors' Notes

- Heavy, solid forms and simple, almost unrealistic, designs typify the first model trains which were produced in the mid-19th century. By the 1890s, companies such as Marklin and Gebrüder Bing had introduced more realistic detail and refinement along with steam and clockwork driven models.
- 'Gauges' and sizes were large, with Marklin introducing defined gauge sizes in 1891. By 1910, large gauges such as 'I', 'II' and 'III', had been replaced, due to the demand for smaller and less expensive toys.
- In 1935, the smaller 'O' gauge was introduced by Marklin, but by then the trains were not as realistic as those made by British makers such as Hornby. As a result, Marklin established the still smaller 'HO' gauge in 1948, with solidly built, die-cast trains. Plastic began to be used for trains from the mid 1950s and was used almost exclusively from the 1960s onward.
- Liveries and couplings can often help to date trains. By 1923, most British train companies had merged into four large companies and liveries were redesigned to match them. Couplings were in the form of tin loops before 1904, hooks from 1904-1913 and sliding drop links after 1913.
- Look for large and well-detailed, realistic trains by major makers. Large, hand-painted tinplate examples, primarily from Germany, are usual y very valuable and sought after. Damage to paintwork and dents caused by play will reduce value. For later trains especially, excellent condition is essential and sets with original boxes will be more desirable.

A Bassett-Lowke O-gauge electric motored 4-4-0 locomotive and six wheel tender, finished in maroon with "RN 417" to cab sides, and LMS tender, minor some wear, refinished overall.

$100-150 **W&W**

A Bing for Bassett-Lowke O-gauge 4-4-0 clockwork locomotive, in LMS dark maroon, George V nameplates added to splashers, yellow/black lining, associated six wheel tender in black with white/red lining, some wear to finish.

$180-220 **W&W**

A Bassett-Lowke O-gauge clockwork 'Prince Charles' 4-4-0 locomotive and tender, in a 3R-lined blue livery, number 62078, with key, good condition, unboxed.

British company W.J. Bassett-Lowke (1899-1969) sold trains supplied by Gebrüder Bing until 1933 and Carette until c1917. After this, they sold trains from their own factory called George Winteringham.

$400-600 **DN**

A Bing O-gauge 4-4-0 electric motored locomotive and tender, RN 1924 in Midland maroon colors with yellow and black lining, LMS to six wheel tender, minor wear, minor age crazing to paintwork.

$220-280 **W&W**

A Bing O-gauge 4-4-0 electric motored locomotive and tender, black all-over finish, transfer double line to boiler, minor wear.

$180-220 **W&W**

A Bing O-gauge 4-4-0 'George the Fifth' clockwork locomotive and tender, in Midland maroon colors with yellow and black lining, 1,000 to six wheel tender, minor wear and loco appears refinished.

$180-220 **W&W**

A Bing Superforce O-gauge clockwork steam locomotive and tender, with one lamp missing and original box.

c1900

$1,200-1,800 **ATK**

A CLOSER LOOK AT A BING LOCOMOTIVE

This was made by German toy maker Gebrüder Bing (1867-1933), whose trains are second only to Marklin in terms of quality and value.

The detailing is excellent and highly realistic, which is typical of top quality Bing trains.

Gauge II is a large and desirable size; large, hand-painted trains were expensive, top of the range toys in their day.

It is steam driven and an early train, partly shown by the hand-painted LSWR livery making it additionally desirable.

A Bing gauge II live steam 4-4-0 LSWR 7096 locomotive and six wheel LSWR tender, hand-painted in green/brown with yellow lining, paint crazed, some denting.

$6,000-9,000 **BonC**

A Hornby 0-gauge 0-4-0 clockwork tank locomotive No. 1 special, finished in Southern 516 green and black livery.

$150-200   W&W

A Hornby 0-gauge 4-4-4 special tank locomotive, a well restored three rail 20v electric, finished in Southern E492 black livery.

$220-280   W&W

A Hornby 0-gauge 4-4-4 tank locomotive, a well restored clockwork No. 2, finished in Southern B604 green and black livery.

$280-320   W&W

A Hornby 0-gauge 4-4-4 tank locomotive, a well restored clockwork No. 2, finished in Southern E492 black livery.

$280-320   W&W

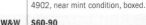

A Hornby 0-gauge 4-4-0 locomotive and tender, a well restored clockwork No. 2 finished in Southern A760 green and black livery.

$280-320   W&W

A Hornby R372 Class A4 'Seagull' locomotive, in LNER blue livery, number 4902, near mint condition, boxed.

$60-90   DN

Hornby

- Frank Hornby began to manufacture trains in 1920, when German imports were unpopular after WWI. The company's trains were sturdy but crudely modeled.
- During the 1930s, it introduced its 'Dublo' range to compete with Marklin's popular 00 range. By then its production had also become realistically modeled, with better detailing.
- Post-WWII 0-gauge trains were of poor quality. They were redesigned but production ceased in 1969. They were replaced with other current ranges which were still popular.
- By 1964 Hornby had been crippled by the introduction of plastic trains and was taken over by Tri-ang.
- Today, its 0-gauge trains make excellent and often affordable collections. As the finer early pieces have become rare, examples from the 1960s to the 1980s have become highly sought-after in mint condition.

A Hornby 0-gauge No. 101 tank passenger set, in the scarce LNER teak livery, comprising 101-type LNER RN 460, 0-4-0 locomotive, clockwork, two 1st/3rd composite four wheel coaches and guards/baggage van, in original blue card set box with inner packing card, circle of rail, two straights, clip box clips and key and packet of four lights, box, minor outer marks, worn.

$180-220   W&W

A Hornby Series E3200 Electric Passenger set, 20-volt electric 4-4-2 Royal Scot engine No. 6100 with smoke detectors and tender in maroon LMS livery, together with three LMS coaches and track, front bogie wheels to engine detached with one wheel missing and one fatigued.

$800-1,200   BonC

A 1960's French Hornby HO-gauge train set, comprising a twin pantograph Bo Bo SNCF locomotive, RN BB16009, plus two coaches with "Paris Lille" destination boards, 1st and 2nd Class examples, with a small, quantity of track, boxed, minor wear.

$300-500   W&W

A Hornby R49 limited edition 'Lord of the Isles' set, comprising GWR 4-2-2 locomotive number 3046 and three chocolate and cream coaches, near mint boxed.

$120-180   DN

A scarce O-gauge Leeds Model Co 0-6-0 compound tender locomotive, in LMS maroon, clockwork powered, well detailed in yellow, RN 4422 with LMS to tender, some refinishing.

$220-280   W&W

An O-gauge Leeds Model Co 2-4-2 tank locomotive in black, LMS to tank and RN 10943 to bunker, electric motored, minor wear, probably refinished.

$180-220   W&W

An O-gauge Leeds Model Co 0-6-0 Southern tank locomotive "Southern 261" to tank sides, finished overall green with yellow and black edge lining, electric motored, replaced mirror wear overall.

$150-200   W&W

An O-gauge Leeds Model Co 0-6-0 Jinty-style tank locomotive, refinished in black, electric motored, some wear to finish.

$150-200   W&W

An O-gauge Leeds 4-4-0 Mainline locomotive in BR black livery, with six wheel tender, RN 60725, red and white lining, electric motored, minor wear overall.

$220-280   W&W

An O-gauge Milbro 4-4-2 Great Western tank locomotive, RN 45, electric motored, tinplate construction with die-cast fittings, finished GW green with yellow lining, some finish loss, minor fatigue to wheels.

$220-280   W&W

An O-gauge Milbro 4-4-2 tank locomotive, finished in green Southern livery, 890 to tank sides, yellow lining, electric motor, some paint wear.

$180-220   W&W

A Tri-ang OO-gauge train set RS1, containing 4-6-2 Princess Victoria in black BR livery RN 4620s, two cream/maroon coaches mainline composite and 3rd brake end, plus an oval of black plastic track, in original box, minor rubs only, servicing leaflet.

$220-280   W&W

$700-1,000   BonC

A Tich 3.5in handbuilt steam driver 0-4-0 tank locomotive, with copper, steel and brass body, in maroon and black livery, the cab with full compliment of controls, saddle water tanks, one with manual water pump, steam whistle and safety valve.

A Tri-ang OO-gauge train set RS1, containing 4-6-2 Princess Victoria in black BR livery RN 4620's, two cream/maroon coaches mainline composite and 3rd brake end, plus an oval of black plastic track in original box, minor rubs only, servicing leaflet.

$100-150   W&W

A Wrenn Railways 4-6-2 streamlined Mallard, RN 4468 in blue eight wheel tender LMER to sides, in original box with packing, coupling and instructions, box minor corner rubs, appears unrun, few minor marks to tender.

After Hornby were sold to Tri-ang in 1964, George Wrenn bought most of Hornby's dies and tooling and produced trains such as this one in liveries and variations not made by Hornby. Many of these are more valuable than the original Hornby versions. This continued until Wrenn's retirement in 1994 when production was continued by Dapol of Wales.

$150-200   W&W

An O-gauge 0-6-2 tinplate and die-cast scratch-built Southern tank locomotive, Southern 2591 to tank sides, green finish and white and black edge lining, electric motored, fine scale wheels, well detailed, minor wear overall.

$180-220 W&W

An O-gauge locomotive and six wheel tender, probably modified Bassett-Lowke body with clockwork mechanism, Onyx name plate transfers to splashers, 5652 to tender sides, finished overall black with LMS crest to cab sides, minor finish wear.

$100-150 W&W

An O-gauge 2-4-2 tank locomotive, scratch-built from mainly brass, with white metal castings, overall black finish WJR and 19 to sides, fitted Bassett-Lowke clockwork mechanism, some wear to finish.

$100-150 W&W

A gauge II 4-6-0 Experiment 66 train, and six wheel tender fitted with stud contact electric motor, black with red/cream lining, lacks some small parts.

$700-1,000 BonC

An O-gauge 4-4-2 clockwork tank locomotive, made mainly from tinplate and L& NWR RN 44 to sides, driving wheels fatigued, minor finish wear.

$120-180 W&W

A 5in gauge scratch-built 0-6-0 PT GWR 5717 Collect tank locomotive, in 1:1 scale, with Stephenson's valve gear.

Scratch-built trains are built by semi-professional amateurs or hobbyists and not by major manufacturers. Due to the care and skill of some of these craftsmen, detailing is often very fine and parts are extremely well engineered. The quality of these two aspects, sophistication of the engine, realism and size all help to define value.

35in (89cm) long

$4,000-6,000 BonC

A 3.5in gauge scratch-built live steam freelance 0-4-0T Helga eight tank Engine, finished in blue.

$700-1,000 BonC

A 3.5in gauge scratch-built live steam London, Brighton and South Coast Railway 0-6-0 A-class tank locomotive No. 57 "Thames".

$2,200-2,800 BonC

An O-gauge scratch built 4-6-2 tank locomotive, in LMS black RN 6978 to tank and crest to bunker, fitted powerful clockwork motor, fine scale wheels, minor wear.

$150-200 W&W

A scratch-built live steam LMS Patriot class 4-6-0 'Illustrious' 5532, finish in black livery.

$1,000-1,500 BonC

An O-gauge Bonds Pullman Car No 74, brown/cream finish with full lining, corridor connectors, good under frame detailing cast bogies, no interior fittings, white roof, minor wear cracking at roof joints.

$120-180 W&W

An O-gauge Pullman car, made using many Bonds parts, brown, cream high gloss finish, well-detailed underframe, cast bogies, fully detailed interior, gray roof, minor wear, few interior seats loose.

$150-200 W&W

An O gauge Pullman coach by Douglas, in brown and cream livery. Undline to sides, yellow lining, underframe detailing, compensating plate and cast bogies, interior detailing and gray roof, corridor connectors, minor wear.

$150-200 W&W

An O-gauge Leeds LBSC, 1st/3rd coach in overall brown finish, paper-covered wood body, white roof, underframe detailing cast and plate bogies, roof refinished, minor wear.

$60-90 W&W

An O-gauge Leeds Model Co. 'Brighton Belle' 1st Class Pullman 'Hazel', in brown/cream livery with corridor connectors fitted, minor wear.

$150-200 W&W

A pair of C-gauge Leeds Model Co. Southern Region bogie coaches 1st/3rd composite and 3rd passenger brake end Suburban stock, finished in green detail printed paper, with guard's buckets to rear of brake end, black underframes and bogies, white roofs, minor wear, roofs refurbished.

$150-200 W&W

An O-gauge wood construction Milbro LMS mainline corridor 3rd coach, fully glazed and with good interior detail with cloth-covered seating and back protectors, removable roof with lighting, cast compensating bogies, corridor connectors, minor wear.

$100-150 W&W

An O-gauge Milbro Pullman coach 'Princess Helen', in brown/cream livery, recessed doors to coach ends, underframe detail, cast brass bogies, corridor connectors, white roof, no interior fittings, minor wear.

$180-220 W&W

An O-gauge Milbro LMS composite dining car, in maroon finish with yellow lining, underframe detail, cast bogie frames, full interior detailing, corridor connectors, gray roof, minor wear overall, bogie frames have lowered running position.

$120-180 W&W

An C-gauge Milbro Pullman 'Princess Helen' coach in brown/cream livery, cream roof factory transfer to one end, corridor connectors, cast brass bogies fully compensating, minor wear.

$150-200 W&W

An O-gauge Pullman car 'Mona', built from commercial parts, finished in brown/cream, gloss finish, minimal underframe detail, cast brass bogies, steel wheels, and fully detailed interior, silver roof, minor wear.

$70-100 W&W

An O-gauge Bing hand colored railway station, with concourse.

10.5in (27cm) wide

$1,500-2,000 ATK

A Hornby Dublo prewar wooden City Station Station Building and Canopy, with side-platform and three green removable panels, good, some retouching, three removable panels missing, replica roof.

$100-150 SAS

A Bing horizontal steam engine, on tin base with colored tiles.

c1926 *10.25in (26cm) wide*

$400-600 ATK

A Bing steam engine, with direct current generator and lamp, carburetor burner and oiler, on metal/timber flooring.

12.25in (31cm) wide

$600-900 ATK

A Bing double hot air engine, pinstriped cast iron engine on wood base with embossed lithographed tin decoration, retains original maker's decal, with original burner and stack, some wear on tin base plate.

Base 10in (25.5cm) wide

$1,000-1,500 NB

A Carette horizontal steam engine, with boiler house, the engine with oiling supply and instrument panels.

26in (65.5cm) high

$2,200-2,800 ATK

A Marklin tinplate model of a vertical steam boiler, with spirit burner.

14.25in (36cm) high

$400-600 Chef

A Frisbie cast iron beam steam engine, with original paint flourish decoration, the walking beam engine mounted over the boiler, marked on top of boiler "Frisbie, Patent 1871".

9in (23cm) high

$3,000-4,000 NB

A Weeden Favourite steam engine, the small painted tin engine with an oscillating cylinder, maker's name embossed on fuel reservoir.

6in (15cm) long

$300-500 NB

Collectors' Notes

- Steam has been used to power models and toys from the late 19th century onward, as an alternative to clockwork. It was largely replaced by battery or electric power in the 20th century, although some toys are still being sold and some models (usually scratch built by amateurs) are still being built.

- There are three primary types of steam engine driven items: stationary toys built for children, moving steam-powered models such as engines, trains and boats and demonstration models made to show how a machine works.

- Stationary engines were made by many of the leading German tinplate manufacturers such as Gebrüder Bing, Marklin, Ernst Plank and Carette. In England, Mamod is the best known maker. They also made moving steam engines.

- Most stationary steam engines drove flywheels that would be attached to other accessories with belts, driving the workings on the accessory. Factories, windmills and other novelty movements can be found.

- Tinplate toys are desirable to tinplate collectors who collect names such as Marklin and Bing. Original paintwork or lithography is important, and damage, often caused by the water and oil used, reduces value. Look for original burners and components.

- Larger demonstration models fetch large sums if sophisticated, well engineered and of a large size. Any finely made 'live steam' pieces such as trains that can be 'ridden' or are larger than a toy will also usually be desirable and valuable.

A Plank vertical hot air engine, early style double flywheel engine mounted on decorative vented cast iron base fitted into a pierced tin housing with ornate embossed maker's plate and original burner, excellent condition.

12in (30.5cm) high

$1,000-1,500 NB

A Wilesco atomic power steam plant, lithographed tin reactor dome and cooling tower, electrically operated, mounted on base with tool platform, excellent condition.

This is an unusual late piece and, despite being steam driven is designed as an atomic power station.

Base 17in (43cm) wide

$120-180 NB

A Doll painted embossed tin elevator steam accessory, some paint loss on base corners where mounting holes were drilled, missing flag.

12in (30.5cm) high

$320-380 NB

A Doll painted tin water elevator with bucket chain, stamped "Made in Germany", some paint loss where mounting holes were installed.

11in (28cm) long

$300-500 NB

A Bing lithographed tin, clown with poodle steam accessory, clown raises stick as poodle lifts paw, some minor flaking on stick and along top edge.

4.5in (11.5cm) high

$320-380 NB

A boxed Mamod SR1 steam roller, in red, green and black livery, complete with burner tray and scuttle, steering rods and a filler funnel.

$80-120 DN

A Mamod TEA1 steam tractor, near mint, box good.

$180-220 Chef

A Weeden live steam road roller, with crank operated steering assembly, makers name embossed on roof, nickel-plated and painted cast iron drive and fly wheels, replaced burner, small area of paint loss on roof.

10in (25.5cm) long

$600-900 NB

A CLOSER LOOK AT A STEAM ENGINE ACCESSORY

The tin is painted, not lithographed, showing it is an early piece, probably before c1906.

It was made for the American market, which is less common, and is still in very good condition.

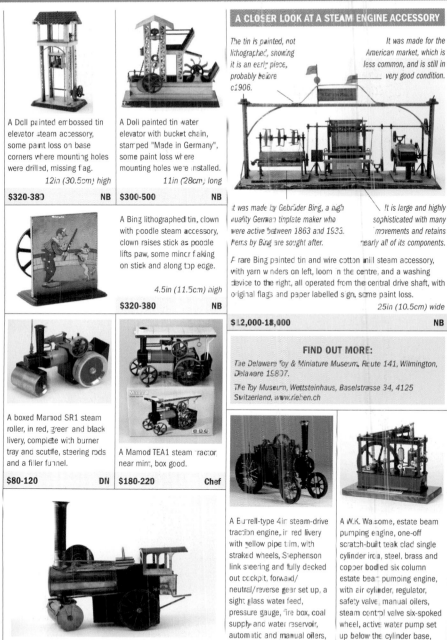

It was made by Gebrüder Bing, a high quality German tinplate maker who were active between 1863 and 1933. Items by Bing are sought after.

It is large and highly sophisticated with many movements and retains nearly all of its components.

A rare Bing painted tin and wire cotton mill steam accessory, with yarn winders on left, loom in the centre, and a washing device to the right, all operated from the central drive shaft, with original flags and paper labelled sign, some paint loss.

25in (10.5cm) wide

$12,000-18,000 NB

FIND OUT MORE:

The Delaware Toy & Miniature Museum, Route 141, Wilmington, Delaware 19807.

The Toy Museum, Wettsteinhaus, Baselstrasse 34, 4125 Switzerland, www.riehen.ch

A Burrell-type 4in steam-drive traction engine, in red livery with yellow pipe trim, with straked wheels, Stephenson link steering and fully decked out cockpit, forward/neutral/reverse gear set up, a sight glass water feed, pressure gauge, fire box, coal supply and water reservoir, automatic and manual oilers, manual handbrake, copper trimmed stack and more.

48in (122cm) long

$3,200-3,800 BonC

A W.K. Watsome, estate beam pumping engine, one-off scratch-built teak clad single cylinder iron, steel, brass and copper bodied six column estate beam pumping engine, with air cylinder, regulator, safety valve, manual oilers, steam control six-spoked wheel, active water pump set up below the cylinder base, with the piston rod continuing into the cylinder and inlet and outlet valves, set to base with plaque by engineer.

9in (23cm) long

$500-700 BonC

A French WWI 'Char d'Assaut tank' , one-off brass bodied clockwork-driven working tank, with metal caterpillar tracks, swivel action side and front mounted guns and a main cannon set up to the front, opening drivers door, incised plate to the roof "Char d'Assaut tank" and incised trade mark to front.

This example was built by St Charmond, French tank manufactures in 1916 as a scale model, probably to provide a visual aid for the French generals, prior to the tank being produced.

A 'Dancing Darkies' by The American Toy Co., the wooden figures dressed in cloth and with strung limbs jig up and down on a key wound, clockwork mechanism.

c1880   *9.75in (25cm) high*

$1,200-1,800   **ET**

A 1920s French fur-covered wind-up drumming monkey, who moves up and down and nods his head whilst drumming.

10.5in (27cm) high

$300-500   **AnaA**

1916   *12in (30.5cm) long*

$1,500-2,000   **BonC**

A Kohler Singing Crow, clockwork lithographed bird with bellows-action, with Kohler key.

6.75in (17.5cm) long

$120-180   **SAS**

A Bassett-Lowke clockwork No. 5 model "P" boat, gray wooden hull, plank effect decks with superstructure, life boats, guns and torpedo chutes, vents and mast, in original carry case.

1929

$800-1,200   **BonC**

A CLOSER LOOK AT AN AUTOMATON

When plugged in to the mains and set off, he raises his hand to eat a spoonful of oats, moves it back down and 'chews' his oats.

This was made to advertise Kirriemuir Milling Co.'s 'Peter Pan Porridge Oats' at an agricultural show and then distributed to retailers. Only 17 examples were made.

It was made in 1947, which is a very late date for an automaton. Most automata had clockwork mechanisms and were made in the 19th century in France.

A Japanese Suzuki celluloid and tinplate wind-up cycling Santa Claus, with ringing bell.

c1946   *4.25in (10.5cm) high*

$150-200   **MAC**

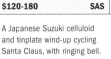

A clockwork rabbit, holding a camera.

A clockwork money, holding a camera.

This example was made by well-known English toy maker Chad Valley, the mechanism by the Fife Engineering Co.

A plastic and composition Chad Valley 'Peter Pan Porridge Oats' monkey automaton.

8in (20cm) high   *c1950*   *7in (18cm) high*

$280-320   **ATK**   **$280-320**   **ATK**

c1947   *20in (50cm) high*

$1,800-2,200   **ET**

A rare Japanese Alps Cragston Great Astronaut, tinplate construction and battery-powered, featuring moving pictures on TV screen, rotating arms and legs with antenna switch, in original box with packing, age wear and tears to box very good condition minor marks.

14in (35.5cm) long

$800-1,200   **W&W**

A Japanese DSK trademark tinplate and plastic Apollo Lunar Module model, battery-powered, boxed.

$220-280   **Chef**

A Japanese plastic clockwork robot.

6.75in (17cm) high

$30-40   **L**

A 1980s TOMY Krakbot. During the 1980s, TOMY released a range of toy robots with individual actions, from racing around the room crashing into things and then racing off in another direction, like the Dingbot and Spotbot to 'serving' drinks, like the Omnibot.

6in (15cm) high

$70-100   **L**

A 1980s TOMY Verbot, with voice transmitter.

9in (23cm) high

$80-120   **L**

A 1980s TOMY Omni Jnr robot.

This was the smaller, more inexpensive version of the Omnibot, the top of the range, remote control toy robot produced by TOMY which could pour drinks.

10.5in (26.5cm) high

$80-120   **L**

A 1980s TOMY Mr DJ Robot radio.

7in (18cm) high

$80-120   **L**

A TOMY Mr Money Automatic Bank.

Place a coin on his hand and this financially aware toy would throw it into his mouth where it would fall into an internal money bank.

c1987   *6in (15cm) wide*

$30-50   **L**

A 1980s TOMY Spotbot.

4in (10cm) long

$40-50   **L**

Collectors' Notes

- Money banks are typically made of painted cast iron. There are two types; mechanical banks with movements started by inserting a coin or pulling a lever, and still banks.

- The first cast iron money bank of this type was patented in 1869, although money banks had existed for centuries. It was made by J&E Stevens & Co of Cromwell, Connecticut, who went on to become a prolific maker. Other known makers include the Hubley Manufacturing Co who also made doorstops, Kyser & Rex (1879-1898) and the Shepard Hardware Co (1882-1892).

- Collectors focus strongly on condition. In terms of grading, the top two grades (eg. 9 and 10) are further subdivided into smaller grades (eg. 9.8) based on the number of chips and level of fading of the paint. A bank in very good condition can be worth over ten times more than one in average condition.

- Mechanisms should work and the coin trap should be original. Repainting devalues a bank, look closely at the paint which should have depth and show signs of crazing from age.

- There are many fakes, especially of mechanical and 'Jolly N' banks. Fakes do not usually 'fit' together well at joins, have rough surfaces and less fine detailing. Internal components are often clearly modern. Some are aged to look 'rusty' and old.

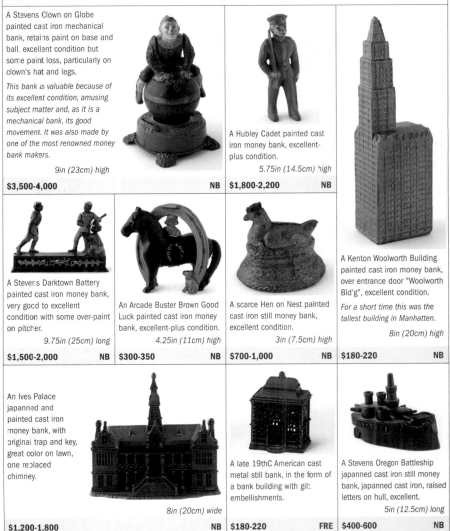

A Stevens Clown on Globe painted cast iron mechanical bank, retains paint on base and ball, excellent condition but some paint loss, particularly on clown's hat and legs.

This bank is valuable because of its excellent condition, amusing subject matter and, as it is a mechanical bank, its good movement. It was also made by one of the most renowned money bank makers.

9in (23cm) high

$3,500-4,000 NB

A Hubley Cadet painted cast iron money bank, excellent-plus condition.

5.75in (14.5cm) high

$1,800-2,200 NB

A Kenton Woolworth Building painted cast iron money bank, over entrance door "Woolworth Bld'g", excellent condition.

For a short time this was the tallest building in Manhatten.

8in (20cm) high

$180-220 NB

A Stevens Darktown Battery painted cast iron money bank, very good to excellent condition with some over-paint on pitcher.

9.75in (25cm) long

$1,500-2,000 NB

An Arcade Buster Brown Good Luck painted cast iron money bank, excellent-plus condition.

4.25in (11cm) high

$300-350 NB

A scarce Hen on Nest painted cast iron still money bank, excellent condition.

3in (7.5cm) high

$700-1,000 NB

An Ives Palace japanned and painted cast iron money bank, with original trap and key, great color on lawn, one replaced chimney.

8in (20cm) wide

$1,200-1,800 NB

A late 19thC American cast metal still bank, in the form of a bank building with gilt embellishments.

$180-220 FRE

A Stevens Oregon Battleship japanned cast iron still money bank, japanned cast iron, raised letters on hull, excellent.

5in (12.5cm) long

$400-600 NB

A 1960s Mickey Mouse Pelham puppet, mint condition, in box.

Pelham Puppets was founded in 1947 in Marlborough, England by Robert Pelham. They acquired the rights to make Disney character puppets in 1953. Pinocchio is one of the most common, but the many versions of Mickey Mouse made over the years make him comparatively common as well. Early puppets generally tend to be rarer and more desirable, but some of the later puppets are the rarest as fewer were made. Condition is critical as many were produced, collectors will only pay high prices for exceptionally rare characters or for those in the best condition, preferably with a box.

c1960   9in (23cm) high

$150-200   **BEJ**

A Pelham Puppet 'Donald Duck', dressed in sailor uniform, complete with strings and operating tree, in original box, very good condition for age, box torn, minor wear to model.

$80-120   **W&W**

A Pelham Puppet type SL 'Noddy', early version with large wooden head, with original control bar and black strings, complete with original instruction sheet, moth damage to felt hat, otherwise generally good condition in poor but original card box, with red and blue label to the lid, inscribed "An Enid Blyton Character by courtesy of Miss Enid Blyton".

$150-200   **DN**

A Pelham Puppet 'Reynardo the Fox', with carved head, hinged mouth with red felt lining, wooden carved hands and shoes, wearing red felt pants and jacket, yellow shirt and white bow tie, in plain box.

Reynardo the Fox is a character from the MGM film 'Lili', released in 1953 and then re-released as a Broadway musical in 1961. Reynardo was a mischievous, thieving character. Pelham Puppets of him are scarce, especially in this condition.

c1954   20in (51cm) high

$800-1,200   **BonC**

Left: A 1960s Pelham Puppet type SL 'Prince Charming', wearing white pants, red jacket and yellow top with white ruff, long silver hair, metal knee joints, standard control, yellow box.

$120-180

Right: A 1960s Pelham Puppet type SS 'Red Riding Hood', wearing a blue and white checked dress, red cloak, and with black hair and metal knee joints, standard control, yellow box.

$60-90   **BonC**

Left: A 1950s Pelham Puppet type SL 'Mr. Turnip', wearing a brown jacket and green pants with blue scarf and copper twirl to head, standard control, in plain brown box.

$100-150

Right: A 1970s Pelham Puppet type SL 'Wicked Witch', wearing a black dress, cape and hat, standard control, in yellow De Luxe window box, some tears and clear window missing to box, end of box stamped "Witch".

$60-90   **BonC**

A 'Mr Turnip Head' puppet, taken from the BBC TV series, in red, green and yellow, strings are detached from bars with box.

$120-180   **Vec**

A papier-mâché clown 'roly poly', a lead clown and puzzle.

$100-150 BonC

A Pelham Puppet type SL 'Sarah Swede', in blue dress and bonnet, pink apron and tartan shawl, with original control bar and black strings, some moth holes in bonnet but generally good condition, in fair, period but possibly incorrect, card box with red and blue label to the lid, one side with tear.

$280-320 DN

A Moko 'Muffin the Mule' metal puppet, complete with original tail, strings and finger rings in original box with graphics, minor wear.

$300-350 W&W

A Meccano Accessory Outfit 4A, with instruction book dated "1.55" and revision of contents list dated "3.55" in original box, slightly sun faded.

$50-80 SAS

A Meccano 'Votre Enchantment' 1937-1938 French Factory Meccano Products Catalogue, small paper tear to rear cover.

$60-90 SAS

A selection of Meccano 'Toys of Quality' Catalogues, including 1952, 1953, 1954-1955 and 1955-1956.

$60-90 SAS

A Scalextric Set 70, by Minimodels Ltd for Triangood, with 'autoscream' unit, two cars, track, accessories and instructions, boxed.

$80-120 Chef

A Meccano No.0 'Aeroplane Constructor' kit, the model made up as 0.3 Light Biplane, complete with unused floats, spanner, instructions and an advertising sheet for "Motor Car Constructor Outfits", box complete with original mounting card, pilot missing, some tape damage.

$300-500 DN

A Chad Valley Fordson Major new-type tractor.

$220-280 Chef

An ERTL 1/16 scale Ford 4000 tractor, unboxed.

$80-120 Chef

An ERTL 1/16 scale Case 2590 tractor, unboxed.

$60-90 Chef

An ERTL John Deere tractor.

$30-40   **Chef**

A Chad Valley green aluminium CW10045 Green Line Double Deck Bus, roof over-painted.

10in (25.5cm) long

$280-320   **SAS**

A Doepke MG TD, in painted cast aluminum with rubber tires, with fine detailing, edge wear.

15in (38cm) long

$300-500   **NB**

A 19thC-style kerbside model Robert E. Lee paddle steamer, with hand-built metal and wood bodies, with black and white livery, metal work to the chimney stacks, paddles and railings, davits and boat, chained loading ramps, chimney supports, flag poles, staircase and windows.

$220-280   **BonC**

A Bassett-Lowke Waterline Model Ships 'Alcantara', and 'Vienna', boxed.

$600-900   **Chef**

A child's wooden dog cart, with wooden spoked wheels and sides, elevated seat to rear for two children, having metal arms back, tow bar to front.

c1880   *40in (102cm) long*

$300-400   **BonC**

A black-painted wood, metal and leather miniature carriage.

31in (79cm) long

$600-900   **SI**

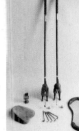

A novelty golf game, by The A. Schoenhut Company, Philadelphia, the golf playing subject operated by a golf club handle mechanism, and each with a series of woods and irons, bunkers, a tee, balls and various accessories.

$1,200-1,800   **LC**

A mid- to late 19thC German painted wooden Noah's ark and animals, with eight painted wooden people and approximately 90 pairs of animals.

Size and the quality of the carving and painting help to dictate value, with larger and finer examples usually being more valuable. It is also important that as many pairs of animals as possible are present and undamaged. Interestingly, many of the 19thC carvers had never seen the animals they were carving and, as there were no photographs or book illustrations to copy. As a result many look oddly shaped or proportioned to our eyes, some with a strong 'folky' feel.

Ark 7.5in (19cm) high

$800-1,200 (set)   **BonC**

Collectors' Notes

- The 19th century saw the largest growth in chess set manufacture, matched by increased interest in this previously 'aristocratic' game. Most chess sets available today date from this period onwards.

- India and China exported many of the sets currently collected. Also significant in the collecting field are British-made Staunton sets and those from other European countries, particularly Germany and Austria.

- Earlier sets dating from the 17th and 18th centuries can be found, but the earlier or finer quality the set, the higher the price. Chess sets do not have to be sold with accompanying boards – collectors may have a large number of sets and only one board.

- As well as the date, the quality of carving and the material used are important indicators of value. Well-executed carving and exotic woods or ivory are highly desirable features. Plain sets in base woods, such as boxwood, usually fetch low values.

- Interest in chess sets is expanding and there is only a limited supply, even of prolifically produced ones. Good quality sets are becoming harder to find and even relatively common examples, such as carved Cantonese sets, are becoming more desirable.

- Condition is very important. Cracks, missing or replaced pieces will devalue a set. Look closely at the colors of stained pieces – it can be difficult to match color exactly when pieces have been replaced.

A 19thC English Jaques Staunton ivory chess set, the white king signed "J. Jaques London" on the base, boxed, label missing.
King 3in (7.5cm) high

$800-1,200 CO

A large English bone Barleycorn-pattern chess set.
c1850 *King 4.5in (11.5cm) high*

$300-500 CO

A 19thC English bone Barleycorn-pattern chess set.
King 4.5in (11.5cm) high

$120-180 CO

A 19thC English Jaques Staunton weighted boxwood and ebony chess set, the white king stamped "Jaques London".
King 3.25in (8.5cm) high

$280-320 CO

A 19thC English Jaques Staunton weighted boxwood and ebony chess set, the white king stamped "Jaques London", in a box with green label marked "J. Jaques & Son, Ltd, London, England".

This set is in excellent, complete condition and retains its box, also in excellent condition, hence the price is higher than that of similar sets.
King 3.5in (9cm) high

$1,000-1,500 CO

An English 'Staunton Pattern' weighted boxwood chess set, the kings with onion-shaped dome and cross, boxed, black king warped.

Although they look like Staunton sets, 'Staunton Pattern' sets were not made by Jaques Staunton and do not bear 'Jaques' stamping.
c1880 *King 3.5in (9cm) high*

$150-200 CO

An English ivory chess set, boxed.
c1860 *King 3.75in (9.5cm) high*

$500-700 CO

An English ivory Barleycorn-pattern chess set.
c1870 *King 3.25in (8.5cm) high*

$500-700 CO

A CLOSER LOOK AT A CHESS SET

Fine quality English Victorian sets, such as this popular Lund-style set, are becoming scarce.

The carving is very well executed and the material used is a good quality ivory.

The set is complete, but some pawns have been re-carved or replaced. The price would have been higher if every piece were original.

An English ivory Lund-style chess set, boxed, some pawns re-carved.

Lund was a retailer in Cornhill, London, who sold an array of stationery, corkscrews, chess sets and many other small pieces.

c1840 King 3.5in (9cm) high

$1,200-1,800 CO

An ivory Edinburgh upright chess set, boxed.
c1860

$800-1,200 CO

An English celluloid chess set.
c1910 King 2in (5cm) high

$280-320 CO

A boxwood Dublin playing chess set, one black pawn replaced.
c1840 King 4.25in (10.5cm) high

$500-700 CO

A 19thC English rosewood and boxwood Old English-pattern chess set, boxed.

King 4.25in (10.5cm) high

$280-320 CO

A rare early 18thC English boxwood playing chess set, incomplete with one rook and four pawns missing, in later box.

Had it been complete, this set would have a much higher value.

King 3.75in (9.5cm) high

$400-600 CO

An unusual English carved boxwood 'Ship's' chess set, with bowl-shaped weighted bases, boxed.

The curved bases allowed the pieces to rock without falling over as the ship moved.

c1950 King 2.25in (6cm) high

$600-900 CO

An English ivory and ebony Washington-type chess set, in associated Indian sandalwood box.
c1800 King 3.5in (9cm) high

$400-600 CO

European Sets

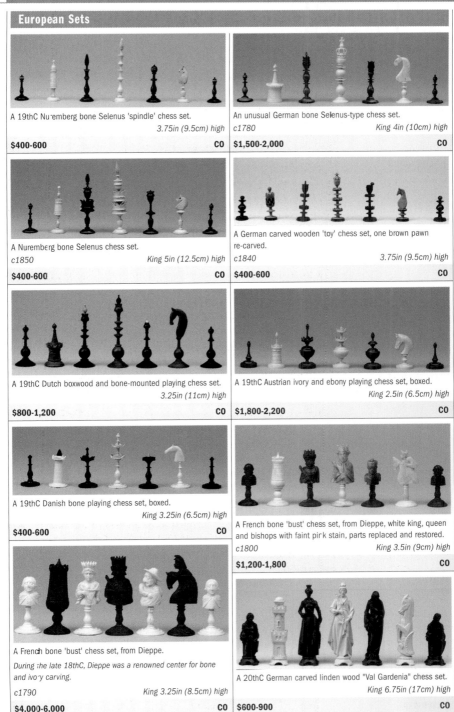

A 19thC Nuremberg bone Selenus 'spindle' chess set.

3.75in (9.5cm) high

$400-600 CO

An unusual German bone Selenus-type chess set.

c1780 *King 4in (10cm) high*

$1,500-2,000 CO

A Nuremberg bone Selenus chess set.

c1850 *King 5in (12.5cm) high*

$400-600 CO

A German carved wooden 'toy' chess set, one brown pawn re-carved.

c1840 *3.75in (9.5cm) high*

$400-600 CO

A 19thC Dutch boxwood and bone-mounted playing chess set.

3.25in (11cm) high

$800-1,200 CO

A 19thC Austrian ivory and ebony playing chess set, boxed.

King 2.5in (6.5cm) high

$1,800-2,200 CO

A 19thC Danish bone playing chess set, boxed.

King 3.25in (6.5cm) high

$400-600 CO

A French bone 'bust' chess set, from Dieppe, white king, queen and bishops with faint pink stain, parts replaced and restored.

c1800 *King 3.5in (9cm) high*

$1,200-1,800 CO

A French bone 'bust' chess set, from Dieppe.

During the late 18thC, Dieppe was a renowned center for bone and ivory carving.

c1790 *King 3.25in (8.5cm) high*

$4,000-6,000 CO

A 20thC German carved linden wood "Val Gardenia" chess set.

King 6.75in (17cm) high

$600-900 CO

Chinese Sets

A 19thC Cantonese export ivory figural chess set, together with a 19thC English leather-covered board/box.

King 4.75in (12cm) high

$320-380 CO

A 19thC ivory Cantonese export ivory 'George III' chess set.

King 4.25in (11cm) high

$500-700 CO

A 19thC Cantonese carved ivory 'George II' figural chess set.

King 4.25in (10.5cm) high

$350-400 CO

A 19thC Cantonese ivory 'puzzleball' figural chess set, together with a 19thC English board box.

King 2.5in (6.5cm) high

$350-400 CO

A 19thC Cantonese export ivory 'puzzleball' set.

King 5.75in (14.5cm) high

$300-400 CO

A Cantonese export ivory chess set.

c1840 King 5in (13cm) high

$1,800-2,200 CO

A Cantonese export ivory 'George III' chess set.

Usually Chinese in origin, 'George III' sets have a King and Queen who resemble King George III and Queen Charlotte.

c1840 King 6.25in (16cm) high

$2,200-2,800 CO

A 19thC Cantonese ivory, Burmese-type, small chess set, in an Indian carved wooden sandalwood box.

King 3.75in (9.5cm) high

$300-350 CO

A 20thC Hong Kong ivory figural chess set.

King 4.5in (11.5cm) high

$2,200-2,800 CO

A 19thC Cantonese carved ivory, Burmese-type, small chess set, some replaced pawns.

King 3.25in (8cm) high

$350-400 CO

Novelty Sets

A 20thC Italian Bussano 'Animal' chess set, together with a ceramic and wood-framed board.

King 5.5in (14cm) high

$1,800-2,200 CO

A 20thC Portuguese pottery 'Rat' figural chess set.

King 3.75in (9.5cm) high

$600-900 CO

A 20thC German Albert Stahl Thuringian porcelain 'Frog' set.

King 2.75in (9.5cm) high

$180-220 CO

A 20thC Royal Dux porcelain figural chess set, signed.

King 4.5in (11.5cm) high

$600-900 CO

A 20thC German Furstenberg biscuit porcelain 'Bust' chess set, each base marked "F", together with a hardstone chessboard.

The design for the pieces was taken from the original 18thC mold to commemorate the bicentenary of the Fürstenberg factory in 1947.

King 3.25in (8.5cm) high

$600-900 CO

A 20thC Javanese Indonesian-style painted wood 'Deity' chess set.

King 4.25in (11cm) high

$120-180 CO

A 20thC Anri carved wooden 'Conquistador' figural chess set.

King 5.5in (14cm) high

$700-1,000 CO

A 20thC Venetian Murano large glass 'Bust' chess set.

$1,200-1,800 CO

A Murano glass chess set, Venetian, together with a glass board.
c1960

King 5.5in (14cm) high

$2,200-2,800 CO

FIND OUT MORE...

'Master Pieces: The Architecture of Chess' by Gareth Williams, Viking Press, 2000, ISBN: 0670893811 (Also published by Apple Press).

Musée International du Jeu d'Echec (The International Museum of Chess) Chateau de Clairvaux, 86140 Scorbe-Clairvaux, France.

U.S. Chess Hall of Fame and Museum, U.S. Chess Center, 1501 M Street NW, Washington DC 20005, U.S.A.

Collectors' Notes

■ Computer games were first produced and sold around 1979 and grew rapidly in popularity during the 1980s. 'Shoot 'em up' and 'beat 'em up' games are very popular and addictive and characterize computer game production.

■ Most computer games were and are produced in Japan with popular names such as Nintendo, TOMY and SEGA becoming household names. Games produced solely for the Japanese market are sought after, but only if they can be played without mastery of the Japanese language.

■ Computer games must be complete and in working order to have a value. Commonly missing parts which reduce value include the battery cover. An original box and instructions add value.

A silver Nintendo 'Vermin MT-03' game and watch.

Nintendo 'Game and Watch' sets are very popular with collectors, with around 65 different games to collect. This is in excellent and complete condition.

c1980   3.75in (9.5cm) wide

$400-600   HLJ

A silver Nintendo 'The Exterminator MT-03' game and watch.
c1980   3.75in (9.5cm) wide
$150-200   HLJ

A Nintendo 'Parachute PR-21' wide-screen game and watch.
c1981   4.25in (11cm) wide
$60-90   HLJ

A Nintendo 'Fire Attack ID-29' wide-screen game and watch.
c1982   4.25in (11cm) wide
$70-100   HLJ

A Nintendo 'Squish MG-61' multi-screen game and watch.
c1983   4.25in (11.5cm) wide
$70-100   HLJ

A Nintendo 'Snoopy SM-91' panorama screen game and watch.

c1983

$120-180   HLJ

A Nintendo 'Zelga ZL-65' multi-screen game and watch.
c1989   4.25in (11.5cm) wide
$50-80   HLJ

A Nintendo 'Micro Vs Donkey Kong III AK-302' game and watch.
c1994   6in (15.5cm) wide
$100-150   HLJ

A Nintendo 'Micro Vs Donkey Kong Hockey HK-303', two-player game and watch.

c1984   6in (15.5cm) wide
$100-150   HLJ

A Nintendo 'Micro Vs Boxing BX-301' two-player game and watch.
c1984   6in (15.5cm) wide
$100-150   HLJ

A TOMY 'Knights Mission' hand-held clockwork game.
c1979   5.75in (14.5cm) wide
$15-25   HLJ

A TOMY 'Monster Burger' hand-held color LSI game
c1983   5.75in (14.5cm) wide
$30-50   HLJ

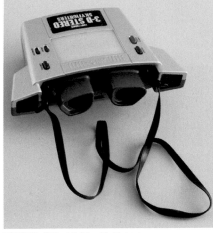

A TOMY 'Skyfighters' 3-D hand-held game.
c1983   8.25in (21cm) wide

$30-50   HLJ

A TOMY 'Mr Go!' hand-held color LSI game.

c1983   4.5in (11.5cm) wide

$30-50   HLJ

A Bambino 'Boxing' tabletop game.
c1979   11.75in (30cm) wide

$40-60   HLJ

A Bambino 'UFO Master-Blaster Station hand-held game.

c1980   5in (13cm) wide

$50-80   HLJ

A CGL 'Earth Invaders' hand-held game.
c1980   7.7in (20cm) wide

$60-90   HLJ

A Grandstand 'Munchman' tabletop game.
c1981   7.7in (20cm) wide

$40-60   HLJ

A Sega Nomad 'Genesis' (Mega Drive) hand-held portable game console.
c1995   7.25in (18.5cm) wide

$150-200   HLJ

A Grandstand 'Pocket Scramble' hand-held game.
c1983   6in (15cm) wide

$50-80   HLJ

A Palitoy 'Alex Higgins Cue Ball' tabletop game.
c1980   6in (15.5cm) wide

$60-90   HLJ

FIND OUT MORE...

'The Ultimate History of Video Games: From Pong to Pokemon – The Story behind The Craze that Touched Our Lives and Changed The World', by Steve L. Kent, published by Prima Publishing, 2001.

'Electronic Plastic', edited by Jaro Gielens, published by Die Gestalten Verlag, 2001, and covering hand-held games only.

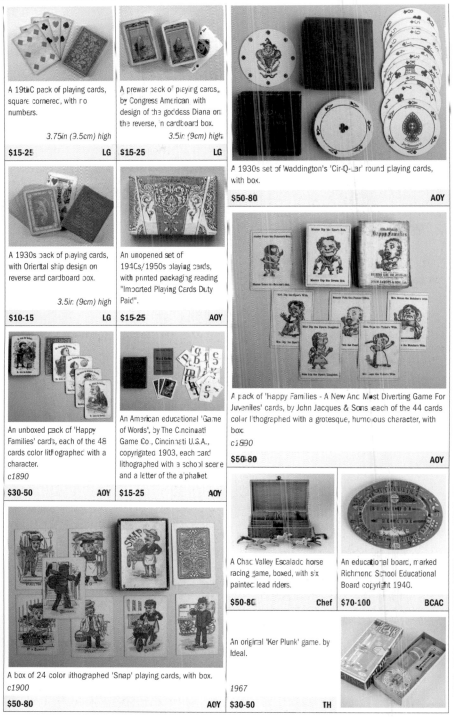

A 19thC pack of playing cards, square cornered, with no numbers.

3.75in (9.5cm) high

$15-25   LG

A prewar pack of playing cards, by Congress American with design of the goddess Diana on the reverse, in cardboard box.

3.5in (9cm) high

$15-25   LG

A 1930s set of Waddington's 'Cir-Q-Lar' round playing cards, with box.

$50-80   AOY

A 1930s pack of playing cards, with Oriental ship design on reverse and cardboard box.

3.5in (9cm) high

$10-15   LG

An unopened set of 1940s/1950s playing cards, with printed packaging reading "Imported Playing Cards Duty Paid".

$15-25   AOY

A pack of 'Happy Families - A New And Most Diverting Game For Juveniles' cards, by John Jacques & Sons each of the 44 cards color lithographed with a grotesque, humorous character, with box.

c1890

$50-80   AOY

An unboxed pack of 'Happy Families' cards, each of the 48 cards color lithographed with a character.

c1890

$30-50   AOY

An American educational 'Game of Words', by The Cincinnati Game Co., Cincinnati U.S.A., copyrighted 1903, each card lithographed with a school scene and a letter of the alphabet.

$15-25   AOY

A Chad Valley Escalado horse racing game, boxed, with six painted lead riders.

$50-80   Chef

An educational board, marked Richmond School Educational Board copyright 1940.

$70-100   BCAC

A box of 24 color lithographed 'Snap' playing cards, with box.

c1900

$50-80   AOY

An original 'Ker Plunk' game, by Ideal.

1967

$30-50   TH

TRIBAL ART

Collectors' Notes

- Tribal art is the work of the peoples of Africa, Oceania, South East Asia and the Americas. It was originally made for cultural, ceremonial or functional purposes, rather than for aesthetic appreciation.
- The atmosphere and climate has meant that most of the older pieces have been destroyed. Most pieces on the market today date from the late 19thC or 20thC. As pieces are not dated or signed, it is very difficult to date them precisely.
- Wear and use will add patination very quickly but patination can be 'applied', so it is not usually an indicator of authenticity, except to a trained eye. View genuine pieces to learn how to tell the difference.
- Many collectors choose to focus on the work of certain cultural areas or particular tribes. Most African masks and figures will originate from western and central areas, while the southern areas mainly produced smaller, utilitarian objects like pots.
- Many pieces found on the market today were made for tourists rather than to be used by tribes. This is due to the subject's increasing popularity and to tourism, both of which grew from the mid-20thC onward.
- Many deem these as tourist pieces, as 'fakes' or 'reproductions', but as they are often inexpensive, an attractive and diverse collection can be built easily.
- To build up a collection of authentic, aged and used pieces, it is best to visit a reputable auction house or dealer.

Figures

A 20thC Bakongo nail fetish figure (nkondi), from Lower Congo, with nails hammered overall, inlaid cowrie shell eyes and bilongo glass box to abdomen.

The Nkondi figures were made with the intention of helping chiefs seek out and punish witches and wrongdoers. Weapons or raised arms represent the ability to kill or strike a person or spirit responsible for a curse or evil.

23in (58.5cm) high

$150-200 RTC

A 20thC fetish figure (nkonci), from D. R. Congo, with metal projections, the upraised arm holding metal dagger, with rectangular glass box and red cloth pouches around neck and ankles, four fang-like teeth and wearing a hat with lozenge pattern.

33in (84cm) high

$180-220 RTC

A 20thC Yoruba Ibeji twin, from Nigeria, with pointed coiffure and scarification on cheeks.

Ibeji twins are amongst the most famous Yoruba figures and represent deceased twins. They are honored with prayers and libations.

12in (30.5cm) high

$50-80 RTC

A 20thC Yoruba Ibeji twin figure, from Nigeria, with pendulous breasts and oversized wedge-shaped feet, wearing a bead necklace, with carved scarification details on face and belly.

10.25in (26cm) high

$60-90 RTC

A Dan ancestor figure, from the Ivory Coast, standing on wedge-shaped feet, with bulbous forehead, carved scarification details on breasts and stomach, and wearing two white beaded belts.

38in (96.5cm) high

$220-280 RTC

A male figure, possibly Sepik, from Papua New Guinea, with cassowary feathers attached to clay shell-embedded head, wearing raffia skirt and anklets, traces of red pigment.

52in (132cm) high

$320-380 RTC

A Dogon mask, from Mali, with female figure wearing pendant cowrie-shell earrings and decorated with red pompoms, sitting atop a helmet-like face painted in red and blue.

36in (91.5cm) high

$300-400 RTC

A Bwa polychrome wood plank dance mask, from Burkina Faso, with a red hooked-nose projection on owl-like face, with opening for a nose between ringed eyes, on flat, black-and-white painted geometric decorated body.

These masks were used in agricultural rituals. The mask is believed to be high enough to 'touch' the sky.

61in (155cm) high

$180-220   RTC

An early 20thC Guro mask, of Gu, from the Ivory Coast.

13in (33cm) long

$800-1,200   SI

An early 20thC Guro mask, of Zamble, from the Ivory Coast.

17in (43cm) long

$1,800-2,200   SI

A Kuba ceremonial helmet mask, from Zaire, the metal sections attached with nails and inlaid beads, the head covered with burlap and hair tufts, with pendant seed pods.

15in (38cm) high

$150-200   RTC

A Kuba helmet mask, from D. R. Congo/Zaire, with raffia beard, carved with two horns curled back over head, the face painted with scarification lines.

42in (116cm) high

$300-400   RTC

A Kuba Ngeende dance mask, from Zaire, with elephant trunk, covered with burlap and cowrie shells, the square-shaped face having animal fur

15in (38cm) high

$400-600   RTC

A Warega wood mask, from D. R. Congo, surrounded with feathers.

5in (13cm) high

$300-500   SI

An early 20thC Pende wood mask, from D. R. Congo.

15in (38cm) high

$3,000-4,000   SI

A Dan mask, from the Ivory Coast, with metal teeth and burlap roll decorated with cowrie shells as hair.

11in (28cm) high

$220-280   FTC

An early 20thC Lega wood mask, from Zaire.

6in (15cm) long

$700-1,000   SI

An African mask, made from carved and painted wood.

44in (111.5cm) high

$300-400   FRE

A Pacific Northwest wood mask, painted with green, black and red paint.

10in (25.5cm) long

$700-1,000 **SI**

An 18thC Hawaiian calabash bowl.

6.5in (16.5cm) high

$1,200-1,800 **JBB**

A Cameroon Grassland mask.
c1870

$2,000-3,000 **JBB**

A 19thC Nepalese mask.

10in (25cm) high

$1,000-1,500 **JBB**

A 1950s Zulu beer pot, from South Africa.

The nomadic Zulu tribes produce few masks and figures, perferring small domestic wares such as pots and spoons.

c1955 6.25in (16cm) high

$220-280 **JBB**

A Taiwanese tribal votive plaque.

c1900 12.5in (31.5cm) high

$600-900 **JBB**

An Asante bronze vessel, from Ghana, with figural scene, the body covered in bands of geometric and floral designs.

These were used to keep valuables and religious offerngs.

9in (23cm) high

$350-400 **RTC**

An African carved wood birthing chair, carved with figures in various pursuits.

30in (76cm) high

$300-500 **SI**

An early 20thC Southern Fang wood ladle, from the Gabon, with figural decoration.

16.5in (42cm) long

$700-1,000 **SI**

An early 20thC Kuba wood sceptre, from D. R. Congo/Zaire

13in (33cm) long

$500-800 **SI**

An early 20thC Austral Islands ritual wood sword, from the South Pacific, with incised decoration.

28in (71cm) long

$300-500 **SI**

A Yoruba beaded crocodile ornament, from Nigeria, with cowrie-shell row down center of back and toes, geometric beaded pattern on tail and colored beaded turtle and fish on back, all attached to white cotton backing, with loop at one end.

39in (99cm) long

$180-220 **RTC**

Collectors' Notes

- The art of the c25,000 Inuit Eskimos in North Canada began being popularly traded from the late 1940s. During the 1950s and 60s, cooperatives were established by those such as the Canadian Art Council to market and sell Inuit artworks. A tuberculosis outbreak in the 1950s meant many artists were relocated to a sanatorium in Hamilton where they continued to sculpt, drawing interest from collectors.

- As they live above the tree-line, stone, bone and tusks are used instead of wood. Stone was not used before the 1950s and most stone sculptures found will be contemporary works, dating from after the 1960s.

- Themes are inspired by the harsh, seminomadic lifestyle and by arctic wildlife as well as mythical or shamanic legends.

- Many pieces are signed with 'disc numbers' usually beginning with an 'E' or 'syllabics', the Inuit pictogram-based language, where shapes mean certain letters and sounds.

- Beware of cast stone or plastic sculptures, which are not unique Inuit sculptures but mass-produced imitations.

A carved green stone Inuit sculpture of a mother with child, in an amaut and stretching a boot, by Josephie Aculiak of Inukjuak (1920-1968), signed with disc number and syllabics to underside.

7.5in (19cm) high

$800-1,200 RTC

A black stone Inuit sculpture of a mother carrying a child in an amaut and weaving, attributed to Alacie Alasnuk, Povungnituk, with separate willow and sinew mat on stone platform, inscribed "Alacie Alashuk" on label to base.

5.5in (14cm) high

$500-800 RTC

A carved black stone Inuit sculpture of a hunter kneeling over a blow hole, holding a sinew fishing line, by an unknown artist, possibly lacks an implement.

4.25in (11cm) high

$500-700 RTC

A carved gray stone Inuit sculpture of a hunter holding carved bone spears, by Simonee Aupaluktaq (b.1926), signed in syllabics and with disc number to base.

9.5in (24cm) high

$400-600 RTC

A carved dark gray stone Inuit sculpture of a hunter spearing a bear, by Charlie Ittusar Mark (b 1926), signed with disc number and syllabics to the underside.

6.5in (16.5cm) high

$320-380 RTC

A carved black stone Inuit sculpture of a bear on top of a seal, by George Palliser of Iunkjuak (b 1927), signed with disc number to the underside.

8.5in (21.5cm) high

$350-400 RTC

A carved white quartz Inuit sculpture of a seated polar bear, by an unidentified artist.

8.5in (21.5cm) high

$1,200-1,800 RTC

A small colorful felt appliqué Inuit wall hanging, depicting an Arctic scene, by an unknown artist, with embroidered borders and signed in syllabics.

$100-150 RTC

A colorful felt applique Inuit wall hanging depicting an Arctic scene, with embroidered borders and signed in syllabics.

38.5in (98cm) high

$100-150 RTC

Lucy Qinnuuyar of Cape Dorset, (1915-1982), "Man Wanting A Seal", print, color stencil, signed, titled and dated numbered 15/50.

1964   17in (43cm) high

$400-600 RTC

A gold-plated Elgin 15-jewel pocket watch, with engraved floral motif to reverse.

2.25in (5.5cm) wide

$120-180 | **AnaA**

A gold-plated Elgin hunter pocket watch.

'Hunter' watches have full hinged covers over the dial. 'Half Hunters' have hinged covers with a hole in the middle allowing partial view of the dial.

c1910 | *2in (5cm) wide*

$150-200 | **TAB**

A 1940s WWII 15-jewel Elgin bomb timer.

Used to time periods between release and detonation.

$100-150 | **ML**

A gold-plated Hamilton 17-jewel pocket watch, with plain reverse.

2in (5cm) wide

$120-180 | **AnaA**

A gold-plated Hampden lady's pocket watch, with engraved floral design to reverse.

1.25in (3cm) wide

$70-100 | **AnaA**

A gold-plated Waltham gentleman's hunter pocket watch.

c1910 | *1.5in (4cm) high*

$80-120 | **TAB**

A 1920s lady's cloisonné enameled spherical fob pin watch, unmarked, with 17-jewel Swiss-made movement.

2in (5cm) long

$70-100 | **TAB**

An 1890s gold-plated lady's pocket watch, unmarked, the hands set with two diamond chips, the case heavily decorated with etched floral pattern.

1.25in (3cm) wide

$80-120 | **TAB**

An Art Deco Movado lady's silver gilt and black enamel decorated purse watch, with square ivory baton dial, the case hallmarked London import, damage to one enameled corner.

1928 | *Case 2in (5cm) wide*

$220-280 | **F**

A 9ct gold pocket watch fob chain, with an older revolving citrine seal fob which is not engraved.

c1900

$180-220 | **TAB**

A Victorian 9ct gold solid 'Trombone and Knot' pattern single Albert chain.

14.5in (37cm) long

$400-600 | **F**

A white metal 'Giraffe' watch stand.

6.5in (16.5cm) high

$220-280 | **BCAC**

Collectors' Notes

- During the early 20thC, the increasing popularity of aviation and driving, coupled with practical requirements of warfare, meant that wristwatches became more popular than the impractical pocket watch, driving it into obscurity.
- The earliest wristwatches look very like small pocket watches, and have wire 'lugs' to hold the strap. The style quickly took off and by the 1930s, wristwatches outnumbered pocket watches many times over. Surprisingly early wristwatches are usually of low value, unless very finely made.
- Watches from the 1920s and 1930s are often shaped in the geometric, clean-lined style of the period. Watches from the 1940s are styled more like the jewelry of the time. Watches made for wartime use are easily recognized by their robust construction, black dials and luminous hands.
- Look for cases in precious metal or embellished with jewels. Complex movements with extra features, such as chronographs, are also more valuable. A high quality maker, such as Rolex, is also desirable.
- Always check the movement to ensure it is correct for the case. With precious metal cases, look for the correct marks as many were coated with rolled gold or gold plated.

A 1990s Breitling Automatic II gentleman's wristwatch, for the European market.

$700-1,000   ML

A 1950s gold-plated Bulova stone-set gentleman's wristwatch.

$100-150   ML

A 1950s 10ct gold-plated Bulova 'Chevrolet' gentleman's logo wristwatch.

These watches were made by Bulova and printed with a company logo for the company to give out as gifts.

$100-150   ML

A 1950s 17-jewel Incablock Buser Precision Explorer gentleman's wristwatch, with unusually shaped gold-plated case.

$150-200   ML

A 1940s Swiss-made Carrol 18ct gold-cased two register chronograph, for the European market.

The dials on a chronograph are known as 'registers'.

$500-700   ML

A 1940s Swiss-made Certina gold-plated wristwatch.

$30-50   TAB

A 1960s stainless steel CWC European military watch, with broad arrow marking.

$120-180   ML

A 1930s gold-plated Elgin gentleman's wristwatch, with stepped case and two-tone dial.

$120-180   ML

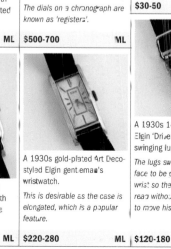

A 1930s gold-plated Art Deco-styled Elgin gentleman's wristwatch.

This is desirable as the case is elongated, which is a popular feature.

$220-280   ML

A 1930s 14ct gold-plated Lord Elgin 'Driver's' watch, with swinging lugs.

The lugs swing and allow the face to be positioned on the wrist so that it can easily be read without the driver needing to move his hand.

$120-180   ML

A 14ct white gold-plated Lord Elgin 'Dunbar' gentleman's wristwatch, with asymmetrical case with original box.

Elgin made two movements – Elgin and Lord Elgin, the latter being the higher quality and more expensive range.

c1950

$220-280   ML

A 1950s Elgin logo watch, with Porsche logo.

$120-180   ML

A 1930s 10ct gold-plated Gruen Curvex wristwatch, with Art Deco-styled case.

$80-120   TAB

A 1930s Swiss nickel-cased Gruen gentleman's wristwatch, with Radium hands and dial.

$150-200   ML

A 1950s Swiss gold-plated cased Gruen 21-jewel movement gentleman's wristwatch, with an unusually shaped case, with original box.

The 21-jewel movement was the higher quality movement by Gruen. This watch is desirable for this reason and for its shape.

$220-280   ML

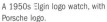

A 1930s 14ct gold-plated Hamilton 'Leicester' gentleman's wristwatch, with original cream Bakelite Art Deco-styled box.

The box alone is worth around $50.

$280-320   ML

A 14ct gold-plated Hamilton Boulton gentleman's wristwatch, with clear crystal.

c1940

$150-200   ML

A 14ct Hamilton Boulton gentleman's wristwatch, with original Art Deco Bakelite box.

The striking blue crystal is highly unusual, making this watch more valuable than other similar Hamilton Boultons.

c1940

$300-400   ML

A 1960s gold-plated cased Hamilton automatic gentleman's wristwatch, with original plastic box.

The box, particularly with its 'atomic' motif, shows the 1960s fascination with futuristic design, outer space and atomic power.

$150-200   ML

A 1930s Hamilton lady's 14ct white gold-cased watch, inset with diamonds, in original Art Deco cream Bakelite box.

$500-700   ML

A 1940s Swiss-made Helvetia 18ct gold-cased two register chronograph, for the European market.

$500-700   ML

A 1970s Heuer gentleman's Carrera automatic chronograph wristwatch, with black finished square case, round black dial, luminous baton markers and fluorescent orange chronograph hands.

This watch was named after the famed Carrera Race and was made before and during the transition of Heuer to Tag Heuer. The high quality '510' movement is still used today.

Case 1.5in (4cm) diam

$400-600   F

A CLOSER LOOK AT A HEUER WATCH

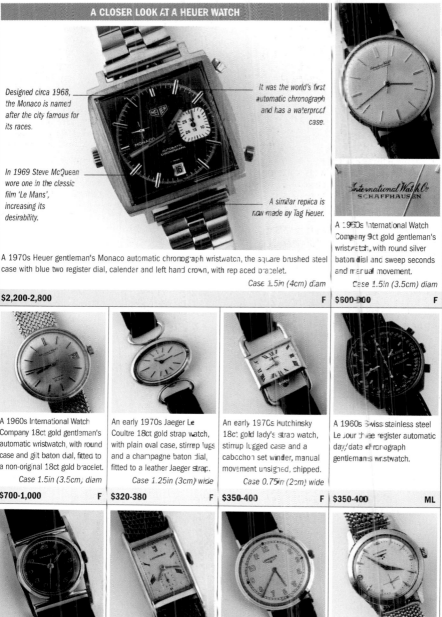

Designed circa 1968, the Monaco is named after the city famous for its races.

It was the world's first automatic chronograph and has a waterproof case.

In 1969 Steve McQueen wore one in the classic film 'Le Mans', increasing its desirability.

A similar replica is now made by Tag Heuer.

A 1970s Heuer gentleman's Monaco automatic chronograph wristwatch, the square brushed steel case with blue two register dial, calendar and left hand crown, with replaced bracelet.

Case 1.5in (4cm) diam

$2,200-2,800   F

A 1960s International Watch Company 9ct gold gentleman's wristwatch, with round silver baton dial and sweep seconds and manual movement.

Case 1.5in (3.5cm) diam

$600-800   F

A 1960s International Watch Company 18ct gold gentleman's automatic wristwatch, with round case and gilt baton dial, fitted to a non-original 18ct gold bracelet.

Case 1.5in (3.5cm) diam

$700-1,000   F

An early 1970s Jaeger Le Coultre 18ct gold strap watch, with plain oval case, stirrup lugs and a champagne baton dial, fitted to a leather Jaeger strap.

Case 1.25in (3cm) wide

$320-380   F

An early 1970s Hutchinsky 18ct gold lady's strap watch, stirrup lugged case and a cabochon set winder, manual movement unsigned, chipped.

Case 0.75in (2cm) wide

$350-400   F

A 1960s Swiss stainless steel Le Jour three register automatic day/date chronograph gentleman's wristwatch.

$350-400   ML

A 1930s 10ct gold-plated Longines gentleman's wristwatch, with an unusual case.

$180-220   ML

A 1930s 14ct gold-cased Longines gentleman's wristwatch.

$280-320   ML

A 1950s 18ct gold-cased Longines gentleman's wristwatch.

$320-380   ML

A 1950s Longines gentleman's manual watch with round steel case, white dial, gilt dagger hands and batons, and subsidiary seconds, fitted to non-original expanding bracelet.

$120-180   F

A CLOSER LOOK AT AN OMEGA WATCH

The Speedmaster has a very high quality chronograph movement and is cased in tough stainless steel.

It is the only wristwatch that has withstood all of NASA's stringent tests for use on space voyages.

In April 1970, when Apollo 13's onboard chronometer broke, the Speedmaster was the only time-keeping instrument on board. Its reliability saved the astronauts' lives.

On July 21, 1969, it became the only watch ever worn on the moon, gaining its 'Moon Watch' nickname.

A mid-1970s Omega Speedmaster Professional 'Moon Watch', on steel bracelet with manual movement, case back with inscription relating to the first space mission.

$700-1,000   F

An Omega gentleman's 9ct gold Seamaster quartz watch, with round case, champagne dial on a 9ct gold bracelet with Omega clasp.

8in (20cm) long

$500-700   F

ROLEX

The Rolex brand was developed in 1905, at Wilsdorf & Davies in London. The founder, Hans Wildorf, trained as a watch-maker. He started his own wristwatch factory, speculating that the wristwatch would become more popular than the dominant pocket watch. By the 1920s, his gamble had paid off – his watches were extremely popular. In 1926, Rolex developed the world's first fully waterproof case, the famed 'Oyster' case. In 1931, it developed the first reliable self-winding 'perpetual' watch.

A Rolex lady's 18ct gold Oyster Perpetual Datejust watch, with gilt dial and Jubilee bracelet, case dial and movement signed "Rolex".

$3,000-4,000   F

An Art Deco Rolex steel-cased cocktail watch, of rectangular geometric design, with ivory dial, case, dial and movement signed "Rolex", non-Rolex crown and bracelet, minute hand missing.

$220-280   F

An early 20thC Rolex lady's 9ct gold wristwatch, with round white Roman enamel dial, skeleton center seconds hand, and the case with hinged back and bezel, case, dial and movement signed "Rolex".

Case 1.25in (3cm) diam

$400-600   F

A 1930s Rolex silver-cased lady's watch, with round case, white enamel full-figure dial, skeleton hands and hinged case back, case, dial and movement signed "Rolex", dial with hairline cracks.

1.25in (3cm) diam

$280-320   F

An early 1900s Rolex silver-cased lady's watch, with round case, white enamel Arabic dial and hinged case back, hallmarked London, case, dial and movement signed "Rolex", dial with hairline crack.

1918 Case 1.25in (3cm) diam

$300-400   F

An early 20thC Rolex lady's watch head, the circular white Roman dial encompassed by a seed-pearl set bezel to front and back, green guilloche enamel decoration.

Case 0.75in (2cm) diam

$300-500   F

A late 1950s Rolex gentleman's steel Oyster Precision wristwatch, with white baton dial, center seconds and milled outer bezel, dial and movement signed, strap non-original.

$600-900   F

A 1950s Rolex gentleman's 9ct gold watch, with circular white dial, mixed markings and manual movement, case marked.

A Tudor gentleman's automatic steel Prince Oysterdate bracelet watch, with round silver baton dial, milled bezel and fitted to integral steel bracelet.

Tudor is another brand name used by Rolex.

A 1950s Tudor lady's steel-cased Oyster Princess bracelet watch, with silver baton dial, automatic movement and Oyster bracelet.

A Tudor lady's steel Oyster Royal on strap, with round silver Arabic dial.

c1950

$400-600　　　F

$350-400　　　F

$220-280　　　F

$110-130　　　F

A 1930s 14ct gold case and band Tiffany & Co. triple date gentleman's wristwatch, with movement by Movado.

A 1930s 14ct gold-cased Tiffany & Co. gentleman's wristwatch, Longines movement.

A 1970s Tissot gentleman's 13ct gold Stylist wristwatch, with oval gold baton dial and date facility, on a woven bracelet, engraving to case back.

A 1950s Universal Geneve gentleman's 18ct gold manual wristwatch, with round silver baton dial, dagger hands and dished bezel.

Case 1.5in (3.5cm) diam

$700-1,000　　　ML

$400-600　　　ML

$500-700　　　F

$500-700　　　F

A Zenith lady's gold-plated manual wristwatch, with square silver baton dial.

Case 0.75in (2cm) diam

$60-90　　　F

An early 20thC gentleman's silver-cased waterproof watch, with black full-figure dial, later movement.

Case 1.5in (3.5cm) diam

An early 20thC lady's 9ct gold wristwatch, with decorative white enamel dial, hinged case back and fitted to the expanding rolled gold bracelet.

An American 1990s stainless steel quartz British military NATO type wristwatch.

A 1990s stainless steel Royal Engineer Regiment Explosive Ordnance Disposal military watch.

$60-90　　　F

$40-60　　　F

$80-120　　　ML

$100-150　　　ML

Collectors' Notes

- Corkscrews can be categorized into 'straight pull' types, where the cork is pulled by strength, and 'mechanical' types, where a mechanism helps to pull the cork. Early straight pull or complex mechanical corkscrews are usually the most desirable and valuable.
- The 'screw' is often known as the 'worm' or 'helix' and is cast or made from shaped wire. Sharpened edges are known as 'ciphered' edges and help to penetrate the cork.
- The 19th century is considered the age of invention and the 'golden age' of the corkscrew. Look for examples marked with a maker's name or patent, or those made from precious materials. Sophisticated mechanisms such as the double helix 'Thomason' types or the 'King's type' are also desirable.

A Dutch silver pocket corkscrew.

c1840   *3.5in (9cm) long*

$500-700   **CSA**

A Henshall button-type corkscrew, with turned walnut handle.

Samuel Henshall registered the first patent for a corkscrew in 1795. The 'button' is the disc of metal at the top of the screw or 'worm' and its purpose was to compress and turn the cork when the worm had been fully inserted, allowing it to be removed more easily.

c1840 5.25in (13.5cm) long

$50-80   **CSA**

A straight pull corkscrew, with dusting brush.

c1860   5.57in (14.5cm) long

$12-18   **CSA**

A corkscrew, with carved bone handle and dusting brush.

c1850   5in (12.5cm) long

$50-80   **CSA**

A combination corkscrew and Codd bottle marble pusher.

'Codd bottles' were developed in 1872 by Hiram Codd. They used a marble 'stuck' inside the top of the neck to seal the bottle. The bottle would be filled upside down and the pressure would force the marble up to the top to seal the bottle. When someone wanted to drink the contents, the marble was pushed down with a finger, but would stay in the neck of the bottle due to an internal protrusion holding it there.

c1890   4.5in (11.5cm) long

$30-40   **CSA**

A Signet type corkscrew, with leather-covered grip.

c1900   4.75in (12cm) long

$70-100   **BS**

A 19thC folding bow steel corkscrew.

The value of these bow corkscrews lies in the number of accessories they have. More complex examples, with a number of accessories, are generally more desirable than simpler ones, such this.

4.75in (12cm) long

$40-60   **BS**

A Welsh cast brass two-finger figural Jenny Jones corkscrew.

c1930   5in (12.5cm) long

$15-25   **CSA**

A German celluloid lady's legs corkscrew, with pink-striped full length stockings.

c1880-90 2.5in (6.5cm) long

$180-220   **CSA**

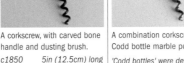

A German plastic 'pair' of shoes' corkscrew, marked "D.R.G.M. 82205".

c1900   2.5in (6.5cm) long

$180-220   **CSA**

A German cast brass key corkscrew, decorated with vine leaves and grapes.
c1930   5in (12.5cm) long
$15-25   **CSA**

An early 19thC Heeley & Sons Thomason-type corkscrew, with turned bone handle and wire helix, the turned brass barrel with an applied label bearing the royal arms and maker's name "HEELEY & SONS", replacement brush, tip of helix broken off.
$300-500   **DN**

A brass Farrow & Jackson-type corkscrew, with open frame and wire helix, the central screw raised by two wing-shaped levers.

Examples marked with Farrow & Jackson's name are more valuable and desirable to collectors, as are silver versions. Their very recognizable design, with its 'butterfly wing' nut' screwing to withdraw the cork, was widely copied.

$80-120   **DN**

A novelty German bone and metal miniature corkscrew.
c1880   2.5in (6.5cm) long
$70-100   **CSA**

A 1920s Monopole steel corkscrew.
$70-100   **BS**

A French 'Perfect' concertina corkscrew.
c1920   8.5in (21.5cm) long
$30-50   **CSA**

An English Magic Lever cork drawer.
c1920   5.5in (14cm) long
$50-80   **CSA**

A 1930s Italian painted aluminum German corkscrew.
10.5in (26.5cm) high
$70-100   **CSA**

A 1950s Danish figural corkscrew and bottle opener stand, in the form of a tramp with a bag of swag over one shoulder, on a marble base.
6.5in (16.5cm) high
$50-80   **CSA**

A CLOSER LOOK AT A CORKSCREW

The 'Rotary Eclipse' or 'Original Eclipse' is considered by many collectors to be the finest bar corkscrew.

It is solidly built from brass and can be firmly anchored to a bar surface. It has clean and handsome lines.

A double threaded screw, first developed by Andrew Muir in 1880, is used to create the worm in two movements.

Turning the handle forces the worm into the cork, and removes it, in a smooth action.

A 1920s 'The Original Eclipse' bar corkscrew, by Gaskell & Chambers.
16in (40.5cm) wide
$400-600   **CSA**

A 1920s 'The Don' brass bar corkscrew by Gaskell & Chambers.
12in (30.5cm) high
$120-180   **CSA**

An panel-shaped "Sherry" label, unmarked.

c1780 2in (5cm) wide

$70-100 CSA

A silver "Sherry" label, by William Brown, London hallmarks.

c1826 2.25in (5.5cm) wide

$80-120 CSA

A pair of 1840s old Sheffield plate spirit labels.

1.75in (4.5cm) wide

$50-80 CSA

A Victorian silver "Sherry" label, by "Y & W", Birmingham hallmarks.

1853 2.75in (7cm) wide

$100-150 CSA

A silver "Whiskey" label, Chester hallmarks.

1896 2in (5cm) wide

$70-100 CSA

A silver Rococo design wine label, possibly by William Hollingshead, Philadelphia, cartouche engraved "WHITE" with grapevine and cherubs, unclear hallmark.

$80-120 AAC

A rare Delft pottery "Port" cellar bin label.

c1750 5.25in (13.5cm) wide

$500-700 CSA

A "Calcavella" pottery cellar bin label, with pink luster script.

c1840 5in (12.5cm) wide

$300-400 CSA

A "13" coat hanger-shaped pottery cellar bin label.

c1850 4.5in (11.5cm) wide

$40-60 CSA

A "Margaux, 1861" pottery cellar bin label.

c1860 5in (12.5cm) wide

$400-600 CSA

A Staffordshire enamel "red-port" label.

c1780 2.5in (6.5cm) wide

$320-380 CSA

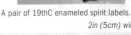

A pair of 19thC enameled spirit labels.

2in (5cm) wide

$70-100 CSA

A combination champagne wire cutter and cork grip.

c1890   7.5in (19cm) long

$15-25   CSA

A champagne tap, with ring-turned ebonized handle.

$50-80   Clv

A 1930s French combination barman's tool, comprising bottle opener, can opener, ice pick and corkscrew.

6.75in (17cm) long

$20-30   CSA

A silver punch ladle, engraved with foliate decoration and turned wooden handle.

c1790   Bowl 2in (5cm) diam

$150-200   CSA

A fine Revere 'Manhattan' bright chrome cocktail shaker designed by Norman Bel Geddes, with raised vertical ribs, good condition, stamped "Revere/Rome N".

Norman Bel Geddes (1893-1958) was an industrial designer who found particular popularity between WWI and WWII, taking America into a new 'modern' age and style.

1936-40   13in (33cm) high

$600-900   DRA

An unusual and rare 'Polar Bear' silver-plated metal cocktail shaker, with formalized features, resting on its haunches with raised head, the head removes and has a separate internal strainer, unmarked.

Novelty cocktail shakers such as this are extremely popular today with a growing group of collectors. Examples like this would have been luxury pieces in their day.

10in (25.5cm) high

$3,500-4,000   DN

An American 1920s painted tin 100lb 'kettleweight', opening to reveal a glass decanter with six shot glasses.

During the Prohibition of the 1920s, many bar ware and drinking accessory manufacturers came up with amusing, witty and inventive ways of hiding drinking accessories.

8.25in (21cm) high

$180-220   DEtc

A 1930s chrome-plated 'Penguin' ice bucket, with mottled brown Bakelite handles and finial by West Bend Aluminum Co. of West Bend, Wisconsin, US.

10.25in (26cm) wide

$40-60   AnaA

A 1950s enameled metal 'Rolls Royce' decanter and glass set, with molded glass decanters and shot glasses.

16.5in (42cm) wide

$180-220   DEtc

A 1920s stoneware "Glen Garry" whisky jug.

7in (17.5cm) high

$50-80   CSA

A Portuguese silver tastevin, with a high relief embossed portrait of the 16thC writer Pietro Aretino, with manuscript, quill pen and floral and foliate designs on the border.

Fietro Aretino (1492-1556) was a prolific Italian writer and poet who lived in Rome and Venice for much of his life.

c1880   4.5in (11.5cm) wide

$300-500   GS

A

Acid Etching A technique using acid to decorate glass to produce a matt or frosted appearance.

Albumen print Photographic paper is treated with egg white (albumen) to enable it to hold more light-sensitive chemicals. After being exposed to a negative, the resulting image is richer with more tonal variation.

Applied Refers to a separate part that has been attached to an object, such as a handle.

B

Baluster A curved form with a bulbous base and a slender neck.

Base metal A term describing common metals such as copper, tin and lead, or metal alloys, that were usually plated in gold or silver to imitate more expensive and luxurious metals. In the US, the term 'pot metal' is more commonly used.

Bébé The French term for a doll that represents a baby rather than an adult.

Bisque A type of unglazed porcelain used for making dolls from c1860 to c1925.

Boards The hard covers of a book.

Brassing On plated items, where the plating has worn off to reveal the underlying base metal.

C

Cabochon A large, protruding, polished, but not faceted, stone.

Cameo Hardstone, coral or shell that has been carved in relief to show a design in a contrasting color.

Cameo glass Decorative glass made from two or more layers of differently colored glass, which are then carved or etched to reveal the color beneath.

Cartouche A framed panel, often in the shape of a shield or paper scroll, which can be inscribed.

Celadon A distinctive grey/green or blue/green glaze for ceramics derived from iron and used to imitate jade in China for over 2,000 years.

Character doll A doll with a face that resembles a real child rather than an idealized one.

Charger A large plate or platter, often for display, but also for serving.

Chromolithography A later development of 'lithography', where a number of printing stones are used in succession, each with a different color, to build up a multi-colored image.

Cloisonné A decorative technique using small cells created by soldering thin strips of metal to an object, which are then filled with colored enamels.

Clubhouse Signature A player's signature that was not actually signed by the player, but by one of his colleagues, such as a batboy.

Composition A mixture including wood pulp, plaster and glue used as a cheap alternative to bisque in the production of dolls' heads and bodies.

Compote A dish, usually on a stem or foot, to hold fruit for the dessert course.

Craze/Crazed/Crazing A network of fine cracks in the glaze caused by uneven shrinking during firing. It also describes plastic that is slowly degrading and has the same surface patterning.

Cultured pearl A pearl formed when an irritant is artificially introduced to the mollusc.

D

Damascened Metal ornamented with inlaid gold or silver, often in wavy lines. Commonly found on weapons or armor.

Diecast Objects made by pouring molten metal into a closed metal die or mold.

Ding A very small dent in metal.

DQ Standing for 'diamond quilted', where a repeated pattern of diamond shapes cover the surface.

E

Earthenware A type of porous pottery that requires a glaze to make it waterproof.

Ebonized Wood that has been blackened with dye to resemble ebony.

E.P.N.S. Found on metal objects and standing for 'electroplated nickel silver', meaning the object is made from nickel which is then electroplated with silver.

Escapement The mechanical part of a clock or watch that regulates the transfer of energy from the weights or spring to the movement of the clock or watch.

F

Faience Earthenware that is treated with an impervious tin glaze. Popular in France from the 16th century and reaching its peak during the 18th century.

Faceted A form of decoration where a number of flat surfaces are cut into the surface of an object such as a gem or a glass vase.

Faux A French word for 'false'. The intention is not to deceive fraudulently but to imitate a more costly material.

Finial A decorative knob at the end of a terminal, or on a lid.

Foliate Leaf and vine motifs.

G

Guilloché An engraved pattern of interlaced lines or other decorative motifs, sometimes enamelled over with translucent enamels.

H

Hallmark The series of small stamps found on gold or silver that can identify the maker, the standard of the metal and the city and year of manufacture. Hallmarks differ for each country and can consist only of a maker's or a city mark. All English silver made after 1544 was required to be fully marked.

IJK

Incised Applied to surface decoration or a maker's mark that has been scratched into the surface of an object with a sharp instrument.

Inclusions Used to describe all types of small particles of decorative materials embedded in glass.

Iridescent A lustrous finish that subtly changes color depending on how light hits it. Often used to describe the finish on ceramics and glass.

L

Lambrequins A shaped decoration derived from the hanging fringes on tents at a jousting competition. Used to describe similarly shaped borders on ceramics, silver and furniture.

Latticinio The Italian term for thin, white strands of glass contained in clear glass and arranged in patterns including spirals. It originated in Venice and is commonly found in glass from Murano.

Lithography A printing technique developed in 1798 and employing the use of a stone upon which a pattern or picture has been drawn with a grease crayon. The ink adheres to the grease and is transferred to the paper when pressed against it.

MNO

Meiji A period in Japanese history dating from 1868-1912.

Millefiori An Italian term meaning 'thousand flowers' and used to describe cut, multi-colored glass canes which are arranged and cased in clear glass. When arranged with the cut side facing the exterior, each circular disc (or short cane) resembles a small flower.

Mint A term used to describe an object in unused condition with no signs of wear and derived from coinage. Truly 'mint' objects will command a premium.

M.O.P. Mother of pearl. The shiny and colored interior of some shells.

Mount A metal part applied to an object made of ceramic, glass or another material, with a decorative or functional use.

Netsuke A small toggle, usually carved from ivory or wood, used to secure pouches and boxes (known as sagemono) hung on cords through the belt of a kimono. They are most often carved as figures or animals.

Opalescent An opal-like, milky glass with subtle gradations of color between thinner more translucent areas and thicker, more opaque areas.

P

Paisley A stylized design based on pinecones and foliage, often with added intricate decoration. It originated in India and is most often found on fabrics, such as shawls.

Paste (jewelry) A hard, bright glass cut the same way as a diamond and made and set to resemble them.

Patera An oval or circular decorative motif often with a fluted or flecal centre. The plural is 'paterae'.

Piqué A decorative technique where small strips or studs of gold are inlaid onto ivory or tortoiseshell on a pattern and secured in place by heating.

Pontil A metal rod to which a glass vessel is attached when it is being worked. When it is removed it leaves a raised disc-shaped 'pontil mark'.

Pot Metal Please see 'Base metal'.

Pounce pot A small pot made of wood (treen), silver or ceramic. Found on inkwells or designed to stand alone, it held a gum dust that was sprinkled over parchment to prevent ink from spreading. Used until the late 18th century.

Pressed (Press Moulded) Ceramics formed by pressing clay into a mould. Pressed glass is made by pouring molten glass into a mould and pressing it with a plunger

R

Reeded A type of decoration with thin raised, convex vertical lines. Derived from the decoration of classical columns.

Relief A form of moulded, pressed or carved decoration that protrudes above the surface of an object. Usually in the form of figures of foliate and foliage designs, it ranges in height from 'low' to 'high'.

Repoussé A French term for the raised, 'embossed' decoration on metals such as silver. The metal is forced into a form from one side causing it to bulge.

S

Satsuma Collective term for potteries on the island of Kyushu, Japan, which made items for export to the West. Their ware is typified by a clear, yellowish glaze, often decorated with colored figures and flowers and gilt decoration.

Sgraffito An Italian word for 'little scratch' and used to describe a decorative technique where the outer surface of an object, usually in glazed or colored ceramic, is scratched away in a pattern to reveal the contrasting colored underlying surface.

Stoneware A type of ceramic similar to earthenware and made of high-fired clay mixed with stone, such as feldspar, which makes it non-porous.

Sweetspot The area of a baseball between the two curving lines of stitching where it is most desirable to find a player's autograph.

T

Tazza A shallow cup with a wide bowl, which is raised up on a single pedestal foot.

Tooled Collective description for a number of decorative techniques applied to a surface. Includes engraving, stamping, punching and incising.

V

Vermeil Gold-plated silver.

Vesta case A small case or box, usually made from silver, for carrying matches.

W

White metal Precious metal that is possibly silver, but not officially marked as such.

Whitework Decorative white embroidery on white fabric, usually cotton. Often said to be the forerunner of lace.

Y

Yellow metal Precious metal that is possibly gold, but not officially marked as such.

CLIENT	PAGE NO		CLIENT	PAGE NO
Live Auctioneers	109		Dorling Kindersley	321
Craftsman Auctions	158		South Street Antiques Center	333
James D. Julia Auctioneers	300		Dorling Kindersley	405

KEY TO ILLUSTRATIONS

EVERY COLLECTIBLE ILLUSTRATED in the DK *Collectibles Price Guide 2004* by Judith Miller has a letter code which identifies the auction house or dealer that sold it. The list below is a key to these codes. In the list, auction houses are shown by the letter Ⓐ and dealers by the letter Ⓓ. Some items may have come from a private collection, in which case the code in the list is accompanied by the letter Ⓟ. Inclusion in this book in no way constitutes or implies a contract or a binding offer on the part of any of our contributors to supply or sell the goods illustrated, or similar items, at the prices stated.

If you wish to have any item valued, it is advisable to contact the dealer or specialist in advance to check that they will carry out this service and whether there is a charge. While most dealers will be happy to help you with an enquiry, do remember that they are busy people. Telephone valuations are not possible. Please mention the DK *Collectibles Price Guide 2004* by Judith Miller when making an enquiry.

AAC Ⓐ
Sanford Alderfer Auction Company
501 Fairgrounds Road, Hatfield PA 19440
Tel: 215 393 3000
Fax: 215 368 9055
info@alderferauction.com
www.alderferauction.com

AAG Ⓓ
Animation Art Gallery
13-14 Great Castle St, London W1W 8LS UK
Tel: +44 (0) 20 7255 1456
Fax: +44 (0) 20 7436 1256
gallery@animaart.com
www.animaart.com

AB Ⓐ Ⓓ
Auction Blocks
P.O. Box 2321, Huntington Station, CT 06484
Tel: 203 924 2802
auctionblocks@aol.com
www.auctionblocks.com

ABij/Abij Ⓓ
Aurora Bijoux
Tel: 215 355 1921
aurora@aurorabijoux.com
www.aurorabijoux.com

AGI Ⓐ
Aurora Galleries International
30 Hackamore Lane, Suite 2, Bell Canyon, CA 91307
Tel: 818 884 6468
Fax: 818 227 2941
vjc@auroragalleriesonline.com
www.auroragalleriesonline.com

AIS Ⓓ
Arthur Ivan Spike
South Street Antiques Center, 615 South 6th Street, Philadelphia, PA 19147
Tel: 215 592 0256

AnaA Ⓓ
Anastacia's Antiques
617 Bainbridge Street, Philadelphia, PA 19147
Tel: 215 928 9111

AOY Ⓓ
All Our Yesterdays
6 Park Road, Kelvinbridge, Glasgow G4 9JG UK
Tel: +44 (0) 141 334 7788
Fax: +44 (0) 141 339 8994
antiques@allouryesterdays.fsnet.co.uk

AS&S Ⓐ
Andrew Smith and Son Auctions,
Hankin's Garage, 47 West Street, New Alresford, Hampshire UK
Tel: +44 (0) 1962 735 988
Fax: +44 (0) 1962 738 87
auctions@andrewsmithandson.fs.business.co.uk

ATA/AtA Ⓓ
Atomic Age
318 E Virginia Road, Fullerton, CA 92831
Tel: 714 446 0736
Fax: 714 446 0436
atomage100@aol.com

ATK Ⓐ
Auction Team Koln
Postfach 50 11 19, Bonner Str. 528-530 50971 Koln, Germany
Tel: +49 (0) 221 38 70 49
Fax: +49 (0) 221 37 48 78
auction@breker.com
www.breker.com

B Ⓐ
Bracketts Fine Art Auctioneers
Auction Hall, The Pantiles, Tunbridge Wells, Kent TN2 5QL UK
Tel: +44 (0) 1892 544 500
Fax: +44 (0) 1892 515 191
www.bfaa.co.uk

BA Ⓓ
Branksome Antiques
370 Poole Road, Branksome, Poole, Dorset BH1 1AW UK
Tel: +44 (0) 1202 763 324/679 932
Fax: +44 (0) 1202 763 643

BAd Ⓓ
Beth Adams
Unit G043/044, Alfie's Antiques Market, 13-25 Church St., London NW8 8DT UK
Tel: +44 (0) 20 7723 5613
Fax: +44 (0) 20 7262 1576
badams@alfies.clara.net

BAR Ⓐ
Bristol Auction Rooms
(Collectors' Saleroom)
Baynton Road, Ashton, Bristol BA7 4HJ UK
(Main Saleroom)
St John's Place, Apsley Road, Clifton, Bristol BS8 2ST UK
Tel: +44 (0) 117 973 7201

BB Ⓓ
Barbara Blau
South Street Antiques Center, 615 South 6th Street, Philadelphia, PA 19147
Tel: 215 739 4995
bbjools@msn.com

BBG Ⓓ
Baubles
South Street Antiques Center, 615 South 6th Street, Philadelphia, PA 19147
Tel: 215 487 0207

BCAC Ⓓ
Bucks County Antique Center
Route 202, Lahaska, PA 18931
Tel: 215 794 9180

BEJ Ⓓ
Bébés & Jouets
c/o Post Office, 165 Restalris Road, Edinburgh EH7 6HW UK
Tel: +44 (0) 131 332 5650
bebesetjouets@u.genie.co.uk

Bev Ⓓ
Beverly
30 Church Street, London, NW8 8EP UK
Tel: +44 (0) 20 7262 1576

Bib Ⓓ
Biblion
1/7 Davies Mews, London W1K 5AB UK
Tel: +44 (0) 20 7629 1374
www.biblion.com

BonC Ⓐ
Bonhams, Knightsbridge
Montpelier Street, London SW7 1HH UK
Tel: +44 (0) 20 7393 3900
Fax: +44 (0) 20 7393 3905
info@bonhams.com
www.bonhams.com

BonL Ⓐ
Bonhams, Leeds
Hepper House, 17A East Parade, Leeds LS1 2BH UK
Tel: +44 (0) 113 244 8011
Fax: +44 (0) 113 242 9875
www.bonhams.com

BonS Ⓐ
Bonhams
101 New Bond Street, London W1S 1SR UK
Tel: +44 (0) 20 7629 6602
Fax: +44 (0) 20 7629 8876
www.bonhams.com

BP Ⓓ
The Blue Pump
178 Davenport Road, Toronto, Canada M5R 1J2
Tel: 001 416 944 1673

BRB Ⓓ
Bauman Rare Books
4535 Madison Ave, between 54th & 55th Streets, New York NY 10022
Tel: 212 751 0011
www.baumanrarebooks.com

BS Ⓓ
Below Stairs of Hungerford
103 High Street, Hungerford, Berkshire RG17 0NB UK
Tel: +44 (0) 1488 682 317
Fax: +44 (0) 1488 684 294
www.belowstairs.co.uk

BW Ⓐ
Biddle & Webb
Icknield Square, Ladywood, Birmingham B16 0PP UK
Tel: +44 (0) 121 455 8042
Fax: +44 (0) 121 454 9615
www.biddleandwebb.co.uk

BY Ⓓ
Bonny Yankauer
bonnyy@aol.com

CA Ⓐ
Chiswick Auctions
1-5 Colville Road, London
W3 8BL UK
Tel: +44 (0) 20 8992 4442
Fax: +44 (0) 20 8892 0541

CAC Ⓓ
Charles Cohn
P.O. Box 8835, Elkins Park, PA
19027
Tel: 215 840 6112
cacint@comcast.net

CamA Ⓐ
Camelot Antiques
7871 Ocean Gateway, Easton,
Maryland 21601
Tel: 410 820 4396
camelot@goeaston.net
www.about-antiques.com/
CamelotAntiques

Cast Ⓓ
Castaside
Unit B037-42, Alfie's Antiques
Market, 13-25 Church St.,
London, NW8 8DT UK
Tel: +44 (0) 20 7723 7686
castaside@alfies.clara.net

CBe Ⓟ
Christina Bertrand
tineke@rcn.com

CCL Ⓓ
Cloud Cuckoo Land
6 Charlton Place, Camden
Passage, London, N1 8AJ UK
Tel: +44 (0) 20 7354 3141

CEC Ⓓ
Chris & Eddie's Collectibles
South Street Antiques Center,
615 South 6th Street,
Philadelphia, PA 19147
Tel: 215 592 0256

CHAA Ⓐ
**Cowan's Historic
Americana Auctions**
673 Wilmer Avenue, Cincinnati,
OH 45226
Tel: 513 871 1670
Fax: 513 871 8670
www.historicamericana.com

Chef Ⓐ
Cheffins
The Cambridge Saleroom, 2
Clifton Road, Cambridge
CB1 4BW UK
Tel:+44 (0) 1223 213 343
Fax: +44 (0) 1223 413 396
www.cheffins.co.uk

Clv Ⓐ
Clevedon Salerooms
The Auction Centre, Kenn Road,
Clevedon, Bristol BS21 6TT UK
Tel: +44 (0) 1934 830 111
Fax: +44 (0) 1934 832 538
www.clevedon-salerooms.com

CO Ⓐ
Cooper Owen
10 Denmark Street, London
WC2H 8LS UK
Tel: +44 (0) 20 7240 4132
Fax: +44 (0) 20 7240 4339
info@cooperowen.com
www.cooperowen.com

COB Ⓓ
Cobwebs
78 Old Northam Road,
Southampton SO14 0PB UK
Tel: +44 (0) 2380 227 458
www.cobwebs.uk.com

CR Ⓕ
Craftsman Auctions
333 North Main
Street,Lambertville, NJ 08530
Tel: 609 397 9374
Fax: 609 397 9377
www.ragoarts.com

CRIS/Cris Ⓓ
Cristobal
26 Church Street, London
NW8 8EF UK
Tel/Fax: +44 (0) 20 7724 7230
www.cristobal.co.uk

CS Ⓓ
Christopher Seidler
Stand G13, Greys Mews Antiques
Market, London W1K 5AB UK
Tel: +44 (0) 20 7629 2851
Fax: +44 (0) 20 7493 9344
tomus@tinyworld.co.uk

CSA Ⓓ
Christopher Sykes Antiques
The Old Parsonage, Woburn,
Milton Keynes MK17 9QL UK
Tel: +44 (0) 1525 290 259/290 467
Fax: +44 (0) 1525 290 061
www.sykes-corkscrews.co.uk

CVS Ⓓ
**Cad Van Swankster at
The Girl Can't Help It**
Alfies Antique Market, Shop
G115, Ground Floor,
13-25 Church Street,
London NW8 8DT UK
Tel: +44 (0) 20 7723 0564
Fax: +44 (0) 20 8809 3923

CW Ⓟ
Christine Wildman Collection
wild123@attcanada.ca

D Ⓐ
Dickins Auctioneers
Claydon Saleroom, Calvert Road,
Middle Clayton,
Bucks, MK18 2EZ UK
Tel: +44 (0) 1296 714 434
Fax: +44 (0) 1296 714 492
www.dickins-auctioneers.com

DAW/Daw Ⓠ
**Dawson's Auctioneers &
Appraisers**
128 American Road, Morris
Plains, NJ C795C
Tel: 973 984 6900
Fax: 973 984 6956
www.dawsons.org

DCC Ⓟ
Dee Carlton Collection
qnoscots@aol.com

DE Ⓓ
The Doll Express
The Antiques Showcase at The
Black Horse, 2222 North Reading
Road, Denver, PA 17517
Tel: 717 335 3300
www.thedollexpress.com

DEtc Ⓒ
Deco Etc
122 West 25th Street, (between
6th & 7th Aves.), New York,
NY 10010
Tel: 212 675 3327
deco_etc@msn.com

DH Ⓓ
Huxtins
11 & 12 The Lipka Arcade, 288
Westbourne Grove, London W11 UK
Tel: +44 (0) 7710 132 200
www.huxtins.com

DN Ⓐ
Dreweatt Neate
Donnington Priory Salerooms,
Donnington, Newbury, Berkshire
RG14 2JE UK
Tel: +44 (0) 1635 553 553
Fax: +44 (0) 1635 553 599
www.auctions.dreweatt-neate.co.uk

DO Ⓓ
DODO
Alfies Antique Market, 1st floor
(F073, 83 & 84), 13-25 Church
Street, Marylebone, London
NW8 8DT UK
Tel: +44 (0) 20 7706 1545
dodoposters@yahoo.com

DRA Ⓐ
Rago Modern Auctions
333 North Main Street,
Lambertville, NJ 08530
Tel: 609 397 9374
Fax: 609 397 9377
info@ragoarts.com
www.ragoarts.com

ET Ⓐ
Early Technology
Monkton House, Old Craighall
Musselburgh, Midlothian,
Scotland EH21 8SF UK
Tel: +44 (0) 131 665 5753
michael.bennett-levy@virgin.net
www.earlytech.com

F Ⓐ
Fellows & Sons
Augusta House, 19 Augusta St,
Hockley, Birmingham B18 6JA UK
Tel: +44 (0) 121 212 2131
Fax: +44 (0) 121 212 1249
info@fellows.co.uk
www.fellows.co.uk

FA Ⓐ
Fraser's Autographs
399 The Strand, London
WC2R 0LX UK
Tel: +44 (0) 20 7836 9325
Sales@frasersautographs.co.uk
www.frasersautographs.com

FFM Ⓓ
Festival
136 South Ealing Road, London
W5 4QJ UK
Tel: + 44 (0) 20 8840 9333
info@festival1951.co.uk

FIS Ⓠ
Dr Fischer
Trappensee-Schlösschen, D-
74074 Heilbronn, Germany
Tel: 00 49 (0) 7131 15 55 70
Fax: C0 49 (0) 7131 15 55 720
www.auctions-fischer.de

FJA Ⓓ
Feljoy Antiques
Shop 3, Angel Arcade, Camden
Passage, London, N1 8EA UK
Tel: +44 (0) 20 7354 5336
Fax: +44 (0) 20 7831 3485
joy@feljoy-antiques.demon.co.uk
www.chintznet.com/feljoy

FM Ⓓ
Francesca Martire
Stand 1, 131-137, First Floor,
Alfie's Antiques Market, 13-25
Church Street, London NW8 0RH UK
Tel: +44 (0) 20 7724 4802
martire@alfies.clara.net

FRE Ⓐ
Freeman's
1808 Chestnut Street,
Philadelphia, PA 19103
Tel: 215 563 9275
Fax: 215 563 8236
info@freemansauction.com
www.freemansauction.com

G Ⓐ
Guernsey's Auctions
108 East 73rd Street, New York,
NY 10021
Tel: 212 794 2280
Fax: 212 794 3638
guernsey@guernseys.com
www.guernseys.com

Gats Ⓐ
The Gatsby Collection
Tel 440 258 2397

GC Ⓟ
Graham Cooley Collection
Tel: +44 (0) 7968 722269
graham.cooley@metalysis.com

GCA Ⓓ
Griffin & Cooper Antiques
South Street Antiques Center,
615 South 6th Street,
Philadelphia, PA 19147
Tel: 215 582 0418/3594

GG Ⓟ
Guest & Gray
1-7 Davies Mews, London
W1K 5AB UK
Tel +44 (0) 20 7408 1252
Fax: +44 (0) 20 7499 1445
info@chinese-porcelain-art.com
www.chinese-porcelain-art.com

GGrt Ⓒ
Gary Grant
18 Arlington Way, London,
EC1R 1UY UK
Tel: +44 (0) 20 7713 1122

GH Ⓓ
Gideon Hatch
1 Port House, Plantation Wharf,
Battersea, London SW11 3TY UK
Tel: +44 (0) 20 7223 3996
Fax: +44 (0) 20 7223 3997
info@gideonhatch.co.uk
www.gideonhatch.co.uk

GN Ⓓ
Gillian Neale Antiques
PO Box 247, Aylesbury, HP20 1JZ UK
Tel: +44 (0) 1296 423754
Fax: +44 (0) 1296 334601
gillianneale@aol.com
www.gilliannealeantiques.co.uk

GorL Ⓐ
Gorringes
15 North Street, Lewes, East
Sussex BN7 2PD UK
Tel: +44 (0) 1273 472 503
auctions@gorringes.co.uk
www.gorringes.co.uk

GS Ⓓ
Goodwins Antiques Ltd
15 & 16 Queensferry Street,
Edinburgh EH2 4QW UK
Tel: +44 (0) 131 225 4717

H&G Ⓓ
Hope and Glory
131A Kensington Church Street,
London W8 7LP UK
Tel: +44 (0) 20 7727 8424

HA Ⓐ
Hunt Auctions
75 E. Uwchlan Ave, Suite 130,
Exton, PA 19341
Tel: 610 524 0822
info@huntauctions.com
www.huntsauctions.com

HamG Ⓐ
Hamptons
Baverstock House, 93 High
Street, Godalming, Surrey
GU7 1AL UK
Tel: +44 (0) 1483 423 567
Fax: +44 (0) 1483 426 392
fineart@hamptons-int.com
www.hamptons.co.uk

HB Ⓓ
Victoriana Dolls
101 Portobello Road, London
W11 2BQ UK
Tel: +44 (0) 1737 249 525
heather.bond@totalserve.co.uk

HC Ⓐ
Heritage Comics
Heritage Plaza, 100 Highland
Park Village, 2nd Floor, Dallas, TX
75205-2788
Tel: 800 872 6467 /
214 528 3500
Fax: 214 520 6968
www.heritagecomics.com

HD Ⓙ
Halcyon Days
14 Brook Street, London
W1S 1BD UK
Tel: +44 (0) 20 7629 8811
info@halcyondays.co.uk
www.halcyondays.co.uk

HERR Ⓐ
**W.G. Herr Art & Auction
House**
Friesenwall 35, D - 50672
Cologne, Germany
Tel: +49 (0) 221 25 45 48
Fax: +49 (0) 221 270 67 42
kunst@herr-auktionen.de
www.herr-auktionen.de

HGS Ⓓ
Harper General Store
10482 Jonestown Rd, Annville, PA
17003
Tel: 717 865 3456
Fax: 717 865 3813
la_wver5@comcast.net
www.harpergeneralstore.com

HLJ Ⓓ
Hugo Lee-Jones
Tel: +44 (0) 1227 375 375
Mob: +44 (0) 7941 187 2027
electroniccollectables@hotmail.com

JBB Ⓐ
Jean-Baptiste Bacquart
www.AfricanAndOceanicArt.com

JBC Ⓟ
James Bridges Collection

JDJ Ⓐ
James D. Julia Inc
P.O. Box 830, Fairfield, Maine
04937
Tel: 20 7453 7125
www.juliaauctions.com

JF Ⓐ
Jill Fenichell
305 East 61st St, New York, NY
Tel: 212 980 9346
jfenichell@yahoo.com

JH Ⓓ
Jeanette Hayhurst Fine Glass
32a Kensington Church St,
London W8 4HA UK
Tel: +44 (0) 20 7938 1539

JHB Ⓓ
Joseph Bonnar
72 Thistle Street, Edinburgh
EH2 1EN UK
Tel: +44 (0) 131 226 2811
Fax: +44 (0) 131 225 9438

JJ Ⓓ
The Junkyard Jeweler
937 West Beach Street, Suite
49,Long Beach, NY 11561
spigner@aol.com
www.tias.com/stores/thejunkyardjeweler

JPA Ⓓ
Jessica Pack Antiques
jpantiqs1@aol.com

JSC Ⓟ
Jean Scott Collection
jean@stanhopes.info
www.stanhopes.info

K&R Ⓓ
Keller & Ross
P.O. Box 783, Melrose, MA 02176
Tel: 978 988 2070
http://members.aol.com/kellerross

KBon Ⓐ
Bonhams, Knowle
The Old House, Station Road,
Knowle, West Midlands B93 0HT UK
Tel: +44 (0) 1564 776 151
info@bonhams.com
www.bonhams.com

KF Ⓓ
Karl Flaherty Collectables
Tel: 02476 445 627
kfckarl@aol.com

KG Ⓓ
Ken Grant
F109-F111 Alfies Antiques
Market, 13 Chapel Street, London
NW8 UK
Tel: +44 (0) 20 7723 137
k-grant@alfies.clara.net

L Ⓓ
Luna
323 George St, Nottingham
NG1 3BH UK
Tel: +44 (0) 115 924 3267
info@luna-online.co.uk

L&T Ⓐ
Lyon and Turnbull Ltd.
33 Broughton Place, Edinburgh
EH1 3RR UK
Tel: +44 (0) 131 557 8844
Fax: +44 (0) 131 557 8668
www.lyonandturnbull.com

LC Ⓐ
**Lawrence's Fine Art
Auctioneers**
The Linen Yard, South St,
Crewkerne, Somerset TA18 8AB UK
Tel: +44 (0) 1460 73041
Fax: +44 (0) 1460 74627
www.lawrences.co.uk

LFA Ⓐ
Law Fine Art Ltd.
Firs Cottage, Church Lane,
Brimpton, Berkshire RG7 4TJ UK
Tel: +44 (0) 118 971 0353
Fax: +44 (0) 118 971 3741
www.lawfineart.co.uk

LG Ⓓ
Legacy
G50/51 Alfie's Antiques Centre,
13-25 Church St, London NW8 UK
Tel: +44 (0) 20 7723 0449
legacy@alfies.clara.net

LH Ⓓ
Lucy's Hat D
South Street Antiques Center,
615 South 6th Street,
Philadelphia, PA 19147
Tel: 215 592 0256
shak06@aol.com

LHS Ⓐ Ⓓ
L.H. Selman Ltd
123 Locust St, Santa Cruz,
CA 950600
Tel: 831 427 1177
lselman@got.net

MA Ⓓ
Manic Attic
Stand S011, Alfies Antiques
Market, 13 Church Street, London
NW8 8DT UK
Tel: +44 (0) 20 7723 6105
manicattic@alfies.clara.ret

MAC Ⓓ
Mary Ann's Collectibles
South Street Antiques Center,
615 South 6th Street,
Philadelphia, PA 19147
Tel: 215 923 3247

MB Ⓓ
Mostly Boxes
93 High Street, Eton, Windsor,
Berkshire SL4 6AF UK
Tel: +44 (0) 1753 858 470

MC Ⓓ
Metropolis Collectibles Inc.
873 Broadway, Suite 201, New
York, NY 10003
Tel: 212 260 4147
Fax: 212 260 4304

MCol Ⓟ
Mick Collins Collection
admin@sylvacclub.com

Men Ⓓ
**Mendes Antique Lace
and Textiles**
Flat 2, Wilbury Lawn, 44 Wilbury
Road, Hove, East Sussex BN3 3PA UK
Tel: +44 (0) 1273 203 317
antiques@mendes.co.uk

MG Ⓓ
Mod-Girl
South Street Antiques Center,
615 South 6th Street,
Philadelphia, PA 19147
Tel: 215 592 0256
Tel: 215 413 0434

MH Ⓓ
Mad Hatter Antiques
Unit 82, Admiral Vernon Antique
Market, 141-149 Portobello Rd,
London W11 UK
Tel: +44 (0) 20 7262 0487
madhatter.portobello@virgin.net

MHC Ⓟ
Mark Hill Collection
Mob: +44 (0) 7798 915 474
stylophile@btopenworld.com

MHT Ⓓ
Mum Had That
Tel: +44 (0) 1442 412 360
www.mumhadthat.com

ML Ⓓ
Mark Laino
South Street Antiques Center,
615 South 6th Street,
Philadelphia, PA 19147
Tel: 215 592 0256

MM Ⓐ
Mullock Madeley
The Old Shippon, Wall-under-
Heywood, Church Stretton,
Shropshire SY6 7DS UK
Tel: +44 (0) 1694 771 771
www.mullock-madeley.co.uk

MSC Ⓟ
Mark Slavinsky Collection

NB Ⓓ
**Noel Barrett Antiques &
Auctions Ltd**
P.O. Box 300, Carversville, PA
18913
Tel: 215 297 5109
www.noelbarrett.com

NBS Ⓟ
New Baxter Society
The New Baxter Society, c/o
Reading Museum & Art Gallery,
Blagrave St, Reading, Berkshire
RG1 1QH UK
www.rpsfamily.demon.co.uk

NWC Ⓟ
Nigel Wright Collection

OACC Ⓓ
**Otford Antiques and Collectors
Centre, 26-28 High Street, Otford,
Kent TN14 5PQ UK
Tel: +44 (0) 1959 522 025
www.otfordantiques.co.uk

P Ⓓ
Posteritati
239 Center St, New York, NY
10013
Tel: 212 226 2207
Fax: 212 226 2102

PB Ⓓ
Petersham Books
Unit 67, 56 Gloucester Rd,
Kensington, London SW7 4UB UK
Tel/Fax: +44 (0) 20 7581 9147
ks@modernfirsts.co.uk
www.modernfirsts.co.uk

PC Ⓟ
Private Collection

Pen Ⓓ
Pendulum of Mayfair
King House, 51 Maddox Street,
London, W1S 2PH UK
Tel: +44 (0) 207629 6606
www.pendulumofmayfair.com

Pook Ⓓ
Pook & Pook
P.O. Box 268, Downington, PA
19335
463 East Lancaster Ave,
Downington, PA 19335
Tel: 610 269 4040
Fax: 610 269 0695
info@pookandpook.com
www.pookandpook.com

PSA Ⓓ
Potteries Specialist Auctions
271 Waterloo Road, Cobridge,
Stoke-on-Trent, ST6 3HR UK
Tel: +44 (0) 7182 286 622
Fax: +44 (0) 1782 213 777
enquiries@potteriesauctions.com
www.potteriesauctions.com

Qu Ⓐ
Quittenbaum
Hohenstaufenstraße 1, D-80801,
München, Germany
Tel: +49 (0) 89 33 00 75 6
Fax: +49 (0) 89 33 00 75 77
dialog@quittenbaum.de
www.quittenbaum.de

RAA Ⓓ
Axtell Antiques
1 River Street, Deposit, NY 13754
Tel: 607 467 2353
Fax: 607 467 4316
rsaxtell@msn.com
www.axtellantiques.com

RBL Ⓓ
Richard Ball Lighters
richard@lighter.co.uk

RdeR Ⓓ
Rogers de Rin
76 Royal Hospital Road, Paradise
Walk, Chelsea, London SW3 4HN UK
Tel: +44 (0) 20 7352 9007
Fax: +44 (0) 7351 94C7
rogersderin@rogersderin.co.uk
www.rogersderin.co.uk

REN/Ren Ⓒ
Rennies
13 Rugby Street, London WC1 3QT UK
Tel: +44 (0) 20 7405 0220
info@rennart.co.uk

RG Ⓓ
Richard Gibbon
34/34a Islington Green, London
N1 8DU UK
Tel: +44 (0) 20 7354 2852
neljeweluk@aol.com

RH Ⓓ
Rick Hubbard Art Deco
3 Tee Court, Bell Street, Romsey,
Hampshire SO51 8GY UK
Tel/Fax: +44 (0) 1794 513 133
www.rickhubbard-artdeco.co.uk

Rox Ⓓ
Roxanne Stuart
Tel. 888 750 8869 /215 750 8868
gemfairy@aol.com

RTC Ⓐ
Ritchie's Auctioneers &
Appraisers
288 King St East, Toronto,
Ontario, Canada M5A 1KA
Tel: 416 364 1864
www.ritchies.com

S&T Ⓓ
Steinberg and Tolkien
193 King's Road, Chelsea,
London SW3 5ED UK
Tel: +44 (0) 20 7373 3660
Fax: +44 (0) 20 7376 3630

SAS Ⓐ
Special Auction Services
Kennetholme, Midgham, Nr.
Reading, Berkshire UK
Tel: +44 (0) 1189 712 949
www.invaluable.com/sas

SCC Ⓟ
Silas Currie Collection

SCG Ⓓ
Gallery 1930 - Susie Cooper
Gallery
18 Church Street, London
NW8 8EP UK
Tel: +44 (0) 20 7723 1555
Fax: +44 (0) 20 7735 8309
www.susiecooperceramics.com

SF Ⓓ
Sandra Fellner
Stand 125/B14, Grays Mews
Antiques Market, Davies Mews,
South Molton Lane, London
W1Y 5AE UK
Tel: +44 (0) 20 8946 5613
fellner-sellers@grays.clara.net

SI Ⓐ
Sloans
Ceased trading

SM Ⓒ
Sparkle Moore at The Girl
Can't Help It
Alfies Antique Market, Shop G100
& G116, Ground Floor, 13-25
Church Street, London NW8 UK
Tel: +44 (0) 20 7724 8984
www.sparklemoore.com

SotT Ⓓ
Sign of the Tymes
2 Morris Farm Rd, Lafayette, NJ
07848
Tel: 973 383 6028
jhap@nac.net
www.millantiques.com

SRA Ⓐ
Sheffield Railwayana
43 Little Norton Lane, Sheffield
S8 8GA UK
Tel/Fax: +44 (0) 114 274 5085
www.sheffieldrailwayana.co.uk

SS Ⓓ
Spencer Swaffer Antiques,
30 High Street, Arundel, West
Sussex, BN18 9AB UK
Tel: 44 (0) 1903 882 132
Fax: 44 (0) 1903 884 564
spencerswaffer@btconnect.com

SSc Ⓟ
Sue Scrivens Collection

STC Ⓓ
Seaside Toy Center,
179 Main Street, Westerly, Rhode
Island C2891
Tel: 401 596 C962

Swa Ⓐ
Swann's Auction Galleries,
104 East 25th Street, New York,
NY 10010
Tel: 212 254 4710
Fax: 212 979 1017
www.swanngalleries.com

TA Ⓐ
333 Auctions LLC
333 North Main St, Lambertville,
NJ 08530
Tel: 609 397 9374
www.333auctions.com

TAB Ⓓ
Take-A-Boo Emporium
1927 Avenue Road, Toronto,
Ontario M5M 4A2 Canada
Tel/Fax: 416 785 4555

Tag Ⓓ
Tagore Ltd
Stand 302, Grays Antiques
Market, 58 Davies Street, London
W1Y 2LP UK
Tel: +44 (0) 20 7499 0158
tagore@grays.clara.net

TBK/TBk Ⓓ
T.C.S. Brooke
The Grange, 51 Norwich Road,
Wroxham, Norfolk NR12 8RX UK
Tel: +44 (0) 1603 782 644

TDG Ⓓ
The Design Gallery
5 The Green, Westerham, Kent
TN16 1AS UK
Tel: +44 (0) 1959 561 234

TEN Ⓐ
Tennants Auctioneers
The Auction Centre, Leyburn,
North Yorkshire DL8 5SG UK
Tel: +44 (0) 1969 623780
Fax: +44 (0) 1969 624281

TGC Ⓟ
Tony Garbarino Collection

TGM Ⓓ
The Glass Merchant
Tel: +44 (0) 7775 683 961
as@titan98.freeserve.co.uk

TH Ⓓ
Toy Heroes
42 Westway, Caterham-on-the-
Hill, Surrey CR3 5TP UK
Tel: +44 (0)1883 348 001
www.toyheroes.co.uk

TK Ⓐ
Auction Team Köln
Postfach 50 11 19, Bonner Str.
528-530, D-50971 Köln, Germany
Tel: +49 (0) 221 38 70 49
www.breker.com

TM Ⓓ
Tony Moran
South Street Antiques Center,
615 South 6th Street,
Philadelphia, PA 19147
Tel: 215 592 0256

TO Ⓓ
Titus Omega
Shop 1E, Ground Floor, Georgian
Village, London, N1 UK
Tel +44 (0) 20 7704 8003
www.titusomega.com

TP Ⓓ
Tenth Planet Ltd
Unit 36 Vicarage Field Shopping
Centre, Ripple Road, Barking
Essex, IG11 8DQ UK
Tel: +44 (0) 20 8591 5357
sales@tenthplanet.co.uk
www.tenthplanet.co.uk

TR Ⓓ
Terry Rodgers & Melody LLC
30 & 31 Manhattan Art and
Antiques Center, 1050 2nd
Avenue, New York, NY 10022
Tel: 212 758 3164
melodyjewelry@aol.com

TRA Ⓓ
Toy Road Antiques
2200 Highland St., Canal
Winchester, OH 43110
Tel: 614 834 1786
toyroad@ao.com

TVH Ⓓ
tvhistory.tv
www.tvhistory.tv

TWC Ⓐ
T. W. Conroy
36 Oswego St, Baldwinsville, NY
13027
Tel: 315 638 6434
www.twconroy.com

V Ⓓ
Ventisero
4 Unit S0C1, Alfies Antique
Market, 13-25 Church Street,
London NW8 8DT UK
Mob: 0+44 (0) 7767 498 766

Vec Ⓓ
Vectis Auctions Limited
Fleck Way, Thornaby, Stockton on
Tees TS17 9JZ UK
Tel: +44 (0) 1642 750 616
www.vectis.co.uk

VV Ⓓ
Vintage to Vogue
228 Milsom Street, Bath, Avon,
BA1 1DG UK
Tel: +44 (0) 1225 337323

W&W Ⓐ
Wallis and Wallis
West Street Auction Galleries,
Lewes, East Sussex BN7 2NJ UK
Tel: +44 (0) 1273 480 208
www.wallisandwallis.co.uk

WAD Ⓐ
Waddingtons,
111 Bathurst Street, Toronto,
Ontario, Canada, M5V 2R1
Tel: 001 416 504 9100
www.waddingtons.ca

Wain Ⓓ
William Wain at Antiquarius
Stand J6, Antiquarius,
135 King's Road,Chelsea,
London, SW3 4PW UK
Tel: +44 (0) 207351 4905

WHA Ⓐ
Willis Henry Auctions Inc
22 Main Street, Marshfield,
MA 02050
Tel: 781 834 7774
www.willishenry.com

WoS Ⓓ
Wheels of Steel
Unit B10-11, Grays Mews Antiques
Market, 1/7 Davies Mews, London
W1Y 2LP UK
Tel: +44 (0) 20 7629 2813
Fax: +44 (0) 20 7493 9344
wheels-of-steel@grays.clara.net

WW Ⓐ
Woolley and Wallis
51-61 Castle Street, Salisbury,
Wiltshire SP1 3SU UK
Tel: +44 (0) 1722 424 500
Fax: +44 (0) 1722 424 508
enquiries@woolleyandwallis.co.uk
www.woolleyandwallis.co.uk

DIRECTORY OF SPECIALISTS

If you wish to have any item valued, it is advisable to contact the dealer or specialist in advance to check that they will carry out this service and whether there is a charge. While most dealers will be happy to help you with an enquiry, do remember that they are busy people.

Telephone valuations are not possible. Please mention DK *Collectibles Price Guide 2004* by Judith Miller when making an enquiry. Specialist Dealers wishing to be listed in the next edition, space permitting, are requested to email info@thepriceguidecompany.com

ADVERTISING

Bill & Rick Kozlowski
Tel: 215 997 2486

The Nostalgia Factory
51 North Margin St, Boston, MA
02113
Tel: 617 720 2211
posters@nostalgia.com
www.nostalgia.com

Toy Road Antiques
2200 Highand St., Canal
Winchester, OH 43110
Tel: 614 834 1786

AMERICANA

Richard Axtell Antiques
1 River St, Deposit, NY 13754
Tel: 607 467 2353
Fax: 607 467 4316
raxtell@msn.com
www.axtellantiques.com

Buck County Antique Center
Route 202, Lahaksa, PA 18931
Tel: 215 794 9180

Fields of Glory
55 York St, Gettysburg, PA 17325
Tel: 717 337 2837
foglory@cvn.net
www.fieldsofglory.com
(Civil War Items)

Olde Hope Antiques
P.O. Box 718, New Hope, PA
18938
Tel: 215 297 0200
Fax: 215 297 0300
info@oldhopeantiques.com
www.oldhopeantiques.com

The Splendid Peasant
Route 23 & Sheffield Rd, P.O. Box
536, South Egremont, MA 01258
Tel: 413 528 5755
folkart@splendidpeasant.com
www.splendidpeasant.com

ANTIQUITIES

Frank & Barbara Pollack
1214 Green Bay Rd, Highland
Park, IL 60035
Tel: 847 433 2213
fpollack@compuserve.com

AUTOGRAPHS

Autographs of America
P.O. Box 461, Provo
UT 84603-0461
tanders3@autographsofamerica.com
www.autographsofamerica.com

Nate's Autograph Hound
10020 Raynor Road, Silver Spring,
MD 20901
autohnd@access.digex.net

Platt Autographs
1040 Bayview Dr #428, Fort
Lauderdale, FL 33306
Tel: 954 564 2002
ctplatt@ctplatt.com
www.ctplatt.com

AUTOMOBILIA

Dunbar's Gallery
76 Haven St, Milford,
MA 01757-3821
Tel: 508 634 8697
Fax: 508 634 8698

BOOKS

Abebooks
www.abebooks.com

Aleph-Bet Books
218 Waters Edge, Valley Cottage,
NY 10989
Tel: 914 268 7410
Fax: 914 268 5942
helen@alephbet.com
www.alephbet.com

Bauman Rare Books
4535 Madison Ave, between 54th
& 55th Streets, New York,
NY 100022
Tel: 212 751 0011
brb@baumanrarebooks.com
www.baumanrarebooks.com

Deer Park Books
609 Kent Rd, Route 7,
Gaylordsville, CT 06755
Tel/Fax: 860 350 4140
deerparkbk@aol.com
www.abebooks.com/home

CAMERAS & PHOTOGRAPHICA

Bryan Ginns
2109 Cty Rte 21, Valatie, NY
12184-6001
Tel: 518 392 805
Fax: 518 392 7925
the3dman@aol.com
www.stereographica.com

The Camera Man
1614 Bethlehem Pike, Flourtown,
PA 19031-2026
Tel/Fax: 215 233 4025

CANES

**Tradewinds Antiques
& Auctions**
24 Magnolia Ave, P.O. Box 249,
Manchester, MA 01944
Tel: 978 768 3327
Fax: 978 526 4085
taron@tiac.com
www.tradewindsantiques.com

CERAMICS

Blue & White Dinnerware
4800 Crestview Dr, Carmichael,
CA 95609
Tel: 916 961 7406
thefourls@aol.com

Fayne Landes Antiques
593 Hansell Road, Wynnewood,
PA 19096
Tel: 610 658 0566

The Perrault-Rago Gallery
65 Ferry Street, Lambertville,
NJ 08530
Tel: 609 397 1802
www.ragoarts.com

The Royal Pair Antiques
12707 Hillcrest Dr, Longmont,
CO 80501-1162
Tel: 303 772 2760

The World of Ceramics
208 Hemlock Dr, Neptune,
NJ 07753
antique208@msn.com
(Cups & Saucers)

Greg Walsh
32 River View Lane, P.O. Box 747,
Potsdam, NY 13676-0747
Tel: 315 265 9111
gwalsh@northnet.org
(Stoneware)

Happy Pastime
P.O. Box 1225, Ellicott City,
MD 21041-1225
Tel: 410 203 1101
hpastime@bellatlantic.net
www.happypastime.com
(Figurines)

Keller & Ross
P.O. Box 783, Melrose, MA 02716,
Tel: 978 988 2070
kellerross@aol.com
http://members.aol.com/kellerross

Ken Forster
5501 Seminary Road, Ste 1311,
South Falls Church, VA 22041
Tel: 703 379 1142
(Art Pottery)

Mellin's Antiques
P.O. Box 1115, Redding, CT 06875
Tel: 203 938 9538
remellin@aol.com

Mark & Marjorie Allen
6 Highland Dr, Amherst,
NH 03031
mandmallen@antiquedelft.com
www.antiquedelft.com

Charles & Barbara Adams
289 Old Main St, South Yarmouth,
MA 02664
Tel: 508 760 3290
adams_2430@msn.com

Stephanie Hull Winters
Classic Treasures, 3232 Morgan
Rd, Temple, GA 30179
Tel: 770 562 1332
swinters@bellsouth.net
(Art Pottery)

COMICS

Carl Bonasera
A1-American Comic Shops, 3514
W. 95th St, Evergreen Park,
IL 60642
Tel: 708 425 7555

Metropolis Collectibles Inc.
873 Broadway, Suite 201,
New York, NY 10003
Tel: 212 260 4147
Fax: 212 260 4304
orders@metropoliscom cs.com
www.metropoliscomics.com

The Comic Gallery
4224 Balboa Ave, San Diego,
CA 92117
Tel: 619 483 4853

COSTUME & ACCESSORIES

Lucy's Hats
South Street Antiques Center,
615 South 6th Street, Philadelphia,
PA 19147
Tel: 215 592 0256
shak06@aol.com

COSTUME JEWELRY

Aurora Bijoux
Tel: 215 855 1921
aurora@aurorabijoux.com
www.aurorabijoux.com

Barbara Blau
South Street Antiques Center,
615 South 6th Street, Philadelphia,
PA 19147
Tel: 215 592 0256
Tel: 215 739 4995

The Junkyard Jeweler
937 West Beach Street, Suite
49,Long Beach, NY 11561
spigner@aol.com
www.tias.com/stores/thejunkyardje
weler

Mod-Girl
South Street Antiques Center,
615 South 6th Street, Philadelphia,
PA 19147
Tel: 215 592 0256

Roxanne Stuart
Tel: 215 750 8868
gemfairy@aol.com

Terry Rodgers & Melody LLC
30 & 31 Manhattan Art and
Antiques Center, 1050 2nd
Avenue, New York, NY 10022
Tel: 212 758 3164
Fax: 212 935 6365
melodyjewelry@aol.com

DOLLS

The Doll Express
The Antiques Showcase at The
Black Horse 2222 North Reading
Road, Denver, PA 17517
Tel: 717 335 3300
thedollexpress@hotmail.com

Treasure & Dolls
518 Indian Rocks Rd, N. Belleair
Bluffs, FL 33770
Tel: 727 584 7277
dolls@antiquedoll.com
www.antiquecoll.com

FIFTIES & SIXTIES

Deco Etc
122 West 25th Street, (between
6th & 7th Aves.), New York,
NY 10010
Tel: 212 675 3327
deco_etc@msn.com

Lois' Collectibles of Antique
Market III, 413 W Main St, Saint
Chares, IL 60174-1815
Tel: 630 377 5599

Steve Colby
Off The Deep End, 712 East St,
Frederick, MD 21701-5239
Tel: 301 698 9006
chilimon@offtheceepend.com
www.offthedeepend.com

FILM MEMORABILIA

STARticles
58 Stewart St, Studio 301, Toronto,
Ontario, M5V 1H6 Canada
Tel: 416 504 8286
info@starticles.com

Norma s Jeans
3511 Turner Lane, Chevy Chase,
MD 20815-2313
Tel: 301 652 4644
Fax: 301 907 0216

George Baker
CollectorsMart, P.O. Box 580466,
Modesto, CA 95358
Tel: 290 537 5221
Fax: 209 531 0233
georgeb1@thevision.net
www.collectorsmart.com

GENERAL

Antiques of Cape May
Tel: 800 224 1687

Bucks County Antique Center
Route 202, Lahaska, PA 18931
Tel: 215 794 9180

Burlwood Antique Center
Route 3, Meredith, NH 03253
Tel: 603 279 6387
rckhprant@aol.com

Manhattan Art & Antiques Center
1050 Second Avenue (between
55th & 56th Street) New York, NY,
10022 Tel: 212-355-4400
Fax: 212-355-4403
info@the-maac.com

The Lafayette Mill Antiques
12 Morris Farm Road (Just off Rte
15), Lafayette NJ 07848
Tel: 973 383 0065
millpatnes@inpro.net
www.millantiques.com

South Street Antiques Center
615 South 5th Street, Philadelphia,
PA 19147
Tel: 215 592 0256

GLASS

C. Lucille Britt
4305 W 78th St, Prairie Village,
KS 66208
Tel: 913 642 3587

Past-Tyme Antiques
Tel: 703 777 8556
pasttymeantiques@aol.com

Jeff E. Purtell
P.O. Box 28, Amherst,
NH 03031-0028
Tel: 603 673 4331
Fax: 603 673 1525
(Steuben)

Paul Reichwein
2321 Hershey Ave, East Petersburg,
PA 17520
Tel: 717 569 7537
paurdg@aol com

Paul Stamati Gallery
1050 2nd Ave, New York,
NY 10022
Tel: 212 754 4533
Fax: 718 271 6658
mail@rene-lalique.com
www.rene-lalique.com

Suzman's Antiques
P.O. Box 301, Rehoboth, MA 02769
Tel: 508 252 5729
suzmanf@ride.ii.net

HOLIDAY MEMORABILIA

Chris & Eddie's Collectibles
South Street Antiques Center,
615 South 6th Street, Philadelphia,
PA 19147
Tel: 215 592 0256

Sign of the Tymes
2 Morris Farm Rd, Lafayette,
NJ 07848
Tel: 973 383 6028
jhap@nac.net
www.millantiques.com

JEWELRY

Arthur Guy Kaplan
P.O. Box 1942, Baltimore,
MD 21203
Tel: 410 752 2090

Tony Laughter
Perry's at SouthPark, SouthPark
Mall, Charlotte, NC 28211
Tel: 704 364 1391

KITCHENALIA & HOUSEHOLD

Dynamite Antiques & Collectibles
Ellen Bercovici
Tel: 301 652 1140

LAMPS & LIGHTING

Deco Etc
122 West 25th Street, (between
6th & 7th Aves.), New York,
NY 10010
Tel: 212 675 3327
deco_etc@msn.com

MECHANICAL MUSIC

The Music Box Shop
7236 E 1st Ave, Scottsdale,
AZ 85251
Tel: 602 945 0428
Fax: 602 200 9365
musicboxshop@home.com
www.themusicboxshop.com

Mechantiques
The Crescent Hotel, 75 Prospect St,
Eureka Springs, AR 72632
Tel: 501 253 9766
mroe@aol.com
www.mechantiques.com

MEDICAL INSTRUMENTS

C. Keith Wilbur
The Doctor's Bag, 397 Prospect St,
Northampton, MA 01060-2047
Tel: 413 584 1440

Armoreak Antiques
531 Doub Rd, Lewisville,
NC 27023
Tel: 336 945 9477
Fax: 336 945 9914
clestuff@armbrookantiques.com
www.armbrookantiques.com

Scientific Medical & Mechanical Antiques
P.O. Box 412, Taneytown,
MD 21787
Tel: 301 447 2580
smma@americanartefacts.com
www.americanartefacts.com/smma

MILITARIA

Articles of War
358 Boulevard, Middletown,
RI 02842
Tel: 401 846 8503
dutch5@ids.com

Stewarts Military Antiques
108 W. Main St, Mesa, AZ 85201
Tel: 602 834 4004

Terry Porter Fine Antique Arms
P.O. Box 53025, Mesquite,
TX 75150
Tel: 214 679 7410
Fax: 972 68 8992
terry.porter@fineantiquearms.com
www.fineantiquearms.com

MARBLES

Auction Blocks
P.O. Box 2321, Huntington Station,
CT 06484
Tel: 203 924 2802
auctionblocks@aol.com
www.auctionblocks.com

OPTICAL INSTRUMENTS

Vintage Eyeware
Tel: 917 721 5546
www.vintage-eyeware.com

ORIENTAL & ASIAN

Oriental Treasures Antiques
159 W. Kenzie Street, Chicago,
IL 60510-4514
Tel: 773 761 2907
Fax: 773 761 0789

Gallery of Fine Netsuke
163 Third Ave, Ste 295, New York,
NY 10003
Tel: 212 533 3666
mspindel@mindspring.com
www.spindel.com

**Oriental Antiques Shop
Miracle Ventures**
P.O. Box 75, Flushing, NY 11363
Tel/Fax: 718 225 1461

Sharon & Arno Ziesnitz
7835 Painted Daisy Dr,
Springfield, VA 22152
Tel: 703 451 1033
Fax: 703 569 4221
ziesnitz@aol.com

PENS & WRITING EQUIPMENT

Fountain Pen Hospital
10 Warren Street, New York,
NY 10007
Tel: 212 964 0580
info@fountainpenhospital.com
www.fountainpenhospital.com

Gary & Myrna Lehrer
16 Mulberry Rd, Woodbridge,
CT 06525-1717
Tel: 203 389 5295
Fax: 203 389 4515
garylehrer@aol.com
www.gopens.com

David Nishimura
Vintage Pens, P.O. Box 41452
Provicence, RI 02940-1452
Tel: 401 351 7607
Fax: 401 351 1168
www.vintagepens.com

Sandra & L. 'Buck' van Tine
Lora's Memory Lane, 13133 North
Caroline St, Chillicothe,
IL 61523-9115
Tel: 309 579 3040
Fax: 309 579 2696
lorasink@aol.com

Sam Fiorella
Pendemonium, 15231 Larkspur
Lare, Dumfries, VA 22026-2075
Tel: 703 670 8549
Fax: 703 670 3875
www.pendemonium.com

PERFUME & SCENT BOTTLES

Oldies But Goldies
P.O. Box 217, Hankins,
NY 12741-0217
Tel: 914 887 5272
oldgood@catskill.net
www.catskill.net/oldgood

Monsen & Baer Inc
P.O. Box 529, Vienna,
VA 22183-0529
Tel: 703 938 2129
monsenbaer@erols.com

PLASTICS

Dee Battle
9 Orange Blossom Trail, Yalaha,
FL 34797
Tel: 352 324 3023

Malabar Enterprises
172 Bush Lane, Ithaca, NY 14850
Tel: 607 255 2905
Fax: 607 255 4179
asn6@cornell.edu

POSTERS

Posteritati
239 Center St, New York,
NY 10013
Tel: 212 226 2207
Fax: 212 226 2102
mail@posteritati.com
www.posteritati.com

Poster America
138 West 18th St, New York,
NY 10011-5403
Tel: 212 206 0499
Fax: 212 727 2495
pfair@dti.net
www.posterfair.com

Vintage Poster Works
P.O. Box 88, Pittford, NY 14534
Tel: 716 218 9483
Fax: 716 218 9035
debra@vintageposterworks.com
www.vintageposterworks.com

La Belle Epoque
11661 San Vincente, 3304 Los
Angeles, CA 90049-5110
Tel: 310 442 0054
Fax: 310 826 6934
ktscicon@ix.netcom.com

ROCK & POP

Heinz's Rare Collectibles
P.O. Box 179, Little Silver,
NJ 07739-0179
Tel: 732 219 1988
Fax: 732 219 5940
(The Beatles)

Tod Hutchinson
P.O. Box 915, Griffith,
IN 46319-0915
Tel: 219 923 8334
toddtcb@aol.com
(Elvis Presley)

SCIENCE & TECHNOLOGY

George Glazer
28 East 2nd St, New York,
NY 10021
Tel: 212 535 5706
Fax: 212 988 3992
worldglobe@aol.com
www.georgeglazer.com

Tesseract
Box 15, Hastings-on-Hudson,
NY 10706
Tel: 914 478 2594
Fax: 914 478 5473
e-mail: coffeen@aol.com
www.etesseract.com

Bob Elsner
Heights Antiques
29 Clubhouse Lane, Boynton
Beach, FL 33436-6056
Tel: 561 736 1362
Fax: 561 736 1914
rjelsner@aol.com
(Barometers)

The Olde Office
68-845 Perez Rd, Ste 30,
Cathedral City, CA 92234
Tel: 760 346 8653
Fax: 760 346 6479
info@thisoldeoffice.com
www.thisoldeoffice.com

Jane Hertz
6731 Ashley Ct, Sarasota,
FL 34241-9696
Tel: 941 925 0385
Fax: 941 925 0487
auction@breker.com
www.breker.com
(Cameras, Office & Technical
Equipment)

SILVER

**Argentum –
The Leopard's Head**
414 Jackson St, Ste 101,
San Francisco, CA 94111
Tel: 415 296 7757
Fax: 415 296 7233
www.argentum-theleopard.com

Gary Neiderkorn Silver
2005 Locust St, Philadelphia,
PA 19103-5606
Tel/Fax: 215 567 2606

Lauren Stanley Gallery
300 E 51st St, New York,
NY 10022
Tel: 212 888 6732
Fax: 212 486 2503
info@laurenstanley.com
www.laurenstanley.com

Jonathan Trace
P.O. Box 418, 31 Church Hill Road,
Rifton, NY 12471
Tel: 914 658 7336

SMOKING

Richard Weinstein
International Vintage Lighter
Exchange, 30 W. 57th St,
New York, NY 10019
vinlighter@aol.com
www.vintagelighters.com

Ira Pilossof
Vintage Lighters Inc., P.O. Box
1325, Fairlawn, NJ 07410-8325
Tel: 201 797 6595
vintageltr@aol.com

Mike Cassidy
1070 Bannock #400, Denver,
CO 80204
Tel: 303 446 2726

Chuck Haley
Sherlock's, 13926 Double Girth
Ct., Matthews, NC 28105-4068
Tel: 704 847 5480
(Pipes)

SPACE MEMORABILIA

Gregg Linebaugh
AVD Services, P.O. Box 604, Glenn
Dale, MD 20769
Tel: 301 249 3895

The Ultimate Space Place
P.O. Box 5411, Merritt Island,
FL 32954
Tel: 407 454 4236
questions@thespaceplace.com
www.thespaceplace.com

SPORTING MEMORABILIA

Classic Rods & Tackle
P.O. Box 288, Ashley Falls,
MA 01222
Tel: 413 229 7988

Larry Fritsch Cards Inc
735 Old Wassau Rd, P.O. Box 863,
Stevens Point, WI 54481
Tel: 715 344 8687
Fax: 715 344 1778
larry@fritschcards.com
www.fritschcards.com
(Baseball Cards)

George Lewis
Golfiana, P.O. Box 291,
Mamaroneck, NY 10543
Tel: 914 835 5100
Fax: 914 835 1715
george@golfiana.com
www.golfiana.com

Golf Collectibles
P.O. Box 4430, Irving, YX 75016
Tel: 972 594 7802
furjanic@directlink.net
www.folfforallages.com

The Hager Group
P.O. Box 952974, Lake Mary,
FL 32795
Tel: 407 788 3865
(Trading Cards)

Hall's Nostalgia
21-25 Mystic St, P.O. Box 408,
Arlington, MA 02174
Tel: 781 646 7757

Tom & Jill Kaczor
1550 Franklin Rd., Langhorne,
PA 19047
Tel: 215 968 5776
Fax: 215 946 6056

Mike's Tackle Box
P.O. Box 5827., Bellingham,
WA 98227
Tel: 360 734 7379
mike@nikestackle.com

TEDDY BEARS & SOFT TOYS

Harper General Store
10482 Jonestown Rd, Annville,
PA 17003
Tel: 717 865 3455
Fax: 717 865 3813
www.harpergeneralstore.com

Marion Weis
Division St Antiques, P.O. Box
374, Buffalo, MN 55313-0374
Tel: 612 682 6453

TEXTILES & COSTUME

Colette Donovan
98 River Road, Merrimacport,
MA 0186C
Tel: 978 346 0614

Fayne Landes Antiques
593 Hansell Road, Wynnewood,
PA 19096
Tel: 610 653 0566
fayne@comcast.net

Sweethaven Lace
4681 Bloomfield Rd, Taylorsville,
KY 40071
Tel: 502 477 8819
sfierbaugh@aem.org

Vintage Clothing Company
P.O. Box 20501, Keizer, OR
97307-0504
retrothreads@aol.com

Yesterday's Threads
206 Meadow St Branford,
CT 06405-3634
Tel: 203 481 6452
Fax: 203 483 7550

TOYS & GAMES

Barry Carter
Knights own Antiques Mall, 136
W. Carey St, Knightstown,
IN 46148-1111
Tel: 765-345 5665
bcarter@spitfire.net

France Antique Toys
Tel: 631 754 1399

Litwin Antiques
P.O. Box 5865, Trenton,
NJ 08638-0865
Tel/Fax: 609 275 1427
(Chess)

Harry R. McKeon, Jr.
18 Rose Lane, Flourtown,
PA 19031-1910
Tel: 215 233 4094
toyspost@aol.com
(Tin Toys)

Jessica Pack Antiques
Chape Hill, NC
Tel: 919 408 0406
jpanls1@aol.com

The Old Toy Soldier Home
977 S. Santa Fe, Ste 1
Vista, CA 92083
Tel: 760 758 5481
Fax: 760 758 5481
info@oldtoysoldierhome.com
www.oldtoysoldierhome.com

Trains & Things
106 East Front St, Traverse City,
MI 49684
Tel: 616 947 1353
Fax: 616 947 1411
tctrains@traverse.net
www.tctrains.com

TRIBAL

Hurst Gallery
53 Mount Auburn St, Cambridge,
MA 02138
Tel: 617 491 6888
nhurst@compuserve.com
www.hurstgallery.com

Marcy Burns American Indian Arts
P.O. Box 181, Glenside,
PA 19038
Tel: 215 576 1559
mbindianart@home.com

Malter Galleries
17005 Ventura Blvd, Encino,
CA 91316-4128
Tel: 818 784 7772
rarearts@earthlink.net
www.maltergalleries.com

Elliot & Grace Snyder
P.O. Box 598, South Egremont,
MA 01258
Tel: 413 528 3581

WATCHES

Finer Times Vintage Timepieces
P.O. Box 273020, Tampa,
FL 33688
Tel: 813 963 5757
Fax: 813 960 5676
dontime@minspring.com www.fine
rtimes.com

Mark Laino
South Street Antiques Center,
615 South 6th Street,
Philadelphia, PA 19147
Tel: 215 592 0256

Temes & Co.
238 N. Charles St, Baltimore,
MD 21201
Tel: 410 347 7600
Fax: 410 685 3299

Texas Time
3076 Waunuta St, Newbury
Park, CA 1320
Tel: 805 498 5644
Fax: 805 480 9514
pearl@dock.net
www.texastime.com

WINE & DRINKING

Derek White
The Corkscrew Pages, 769
Sumter Dr, Morrisville, PA 19067
Tel: 215 493 4143
Fax: 609 860 5380
cswrite@marketsource.com
www.caponfine.com

Donald A. Bull
P.O. Box 596, Wirtz, VA 24184
Tel: 540 721 1128
Fax: 540 721 5468
corkscrue@aol.com

Steve Visakay Cocktail Shakers
P.O. Box 1517 West Caldwell, NJ
07007-1517
Tel: 914 352 5640
svisakay@aol.com

DIRECTORY OF AUCTIONEERS

Auctioneers who wish to be listed in this directory for our next edition, space permitting, are requested to
email info@thepriceguidecompany.com

ALABAMA

Flomaton Antique Auctions
P.O. Box 1017, 320 Palafox Street,
Flomaton, AL 36441
Tel: 334 296 3059
Fax: 334 296 3710

ARIZONA

Dan May & Associates
4110 N. Scottsdale Road,
Scottsdale, AZ 85251
Tel: 602 941 4200

ARKANSAS

Ponders Auctions
1504 South Leslie, Stuttgart,
AR 72160
Tel: 501 673 6551

CALIFORNIA

Aurora Galleries International
30 Hackamore Lane, Ste 2,
Bell Canyon, CA 91307
Tel: 818 884 6468

Fax: 818 227 2941
vjc@auroragalleriesonline.com
www.auroragalleriesonline.com

Butterfield & Butterfield
7601 Sunset Blvd Los Angeles,
CA 90046
Tel: 323 850 7500
Fax: 323 850 5843
info@butterfields.com
www.butterfields.com

Butterfield & Butterfield
220 San Bruno Ave, San
Francisco, CA 94103
Tel: 415 861 7500
Fax: 415 861 8951
info@butterfields.com
www.butterfields.com

Clark Cierlak Fine Arts
14452 Ventura Blvd,
Sherman Oaks, CA 91423
Tel: 818 783 3052
Fax: 818 783 3162
clark@estateauctionservice.com
www.estateauctionservice.com

I.M. Chait Gallery
9330 Civic Center Dr, Beverly Hills,
CA 90210
Tel: 310 285 0182
Fax: 310 285 9740
imchait@aol.com
www.chait.com

Cuschieri's Auctioneers & Appraisers
863 Main Street, Redwood City,
CA 94063
Tel: 650 556 1793
Fax: 650 556 9805
www.cuschieris.com

eBay, Inc
2005 Hamilton Ave, Ste 350
San Jose, CA 95125
Tel: 408 369 4839
www.ebay.com

L.H. Selman
123 Locust St, Santa Cruz,
CA 95060
Tel: 800 538 0766
Fax: 408 427 0111
leselman@gct.net

Malter Galleries
17003 Ventura Blvd, Encino,
CA 91316
Tel: 818 784 7772
Fax: 818 784 4726
www.maltergalleries.com

Poster Connection Inc
43 Regency Dr, Clayton, CA 94517
Tel: 925 673 3343
Fax: 925 673 3355
sales@posterconnection.com
www.posterconnection.com

Profiles in History
110 North Doheny Dr, Beverly
Hills, CA 90211
Tel: 310 859 7701
Fax: 310 859 3842
www.profilesinhistory.com

San Rafael Auction Gallery
634 Fifth Avenue San Rafael,
CA 9490
Tel: 415 457 4458
Fax: 415 457 4899
www.sanrafael-auction.com

Slawinski Auction Co.
6221 Graham Hill Road, Ste C,
Felton, CA 95018
Tel: 831 335 9300
Fax: 831 335 6933
antiques@slawinski.com
www.slawinski.com

CONNECTICUT

Alexander Autographs
100 Melrose Ave, Greenwich,
CT 06830
Tel: 203 622 8444
Fax: 203 622 8765
peter@alexautographs.com
www.alexautographs.com

**Norman C. Heckler &
Company**
79 Bradford Corner Road,
Woodstock Valley, CT 0682
Tel: 860 974 1634
Fax: 860 974 2003
www.hecklerauction.com

Lloyd Ralston Gallery
250 Long Beach Blvd, Stratford,
CT 016615
Tel: 203 386 9399
Fax: 203 386 9519
lrgallery@aol.com
www.lloydralstontoys.com

DELAWARE

**Remember When
Auctions Inc.**
42 Sea Gull Rd, Swann Estates,
Selbyville, DE 19975
Tel: 302 436 8869
Fax: 302-436-6144
sales@history-attic.com
www.history-attic.com

FLORIDA

Auctions Neapolitan
995 Central Avenue, Naples,
FL 34102
Tel: 941 262 7333
kathleen@auctionsneapolitan.com
www.auctionsneapolitan.com

Burchard Galleries
2523 30th Ave N, St Petersburg,
FL 33713
Tel: 727 821 11667
mai.@burhcardgalleries.com
www.burchardgalleries.com

Dawson's
P.O. Box 646, Palm Beach,
FL 33480
Tel: 561 835 6930
Fax: 561 835 8464
info@dawsons.org
www.dawsons.org

Arthur James Galleries
615 E. Atlantic Ave, Delray Beach,
FL 33483
Tel: 561 278 2373
Fax: 561 278 7633
www.arthurjames.com

Kincaid Auction Company
3214 E Hwy 92, Lakeland,
FL 3381
Tel: 800 970 1977
kincaid@kincaid.com
www.kincaid.com

Sloan's Auction Galleries
8861 NW 19th Terace, Ste 100,
Miami, FL 33172
Tel: 305 751 4770
sloans@sloansauction.com
www.sloansauction.com

GEORGIA

Great Gatsby's
5070 Peachtree Industrial Blvd,
Atlanta, GA
Tel: 770 457 1905
Fax: 770-457-7250
internet@greatgatsbys.com
www.gatsbys.com

My Hart Auctions Inc
P.O. Box 2511, Cumming,
GA 30028
Tel: 770 888 9006
myhart@prodigy.net
www.myhart.net

IDAHO

The Coeur D'Alene Art Auction
P.O. Box 310, Hayden, ID 83835
Tel: 20 8772 9009
Fax: 20 8772 8294
cdaartauction@cdaartauction.com
www.cdaartauction.com

ILLINOIS

Joy Luke
300 East Grove Street,
Bloomington, IL 61701
Tel: 309 828 5533
Fax: 309 829 2266
robert@joyluke.com
www.joyluke.com

INDIANA

**Curran Miller Auction & Realty
Inc**
4424 Vogel Rd, Ste 400,
Evansville, IN 47715
Tel: 812 474 6100
Fax: (812) 474-6110
cmar@curranmiller.com
www.curranmiller.com

Kruse International
5540 County Rd 11A, Auburn,
IN 46706
Tel: 800 968 4444
info@kruseinternational.com
www.kruse.com

Lawson Auction Service
923 Fourth Street, Columbus,
IN 47265
Tel: 812 372 2571
dlawson@lawson-auction.com
www.lawson-auction.com

Slater's Americana
5335 N. Tacoma Ave, Ste 24,
Indianapolis, IN 46220
Tel: 317 257 0863

Stout Auctions
529 State Road 28 East,
Willamsport, IN 47993
Tel: 765 764 6901
Fax: 765-764-1516
stoutauctions@hotmail.com
www.stoutauctions.com

IOWA

Gene Harris Auctions
2035 18th Ave, Marshalltown,
IA 50158
Tel: 641 752 0600
ghaac@geneharrisauctions.com
www.geneharrisauctions.com

**Jackson's Auctioneers &
Appraisers**
2229 Lincoln St, Cedar Falls,
IA 50613
Tel: 319 277 2256
sandim@jacksonsauction.com
www.jacksonsauction.com

Tubaugh Auctions
1702 8th Ave, Belle Plaine,
IA 52208
Tel: 319 444 2413
www.tubaughauctions.com

KANSAS

**Manions International Auction
House**
P.O. Box 12214, Kansas City,
KS 66112
Tel: 913 299 6692
Fax: 913 299 6792
collecting@manions.com
www.manions.com

CC Auctions
416 Court St, Clay Center,
KS 67432
Tel: 785 632 6021
dhamilton@cc-auctions.com
www.cc-auctions.com

Spielman Auctions
2259 Homestead Rd, Lebo,
KS 66856
Tel: 316 256 6558

KENTUCKY

Hays & Associates Inc
120 South Spring Street,
Louisville, KY 40206
kenhays@haysauction.com
www.haysauction.com

Steffens Historical Militaria
P.O. Box 280, Newport, KY 41072
Tel: 859 431 4499
Fax: 859 431 3113
www.steffensmilitaria.com

LOUSIANA

**Morton M. Goldberg
Auction Galleries**
547 Baronne Street
New Orleans, LA 70113
Tel: 504 592 2300
Fax: 504 592 2311

New Orleans Auction Galleries
801 Magazine Street. New
Orleans, LA 70130
Tel: 504 566 1849
Fax: 504 566 1851
info@neworleansauction.com
www.neworleansauction.com

MAINE

Guyette & Schmidt
P.O. Box 522, West Farmington,
ME 04992
Tel: 20 7778 6256
Fax: 20 7778 6501
decoys@guyetteandschmidt.com

**James D. Julia
Auctioneers Inc.**
P.O. Box 830, Fairfield
ME 04937
Tel: 207 453 7125
Fax: 207 453 2502
jjulia@juliaauctions.com
www.juliaauctions.com

**Thomaston Place
Auction Galleries**
P.O. Box 300, 51 Atlantic Highway,
US Rt 1 Thomaston ME 04861
Tel: 207 354 8141
Fax: 207 354 9523
barbara@kajav.com
www.thomastonauction.com

MARYLAND

DeCaro Auction Sales Inc.
117A Bay Street, Ste D, Easton,
MD 21601
Tel: 410 820 4000
Fax: 410 820 4332
info@decaroauctions.com
www.decaroauctions.com

**Hantman's Auctioneers &
Appraisers**
P.O. Box 59366, Potomac, MD
20859
Tel: 301 770 3720
Fax: 301 770 4135
hantman@hantmans.com
www.hantmans.com

**Isennock Auctions &
Appraisals**
Isennock Auction Services, Inc.
4106B Norrisville Road, White
Hall, MD 21161
Tel: 410-557-8052
Fax 410-692-6449
info@isennockauction.com
www.isennockauction.com

Sloans & Kenyon
4605 Bradley Boulevard,
Bethesda, Maryland 20815
Tel: 301 634-2330
Fax: 301 656-7074
info@sloansandkenyon.com
www.sloansandkenyon.com

MASSACHUSETTS

Eldred's
P.O. Box 796, 1483 Route 6A
East Dennis, MA 02641
Tel: 508 385 3116
Fax: 508 385 7201
info@eldreds.com
www.eldreds.com

Grogan & Company
22 Harris St, Dedham, MA 02026
Tel: 800-823 1020
Fax: 781 461 9625
grogans@groganco.com
www.groganco.com

Simon D. Hill & Associates
420 Boston Turnpike, Shrewsbury,
MA 01545
Tel: 508 845 2400
Fax: 978 928 4129
simondhill@earthlink.net
www.simondhillaucts.com

Skinner Inc
The Heritage on the Garden, 63
Park Plaza, Boston, MA 02116
Tel: 617-350-5400
Fax: 617-350-5429
info@skinnerinc.com
www.skinnerinc.com

Willis Henry Auctions
22 Main St, Marshfield,
MA 02050
Tel: 781 834 7774
Fax: 781 826 3520
wha@willishenry.com
www.willishenry.com

MICHIGAN

DuMouchelles
408 East Jefferson Ave, Detroit,
MI 48226
Tel: 313 963 6255
Fax: 313 963 8199
info@dumouchelles.com
www.dumouchelles.com

MINNESOTA

Buffalo Bay Auction Co
5244 Quam Circle, Rogers,
MN 55374
Tel: 612 428 8480
buffalobayauction@hotmail.com
www.buffalobayauction.com

Rose Auction Galleries
2717 Lincoln Dr, Roseville,
MN 55113
Tel: 651 484 1415
Fax: 651 636 3431
auctions@rosegalleries.com
www.rosegalleries.com

MISSOURI

Ivey-Selkirk
7447 Forsyth Blvd, Saint Louis,
MO 63105
Tel: 314 726 5515
Fax: 314 726 9908
www.iveyselkirk.com

MONTANA

Allard Auctions Inc
P.O. Box 460 St Ignatius,
MT 59865
Tel: 406 745 0500
Fax: 406 745 0502
info@allardauctions.com
www.allardauctions.com

NEW HAMPSHIRE

Northeast Auctions
93 Pleasant St, Portmouth,
NH 03801-4504
Tel: 603 433 8400
Fax: 603 433 0415
www.northeastauctions.com

NEW JERSEY

Bertoia Auctions
2141 Demarco Dr, Vineland,
NJ 08360
Tel: 856 692 1881
Fax: 856 692 8697
bil@bertoiaauctions.com
www.bertoiaauctions.com

Craftsman Auctions
333 North Main St, Lambertville
NJ 08530
Tel: 609 397 9374
Fax: 609 397 9377
www.ragoarts.com

Dawson's
128 American Rd, Morris Plains,
NJ 07950
Tel: 973 984 6900
Fax: 973 984 6956
info@dawsons.org
www.dawsons.org

Greg Manning Auctions Inc
775 Passaic Ave, West Caldwell,
NJ 07006
Tel: 973 883 0004
Fax: 973 882 3499
www.gregmanning.com

Rago Modern Auctions LLP
333 North Main St, Lambertville,
NJ 08530
Tel: 609 397 9374
Fax: 609 397 9377
info@ragoarts.com
www.ragoarts.com

NEW MEXICO

Parker-Braden Auctions
P.O. Box 1897, 4303 National
Parks Highway, Carlsbad
NM 88220
Tel: 505 885 4874
Fax: 505 885 4622
www.parkerbraden.com

NEW YORK

Christie's
20 Rockefeller Plaza, New York,
NY 10020
Tel: 212 636 2000
Fax: 212 636 2399
info@christies.com
www.christies.com

TW Conroy
36 Oswego St, Baldwinsville,
NY 13027
Tel: 315 638 6434
Fax: 315 638 7039
brad@twconroy.com
www.conroy.com

Samuel Cottone Auctions
15 Genesee St, Mount Morris,
NY 14510
Tel: 585 658 3119
Fax: 585 658 3152
scottone@rochester.rr.com
www.cottoneauctions.com

William Doyle Galleries
175 E. 87th St, New York
NY 10128
Tel: 212 427 2730
Fax: 212 369 0892
www.doylenewyork.com

Guernsey's Auctions
108 East 73rd St, New York,
NY 10021
Tel: 212 794 2280
Fax: 212 744 3638
auctions@guernseys.com
www.guernseys.com

**Phillips, De Pury &
Luxembourg**
450 West 15 Street, New York
NY 10011
Tel: 212 940 1200
Fax: 212 688 1647
inquiry.desk@phillips-dpl.com
www.phillips-dpl.com

Sotheby's
1334 York Ave at 72nd St,
New York, NY 10021
Tel: 212 606 7000
Fax: 212 606 7107
info@sothebys.com
www.sothebys.com

Swann Galleries Inc
104 E. 25th St, New York,
NY 10010
Tel: 212 254 4710
Fax: 212 979 1017
swann@swanngalleries.com
www.swanngalleries.com

NORTH CAROLINA

Robert S. Brunk
P.O. Box 2135, Asheville,
NC 28802
Tel: 828 254 6846
Fax: 828 254 6545
www.brunkauctions.com

Historical Collectible Auctions
P.C. Box 975 Burlington,
NC 27215
Tel: 336 570 2803
bids4hca@aol.com
www.hcaauctions.com

NORTH DAKOTA

**Curt D Johnson Auction
Company**
P.O. Box 135, Grand Forks,
SC 58201
Tel: 701 746 1378
merfeld@rrv.net
www.curtdjohnson.com

OHIO

Cowans Historic Americana
673 Wilmer Avenue, Cincinnati,
OH 45226
Tel: 513 871 1670
Fax: 513 871 8670
www.historicamericana.com

DeFina Auctions
1591 State Route 45 Sth,
Austinburg, OH 44010
Tel: 440 275 6674
info@definaauctions.com
www.definaauctions.com

Garth's Auctions
2690 Stratford Rd, Box 369,
Delaware, OH 43015
Tel: 740 362 4771
Fax: 740 363 0164
info@garths.com
www.garths.com

PENNSYLVANIA

Alderfer Auction Gallery
501 Fairgrounds Rd, Hatfield,
PA 19440
Tel: 215 393 3000
info@alderferauction.com
www.alderferauction.com

Noel Barrett
P.O. Box 300, Carversville,
PA 18913
Tel: 215 297 5109
toys@noelbarrett.com
www.noelbarrett.com

Dargate Auction Galleries
214 North Lexington, Pittsburgh,
PA 15208
Tel: 412 362 3558
info@dargate.com
www.dargate.com

Freeman's
1808 Chestnut Ave, Philadelphia,
PA 19103
Tel: 610 563 9275
info@freemansauction.com
www.freemansauction.com

Hunt Auctions
75 E. Uwchlan Ave, Ste 1, 30
Exton, PA 13341
Tel: 610 524 0822
Fax: 610 524 0826
www.huntauctions.com

Pook & Pook Inc
463 East Lancaster Ave,
Downington, PA 19335
Tel: 610 269 4040
Fax: 610 269 9274
info@pookandpook.com
www.pookandpook.com

Skinner's Auction Co.
170 Northampton St, Easton,
PA 18042
Tel: 610 330 6933
skinnaucti@aol.com
www.skinneraust.baweb.com

Stephenson's Auctions
1005 Industrial Blvd,
Southampton, PA 18966
www.stephensonsauction.com

RHODE ISLAND

WebWilson
P.O. Box 506, Portsmouth,
RI 02871
Tel: 800 508 0022
hww@webwilson.com
www.webwilson.com

SOUTH CAROLINA

Charlton Hall Galleries
912 Gervais St Columbia,
SC 29201
Tel: 803 799 5678
info@charltonhallgalleries.com
www.hcharltonhallgalleries.com

TENNESSEE

Berenice Denton Estates
4403 Murphy Road, Nashville,
TN 37209
Tel: 615 292 5765
lnichols66@home.com

Kimball M. Sterling Inc
125 W. Market St, Johnson City,
TN 37604
Tel: 423 928 1471
kimsold@tricon.net
www.sterlingsold.com

TEXAS

Austin Auctions
8414 Anderson Mill Rd, Austin,
TX 78729-4702
Tel: 512 258 5479
Fax: 512 219 7372
austinauction@cs.com
www.austinauction.com

Dallas Auction Gallery
1518 Socum St, Dallas,
TX 75207
Tel: 213 653 3900
Fax: 213 653 3912
info@dallasauctiongallery.com
www.dallasauctiongallery.com

Heritage Comics
Heritage Plaza, 100 Highland
Park Village, 2nd Floor, Dallas,
TX 75205-2788
Tel: 214 528 3500
Fax: 214 520 6968
jsmith@heritagecomics.com
www.heritagecomics.com

UTAH

America West Archives
P.O. Box 100, Cedar City,
UT 84721
Tel: 435 586 9497
awa@utah.net
www.americawestarchives.com

VERMONT

Eaton Auction Service
RR1 Box 333, Fairlee, VT 05045
Tel: 802 333 9717

VIRGINIA

**Ken Farmer Auctions &
Estates**
105A Harrison St, Radford,
VA 24141
Tel: 540 639 0939
Fax: 540 639 1759
info@kfauctions.com
www.kfauctions.com

Phoebus Auction Gallery
14-16 E. Mellen St, Hampton,
VA 23663
Tel: 757 722 9210
Fax: 757 723 2280
bwelch@phoebusauction.com
www.phoebusauction.com

Signature House
407 Liberty Ave, Bridgeport,
WV 25330
Tel: 304 842 3386
Fax: 304 842 3001
www.signaturehouse.net

WASHINGTON DC

Weschlers
909 E St, NW Washington,
DC 20004
Tel: 202 628 1281
Fax: 202 628 2366
fineart@weschlers.com

WISCONSIN

Krueger Auctions
P.O. Box 275, Iola,
WI 54945-0275
Tel: 715 445 3845

Schrager Auction Galleries
2915 North Sherman Blvd, P.O.
Box 100043, Milwaukee,
WI 53210
Tel: 414 873 3738
Fax: 414 873 5229
askus@schragerauction.com
www.schragerauction.com

WYOMING

**Cody Old West Show
& Auction**
1215 Sheridan Ave, Cody,
WY 82414
Tel: 317 587 9014
Fax: 307 587 3979
oldwest@codyoldwest.com
www.codyoldwest.com

Manitou Gallery
1715 Carey Ave, Cheyenne,
WY 82001
Tel: 307 635 7670
Fax: 307 778 3926
ptassi@aol.com

CLUBS AND SOCIETIES

ADVERTISING

**Antique Advertising
Association of America**
P.O. Box 1121, Morton Grove,
IL 60053
Tel: 708 446 0904
www.pastimes.org

**Coca Cola Collectors Club
International**
P.O. Box 49166, Atlanta, GA
30359-1166

**Tin Container Collectors
Association**
P.O. Box 440101 Aurora,
CO 80044

AMERICANA

Folk Art Society of America
P.O. Box 17041, Richmond,
VA 23226-70

**American Political Items
Collectors**
P.O. Box 340339 San Antonio,
TX 8234-0339
http://www.collectors.org/apic

AUTOGRAPHS

**International Autograph
Collectors Club & Dealers'
Alliance**
4575 Sheridan St, Ste 111,
Hollywood, FL 33021-3515
Tel: 561 736 8409
www.iacc-da.com

**Universal Autograph Collectors
Club**
P.O. Box 6181, Washington,
DC 20044
Tel: 202 332-7388
http://www.uacc.com

AUTOMOBILIA

Automobile Objets d'Art Club
252 N. 7th St. Allentown,
PA 18102-4204
Tel: 610 432 3355
oldtoy@aol.com

BOOKS

**Antiquarian Bookseller's
Association of America**
20 West 44th St, 4th Floor,
New York, NY 10036
Tel: 212 944 8291

CAMERAS

**American Society of
Camera Collectors**
7415 Reseda Blvd, Reseda,
CA 91335
Tel: 818 345-2660.

**American Photographic
Historical Society Inc.**
1150 Avenue of the Americas,
New York, NY 10036
Tel: 212 575 0483
gfine@monmouth.com

CERAMICS

**American Art Pottery
Association**
P.O. Box 834, Westport,
MA 02790-0697
www.amartpot.com

American Ceramics Circle
520 16th St, Brooklyn, NY 11215
Tel: 718 832 5446
nlester@earthlink.net

**American Cookie Jar
Association**
1600 Navajo Rd, Norman,
OK 73026
davismj@ionet.net

Style 1900
David Rago, 9 Main St,
Lambertville, NJ 08530

The Belleek Collectors Society
144 West Britannia Street,
Taunton, MA 02780
Tel: 508 824-6611
Fax: 508 822-7269.

Blue & White Pottery Club
224 12th Street N.W., Cedar
Rapids, IA 52405
Tel: 319 362-8116.

U.S. Chintz Collectors Club
P.O. Box 50888, Pasadena,
CA 91115
Tel: 626 441-4708
Fax: 626 441-4122
http://www.chintznet.com

Clarice Cliff Collectors' Club
1 Foxtell Way, Chellaston, Derby,
Derbyshire DE73 1PU UK
webmaster@claricecliff.com
www.claricecliff.com

Dedham Pottery Collectors Society
248 Highland St, Dedham,
MA 02026
Tel: 800 283-8070
dpcurator@aol.com

Goebel Networkers.
P.O. Box 396, Lemoyne, PA 17043

**Homer Laughlin China
Collectors Association
(Fiesta ware)**
P.O. Box 1093
Corbin KY 40702-1093
www.hlcca.org

Hummel Collectors Club
1261 University Dr, Yardley, PA
19067-2857
Tel: 888 548 6635
Fax: 215 321 7367
http://www.hummels.com

**Roseville of The Past
Pottery Club**
P.O. Box 656 Clarcona, FL 32710-
0656
Tel: 407 294 3980
Fax: 407 294 7836
rosepast@bellsouth.net

**Royal Bayreuth Collectors
Club**
926 Essex Circle, Kalamazoo,
MI 49008
Tel: 616 343-6066
judykazoo@aol.com

**Royal Doulton International
Collectors' Club**
700 Cottontail Lane, Somerset,
NJ 08873
Tel: 800 682-4462
Fax: 732 764-4974

Stangl & Fulper Club
P.O. Box 538, Flemington,
NJ 08822
Tel: 908 995 2696
kenlove508@aol.com

American Stoneware
Collectors Society
P.O. Box 281, Bay Head, NJ 08742
Tel: 732 899 8707

Susie Cooper Collectors Group
Panorama House, 18 Oaklea
Mews, Aycliffe Village, County
Durham DL5 6JP UK
www.susiecooper.co.uk

DECOYS

East Coast Decoy Collectors Association
1116 Morningside Lane,
Alexander, VA 22308
potomacduck@cox.net

Midwest Decoy Collectors Association
6e Scott Street, Chicago, IL 60610
Tel: 312 337 7957

New Jersey Decoy Collectors Association
1745 Silverton Road, Tom's River,
NJ 0875

DISNEYANA

National Fantasy Club For Disneyana Collectors & Enthusiasts
P.O. Box 106 Irvine,
CA 92713-9212
Tel: 714 731 4705
info@nffc.org
http://www.nffc.org

Walt Disney Collectors' Society
500 South Buena Vista St,
Burbank, CA 91521-8028
Tel: 800 932 5749

EPHEMERA

Ephemera Society of America
P.O. Box 95, Cazenovia,
NY 13035-0095
Tel: 315 655-2810
Fax: 315 655-1078
info@ephemerasociety.org
http://www.ephemerasociety.org

National Valentine Collectors Association
P.O. Box 1404, Santa Ana,
CA 92702
Tel: 714 547 1355

FIFTIES & SIXTIES

Head Hunters Newsletters
P.O. Box 83H, Scarsdale,
NY 10583.
Tel: 914 472 0200

FILM & TV MEMORABILIA

The Animation Art Guild
330 W. 45th St, Ste 9D, New York,
NY 10036-3864
Tel: 212 765 3030
theaagltd@aol.com

James Bond 007 Fan Club & Archive
P.O. Box 007, Surrey KT15 IDY UK
Tel: +44 (0) 1483 756007

Lone Ranger Fan Club
19205 Seneca Ridge Court,
Gaithersburg MD 20879-3135

GLASS

American Carnival Glass Association
9621 Springwater Lane,
Miamisburg, OH 45342

Land of Sunshine Depression Glass Club
P.O. Box 560275, Orlando
FL 32856-0275
Te : 407 298 3355

Lalique Collectors Society
400 Veterans Blvd, Carlstadt,
NJ 07072-2704
Tel: 800 274 7825
info@lalique.com
www.lalique.com

Vaseline Glass Collectors
P.O. Box 125, Russellville,
MO 35074
vgci@hotmail.com
www.cnet.net/users/davepeterson/

JEWELRY

Cuff Link Society
P.O. Box 5700 Vernon Hills,
IL 60061
Tel: 847 816 0035

Leaping Frog Antique Jewelry & Collectible Club
4841 Martin Luther King Blvd,
Sacramento, CA 95820-4932
Tel: 916 452 6728
pandora@cwia.com

Vintage Fashion & Costume Jewelry Club
P.O. Box 265, Glen Oaks,
NY 11004-0265
Tel: 718 939 3095
vfcj@aol.com

KITCHENALIA

Kitchen Antiques & Collectibles News
4645 Laurel Ridge Dr Harrisburg
PA 17119

MECHANICAL MUSIC

Musical Box Society International
700 Walnut Hill Rd, Hockessin
DE 19707
Tel: 302 239 5658
cotps@aol.com
http://www.mbsi.org

MILITARIA

Civil War Collectors & The American Militaria Exchange
5970 Toylor Ridge Dr, West
Chester, OH 45069
Te : 513 874 0443
rwmorgan@aol.com
www.civiwar-collectors.com

OPTICAL, MEDICAL, SCIENTIFIC & TECHNICAL

International Association of Calculator Collectors
P.O. Box 345, Tustin,
CA 92781-0345
Tel: 714 730 6140
Fax: 714 730 6140
mrcalc@usa.net
http://www.geocities.com/siliconv
alley/park/7227.

ORIENTAL & ASIAN

International Chinese Snuff Bottle Society
2601 North Charles St, Baltimore,
MD 21218-4514
Tel: 410 467 9400
www.snuffbottle.org

International Netsuke Society
P.O. Box 161269, Altamonte
Springs, FL 32716-1269
Tel: 407 772 1906
odanuk@worldnet.att.net
http://www.netsuke.org/

PENS & WRITING

The Society of Inkwell Collectors
P.O. Box 324, Mossville, IL 61552
Tel: 309 579 3040
director@soic.com
www.soic.com

Pen Collectors of America
P.O. Box 80, Redding Ridge,
CT 06876
www.pencollectors.com

PERFUME BOTTLES

International Perfume Bottle Association
395 Croton Rd., Wayne, PA 19087
Tel: 610-995-9051
jcabbott@bellatlantic.net
http://www.perfumebottles.org

PEZ

Pez Collectors News
P.O. Box 14956, Surfside Beach,
SC 29587
info@pezcollectorsnews.com
www.pezcollectorsnews.com

ROCK N ROLL

Elvis Forever TCB Fan Club
P.O. Box 1066, Miami,
FL 33730-1066

Working Class Hero Beatles Club
3311 Niagara St, Pittsburgh,
PA 1213-4223

SMOKING

Cigarette Lighter Collectors Club
SPARK International
rainer.kytzia@hamburg.sc.philips.com
http://members.aol.com/intspark

Pocket Lighter Preservation Public & Historical Society, Inc.
P.O. Box 1054, Addison,
IL 60101-8054
Tel: 703 543 9120

The Society for Clay Pipe Research
2 Combe Avenue, Portishead,
Bristol BS20 6JR UK

SNOWDOMES

Snowdome Collectors Club
P.O. Box 53262, Washington,
DC 20039-9262

SPORTING MEMORABILIA

Boxing & Pugilistica Collectors International
P.O. Box 83135, Portland,
OR 97283-0135
Tel: 503 286 3597

Golf Collectors Society
P.O. Box 24102, Cleveland,
OH 44124
Tel: 216 861 1615
www.golfcollectors.com

National Fishing Lure Collectors Club
H.C. 33, Box 4012, Reeds Spring,
MO 65737
spurr@fishgfisner.com

Society for American Baseball Research
812 Huron Rd, E. 719, Cleveland,
OH 44115
info@sabr.org
www.sabr.org

SPACE MEMORABILIA

National Space Society
600 Pennsylvania Ave SE., Ste
201, Washington DC 20003-4316
Tel: 202 543 1900
nsshq@nss.org

TEXTILES & COSTUME

The Costume Society of America
55 Edgwater Dr, P.O. Box 73,
Earleville, MD 21919-0073
Tel: 410 275 1619
www.costumesocietyamerica.com

American Fan Collectors' Association
P.O. Box 5473, Sarasota,
FL 34277-5473
Tel: 817 267 9951
Fax: 817 267 0387

International Old Lacers
P.O. Box 554, Flanders NJ 07836
iolinc@aol.com

TOYS & GAMES

Annalee Doll Society
P.O.Box 1137, Meredith,
NH 03253
Tel: 800 433-6557
Fax: 603 279-6659

The Antique Toy Collectors of America, Inc
c/o Carter, Ledvard & Milburn,
Two Wall St – 13th Floor, New York,
NY 10005

Chess Collectors' International
P.O. Box 166, Commack,
NY 11725-0166
Tel: 516 543 1330
lichness@aol.com

Effanbee Doll Club
Tel: 888 272 2363
pacenet@pacenetinc.com
www.effnbeedolls.com

The Matchbox International Collectors Association
13a Lower Bridge Street, Chester
CH1 1RS UK

National Model Railroad Association
4121 Cromwell Rd, Chattanooga,
TN 37421
Tel: 423 892 2846
nmra@tttrains.com

Toy Soldier Collectors of America
5340 40th Ave N, Saint
Petersburg, FL 33709
Tel: 727 527 1430

United Federation of Doll Clubs
10920 N. Ambassador Dr, Kansas
City, MO 64153
Tel: 816-891-7040
ufdc@aol.com

TREEN & BOXES

Mauchline Ware Collectors' Club
14 Blake Ter. SE, Cedar Rapids,
IA 52403
Tel: 319-362-2643
tknyc@earthlink.net

TRIBAL ART

The Antique Tribal Art Dealers Association
P.O. Box 620278, Woodside,
CA 94062
Tel: 415 851 8670.
Fax: 415 851 3508.

WATCHES

Early American Watch Club
P.O. Box 81555, Wellesley Hills,
MA 02481-1333

National Association of Watch & Clock Collectors
514 Poplar St, Columbia,
PA 17512-2130
Tel: 717 684 8261
www.nawacc.org

WINE & DRINKING

International Correspondence of Corkscrew Addicts
670 Meadow Wood Road
Mississauga Ontario, L5J 2S6
Canada
Dugohuzo@aol.com
www.corkscrewnet.com/icca

Using the Internet

THE INTERNET HAS REVOLUTIONIZED the trading of collectibles as most are easily described and photographed and shipping is comparatively easy, due to average size and weight. Prices are also generally more affordable. Millions of collectibles are traded daily, with sites varying from global marketplaces, such as eBay, to specialist dealers' websites.

When searching online, remember that some people may not know how to describe their item. General category searches, although more time consuming, and even purposefully misspelling a name, can yield results. Also, if something looks too good to be true, it probably is. Use this book to get to know your market visually, so you can tell the difference between a real bargain and something that sounds like one.

As you will understand from buying this book, color photography is vital – look for online listings that include as many images as possible and check them carefully. Be aware that colors can appear differently, even between computer screens.

Always ask questions about the object, particularly regarding condition. If there is no image, or you want to see another view – ask. Most sellers want to realise the best price for their items, so they will be happy to help – if approached politely and sensibly.

As well as the "e-hammer" price, you will probably have to pay additional fees such as packing, shipping and, possibly, taxes. Ask for an estimate for these before leaving a bid to give you an idea of the maximum the item will cost if you are successful and so help you to tailor your bid.

As well as the well-known online auction sites, such as eBay, there are a host of other online resources for buying and selling, such as fair and auction listings.

Internet Resources

Live Auctioneers
www.liveauctioneers.com
A free service which allows users to search catalogs from auction houses in Europe, the US and the UK. Through its connection with eBay, users can bid live via the internet into salerooms as auctions happen. Registered users can search an archive of past catalogues.

invaluable.com
www.invaluable.com
A subscription service allowing users to search auction house catalogs from the UK and Europe. Offers an extensive archive.

The Antiques Trade Gazette
www.atg-online.com
The online version of the UK trade newspaper, comprising auction and fair listings, news and events.

Maine Antiques Digest
www.maineantiquesdigest.com
The online version of America's trade newspaper including news, articles, fair and auction listings and more.

La Gazette du Drouot
www.drouot.com
The online home of the magazine listing all auctions to be held in France.

Auctionnet.com
www.auctionnet.com
Simple online resource listing over 500 websites related to auctions online.

AuctionBytes
www.auctionbytes.com
Auction resource with community forum, news, events, tips and a weekly newsletter.

Auctiontalk
www.auctiontalk.com
Auction news, online and offline auction search engines and live chat forums.

Go Antiques/Antiqnet
www.goantiques.com
www.antiqnet.com
An online global aggregator for antiques, art and collectibles dealers who showcase their stock for users to browse and buy.

eBay
www.ebay.com
The largest and most diverse online auction site with over 52 million registered users. At eBay Live Auctions (www.ebayliveauctions.com) traditional auctions are combined with realtime, online bidding allowing users to interact with the saleroom as the auction takes place.